Organizational Stress and Well-Being

In this Cambridge Companion, global thought leaders in the fields of workplace stress and well-being highlight how theory and research can improve employee health and well-being. The volume explains how and why the topics of workplace stress and well-being have evolved and continue to be highly relevant, and why line managers have great influence over employees' quality of working life. It includes the latest research findings on stress and well-being and their impact on organizations, as well as up-to-date findings on the effectiveness of workplace interventions focused on these issues. It also explores important and emerging issues relating to organizational stress and well-being, including the ongoing effects of the global coronavirus pandemic. This is an ideal reference for students and researchers in the areas of human resources management, occupational health psychology, and organisational behaviour.

LAURENT M. LAPIERRE is the Ian Telfer Professor of Workplace Behaviour and Health, Telfer School of Management, University of Ottawa, Canada. He has published in several leading management and organizational psychology journals, including *Journal of Management, Leadership Quarterly, Journal of Organizational Behavior*, and *Personnel Psychology*. He was recognized in 2018 as an "Extraordinary Contributor to Work and Family Research" by the Work and Family Researchers Network (WFRN).

SIR CARY COOPER, CBE, is the 50th Anniversary Professor of Organizational Psychology and Health, Alliance Manchester Business School, University of Manchester, UK; Outgoing President of the Chartered Institute of Personnel Development (CIPD); President of the Institute of Welfare; and Chair of the National Forum for Health and Well-Being at Work. Sir Cary was knighted by the Queen in 2014 for his contribution to the social sciences. He is author/editor of more than 200 books and 150 scholarly articles and chapters.

Cambridge Companions to Management provide an essential resource for academics, graduate students, and reflective business practitioners seeking cutting-edge perspectives on managing people in organizations. Each Companion integrates the latest academic thinking with contemporary business practice, dealing with real-world issues facing organizations and individuals in the workplace, and demonstrating how and why practice has changed over time. World-class editors and contributors write with unrivalled depth on managing people and organizations in today's global business environment, making the series a truly international resource.

Organizational Stress and Well-Being

Edited by

LAURENT M. LAPIERRE
University of Ottawa

SIR CARY COOPER
University of Manchester

CAMBRIDGE
UNIVERSITY PRESS

CAMBRIDGE
UNIVERSITY PRESS

Shaftesbury Road, Cambridge CB2 8EA, United Kingdom

One Liberty Plaza, 20th Floor, New York, NY 10006, USA

477 Williamstown Road, Port Melbourne, VIC 3207, Australia

314–321, 3rd Floor, Plot 3, Splendor Forum, Jasola District Centre, New Delhi – 110025, India

103 Penang Road, #05–06/07, Visioncrest Commercial, Singapore 238467

Cambridge University Press is part of Cambridge University Press & Assessment, a department of the University of Cambridge.

We share the University's mission to contribute to society through the pursuit of education, learning and research at the highest international levels of excellence.

www.cambridge.org
Information on this title: www.cambridge.org/9781009268301

DOI: 10.1017/9781009268332

© Cambridge University Press & Assessment 2023

First published 2023
First paperback edition 2024

A catalogue record for this publication is available from the British Library

Library of Congress Cataloging-in-Publication data
Names: Cooper, Cary L., editor. | Lapierre, Laurent, editor.
Title: Organizational stress and well-being / Sir Cary Cooper, University of Manchester, Laurent M. Lapierre, University of Ottawa.
Description: 1 Edition. | New York, NY : Cambridge University Press, 2022. | Series: CACM Cambridge companions to management | Includes bibliographical references and index.
Identifiers: LCCN 2022033783 (print) | LCCN 2022033784 (ebook) | ISBN 9781009268332 (epub) | ISBN 9781009268318 (hardback) | ISBN 9781009268301 (paperback)
Subjects: LCSH: Job stress. | Work environment. | Psychology, Industrial.
Classification: LCC HF5548.85 (ebook) | LCC HF5548.85 .O743 2023 (print) | DDC 331.25/6 23/eng/20220–dc22
LC record available at https://lccn.loc.gov/2022033783

ISBN   978-1-009-26831-8   Hardback
ISBN   978-1-009-26830-1   Paperback

Contents

Figures

Tables

Contributors

Shalene J. Allen, *Portland State University, USA*

Kara A. Arnold, *Memorial University of Newfoundland, Canada*

Terry A. Beehr, *Central Michigan University, USA*

Wendy J. Casper, *University of Texas at Arlington, USA*

Huijun Chen, *Nottingham Trent University, UK*

Peter Y. Chen, *Auburn University, USA*

Sara Connolly, *University of East Anglia, UK*

Kevin Daniels, *University of East Anglia, UK*

Hope Dodd, *University of Georgia, USA*

Leslie B. Hammer, *Portland State University, USA*

Amanda J. Hancock, *Memorial University of Newfoundland, Canada*

Dorian Hartlaub, *Goethe University Frankfurt, Germany*

Alina S. Hernandez Bark, *Goethe University Frankfurt, Germany*

Ilke Inceoglu, *University of Exeter Business School, UK*

Maria Karanika-Murray, *Nottingham Trent University, UK*

Ronit Kark, *Bar-Ilan University, Israel; University of Exeter Business School, UK*

E. Kevin Kelloway, *St Mary's University, Canada*

Laurent M. Lapierre, *University of Ottawa, Canada*

Rose LeFevre-Levy, *University of Georgia, USA*

Jordyn J. Leslie, *Portland State University, USA*

Yiqiong Li, *University of Queensland, Australia*

George Michaelides, *University of East Anglia, UK*

Nora Elena Daher-Moreno, *Memorial University of Newfoundland, Canada*

Emike Nasamu, *University of Chester, UK*

Kimberly E. O'Brien, *Central Michigan University, USA*

Henri Pirkkalainen, *Tampere University, Finland*

Daniel Quintal-Curcic, *University of Ottawa, Canada*

Frederick Rice, *University of Texas at Arlington, USA*

Emma Russell, *University of Sussex, UK*

Marisa Salanova, *Universitat Jaume I, Spain*

Markus Salo, *University of Jyvaskyla, Finland*

Wilmar Schaufeli, *Utrecht University, the Netherlands*

Kristen M. Shockley, *University of Georgia, US*

Johannes Siegrist, *Heinrich Heine University Düsseldorf, Germany*

Paul E. Spector, *University of South Florida, USA*

Monideepa Tarafdar, *University of Massachusetts Amherst, USA*

Hoda Vaziri, *University of North Texas, USA*

Julie Holliday Wayne, *Wake Forest University, USA*

Zara Whysall, *Nottingham Trent University, UK*

Haibo Wu, *South China University of Technology, China*

Introduction

With the COVID-19 pandemic in its third year, the topic of this book cannot be more relevant. Before the onset of the pandemic, the strains experienced by managers and employees had been rising for years. Various factors can account for this rise, such as the intensifying pace of work, growing job insecurity in the gig economy, increasing globalization, information technology's steady invasion of all aspects of life, and heightened incompatibilities between individuals' work and personal lives. The pandemic has made things dramatically worse for many.

Setting the stage for the rest of the book, its first section describes the evolution and continued relevance of the study of organizational stress and well-being. In Chapter 1, Paul Spector provides an account of how the field's theories and topics of study have evolved since its origins in the United Kingdom during World War I. In Chapter 2, Peter Chen, Yiqiong Li, and Haibo Wu provide an overview of research findings illustrating why the field's topics continue to be of utmost salience to organizations and to societies more broadly. In Chapter 3, Johannes Siegrist helps readers understand the differences and similarities among four theorical models explaining the adverse effects of work on individuals' health, each having been the subject of considerable international research over the last few decades.

The second section focuses on line managers. People in such positions are typically responsible for supervising front-line employees and interfacing between those employees and higher levels of management. Given the nature of their positions, line managers can experience a considerable amount of stress while also having profound positive and negative effects on the well-being of those they supervise. In Chapter 4, Dorian Hartlaub, Ilke Inceoglu, Alina Hernandez Bark, and Ronit Kark discuss key stressors that line managers face in a globalized economy, how these stressors can change during a major crisis like the current COVID-19 pandemic, and how line managers can potentially cope with them. In Chapter 5, Amanda Hancock, Nora Moreno, and Kara Arnold address how, why, and when line managers can influence their subordinates' well-being by reviewing and critiquing research linking the leadership styles most frequently studied among line managers to their employees' well-being.

The third section delves into well-known topics of organizational stress and well-being that persist in their organizational and societal relevance, including work–nonwork balance, presenteeism, burnout, work engagement, gender differences in the experience of stress and well-being, and issues relating to the measurement of well-being. In Chapter 6, Wendy Casper, Julie Wayne, Frederick Rice, and Hoda Vaziri explain how the conceptualization of work–nonwork balance has evolved over time, how the notion is currently defined, and how it can more accurately be measured. In Chapter 7, Zara Whysall, Maria Karanika-Murray, and Huijun Chen fill a significant gap in the presenteeism literature by advancing a model of presenteeism decision-making, which encapsulates both absenteeism and presenteeism as potential outcomes of the same decision-making process. In Chapter 8, Wilmar Schaufeli provides an historical account of scholarship on burnout, how burnout has been measured, what seems to cause it, and what it can lead to, and identifies important questions that remain unanswered. Chapter 9 shifts to more positive work experiences, in which Marisa Salanova presents a framework for understanding how and why work engagement is experienced by employees, and how it is conceptually linked to different facets of well-being in organizations. In Chapter 10, Hope Dodd, Rose LeFevre-Levy, and Kristen Shockley address differences between men and women's experience of stress by examining how they can vary in terms of the stressors they are exposed to. The section ends with Chapter 11, in which Kevin Daniels, Emma Russell, George Michaelides, Emike Nasamu, and Sara Connolly provide insight into concepts relating to the measurement of well-being, describe the monetary implications of measured changes in well-being, and discuss why it is important to consider variation in well-being both within and between individuals.

The book's fourth section addresses workplace interventions aimed at reducing employee stress and ameliorating their well-being. In Chapter 12, Leslie Hammer, Shalene Allen, and Jordyn Leslie provide a systematic review of research on the efficacy of interventions in which managers or supervisors are trained on how to help their employees experience less stress and greater well-being. In Chapter 13, Kimberly O'Brien and Terry Beehr describe various empirically supported job stress interventions that directly involve employees (rather than their superiors) and train them on how to better manage their own stress and well-being.

The final section deals with two emerging topics in the field. In Chapter 14, Monideepa Tarafdar, Henri Pirkkalainen, and Markus Salo speak to the ubiquitous presence of information technology, why it can induce stress ("technostress"), and how people can better cope with it. In Chapter 15, Laurent Lapierre, Kevin Kelloway, and Daniel Quintal-Curcic discuss mental health and how it can be conceptualized and measured among employed individuals, and then draw on various empirical literatures in explaining how senior managers (e.g., executives) and especially employees' immediate managers can most effectively support employees' mental health.

In sum, this volume provides invaluable insights into the past, present, and future of scholarship addressing the stress and well-being of the many millions of people working in organizations. These insights can serve as a guide not only to policy makers and managers wanting to develop more effective ways of ensuring a healthy workforce, but also to scholars aiming to push the frontiers of the field.

PART I

Historical Evolution and Continued Relevance of the Study of Organizational Stress and Well-Being

1 | From Occupational Fatigue to Occupational Health

PAUL E. SPECTOR

The scientific study of the human side of organizations is barely into its second century. The initial focus in the early days of industrial-organizational (I-O; then called industrial) psychology and the associated field of management was on organizational productivity by maximizing employee job performance and making the most of human resources (then termed personnel). The study of employee well-being distinct from job performance has had a comparatively short history, particularly in North America. When I wrote the first chapter of my I-O psychology textbook in the middle 1990s, one reviewer commented that my chapter on worker health and safety did not belong in the book as it was not part of the field. The evolution of thinking about the ethical treatment of employees has occurred rather rapidly since then and is reflected in the rich literature on occupational stress and health.

As an American I-O psychology doctoral student in the middle 1970s, it was made clear to me that if I studied worker well-being, which in those days was almost entirely about job satisfaction, I needed to justify it by linking to job performance and the bottom line. After all, no competent manager would consider employee well-being to be a valid concern unless it had direct ties to costs. Thus, I was to justify each research report on job satisfaction by noting how having dissatisfied employees would lead to detrimental outcomes like low productivity or costly turnover. Elements of that sort of thinking can still be found today – how many of us still cite scary statistics about the cost of stress in our occupational stress papers? However, it has become increasingly acceptable for us to study employee well-being purely on ethical grounds.

This chapter will provide a historical perspective on the scientific study of worker well-being in its own right. The earliest studies took an occupational stress perspective, linking working conditions or stressors to physical and psychological strain outcomes, such as negative emotions and physical symptoms. The emergence of the interdisciplinary occupational health psychology field, which evolved from the study of stress, broadened interest into related topics such as accidents, injuries, mistreatment, and violence. The study of occupational stress became the study of occupational health, safety, and well-being.

Historical Roots

The history of scientific research on worker well-being is very much the history of industrial (and later industrial-organizational) psychology, although there are major contributions of researchers from other fields. Whereas the traditional academic literature on industrial psychology in general was dominated by North Americans, the same was not the case for the study of worker well-being that had its initial development primarily in Europe. There are three streams of research that serve as the foundation for the study of worker well-being in Europe.

- Early industrial psychology research on fatigue beginning during World War I in Britain.
- Trist and Bamforth's (1951) classic paper on technological disruption.
- Scandinavian research on occupational stress.

In North America, as the field matured, it started to shift focus toward worker well-being, but it would be decades until it became mainstream.

Industrial Psychology and the Study of Fatigue in Britain

The scientific study of employee well-being can be traced to the founding of the Health of Munition Workers' Committee (HMWC) in Britain during World War I (Kreis, 1995). As discussed by Kreis, a major activity of the HMWC was to investigate working conditions that would contribute to fatigue and lost productivity. Whereas counterparts in the United States were focused almost entirely on maximizing efficiency, the HMWC researchers were interested in how working conditions that led to fatigue would affect the well-being of employees, for example by increasing anxiety and boredom. At the end of the war, the HMWC was replaced by the Industrial Health Research Board that continued the study of worker well-being.

The leading figure who helped shape early British industrial psychology was Charles Myers, whose writing provided a more balanced treatment of efficiency and well-being than was seen across the

Atlantic. His book *Mind and Work* (Myers, 1920) dealt with employee accidents, boredom, fatigue, and mental health. He described research on rest pauses showing that they could increase productivity even though the amount of time spent working was less. Myers's (1926) industrial psychology textbook included many topics that are prominent in modern occupational health psychology, including accidents, mental health, negative emotions particularly anxiety and boredom, and withholding of output (today counterproductive work behavior). Some of the topics in his text were those a reviewer suggested I remove from mine nearly 70 years later.

Socio-technical Systems

One of the most influential papers in the evolution of thinking about employee well-being was written by Trist and Bamforth (1951). Their paper documented how the social disruption of technological change adversely affected coal miners in Britain. This classic paper talks about how increased isolation and insufficient autonomy were stressful and led to strains of emotional distress and absence. It serves as a foundation for the study of working conditions as stressors, and for socio-technical systems theory that has dominated British organizational research ever since.

Socio-technical systems theory provides a point of view in which the social system and technological system are considered together. The principle of joint optimization suggests that in the ideal workplace, the social and technical systems are designed in a way that best fits with one another. This extends the purpose of human factors from designing technology to fit people to the idea that you have to consider elements of both in designing ideal systems. This allows employees to perform tasks efficiently while reducing strain. A number of established practices such as autonomous work groups and job enrichment can be considered from the point of view of social-technical systems.

The Rise of Stress Research in Scandinavia

Researchers in Scandinavian counties, particularly Norway and Sweden, became early leaders in the study of general and occupational stress (Barling & Griffiths, 2011). This work on stress began in the 1960s and 1970s, underscoring the importance of the workplace

(Cooper & Dewe, 2004). One particular focus was on the link between occupational stress and cardiovascular disease, particularly the impact of life changes, such as increased responsibility at work (Theorell, 2019). A number of prominent researchers contributed to the foundation upon which occupational stress research would be built.

During the 1980s most of the research on occupational stress was coming from Europe and particularly Scandinavia. A content analysis by Erez (1994) examined the topics in applied psychology articles by country. She found that the majority of Swedish workplace research involved employee health and well-being, whereas only 5% of American articles covered those topics. The number of researchers in the United States who were studying employee health and stress was small, and it would be more than a decade before this topic became mainstream in the United States.

Developments in North America

American industrial psychology developed at the same time as its British counterpart, beginning during World War I. Whereas the British linked employee productivity and employee well-being, Americans focused primarily on productivity. Their study of worker well-being would take decades to fully develop, beginning with the study of job satisfaction and eventually embracing a broader focus on employee health.

Job Satisfaction

Early studies of worker well-being in the United States focused on job attitudes, often using the newly developed methods for job attitude assessment. Of particular note are the scientific job satisfaction studies by Robert Hoppock. His book *Job Satisfaction* (Hoppock, 1935) described three studies he conducted on the topic that had considerable impact on the field (Bowling & Cucina, 2015). One important contribution was the job satisfaction scale that he included, which provided a standard instrument that researchers began to use. Many of the early studies of job satisfaction, at least in North America, were concerned primarily with how it might affect employee productivity, but over time job satisfaction began to be studied as an important factor in employee health and well-being. One of the early controversies that continues today is whether or not job satisfaction is linked to job performance. Some reviewers of the literature concluded that it was not (Iaffaldano & Muchinsky, 1985; Vroom, 1964), whereas others reached the opposite conclusion (Judge et al., 2001; Petty et al., 1984).

Job satisfaction has become one of the most studied organizational variables, with more than 31,000 sources contained in both the PsycInfo and Web of Science databases as of December 2020. It is significantly related to hundreds of organizational variables and might be considered a universal outcome. It is an indicator of work adjustment and well-being by showing that people are satisfied with their jobs and aspects of work. It is not sufficient as a measure of worker health and broader well-being. For that, we have to look to other variables.

Mental Health of the Worker

One of the leading figures in the early American work on employee well-being is Arthur Kornhauser. As discussed in Zickar's (2003) Kornhauser biography, worker attitudes was a new topic in the early days of American I-O psychology that interested Kornhauser. In the 1930s, Kornhauser grew critical of the field for being too management-oriented, to the neglect of worker well-being. He became interested in the mental health of workers, which led him to conduct a large-scale interview study of Detroit auto workers (Kornhauser, 1965). The study showed a link between working conditions and negative emotions, and that experiences of work would spill over to the family. This study provided a foundation for later work on occupational stress and work–family conflict.

Occupational Stress: The Explosion

The study of employee well-being began slowly, with the main interest in Britain and Scandinavia. The topic got off to a slower start in North America, but by the end of the twentieth century, research had exploded. During the 1980s, a handful of researchers in North America and elsewhere became interested in the connection between working conditions and employee health/well-being from the perspective of occupational stress. By the 1990s, the study of this topic took off, and interest has accelerated since. Figure 1.1 shows the number of papers published on occupational stress from 1950 through 2019. I queried the Web of Science (WoS) database using the search term

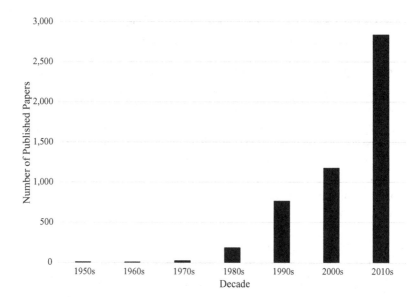

Figure 1.1

"occupational health" to get a count of papers published each year. I combined yearly counts into decades from the 1950s to the 2010s. As the figure shows, there were very few papers published until the 1980s, with a rapid acceleration after that. Fifty-seven percent of occupational stress papers in the WoS database were published between 2010 and 2019. In 2019 alone, there were as many papers as in all the years up to 1993. Clearly, occupational stress is a major topic of study worldwide.

Occupational Stress as a Discipline

In many ways, the study of occupational stress can be considered a discipline in its own right because it shares many of the features with recognized disciplines.

- **It is interdisciplinary.** Occupational stress researchers come from many disciplines, including I-O psychology and other areas of psychology, management, and the health sciences. Papers on occupational stress are published in journals from many different disciplines.
- **It has its own journals.** *Work & Stress* was founded in 1981 by Tom Cox at the University of Nottingham in the UK. Although the focus at the time was occupational stress, today it has broadened to

incorporate all topics in occupational health psychology. Other journals focus on stress in general, including occupational stress (e.g., *International Journal of Stress Management*), whereas occupational health psychology journals such as *Journal of Occupational Health Psychology* and *Occupational Health Science* are major outlets for occupational stress research.

- **It has its own conference.** The biannual Work, Stress, and Health conference in North America began with a main focus on occupational stress, although in recent years it has broadened to include other occupational health psychology (OHP) topics.
- **There are books on the topic.** Many books, including this one, are concerned entirely or mainly with occupational stress. There is even the *Handbook of Work Stress*, published in 2005 by Sage Publications, and an annual book series, *Research in Occupational Stress and Well-Being*, published since 2001 by JAI.

Early Occupational Stress Contributions

There are many contributions to the field of occupational stress coming from Europe and the United States. One that linked the early focus on job satisfaction to the broader concern with stress was the book *Work and Well-being* (Warr & Wall, 1975). Although most of the book reviewed research on job satisfaction, there was a chapter devoted to occupational stress. This book was my introduction to the topic of occupational stress and inspired my lifelong interest in the topic. There are many early contributions to the study of occupational stress, but three deserve mention based on their impact in shaping the study of occupational stress and occupational health:

- **Contributions by the Institute for Social Research.** The Institute for Social Research at the University of Michigan began a program of research on employee well-being at the end of the 1950s (Cooper & Dewe, 2004). This program produced many influential products that helped shape the field of occupational stress and broader occupational health. One of the most significant was Katz and Kahn's (1966) *The Social Psychology of Organizations*. In this book, they discuss the role stressors of role ambiguity, role conflict, and role overload that came to dominate the study of occupational stress research for quite some time. Another is the *Job Demands and*

Worker Health study (Caplan et al., 1975), funded by the National Institute of Occupational Safety and Health (NIOSH). This large-scale study of high stress occupations showed a clear link between stressors and strains.

- **Beehr and Newman's (1978) Occupational Stress Model.** One of the most influential papers published in the early days of occupational stress research was Beehr and Newman's (1978) review of the newly emerging literature on occupational stress. One of their major contributions was the inclusion of a model that outlines the complex stress process involving environmental characteristics, individual differences, and both short-term and long-term outcomes for employees and organizations.

- **The Demand-Control Model.** The Demand-Control Model (Karasek, 1979), built on the idea that stressful working conditions (stressors) would lead to poor health and well-being (strains). It suggested that control would buffer the adverse effects of demands and reduce their negative impact. This provided an important stressor-strain framework that would drive much subsequent research and led to the more complex Demand-Control-Support model, which added a buffering effect of social support (Karasek & Theorell, 1990). These models drew attention to the prominence of control in the occupational stress process, and although the buffering effect of both control and support have proven to be elusive (de Lange et al., 2003), there is little doubt that control and support play important roles.

Twenty-First Century Developments

As the study of occupational stress expanded into the twenty-first century, it developed in several directions. Some directions were derived from the general stress literature, whereas others built on work from the occupational domain.

Resource Approaches

Most occupational stress papers rely on resource theories as their underlying frameworks. Initially authors cited Conservation of Resources (COR) Theory (Hobfoll, 1989), which explains how the loss of resources or threat of loss is stressful, leading to strain. Stressors are considered conditions at work that consume resources, which explains their link to strains. According to this view, resources are things that a person values, and activities that drain resources are stressful.

Two limitations with COR Theory, its lack of work focus and a general and rather vague definition of resources, left an opening for widespread adoption of the work-specific Job Demand-Resource Theory (Bakker & Demerouti, 2014). This theory defines resources as things that enable a person to perform job tasks and suggests that strains occur when job demands exceed available resources. When resources are sufficient to perform job tasks, motivation (engagement) and positive well-being are enhanced. The more specific JD-R Theory has begun to replace COR Theory as a foundation for occupational stress research as it specifies a more specific connection between working demands and strains.

Cross-cultural and Cross-national Issues

Early occupational stress research was concerned with basic principles linking stressors to strains. As globalization expanded into the twenty-first century, there was increasing interest in cross-cultural and cross-national differences in occupational stress. As information technologies made international collaboration easier, researchers in different countries began pooling their resources to conduct comparative occupational stress studies.

One of the largest-scale efforts was the Collaborative International Study of Managerial Stress (CISMS). This two-phase study involved 46 researchers from 39 countries who collected data from more than 14,000 managers. CISMS produced more than two dozen journal articles, most of which dealt with country differences (Spector et al., 2002) and culture differences (Spector et al., 2001).

Other, more modest programs have taken a more precise look at country/culture differences in occupational stress. A notable example is the work of Cong Liu and colleagues, who in a series of studies have investigated differences between Americans and Chinese, focusing on the stressors of interpersonal conflict (e.g., Liu et al., 2015) and organizational constraints (e.g., Liu et al., 2010).

Organizational Climates

The psychological literature on accidents and injuries has been dominated by a focus on safety climate (Zohar, 2010). Safety climate is the individual perception (perceived climate) or shared perception (organizational climate) that policies and practices of the organization support safety. In other words, following safety protocols is encouraged by management. The idea of climate being linked to occupational stress began to take hold in the new century as researchers noted that climates could be related to strains (Spector et al., 2007).

Of the many climates studied, the one that has the closest link to occupational stress is psychosocial safety climate (Dollard et al., 2012; Idris et al., 2012). This type of climate describes organizations where employees feel safe from mistreatment and psychological aggression. People are free to be themselves in an environment of acceptance. Such climates have lower levels of social stressors, such as bullying (Law et al., 2011), and strains such as burnout (Idris et al., 2014).

From Occupational Stress to Occupational Health

As the study of occupational stress and worker well-being developed, it became clear that it dealt with a very broad and complex set of issues. Researchers who studied these issues, many of whom were not psychologists, became convinced that it was large enough to represent a separate field within psychology, and the field of OHP emerged. Quick (1999) credits Raymond et al. (1990) as using the term for the first time in print. Their vision was to integrate the training of OHP practitioners and researchers across a variety of fields, including business, medicine, nursing, occupational health, and psychology. The extent to which this integration has been successful is debatable, as most training is focused mainly in psychology, but there is no doubt that the field of OHP has emerged, initially in Europe and then in North America.

OHP is a field concerned with psychological factors in employee health, safety, and well-being. Much of its attention focuses on the psychosocial aspects of the physical and social working environment. Occupational stress is central to the field of OHP, but OHP covers more territory than stress, and its point of view is broader. It connects with fields concerned with occupational health and safety, investigating how psychosocial aspects of the workplace contribute to accidents, injuries, and illness. It takes a public health perspective in being concerned with exposures to both physical and psychological risks in the workplace, and in recognizing the distinction between primary prevention (changing the job), secondary prevention (giving employees tools), and tertiary prevention (treating illness and injury).

The field got its early impetus in the United States from a partnership between the American Psychological Association and NIOSH. Over a period of about six years, they awarded small seed grants to more than a dozen graduate programs in the United States, most of them I-O psychology doctoral programs, to stimulate the training of OHP. Five of these programs received NIOSH training grants: Colorado State University, Ohio University, Portland State University, University of Connecticut, and University of South Florida. The partnership also supported two small conferences at Portland State University and University of South Florida where ideas for developing the field in the United States were discussed. This resulted in the founding of the Society of Occupational Health Psychology in the United States.

OHP can be considered a major subfield within psychology, although it is interdisciplinary and goes beyond psychology. There are several characteristics that define it as an established field.

- **OHP Societies.** There are societies devoted entirely to OHP. The UK has the European Academy of Occupational Health Psychology (EAOHP); in the United States, there is the Society for Occupational Health Psychology (SOHP).
- **OHP Graduate Training.** There are more than two dozen universities in both Europe and North America that provide graduate training in OHP. Most are attached to I-O psychology graduate programs, but some are attached to other programs, such as cognitive or social psychology.
- **OHP Journals.** APA has supported the development of OHP by publishing *Journal of Occupational Health Psychology*. In 2016, SOHP launched *Occupational Health Science* to be an interdisciplinary OHP journal. *Work & Stress* originally devoted to occupational stress evolved into a broader OHP journal as it became affiliated with the EAOHP (Cox & Tisserand, 2006).
- **OHP Conferences.** Europe has an annual OHP conference, and as mentioned earlier, the Work, Stress, and Health conference sponsored initially by APA and NIOSH has broadened its purview to OHP and is now cosponsored by SOHP.
- **OHP Books.** There are many books dealing with OHP topics, but most notable is the *Handbook of Occupational Health Psychology*,

edited by James Quick and Lois Tetrick, and OHP textbooks *Occupational Health Psychology*, written by Irvin Schonfeld and Chu-Hsiang (Daisy) Chang (2017), and *Essentials of Occupational Health Psychology*, by Chris Cunningham and Kristen Black (2021).

Today the OHP field is rapidly growing within Europe, the United States, and many other parts of the world as concern for employee health and well-being becomes increasingly recognized. This is reflected in job ads for psychologists that list OHP as a research focus of interest, and in the personal statements of prospective graduate students who note OHP interests. It can be seen in the programs of I-O psychology conferences (European Association of Work and Organizational Psychology and Society for Industrial and Organizational Psychology) and management conferences (Academy of Management, European Academy of Management, Southern Management Association) as OHP topics are frequent topics of sessions. All of this research attention has taught us much about the connection between the work environment and employee health, but also where more work is needed on how best to manage organizations to maximize employee health and well-being.

Creating Healthy Workplaces

A truly healthy workplace is one in which both the employee and the organization can thrive. This means not only the absence of ill health but also continued growth and positive well-being (Spreitzer et al., 2005). Healthy employees are best positioned to contribute to organizational functioning, and healthy organizations have the resources to provide good working conditions and make contributions to the broader society. The health of one cannot be sustained if the other is ignored. The duality of health – employee and organization – is recognized by the concept of the healthy work organization (Sauter et al., 1996). Such organizations have management practices that jointly promote employee and organizational health.

There are a number of management practices and ways of running organizations that contribute to organizational health. Such practices treat employees as valuable resources to be developed and protected rather than exploited. This means providing employees with the resources and tools to efficiently do their jobs while avoiding unnecessary stress. It requires running organizations efficiently and developing organizational climates that minimize stress while facilitating key organizational goals. The remainder of this chapter will provide specific management recommendations or best practices for building a healthy organization.

Realign Management Thinking

There is a tendency to think of human resources as costs, both the direct costs of salary and benefits and indirect costs of resources provided to employees. This is wrong thinking and should be replaced with the idea of human resource investments that will provide future returns in productivity, quality, and reputation. One of the early insights provided by Myers (1920) was that working fewer hours often resulted in greater total output. Thus, investing in employees by providing rests can lead to a return of even more performance without overly straining the employees. Many other human resource investments can provide impressive returns.

Build a General Safety Climate

A healthy organization has a climate that protects employees from both physical and psychological risks. This means having a general safety climate that includes elements of safety climate (focus on accidents/injuries) and psychosocial safety climate (focus on mistreatment). There are several steps organizations can take in dealing with such climates (Spector, 2019b).

1 **Make Climate a Goal**. Top management needs to adopt the development of a general safety climate as a strategic goal. This means investing resources into safety and considering it a worthwhile investment. It should be considered okay to take time to be safe, even if it means slowing production a little.
2 **Communicate Policies**. Policies concerning climate need to be disseminated throughout the organization. This involves messaging from not only the top but also all levels of management. Safety, both physical and psychological, should be a common topic of discussion throughout the organization.
3 **Model Safety**. Safety policies and practices are for everyone. All managers should follow safety rules (e.g., wearing safety gear) and

not assume that telling employees is sufficient without modeling that behavior (Kessler et al., 2020).

4 **Take Corrective Action.** Direct supervisors need to monitor employee behavior and take corrective action when necessary. Employees should be recognized for safe behavior and corrected for unsafe actions. This means progressive discipline of starting with gentle reminders and escalating to more punitive measures if unsafe behaviors persist.

Select the Right People

It is important to match people's capabilities to the demands of the job in order to maximize organizational health. Mismatches will not only result in substandard performance but also create undue stress as individuals struggle to perform job tasks. Effective selection systems focus on hiring the best talent for the specific job by identifying job requirements and then using selection tools to assess job applicants. Those tools can minimize personal biases of decision-makers and achieve greater workforce diversity and a more capable workforce that performs better with less effort and stress.

Develop Your Talent

Training and other developmental activities should be considered investments that can not only improve the performance of employees in their current positions but also provide a talent pool from which to draw for higher level positions. An effective training and development program focuses on three elements (Spector, 2021).

1 **Training Needs Assessment.** Training resources are always limited, so they should be invested wisely so they will have the most impact. Needs assessment means conducting research to determine where knowledge and skill gaps exist for employees, and what future knowledge and skill will be needed. This means first identifying gaps and then prioritizing what and who are to be trained.
2 **Training Design.** Training needs to incorporate known principles that maximize effectiveness. The common approach to corporate training of having employees attend all-day presentations might be

practical, but it is not particularly effective in most cases. Well-designed training needs to incorporate the following principles.

- **General Principles**. This means providing the big picture to put the training in context. A training program on a particular application for individuals new to computing should begin with a brief overview of the computer, its main components, and applications in general. Trainees will better understand the particular application they are being taught if they have a general sense of what a computer is and how it works.
- **Spaced Training**. Learning is retained better when training occurs in shorter sessions spread over time rather than one long session. Further, the longer the interval between training sessions, the longer trainees will remember what was trained (Cepeda et al., 2009).
- **Feedback**. In order to learn effectively, people need feedback. They need to know if what they have learned is correct. With training that teaches knowledge, quizzes can be used to show trainees that they understand the material correctly. Skills training should allow practice sessions that include feedback to indicate if something was done correctly.
- **Match Practice With the Job**. The best training allows practice on tasks that are as close as possible to the job itself. For example, flight training makes use of simulators that include elements that match aircraft on the features being trained. High fidelity simulators have cockpits that mimic the real thing and can simulate the motions of an aircraft in response to the actions taken by the trainee.

3 **Training Evaluation**. It should not be assumed that training was effective just because it was completed. Training needs to be evaluated to see if employees felt it was worthwhile, if they learned anything (e.g., by use of a quiz at the end of training), if they apply what was learned on the job, and if the training resulted in improvements in employee or organizational outcomes (Kirkpatrick, 1977). Evaluation means conducting research and collecting data that can be used to determine if training can be improved, or if it is worthwhile to do at all. An effective strategy is to do a pilot test of new training on a small group of employees to determine if the training is effective before rolling it out to all employees who will be trained.

Leadership

One of the key elements in a healthy work organization is leadership. Perhaps the two most important functions of leaders, recognized as far back as the Ohio State Leadership Studies (Fleishman & Harris, 1962), are providing structure and providing support. Structure concerns the organization of work and the coordination of effort across employees and functions. It helps clarify to employees what their roles are and where to put their efforts. Support means paying attention to employees and providing assistance to them in dealing with the demands of the job. Leaders vary in the extent to which they provide each function, but they are both vital to good leadership.

Work needs to be structured, and the costs of a passive leader who does not perform the structuring function can be substantial in terms of both employee poor performance and stress. Effective structure can minimize many stressors, including role ambiguity, role conflict, and work overload, because it clarifies expectations and balances workload to be most efficient.

Support comes in two broad forms. Instrumental support provides assistance in getting jobs done. This includes showing employees how to perform tasks and taking on some tasks when employees are overloaded. Emotional support helps employees cope with the stress of the job and, in some cases, stress off the job. Emotionally supportive leaders consider the impact of decisions on employees and build trusting relationships. Their support can help buffer the negative impact of stressful jobs and is particularly vital in industries where jobs are inherently stressful, such as first responders and healthcare. Paying attention to employee health, safety, and well-being is important for providing a general safety climate as it makes clear to employees that their health, safety, and well-being are priorities.

Although it is widely acknowledged that support is a vital leadership function, there has been surprisingly little attention paid to how it can best be accomplished. A new line of research has shown that well-intentioned but poorly delivered support can add to employee stress rather than making it better. Gray et al. (2019) identified ten ways in which workplace support by supervisors and others can be counterproductive. For example, support might be unwanted, delivered in a way that is insulting, or not provide what the employee needs. Gray et al.'s research suggests that managers should consider the following.

- **Communicate with Employees.** Be sure that you understand what support is needed and that the support is wanted. Sometimes an employee needs to struggle to learn how to perform a task and to build confidence. Unless consequences of failure are severe, which can be the case in healthcare, allow employees to figure it out themselves if they wish.

- **Explain Rather Than Do.** If an employee does not know how to do a task, it is better to teach that employee how to do it than to step in and do it for him or her. In the long run, it can be more effective to explain how to do something and sit with an employee while they try, than to do it and have him or her watch. Learning requires doing and feedback.

- **Do Not Be Critical.** Often offers of support can be interpreted as criticism. After all, if you are offering to help an employee with a problem, it implies that the employee is not capable of doing the job. Be tactful in approaching employees and do not assume help is needed. An approach like, "How is it going today?" is better than "You look like you could use some help".

- **Support, Don't Dismiss.** When employees are dealing with difficult events, either on or off the job, it can be tempting to try to make them feel better by looking on the bright side, for example telling them that it happened to you once and everything came out all right. This approach can often make someone feel worse by discounting their feelings. Sometimes it is best to say you are sorry they are having the problem, and just be willing to listen.

Provide Rewards for Contributions

Rewards for performance are important because they provide feedback that employee efforts are recognized and worthwhile to management. One of the major stress theories, the Effort-Reward Imbalance Theory, recognizes that unrewarded effort can be stressful (Siegrist, 1996). People whose efforts are unrewarded can feel exploited and unfairly treated.

There are many ways to reward employees, not all of which are monetary. Pay-for-performance systems can be effective if administered in a fair and transparent way, but systems in which most pay is linked to output (e.g., commission sales) can be stressful. Nonmonetary rewards can be as effective in terms of feedback and motivation. It is not a stretch to suggest that employees will work for praise, although obviously they will not work for praise alone. Providing praise and showing appreciation can enhance employee motivation because it provides feedback that their performance is good, and it signals that the employee is having a positive impact.

Praising employees and showing appreciation does not always come naturally to supervisors. Spector (2019a) offers five tips for using these sorts of rewards.

- Show appreciation for both effort and results. Results ultimately come from effort, so you want to encourage employees to remain motivated even when they have not yet accomplished their goals. Rewarding effort can be used to motivate employees by acknowledging improved performance over time.
- Appreciation can be shown with a simple "thank you".
- Be clear about what you are rewarding. Thank employees for specific efforts or accomplishments (e.g., a new person best for monthly sales), rather than providing vague statements not tied to particular actions.
- Use rewards to develop people. You can use the principle of successive approximations to reward employees for getting closer and closer to the level of performance you need. Reward an employee for initial efforts, and as performance improves over time, give occasional praise for doing better.
- Rewards need to be fair. Set your own standards and process for providing rewards and then apply them equally to all employees. Praising one employee and ignoring others can create bad feelings and conflict within a group. You need to acknowledge your stars, but average performers also need appreciation and recognition to maintain efforts to improve.

From Fatigue to Health

The scientific field of employee health and well-being is barely one hundred years old. It began with a focus on fatigue during a war in Europe when understanding what drives employee efforts was a matter of survival. In Britain, there was an immediate recognition that employee health and well-being were tied to job conditions that led at least in part to an employee-centered approach to understanding the human side of the workplace moving forward. At the same time, in the

United States, there was a focus primarily on factors that would lead to job performance, with little regard for the impact on employees. Thus, Taylor's *Scientific Management*, which used evidence-based approaches to maximize productivity, was more embraced in North America than in Britain (Kreis, 1995).

They may have followed different paths across the Atlantic, but by the twenty-first century, the importance of worker health and safety was recognized not only in Europe and North America, but by researchers across the world. The study of the psychosocial aspects that are the heart of the field of OHP has become almost universal. This can be seen in the rapid expansion of this field in terms of the research being published and the number of outlets available.

An exclusive focus on organizational efficiency to the exclusion of the well-being of people is bound to be unproductive. Healthy organizations are not only efficient but also have members who enjoy good physical and psychological health and well-being. We know a great deal about the characteristics and practices of such organizations, and examples can be found by consulting lists that recognize the best places to work. Creating such organizations requires effort and expertise in order to jointly optimize conditions that enhance organizations with conditions that enhance their people.

References

Bakker, A. B., & Demerouti, E. (2014). Job demands-resources theory. In P. Y. Chen & C. L. Cooper (Eds.), *Work and wellbeing* (Vol. 3, pp. 37–64). Wiley-Blackwell.

Barling, J., & Griffiths, A. (2011). A history of occupational health psychology. In L. E. Tetrick & J. C. Quick (Eds.), *Handbook of occupational health psychology* (pp. 21–34). American Psychological Association.

Beehr, T. A., & Newman, J. E. (1978). Job stress, employee health, and organizational effectiveness: A facet analysis, model, and literature review. *Personnel Psychology, 31*(4), 665–699.

Bowling, N. A., & Cucina, J. M. (2015). Robert Hoppock: Early job satisfaction and vocational guidance pioneer. *The Industrial-Organizational Psychologist, 53*, 109–116.

Caplan, R. D., Cobb, S., French, J. R. P., Jr., Van Harrison, R., & Pinneau, S. R., Jr. (1975). *Job demands and worker health: Main effects and occupational differences.* U.S. Department of Health, Education, and Welfare.

Cepeda, N. J., Coburn, N., Rohrer, D., Wixted, J. T., Mozer, M. C., & Pashler, H. (2009). Optimizing distributed practice: Theoretical analysis and practical implications. *Experimental Psychology*, 56(4), 236–246. http://doi.org/10.1027/1618-3169.56.4.236

Cooper, C. L., & Dewe, P. (2004). *Stress: A brief history*. Blackwell.

Cox, T., & Tisserand, M. (2006). *Work & Stress* comes of age: Twenty years of occupational health psychology. *Work & Stress*, 20(1), 1–5. http://doi.org/10.1080/02678370600739795

Cunningham, C. J. L., & Black, K. J. (2021). *Essentials of occupational health psychology*. Routledge.

Dollard, M. F., Tuckey, M. R., & Dormann, C. (2012). Psychosocial safety climate moderates the job demand-resource interaction in predicting workgroup distress. *Accident Analysis and Prevention*, 45, 694–704. https://doi.org/10.1016/j.aap.2011.09.042

Erez, M. (1994). Toward a model of cross-cultural industrial and organizational psychology. In H. C. Triandis, M. D. Dunnette, & L. Hough (Eds.), *Handbook of industrial and organizational psychology* (Vol. 4, pp. 559–607). Consulting Psychologists Press.

Fleishman, E. A., & Harris, E. F. (1962). Patterns of leadership behavior related to employee grievances and turnover. *Personnel Psychology*, 15, 43–56.

Gray, C. E., Spector, P. E., Lacey, K. N., Young, B. G., Jacobsen, S. T., & Taylor, M. R. (2019). Helping may be harming: Unintended negative consequences of providing social support. *Work & Stress*, 1–27. http://doi.org/10.1080/02678373.2019.1695294

Hobfoll, S. E. (1989). Conservation of resources: A new attempt at conceptualizing stress. *American Psychologist*, 44(3), 513–524. http://doi.org/10.1037/0003-066X.44.3.513

Hoppock, R. (1935). *Job satisfaction*. Harper and Brothers.

Iaffaldano, M. T., & Muchinsky, P. M. (1985). Job satisfaction and job performance: A meta-analysis. *Psychological Bulletin*, 97(2), 251–273. http://doi.org/10.1037/0033-2909.97.2.251

Idris, M. A., Dollard, M. F., Coward, J., & Dormann, C. (2012). Psychosocial safety climate: Conceptual distinctiveness and effect on job demands and worker psychological health. *Safety Science*, 50(1), 19–28. http://doi.org/10.1016/j.ssci.2011.06.005

Idris, M. A., Dollard, M. F., & Yulita. (2014). Psychosocial safety climate, emotional demands, burnout, and depression: A longitudinal multilevel study in the Malaysian private sector. *Journal of Occupational Health Psychology*, 19(3), 291–302. http://doi.org/10.1037/a0036599

Judge, T. A., Thoresen, C. J., Bono, J. E., & Patton, G. K. (2001). The job satisfaction–job performance relationship: A qualitative and

quantitative review. *Psychological Bulletin*, 127(3), 376–407. http://doi
.org/10.1037/0033-2909.127.3.376

Karasek, R. A., Jr. (1979). Job demands, job decision latitude, and mental
strain: Implications for job redesign. *Administrative Science Quarterly*,
24(2), 285–308. http://doi.org/10.2307/2392498

Karasek, R. A., Jr., & Theorell, T. (1990). *Healthy work: Stress, productivity
and the reconstruction of work life*. Basic Books.

Katz, D., & Kahn, R. L. (1966). *The social psychology of organizations*.
John Wiley.

Kessler, S. R., Lucianetti, L., Pindek, S., & Spector, P. E. (2020).
"Walking the talk": The role of frontline supervisors in preventing
workplace accidents. *European Journal of Work and Organizational
Psychology*, 29(3), 1–12. http://doi.org/10.1080/1359432X.2020
.1719998

Kirkpatrick, D. L. (1977). Evaluating training programs: Evidence versus
proof. *Training and Development Journal*, 31, 9–12.

Kornhauser, A. (1965). *Mental health of the industrial worker*. John Wiley.

Kreis, S. (1995). Early experiments in British scientific management: The
Health of Munitions Workers' Committee, 1915–1920. *Journal of
Management History*, 1, 65–78.

de Lange, A. H., Taris, T. W., Kompier, M. A., Houtman, I. L., & Bongers,
P. M. (2003). "The very best of the millennium": Longitudinal research
and the demand-control-(support) model. *Journal of Occupational
Health Psychology*, 8(4), 282–305.

Law, R., Dollard, M. F., Tuckey, M. R., & Dormann, C. (2011).
Psychosocial safety climate as a lead indicator of workplace bullying
and harassment, job resources, psychological health and employee
engagement. *Accident Analysis and Prevention*, 43(5), 1782–1793.
http://doi.org/10.1016/j.aap.2011.04.010

Liu, C., Li, C., Fan, J., & Nauta, M. M. (2015). Workplace conflict and
absence/lateness: The moderating effect of core self-evaluation in China
and the United States. *International Journal of Stress Management*, 22
(3), 243–269. http://doi.org/10.1037/a0039163

Liu, C., Nauta, M. M., Li, C., & Fan, J. (2010). Comparisons of organizational constraints and their relations to strains in China and the United
States. *Journal of Occupational Health Psychology*, 15(4), 452–467.
http://doi.org/10.1037/a0020721

Myers, C. S. (1920). *Mind and work: The psychological factors in industry
and commerce*. University of London Press.

(1926). *Industrial psychology in Great Britain*. Jonathan Cape.

Petty, M. M., McGee, G. W., & Cavender, J. W. (1984). A meta-analysis of
the relationships between individual job satisfaction and individual

performance. *The Academy of Management Review*, 9(4), 712–721. www.jstor.org/stable/258493

Quick, J. C. (1999). Occupational health psychology: The convergence of health and clinical psychology with public health and preventive medicine in an organizational context. *Professional Psychology: Research and Practice*, 30(2), 123–128. http://doi.org/10.1037/0735-7028.30.2 .123

Raymond, J. S., Wood, D. W., & Patrick, W. K. (1990). Psychology doctoral training in work and health. *American Psychologist*, 45(10), 1159–1161. http://doi.org/10.1037/0003-066X.45.10.1159

Sauter, S. L., Lim, S. Y., & Murphy, L. R. (1996). Organizational health: A new paradigm for occupational stress research at NIOSH. *Japanese Journal of Occupational Mental Health*, 4(4), 248–254.

Schonfeld, I. S., & Chang, C.-H. (2017). *Occupational Health Psychology*. Springer.

Siegrist, J. (1996). Adverse health effects of high-effort/low-reward conditions. *Journal of Occupational Health Psychology*, 1(1), 27–41. http://doi.org/10.1037/1076-8998.1.1.27

Spector, P. E. (2019a). People work for praise. https://paulspector.com/people-work-for-praise/

(2019b). What is organizational climate? https://paulspector.com/what-is-organizational-climate/

(2021). *Industrial and organizational psychology: Research and practice*. John Wiley.

Spector, P. E., Cooper, C. L., Sanchez, J. I., O'Driscoll, M., Sparks, K., Bernin, P., Büssing, A., Dewe, P., Hart, P., Lu, L., Miller, K., de Moraes, L. F. R., Ostrognay, G., Pagon, M., Pitariu, H., Poelmans, S., Radhakrishnan, P., Russinova, V., Salamatov, V., ... Yu, S. (2001). Do national levels of individualism and internal locus of control relate to well-being: An ecological level international study. *Journal of Organizational Behavior*, 22(8), 815–832. http://doi.org/10.1002/job .118

Spector, P. E., Cooper, C. L., Sanchez, J. I., O'Driscoll, M., Sparks, K., Bernin, P., ... Yu, S. (2002). Locus of control and well-being at work: How generalizable are Western findings? *Academy of Management Journal*, 45(2), 453–466. https://doi.org/10.5465/3069359

Spector, P. E., Coulter, M. L., Stockwell, H. G., & Matz, M. W. (2007). Perceived violence climate: A new construct and its relationship to workplace physical violence and verbal aggression, and their potential consequences. *Work & Stress*, 21(2), 117–130. http://doi.org/10.1080/02678370701410007

Spreitzer, G., Sutcliffe, K., Dutton, J., Sonenshein, S., & Grant, A. M. (2005). A socially embedded model of thriving at work. *Organization Science*, 16(5), 537–549. http://doi.org/10.1287/orsc.1050.0153

Theorell, T. (2019). A long-term perspective on cardiovascular job stress research. *Journal of Occupational Health*, 61(1), 3–9. http://doi.org/10.1002/1348-9585.12032

Trist, E. L., & Bamforth, K. W. (1951). Some social and psychological consequences of the longwall method of coal-getting: An examination of the psychological situation and defences of a work group in relation to the social structure and technological content of the work system. *Human Relations*, 4(1), 3–38. http://doi.org/10.1177/001872675100400101

Vroom, V. H. (1964). *Work and motivation*. John Wiley.

Warr, P., & Wall, T. D. (1975). *Work and well-being*. Penguin.

Zickar, M. J. (2003). Remembering Arthur Kornhauser: Industrial psychology's advocate for worker well-being. *Journal of Applied Psychology*, 88(2), 363–369. http://doi.org/10.1037/0021-9010.88.2.363

Zohar, D. (2010). Thirty years of safety climate research: Reflections and future directions. *Accident Analysis and Prevention*, 42(5), 1517–1522. https://doi.org/10.1016/j.aap.2009.12.019

2 | *Impacts of Stress and Well-Being on Organizations and Societies*
A Global Perspective

PETER Y. CHEN, YIQIONG LI, AND HAIBO WU

It has been estimated that full-time employees spend approximately 8.5 hours at work per day (US Bureau of Labor Statistics, 2019a) during the course of a 50-year working life (assuming employment occurs from 18 to 67). The devotion of time and energy to working life reflects not only societal and cultural values (e.g., being dependable, resourceful, or productive), but also individual beliefs, values, motivations, and attitudes (e.g., belongingness, pride, calling, achievement, and admiration).

Yet, workplaces are filled with physical and psychological hazards and risks that often lead to workers' suffering in the course of working life. One major occupational health and safety problem faced by workers is frequent exposure to stressful events or conditions at work (i.e., occupational stressors). According to 2019 survey conducted by the American Psychological Association (APA, 2019), more than 60% of employed adults identified work as a major source of stress. Furthermore, more than 56% of employed adults are concerned about job stability during the COVID-19 pandemic crisis (APA, 2020).

Exposure to occupational stressors could have devastating or even life-threatening effects on employees' health and well-being. Imagine a waitress in Victoria, Australia, being constantly spat on, insulted, ridiculed, called ugly and fat, along with having poison put in her bag by her coworkers and fish sauce poured all over her hair and clothes. That is what it is like to be a victim of workplace bullying, as continually experienced by 19-year-old waitress Brodie Panlock, who subsequently died by suicide (Brodie's Law, 2011). Also imagine sanitation workers in Alabama, United States, being denied bathroom breaks outside of their sole 30-minute break per eight-hour shift and wearing diapers to work at dangerously fast speeds in a poultry processing site (Southern Poverty Law Center, 2016). As Smallwood

(2007) expressed the anguish workers' experience, "No one should die while trying to make a living. No one should have to die while trying to make a living."

Recognizing prevalence of occupational stressors as well as severe consequences, the World Health Organization in 2019 finally included occupational stressors as well as adverse outcomes in the eleventh revision of the International Classification of Diseases. Furthermore, a new diagnostic category, "Trauma and Stress-Related Disorders" (e.g., adjustment disorders and posttraumatic stress disorders) caused by traumatic events at work (e.g., bullying, toxic working environment) has been added to the *Diagnostic and Statistical Manual of Mental Disorders* (*DSM-5*, American Psychiatric Association, 2013).

Stress research has consistently shown that stressful experience adversely affects individuals' immune systems (Cohen et al., 1991; Stone et al., 1994), physical illness (Broadley et al., 2005), and mental illness (Lazarus & Folkman, 1987; Richardson et al., 2013). In the context of the work environment, similar impacts have also been reported by multiple meta-analyses. For instance, occupational stressors such as overtaxing job demands, hostile working environments, insecure jobs, unfair treatments, or interpersonal conflicts have consistently been shown to be associated with workers' physical health problems such as cardiovascular disease, obesity, sick leaves, depression, anxiety, somatic symptoms, and risk behaviors such as alcohol abuse, smoking, lack of sleep (Kivimäki et al., 2006; Landsbergis et al., 2013), and psychological well-being (Bonde, 2008; McKee-Ryan et al., 2005; Sparks et al., 1997; Stansfeld & Candy, 2006; Sverke et al., 2002).

Poor worker health not only adversely affects individuals and their families (emotions, family and social relationships, career development, etc.) but also disrupts long-term growth (productivity, health, tax revenues, etc.) of organizations and nations (Goh et al., 2019; Hassard et al., 2018a; Jiang & Lavaysse, 2018). In the present chapter, we focus on negative impacts of occupational stressors on organizations and nations. First, we review adverse impacts, such as productivity loss, health care cost, morbidity, or mortality of occupational stressors at macro levels. To examine how these impacts are addressed from a broader perspective, we then survey legislation across nations that address workers' compensation due to mental stress, and five specific occupational stressors, including age discrimination, racial discrimination, sex discrimination, sexual harassment, and bullying occurring at the workplace. After that, we summarize the above review and offer recommendations for future research and practices.

Impacts of Occupational Stressors at Macro Levels

We present impacts of occupational stressors at macro levels (e.g., organizations, industries, or nations) by following three inclusion criteria. First, the present review mainly reviews research that has been conducted based on national data as well as meta-analytic studies. We exclude studies focusing on an individual organization, such as a pharmaceutical company (Schmidt et al., 2019), because the results of these studies may not provide a comparable and comprehensive picture pertaining to astronomical impacts of occupational stressors. Second, our review focuses on articles published in the last five years (2015–2020) to provide up-to-date, comparable results. Past reviews about costs of occupational stressors can be referred to Sauter et al. (1990), Matrix (2012), and EU-OSHA (2014). Finally, we review research that provides evidence that outcomes are associated with (or attributed to) occupational stressors. We hasten to emphasize that research designs at the macro level are not able to make causal inferences.

Impacts in Terms of Economic Costs

Financial impact is often included while assessing impacts of organizational stressors at the organizational or national level. Criteria such as productivity loss, sickness absenteeism, presenteeism, medical claim, or health care cost have been used to estimate direct and indirect costs in past cost-of-illness research (e.g., Hassard et al., 2018a, 2018b, 2019). It should be emphasized that direct and indirect costs merely reflect a myopic snapshot of much broader impacts. Intangible costs to societies as a whole – such as physical and psychological sufferings, reduced quality of individual and family lives, and loss of lives (Goh et al., 2015, 2016) attributed to occupational stressors, and violation of right to work in just and favorable conditions and right to have adequate living for the health and well-being of workers and their family (United Nations, 1948) – are often not adequately estimated. Thus, keep in mind that estimated economic costs of organizational stressors are likely grossly underestimated.

Productivity losses, manifested as sickness absenteeism, turnover, and presenteeism, etc., are one of the key outcomes while investigating adverse impacts of occupational stressors at the macro level. For example, based on 1513 participants of a Swiss workforce two-wave survey, Brunner et al. (2019) found associations between occupational stressors and productivity losses due to sickness absenteeism and presenteeism. Their results revealed that occupational stressors accounts for 23.8% of the total health-related production losses. The losses correspond to 195 Swiss francs per worker each month, or 3.2% of the average monthly earnings in Switzerland.

Kline and Lewis (2019) focused on one type of occupational stressor, bullying and harassment, and estimated its related cost from staff in the National Health Service (NHS), which is responsible for health care delivery in England. The total estimated cost attributed to bullying and harassment is £2.281 billion annually, of which sickness absenteeism costs £483.6 million, turnover costs £231.9 million, productivity loss costs £575.7 million, presenteeism costs £604.4 million, and compensation and litigation cost £83.5 million.

To inform the Australian Human Rights Commission's national inquiry into sexual harassment in Australian workplaces, Deloitte Access Economics (2019) estimated cost of workplace sexual harassment in 2018 to be $3.5 billion, of which productivity losses account for $2.6 billion. Among those $2.6 billion, 70% of the cost is lost by organizations, 23% of the cost is tax revenue loss, and 7% of the cost accounts for income loss of employees.

Discrimination at work is a major occupational stressor (Mays et al., 1996) experienced by disadvantaged social groups. In 2019, a total of 72,675 charges of workplace discrimination were received by the Equal Employment Opportunity Commission in US, leading to $486 million in monetary relief for victims of discrimination (US Equal Employment Opportunity Commission, 2020a). The economic cost of workplace discrimination to the UK economy is estimated at £127 billion every year, of which £123 billion is due to gender discrimination; £2.6 billion to discrimination against ethnic minorities; and £2 billion to discrimination against sexual orientation (Centre for Economic and Business Research, 2018).

Depression has been shown to be related to productivity loss, sickness absenteeism, and presenteeism (Bonde, 2008). To estimate the economic cost of work-related depression, Cocker et al. (2017) first estimated 13.2% (men) and 17.2% (women) of depression cases were attributed to job strain (i.e., high job demands and low job control) based on Australian population data. After that, they conducted a Markov modeling to simulate the economic benefits of removing job strain-related depression. Estimated average benefit to eliminate depression attributed to job strain in Australia is $730 million in one year, with a confidence level ranging from $425 million to $882 million; and $11.8 billion over a lifetime, with a confidence level ranging from $6.9 billion to $14.3 billion.

Now we switch to a systematic review (Hassard et al., 2018a) that estimates annual cost of work stress, adjusted in 2014-valued US dollars, based on 15 cost-of-illness studies conducted in eight countries. Because different outcome criteria and approaches were used by each of 15 studies, annual estimated cost of occupational stress substantially varied within as well as across countries: Australia ($0.22 to $3.98 billion; cost per worker: $17.79 to $320.14), Canada ($2.59 to $9.59 billion; $131.31 and $486.33), Denmark ($0.379 to $2.27 billion; $130.07 to $777.26), France ($1.83 to $4.36 billion; $60.95 to $145.03), Sweden ($703.12 million; $136.71), Switzerland ($3.33 billion; $701.14), United Kingdom ($2.18 billion to 23.63 billion; $66.35 to $716.58), and the United States ($187 billion; $1211.84). Overall, the annual estimated cost of work-related stressful experience at a national level ranged from $221.13 million to $187 billion, of which productivity loss accounts for 70–90% and health care cost accounts for 10–30%.

There are a few comparative evaluation studies that focus on a specific type of occupational stressor. For example, Hassard et al. (2018b) estimated annual costs attributed to psychosocial workplace aggression at a national level. Workplace aggression is defined as interpersonal and harmful behaviors such as bullying, mobbing, harassment, interpersonal conflict, discrimination, incivility, abusive supervision, or mistreatment. Based on 12 studies conducted in five nations – Australia, Italy, Spain, the United Kingdom (UK), and the United States (US) – the authors estimated the annual costs attributed to psychosocial workplace aggression ranged between $114.64 million and $35.9 billion across the five countries, adjusted to 2014 US dollar rates. Similarly, Hassard et al. (2019) estimated costs attributed to work-related violence (behaviors that are physical in nature such as homicide or assault) in the US (nine studies) and UK (one study). The annual estimated costs attributed to work violence, primarily in the US, varies from $2.36 million to $55.86 billion, adjusted to 2017 US dollar rates.

Impacts in Terms of Health Outcomes

In this section, we focus on epidemiological evidence in relation to health consequences of occupational stressors. Goh et al. (2015) meta-analyzed 228 studies reporting relationships of occupational stressors (i.e., low job control, job insecurity, unemployment, job demand, organizational injustice, low social support at work, work–family conflict, long work hours, and shift work) with four health outcomes (morbidity or physician-diagnosed medical conditions, mortality, perceived poor physical health, and perceived poor mental health). They found that unemployment and low job control were significantly related to all of the health outcomes. In addition, all of the occupational stressors, except for work–family conflict, were significantly associated with morbidity.

To meaningfully interpret the above relationships, Goh et al. (2015) used the odds ratio of secondhand smoking for the above four health outcomes as a frame of reference (i.e., 1.3 for morbidity, 1.15 for mortality, 1.47 for perceived poor physical health, 1.49 for perceived poor mental health, respectively). Tobacco is one of the health indicators in Health People 2020 (US Department of Health and Human Services, 2020). Regarding morbidity, it was found that organizational injustice, job demands, shift work, and unemployment exhibited stronger effects than secondhand smoking. Similarly, low job control, unemployment, long work hours, and work–family conflict exhibited stronger effects on mortality than secondhand smoking; work–family conflict, unemployment, and job insecurity showed stronger effects on poor physical health than secondhand smoking; and work–family conflict, unemployment, job demands, and organizational injustice showed stronger effects on poor mental health than secondhand smoking.

Goh et al. (2016) further estimated mortality and health care cost attributed to an absence of health insurance and the occupational stressors described in the previous section. Based on their conservative estimates, there are more than 120,000 deaths and more than $110 billion spent in health care per year in the United States. Lately, Goh et al. (2019) estimated 17,000 preventable deaths each year attributed to occupational stressors in the United States. They also estimated $44 billion in preventable health care costs each year attributed to occupational stressors in the United States. This cost is much higher than the annual direct/indirect health care cost, $10 billion, of second-hand smoke.

Suicide Attributed to Unemployment

Chen and Stallones (2011) have argued that self-inflicted fatality, or suicide, is a hidden occupational fatality for three reasons. According to the US Bureau of Labor Statistics, BLS (2019b), suicide is included in the BLS Census of Fatal Occupational Injuries if (1) the suicide occurred on the work premises, or (2) the suicide occurred off the work premises but can be definitively linked back to work. However, about 75% of suicides occur in a house or apartment, followed by natural areas, streets or highways, or in motor vehicles (Colorado Department of Public Health and Environment, 2007). Of 5,333 occupational fatalities in 2019, furthermore, there are only 12 fatalities coded as suicide. In addition, suicide has been a major public health concern and was ranked 2, 4, and 8 among the top 10 leading causes of death in 2018 for working age groups 25–34, 35–54, and 55–64, respectively, in the United States (US National Institute of Mental Health, 2020). Finally, suicide rates tend to be disproportionately higher in some industries than those in the general population (see Chen & Stallones, 2011).

Unemployment has been shown to be associated with suicide. Loss of employment is a major stressful work and life event which has shown detrimental impacts on the physical and psychological well-being of workers and their families (McKee-Ryan et al., 2005; Paul & Moser, 2009). Nordt et al. (2015) tracked trends of suicide and unemployment between 2000 and 2011 in 63 countries across the Americas, Europe, Africa, and Asia and found an increase in suicide rate approximately six months after a rise in unemployment. They further estimated around 45,000 out of 233,000 suicides per year are likely related to loss of employment. Similarly, a study of suicide rate and business cycle from 1928 to 2007 in the US reveals that suicide rates generally rise during recessions (Luo et al., 2011). Similar results were reported in Japan and European countries (Breuer, 2015).

Legislations Related to Occupational Stressors across Nations

In this section, we survey a sample of legislation that addresses some of the occupational stressors across nations with diverse geopolitical backgrounds and cultures, including Australia, Canada, China, France, Germany, Russia, Singapore, Slovakia, South Africa, South Korea, the United Kingdom, and the United States. The countries reviewed in the following sections have been selected approximately based on three inclusion criteria: (1) we chose one or two countries from each continent/ geopolitical region, (2) we balanced both common laws and civil laws, and (3) we focused on countries with the latest legislation related to the occupational stressors reviewed below.

We will first briefly discuss workers' compensation legislation, although occupational stressors were not clearly defined. Workers' compensation legislation is closely related to occupational safety and health issues such as mental stress caused by injury, traumatic events, or occupational disease (Barth, 1990) and has been addressed by legislation such as the Health and Safety at Work Act 1974 (UK), Occupational Health and Safety Act 1979 (Canada), Occupational Health and Safety Act 1984 (Australia), or Occupational Safety and Health Act 1970 (USA).

After that, we review work-related legislation specifically addressing age discrimination, racial discrimination, sex discrimination, sexual harassment, and workplace bullying. The late Ronald J. Burke (2019) identified bullying, incivility, and discrimination at work as key organizational characteristics associated with unhealthy workplaces.

Workers' Compensation Legislation

Workers' compensation legislation usually does not define occupational stress or specific occupational stressors because occupational stress is not a medical condition, even though it may be a cause or trigger of a medical condition. Occupational health and safety legislation in the United Kingdom, Canada, Denmark, and Australia places general duties upon all employers to ensure the health, safety, and welfare at work of all employees as long as it is reasonably practical. In Denmark, under the law on occupational safety and health (The Danish Working Environment Act), employers bear responsibility for workers not being exposed to any form of strain/harassment/

discrimination at work. Typically, a workers' compensation claim requires workers to establish that they have suffered from an "injury," including illness, disease, and/or body injuries.

Claims in which a worker has suffered a recognized injury or disease caused by a work-related stressor are generally referred to by practicing lawyers as "mental stress" or "work-related stress" claims. For instance, in a decision of the High Court of Australia in *Koehler v Cerebos (Australia) Ltd.* (2005), the employee's psychiatric injury was held not to have been foreseeable by the employer. Whilst Mrs. Koehler had frequently complained about her workload, it was found that her complaints were all "...directed to whether the work could be done; [and] none [of the complaints] suggested that the difficulties she was experiencing were affecting her health." Given that the employee's psychiatric injury was not foreseeable by the employer, there could be no duty of care (and, thus, no damages awarded). The High Court found that Mrs. Koehler had "voluntarily" accepted the position as a part-time merchandiser and by doing so had agreed to perform the duties that she later complained of as excessive. This decision therefore reflects a judicial view that employees and employers are free to contract as they agree about the work one party will do for the other party.

Age Discrimination Legislation

Over 50 countries have similar legislation for age discrimination (Lewis Silkin LLP, 2020). A sample of age discrimination legislation is described in Table 2.1. The US Age Discrimination in Employment Act 1967 (amended in 1974 and 1978) aims to promote employment decisions based on employees' or job applicants' qualifications rather than age, and age is specifically defined as 40 or older. Yet, the Act does not protect workers under the age of 40, although some states have laws that protect younger workers from age discrimination.

In contrast, other age discrimination legislation, such as the UK Equality Act 2010 or the Slovakia Labour Code & Antidiscrimination Act, emphasizes fair treatments regardless of age. In *Hendrick v. Hercules, Inc.* (1981), a reorganizational planning committee in Hercules determined that Hendrick did not possess the necessary qualifications for the new position, and he was terminated in April 1978 because his position as Plant Manager had been eliminated. Hedrick testified that Director of Operations in Hercules told him that

Table 2.1 *Age discrimination legislation*

Age discrimination legislation	Definition
UK (Equality Act 2010)	Direct discrimination happens when employers treat persons worse than another in a similar situation because of age. Indirect discrimination happens when an organization has a particular policy or way of working that applies to everyone but which puts people of an age group at a disadvantage.
US (Age Discrimination in Employment Act 1967)	The Act forbids age discrimination against people who are age 40 or older. The law prohibits discrimination in any aspect of employment, including hiring, firing, pay, job assignments, promotions, layoff, training, benefits, and any other term or condition of employment. However, it does not protect workers under the age of 40, although some states have laws that protect younger workers from age discrimination. It is not illegal for an employer or other covered entity to favor an older worker over a younger one, even if both workers are age 40 or older. Discrimination can occur when the victim and the person who inflicted the discrimination are both over 40.
Australia (Age Discrimination Act 2004)	Direct discrimination occurs when someone treats, or proposes to treat, the aggrieved person less favorably than it treats, or would treat, a person of a different age under circumstances that are the same or materially the same, if the discriminator does so because of the aggrieved person's age or a characteristic that appertains or is generally imputed to a person of that age. Indirect discrimination occurs when someone discriminates against the aggrieved person on the group of their age by: (a) imposing or proposing to impose a condition, requirement or practice; (b) the condition, requirement or practice is not reasonable; and (c) the condition, requirement or practice has or is likely to have the effect of disadvantaging persons of that age.

Table 2.1 (*cont.*)

Age discrimination legislation	Definition
Germany (General Equal Treatment Act 2006)	Direct discrimination arises when an individual is treated less favorably than another individual in a comparable situation. Indirect discrimination concerns apparently neutral measures, criteria or practices which may appear neutral but may confer a disadvantage on an individual compared to others, unless these measures, criteria or practices can be objectively justified by a legitimate purpose and if the means used to achieve that purpose are necessary and appropriate. Note. Soldiers are not protected by the Act, but by a separate Equal Treatment Act which does not protect them against age discrimination.
France (Labour Code & Criminal Code)	Direct discrimination arises when an individual is treated less favorably than another individual in a comparable situation. Indirect discrimination concerns apparently neutral measures, criteria or practices which may appear neutral but may confer a disadvantage on an individual compared to others, unless these measures, criteria or practices can be objectively justified by a legitimate purpose and if the means used to achieve that purpose are necessary and appropriate.
Slovakia (Labour Code & Antidiscrimination Act)	Conditions considered as discrimination are: (a) a minimum or maximum age limit as a condition for access to employment; (b) special conditions for access to employment or vocational training and special conditions for work performance, including remuneration and dismissal, if it concerns persons of a certain age category and if the aim of these special conditions is to support the incorporation of such persons in the workforce or their protection; (c) minimum age conditions, professional experience, or a specified number of years worked for access to employment or to certain advantages in

Table 2.1 (*cont.*)

Age discrimination legislation	Definition
	employment; (d) stipulating different age concerning entitlements in retirement or disability pension schemes for employees or groups of employees; and (e) use of a different calculation for pension allowances depending on the age.
Russia (Labour Code, Retirement Age Increased and Age Discrimination Law & Criminal Act)	Certain age-based variations in employment conditions, limitations, preferences, etc. are established by the Labour Code or other federal laws in view of the job requirements and workplace conditions.

"Hercules was going to get rid of the good 'ole Joes and get some younger folks in." The court awarded Hedrick $52,887 for wage losses and $26,443.50 in liquidated damages.

A significant ruling highlights that EU member states (i.e., Germany in this case) and EU legislation were challenged when an organization failed to comply with the general principle of equal treatment. In *Mangold v. Helm* (2005), Mangold was a 56-year-old German man employed on a fixed term contract in a permanent full-time job. According to Sec. 14 para. 3 of the German Part-Time Work and Fixed-Term Employment Contracts Act, no objective reason is necessary to enter into an employment contract of limited duration if the employee has reached the age of 52. Mangold claimed that the lack of protection, over age 52, was age discrimination. The European Court of Justice sided with Mangold and held this provision as violating the Employment Equality Framework (Directive 2000/78/EC). Specifically, the European Court of Justice ruled that

Community law and, more particularly, Article 6(1) of Council Directive 2000/78/EC of 27 November 2000 establishing a general framework for equal treatment in employment and occupation must be interpreted as precluding a provision of domestic law such as that at issue in the main proceedings which authorizes, without restriction, unless there is a close connection with an earlier contract of employment of indefinite duration concluded with the same employer, the conclusion of fixed-term contracts of employment once the worker has reached the age of 52. It is the responsibility of the national court to guarantee the full effectiveness of the general principle of non-discrimination in respect of age, setting aside any provision of national law which may conflict with Community law, even where the period prescribed for transposition of that directive has not yet expired.

Racial Discrimination Legislation

Over 169 countries have developed legislation for elimination of discrimination (racial/gender) to meet the standards set in Conventions of International Labour Organization (Fredman, 2012).

Title VII in the US Civil Right Act 1964 promotes equal employment opportunity and prohibits employment discrimination based on race, color, religion, sex, or national origin. In very narrowly defined situations, an employer is permitted to discriminate based on a reasonably needed trait that is a bona fide occupational qualification such certain knowledge, skills, and abilities needed to perform a job. Prior to 1972, Title VII lacked any strong enforcement provisions. After the US Congress passed the Equal Employment Opportunity Act 1972, the Act amended Title VII and gave Equal Employment Opportunity Commission (EEOC) authority to initiate its own enforcement litigation.

A landmark case, *Griggs v. Duke Power Co* (1971), argued before the US Supreme Court, has been considered the first employment discrimination case based on race. The Supreme Court ruled, under Title VII of the Civil Rights Act 1964, that Duke Power Co's employment requirements (high school diploma, Bennett Mechanical Comprehension Test, and Wonderlic Cognitive Ability Test) not only showed disparate treatment of black employees but also that these did not pertain to applicants' ability to perform the job. Thus, employment requirements unintentionally discriminate against black employees.

In contrast to other countries' legislation, described in Table 2.2, the Australian Parliament passed an Act that specifically addressed racial discrimination, the Racial Discrimination Act 1975. The Act prohibits treating someone less fairly than someone else in a similar situation because of his/her race, color, descent, or national or ethnic origin. The Act covers areas including employment, land, housing or accommodation, provision of goods and services, access to places and facilities for use by the public, advertising, or joining a trade union. In *Bligh and*

Table 2.2 *Racial discrimination legislation*

Racial discrimination legislation	Definition
UK (Equality Act 2010)	Direct discrimination happens when someone treats a person worse than another in a similar situation because of race. Indirect discrimination happens when an organization has a particular policy or way of working that puts people of their racial group at a disadvantage.
US (Civil Rights Act 1964, amended in 1991)	Race discrimination involves treating someone (an applicant or employee) unfavorably because he/she is of a certain race or because of personal characteristics associated with race (such as hair texture, skin color, or certain facial features). Color discrimination involves treating someone unfavorably because of skin color complexion. Race discrimination also can involve treating someone unfavorably because the person is married to (or associated with) a person of a certain race or color.
Australia (Racial Discrimination Act 1975, amended in 2013)	It is unlawful for a person to do any act involving a distinction, exclusion, restriction or preference based on race, color, descent or national or ethnic origin which has the purpose or effect of nullifying or impairing the recognition, enjoyment or exercise, on an equal footing, of any human right or fundamental freedom in the political, economic, social, cultural or any other field of public life.
France (Labour Code & Criminal Code)	Direct discrimination is a situation where one person is treated less favorably than another is, has been or would be treated in a comparable situation on grounds of racial or ethnic origin. Indirect discrimination occurs where an apparently neutral provision, criterion or practice would put persons of a racial or ethnic origin at a particular disadvantage when compared with other persons, unless that provision, criterion or practice is objectively justified by a legitimate aim and the means of achieving that aim are appropriate and necessary.

Table 2.2 (*cont.*)

Racial discrimination legislation	Definition
Germany (Antidiscrimination Law (Berlin), 2020)	The law explicitly bars public authorities – including police and public schools – from discriminating based on skin color and race. People can also not be discriminated against based on a lack of German language skills.
Singapore (Article 12, Constitution of the Republic of Singapore)	There shall be no discrimination against citizens of Singapore on the grounds only of religion, race, descent or place of birth in any law or in the appointment to any office or employment under a public authority or in the administration of any law relating to the acquisition, holding or disposition of property or the establishing or carrying on of any trade, business, profession, vocation or employment.
South Africa (Section 7 of the Constitution)	No person may unfairly discriminate against any person on the ground of race, including the exclusion of persons of a particular race group under any rule or practice that appears to be legitimate but which is actually aimed at maintaining exclusive control by a particular race group; and the provision or continued provision of inferior services to any racial group, compared to those of another racial group.

Ors v. State of Queensland (1996), the Australian Human Rights Commission found past Aboriginal employees were underpaid by the Queensland Government, and A\$7,000 was awarded to each plaintiff.

Although a definition of racial discrimination is absent from German General Equal Treatment Act, Berlin passed the first German state antidiscrimination law on June 4, 2020. This is the first antidiscrimination law to include discrimination factors of race, skin color, and German language skill.

Racial discrimination in employment is prohibited in Article 12 of the Constitution of the Republic of Singapore:

Except as expressly authorised by this Constitution, there shall be no discrimination against citizens of Singapore on the ground only of religion, race, descent or place of birth in any law or in the appointment to any office or employment under a public authority or in the administration of any law relating to the acquisition, holding or disposition of property or the establishing or carrying on of any trade, business, profession, vocation or employment.

Similarly, racial discrimination is prohibited in Section 7 of the Constitution of South Africa.

Sex Discrimination Legislation

Title VII in the US Civil Rights Act promotes equal employment opportunity and prohibits employment discrimination based on race, color, religion, sex, or national origin. In *United Automobile Workers v. Johnson Controls, Inc.* (1991), the US Supreme Court ruled that Johnson Controls' policy to exclude women with childbearing capacity from lead-exposed jobs explicitly discriminated against women based on their sex. In contrast to other countries' legislation, described in Table 2.3, the Australian Parliament passed an Act that specifically addressed sex discrimination, the Sex Discrimination Act 1984.

In section 12, the Constitution of the Republic of Singapore defined that discrimination against women (only for discriminatory behaviors against women) shall

mean any distinction, exclusion or restriction made on the basis of sex which has the effect or purpose of impairing or nullifying the recognition, enjoyment or exercise by women, irrespective of their marital status, on a basis or equality of men and women, of human rights and fundamental freedoms in the political, economic, social, cultural, civil or any other field.

In France, any discrimination is considered as a criminal issue. Under the Criminal Code, where a legal entity has been found to have discriminated against an employee, it may be liable to a fine of €225,000 and possibly some additional sanctions such as the dissolution of the legal entity, the publication of the judgment, the ban of the exercise of a determined professional activity, or the closure of the company's entities.

Table 2.3 *Sex discrimination legislation*

Sex discrimination legislation	Definition
UK (Equality Act 2010)	Direct discrimination happens when, because of sex, people treat someone worse than another of the opposite sex who is in a similar situation. Indirect discrimination happens when an organization has a particular policy or way of working that applies in the same way to both sexes but which puts a person at a disadvantage because of sex.
US (Civil Rights Act 1964)	Sex discrimination involves treating someone (an applicant or employee) unfavorably because of that person's sex. Discrimination against an individual because of gender identity, including transgender status, or because of sexual orientation is discrimination because of sex.
Australia (Sex Discrimination Act 1984)	It is unlawful for an employer to discriminate against a person on the ground of the person's sex, sexual orientation, gender identity, intersex status, marital or relationship status, pregnancy or potential pregnancy, breastfeeding or family responsibilities: (a) in the arrangements made for the purpose of determining who should be offered employment; (b) in determining who should be offered employment; or (c) in the terms or conditions on which employment is offered.
Germany (General Equal Treatment Act 2006)	Direct discrimination shall be taken to occur where one person is treated less favorably than another is, has been or would be treated in a comparable situation on any of the grounds. Indirect discrimination shall be taken to occur where an apparently neutral provision, criterion or practice would put persons at a particular disadvantage compared with other persons on any of the grounds.
France (Labor Code & Criminal Code)	Direct discrimination is a situation where one person is treated less favorably than another is, has been or would be treated in a comparable situation on grounds of gender. Indirect discrimination occurs where an apparently neutral provision, criterion or practice would put persons of a gender origin at a particular disadvantage when compared with other

Table 2.3 (*cont.*)

Sex discrimination legislation	Definition
	persons, unless that provision, criterion or practice is objectively justified by a legitimate aim and the means of achieving that aim are appropriate and necessary.
Singapore (Section 12 (1) (2) Constitution of the Republic of Singapore)	Discrimination against women shall mean any distinction, exclusion or restriction made on the basis of sex which has the effect or purpose of impairing or nullifying the recognition, enjoyment or exercise by women, irrespective of their marital status, on a basis or equality of men and women, of human rights and fundamental freedoms in the political, economic, social, cultural, civil or any other field.

Sexual Harassment Legislation

In 2020, there are 140 countries with similar legislation for preventing and redressing sexual harassment (Arekapudi & Recavarren, 2020). According to Quick and McFadyen (2017), there is no universal legal definition of sexual harassment, although most definitions contain description of unwanted or unwelcome conduct that intimidates and humiliates victims, as shown in Table 2.4. US EEOC (2020b) defined sexual harassment as "unwelcome sexual advances, requests for sexual favors, and other verbal or physical harassment of a sexual nature." Sexual harassment can include offensive remarks about a person's sex; even harassment does not have to be a sexual nature. Furthermore, both victim and the harasser can be either a woman or a man, and the victim and harasser can also be the same sex. The US Supreme Court and federal courts support coverage of LGBT-related discrimination under Title VII of the Civil Rights Act (US EEOC, 2020c).

In Quick and McFadyen's (2017) review, concerns about sexual harassment worldwide have also been addressed by the International Labor Organization, the International Confederation of Free Trade Unions, the European Union, and the United Nations Committee on the Elimination of Discrimination Against Women.

Table 2.4 *Sexual harassment legislation*

Sexual harassment legislation	Definition
UK (Equality Act 2010)	Sexual harassment is unwanted behavior of a sexual nature which: (a) violates your dignity; (b) makes you feel intimidated, degraded or humiliated; or (c) creates a hostile or offensive environment.
US (section 703 of Title VII, Civil Right Act, 1964)	Harassment on the basis of sex is unwelcome sexual advances, requests for sexual favors, and other verbal or physical conduct of a sexual nature, which constitute sexual harassment when (1) submission to such conduct is made either explicitly or implicitly a term or condition of an individual's employment, (2) submission to or rejection of such conduct by an individual is used as the basis for employment decisions affecting such individual, or (3) such conduct has the purpose or effect of unreasonably interfering with an individual's work performance or creating an intimidating, hostile, or offensive working environment.
Australia (Sex Discrimination Act 1984)	A person sexually harasses another person (the person harassed) if: (a) the person makes an unwelcome sexual advance, or an unwelcome request for sexual favors, to the person harassed; or (b) engages in other unwelcome conduct of a sexual nature in relation to the person harassed.
Germany (Act to establish equality for men and women)	Sexual harassment includes unwanted physical contact, leering, lewd looks, sexual comments, sexist jokes or the displaying of pornographic material. A single action may constitute sexual harassment.
France (Labor Code & Criminal Code)	Sexual harassment includes repeated acts or conduct with a sexual connotation that either violate the dignity of the employee because of its degrading or humiliating nature or create an intimidating, hostile, or offensive situation against him/her. It also includes the act of

Table 2.4 (*cont.*)

Sexual harassment legislation	Definition
	exerting any form of serious pressure, even if not repeated, for the real or apparent purpose of obtaining an act of a sexual nature, whether it is sought for the benefit of the perpetrator or for the benefit of a third party.
China (Civil Act 2020)	Unwelcome behavior from a person against another by sexual language or actions or by sexual advances against a subordinate.

Similar to sexual discrimination legislation in France, sexual harassment is considered a criminal issue, and a legal entity may be liable to a fine of €225,000 and some additional sanctions, as described earlier. In contrast to other countries, the Australian court considers sexual harassment (covered under the Sex Discrimination Act 1984) in a much broader context, including social functions, work conferences, work-related trips, etc. In *South Pacific Resort Hotels Pty Ltd v. Trainor* (2005), the Full Court of the Federal Court of Brisbane confirmed that the conduct of a hotel worker constituted sexual harassment, despite the conduct occurring after hours. The case involved island hotel workers, residing in accommodation provided by the employer, at which no visitors were permitted to enter. A coworker entered a colleague's bedroom uninvited on two occasions, while both employees were off duty. The Full Court held that the sexual harassment took place because of their common employment and subsequent accommodation and that it could not be said that the common employment was "unrelated or merely incidental to the sexual harassment of one by the other." Ms. Trainor was awarded $5,000 in general damages and $7,500 in past and future economic loss.

Workplace Bullying Legislation

Finally, workplace bullying is a persistent pattern of mistreatment from others in the workplace that causes either physical or emotional harm.

Currently, Cobb (2017) has reviewed workplace bullying legislation from 50 countries across Europe, the Asia Pacific region, the Americas, and the Middle East and Africa. Comprehensive workplace bullying legislation in the United States has not been passed by the federal government, although some state legislatures have considered bills related to workplace bullying, such as Nevada, New York, Washington, Illinois, etc.

In the United Kingdom, although bullying is not specifically mentioned in workplace legislation, there are means such as the Protection From Harassment Act 1997 to obtain legal redress for bullying. Workplace bullying, or an employer tolerating bullying, is typically viewed as breaching contractual terms in the United Kingdom. Parties to the employment contract have a (legal) duty of trust and confidence to each other. Such a breach creates circumstances entitling an employee to terminate his or her contract of employment without notice, and an Employment Tribunal considers the termination as an unfair dismissal. An employee bullied in response to asserting a statutory right can be compensated for the damage under Part V of the Employment Rights Act 1996, and if dismissed, Part X of the same Act provides that the dismissal is automatically unfair. In *Majrowski v. Guy's and St Thomas's NHS Trust* (2006), William Majrowski (M) was formerly employed by St Thomas's NHS Trust (D). M claimed that he had been bullied by his manager (L), which M claimed amounted to harassment under the Protection From Harassment Act 1997. It was held that D was vicariously liable for the offense committed by L. D appealed and the appeal was dismissed for the reason of breaching contract.

In Canada, under the Ontario Occupational Health and Safety Act 1979, all employers should take precaution to protect their workers in reasonable circumstances. In 2007, Ontario passed a new bill (Bill-29), which made an amendment to the Ontario Occupational Health and Safety Act. Bill-29 proposed that employees should be protected from harassment and violence in the workplace. In addition, protection for employees will include psychological abuse and bullying behaviors. Moreover, the Province of Quebec passed legislation addressing workplace bullying in 2004. Summaries of workplace bullying legislation are shown in Table 2.5.

Table 2.5 *Workplace bullying legislations*

Sexual harassment legislation	Definition
UK (Protection from Harassment Act 1997)	Bullying and harassment is behavior that makes someone feel intimidated or offended.
Canada (Occupational Health and Safety Act 1979)	The attempted or actual exercise of any intentional physical force that causes or may cause physical injury to a worker. It also includes any threats which give a worker reasonable grounds to believe he or she is at risk of physical injury.
Australia (Fair Work Act 2009)	A worker is bullied at work if: (a) while the worker is at work in a constitutionally covered business: (i) an individual; or (ii) a group of individuals; repeatedly behaves unreasonably towards the worker, or a group of workers of which the worker is a member; and (b) that behavior creates a risk to health and safety.
South Korea (Labor Standards Act)	An act of an employer (or business owner) or employee (or worker) that causes physical or mental suffering or worsens the working environment of another employee/worker by taking advantage of his/her status or relationship within the workplace beyond the appropriate scope of work.

Conclusions

Our review shows that workers continue reporting stressful experiences at work. During the 1970s, about one-fourth to one-third of Swedish workers reported their job as often "stressful" or moderate to high levels of "stress" at work (cited in Sauter et al., 1990). By the 1990s, there were about 40% of respondents (Northwestern National Life Insurance Company, 1991) who considered their job as being very or extremely stressful. In the twenty-first century, American Psychological Association (2019) reported about 60% of employees perceiving their work as a major source of stress.

Work-related stress was considered as a national health problem in a national strategy proposed by the US National Institute for Occupational Safety and Health (Sauter et al., 1990). Our review shows occupational stress remains a major concern raised by labor experts of 54 countries (International Labour Organization, 2016) and the European Agency for Safety and Health at Work (EU-OSHA, 2018).

Adverse impacts of occupational stressors on individuals and families have been consistently reported in the literature of occupational health psychology (see the 2017 special issue of *Journal of Occupational Health Psychology*). Reports about negative consequences of occupational stressors on organizations, societies, and nations have also been documented (e.g., EU-OSH, 2014; Ganster et al., 2001; Matrix, 2012). Our review shows continuing research examining adverse impacts at macro levels (e.g., Goh et al., 2015, 2016, 2019; Hassard et al., 2018a, 2018b, 2019) and these impacts, such as loss of organizational productivity, government tax revenue, workers' income and health, as well as mortality, have been staggering over years (e.g., EU-OSHA, 2009 vs. EU-OSHA 2014).

Our survey of legislation related to specific occupational stressors reflects a growing awareness as well as an indisputable testimony regarding adverse impacts of occupational stressors on people's lives. A recent example is Japan's Work Style Reform Bill, passed in 2018, which addresses Japan's extreme overwork culture that led to Karoshi (death from overwork).

There is no definitive data to show that an increase of workplace protection legislation such as antidiscrimination or sexual harassment is associated with a decrease of economic impact attributable to occupational stressors. However, one may infer beneficial effects resulting from workplace protection legislation (US CDC, 1999) For instance, US workplace fatalities have significantly fallen since OSHA was enacted, from 14,000 (38 worker deaths a day) in 1970 to 5,333 in 2019 (15 worker deaths a day) (US Department of Labor, 2021).

While comparing the United States with similar European counterparts regarding impacts of occupational stressors, Goh et al. (2019) found that if the United States had similar workplace protection policies implemented by European counterparts, it would have reduced about $40 billion on health care cost attributed to occupational stressors. Their findings highlighted the critical role of workplace protection legislation and policies in reducing health tolls.

However, it should be emphasized that complaints of violating workplace protection legislation and policies continue. For instance, we have witnessed a series of sexual harassment cases since the 2016 Me Too movement, including cases like Roger Ailes and Bill O'Reilly at Fox News, Charlie Rose at PBS and Bloomberg, Matt Lauer at NBC, the Royal Canadian Mounted Police, and the US Army Fort Hood. Regarding broad psychosocial risks at work, Leka et al. (2015) evaluated 34 EU regulatory policies related to mental health or psychosocial risks at work. Based on a rating from 0 (not covered or no reference to) to 5 (comprehensive coverage) used to assess five dimensions (e.g., coverage of exposure factors in relation to mental health in the workplace, coverage of mental health problems/ disorders at work, or coverage of risk assessment aspects in relation to mental health in the workplace), Leka et al. scored 23 (68%) regulatory policies 5 or less out of a maximum of 25, and the highest score was only 13. Their result indicated these regulatory policies generally lacked coverage, specificity, and assessment in relation to psychosocial risks at work.

Considering the prevalence and severity of occupational stress, our fifth observation includes increases of occupational stress research, more journals devoted to occupational stress research, and advancement in occupational stress interventions. For instance, Bliese et al. (2017) tracked occupational stress research published from 1917 to 2017 in the *Journal of Applied Psychology* and documented an increase from a 50-year period between 1917 and 1966 (173 articles), a 30-year period between 1967 and 1996 (213 articles), to a 20-year period between 1997 and 2017 (220 articles). Since *Work & Stress* was established in 1987, the *Journal of Occupational Health Psychology*, *International Journal of Stress Management*, and *Occupational Health Science* have been subsequently established, in 1997, 2003, and 2017, respectively. Furthermore, evidence-based interventions to combat adverse impact of occupational stressors have gradually increased (e.g., Bakker & van Wingerden, in press; Bambra et al., 2009; Bartlett et al., 2019; Beehr, 2019; Brady et al., in press; Falon et al., in press; Gonzalez-Morales et al., 2018; LaMontagne et al., 2007; Odle-Dusseau et al., 2016; Richardson & Rothstein, 2008).

In sum, the progress described above has clearly documented the prevalence and severity of occupational stressors and has established evidence of linking occupational stressors with morbidity, mortality, and economic costs borne out of individuals, families, organizations, and nations. The progress also highlights that occupational stress remains a major health concern around the globe, as well as a research focus among journals in economics, law, management, medicine, policy, psychology, public health, and safety science. Furthermore, a growing awareness of occupational stress is highlighted by a variety of legislation and regulatory policies. Considering these significant progresses and advancements, where shall we go from here?

Look Forward

We conclude our review by emphasizing preventive strategies applicable to workers, organizations, and nations. First, there have been more stress management interventions designed to reduce stress symptoms. These interventions, such as mindfulness training, cognitive-behavioral intervention, relaxation, personal resources training, or resilience-strengthening intervention, have generally shown expected outcomes (Bakker & van Wingerden, in press; Bartlett et al., 2019; Beehr, 2019; Falon et al., in press). In contrast, there are relatively fewer stress management interventions designed to modify occupational stressors (e.g., reducing abusive supervision; Gonzalez-Morales et al., 2018), increase support (e.g., family-supportive supervisor behaviors, Odle-Dusseau et al., 2016; supervisor support behaviors, Brady et al., in press), or modify work contexts (e.g., increasing employee control through task restructuring, Bambra et al., 2009). Whatever the foci are, these evidence-based interventions tend to be highly intensive (i.e., time demands, high cost, required expertise). As a result, implementing a stress management intervention with high intensity, which is typically found in academic journals, is unlikely to align well with daily operations in organizations. It would also be a challenge for workers to sustain practicing individual-focused stress management interventions.

We argued that future intervention research shall not only ask "how does it work" and "does it work" but also answer "does it work with minimal intensity?" (Glasgow & Emmons, 2007) or "does or can it work under real-world conditions?" (Glasgow et al., 2003). Understandably, the latter questions raise the bar for future intervention research. Yet, these questions are indispensable to substantially advance occupational stress research and practices. Answers to these questions are also needed considering that most businesses establishments are small (defined as fewer than 500 employees). For instance, 99.9% of US businesses are small businesses with an average of ten employees (US Small Business Administration, 2019). It is well known that small establishments tend not to manage occupational safety and health (OSH) well, and often show low level of compliance in relation to OSH regulations (EU-OSHA, 2018). It should be emphasized that even large establishments such as National Health Service England (Health Education England, 2019) acknowledge the difficulty of implementing interventions because OSH interventions tend to be costly and time consuming and require considerable commitments from management. This sentiment was also echoed by progressive executives (Pfeffer et al., 2020), described below.

Research has consistently shown that management commitment plays a vital role to manage safety and health concerns (EU-OSHA, 2018; Schall & Chen, in press). Pfeffer et al. (2020) interviewed executives from 20 progressive companies. Overall, these executives viewed themselves being responsible for well-being of employees and their families, and most of them viewed a healthy workplace as a means to gain profits. Similar to conventional view, they viewed occupational stressors as inevitable, a strong focus on productivity in business as imperative, and modifying sources of stress as unfeasible. These views highlight stiff challenges in future research and practice in managing or preventing stress. Kotter (1995), in a seminal essay, pointed out that most organizational change initiatives fail because management fails to develop a sense of urgency, or to communicate the urgency broadly with key constituencies. Without the sense of urgency shared by the majority of managers/supervisors and employees pertaining to prevalence and severity of occupational stressors, management teams are less likely to commit and prioritize resources to minimize psychosocial risks, are less likely to institutionalize preventive strategies as daily, routine operations, and are less inclined to create shared values and norms with regard to healthy workplaces. To advance preventive stress management in future research and practice, it is essential to connect the urgency with impacts of occupational stressors. We acknowledge that it is a challenging goal in stress management. Next, we shall also consider some "low hanging fruit."

Burke (2019) identified several organizational characteristics associated with unhealthy workplaces. These characteristics include toxic leadership, bullying, organizational politics that promote actors' interest, uncivil behaviors at work, and discrimination. With relatively inexpensive strategies, organizations can build psychologically healthy workplace by creating climates for fairness and civility with follow-through, actionable polices guided by legislation, and utilizing evidence-based HR tools to select, monitor, appraise, and develop managers, supervisors, and employees. Scientific advancements over the past century in recruitment, selection, leadership, performance management and appraisal, or development (see Kozlowski et al., 2017) offer invaluable insights that occupational stress research and practices can tag along.

Occupational stress research has continued identifying timely occupational stressors such as telepressure (Barber & Santuzzi, 2015) and illegitimate tasks (Sonnentag & Lischetzke, 2018). Of occupational stressors studied over the past century (Beehr & Newman, 1978; Bliese et al., 2017), some could be relatively easier to modify and use interventions such as those identified by the US NIOSH panel (Wiegand et al., 2012). Without utilizing many resources, organizations may gather surveillance data pertaining to these stressors. Accordingly, organizations can efficiently and effectively modify and intervene with these stressors.

Finally, governments should view occupational stress as a key public health concern. Goh et al. (2015) has shown that negative impacts of occupational stressors are worse than those of tobacco uses, a health indicator in Health People 2020 (US Department of Health and Human Services, 2020). Health People 2020 identified 26 health indicators – injury and violence, access to health services (e.g., health insurances), clinical preventive services to treat cardiovascular diseases, mental health (e.g., suicide and depression), substance abuse (e.g., drinking) – which have been linked to occupational stressors. Yet, key occupational stressors, leading indicators that are responsible for mental health and physical health, are not included in Health People 2020, nor in US public health surveillance systems. Similarly, Leka et al. (2015) concluded that risk assessments were often not covered in most EU regulatory policies. Should key occupational stressors be monitored nationally and globally, surveillance data regarding these stressors will be extremely helpful to guide regulatory and organizational policies and raise awareness of urgency among the public. After all, it is inconceivable to expect nations, organizations, and individuals to diligently manage what has not been measured!

References

American Psychological Association (2019). *Stress in America: Stress and current events. Stress in America™ survey.* www.apa.org/news/press/releases/stress/2019/stress-america-2019.pdf

    (2020). *Stress in America™ 2020: A national mental health crisis.* www.apa.org/news/press/releases/stress/2020/sia-mental-health-crisis.pdf

American Psychiatric Association (2013). *Diagnostic and statistical manual of mental disorders* (5th ed.). https://doi.org/10.1176/appi.books.9780890425596

Arekapudi, N., & Recavarren, I. S. (2020). Sexual harassment is serious business. *World Bank Blog.* https://blogs.worldbank.org/developmenttalk/sexual-harassment-serious-business

Bakker, A. B., & Van Wingerden, J. (in press). Do personal resources and strengths use increase work engagement? The effects of a training intervention. *Journal of Occupational Health Psychology.*

Bambra, C., Gibson, M., Sowden, A. J., Wright, K., Whitehead, M., & Petticrew, M. (2009). Working for health? Evidence from systematic reviews on the effects on health and health inequalities of organizational changes to the psychosocial work environment. *Preventive medicine, 48,* 454–461.

Barber, L. K., & Santuzzi, A. M. (2015). Please respond ASAP: Workplace telepressure and employee recovery. *Journal of Occupational Health Psychology, 20,* 172–189.

Barth, P. S. (1990). Workers' compensation for mental stress cases. *Behavioral Sciences and the Law, 8,* 349–360.

Bartlett, L., Martin, A., Neil, A. L., Memish, K., Otahal, P., Kilpatrick, M., & Sanderson, K. (2019). A systematic review and meta-analysis of workplace mindfulness training randomized controlled trials. *Journal of Occupational Health Psychology, 24,* 108–126.

Beehr, T. A. (2019). Interventions in occupational health psychology. *Journal of Occupational Health Psychology, 24,* 1–3.

Beehr, T. A., & Newman, J. E. (1978). Job stress, employee health, and organizational effectiveness: A facet analysis, model, and literature review. *Personnel Psychology, 31*, 665–699.

Bliese, P. D., Edwards, J. R., & Sonnentag, S. (2017). Stress and well-being at work: A century of empirical trends reflecting theoretical and societal influences. *Journal of Applied Psychology, 102*, 389–402.

Bligh and Ors v. State of Queensland. (1996). HREOCA 28.

Bonde, J. P. E. (2008). Psychosocial factors at work and risk of depression: A systematic review of the epidemiological evidence. *Occupational and Environmental Medicine, 65*, 438–445.

Brady, J. M., Hammer, L. B., Mohr, C. D., & Bodner, T. E. (in press). Supportive supervisor training improves family relationships among employee and spouse dyads. *Journal of Occupational Health Psychology*.

Breuer, C. (2015). Unemployment and suicide mortality: Evidence from regional panel data in Europe. *Health Economics, 24*, 936–950.

Broadley, A. J., Korszun, A., Abdelaal, E., Moskvina, V., Jones, C. J., Nash, G. B., Ray, C., Deanfield, J., & Frenneaux, M. P. (2005). Inhibition of cortisol production with metyrapone prevents mental stress-induced endothelial dysfunction and baroreflex impairment. *Journal of the American College of Cardiology, 46*, 344–350.

Brodie's Law. (2011). www.justice.vic.gov.au/safer-communities/crime-prevention/bullying-brodies-law

Brunner, B., Igic, I., Keller, A. C., & Wieser, S. (2019). Who gains the most from improving working conditions? Health-related absenteeism and presenteeism due to stress at work. *The European Journal of Health Economics, 20*, 1165–1180.

Burke, R. J. (2019). Creating psychologically healthy workplaces. In R. J. Burke and A. M. Richardsen (Eds.), *Creating psychologically healthy workplaces* (pp. 2–41). Edward Elgar Publishing.

Centre for Economic and Business Research. (2018). *The value of diversity*. https://cebr.com/reports/cebr-research-with-involve-on-the-value-of-diversity/

Chen, P. Y., & Stallones, L. (2011). Hidden occupational fatalities in the agricultural industry. In E. K. Kelloway and C. L. Cooper (Eds.), *Occupational health and safety in small and medium sized enterprises* (pp. 69–80). London: Elgar.

Cobb, E. P. (2017). *Workplace bullying and harassment: New developments in international law*. Taylor & Francis.

Cocker, F., Sanderson, K., & LaMontagne, A. D. (2017). Estimating the economic benefits of eliminating job strain as a risk factor for depression. *Journal of Occupational and Environmental Medicine, 59*, 12–17.

Cohen, S., Tyrrell, D. A., & Smith, A. P. (1991). Psychological stress and susceptibility to the common cold. *New England Journal of Medicine, 325*, 606–612.

Colorado Department of Public Health and Environment. (2007). *Colorado violent death reporting system (COVDRS): Highlights from 2004–2006.*

Deloitte Access Economics. (2019). *The economic costs of sexual harassment in the workplace – final report.* https://www2.deloitte.com/content/dam/Deloitte/au/Documents/Economics/deloitte-au-economic-costs-sexual-harassment-workplace-240320.pdf

EU-OSHA. (2009). *OSH in figures: Stress at work – facts and figures.* European Agency for Safety and Health at Work. https://osha.europa.eu/en/publications/osh-figures-stress-work-facts-and-figures

(2014). *Calculating the costs of work-related stress and psychosocial risks.* European Agency for Safety and Health at Work. https://osha.europa.eu/en/tools-and-publications/publications/literature_reviews/calculating-the-cost-of-work-related-stress-and-psychosocial-risks.

(2018). *Management of psychosocial risks in European workplaces – evidence from the second European survey of enterprises on new and emerging risks.* European Agency for Safety and Health at Work. https://osha.europa.eu/en/publications/management-psychosocial-risks-european-workplaces-evidence-second-european-survey

Falon, S. L., Karin, E., Boga, D., Gucciardi, D. F., Griffin, B., & Crane, M. F. (in press). A clustered-randomized controlled trial of a self-reflection resilience-strengthening intervention and novel mediators. *Journal of Occupational Health Psychology.*

Fredman, S. (2012). *Anti-discrimination laws and work in the developing world: A thematic overview.* Background paper for the world development report 2013. http://adapt.it/adapt-indice-a-z/wp-content/uploads/2015/01/wdr_anti-discrimination_laws_2013.pdf

Ganster, D. C., Fox, M. L., & Dwyer, D. J. (2001). Explaining employees' health care costs: A prospective examination of stressful job demands, personal control, and physiological reactivity. *Journal of Applied Psychology, 86*, 954–964.

Glasgow, R. E., & Emmons, K. M. (2007). How can we increase translation of research into practice? Types of evidence needed. *Annual Review of Public Health, 28*, 413–433.

Glasgow, R. E., Lichtenstein, E., & Marcus, A. C. (2003). Why don't we see more translation of health promotion research to practice? Rethinking the efficacy-to-effectiveness transition. *American Journal of Public Health, 93*, 1261–1267.

Goh, J., Pfefer, J., & Zenios, S. A. (2015). Workplace stressors & health outcomes: Health policy for the workplace. *Behavioral Science & Policy*, *1*, 43–52.

Goh, J., Pfeffer, J., & Zenios, S. A. (2016). The relationship between workplace stressors and mortality and health costs in the United States. *Management Science*, *62*, 608–628.

(2019). Reducing the health toll from US workplace stress. *Behavioral Science & Policy*, *5*, 2–13.

Gonzalez-Morales, M. G., Kernan, M. C., Becker, T. E., & Eisenberger, R. (2018). Defeating abusive supervision: Training supervisors to support subordinates. *Journal of Occupational Health Psychology*, *23*, 151–162.

Griggs v. Duke Power Co. (1971). 401 U.S. 424.

Hassard, J., Teoh, K. R., & Cox, T. (2019). Estimating the economic burden posed by work-related violence to society: A systematic review of cost-of-illness studies. *Safety Science*, *116*, 208–221.

Hassard, J., Teoh, K. R., Visockaite, G., Dewe, P., & Cox, T. (2018a). The cost of work-related stress to society: A systematic review. *Journal of Occupational Health Psychology*, *23*, 1–17.

(2018b). The financial burden of psychosocial workplace aggression: A systematic review of cost-of-illness studies. *Work & Stress*, *32*, 6–32.

Health Education England. (2019). *NHS staff and learners' mental wellbeing commission*. www.hee.nhs.uk/sites/default/files/documents/NHS%20%28HEE%29%20-%20Mental%20Wellbeing%20Commission%20Report.pdf

Hendrick v. Hercules, Inc. (1981). 27 FEP Cases 1616.

Jiang, L., & Lavaysse, L. M. (2018). Cognitive and affective job insecurity: A meta-analysis and a primary study. *Journal of Management*, *44*, 2307–2342.

Kivimäki, M., Virtanen, M., Elovainio, M., Kouvonen, A., Väänänen, A., & Vahtera, J. (2006). Work stress in the etiology of coronary heart disease – a meta-analysis. *Scandinavian Journal of Work, Environment & Health*, *32*, 431–442.

Kline, R., & Lewis, D. (2019). The price of fear: Estimating the financial cost of bullying and harassment to the NHS in England. *Public Money & Management*, *39*, 166–174.

Koehler v Cerebos (Australia) Ltd. (2005). HCA 15.

Kotter, J. P. (1995, March–April). Leading change: Why transformation efforts fail? *Harvard Business Review*, 59–67.

Kozlowski, S. W., Chen, G., & Salas, E. (2017). One hundred years of the Journal of Applied Psychology: Background, evolution, and scientific trends. *Journal of Applied Psychology*, *102*, 237–253.

LaMontagne, A. D., Keegel, T., Louie, A. M., Ostry, A., & Landsbergis, P. A. (2007). A systematic review of the job-stress intervention evaluation literature, 1990–2005. *International Journal of Occupational and Environmental Health, 13,* 268–280.

Landsbergis, P. A., Dobson, M., Koutsouras, G., & Schnall, P. (2013). Job strain and ambulatory blood pressure: A meta-analysis and systematic review. *American Journal of Public Health, 103,* e61–e71.

Lazarus, R. S., & Folkman, S. (1987). Transactional theory and research on emotions and coping. *European Journal of Personality, 1,* 141–169.

Leka, S., Jain, A., Iavicoli, S., & Di Tecco, C. (2015). An evaluation of the policy context on psychosocial risks and mental health in the workplace in the European Union: Achievements, challenges, and the future. *BioMed Research International, 25.* https://doi.org/10.1155/2015/213089

Lewis Silkin LLP (2020). International age discrimination. www.agediscrimination.info/international

Luo, F., Florence, C. S., Quispe-Agnoli, M., Ouyang, L., & Crosby, A. E. (2011). Impact of business cycles on US suicide rates, 1928–2007. *American Journal of Public Health, 101,* 1139–1146.

Majrowski v. Guy's and St Thomas' NHS Trust. (2006). UKHL 34.

Mangold v. Helm. (2005). Case C-144/04.

Matrix. (2012). Economic analysis of workplace mental health promotion and mental disorder prevention programmes and of their potential contribution to EU health, social and economic policy objectives, Executive Agency for Health and Consumers, Specific Request EAHC/2011/Health/19 for the Implementation of Framework Contract EAHC/2010/Health/01 Lot 2. www.mentalhealthpromotion.net/resources/matrix_2012-economic-analysis-of-wmhp-programmes.pdf

Mays, V. M., Coleman, L. M., & Jackson, J. S. (1996). Perceived race-based discrimination, employment status, and job stress in a national sample of black women: Implications for health outcomes. *Journal of Occupational Health Psychology, 1,* 319–329.

McKee-Ryan, F., Song, Z., Wanberg, C. R., & Kinicki, A. J. (2005). Psychological and physical well-being during unemployment: A metanalytic study. *Journal of Applied Psychology, 90,* 53–76.

Nordt, C., Warnke, I., Seifritz, E., & Kawohl, W. (2015). Modelling suicide and unemployment: A longitudinal analysis covering 63 countries, 2000–11. *The Lancet Psychiatry, 2,* 239–245.

Northwestern National Life Insurance Company. (1991). *Employee burnout: America's newest epidemic.* Northwestern National Life Insurance Company. www.cdc.gov/niosh/docs/99-101/#What%20Workers%20Say%20About%20Stress%20on%20the%20Job

Odle-Dusseau, H. N., Hammer, L. B., Crain, T. L., & Bodner, T. E. (2016). The influence of family-supportive supervisor training on employee job performance and attitudes: An organizational work–family intervention. *Journal of Occupational Health Psychology, 21,* 296–308.

Paul, K. I., & Moser, K. (2009). Unemployment impairs mental health: Meta-analyses. *Journal of Vocational Behavior, 74,* 264–282.

Pfeffer, J., Vilendrer, S., Joseph, G., Kim, J., & Singer, S. J. (2020). Employers' role in employee health: Why they do what they do. *Journal of Occupational and Environmental Medicine, 62,* e601–e610.

Quick, J. C., & McFadyen, M. (2017). Sexual harassment: Have we made any progress? *Journal of Occupational Health Psychology, 22,* 286–298.

Richardson, T., Elliott, P., & Roberts, R. (2013). The relationship between personal unsecured debt and mental and physical health: A systematic review and meta-analysis. *Clinical Psychology Review, 33,* 1148–1162.

Sauter, S. L., Murphy, L. R., & Hurrell, J. J. (1990). Prevention of work-related psychological disorders: A national strategy proposed by the National Institute for Occupational Safety and Health (NIOSH). *American Psychologist, 45,* 1146–1158.

Schmidt, B., Schneider, M., Seeger, P., van Vianen, A., Loerbroks, A., & Herr, R. M. (2019). A comparison of job stress models: Associations with employee well-being, absenteeism, presenteeism, and resulting costs. *Journal of Occupational and Environmental Medicine, 61,* 535–544.

Schall, M., & Chen, P. Y. (in press). Evidence-based strategies for improving occupational safety and health among teleworkers during and after the Coronavirus pandemic. *Human Factors.*

Smallwood, S. (2007). *Poetry performance on the occasion of Workers' Memorial Day 2007.* CDC. www.cdc.gov/niosh/docs/video/osh_poem.html

Sonnentag, S., & Lischetzke, T. (2018). Illegitimate tasks reach into after-work hours: A multilevel study. *Journal of Occupational Health Psychology, 23,* 248–261.

South Pacific Resort Hotels Pty Ltd v. Trainor. (2005). FCAFC 130.

Southern Poverty Law Center. (2016). *SPLC files federal safety complaints against poultry plant that fired whistleblowers.* www.splcenter.org/news/2016/07/26/splc-files-federal-safety-complaints-against-poultry-plant-fired-whistleblowers

Sparks, K., Cooper, C., Fried, Y., & Shirom, A. (1997). The effects of hours of work on health: A meta-analytic review. *Journal of Occupational & Organizational Psychology, 70,* 391–408.

Stansfeld, S., & Candy, B. (2006). Psychosocial work environment and mental health – A meta-analytic review. *Scandinavian Journal of Work, Environment & Health, 32,* 443–462.

Stone, A. A., Neale, J. M., Cox, D. S., Napoli, A., Valdimarsdottir, H., & Kennedy-Moore, E. (1994). Daily events are associated with a secretory immune response to an oral antigen in men. *Health Psychology, 13,* 440–446.

Sverke, M., Hellgren, J., & Näswall, K. (2002). No security: A meta-analysis and review of job insecurity and its consequences. *Journal of Occupational Health Psychology, 7,* 242–264.

United Automobile Workers v. Johnson Controls. (1991). 499 U.S. 187.

United Nations. (1948). *Universal declaration of human rights.* www.un .org/en/universal-declaration-human-rights/index.html

US Bureau of Labor Statistics. (2019a). *American time use survey.* www.bls .gov/tus/

   (2019b). *Fatal occupational injuries by event.* www.bls.gov/charts/census-of-fatal-occupational-injuries/fatal-occupational-injuries-by-event-drilldown.htm

US Centers for Disease Control and Prevention. (1999). Achievements in public health, 1900–1999: Improvements in workplace safety – United States, 1900–1999. *Morbidity and Mortality Weekly Report, 48,* 461–469.

US Department of Health and Human Services. (2020). *2020 leading health indicator topics.* www.healthypeople.gov/2020/leading-health-indica tors/2020-LHI-Topics

US Department of Labor. (2021). *Commonly used statistics.* www.osha.gov/ data/commonstats

US Equal Employment Opportunity Commission. (2020a). *EEOC issues fiscal year 2019 agency financial report.* www.eeoc.gov/newsroom/ eeoc-issues-fiscal-year-2019-agency-financial-report

   (2020b). *Sexual harassment.* www.eeoc.gov/sexual-harassment

   (2020c). *Examples of court decisions supporting coverage of LGBT-related discrimination under Title VII.* www.eeoc.gov/wysk/examples-court-decisions-supporting-coverage-lgbt-related-discrimination-under-title-vii

US National Institute of Mental Health (2020). *Suicide.* www.nimh.nih.gov/ health/statistics/suicide.shtml

US Small Business Administration. 2019 *Small business profile.* https://cdn. advocacy.sba.gov/wp-content/uploads/2019/04/23142719/2019-Small-Business-Profiles-US.pdf

Wiegand, D. M., Chen, P. Y., Hurrell, J. J. Jr., Jex, S., Nakata, A., Nigam, J., Robertson, M., & Tetrick, L. (2012). A consensus method for updating psychosocial measures used in NIOSH health hazard evaluations. *Journal of Occupational and Environmental Medicine, 54*, 350–355.

World Health Organization. (2019). *International statistical classification of diseases and related health problems* (11th ed.). www.who.int/classifica tions/icd/en/

3 | Theories of Organizational Stress and Well-Being

A Comparative Perspective

JOHANNES SIEGRIST

Within a society's social structure, organizations aim at achieving specific goals through formalized action programs. These programs share several common features, such as division of labor, social roles and norms, and a common frame of collaboration among members, in either real or virtual settings. In modern societies, each institutional domain has developed its own distinct organizations, such as schools and universities (education), courts (law), churches (religion), and businesses or enterprises (economy). In organizational research, businesses and enterprises represent the type of organizations that received most attention, and this holds particularly true for studies exploring links with stress and well-being. This preference seems well justified, given the importance of economic productivity for societal progress in general, and given the significance of paid work for welfare and well-being in adult human life. Theories addressing this topic need to take into account far-reaching changes in the nature of work and employment within these organizations that occurred in the context of economic globalization, in conjunction with groundbreaking technological advances. At the level of employment sectors, a shift from industrial mass and lean production towards service delivery and information/communication technology-driven jobs is observed. With this shift, physically strenuous workplaces with exposure to noxious physical, chemical, and biological hazards were reduced, whereas more jobs were – and are – characterized by psychomental and socioemotional demands. At the level of employment relations, a rise in nonstandard employment resulted from several developments. They include more diversified and flexible working-time arrangements and mobile (including home-based) work in response to advanced telecommunication and a growing service sector. In addition, with an expanding transnational labor force, national legal regulations protecting formal long-term employment were weakened where many public enterprises were privatized and where a variety of nonstandard work arrangements were on the rise, such as temporary agency-based work, parttime work, fixed-term contingent work, self-employment, and independent contracting (Kalleberg, 2009). Moreover, at the level of quality of work, a heightened amount of work pressure has been observed more recently in businesses and enterprises of many high-income countries (Gallie, 2013). With growing economic competition, employers are forced to reduce labor costs by intensifying work and by implementing restructuring strategies, such as offshoring, downsizing, or outsourcing (Cooper et al., 2012). As a result, a substantial part of the workforce is experiencing job instability, insecurity, involuntary parttime work, and periods of unemployment (Eurofound, 2018). It is important to understand how these three developments – changes in employment sectors, employment relations, and quality of work – affect the well-being of workers. This scientific task has now become even more important with the advent of the new pandemic of COVID-19 with its deleterious direct and indirect effects on working people's health and well-being.

As mentioned, with the shift to a postindustrial, service, and information-based economy, many more jobs are now defined by distinct features of a psychosocial work environment, rather than by those aspects of a material work environment that dominated the period of industrial production. Accordingly, the scientific challenges of studying the links between work performed in organizations and the well-being of working people need now to be tackled primarily by social and behavioral scientists, extending the traditional paradigm of occupational medicine with its focus on toxicology, chemistry, physics, and clinical science. In this chapter, I discuss the contribution of selected theoretical models of organizational stress, and more specifically of a critical psychosocial work environment, to the explanation of working people's health and well-being. These models represent main approaches of recent international research in this field. Using a set of quality criteria, their similarities and differences are elucidated in a comparative perspective. The chapter ends with some suggestions for future research along these lines and a reflection on how its policy impact might be strengthened.

The Role of Theory in Occupational Stress Research

It is the aim of a theory to provide an explanation or prediction of unknown or poorly understood relations between a set of phenomena. Different from general laws discovered by basic sciences, the degree of generalization of theories in the social and behavioral sciences is limited, given their dependence on sociocultural and socioeconomic contexts of human behavior and the many changes over time and place. Therefore, claims of general theories in these latter sciences are rare, in contrast to an extended number of theoretical models with a restricted explanatory scope. One type of such restricted theoretical models is concerned with the identification of health-related features of a psychosocial work environment. The term 'psychosocial work environment' represents an umbrella concept that bridges the social opportunity structure at work with the working people's needs of functioning and well-being (Levi, 1971). These needs include, among others, a sense of security, trust and belonging, and recurrent experiences self-efficacy and self-esteem (Siegrist & Marmot, 2004). In view of the complexity and variability of psychosocial working conditions, models aim at reducing this complexity by selectively focusing on a restricted set of elements. These elements are delineated at a level of generalization that allows for their identification in a wide range of different occupations and contexts. At the same time, these elements are assumed to provide an explanation of the links between the psychosocial work environment and the working person's health and well-being. Obviously, within this link, the human brain with its cognitions, emotions, motivations, and their bodily and behavioral responses defines the crucial pathway. Therefore, the explanatory elements of a theoretical model need to be embedded in psychobiologically and behaviorally grounded concepts of stress and well-being (see below). Hence, a theoretical model of a psychosocial work environment with relevance to health and well-being proposes an explanatory concept. This concept calls for a standardized assessment and, once operationalized, is subject to extensive empirical testing of its propositions.

During the past decades, a number of theoretical models of a health-related psychosocial work environment were proposed by social and behavioral scientists. This raises the question of how to cope with this development. Is a diversity of models justified? To what extent are they independent of each other or, at least partially, overlapping? How can their scientific quality be evaluated? These questions have rarely been answered in a systematic way, although a comparative discussion seems timely. This chapter presents such a discussion. To this end, it is mandatory to clarify what aspects of scientific quality of respective research are considered in selecting and comparing theoretical models. Using the following five criteria, four theoretical models will be selected.

Explanatory Contribution

The first criterion concerns the model's disciplinary background and its theoretical fundament. Does the concept define pathways linking the work environment with health and well-being, thus offering explanations of statistical associations? This also implies that features of the work environment are consistently measured within the model.

Assessment

These models are most often investigated using psychometrically validated scales of questionnaires or interviews. It is therefore important to include concepts based on scales that meet internationally established quality criteria.

Strength of Evidence

How extensive have these models been empirically tested? Were findings derived from appropriate study designs? How consistent is the body of evidence?

Generalization

This aspect concerns (a) the range of health and behavioral outcomes under study; (b) the model's suitability for different types of occupations and employment sectors; and (c) its extension to the analysis of productive activities beyond paid work.

Policy Impact

As it is the overarching aim of related scientific knowledge to promote healthy work, it seems appropriate to explore the model's policy impact.

Within a rich and extensive scientific literature dealing with psychosocial aspects at work and well-being, the following theoretical models made significant contributions to the advancement of knowledge and inspired new directions of analysis but were judged to provide insufficient evidence on one of the five criteria mentioned: 'burnout' (Maslach & Leiter, 2017), 'sense of coherence' (Antonovsky, 1987), 'stressor-detachment' (Sonnentag & Fritz, 2015), 'stress as offense of self' (Semmer, 2020), 'person-environment-fit' (Edwards et al., 1998), 'conservation of resources' (Hobfoll, 1989), and 'vitamin model' (Warr, 2017). For instance, the strength of prospective evidence on adverse effects on health was considered to be restricted ('stress as offense of self'; 'stressor-detachment'; 'person–environment fit'), or the elaboration of work-specific explanatory links was not obvious ('burnout'; 'vitamin model'; 'sense of coherence'), or the operational measurement of the concept was not specific enough (for a critical appraisal of 'conservation of resources', see e.g. Halbersleben et al., 2014). As a result of this selection process, the following four theoretical models were judged to meet all five criteria to a sufficient extent: 'demand-control' (DC) or 'job strain' (Karasek, 1979; Karasek & Theorell, 1990), 'effort-reward imbalance' (ERI) (Siegrist, 1996; Siegrist & Wahrendorf, 2016), 'organizational justice' (OJ) (Greenberg & Cohen, 1982; Elovainio et al., 2002), and 'job demands-resources' (JD-R) (Demerouti et al., 2001; Bakker & Demerouti, 2017). In the next section, these models are briefly described, followed by a comparative discussion of their similarities and differences.

Four Theoretical Models: Similarities and Differences

Demand-Control

The demand-control (DC) model is one of the most widely applied and most well-known models of psychosocial stress at work. It was first proposed by American sociologist Robert Karasek (1979), with elaborated links to psychobiological stress theory, as applied to cardiovascular disease (Karasek & Theorell, 1990), and with an extension to include social support at work as a third dimension (Johnson & Hall, 1988). Its scientific roots are grounded in sociological alienation theory, where low control among workers was studied in relation to their well-being and personal development (Kornhauser, 1965), and in occupational health research on high workload (Frankenhaeuser & Gardell, 1976). Karasek's original idea of combining the two dimensions of psychological demands and decision latitude (or control) to explain elevated health risks was supported by survey data. Soon, it became apparent that the control dimension was composed of two different aspects, the worker's influence on performing the work (decision authority) and his or her ability to use own resources (skill level). Jobs defined by high psychological demands and low decision latitude or skill level were proposed to generate stress and to reduce health and well-being, whereas demanding jobs with a high level of control and autonomy were thought to buffer stress and to strengthen the experience of mastery and active learning (Karasek & Theorell, 1990). A close link of these sociological components with psychobiological stress theory is considered a particular strength of this model. Specifically, conditions of high demand and low control were shown to simultaneously activate two stress axes within the organism, the sympatho-adrenal medullary and the hypothalamic-pituitary-adrenocortical axis, and this synergistic activation contributes to the pathology of stress-related disorders, such as ischemic heart disease (Henry & Stephens, 1977). Recently, Karasek has proposed a substantial multilevel extension of the original DC model, termed 'associationalist demand-control theory' (Karasek, 2020). As empirical data on this new version are currently not available, it will not be included in this comparison.

The DC model is measured by different approaches, self-reported questionnaires, observational ratings, or features of administrative job classifications ('job exposure matrices'). Yet, the job strain questionnaire (JCQ) has been established as the standard method. It is composed of five items measuring psychological demands, six items measuring decision authority, and four items measuring skill discretion. Items are assessed on a 5-point Likert scale according to experienced intensity (Karasek et al., 1998). Psychometric properties of the scales and factorial validity of the model were tested in a number of methodological studies (e.g. Chungkham et al., 2013). An additional scale measuring social support at work was constructed in a similar way, but many epidemiological studies did not include this scale in their model tests. The main approach of analyzing the model is based on the 'split half' method, where scores of job demands above the median are scored 'high' and scores of job control below the median are scored 'low'. However, additional analyses of the combined effect of the two dimensions were performed, applying additive or multiplicative interaction. It should also be mentioned that many investigations studied the effects of single scales rather than their combination. Overall, there is considerable variation in exploring the model's propositions.

Strong evidence exists on the contributions of the DC model towards explaining elevated risks of stress-related disorders and ill health. This has been documented by several systematic reviews and meta-analyses of prospective cohort studies. They include the effects of job strain on ischemic heart disease (Theorell et al., 2016), high blood pressure (Gilbert-Ouimet et al., 2014), and depression (Madsen et al., 2017). A variety of additional reports demonstrate associations with metabolic disorders, musculoskeletal disorders, poor cognitive functioning, sickness absence, disability, and life years lost. It is beyond the scope of this chapter to give a representative account of this knowledge, but some recent reports from the original authors illustrate its significance (Theorell, 2020; Karasek, 2020). On balance, it seems that the single component 'job control' exerts relatively strongest effects on disease risks, and that the claim of a synergistic effect of high demand and low control is not consistently confirmed. On the other hand, some studies show that, according to the model, 'active jobs' defined by high demand and high control exert some beneficial health effect. Whereas abundant research on the DC model was conducted by epidemiologists, fewer findings are available from experimental and quasi-experimental studies, such as naturalistic studies of physiological activity in everyday working life. They provide some support with regard to increased blood pressure, reduced heart rate variability, elevated secretion of stress hormones, and impaired immune function (e.g. Steptoe & Kivimäki, 2012; Jarczok et al., 2013; Theorell, 2020).

In summary, the DC model has been investigated more thoroughly than any other similar concept, and its components, in particular job control, demonstrate robust effects on working people's health and well-being. The model was applied to a wide range of health outcomes, including health-related behaviors (Kivimäki et al., 2018), and the notion of low control was extended to explore health effects related to work at home (Chandola et al., 2004) and to school work (Gädin & Hammarström, 2000). To some extent, this latter information indicates that the model's core notions can be generalized beyond the context of paid work. Finally, concerning policy impact, the DC model was investigated in a number of intervention studies, with a focus on job task redesign and other organizational improvements at the level of enterprises and businesses. Several such interventions resulted in positive effects on workers' well-being (Brisson et al., 2016).

Effort-Reward Imbalance

The effort-reward imbalance (ERI) model represents a complementary approach towards analyzing a health-adverse psychosocial environment. It focuses on the employment contract as the core element of employment relations, emphasizing the role of social reciprocity in costly transactions for health and well-being (Siegrist, 1996). Rooted in sociological and social psychological theories of exchange and equity (Gouldner, 1960; Adams, 1965), and referring to sociological role theory (Merton, 1968), the model assumes that the principle of equivalent reward in return for effort spent at work is often violated, such that workers are exposed to 'high cost–low gain' conditions (imbalance) in a core social role. Importantly, three basic types of reward are transmitted, salary or wage (financial reward), career promotion or job security (status-related reward), and esteem or recognition (socioemotional reward). Imbalance is likely to occur if workers have no alternative choice in the labor market and if they are exposed to heavy competition. In addition to these extrinsic factors, an intrinsic motivational factor, the working person's inability to withdraw from work obligations and excessive striving ('overcommitment'), contributes to this imbalance. This risky pattern of coping may be due to an underlying need for approval and esteem at work, but it can also be reinforced by group pressure at work. The model's central proposition states that each component, high effort, low reward, and high overcommitment, is associated with an elevated health risk, and that the combined effect of high effort and low reward contributes to adverse health in addition to the main effects. The ERI model has a strong transdisciplinary link to neuroscience-based stress theory as sustained experience of reward deficiency at work activates distinct brain reward circuits, including nucleus accumbens, anterior cingulate cortex, and insula (Schultz, 2006). This threat or loss of significant social reward is associated with sustained activation of the stress axes mentioned above, and it may additionally stimulate addictive behavior. In the long run, allostatic load is triggered within several regulatory systems of the body, thus precipitating the development of stress-related disorders (McEwen, 1998).

The ERI model is measured by the three scales 'effort', 'reward', and 'overcommitment', containing 4-point Likert-scaled items. The original version has been supplemented by a short version with a total of 16 items. Extensive psychometric tests of both versions were performed in several languages. The factorial validity was tested by confirmatory factor analysis, and the model fit was recurrently improved when a second order model representing the theoretical structure underlying the scales was analyzed (e.g. Leineweber et al., 2010). Additionally, longitudinal measurement invariance of the model's scales was demonstrated (Montano et al., 2016). Hypotheses were tested using regression analyses with single scales, and additionally with their combination. To this end, a logarithmic ratio of the scales 'effort' and 'reward' was constructed that quantifies the imbalance at the individual level. Alternative approaches include additive and multiplicative interaction analysis of scales.

The evidence of prospective associations of ERI with elevated risks of stress-related disorders concurs with the one demonstrated for the DC model. Although based on a lower number of studies, the effect sizes of relative risks or odds ratios are comparable in the case of ischemic heart disease (Siegrist & Li, 2020), depression (Rugulies et al., 2017), and high blood pressure (Gilbert-Ouimet et al., 2014). Again, a broad spectrum of additional indicators of health and well-being were examined with regard to effort and reward at work (Siegrist & Wahrendorf, 2016). Further support of the model's hypotheses comes from a series of experimental and quasi-experimental studies using cardiovascular and autonomic nervous system markers, measures of stress hormone release, and measures of inflammatory and immune function (Eddy et al., 2018; Siegrist & Li, 2020). When summarizing the results, the model's propositions are mainly supported, yet to a different extent. Concerning the effects of single scales, 'low reward' exerts relatively strongest effects on health, followed by 'effort' and 'overcommitment'. The summary measure combing the two extrinsic components is associated with health in a majority of studies, but adjusting for the effects of single scales has often not been performed or reported in publications, thus leaving room for further analyses. Few studies so far have tested the moderating role of 'overcommitment' in this latter association with health.

Given a fundamental role of the norm of reciprocity in social exchange, the ERI model has been applied to several types of costly social transactions other than paid work. Associations with well-being were observed in household and family work, voluntary work, caregiving, and informal help, and among students in the context of educational work (Siegrist & Wahrendorf, 2016). It is therefore assumed that the model's hypotheses are valid for a larger range of productive social activities. Concerning policy impact, the ERI model was investigated in several intervention studies, in combination either with or without the DC model, with effects similar to those reported (Brisson et al., 2016). Yet, the model's significance for policy is not restricted to the organizational level but extends to the level of national labor and social policies. Cross-country investigations demonstrated that lower levels of effort-reward imbalance at work were documented in countries with high investments in active labor market policies, thus pointing to their potential mitigating effect (Lunau et al., 2015). In conclusion, research based on the ERI model has extended the evidence of health-adverse psychosocial work environments above and beyond the demand-control approach.

Organizational Justice

The third concept selected for this contribution, organizational justice (OJ), has a long tradition in research on social and organizational psychology, where three basic notions of justice are distinguished: distributive, procedural, and relational justice (Greenberg & Cohen, 1982). The first notion points to the fairness of distribution of resources and rewards between members of a group, whereas the second notion stresses fair decision-making procedures and equal application of rules in organizational behavior. The third notion concerns respectful and trusting behavior between colleagues, and specifically between leaders or managers and employees within the organization, thus avoiding prejudice, bullying, and discrimination.

Through the decades, research on organizational justice was devoted to the study of its effects on working people's behavior within their companies and businesses. Analyses revealed that perceived injustice within organizations increased the likelihood of dissatisfaction, absenteeism, turnover intention, and attitudes of disengagement or even revenge (Greenberg & Colquitt, 2005). Therefore, these findings were of direct practical interest for improving leadership behavior, management styles, teamwork collaboration, and work motivation. In 2002, Finnish psychologist Marko Elovainio and his team applied this model to the explanation of stress-related ill health and disease, documenting associations with mental health and sickness absence (Elovainio et al., 2002). The hypothesis states that all three notions of perceived injustice in an organization weaken employees' sense of security, trust, and control, even in the absence of personally experienced offense, thus eliciting feelings of anxiety, tension, and resulting physiological stress reactions.

The OJ model is commonly measured by a set of standardized questionnaire items developed in 1991 (Moorman, 1991), but additional operationalizations have been used. Compared with the measurement of the DC and the ERI models, fewer reports on the scales' psychometric properties have been published so far. The empirical evidence of associations of organizational justice with health and well-being has been summarized in two reviews, one focusing on mental health (Ndjaboué et al., 2012), and one providing a general overview (Elovainio & Virtanen, 2020). Solid prospective evidence was reported for effects of relational and procedural injustice on reduced mental health, where effect sizes were comparable to those reported by the other two models. In addition, several investigations document an association with cardiovascular disease risk (Theorell et al., 2016). As preliminary evidence points to links with behavioral risk factors and with inflammatory markers (blood-based indicators of disease), there is reason to assume that perceived injustice affects the cardiovascular and other bodily systems via enhanced stress reactions and negative emotions threatening people's sense of integrity and self (Elovainio & Virtanen, 2020).

Given the general significance of perceptions of organizational injustice, one can assume that health effects are observed in organizations other than companies and businesses. In fact, at least for one different type of organizations, schools, this assumption has been successfully tested (Elovainio & Virtanen, 2020). Overall, relational and procedural injustice are considered independent predictors of reduced mental health and increased cardiovascular risk, while the contribution of distributive justice deserves further clarification. Additional prospective investigations using a standardized assessment and including interventions are desirable to increase the impact of this promising conceptual approach.

Job Demands-Resources

As a shared characteristic, the models discussed so far define particular organizational features that affect human health and well-being. With their hypotheses, they offer explanations that can be empirically supported or falsified. The job demands-resources (JD-R) model provides a more general conceptual framework that includes a wider set of job demands and job resources and that addresses negative (impaired health) as well as positive motivational outcomes (performance, personal growth). This model was developed in several steps, starting as a concept that aimed at explaining burnout (Demerouti et al., 2001), being extended to include work engagement as a motivational process stimulated by job resources, and finally integrating personal resources as mediators and moderators of relations between job characteristics and well-being (Schaufeli & Taris, 2014). As a general framework, the JD-R model calls on distinct psychological theories of coping with demands and of strengthening resilience and recovery in order to explain the observed associations. Such approaches include conservation of resources, social cognitive, and self-determination theories (Schaufeli & Taris, 2014). The model has also inspired more specific applications, in particular the concept of psychosocial safety climate, a concept maintaining that managerial investments into psychosocial safety are instrumental in reducing job demands, increasing job resources, and promoting workers' well-being (Dollard et al., 2019). With its emphasis on direct and indirect effects of job resources on personal and organizational outcomes, the JD-R model adds an important dimension to the field of occupational health research, and it links this field with research on job design and human resource management (Bakker & Demerouti, 2017).

Abundant empirical support was documented for the model's central hypotheses of direct positive effects of job resources on work engagement and of job demands on reduced well-being, while job resources also protect against reduced well-being. Fewer studies tested moderation and mediation effects, including personal resources. A recent meta-analytic review of 74 longitudinal studies found substantial support for the central hypotheses (Lesener et al., 2019). Similar to previously discussed concepts, demands and resources were also analyzed in contexts other than paid work, in particular with respect to home and family work (Bakker et al., 2011). Despite its strengths, a general limitation of the model concerns the use of self-report measures in assessing work aspects and well-being, the latter being measured in terms of burnout in most studies. Therefore, the findings are subject to the bias of common method variance, and independent prospective epidemiologic cohort studies with objectively assessed health outcomes are still needed to overcome this limitation. In summary, with its broad application, the JD-R model has produced considerable practical impact, for instance as a monitoring tool for evaluating organizational performance, and as a frame of reference for developing job redesign or job crafting interventions. With the differentiation between organizational and personal resources, and with the dual concept of positive and negative outcomes, this model has substantially enriched research in this field. A controversial issue concerns its epistemological status, i.e. the question whether it serves as an open, heuristic framework that includes any type of demands and resources, or whether it aims at reducing the potential complexity to more specific analytic dimensions, with an inherent benefit of increasing the model's predictive power (Schaufeli & Taris 2014).

A Comparative Discussion

Do these concepts represent distinct theoretical approaches or are they, at least partially, redundant? There is some obvious overlap between 'demand' and 'effort' in the DC and ERI models, between 'relational justice' and 'social support' in the OJ and extended DC model, and between the notions of effort-reward imbalance and distributive justice in the ERI and OJ models. Moreover, the JD-R model draws on a general idea of balance that is inherent in the DC and ERI models, and every dimension of the three other models can easily be labeled a feature of 'demand' or of 'resource' within the JD-R model. One way of clarifying redundancy concerns statistical adjustment in studies exploring health outcomes. For instance, many investigations dealing with organizational justice adjusted for the effects of DC and/or ERI variables, and it turned out that statistically independent results were observed in a majority of cases (Ndjaboué et al., 2012). Similarly, a large number of studies testing the ERI model adjusted for the effects of DC variables, with similar evidence of independent results (Siegrist & Wahrendorf, 2016). These adjustments were less often performed in studies inaugurated by the proponents of the DC and the JD-R models.

Elaborating theoretical differences between the models represents another way of dealing with redundancy. For instance, importantly, distributive justice addresses inequity of distribution of rewards and resources between members of an organization, thus explicitly incorporating social comparison processes, whereas the notion of effort-reward imbalance highlights inequity within individual cost and gain, thus identifying justice of exchange as the core stress-theoretical mechanism. There is also an obvious conceptual difference between procedural justice and the decision authority or control component of the DC model. The former focuses on the application of rules in interactions and decisions between superiors and subordinates, whereas the latter addresses the hierarchical structure of job tasks and the division of labor. Similarly, social support at work delineates more strongly the instrumental than the emotional aspects of social interaction at work, both among colleagues and between subordinates and superiors, whereas relational justice stresses the socioemotional quality of exchange in terms of respect and dignity. In conclusion, it turns out that there is sufficient independence between the four theoretical models, as each model offers some innovative element that enriches our understanding of the impact of organizational features on employees' health and well-being. This conclusion is supported by additional observations indicating that two concepts, the DC and OJ models, focus on the work environment without taking person characteristics into account, whereas the other two concepts integrate person characteristics into their model. A further difference relates to the theoretical emphasis on instrumental, task-oriented aspects (DC and JD-R models) versus social exchange-related aspects (ERI and OJ models). On the other hand, similarities, to some extent, become visible if the criteria of stress-theoretical foundation and of generalization beyond paid work are considered (see Table 3.1).

Table 3.1 *Similarities and differences between theoretical models*

	Demand-control	Effort-reward imbalance	Organizational justice	Job demands-resources
Conceptual focus	▪ Environment ▪ Instrumental behavior	▪ Environment and person ▪ Social exchange	▪ Environment ▪ Social exchange	▪ Environment and person ▪ Instrumental behavior
Stress-theoretical basis	▪ Threat to personal control	▪ Threat to social reward	▪ Threat to integrity/self	▪ Threat to mobilization of resources
Conceptual overlap	▪ Demand ≈ effort ▪ Control ≈ procedural justice	▪ Effort ≈ demand ▪ Reward ≈ distributive justice	▪ Relational justice ≈ social support ▪ Procedural justice ≈ control	▪ Demand and resources may include variables from other models
Extension beyond paid work	▪ Home and family work ▪ Educational work	▪ Voluntary work and caring ▪ Home and family work ▪ Educational work	▪ Educational work	▪ Educational work ▪ Home and family work

Viewed from a perspective of scientific development, it is evident that in a first stage of enquiry, single theoretical models are developed, tested, and compared with the aim of ensuring their original and distinctive nature. However, in a second stage, these models are subject to combined analyses with two scientific interests. In a competitive perspective, one such interest aims at assessing the strengths of evidence attributed to each separate model. Another interest relates to the exploration of cumulative effects of a co-manifestation of stress-enhancing working conditions within occupational groups. It is currently premature to review available evidence on these two aspects, but each aspect is illustrated by findings from one study that includes information on the DC, ERI, and OJ models. In an attempt to identify the relative strength of associations between the three concepts and the risk of sickness absence due to a diagnosed mental disorders, a Canadian team conducted a systematic review and meta-analysis of 13 prospective epidemiologic studies representing 130,056 participants (Duchaine et al., 2020). Risk ratios of the respective work predictors were 1.47 (95% confidence interval (CI) 1.24; 1.74) for job strain (the combined effect of high demand and low control) and 1.66 (95% CI: 1.37; 2.00) for effort-reward imbalance. Using the single model components, 'low reward' was associated with the relatively strongest risk elevation, 1.76 (95% CI 1.49; 2.08). Due to a low number of studies measuring the OJ model, no meta-analysis could be performed with this model, but a protective effect of relational, procedural, and organizational justice was observed in single studies (Duchaine et al., 2020). The second approach assessing the clustering effect of the DC, ERI, and OJ models on the risk of work disability was analyzed by a Finnish team (Juvani et al., 2018). Results shown in Figure 3.1 are based on data from 41,862 Finnish employees included in a survey in 2008, whose subsequent disability pensions up to 2011 were identified through national record linking. Three outcomes of disability pension were analyzed: any cause, depression as cause, and musculoskeletal disorder as cause. As depression-related disability is the outcome of major interest in stress-theoretical terms, results are given for this outcome. In this study, about half of the sample was free from any type of work stress, 27.4% experienced one stressor, 17.7% reported two stressors, and 6.4% indicated exposure to all three stressors. After adjusting for relevant confounds, the hazard ratio of depression-caused work disability was 4.7 times elevated

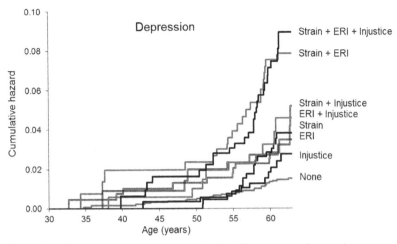

Figure 3.1 Cumulative hazard curves of disability pension due to depression by combination of self-reported work stressors

(95% CI: 2.9; 7.7) in the group exposed to all three stressors compared to the risk in the stress-free group. Respective cumulative hazards are indicated in Figure 3.1. This study demonstrates the health-adverse effects of cumulative risk exposure, and it supports the notion that occupational high-risk groups deserve special preventive attention.

In sum, all four theoretical models of a psychosocial work environment with relevance to health and well-being have scientific validity and practical usefulness. Benefits are expected from strategies of application, their single analysis, and their combined examination. Obviously, further conceptual and methodological developments in this field of research are required. The final section briefly discusses three such developments.

Future Considerations

With the powerful extension of digitalization and automated production, many more jobs are – and will be – performed without physical presence of workers in the traditional organizations of businesses and companies. Telework, work from home, and other forms of distant work, flexible work arrangements with parttime physical presence, and extended virtual meetings are becoming more common. The COVID-19 pandemic has forced large parts of the workforce into working from home as a preventive measure against infection, and this health shock is accelerating a general trend towards distant work. With this change, new risks as well as new opportunities evolve, and the theoretical models discussed here may not be suited to tackle them in an appropriate way because they were conceptualized in times when mainstream work occurred within organizations. Importantly, relevant notions such as supervision; decision-making and control; teamwork; and social relations at work, including support, advice, and positive and negative feedback, have to be adapted to the virtual reality. At the same time, new risks emerge, such as the management of boundaries between working life and private life, including the dangers of overwork and presenteeism, or problems of dealing with obstacles and difficulties during task performance, problems with electronic monitoring and surveillance systems, and the burden of coping with monotony and workplace isolation, in addition to the fear of job loss or job deterioration due to the pandemic (Diebig et al., 2020; Kniffin et al., 2020).

As a related second development, substantial changes in the nature of employment relations, triggered by economic globalization, need to be considered in future research on work environments and health. Again, a majority of models discussed in this chapter were conceptualized in times when employment relations were mainly defined by standard fulltime work contracts. More recently, with increased competition in transnational markets and growing pressure on return on investment among employers, strategies of reducing labor costs and increasing flexibility were implemented, with a substantial rise in nonstandard employment (see above). Therefore, a shift in analysis is required from distinct job profiles and stable work arrangements to employment trajectories along the life course. With this shift of analysis, the dynamic nature of occupational histories with its discontinuities, interruptions, and afflictions on health and well-being becomes apparent. Interestingly, this analytical shift has recently been applied to two of the theoretical models discussed here, the job strain or DC model and the ERI model. In a first report, a Canadian group developed the notion of 'employment strain', where the core notion of low job task control was extended to low employment control over the life course (Lewchuk et al., 2003). Relevant features of low employment control include access to work, work schedule, hours and location, assignment of job tasks and opportunities of using skills, earnings, and employment continuity. Occupational careers are characterized by different patterns of employment control. A different approach was developed in our group, based on retrospective information on employment histories with data on exposure duration, timing, and its sequential character over the life course. Using central stress-theoretical notions such as 'threat to reward' and 'threat to security', three constructs of adverse employment histories were proposed, and their relations with indicators of reduced health functioning were demonstrated: (a) precarious careers (e.g. temporary contracts, repeated job changes); (b) discontinuous working careers (involuntary interruptions); (c) cumulative disadvantage (continued low occupational position) (Wahrendorf et al., 2019). Recurrent instability, disruption, and frustrated career advancement in jobs experienced during early and mid-adult life are associated with poorer quality of work in older age, in addition to their health-detrimental effects (Hoven et al., 2020).

In view of an alarming situation of poor working and employment conditions in developing and emerging economies, and in view of global challenges of providing and securing healthy work to a large disadvantaged workforce in advanced societies, future research on work and health is expected to address these concerns in a more coordinated way. Coordination is not restricted to the development of cross-national and cross-continental comparative studies, using standardized measures, but involves a reliable cooperation with international organizations, such as the International Labour Organization and the World Health Organization. In addition to the production of scientific reviews and evidence-based policy recommendations proposed to governments and economic stakeholders, scientists are expected to strengthen their activities towards reducing the gap between available research knowledge and its implementation into practice (Marmot & Siegrist, 2016). Collaboration with occupational health and safety professionals, promotion of initiatives to improve their competencies and impact through education, training and human resource development, dissemination of public media campaigns to raise awareness, and support of civil society activities to call for action and to develop targeted initiatives are examples of this engagement. Occupational health researchers can learn from the successful collaboration between an international network of scientists engaged in climatic and environmental research and informal as well as formal political movements. The United Nation's Sustainable Development Goals initiative offers a promising opportunity for coordinated efforts. Lastly, there is some hope that healthy work will be moved up on the political agenda and will be available to all those in urgent need.

References

Adams, J. S. (1965). Inequity in social exchange. In B. Leonard (Ed.), *Advances in experimental social psychology* (Vol. 2, pp. 267–299). Academic.

Antonovsky, A. (1987). *Unravelling the mystery of health: How people manage stress and stay well*. Jossey Bass.

Bakker, A. B., & Demerouti, E. (2017). Job demands-resources theory: Taking stock and looking forward. *Journal of Occupational Health Psychology, 22*, 273–285. https://doi.org/10.1037/ocp0000056

Bakker, A. B., Ten Brummelhuis, L. L., Prins, J. T., & Van Der Heijden, F. M. M. A. (2011). Applying the job demands-resources model to the work-home interface: A study among medical residents and their partners. *Journal of Vocational Behavior, 79*, 170–180. https://doi.org/10.1016/j.jvb.2010.12.004

Brisson, C., Gilbert-Ouimet, M., Duchaine, C., Trudel, X., & Vézina, M. (2016). Workplace interventions aiming to improve psychosocial work factors and related health. In J. Siegrist & M. Wahrendorf (Eds.), *Work stress and health in a globalized economy: The model of effort-reward imbalance* (pp. 333–363). Springer International Publications.

Chandola, T., Kuper, H., Singh-Manoux, A., Bartley, M., & Marmot, M. (2004). The effect of control at home on CHD events in the Whitehall II study: Gender differences in psychosocial domestic pathways to social inequalities in CHD. *Social Science & Medicine, 58*(8), 1501–1509. https://doi.org/10.1016/S0277-9536(03)00352-6

Chungkham, H. S., Ingre, M., Karasek, R., Westerlund, H., & Theorell, T. (2013). Factor structure and longitudinal measurement invariance of the demand control support model: An evidence from the Swedish Longitudinal Occupational Survey of Health (SLOSH). *PLoS ONE, 8* (8), e70541. https://doi.org/10.1371/journal.pone.0070541

Cooper, C. L., Pandey, A., & Quick, J. (2012). *Downsizing: Is less still more?* Cambridge University Press.

Demerouti, E., Bakker, A. B., Nachreiner, F., & Schaufeli, W. B. (2001). The job demands-resources model of burnout. *Journal of Applied Psychology, 86*(3), 499–512. https://doi.org/101037//0021-9010863499

Diebig, M., Müller, A., & Angerer, P. (2020). Impact of the digitalization in the industry sector on work, employment, and health. In T. Theorell (Ed.) *Handbook of socioeconomic determinants of occupational health* (pp. 305–319). Springer Nature International Publications.

Dollard, M. F., Dormann, C., & Idris, M. A. (2019). *Psychosocial safety climate: A new work stress theory.* Springer International Publishing.

Duchaine, C. S., Aubè, K., Gilbert-Ouimet, M., Vézina, M., Ndjaboué, R., Massamba, V., Talbot, D., Lavigne-Robichaud, M., Trudel, X., Bruno Pena-Gralle, A.-P., Lesage, A., Moore, L., Milot, A., Laurin, D., & Brisson, C. (2020). Psychosocial stressors at work and the risk of sickness absence due to a diagnosed mental disorder. *JAMA Psychiatry, 77* (8), 842–851. https://doi.org/10.1001/jamapsychiatry.2020.0322

Eddy, P., Wertheim, E. H., Hale, M. W., & Wright, B. (2018). A systematic review and meta-analysis of the effort-reward imbalance model of workplace stress and hypothalamic-pituitary-adrenal axis measures of stress. *Psychosomatic Medicine, 80*(1), 103–113. https://doi.org/10.1097/PSY.0000000000000505

Edwards, J. R., Caplan, R. D., & Van Harrison, R. (1998). Person-environment-fit theory. In C. Cooper (Ed.), *Theories of organizational stress* (pp. 28–67). Oxford University Press.

Elovainio, M., & Virtanen, M. (2020). Organizational justice and health. In T. Theorell (Ed.), *Handbook of socioeconomic determinants of occupational health* (pp. 383–396). Springer Nature International Publications.

Elovainio, M., Kivimäki, M., & Vahtera, J. (2002). Organizational justice: Evidence of a new psychosocial predictor of health. *American Journal of Public Health, 92,* 105–108. https://doi.org/10.2105/AJPH.92.1.105

Eurofound. (2018). *Living and working in Europe 2017.* Publication Office of the European Union.

Frankenhaeuser, M., & Gardell, B. (1976). Underload and overload in working life: Outline of a multidisciplinary approach. *Journal of Human Stress, 2*(3), 35–46 https://doi.org/10.1080/0097840X.1976.9936068

Gadin, K. G., & Hammarström, A. (2000). School-related health – a cross-sectional study among young boys and girls. *International Journal of Health Services, 30*(4), 797–820. https://doi.org/10.2190/K3EN-EAY9-GDTD-002Q

Gallie, D. (2013). *Economic crisis, quality of work, and social integration: The European experience.* Oxford University Press.

Gilbert-Ouimet, M., Trudel, X., Brisson, C., Milot, A., & Vézina, M. (2014). Adverse effects of psychosocial work factors on blood pressure: Systematic review of studies on demand-control-support and effort-reward imbalance models. *Scandinavian Journal of Work, Environment and Health, 40*(2), 109–132. https://doi.org/10.5271/sjweh.3390

Gouldner, A. W. (1960). The norm of reciprocity: A preliminary statement. *American Sociological Review*, *25*(2), 161–178. https://doi.org/10.2307/2092623

Greenberg, J., & Cohen, J. R. (Eds.). (1982). *Equity and justice in social behavior*. Academic Press.

Greenberg, J., & Colquitt, J. A. (2005). *Handbook of organizational justice*. LEA.

Halbesleben, J. R. B., Neveu, J.-P., Paustian-Underdahl, S. C., & Westman, M. (2014). Getting to the 'COR': Understanding the Role of Resources in Conservation of Resources Theory. *Journal of Management*, *40*, 1334–1364. https://doi.org/10.1177%2F0149206314527130

Henry, J. P., & Stephens, P. M. (1977). *Stress, health, and the social environment*. Springer.

Hobfoll, S. E. (1989). Conservation of resources: A new attempt at conceptualizing stress. *The American Psychologist*, *44*(3), 513–524.

Hoven, H., Wahrendorf, M., Goldberg, M., Zins, M., & Siegrist, J. (2020) Cumulative disadvantage during employment careers: The link between employment histories and stressful working conditions. *Advances in Life Course Research*, *46*, 100358. https://doi.org/10.1016/j.alcr.2020.100358

Jarczok, M. N., Jarczok, M., Mauss, D., Koenig, J., Li, J., Herr, R. M., & Thayer, J. F. (2013). Autonomic nervous system activity and workplace stressors: A systematic review. *Neuroscience and Biobehavioral Reviews*, *37*(8), 1810–1823. https://doi.org/10.1016/j.neubiorev.2013.07.004

Johnson, J, V., & Hall, E. M. (1988). Job strain, work social support, and cardiovascular disease: A cross-sectional study of a random sample of the Swedish working population. *American Journal of Public Health*, *78*(10), 1336–1342. https://doi.org/10.2105/AJPH.78.10.1336

Juvani, A., Oksanen, T., Virtanen, M., Salo, P., Pentti, J., Kivimäki, M., & Vahtera, J. (2018). Clustering of job strain, effort-reward imbalance, and organizational injustice and the risk of work disability: A cohort study. *Scandinavian Journal of Work, Environment and Health*, *44*(5), 485–495. www.jstor.org/stable/26567032

Kalleberg, A. (2009). Precarious work, insecure workers: Employment relations in transition. *American Sociological Review*, *74*(1), 1–22. https://doi.org/10.1177/000312240907400101

Karasek, R. (1979). Job demands, job decision latitude, and mental strain: Implications for job redesign. *Administrative Science Quarterly*, *24*(2), 285–308. https://doi.org/10.2307/2392498

(2020). The associationalist demand-control (ADC) theory. In T. Theorell (Ed.), *Handbook of socioeconomic determinants of occupational health* (pp. 573–610). Springer Nature International Publications.

Karasek, R., & Theorell, T. (1990). *Health work: Stress, productivity, and the reconstruction of working life*. Basic Books.

Karasek, R., Brisson, C., Kawakami, N., Houtman, I., Bongers, P., & Amick, B. (1998). The job content questionnaire (JCQ): An instrument for internationally comparative assessment of psychosocial job characteristics. *Journal of Occupational Health Psychology, 3*(4), 322–355. https://doi.org/10.1037/1076-8998.3.4.322

Kivimäki, M., Pentti, J., Ferrie, J. E., Batty, D. Nyberg, S. T., Jokela, M., Virtanen, M., Alfredsson, L., Dragano, N., Fransson, E. I., Goldberg, M., Knutsson, A., Koskenvuo, M., Koskinen, A., Kouvonen, A., Luukkonen, R., Oksanen, T., Rugulies, R. … Deanfield, J. (2018). Work stress and risk of death in men and women with and without cardiometabolic disease: A multicohort study. *Lancet, 6*(9), 705–713. https://doi.org/10.1016/S2213-8587(18)30140-2

Kniffin, K. M., Narayanan, J., Anseel. F., Antonakis, J., Ashford, S. J., Bakker, A. B., Bamberger, P., Bapuji, H., Bhave, D. P., Choi, V., Creary, S., Demerouti, E., Flynn, F., Gelfand, M., Greer, L., Johns, G., Kesebir, S., Klein, P. G., Lee, S. … van Vugt, M. (2020). COVID-19 and the workplace: Implications, issues, and insights for future research and action. *American Psychologist*. Advance online publication. http://doi.org/10.1037/amp0000716

Kornhauser, A. (1965). *The mental health of the industrial worker*. John Wiley & Sons.

Leineweber, C., Wege, N., Westerlund, H., Theorell, T., Wahrendorf, M., & Siegrist, J. (2010). How valid is a short measure of effort-reward imbalance at work? A replication study from Sweden. *Occupational and Environmental Medicine, 67*, 526–531. http://doi.org/10.1136/oem.2009.050930

Lesener, T., Gusy, B., & Wolter, C. (2019). The job demands-resources model: A meta-analytic review of longitudinal studies. *Work & Stress, 33*(1), 76–103. https://doi.org/10.1080/02678373.2018.1529065

Levi, L. (Ed.). (1971). *Society, stress, and disease: Volume 1. The psychosocial environment and psychosomatic diseases*. Oxford University Press.

Lewchuk, W., de Wolff, A., King, A., & Polanyi, M. (2003). From job strain to employment strain: Health effects of precarious employment. *Just Labour, 3*, 23–35. https://doi.org/10.25071/1705-1436.165

Lunau, T., Siegrist, J., Dragano, N., & Wahrendorf, M. (2015). The association between education and work stress: Does the policy context matter? *PLoS ONE, 10*(3), e0121573. https://doi.org/10.1371/journal .pone.0121573

Madsen, I. E. H., Nyberg, S. T., Magnusson Hanson L. L., Ferrie, J. E. (2017). Job strain as a risk factor for clinical depression: Systematic review and meta-analysis with additional individual participant data. *Psychological Medicine, 47*(8), 1342–1356. https://doi.org/10.1017/ S003329171600355X

Marmot, M., & Siegrist, J. (2016). Challenges to national and international policies. In J. Siegrist & M. Wahrendorf (Eds.), *Work stress and health in a globalized economy: The model of effort-reward imbalance* (pp. 365–378). Springer International Publications.

McEwen, B. P. (1998). Protective and damaging effects of stress mediators. *New England Journal of Medicine 338*, 171–179. https://doi.org/10 .1056/NEJM199801153380307

Merton, R. K. (1968). *Social theory and social structure.* Free Press.

Montano, D., Li, J., & Siegrist, J. (2016). The measurement of effort-reward imbalance (ERI). In J. Siegrist & M. Wahrendorf (Eds.), *Work stress and health in a globalized economy: The model of effort-reward imbalance* (pp. 21–42) Springer International Publications.

Moorman, R. (1991). Relationship between organizational justice and organizational citizenship behavior: Do fairness perceptions influence employee citizenship? *Journal of Applied Psychology, 76*(6) 845–855. https://doi.org/10.1037/0021-9010.76.6.845

Ndjaboué, R., Brisson, C., & Vézina, M. (2012). Organizational justice and mental health: A systematic review of prospective studies. *Occupational and Environmental Medicine, 69*(10), 694–700. https://doi.org/10 .1136/oemed-2011-100524

Rugulies, R., Aust, B., & Madsen, I. E. H. (2017). Effort-reward imbalance at work and risk of depressive disorders: A systematic review and meta-analysis of prospective cohort studies. *Scandinavian Journal of Work Environment and Health 43*(4), 294–306. https://doi.org/10.5271/ sjweh.3632

Schaufeli, W. B., & Taris, T. W. (2014). A critical review of the job demands-resources model: Implications for improving work and health. In G. F. Bauer & O. Hämmig (Eds.), *Bridging occupational, organizational and public health* (pp. 43–68). Springer.

Schultz W. (2006). Behavioral theories and the neurophysiology of reward. *Annual Review of Psychology, 57,* 87–115. https://doi.org/10.1146/ annurev.psych.56.091103.070229

Semmer, N. K. (2020). Conflict and offence to self. In T. Theorell (Ed.), *Handbook of socioeconomic determinants of occupational health* (pp. 423–452). Springer Nature International Publications.

Siegrist, J. (1996). Adverse health effects of high effort-low reward conditions at work. *Journal of Occupational Health Psychology, 1*(1), 27–41. https://doi.org/10.1037/1076-8998.1.1.27

Siegrist, J., & Wahrendorf, M. (Eds.). (2016). *Work stress and health in a globalized economy. The model of effort-reward imbalance.* Springer International Publishing.

Siegrist, J., & Li, J. (2020). Effort-reward imbalance and occupational health. In T. Theorell (Ed.), *Handbook of socioeconomic determinants of occupational health* (pp. 355–382). Springer Nature International Publications.

Siegrist, J., & Marmot, M. (2004). Health inequalities and the psychosocial environment – two challenges. *Social Science & Medicine, 58*(8), 1463–1473. https://doi.org/10.1016/S0277-9536(03)00349-6

Sonnentag, S., & Fritz, C. (2015). Recovery from job stress: The stressor-detachment model as an integrative framework. *Journal of Organizational Behavior, 36*(S1), S72–S103. https://doi.org/10.1002/job.1924

Steptoe, A., & Kivimäki, M. (2012). Stress and cardiovascular disease. *Nature Reviews Cardiology, 9,* 360–370. https://doi.org/10.1038/nrcardio.2012.45

Theorell, T., Jood, K., Järvholm, L. S., Vingård, E., Perk, J., Östergren, P. O., & Hall, C. (2016). A systematic review of studies in the contributions of the work environment to ischaemic heart disease development. *European Journal of Public Health, 26*(3), 470–477. https://doi.org/10.1093/eurpub/ckw025

Theorell, T. (2020). The demand control support work stress model. In T. Theorell (Ed.), *Handbook of socioeconomic determinants of occupational health* (pp. 339–353). Springer Nature International Publications.

Wahrendorf, M., Hoven, H., Goldberg, M., Zins, M., & Siegrist, J. (2019). Adverse employment histories and health functioning: The CONSTANCES study. *International Journal of Epidemiology, 48*(2), 402–414. https://doi.org/10.1093/ije/dyy235

Warr, P. (2017). Happiness and mental health. In C. L. Cooper & J. C. Quick (Eds.), *The handbook of stress and health* (pp. 57–74). Wiley & Sons.

PART II

Line Managers

4 Is It Stressful at the Top?

The Demands of Leadership in Times of Stability and Crisis

DORIAN HARTLAUB, ILKE INCEOGLU,
ALINA S. HERNANDEZ BARK, AND RONIT
KARK

A textbook on organizational stress and well-being wouldn't be complete without taking a closer look at the stress and well-being of line managers, the formal leaders within organizations. It seems almost intuitive to identify leadership with stress since high demands, such as long working hours and complex decision-making, seem to be linked to the job description of an organization's leadership roles. Interest in leaders' stress (and well-being more generally) has increased – in recognition of the fact that leaders' physical and psychological health can decline, partly due to the demands of their jobs (Barling & Cloutier, 2017; Zwingmann et al., 2016). Furthermore, leaders' psychological well-being is of high importance since it affects not only their own leadership behaviors (Kaluza et al., 2020) but also the well-being of their employees (e.g. Arnold, 2017; Inceoglu et al., 2018). However, leaders are an ambiguous case when it comes to stress, and it is difficult to form a generalized judgment about whether it is stressful at the top. While the job demands of a leadership position are higher than those of other employees, leaders typically have more access to various types of resources than their employees and therefore may show lower levels of stress (Sherman et al., 2012) and higher levels of well-being (e.g. Warr & Inceoglu, 2018). Leaders do enjoy a great deal of job control and autonomy, which are well-established stress buffers (e.g. Wall et al., 1990; Warr, 2007), and seem motivated to work long hours, due to financial and psychological rewards (Brett & Stroh, 2003). In this chapter, we assess whether it is indeed more stressful at the top or not. We also attempt to understand the impact of context by contrasting times of stability with times of crises.

Drawing on the current scientific literature, we begin this chapter by briefly addressing the stressor–strain relationship (e.g. De Jonge &

Dormann, 2006), taking the demands-resources perspective (e.g. Demerouti et al., 2001), and explaining why it is important to consider context when discussing the demands leaders face today. The impact of stress on their well-being and behavior in contexts that are character-ized by a fast-paced but generally stable environment is further described. We then discuss how the altered context of a major crisis can shift leaders' experience of work demands. To that end, we refer to the COVID-19 pandemic and the various effects it has had on leaders' roles (Higgins et al., 1994).

Leaders nowadays generally work in fast changing times and work environments with high demands, which can be stressful. However, (effective) leadership is even more relevant during times of high pres-sure for organizations and in times of crisis, with decisions having potentially significant consequences for organizations, employees, and even society more broadly. Especially in these contexts, organiza-tions need leaders who handle demands well, make good decisions, and hold the reins (Van Vugt et al., 2008).

The chapter concludes by giving some suggestions on how to cope with stress by looking at two potential strategies for leaders to use – mindfulness and the social identity approach. Both have been shown to be beneficial for health and well-being as well as reducing stress (Haslam et al., 2016; Khoury et al., 2015). Moreover, recent literature suggests the "fruitful" combination of mindfulness and social identity processes when delivering well-being programs in high-stress environ-ments (Adarves-Yorno et al., 2020).

Mindfulness refers to the ability to willingly bring one's awareness to the present moment, while maintaining a nonjudgmental attitude (e.g. Kabat-Zinn, 2006). The literature linking an individual's dispos-ition for and practice of mindfulness to stress relief and positive effects on psychological health and well-being has long featured in organiza-tional research (Bartlett et al., 2019; Khoury et al., 2015; Tomlinson, 2018). However, besides the individual approach for stress coping that mindfulness provides, leaders in organizations may also rely on social strategies to cope with stress. Just like mindfulness, social iden-tity processes are important predictors of psychological well-being (Adarves-Yorno et al., 2020; Haslam et al., 2019; Steffen et al., 2021). Leaders are part of the team they lead, as well as the group of peer level leaders. Cultivating a sense of belonging to a social group has proven to have tremendous health boosting and stress buffering effects (e.g. Haslam et al., 2009, 2016). Fostering their own attachment to the groups and strengthening their followers' social identification with the organization may therefore constitute another way to counter stress and improve high-level leaders' well-being. Thus, while mindfulness provides a strategy for an individual leader's self-care, the social identity approach considers the leader within the social context of the organization. We focus on these two approaches because they are supported by evidence, although we are well aware that there are alternative ways of coping with the demands that come with a leadership position.

Demands of Leadership and Impact on Well-Being

We experience stress (psychologically and physically) in response to appraising specific events or demands (e.g. Folkman et al., 1986). According to cognitive appraisal theory, in the transaction between an individual and their environment, the individual first assesses whether the situation contains well-being relevant demands (primary appraisal) and then appraises the resources available to overcome the posed demands (Folkman et al., 1986). Leaders are no exception to this process. If both a leader's well-being is threatened as demands are too high and a leader's resources to confront those demands are scarce or unavailable, the leader will most probably feel stressed according to the job demands-resources model (Demerouti et al., 2001). Recent approaches of job demands and well-being (e.g. Crawford et al., 2010) have built on this theory and differentiate between challenge demands, which promote personal growth (e.g. high levels of job responsibility, time pressure) and hindrance demands (e.g. role conflict, red tape, organizational politics), which interfere with goal attainment and are typically perceived as more stressful (e.g. Cavanaugh et al., 2000; LePine et al., 2004). Mindfulness and the social identity approach both seem to be important factors influencing this appraisal process. For instance, mindfulness has been shown to positively affect the ability to cognitively reappraise an event, and social identity processes strengthen the perceived social support, which has soothing effects on individual stress experience (Haslam et al., 2005; Troy et al., 2013).

Leading in the Context of Today's World of Work

As the interaction between a leader and the environment or context he or she operates in influences a leader's cognitive appraisal of workplace demands, contextual factors may help us understand whether leaders are in a stressful role at the top. Let us therefore review the importance of context, which helps us to consider the relationships between leadership and well-being (e.g. Inceoglu et al., 2021) and ultimately performance. Context has been defined by Johns (2006, p. 386) as "situational opportunities and constraints that affect the occurrence and meaning of organizational behavior as well as functional relationships between variables". Oc (2018) added to this that with regard to leadership, it is important to consider in which context leadership is taking place and how leadership processes (e.g. perceptions of leaders, leader–member exchange) unfold within a specific context.

The fast changing and globalized world of work implies that leadership has existed in a context aptly described as a "global rat race". While business opportunities have grown all around the world with continuing globalization, so too have volatility, uncertainty, complexity, and ambiguity (VUCA) in business environments. This has been felt strongly among those leading teams, departments, or even organizations. Having found its way into the business dictionary, the "catchy" acronym VUCA is a poignant description of the context of leadership, which is particularly pertinent to organizations participating in the global economic market across different countries. This context involves challenges such as having to lead internationally located and culturally diverse teams, traveling to attend global strategy meetings, or leading teams virtually. VUCA originated from the military vocabulary (introduced by the US Army War College in the 1990s, describing the post–Cold War circumstances in warfare; Jamil & Humphries-Kil, 2017). The comparison of today's globalized world of work to a modern-day warzone clearly indicates the high demands and the stress mentality prevailing in the managerial environment. In fact, scholars have claimed that one consequence of the financial crisis at the end of the first decade of this century is that a cocktail of high stakes, urgency, and uncertainty form the new norm in terms of demands on leaders in organizations (Heifetz et al., 2009). With that in mind, we first consider the specific job demands leaders face in the context of this "global rat-race" before examining how they can change during a global crisis like the COVID-19 pandemic.

Leader Job Demands in Today's World of Work

Job demands refer to aspects of one's work requiring some type of continued physical or psychological effort (e.g. Demerouti et al., 2001). Job resources refer to aspects that are key to goal achievement and can help reduce the strenuous impact of job demands (Crawford et al., 2010; Demerouti et al., 2001). As stated above, it is the individual's (i.e. the leader's) appraisal that determines whether a demand will be experienced as a challenge or a hindrance. What are the common job demands currently faced by leaders, and are they experienced more as challenges or hindrances?

Leaders' Workload

A major influence on well-being and health at the workplace is the workload, which can either cause individuals to thrive or, when it's too high or too low, impair their performance and stress levels (Alsuraykh et al., 2019). Naturally, workload is a major job demand in a leadership position. Leaders' high workload is tied to the expectation that they coordinate and navigate their organization toward goal achievement (Hogg & Vaughan, 2011). They have to prepare for the unexpected and make sure information is gathered, evaluated, and communicated in order to deal with high VUCA (Bennett & Lemoine, 2014). To do so, they typically spend a large amount of time in meetings, often back-to-back, sharing information, communicating tasks, and coordinating the goals to be achieved. They often have a tight schedule due to traveling and attending meetings in different places, while still carrying important operative responsibilities. Such high workload often results in long working hours.

Workload is likely to be perceived as a challenge demand (Crawford et al., 2010). Viewing workload as a challenge demand goes along with a higher work engagement, which in turn lowers perceived stress (Crawford et al., 2010). However, leaders described as transformational might overstretch themselves, going the extra mile while already feeling exhausted (Zwingmann et al., 2016). This greater engagement can take its toll and lead to work–nonwork conflict (e.g. Halbesleben et al., 2009), with leaders finding it difficult to balance the demands at work with possible demands arising from their parenting or other nonwork role commitments. High workload can therefore negatively impact leaders' health, despite leaders viewing it as a challenge demand or having greater access to health-ameliorating resources, such as more job autonomy (Crawford et al., 2010; Ilies et al., 2010; Smith & Cooper, 1994).

Leaders' Job Complexity

Another demand that could be stressful to leaders is the tremendous complexity they encounter in their jobs. The globalized world of work exposes them to an environment in which there is a high interconnectivity and interdependence among multiple dimensions in a system, which causes complexity (Sinha & Sinha, 2020). High job complexity refers to jobs with difficult tasks, requiring many cognitive resources (Rosopa et al., 2019). The example of leaders having to lead culturally diverse teams that are dispersed over different localities and doing so in virtual work settings has been mentioned before. This can be very demanding on leaders' cognitive resources (Salas et al., 2004). Many leaders also face complex tasks as they are leading within contexts of foreign market regulations and laws. Today's fast changing environments require strong mental effort. Alongside their other job demands, leaders could see such complexity as a threat to their well-being (Chung-Yan, 2010; Folkman et al., 1986).

Yet, even though job complexity is a highly demanding aspect of work, it can be positively associated with job satisfaction and work engagement (Crawford et al., 2010; Srivastava et al., 2010). Job complexity calls for strong mental effort, abilities, and skillfulness, which all tend to be motivating when perceived as challenge (Ali et al., 2014; Crawford et al., 2010). This is especially true if individuals experience the possibility of learning and high levels of autonomy, as would be the case for leaders (Ali et al., 2014; Chung-Yan, 2010; Nurmi & Hinds, 2016). The complexity of a job has furthermore been shown to be crucial in the alleviation of burnout (Kubicek & Korunka, 2015). Job complexity therefore has the potential to benefit a leader's well-being.

Communication When Leading Virtual Teams

Years ago, Fiedler (1992) noted that besides job tasks, interpersonal interactions at work, and difficult ones in particular, can be highly demanding. Leaders carry great responsibility for the relationships among their personnel, their well-being, and how they work together. Globalization has implied that leaders increasingly oversee geographically dispersed teams, adding complexity to their job. Poor communication can be more prevalent in virtual teams, especially when work is characterized by volatility, uncertainties, complexity, and ambiguities. Resulting conflicts can easily be perceived as a hindrance demand (Smith & Cooper, 1994).

Virtual communication channels tend to be less rich, making communication more ambiguous, especially when it involves highly complex or emotional-laden content (Daft & Lengel, 1986). Virtual communication is also less direct, less frequent, and less conducive to being openly shared (Schulze & Krumm, 2017) and has been associated with higher levels of fatigue (Shockley et al., 2021; Shoshan & Wehrt, 2022). As a result, it can be more difficult to build relationships and trust in teams that primarily work together virtually and over distance (Powell et al., 2004). Also, as organizations and teams become increasingly diverse (e.g. Roberson & Stevens, 2006), ambiguity in communication due to virtuality may be compounded by greater diversity in norms, backgrounds, knowledge, and culture.

Leaders' Role Ambiguity

The high VUCA world (Bennett & Lemoine, 2014) also affects the context of organizational leadership through its volatility, meaning the fast pace of change. This may affect specific tasks or even the market situation unexpectedly and unpredictably. Irrespective of whether changes are small, big, negative, or positive, they appear to cause uncertainty (Sinha & Sinha, 2020). In fact, the situation might change faster than information can be communicated to decision-makers, further exposing leaders to uncertainties. Leaders' role can thus become more ambiguous to them. Typically, work role ambiguity negatively affects individuals (Garst et al., 2000). It is linked to poor mental health, such as increased depression (Schmidt et al., 2014). As such, it can easily constitute a hindrance demand for leaders (Garst et al., 2000; LePine et al., 2004).

Organizational Politics

The high VUCA world has significantly transformed the way professional careers have to be approached, laying a greater responsibility on individuals to be their own career brokers (Shaffer & Zalewski, 2011).

Therefore, being strategic and skillful in organizational politics, especially when it comes to positioning oneself for a next career step in the VUCA world, may be very important. Organizational politics denote self-interested attempts to influence others. They can range from self-promoting behavior and ingratiation, occasional rule bending for the sake of goal achievement, to backstabbing (e.g. Landells & Albrecht, 2017). Such actions can be demanding on leaders in a hindering or a challenging way.

Employees who start politicking can be a hindrance. Seeking informal relationships with their leaders with the aim of paving the way to personal advantages may be a problematic demand to handle for leaders (Guo et al., 2019). Highly engaged employees, who typically are less involved in organizational politics, tend to react quite poorly to perceived politicking within the team, perceiving it as unfair (Guo et al., 2019; Rosen et al., 2009). Perceived organizational politics may consequently cause a toxic atmosphere, and interpersonal conflicts in the manipulated leader's team can negatively impact team performance and become a hindrance to the leader (Fiedler, 1992; Guo et al., 2019; Rosen et al., 2009; Zulfadil et al., 2020).

On the other hand, leaders who are more politically skilled can experience less stress and better personal well-being (Cullen et al., 2018). Their skill can lead to recognition by superiors, which would build well-being and health (Grebner et al., 2010; Landells & Albrecht, 2017). Furthermore, being more politically skilled can be beneficial to informal relationships with influential peers and leaders, which could increase the availability of social support. More politically skilled leaders could also get more opportunities to promote their own ideas, which can generate feelings of autonomy and control, and experience greater career advancement, all of which can counter perceived stress (Grebner et al., 2010; Landells & Albrecht, 2017). As such, leaders' political skill could help them view their organization's politics more as a challenge than a hindrance.

Leaders' Loneliness

Loneliness appears to be a professional hazard growing with the level of leadership (Zumaeta, 2019). This seems to be especially true for leaders in the VUCA world, which itself can be described as demanding and lonely for leaders (e.g. Waller et al., 2019). Especially, in times of situational uncertainties, employees expect more guidance and decision-making of their leaders, and social support decreases the higher the leadership level is (e.g. Kark & Van Dijk, 2019; Zumaeta, 2019). Although political skill can contribute to the formation of informal relationships with peers and supervisors that are beneficial for a leaders' career advancement, it may not help with their popularity among peers in general (Guo et al., 2019; Landells & Albrecht, 2017). Being at the "top" may be a lonely place.

The competitiveness that goes along with career advancement can create animosity that stands in the way of closeness to peers or subordinates (Rokach, 2014). Extending on the aspect of strategically seeking out social contacts that may serve a specific egocentric agenda, these contacts don't equal intimate connections and therefore the quality of such relationships might be experienced as poor (Rokach, 2014; Szostek, 2019; Zumaeta, 2019). Once the relationship no longer serves a purpose, it is likely to be dropped by one of the involved parties, as it has become a liability, losing its benefits and leading to disengagement, which consequently may contribute to social distance (Rokach, 2014).

Also, while leaders can be effective at creating a common vision and uniting a team of employees, they may not necessarily feel part of that team. Leaders' relationships with followers typically are imbalanced. This may be due to subordinates conveying an expectation of leaders having to support them without any obvious need to reciprocate (Rokach, 2014). As a result, leaders may develop feelings of being ostracized and lonely. Silard and Wright (2020) proposed that this can be due to status differences between leaders and their followers and that it may be especially true for leaders new to their role and those who are less likely to share their emotions. As loneliness has so many known negative effects on mental health and well-being, it can be seen as another hindrance demand on leaders.

Above we have charted the major demands faced by those in formal positions of leadership in a context of relative economic stability. These demands can sometimes be viewed as challenges, which could benefit leaders' well-being. Others can be seen as hindrances, thus hampering their well-being. Leader job demands like job complexity appear to be challenge demands, which have positive and motivating effects, potentially buffering the stress of leadership. Having to lead virtual teams, greater role ambiguity stemming from the fast pace of change, and loneliness seem to be hindrance demands potentially increasing stress for leadership – with workload and organizational politics potentially having both challenging and hindering effects in a context of relative economic stability. Below we turn our attention to leader job demands in the context of a major crisis.

Demands of Leadership and Impact on Well-Being in Times of Crisis

Leader Job Demands in Times of Crisis

Job demands that leaders face in times of crisis are amplified, while access to resources that buffer stress decreases. The VUCA acronym provides an accurate description for the globalized context of the world of work we have come to know throughout the second decade of the twenty-first century. In fact, globalization has turned aspects of past crises into permanent demands of the working world ever since the financial crisis in the early 2000s (Heifetz et al., 2009). To make matters worse, the spread of COVID-19 in late 2019 and throughout 2020 and 2021 has further elevated those demands to new crisis levels. These heightened demands are likely to stay as greater reliance on remote working and virtual communication have become the "new normal".

A crisis can be seen as a particular episode, unexpectedly and strongly affecting contextual factors. Scholars define organizational crisis as a "low-probability, high-impact event that threatens the viability of the organization and is characterized by ambiguity of cause, effect, and means of resolution, as well as by a belief that decisions must be made swiftly" (Pearson & Clair, 1998, p. 60). The COVID-19 pandemic is such an event. It has impacted nations across the globe, costing the lives of millions of people and threatening the health of even more. Governments had to impose drastic measures such as forcing their citizens into confinements and lockdown in order for people to remain socially distanced and flatten the infection curves. For some periods, only professionals involved in essential services were able to leave their households. Everybody else stayed home until further notice. Children had to be homeschooled and remote work turned the homes of many into offices, substantially blurring the lines between work and personal lives (e.g. Allen et al., 2021; Wood et al., 2021). The unpredictability of spread, mutations, and measures to combat the virus have shocked all areas of societal life, also affecting the context of leadership in organizations within the global economy (Buckley, 2020). The previously mentioned demands of leadership and their impact on leader well-being were clearly affected. Similarly, like after the financial crisis at the beginning of the millennium, the demands heightened since the COVID-19 crisis have led to changes in work flexibility, mobility and a greater reliance on virtual work. We address how the earlier-mentioned demands of leadership can be affected in times of crisis by using the particular context of COVID-19 as an example.

Leaders' Workload: In Times of Crisis

Workload has been described as a possible source for leaders to thrive on or as a hinderance, depending on whether the demands are too high or too low (Alsuraykh et al., 2019). We had concluded that under noncrisis circumstances workload could be seen as a challenge, although this can occur at the expense of well-being and work–nonwork commitments. We know that resources such as job control can potentially buffer the effects of workload on stress (Alsuraykh et al., 2019; Ilies et al., 2010; Rigotti et al., 2020).

In times of crisis, employees need a comforting vision and orientation from their leaders (Day et al., 2004; Jetten et al., 2020; Kark & Van Dijk, 2019; Shamir & Howell, 1999; Stam et al., 2018; Van Vugt et al., 2008). As a result, leaders could experience more subordinate endorsement and perceive more decision-making freedom. Experiencing more job control and autonomy could mitigate the negative effects of leaders' increased workload.

However, psychological detachment from work, sleep quality, and positive work–family interaction in the safe space of home are all important for workload recovery (e.g. Ilies et al., 2015; Sanz-Vergel et al., 2011; Sonnentag & Fritz, 2015), but have been curtailed during the COVID-19 pandemic (Rigotti et al., 2020). The situation at home during the COVID-19 pandemic was demanding in and of itself. Lockdowns forced parents to work from home while taking on extraordinary caring and teaching responsibilities for their children (Rigotti et al., 2020; Shockley et al., 2020). So, if under normal circumstances it has been shown that workload can cause strain-inducing work–family conflict, it is fair to assume that this has been even more the case during the COVID-19 crisis.

In conclusion, leader's workload in times of crisis is heightened, although the stress experience through this increased demand may be mitigated by the greater experience of decision-making freedom. In the particular case of the COVID-19 crisis; however, a leader's workload was likely to be amplified by nonwork commitments and limited possibilities to create psychological detachment from work. Workload was therefore likely to be perceived as hindrance.

Leaders' Job Complexity: In Times of Crisis

Job complexity is generally associated with better well-being, suggesting that it is typically viewed more as a challenge than a hinderance. During a crisis, job complexity increases. More cognitive resources are required to perform the job of a leader as many new and swiftly changing contextual variables manifest themselves.

During the COVID-19 pandemic, the already complex task of leading international and virtual teams has increased further in complexity. Infection varied across locations; governments varied in the strategies and measures used to combat the virus. Leaders had to keep those factors in mind when thinking about how tasks could be assigned. Team members' reduced availability due to homeschooling or other personal issues made task assignments more difficult. Personal issues or tragedies had to be made a priority in order to keep teams performing effectively (Hu et al., 2020). In situations that require high emotional and task complexity, leaders' cognitive resources might suffer, especially with the complexity of leading in a crisis such as COVID. Awareness of shortcomings in leading and not being able to make satisfactory decisions would have easily resulted in stress and ill-health (Folkman et al., 1986). Hence, complexity in times of crisis could become a hindrance demand to leaders.

Communication When Leading Virtual Teams: In Times of Crisis

Clear communication has been described as a crucial skill when leading virtual teams (Schulze & Krumm, 2017) and is even more important in times of crisis (Eldridge et al., 2020). The acute levels of stress experienced during the COVID-19 pandemic, coupled with the dramatic increase in virtual work (D'Auria & De Smet, 2020), exacerbated demands placed on leaders. Not only were more leaders forced to lead virtually, but they were tasked with doing so in a context where many employees were in greater distress than usual.

This abrupt change likely had overwhelming effects on leaders. Many leaders had been thrown into the deep end, having to catch up on many skills (e.g. Schulze & Krumm, 2017) to make their virtual teams work effectively, likely causing role ambiguity or conflict. New structures and methods of communicating had to be established. New ways of keeping team members engaged and connected had to be developed, all on the fly, further adding to leaders' workload and job complexity. Such circumstances were likely experienced more as a hindrance than a challenge.

Leaders' Role Ambiguity: In Times of Crisis
The (noncrisis) context of VUCA has been described as consisting of constant volatile and unpredictable changes, exposing leaders to a prevailing uncertainty on many levels (Sinha & Sinha, 2020). This is likely to increase leaders' role ambiguity. Its negative effects on mental health clearly makes it a hindrance demand for leaders (Garst et al., 2000; LePine et al., 2004; Schmidt et al., 2014). Uncertainties and ambiguities increase in times of crisis by definition (Pearson & Clair, 1998), giving to assume that leaders' role ambiguity does so as well.

Interestingly enough, it can be argued that in times of crisis the leaders' role ambiguity increase might be compensated by several challenge demands like job control and autonomy. Followers explicitly seek for guidance from their superiors, desiring to reduce subjective uncertainties prevailing in times of crisis (Cicero et al., 2010; Day et al., 2004; Jetten et al., 2020; Shamir & Howell, 1999; Van Vugt et al., 2008). The leader becomes the designated decision-maker, typically being less restricted, which favors those who prefer autonomy (Day et al., 2004; Parker et al., 2014). During the COVID-19 crisis, leaders certainly had more freedom, such as trying out and choosing new online tools to enable virtual teamwork or allocate rotations for office hours. The pandemic brought a welcome trend for reduction in organizational bureaucracy and red tape, reducing burdensome rules and regulations and increasing employee ownership (Ellerman & Gonza, 2020; Wise, 2020). In general, leaders tend to receive more endorsement for quick decisions by followers during a crisis, in particular when a leader's communication is opportunity-oriented (Dirani et al., 2020; Kark & Van Dijk, 2019; Stam et al., 2018).

Under different circumstances, leaders might not have so easily been able to take the decisions they did during the COVID crisis, or they at least wouldn't have had the necessary follower support for successful implementation. This fuels a leader's perception of higher amount of freedom in a crisis, which can counter leader stress and potentially increase leader well-being even though the economy is in dire straits (Smith & Cooper, 1994).

Organizational Politics: In Times of Crisis

As times of crisis often provide an opportunity for leaders to arise, being more politically skilled could be quite helpful. Earlier we mentioned that leaders' political skill can facilitate relationships with influential individuals within the organization. This can enhance opportunities for social support that can relieve leaders' stress (Haslam et al., 2005), which would be especially welcome in times of crisis when expectations of the leader are high. Nonetheless, the self-interested nature of politically skilled individuals could be poorly looked upon by subordinates during a crisis, as implied by Haslam and colleagues (2021). While followers are particularly receptive to charismatic leaders in times of crisis, leader behavior seen in such a context as motivated by self-interest is likely to result in poor leader–follower or leader–peer relationships, which can in turn increase leaders' stress (Fiedler, 1992).

Leaders' Loneliness: In Times of Crisis

Due to employees' insecurities and desire for charismatic leadership during times of crisis, leaders may actually feel that during such times, they are shouldering an even greater burden (Stam et al., 2018). Despite any insecurities or fears they could be feeling themselves, leaders might continue to refrain from sharing negative emotions (Silard & Wright, 2020) to serve the interests of followers needing "the woman or man of the hour" to lead them out of the crisis (Shamir & Howell, 1999; Stam et al., 2018). This could have exacerbated leaders' hindering feelings of loneliness (Silard & Wright, 2020).

Table 4.1 provides an overview of the differences between leaders' challenge and hindrance demands in times of stability and those in times of crisis.

Table 4.1 *Leaders' challenge and hindrance demands*

Leader job demand	Times of stability		Times of crisis	
	Challenge[a]	Hindrance[b]	Challenge[a]	Hindrance[b]
Leaders' workload	X	X		X
Leaders job complexity	X			X
Communication when leading virtual teams		X		X
Leaders' role ambiguity		X	X	
Organizational politics	X	X		X
Leaders' loneliness		X		X

[a] *Challenge: Demands that promote personal growth*
[b] *Hindrance: Typically, more stressful and in the way of goal attainment*

What Can Be Done?

Leader Resources
The literature on job resources states that aspects like autonomy, task significance, variety of tasks, the ability to take part in decision-making, and many more spark motivation and negatively affect stress and burnout (Demerouti & Nachreiner, 2019). These aspects may all be associated with leadership positions. A growing body of literature therefore argues that leaders may actually experience less stress than subordinates (e.g. Sherman et al., 2012). Leaders dispose of resources like autonomy, power, or recognition more than followers typically do. Autonomy, decision-making, and job control, for instance, are all inherent to the leadership position. They have been linked to workplace health and performance (Bond & Bunce, 2003; Boswell et al., 2004; Rigotti et al., 2020).

Sometimes however, these leader role-related characteristics are not sufficient to prevent stress, and leaders require support through training and interventions. Leadership training and interventions targeting stress reduction have been proven to effectively foster intra- and interpersonally relevant skills (e.g. Lacerenza et al., 2017). The two approaches we want to focus on for that matter have been introduced already: mindfulness and the social identity approach. Both are salient to the leader job demands discussed in this chapter.

Mindfulness and Social Identity Processes

Mindfulness and social identity processes affect individuals' stress experience through intra- and interpersonal processes, respectively. Mindfulness, referring to the dispositional or trained ability to practice present-moment awareness with a nonjudgmental attitude can be considered an intrapersonal resource for leaders to cope with stress. The social identity approach, on the other hand, seems to influence interpersonal aspects like social support, which is crucial when facing stress.

Mindfulness and Stress. Individuals with a well-developed mindfulness are typically able to better deal with stress. They possess a wide set of skills (internal and external observation, acceptance without judgment, acting with awareness, cognitive diffusion, etc.; e.g. Baer et al., 2004; Hayes et al., 2006), that directly or indirectly affect how they appraise demands that they face. Mindfulness facilitates cognitive reappraisal (Garland et al., 2011), which can help to reevaluate stressors as challenges instead of hindrances. Cognitive reappraisal is defined as changing the way emotional stimuli are thought of, with the aim of changing the emotional impact of an event, thus helping to reduce the intensity of the strain experienced (Garland, 2007; Gross & John, 2003; Gross & Thompson, 2007; Troy et al., 2013). Higher mindfulness goes along with higher positive cognitive reappraisal, and more mindful individuals allocate more positive meaning to stressful events, using benefit-finding as a coping strategy (Garland, 2007; Garland et al., 2011; Troy et al., 2013).

Looking at stress from a challenge–hindrance perspective, positive reappraisal fostered by mindfulness may help leaders to perceive stressors as challenges rather than hindrances. Mindfulness skills contribute to the ability to prevail in a metacognitive state of disengagement with thoughts and feelings (Troy et al., 2013). More mindful leaders are likely to benefit from a greater cognitive flexibility, making it easier for them to disengage and reappraise, rather than identifying with stressful feelings caused by the initial appraisal of demands (Baer et al., 2004; Fletcher & Hayes, 2005; Troy et al., 2013). Garland (2011) found support for an upwards spiraling process of mindfulness leading to positive reappraisal and thereby stress reduction. After the stress appraisal occurred, disengagement from the negative first appraisal is crucial in order to reappraise the situation, and mindfulness helps the internal process to achieve this. Hence, leaders who develop their mindfulness can thereby reduce their perceived stress or even avoid the development of feelings of distress.

In terms of stress reduction and stress prevention, developing leader mindfulness certainly isn't the only existing remedy, but it appears to be a key element from an intrapersonal perspective.

Social Identity and Stress. Tajfel and Turner developed the theory of social identity in the late 1970s which, extended by the theory of self-categorization by Turner and colleagues in the 1980s, forms the social identity approach (Jetten et al., 2020). One of the key statements the social identity approach makes is that people define themselves as "we and us" rather than "I and me", in diverse social contexts, through an internalization of their group membership. As a consequence, social identity affects the mental, cognitive, and physical well-being of individuals, and consequently, a person's psyche is under the influence of the state of the group with which they identify (Haslam et al., 2009; Häusser et al., 2012; Jetten et al., 2014).

The interpersonal effects of social identification on cognitive appraisal processes are as follows. With a salient social identification, the appraisal taking place will be based on whether the ingroup's well-being is threatened. If so, then social support will be included in the evaluation of available resources to confront this threat (van Dick, 2015). The social support within a group of people who strongly identify with each other increases in the face of adversity, which is a helpful mechanism for eventually overcoming a problem and buffering stress (Haslam et al., 2005).

Thereby, the interpersonal component of the social identity approach explains how leaders who strongly identify with their organization, their peers, and their team may actually feel social support, as well as an abundance of resources to overcome stressors.

How Mindfulness and Social Identity Help Leaders Cope with Job Demands

Mindfulness and social identity processes are both helpful in predicting well-being and alleviating stress and can be combined in interventions designed to help people cope with highly stressful environments (Adarves-Yorno et al., 2020). Both mindfulness and social identity impact the cognitive appraisal processes and can add to leaders' resources for coping with the demands they face.

To improve intrapersonal processing, leaders can bolster their mindfulness skills by introducing a regular mindfulness practice to their daily routine. Of course, organizational programs providing mindfulness training to employees and leaders are helpful as well and have become increasingly popular (Reb et al., 2020).

To use the social identity approach to coping, leaders could look at their leadership role as one of social identity management. Such identity leadership is built around the development of a shared social identity surrounding the leader and his or her team, peers, and organization (Steffens et al., 2014). Identity leadership involves leaders clearly showing that they are "of the group" (identity prototypicality), that what they do is done with the best interests of the team at heart (identity advancement), that they craft a clear sense of "us" (identity entrepreneurship) and make it matter to be part of the team (identity impresarioship). A social identity approach to leadership that provides leaders and their followers a stronger social identity is very likely to lower stress for all concerned. Combining mindfulness and identity leadership principles in training programs on leader coping strategies seems promising as both mindfulness and social identity–oriented trainings have been shown to be effective in high-stress environments (Adarves-Yorno et al., 2020).

Leaders with a stronger social identity would more easily feel like they have more social support and therefore more resources to deal with workload, job complexity, or the uncertainties of the fast-paced change of today's world of work. Leader loneliness would be less of a stressor as social identity provides a sense of social and emotional belonging (Peterson, 2005). Social identification could also buffer against organizational politics by fostering social support and engagement. Furthermore, shared identity is a key aspect of good communication, which helps to prevent hindrance stress through virtual collaboration (Greenaway et al., 2015).

Leader mindfulness provides leaders with the ability to be more accepting of circumstances and less rigidly tied to the first appraisal, allowing for more positive reappraisal resulting in stress reduction (Garland et al., 2011). More mindful leaders should more easily view workload, job complexity, the fast pace of change, and uncertainty as well as virtual leadership as challenge rather than hindrance demands. Furthermore, mindfulness has been related to the reduction of loneliness (Lindsay et al., 2019) and the reduction of destructive, deviant, or unethical pro-organizational politicking behavior (Wan et al., 2020), which would both reduce the stress of leadership.

Not All That Glitters Is Gold

We caution readers not to consider mindfulness and social identity as panaceas for leaders' stress. Even though these seem promising, more research, specifically looking at the proposed relationships, is necessary to understand how to best make use of both coping strategies and especially on how to best combine them. Leader mindfulness and social identity processes are neither a guarantee against stress at the top, nor the only way to alleviate or prevent it. For example, job design remains an important consideration for alleviating or preventing stress in leadership (and other) roles.

Today's world of work poses many demands on both leaders and followers, and the price of the wear and tear of such a stressful work environment is high. Leaders do in fact hold a great responsibility for the stress their employees experience and play a crucial role in occupational health (Montano et al., 2017). Leaders have to be aware that they are role models and set the tone for their subordinates to follow (Inceoglu et al., 2018). This means that leaders must set an example by taking their self-care seriously.

References

Adarves-Yorno, I., Mahdon, M., Schueltke, L., Koschate-Reis, M., & Tarrant, M. (2020). Mindfulness and social identity: Predicting well-being in a high-stress environment. *Journal of Applied Social Psychology, 50*(12), 720–732. https://doi.org/10.1111/jasp.12708

Ali, S. A. M., Said, N. A., Yunus, N. M., Kader, S. F. A., Latif, D. S. A., & Munap, R. (2014). Hackman and Oldham's job characteristics model to job satisfaction. *Procedia – Social and Behavioral Sciences, 129*, 46–52. https://doi.org/10.1016/j.sbspro.2014.03.646

Allen, T. D., Merlo, K., Lawrence, R. C., Slutsky, J., & Gray, C. E. (2021). Boundary management and work–nonwork balance while working from home. *Applied Psychology, 70*(1), 60–84. https://doi.org/10.1111/apps.12300

Alsuraykh, N. H., Wilson, M. L., Tennent, P., & Sharples, S. (2019). How stress and mental workload are connected. *Proceedings of the 13th EAI International Conference on Pervasive Computing Technologies for Healthcare*, 371–376. https://doi.org/10.1145/3329189.3329235

Arnold, K. A. (2017). Transformational leadership and employee psychological well-being: A review and directions for future research. *Journal of Occupational Health Psychology*, 22(3), 381–393. https://doi.org/10 .1037/ocp0000062

Baer, R. A., Smith, G. T., & Allen, K. B. (2004). Assessment of mindfulness by self-report: The Kentucky inventory of mindfulness skills. *Assessment*, 11(3), 191–206. https://doi.org/10.1177/1073191104268029

Barling, J., & Cloutier, A. (2017). Leaders' mental health at work: Empirical, methodological, and policy directions. *Journal of Occupational Health Psychology*, 22(3), 394–406. https://doi.org/10.1037/ocp0000055

Bartlett, L., Martin, A., Neil, A. L., Memish, K., Otahal, P., Kilpatrick, M., & Sanderson, K. (2019). A systematic review and meta-analysis of workplace mindfulness training randomized controlled trials. *Journal of Occupational Health Psychology*, 24(1), 108–126. https://doi.org/10 .1037/ocp0000146

Bennett, N., & Lemoine, G. J. (2014). What a difference a word makes: Understanding threats to performance in a VUCA world. *Business Horizons*, 57(3), 311–317. https://doi.org/10.1016/j.bushor.2014.01.001

Bond, F. W., & Bunce, D. (2003). The role of acceptance and job control in mental health, job satisfaction, and work performance. *Journal of Applied Psychology*, 88(6), 1057–1067. https://doi.org/10.1037/0021-9010.88.6.1057

Boswell, W. R., Olson-Buchanan, J. B., & LePine, M. A. (2004). Relations between stress and work outcomes: The role of felt challenge, job control, and psychological strain. *Journal of Vocational Behavior, 64* (1), 165–181. https://doi.org/10.1016/S0001-8791(03)00049-6

Brett, J. M., & Stroh, L. K. (2003). Working 61 plus hours a week: Why do managers do it? *Journal of Applied Psychology*, 88(1), 67–78. https:// doi.org/10.1037/0021-9010.88.1.67

Buckley, P. J. (2020). The theory and empirics of the structural reshaping of globalization. *Journal of International Business Studies, 51*(9), 1580–1592. https://doi.org/10.1057/s41267-020-00355-5

Cavanaugh, M. A., Boswell, W. R., Roehling, M. V., & Boudreau, J. W. (2000). An empirical examination of self-reported work stress among U.S. managers. *Journal of Applied Psychology, 85*(1), 65–74. https://doi .org/10.1037/0021-9010.85.1.65

Chung-Yan, G. A. (2010). The nonlinear effects of job complexity and autonomy on job satisfaction, turnover, and psychological well-being.

Journal of Occupational Health Psychology, 15(3), 237–251. https://doi.org/10.1037/a0019823

Cicero, L., Pierro, A., & Knippenberg, D. V. (2010). Leadership and uncertainty: How role ambiguity affects the relationship between leader group prototypicality and leadership effectiveness. *British Journal of Management, 21*(2), 411–421. https://doi.org/10.1111/j.1467-8551.2009.00648.x

Crawford, E. R., LePine, J. A., & Rich, B. L. (2010). Linking job demands and resources to employee engagement and burnout: A theoretical extension and meta-analytic test. *Journal of Applied Psychology, 95*(5), 834–848. https://doi.org/10.1037/a0019364

Cullen, K. L., Gerbasi, A., & Chrobot-Mason, D. (2018). Thriving in central network positions: The role of political skill. *Journal of Management, 44*(2), 682–706. https://doi.org/10.1177/0149206315571154

Daft, R. L., & Lengel, R. H. (1986). Organizational information requirements, media richness and structural design. *Management Science, 32*(5), 554–571. https://doi.org/10.1287/mnsc.32.5.554

D'Auria, G., & De Smet, A. (2020, March). *Leadership in a crisis: Responding to the coronavirus outbreak and future challenges.* https://mck.co/3vilcqE

Day, D. V., Sin, H.-P., & Chen, T. T. (2004). Assessing the burdens of leadership: Effects of formal leadership roles on individual performance over time. *Personnel Psychology, 57*(3), 573–605. https://doi.org/10.1111/j.1744-6570.2004.00001.x

De Jonge, J., & Dormann, C. (2006). Stressors, resources, and strain at work: A longitudinal test of the triple-match principle. *Journal of Applied Psychology, 91*(6), 1359–1374. https://doi.org/10.1037/0021-9010.91.5.1359

Demerouti, E., Bakker, A. B., Nachreiner, F., & Schaufeli, W. B. (2001). The job demands-resources model of burnout. *Journal of Applied Psychology, 86*(3), 499–512. https://doi.org/10.1037/0021-9010.86.3.499

Demerouti, E., & Nachreiner, F. (2019). Zum Arbeitsanforderungen-Arbeitsressourcen-Modell von Burnout und Arbeitsengagement – Stand der Forschung. *Zeitschrift für Arbeitswissenschaft, 73*(2), 119–130. https://doi.org/10.1007/s41449-018-0100-4

van Dick, R. (2015). *Stress lass nach! Wie Gruppen unser Stresserleben beeinflussen.* Springer. https://doi.org/10.1007/978-3-662-46573-8

Dirani, K. M., Abadi, M., Alizadeh, A., Barhate, B., Garza, R. C., Gunasekara, N., Ibrahim, G., & Majzun, Z. (2020). Leadership competencies and the essential role of human resource development in times of crisis: A response to Covid-19 pandemic. *Human Resource Development*

International, *23*(4), 380–394. https://doi.org/10.1080/13678868.2020 .1780078

Eldridge, C. C., Hampton, D., & Marfell, J. (2020). Communication during crisis. *Nursing Management*, *51*(8), 50–53. https://doi.org/10.1097/01 .NUMA.0000688976.29383.dc

Ellerman, D. P., & Gonza, T. (2020). Coronavirus crisis: Government aid that also promotes employee ownership. *Intereconomics*, *55*(3), 175–180. https://doi.org/10.1007/s10272-020-0898-9

Fiedler, F. E. (1992). Time-based measures of leadership experience and organizational performance: A review of research and a preliminary model. *The Leadership Quarterly*, *3*(1), 5–23. https://doi.org/10.1016/ 1048-9843(92)90003-X

Fletcher, L., & Hayes, S. C. (2005). Relational frame theory, acceptance and commitment therapy, and a functional analytic definition of mindfulness. *Journal of Rational-Emotive & Cognitive-Behavior Therapy*, *23* (4), 315–336. https://doi.org/10.1007/s10942-005-0017-7

Folkman, S., Lazarus, R. S., Dunkel-Schetter, C., DeLongis, A., & Gruen, R. J. (1986). Dynamics of a stressful encounter: Cognitive appraisal, coping, and encounter outcomes. *Journal of Personality and Social Psychology*, *50*(5), 992–1003. https://doi.org/10.1037/0022-3514.50.5.992

Garland, E. L. (2007). The meaning of mindfulness: A second-order cybernetics of stress, metacognition, and coping. *Complementary Health Practice Review*, *12*(1), 15–30. https://doi.org/10.1177/ 1533210107301740

Garland, E. L., Gaylord, S. A., & Fredrickson, B. L. (2011). Positive reappraisal mediates the stress-reductive effects of mindfulness: An upward spiral process. *Mindfulness*, *2*(1), 59–67. https://doi.org/10 .1007/s12671-011-0043-8

Garst, H., Frese, M., & Molenaar, P. C. M. (2000). The temporal factor of change in stressor–strain relationships: A growth curve model on a longitudinal study in East Germany. *Journal of Applied Psychology*, *85*(3), 417–438. https://doi.org/10.1037/0021-9010.85.3.417

Grebner, S., Elfering, A., & Semmer, N. K. (2010). The success resource model of job stress. In P. L. Perrewé & D. C. Ganster (Eds.), *Research in Occupational Stress and Well-being* (Vol. 8, pp. 61–108). Emerald Group Publishing Limited. https://doi.org/10.1108/S1479-3555(2010) 0000008005

Greenaway, K. H., Wright, R. G., Willingham, J., Reynolds, K. J., & Haslam, S. A. (2015). Shared identity is key to effective communication. *Personality and Social Psychology Bulletin*, *41*(2), 171–182. https://doi .org/10.1177/0146167214559709

Gross, J. J., & John, O. P. (2003). Individual differences in two emotion regulation processes: Implications for affect, relationships, and well-being. *Journal of Personality and Social Psychology, 85*(2), 348–362. https://doi.org/10.1037/0022-3514.85.2.348

Gross, J. J., & Thompson, R. A. (2007). Emotion regulation: Conceptual foundations. In J. J. Gross (Ed.), *Handbook of emotion regulation* (pp. 3–24). Guilford Press.

Guo, Y., Kang, H., Shao, B., & Halvorsen, B. (2019). Organizational politics as a blindfold: Employee work engagement is negatively related to supervisor-rated work outcomes when organizational politics is high. *Personnel Review, 48*(3), 784–798. https://doi.org/10.1108/PR-07-2017-0205

Halbesleben, J. R. B., Harvey, J., & Bolino, M. C. (2009). Too engaged? A conservation of resources view of the relationship between work engagement and work interference with family. *Journal of Applied Psychology, 94*(6), 1452–1465. https://doi.org/10.1037/a0017595

Haslam, C., Cruwys, T., Haslam, S. A., Dingle, G., & Chang, M. X.-L. (2016). Groups 4 Health: Evidence that a social-identity intervention that builds and strengthens social group membership improves mental health. *Journal of Affective Disorders, 194*, 188–195. https://doi.org/10.1016/j.jad.2016.01.010

Haslam, S. A., Jetten, J., Postmes, T., & Haslam, C. (2009). Social identity, health and well-being: An emerging agenda for applied psychology. *Applied Psychology, 58*(1), 1–23. https://doi.org/10.1111/j.1464-0597.2008.00379.x

Haslam, S. A., O'Brien, A., Jetten, J., Vormedal, K., & Penna, S. (2005). Taking the strain: Social identity, social support, and the experience of stress. *British Journal of Social Psychology, 44*(3), 355–370. https://doi.org/10.1348/014466605X37468

Haslam, S. A., Steffens, N. K., & Peters, K. (2019). The importance of creating and harnessing a sense of "us": Social identity as the missing link between leadership and health. In D. Maughan, R. Williams, V. Kemmp, S. A. Haslam, C. Haslam, K. S. Bhui, & S. Bailey (Eds.), *Social scaffolding: Applying the lessons of contemporary social science to health and healthcare* (pp. 302–311). Cambridge University Press. https://doi.org/10.1017/9781911623069.029

Haslam, S. A., Steffens, N. K., Reicher, S. D., & Bentley, S. V. (2021). Identity leadership in a crisis: A 5R framework for learning from responses to COVID-19. *Social Issues and Policy Review, 15*(1), 35–83. https://doi.org/10.1111/sipr.12075

Häusser, J. A., Kattenstroth, M., van Dick, R., & Mojzisch, A. (2012). "We" are not stressed: Social identity in groups buffers neuroendocrine stress reactions. *Journal of Experimental Social Psychology*, *48*(4), 973–977. https://doi.org/10.1016/j.jesp.2012.02.020

Hayes, S. C., Luoma, J. B., Bond, F. W., Masuda, A., & Lillis, J. (2006). Acceptance and commitment therapy: Model, processes and outcomes. *Behavior Research and Therapy*, *44*(1), 1–25. https://doi.org/10.1016/j .brat.2005.06.006

Heifetz, R., Grashow, A., & Linsky, M. (2009). Leadership in a (permanent) crisis. *Harvard Business Review*, *11*, 2–7.

Higgins, E. T., Roney, C. J. R., Crowe, E., & Hymes, C. (1994). Ideal versus ought predilections for approach and avoidance distinct self-regulatory systems. *Journal of Personality and Social Psychology*, *66*(2), 276–286. https://doi.org/10.1037/0022-3514.66.2.276

Hogg, M. A., & Vaughan, G. M. (2011). *Social psychology* (6th ed.). Prentice Hall.

Hu, J., He, W., & Zhou, K. (2020). The mind, the heart, and the leader in times of crisis: How and when COVID-19-triggered mortality salience relates to state anxiety, job engagement, and prosocial behavior. *Journal of Applied Psychology*, *105*(11), 1218–1233. https://doi.org/10.1037/ apl0000620

Ilies, R., Dimotakis, N., & De Pater, I. E. (2010). Psychological and physiological reactions to high workloads: Implications for well-being. *Personnel Psychology*, *63*(2), 407–436. https://doi.org/10.1111/j.1744-6570.2010.01175.x

Ilies, R., Keeney, J., & Goh, Z. W. (2015). Capitalising on positive work events by sharing them at home: Work–family capitalisation. *Applied Psychology*, *64*(3), 578–598. https://doi.org/10.1111/apps.12022

Inceoglu, I., Arnold, K. A., Leroy, H., Lang, W. B., & Stephan, U. (2021). From microscopic to macroscopic perspectives: The study of leadership and health/well-being. *Journal of Occupational Health Psychology*, *26* (6), 459–468. https://doi.org/10.1037/ocp0000316

Inceoglu, I., Thomas, G., Chu, C., Plans, D., & Gerbasi, A. (2018). Leadership behavior and employee well-being: An integrated review and a future research agenda. *The Leadership Quarterly*, *29*(1), 179–202. https://doi.org/10.1016/j.leaqua.2017.12.006

Jamil, N., & Humphries-Kil, M. (2017). Living and leading in a VUCA world: Response-ability and people of faith. In S. S. Nandram & P. K. Bindlish (Eds.), *Managing VUCA through integrative self-management* (pp. 65–79). Springer International Publishing. https://doi.org/10.1007/ 978-3-319-52231-9_5

Jetten, J., Haslam, C., Haslam, S. A., Dingle, G., & Jones, J. M. (2014). How groups affect our health and well-being: The path from theory to policy:

Groups, health, and well-being. *Social Issues and Policy Review*, *8*(1), 103–130. https://doi.org/10.1111/sipr.12003

Jetten, J., Reicher, S. D., Haslam, S. A., & Cruwys, T. (2020). *Together apart: The psychology of COVID-19*. SAGE.

Johns, G. (2006). The essential impact of context on organizational behavior. *Academy of Management Review*, *31*(2), 386–408. https://doi.org/10.5465/amr.2006.20208687

Kabat-Zinn, J. (2006). Mindfulness-based interventions in context: Past, present, and future. *Clinical Psychology: Science and Practice*, *10*(2), 144–156. https://doi.org/10.1093/clipsy.bpg016

Kaluza, A. J., Boer, D., Buengeler, C., & van Dick, R. (2020). Leadership behavior and leader self-reported well-being: A review, integration and meta-analytic examination. *Work & Stress*, *34*(1), 34–56. https://doi.org/10.1080/02678373.2019.1617369

Kark, R., & Van Dijk, D. (2019). Keep your head in the clouds and your feet on the ground: A multifocal review of leadership–followership self-regulatory focus. *Academy of Management Annals*, *13*(2), 509–546. https://doi.org/10.5465/annals.2017.0134

Khoury, B., Sharma, M., Rush, S. E., & Fournier, C. (2015). Mindfulness-based stress reduction for healthy individuals: A meta-analysis. *Journal of Psychosomatic Research*, *78*(6), 519–528. https://doi.org/10.1016/j.jpsychores.2015.03.009

Kubicek, B., & Korunka, C. (2015). Does job complexity mitigate the negative effect of emotion-rule dissonance on employee burnout? *Work & Stress*, *29*(4), 379–400. https://doi.org/10.1080/02678373.2015.1074954

Lacerenza, C. N., Reyes, D. L., Marlow, S. L., Joseph, D. L., & Salas, E. (2017). Leadership training design, delivery, and implementation: A meta-analysis. *Journal of Applied Psychology*, *102*(12), 1686–1718. https://doi.org/10.1037/apl0000241

Landells, E. M., & Albrecht, S. L. (2017). The positives and negatives of organizational politics: A qualitative study. *Journal of Business and Psychology*, *32*(1), 41–58. https://doi.org/10.1007/s10869-015-9434-5

LePine, J. A., LePine, M. A., & Jackson, C. L. (2004). Challenge and hindrance stress: Relationships with exhaustion, motivation to learn, and learning performance. *Journal of Applied Psychology*, *89*(5), 883–891. https://doi.org/10.1037/0021-9010.89.5.883

Lindsay, E. K., Young, S., Brown, K. W., Smyth, J. M., & Creswell, J. D. (2019). Mindfulness training reduces loneliness and increases social contact in a randomized controlled trial. *Proceedings of the National Academy of Sciences*, *116*(9), 3488–3493. https://doi.org/10.1073/pnas.1813588116

Montano, D., Reeske, A., Franke, F., & Hüffmeier, J. (2017). Leadership, followers' mental health and job performance in organizations: A comprehensive meta-analysis from an occupational health perspective. *Journal of Organizational Behavior, 38*(3), 327–350. https://doi .org/10.1002/job.2124

Nurmi, N., & Hinds, P. J. (2016). Job complexity and learning opportunities: A silver lining in the design of global virtual work. *Journal of International Business Studies, 47*(6), 631–654. https://doi.org/10 .1057/jibs.2016.11

Oc, B. (2018). Contextual leadership: A systematic review of how contextual factors shape leadership and its outcomes. *The Leadership Quarterly, 29*(1), 218–235. https://doi.org/10.1016/j.leaqua.2017.12.004

Parker, S. L., Laurie, K. R., Newton, C. J., & Jimmieson, N. L. (2014). Regulatory focus moderates the relationship between task control and physiological and psychological markers of stress: A work simulation study. *International Journal of Psychophysiology, 94*(3), 390–398. https://doi.org/10.1016/j.ijpsycho.2014.10.009

Pearson, C. M., & Clair, J. A. (1998). Reframing crisis management. *Academy of Management Review, 23*(1), 59–76. https://doi.org/10 .2307/259099

Peterson, C. N. (2005). *How social identity influences social and emotional loneliness.* Walden University ScholarWorks. https://scholarworks .waldenu.edu/cgi/viewcontent.cgi?article=7051&context=dissertations

Powell, A., Piccoli, G., & Ives, B. (2004). Virtual teams: A review of current literature and directions for future research. *ACM SIGMIS Database: The DATABASE for Advances in Information Systems, 35*(1), 6–36. https://doi.org/10.1145/968464.968467

Reb, J., Allen, T., & Vogus, T. J. (2020). Mindfulness arrives at work: Deepening our understanding of mindfulness in organizations. *Organizational Behavior and Human Decision Processes, 159*, 1–7. https://doi.org/10.1016/j.obhdp.2020.04.001

Rigotti, T., De Cuyper, N., & Sekiguchi, T. (2020). The corona crisis: What can we learn from earlier studies in applied psychology? *Applied Psychology, 69*(3), 1–6. https://doi.org/10.1111/apps.12265

Roberson, Q. M., & Stevens, C. K. (2006). Making sense of diversity in the workplace: Organizational justice and language abstraction in employees' accounts of diversity-related incidents. *Journal of Applied Psychology, 91* (2), 379–391. https://doi.org/10.1037/0021-9010.91.2.379

Rokach, A. (2014). Leadership and loneliness. *International Journal of Leadership and Change, 2*(1), 49–58. http://digitalcommons.wku.edu/ ijlc/vol2/iss1/6

Rosen, C. C., Chang, C.-H., Johnson, R. E., & Levy, P. E. (2009). Perceptions of the organizational context and psychological contract breach: Assessing competing perspectives. *Organizational Behavior and Human Decision Processes*, *108*(2), 202–217. https://doi.org/10.1016/j .obhdp.2008.07.003

Rosopa, P. J., McIntyre, A. L., Fairbanks, I. N., & D'Souza, K. B. (2019). Core self-evaluations, job complexity, and net worth: An examination of mediating and moderating factors. *Personality and Individual Differences*, *150*, Article 109518. https://doi.org/10.1016/j.paid.2019 .109518

Salas, E., Burke, C., Fowlkes, J., & Wilson, K. (2004). Challenges and approaches to understanding Leadership Efficacy in multi-cultural teams. In M. Kaplan (Ed.), *Advances in Human Performance and Cognitive Engineering Research: Volume 4. Cultural Ergonomics* (pp. 341–384). Emerald. https://doi.org/10.1016/S1479-3601(03)04012-8

Sanz-Vergel, A. I., Demerouti, E., Mayo, M., & Moreno-Jiménez, B. (2011). Work–home interaction and psychological strain: The moderating role of sleep quality. *Applied Psychology*, *60*(2), 210–230. https://doi.org/10 .1111/j.1464-0597.2010.00433.x

Schmidt, S., Roesler, U., Kusserow, T., & Rau, R. (2014). Uncertainty in the workplace: Examining role ambiguity and role conflict, and their link to depression – a meta-analysis. *European Journal of Work and Organizational Psychology*, *23*(1), 91–106. https://doi.org/10.1080/ 1359432X.2012.711523

Shoshan, H. N., & Wehrt, W. (2022). Understanding "Zoom fatigue": A mixed-method approach. *Applied Psychology*, *71*(3), 827–852.

Schulze, J., & Krumm, S. (2017). The "virtual team player": A review and initial model of knowledge, skills, abilities, and other characteristics for virtual collaboration. *Organizational Psychology Review*, *7*(1), 66–95. https://doi.org/10.1177/2041386616675522

Shaffer, L. S., & Zalewski, J. M. (2011). Career advising in a VUCA environment. *NACADA Journal*, *31*(1), 64–74. https://doi.org/10.12930/0271-9517-31.1.64

Shamir, B., & Howell, J. M. (1999). Organizational and contextual influences on the emergence and effectiveness of charismatic leadership. *The Leadership Quarterly*, *10*(2), 257–283. https://doi.org/10.1016/S1048-9843(99)00014-4

Sherman, G. D., Lee, J. J., Cuddy, A. J. C., Renshon, J., Oveis, C., Gross, J. J., & Lerner, J. S. (2012). Leadership is associated with lower levels of stress. *Proceedings of the National Academy of Sciences*, *109*(44), 17903–17907. https://doi.org/10.1073/pnas.1207042109

Silard, A., & Wright, S. (2020). The price of wearing (or not wearing) the crown: The effects of loneliness on leaders and followers. *Leadership*, *16*(4), 389–410. https://doi.org/10.1177/1742715019893828

Sinha, D., & Sinha, S. (2020). Managing in a VUCA world: Possibilities and pitfalls. *Journal of Technology Management for Growing Economies*, *11*(1), 17–21. https://doi.org/10.15415/jtmge.2020.111003

Smith, M., & Cooper, C. (1994). Leadership and stress. *Leadership & Organization Development Journal*, *15*(2), 3–7. https://doi.org/10.1108/01437739410055290

Srivastava, A., Locke, E. A., Judge, T. A., & Adams, J. W. (2010). Core self-evaluations as causes of satisfaction: The mediating role of seeking task complexity. *Journal of Vocational Behavior*, *77*(2), 255–265. https://doi.org/10.1016/j.jvb.2010.04.008

Stam, D., van Knippenberg, D., Wisse, B., & Nederveen Pieterse, A. (2018). Motivation in words: Promotion- and prevention-oriented leader communication in times of crisis. *Journal of Management*, *44*(7), 2859–2887. https://doi.org/10.1177/0149206316654543

Steffens, N. K., LaRue, C. J., Haslam, C., Walter, Z. C., Cruwys, T., Munt, K. A., ... & Tarrant, M. (2021). Social identification-building interventions to improve health: A systematic review and meta-analysis. *Health Psychology Review*, *15*(1), 85–112.

Steffens, N. K., Haslam, S. A., Reicher, S. D., Platow, M. J., Fransen, K., Yang, J., Ryan, M. K., Jetten, J., Peters, K., & Boen, F. (2014). Leadership as social identity management: Introducing the Identity Leadership Inventory (ILI) to assess and validate a four-dimensional model. *The Leadership Quarterly*, *25*(5), 1001–1024. https://doi.org/10.1016/j.leaqua.2014.05.002

Szostek, D. (2019). The impact of the quality of interpersonal relationships between Employees on counterproductive work behavior: A study of employees in Poland. *Sustainability*, *11*(21), 5916. https://doi.org/10.3390/su11215916

Shockley, K. M., Gabriel, A. S., Robertson, D., Rosen, C. C., Chawla, N., Ganster, M. L., & Ezerins, M. E. (2021). The fatiguing effects of camera use in virtual meetings: A within-person field experiment. *Journal of Applied Psychology*, *106*(8), 1137–1155. https://doi.org/10.1037/apl0000948

Shockley, K. M., Clark, M. A., Dodd, H., & King, E. B. (2020). Work–family strategies during COVID-19: Examining gender dynamics among dual-earner couples with young children. *Journal of Applied Psychology*. Advance online publication. http://doi.org/10.1037/apl0000857

Sonnentag, S., & Fritz, C. (2015). Recovery from job stress: The stressor-detachment model as an integrative framework. *Journal of Organizational behavior, 36*(S1), S72–S103.

Tomlinson, E. R., Yousaf, O., Vittersø, A. D., & Jones, L. (2018). Dispositional mindfulness and psychological health: A systematic review. *Mindfulness, 9*(1), 23–43. https://doi.org/10.1007/s12671-017-0762-6

Troy, A. S., Shallcross, A. J., Davis, T. S., & Mauss, I. B. (2013). History of mindfulness-based cognitive therapy is associated with increased cognitive reappraisal ability. *Mindfulness, 4*(3), 213–222. https://doi.org/10.1007/s12671-012-0114-5

Van Vugt, M., Hogan, R., & Kaiser, R. B. (2008). Leadership, followership, and evolution: Some lessons from the past. *American Psychologist, 63*(3), 182–196. https://doi.org/10.1037/0003-066X.63.3.182

Wall, T. D., Corbett, J. M., Martin, R., Clegg, C. W., & Jackson, P. R. (1990). Advanced manufacturing technology, work design, and performance: A change study. *Journal of Applied Psychology, 75*(6), 691–697. https://doi.org/10.1037/0021-9010.75.6.691

Waller, R. E., Lemoine, P. A., Mense, E. G., Garretson, C. J., & Richardson, M. D. (2019). Global higher education in a VUCA world: Concerns and projections. *Journal of Education and Development, 3*(2), 73. https://doi.org/10.20849/jed.v3i2.613

Wan, M., Zivnuska, S., & Valle, M. (2020). Examining mindfulness and its relationship to unethical behaviors. *Management Research Review, 43*(12). https://doi.org/10.1108/MRR-01-2020-0035

Warr, P. (2007). Searching for happiness at work. *The Psychologist, 20*(12), 726–729.

Warr, P., & Inceoglu, I. (2018). Work orientations, well-being and job content of self-employed and employed professionals. *Work, Employment and Society, 32*(2), 292-311.

Wise, J. (2020). GPs call for cut in red tape to manage aftermath of Covid-19. *BMJ.* https://doi.org/10.1136/bmj.m2729

Wood, S. J., Michaelides, G., Inceoglu, I., Hurren, E. T., Daniels, K., & Niven, K. (2021). Homeworking, well-being and the Covid-19 pandemic: A diary study. *International Journal of Environmental Research and Public Health, 18*(14), 7575.

Zulfadil, Hendriani, S., & Machasin. (2020). The influence of emotional intelligence on team performance through knowledge sharing, team conflict, and the structure mechanism. *Journal of Management Development, 39*(3), 269–292. https://doi.org/10.1108/JMD-12-2018-0354

Zumaeta, J. (2019). Lonely at the top: How do senior leaders navigate the need to belong? *Journal of Leadership & Organizational Studies, 26*(1), 111–135. https://doi.org/10.1177/1548051818774548

Zwingmann, I., Wolf, S., & Richter, P. (2016). Every light has its shadow: A longitudinal study of transformational leadership and leaders' emotional exhaustion: Every light has its shadow. *Journal of Applied Social Psychology, 46*(1), 19–33. https://doi.org/10.1111/jasp.12352

5 | The Role of Line Managers in Promoting and Protecting Employee Well-Being

AMANDA J. HANCOCK, NORA ELENA
DAHER-MORENO, AND KARA A. ARNOLD

The integral role that leaders play in employee well-being has been the subject of numerous systematic reviews and meta-analyses in recent years (see for example Harms et al., 2017; Inceoglu et al., 2017; Montano et al., 2017). Due to this impressive body of work, it has become generally accepted that constructive styles of leadership promote positive employee well-being and mitigate negative employee well-being, while the opposite can be said for destructive styles of leadership (e.g., Arnold, 2017; Tepper et al., 2017).

Even with this expansive body of literature, many questions remain unanswered. Leaders of present-day organizations are challenged to support employee well-being amid contextual forces such as an increasingly globalized economy, changing gender norms, an unprecedented pace of technological change, and global crises such as the Covid-19 pandemic. Thus, the field has emphasized the need to begin to address questions of 'how', 'why', and 'when' certain leadership behaviors can affect employee well-being using robust research designs and innovative methodologies (e.g., Fischer et al., 2017). Furthermore, given the extensive range of constructive and destructive leadership styles and behaviors in the extant literature (e.g., Dinh et al., 2014), researchers have called for examining patterns of leadership characteristics, styles, and behaviors to understand if, and how, they cooccur (e.g., Arnold et al., 2017) and how these combinations are related to employee well-being (e.g., Mäkikangas et al., 2016).

To consolidate the latest research on how line managers affect employee well-being, we examined empirical work published in the last decade focused on constructive and destructive leadership styles, behaviors, and characteristics as predictors of employee well-being. In this chapter, we summarize this recent literature, describe its strengths and limitations, and highlight areas for future work. Based on the results of a comprehensive literature review, we offer frameworks linking constructive and destructive leadership to employee well-being, including a summary of explanatory processes and contextual factors affecting these relationships.

We begin with an outline of leadership in organizations as both constructive and destructive. Then we position the concept of a line manager within the broader leadership literature and outline the definition of employee well-being considered in our review. Next, we explain two research-supported frameworks linking leadership and employee well-being (see Figures 5.1 and 5.2). Finally, we integrate findings into key themes, discuss methodological issues, and future research directions which, if pursued, would advance our understanding in this area.

Construct Clarity: Leadership, Line Managers, and Employee Well-Being

Constructive and Destructive Leadership

Constructive and destructive leadership are typically viewed at opposite ends of the leadership continuum. Constructive leaders are said to enhance the motivation and well-being of followers by using engaging behaviors and encouraging involvement and participation in decision processes (Einarsen et al., 2007). As indicated by previous work on the desirable characteristics of leadership, constructive leaders are concerned with the welfare of their employees (e.g., Bass, 1985).

Destructive leadership, on the other hand, describes repeatedly harmful and/or deviant behaviors targeted towards followers, which may be either physical or verbal, active or passive, direct or indirect (Schyns & Schilling, 2013). These behaviors tend to take a toll on employee psychological well-being and motivation by depleting the stores of personal resources that allow individuals to cope with adversity and have negative associations with employee physical health (e.g., Barling & Frone, 2017; Einarsen et al., 2007; Hobfoll, 1989). The introduction of Tepper's (2000) abusive supervision measure over 20 years ago was an important development in the destructive leadership literature, but this work is still relatively new in comparison to over a century of research on constructive aspects of leadership.

Line Managers as Leaders: Direct Supervisors Matter

Leadership behavior at all levels of the organization is important, but the actions of immediate (i.e., direct) supervisors and/or managers are probably most salient to the well-being of those reporting to them (Kozlowski & Doherty, 1989; Nielsen, 2013). This is likely due to the fact that an immediate supervisor is one of the most influential people in an employee's work environment (e.g., Kozlowski & Doherty, 1989).

Within this area of research, the term *line manager* is used in several different ways. Without a specific description of the *level* of leadership under study, this ambiguous pattern of usage can lead to confusion. For example, in a qualitative study of employees with depression, Sallis and Birkin (2014) described any direct supervisor below the senior management level as a line manager, effectively eliminating the middle manager category (e.g., Yammarino et al., 2005). Another study suggests a line manager can be anyone's immediate supervisor (Lundmark et al., 2017). In other cases, line manager is equated with team leader (e.g., Nielsen, 2013) or middle manager (e.g., Nielsen & Randall, 2009). Finally, in an examination of the mental health of Executive Directors in the nonprofit sector, the 'line manager' or the individual(s) to whom the Executive Director reports directly, was a representative of the Board of Directors (Olinske & Hellman, 2017).

Despite this lack of clarity, in much of the research in the area of leadership and employee well-being, researchers ask participants to rate their direct supervisors' leadership style or report frequencies of their supervisors' behaviors. This approach recognizes that actions taken by direct supervisors (as perceived and rated by employees) have implications for employee well-being. Throughout this chapter, the term line manager is used synonymously with direct or immediate manager/supervisor and leader, and where available, details are provided on the level of organizational hierarchy in each study. We revisit this issue later in the chapter.

Employee Well-Being

Well-being is a multidimensional phenomenon with a range of positive and negative states that relate to employees both at work and outside of work (e.g., Danna & Griffin, 1999; Ganster & Rosen,

2013; Mäkikangas et al. 2016; Montano et al., 2017). It is measured using a broad range of self- and other report scales and physiological measures. Warr (1999) described context-specific well-being as a limited view of people's feelings in relation to their job through focused measurements. Examples of context-specific constructs in well-being research include burnout, job satisfaction and engagement, employee performance, and others.

Context-free well-being is a broader concept that takes into consideration the 'whole person' by measuring life experiences that are not specific to one domain, such as work (Danna & Griffin, 1999). For example, the context-free equivalent of job satisfaction would be life satisfaction (Warr, 1999). Positive indicators of context-free well-being could include high ratings on indicators of psychological functioning or physical health, while negative context-free well-being is often conceptualized as stress, strain, negative affect, and a range of physical and psychological conditions (e.g., depression, anxiety, substance abuse). Generally, there is a positive and reciprocal relationship between context-specific and context-free well-being, with some variation between individuals and contexts. This is grounded in the reality that experiences at work affect the overall person even when they are not at work, referred to as a 'spillover effect'. Indeed, recent studies show that high general, context-free well-being is associated with job-specific well-being (Liang et al., 2018; Weziak-Bialowolska et al., 2020).

In this chapter, we focus on summarizing empirical research predicting *context-free* psychological and physical well-being. This approach emphasizes the importance of line managers in their employees' overall wellness – a phenomenon that is not limited to inside the (virtual) walls of organizations. Given these criteria, important context-specific outcomes such as burnout, job engagement, and other domain-specific variables are not reflected in this review.

Linking Line Managers' Behaviors with Employee Well-Being

Literature Search

Through examination of the literature in this area, we developed two frameworks that summarize the published research on leadership styles, behaviors, and characteristics as predictors of psychological and physical well-being. These frameworks are based on a comprehensive literature search of peer-reviewed articles in 90 databases published in English between January 2010 and May 2020. An initial search retrieved a total of 615 titles. Our inclusion criteria required papers to be empirical studies in which leadership was a predictor and context-free well-being was an outcome. After eliminating duplicates and studies that were unrelated to the topic of interest, such as papers focused on the well-being of leaders themselves (see Chapter 4 of this book), or examinations of a leadership style without employee well-being outcomes, we retained 322 articles.

Consistent with literature emphasizing the need for employee well-being to extend beyond job-focused measures (Inceoglu et al., 2017; Mäkikangas et al., 2016; Montano et al., 2017), we excluded articles focused on outcome variables that were not aligned with our definition of well-being (job satisfaction, turnover intentions, employee performance, etc.). To supplement our initial search, we also performed searches of reference lists of systematic reviews and meta-analyses on related topics. Based on these further criteria, 76 papers were identified for inclusion in the present review.

Description of Studies Included for Review

Most of these studies employed quantitative methods (N = 71), followed by mixed methods (N = 3), with qualitative studies being the minority (N = 2). Of the 76 papers included in our review, nearly one-third (N = 25) drew samples of individuals from diverse or varied industries, while others did not indicate the context from which the sample was drawn (N = 5). Where industry was specified, healthcare (N = 13), manufacturing / technology industries (N = 5), and education (N = 4) were the most frequently studied industries. The majority of studies took place in western settings (North America [N = 27]; European Union [N = 26]), with another 21 in an Asian context.

In terms of analytic approach, 36 of 76 papers examined mediators using either simple mediation (N = 23) or moderated mediation (N = 13). Of these articles, 23 looked at one mediator, while the rest analyzed two or more. To understand the mediational processes through which leadership behavior affects context-free well-being, we used the five mediator groupings proposed in a recent qualitative review of leadership and well-being research by Inceoglu et al. (2017). These categories included: (1) social-cognitive, which is grounded in social learning theory or social information processing and includes variables such as self-efficacy, confidence, perceptions of one's own abilities, and psychological empowerment; (2) motivational, which is rooted in self-determination theory and includes variables associated with job design, such as job autonomy and task variety; (3) affective, which is based on affective events theory and consists of emotional variables such as thriving, engagement, and vigor; (4) relational, which relies on social exchange theory and includes concepts such as justice, trust, and employee perceptions of leader–member exchange; and (5) identification, which is rooted in social identity theory and includes concepts relating to how employees identify with their leader, work group, or organization (e.g., job involvement and group identification). The theoretical rationale for when or why variables were found to occupy the positions of predictor, mediator, or moderator was often lacking or unclear, which at times made it challenging to assign mediators to the appropriate categories. Where a case could be made for assigning one variable to multiple categories (e.g., emotional intelligence), the three authors discussed alternative categorizations and eventually reached consensus. Challenges associated with categorizing mediating variables are discussed in a later section.

Of the 36 papers examining mediators, 15 studied relational mediators, 13 focused on social-cognitive variables, 13 on affective constructs, 6 analyzed motivational variables and 1 article explored a mediator that fell under the identification category. Moderators are discussed according to level, where micro includes individual factors pertaining to either the employee or the line manager, meso includes group/team factors, and macro encompasses factors at the organizational, industry, or national level (Miner, 2002). Twenty-nine of the 76 articles examined moderators. Of these, 21 focused on one moderator while the rest included two or more; 15 focused on micro, 12 looked at meso, and 4 analyzed macrolevel variables (sum of mediator and moderator categories greater than totals of 36 and 29 due to multiple mediators and moderators in some studies).

Constructive Leadership Studies

The most frequently studied constructive leadership styles were transformational and leader–member exchange. Constructive leadership behaviors, in general, have been associated with a number of social-cognitive, motivational, affective, relational, and identification mediators. Relational mediators were studied most frequently. In this category, leadership behaviors that were positively associated with work–family enrichment and negatively related to employee perceptions of work–life/family conflict, related positively to employee well-being (Hill et al., 2016; Munir et al., 2012; Zhang & Tu, 2018). Other relational mediators include team cooperation (Diebig et al., 2017), relational social capital (Read & Laschinger, 2015), trust (Alilyyani et al., 2018), positive relationships with colleagues (Karanika-Murray et al., 2015), less bullying and incivility (Alilyyani et al., 2018), justice perceptions (Kiersch & Byrne, 2015; Tripathi & Ghosh, 2018), and attachment insecurity (Rahimnia & Sharifirad, 2015). It is important to note here that studies focused on mediation (regarding both constructive and destructive leadership) did not always utilize methodology appropriate to testing mediation (i.e., data collected over time to meet the temporal occurrence criteria). Hence, the relationships outlined in the following paragraphs and Figures 5.1 and 5.2 should not necessarily be interpreted as causal.

The second most frequently studied category of mediators was social-cognitive. This included different forms of personal resources such as: psychological capital (Alilyyani et al., 2018), empowerment

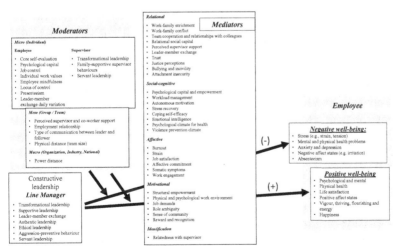

Figure 5.1 Summary of research linking constructive leadership and employee well-being

(Audenaert et al., 2017), autonomous motivation (Pauli et al., 2018), emotional intelligence (Rajesh et al., 2019), coping self-efficacy (Laschinger et al., 2015), stress recovery (Dunkl et al., 2015), psychological climate for health (Gurt et al., 2011) and violence-prevention climate (Yang & Caughlin, 2017). Thus, constructive leadership behaviors have a positive association with employees' personal resources and their psychological well-being.

In terms of affective mediators, both positive and negative states appear to play a role in explaining the relationship between constructive leadership and employee well-being. Context-specific well-being factors such as work engagement (Adil & Kamal, 2016), job satisfaction (Gurt et al., 2011), as well as negative affective factors, such as burnout (Kara et al., 2013) and context-free well-being factors such as stress (Dunkl et al., 2015), have been proposed to explain this relationship. The most frequently studied affective mediators were burnout and satisfaction, followed by stress and affective commitment. Constructive leadership appears to facilitate employee well-being by decreasing levels of stress (Wang et al., 2019), burnout (Alilyyani et al., 2018; Laschinger et al., 2015), and somatic symptoms (Biron, 2013), which was positively related to levels of satisfaction (Rajesh et al., 2019; Yang, 2014), mental health (Laschinger et al., 2015), and well-being (Adil & Kamal, 2016).

In the motivational category, the literature focused on the mediating role of variables that were either inherent to one's role at work or related to factors that might be considered social but associated with the motivational aspect of job design. Thus, the positive relationship between constructive leadership and employee well-being has been found to be mediated by factors including structural empowerment (Alilyyani et al., 2018; Read & Laschinger, 2015), physical work environment (Karanika-Murray et al., 2015), psychological work environment (e.g., social support, meaningful work: Nielsen & Daniels, 2012; relationships with colleagues: Karanika-Murray et al., 2015), job demands (Ogbonnaya & Messersmith, 2019), role ambiguity (Gurt et al., 2011), sense of community (McKee et al., 2011), and reward and recognition systems (Karanika-Murray et al., 2015).

Finally, one article addressed an identification mediator by studying how relatedness with one's supervisor mediates the positive relationship between leader–member exchange and employees' well-being (Ellis et al., 2019). When employees perceived a higher quality relationship with their supervisor, they reported a sense of belonging-ness and felt more vigorous.

In addition to these mediators, there were also a number of micro, meso, and macro factors that have been found to moderate the positive relationship between constructive leadership and employee well-being. Micro moderators were most commonly studied under the individual category of employee or supervisor. Some of these variables were related to employees' psychological states, for example, psychological capital (Adil & Kamal, 2016; Agarwal, 2019), core self-evaluation (Beattie & Griffin, 2014; Wang et al., 2019), employee mindfulness (Walsh & Arnold, 2020), locus of control (Huyghebaert et al., 2017), and job control (Steiner & Wooldredge, 2015).

Generally speaking, higher ratings on followers' positive psycho-logical states, such as employee mindfulness (Walsh & Arnold, 2020), core self-evaluations (Booth et al., 2020), internal locus of control (Huyghebaert et al., 2017), and job control (Steiner & Wooldredge, 2015), have been found to enhance the positive relationship between constructive leadership and employee well-being. On the other hand, follower ratings on external locus of control (Huyghebaert et al., 2017) and presenteeism (Nielsen & Daniels, 2016) tend to weaken this rela-tionship. With regard to supervisor micro moderators, heightened employee perceptions of servant leadership (Wang et al., 2019) and supervisors who displayed family-supportive behaviors (e.g., Zhang & Tu, 2018) strengthened the positive relationship between constructive leadership and employee well-being. Similarly, employees who per-ceived low day-to-day variation in the quality of their relationship with their supervisor reported higher vigor (Ellis et al., 2019).

With regard to meso-level moderators, most studies focused on social support provided by either colleagues or supervisors and how this can bolster the well-being of employees who perceive their leader as constructive (Beattie & Griffin, 2014; Biron, 2013; Hammer et al., 2019; Mohr & Wolfram, 2010; Steiner & Wooldredge, 2015). Other factors in this category included leader–member exchange, employ-ment relationship, communication, and team size. Likewise, mutual investment employment relationships (Audenaert et al., 2017), indirect communication between leaders and followers (Diebig et al., 2017), and a small team size (Vignoli et al., 2018) increased the positive association between constructive leadership and employee well-being. Finally, Zwingmann et al. (2014) studied power distance as a macrolevel moderator and found that the positive association between constructive leadership and employee well-being was even stronger in high-power distance cultures.

Destructive Leadership Studies

Our review showed that abusive supervision was the most frequently studied destructive leadership style. The study of variables that mediate the negative relationship between destructive leadership and employees' well-being has received less attention than mediators associated with constructive leadership. Within destructive leadership, social-cognitive mediators appeared most frequently and included a range of measures of employees' personal resources. Thus, as shown in Figure 5.2, destructive leadership behaviors have been reported to decrease employees' well-being through employee personal resources such as coping strategies (Yagil et al., 2011), psychological capital (Agarwal, 2019; Li et al., 2016), and perceptions of safety climate (Mullen, 2018). Moreover, the literature also explored other social-cognitive mediators that explained the negative relationship between destructive leadership and positive well-being whereby destructive supervisor behaviors were mediated by factors such as employee perceptions of psychological distress (Rafferty et al., 2010) and surface acting (Adams & Buck, 2010). These mediators were then positively

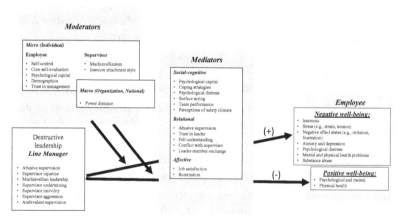

Figure 5.2 Summary of research linking destructive leadership and employee well-being

associated with increases in insomnia and strain and negatively associated with psychological health.

Under the umbrella of relational mediators, the literature suggests that destructive leadership has negative implications for employee well-being through a decrease in the quality of their relationships at work. Destructive behavior from leaders is associated with reduced levels of employee trust in their leader (Belschak et al., 2018), as well as lower perceptions of felt understanding from the supervisor (Booth et al., 2020) and leader–member exchange (Agarwal, 2019). Similarly, destructive forms of leadership were positively associated with conflict with one's supervisor (Liu et al., 2013) and abusive supervision (Li et al., 2016), which can be detrimental to well-being. The motivational and affective categories were the least frequently studied mediating processes of destructive leadership. This category includes job satisfaction (Peltokorpi & Ramaswami, 2019) and rumination (Liang et al., 2018), such that destructive leadership relates to lower job satisfaction and greater rumination, each of which would have unfavorable outcomes for employee well-being. Finally, no mediators in the identification category were reported in the review of destructive leadership.

In terms of moderators, Figure 5.2 shows that the destructive leadership literature has explored mostly microlevel factors along with a handful of meso and macro moderators. There was some overlap with moderators that were studied in the context of constructive leadership (i.e., employee mindfulness, core self-evaluation, and psychological capital), and other moderating factors were specific to destructive literature, such as gender and trait self-control (Abubakar, 2018; Jimmieson et al., 2017). When employees perceived that their job was enriched along different aspects such as high trust in management (Booth et al., 2020) and supportive coworkers (Blomberg & Rosander, 2019), the negative relationship between destructive leadership and employees' well-being was buffered. It appears that gender affects this relationship such that women experience greater detrimental effects on their well-being when they are exposed to destructive leaders than men (Abubakar, 2018). Furthermore, when employees perceive their supervisor as unsupportive (Blomberg & Rosander, 2019), or when leaders rate highly on Machiavellian personality type (Belschak et al., 2018), the already detrimental relationship between destructive leadership and employee well-being is worsened. Counterintuitively, employee mindfulness seems to amplify the already damaging relationship between abusive supervision and vigor (Walsh & Arnold, 2020).

At the meso-level, outcomes of abusive supervision were more destructive when team performance was lower in comparison to higher-performing teams (Li et al., 2016). Investigations of the macro moderator, power distance, illustrated the negative relationship between destructive leadership and employee well-being was stronger when power distance orientation was low (Liu et al., 2013; Peltokorpi & Ramaswami, 2019; Zhang & Liao, 2015).

Summary and Future Directions

Towards a Model Linking Leadership and Employee Well-Being

Upon examination of the two frameworks (Figures 5.1 and 5.2) that were developed based on recent research, it is evident that certain constructs occupy multiple positions. For example, some variables have been positioned as *both* predictors and moderators (servant leadership and Machiavellian leadership); predictors and mediators (abusive supervision); mediators and moderators (psychological capital, perceived supervisor, and coworker support); mediators and outcomes (stress); or predictors, mediators, and moderators (leader–member exchange). This illustrates the complexity of this area of research and a clear need for a unifying theoretical model. Such a model would ideally provide a basis for examining and clarifying the roles that the different constructs measured in the reviewed literature could play in these relationships.

Another observation that resulted from examining constructive and destructive leadership categories as separate predictors of employee well-being was the overlap between these two frameworks. We found five common mediating variables (i.e., trust, LMX, psychological capital, job satisfaction, and coping) and four common moderating variables (i.e., employee mindfulness, core self-evaluation, psychological capital, and power distance), which suggests that these variables operate similarly in positive and negative leadership contexts. However, there were also some interesting differences noted between these two research streams. For example, the mediators most commonly studied in constructive leadership research were relational versus social-cognitive in destructive leadership research. Below we elaborate on these observations, discuss limitations, and highlight additional areas for future research.

Predictors: Construct Validity

Our review illustrates that transformational leadership and leader–member exchange continue to dominate this area of research, which is consistent with previous leadership reviews (e.g., Barling et al., 2011; Dinh et al., 2014; Meuser et al., 2016). Both transformational leadership and leader–member exchange have been criticized for a lack of a clear conceptual definitions and problematic measurement scales (e.g., Gottfredson et al., 2020; Van Knippenberg & Sitkin, 2013). To some degree this issue is reflected in the current review, where leader–member exchange was investigated as a predictor, moderator, and a mediator. This suggests a lack of parsimony and potential for construct redundancy, which may limit the potential of research to advance theory in this area (Banks et al., 2018).

Comparable theoretical and conceptual concerns were also present in the destructive leadership literature where abusive supervision remains a central construct that overlaps with related constructs, such as bullying (e.g., Krasikova et al., 2013; Schyns & Schilling, 2013; Tepper et al., 2017). To introduce greater parsimony in both constructive and destructive leadership research, scholars are encouraged to perform thorough literature reviews before launching investigations, to conduct factor analyses to demonstrate that constructs are empirically distinct, and to focus on identifying conceptually distinct moderating factors to explain contextual differences before introducing new predictor variables (e.g., Meuser et al., 2016).

Setting these concerns aside, the research continues to support the broad premise that constructive leadership is associated with positive employee well-being, and destructive leadership is associated with reduced employee well-being. Arguably, the most interesting aspect of this research is not the direct relationships between predictor and outcome. It is the who, how, and when of these relationships that offer a more compelling focus for future research.

Mediators: How Is Leadership Linked to Employee Well-Being?

A theoretically driven categorization system was used to organize mediators, which allowed us to compare our findings with a recent review in terms of how frequently each mediator was examined

(Inceoglu et al., 2017). Mediators included in the relational category present a particular limitation. By definition, exchange-based constructs should require data from both parties in a dyad. Yet, the relational category includes mediating variables measured from one party's perspective (Inceoglu et al., 2017). While reflective of the current practice for researchers in this area to rely only on the follower perspective, this practice has been described as 'theoretically deficient' (Krasikova & LeBreton, 2012, p. 741). It represents a departure from (intended) theoretical roots of exchange constructs (Gottfredson et al., 2020; Krasikova & LeBreton, 2012) and introduces high potential for bias, redundancy, and error. We return to this issue in a subsequent section.

Grouping similar mediators allowed us to infer that social-cognitive mediators were frequently examined in the destructive leadership literature, potentially due to the substantial personal resources required to respond to and/or protect oneself from destructive leadership. Similarly, the strong focus on relational mediators in the constructive literature may be reflective of the relationship focus that is a consistent theme throughout constructive leadership paradigms. As empirical investigation of mediators progresses, it would be desirable to reach a stage where results pertaining to one variable have been studied enough to allow for meta-analysis. Currently, the infrequency with which many of these intervening variables are studied makes it difficult to draw broad conclusions on how leadership is related to employee well-being. For now, this area of research will continue to benefit from integrative, systematic, and comprehensive study (both qualitative and quantitative) of mediating and moderating factors. Studies that test multiple categories of mediators in the same study that help us begin to understand whether certain categories are more important than others would be beneficial.

The least frequently studied mediating pathways fell into the affective and identification categories. Both categories would benefit from future studies that examine mediators within these currently understudied areas, such as leader–follower affect (e.g., mood and emotions) and personal identification with the leader, group, and organization. There is a theoretical rationale to support the notion that employees would be affected by constructs related to affect and identity in both constructive and destructive streams. For example, transformational leadership emphasizes the value of energizing and inspiring followers to pursue a future state (i.e., vision) and the possibility of emotional contagion between leaders and followers (e.g., Huang et al., 2016). Similarly, in destructive literature, identity threat is a known predictor of abusive supervision and supervisor's displaced aggression (Tepper et al., 2017).

Moderators: The 'Who' and 'When' of Well-Being

Almost half of the published papers in our review examined moderating factors, which are critical to addressing questions of context. Of these studies, most were focused on microlevel characteristics of either leaders or followers, followed by meso-level factors. Compared to the micro and meso categories, macrolevel moderators were the least frequently examined. High-power distance was found to enhance well-being of employees with constructive leaders and protect well-being of employees with destructive leaders (Liu et al., 2013; Peltokorpi & Ramaswami, 2019; Zhang & Liao, 2015; Zwingmann et al., 2014). Gender and culture are known to play an important moderating role at the individual level of abusive supervisory behavior, and it would be worthwhile to investigate these as moderators of well-being outcomes at the meso and macro levels in future studies of this destructive behavior (e.g., Mackey et al., 2015; Vogel et al., 2015).

Outcomes: What Types of Well-Being Are Studied?

Sixty of the reviewed papers focused on negative well-being, while 32 investigated positive well-being (total is greater than 76 due to 13 papers that examined positive and negative indicators of well-being). Regardless of whether the focus was on constructive or destructive leadership, negative well-being outcomes were more frequently studied than positive well-being outcomes, and psychological well-being was studied more frequently than physical well-being.

Given the relatively novel conceptualization of well-being as having both positive and negative indicators (e.g., Danna & Griffin, 1999; Inceoglu et al., 2017; Mäkikangas et al. 2016; Montano et al., 2017), this area of research could become more balanced by including more focus on positive indicators of eudaimonic well-being and health-related occupational outcomes, such as thriving and vigor. Recent studies also suggest that other constructs from positive psychology, such as employee mindfulness, do not necessarily protect employees' psychological well-being from abusive supervision (Walsh & Arnold,

2020). At present, understanding the positive effects of leadership on employee well-being is limited by an abundance of research on negative well-being outcomes. It was encouraging to see use of both subjective and objective measures, indicative of a shift away from reliance on subjective self-report measures and increased focus on physical well-being (e.g., blood pressure, psychosomatic complaints; Busch et al., 2017).

Theory

From a theoretical perspective, most articles derived hypotheses from an integrated perspective consisting of both focal and supporting theories. Focal theories are the central phenomenon of interest, while supporting theories provide alternative and/or additional insights such as conceptualizing antecedents, outcomes, or moderators/mediators (Meuser et al., 2016). Approaching this area of research using both focal and supporting theories is useful for advancing this work given recent efforts to distinguish employee well-being from job-specific constructs, such as job satisfaction, and to treat well-being as a multidimensional construct with both positive and negative states.

As is common in employee well-being research, resource-based frameworks such as Hobfoll's (1989) Conservation of Resources and the Job Demands-Resources model (Bakker & Demerouti, 2007) were the most commonly used focal theories to predict outcomes of both constructive and destructive leadership behaviors. There was noticeable variety in the supporting theories used to justify predictions about outcomes of leadership styles, behaviors, and characteristics with some secondary theories appearing only once (e.g., functional leadership theory, Fiset & Boies, 2018; uncertainty management theory, Herr et al., 2019). In the name of parsimony and theoretical integration, more consideration should be given to the selection of appropriate theoretical frameworks to justify inclusion of mediators, moderators, and outcomes. Furthermore, research design and methodological approach should be informed by theory.

Methodological Directions

Research Design: Increasing Methodological Diversity

When selecting a study design and method of analysis, researchers should be guided by the research question(s) (e.g., Howard &

Hoffman, 2018). Complex issues in modern-day organizations are yielding new and different research questions that may require researchers to consider the full range of research designs and methodological approaches to address relevant questions in leadership and employee well-being research.

It was encouraging to see diverse methodological approaches such as experience sampling methodology (ESM), intervention studies, and experimental vignettes with increased frequency compared to a similar review completed a decade ago (Skakon et al. 2010). For example, consistent with calls for leadership research to recognize the dynamic (changing) nature of leader–follower relationships (Van Knippenberg & Sitkin, 2013), ESM approaches have illustrated that follower perceptions of the quality of their relationship with their leader (Ellis et al., 2019) and of transformational leadership can change throughout a workday (Diebig et al., 2017).

Similarly, intervention studies that embrace a participatory design show great potential to improve employee well-being (Nielsen, 2013) and provide causal evidence related to these relationships. As a highly salient local influence, line managers are in a position to encourage adoption of interventions targeted at employee health and well-being; ensuring buy-in of line managers can make or break the success of an intervention. For example, Busch et al. (2017) determined that line managers were less effective than senior managers at encouraging employees to participate in well-being intervention because the line managers felt too stressed about their own work situation and well-being to dedicate time to improving the health and well-being of their direct reports (see Chapter 4 of this book). This relates to the importance of specifying the level of leadership in this research area. There is also opportunity for qualitative methods to advance research questions of an exploratory nature (e.g., Sallis & Birkin, 2014) and progress towards theoretical integration (e.g., Meuser et al., 2016). Finally, increased usage of mixed methods approaches will be positioned to offer the empirical rigor required to match the complexity of organizational phenomenon (Molina-Azorin et al., 2017).

Despite these notable changes over the past decade, and consistent with previous reviews of leadership and employee well-being, quantitative survey methodology was still the most common methodology, and most papers in our review were based on cross-sectional data (N = 62) collected from followers about their perceptions of leadership (i.e., single source). Of particular concern is that many of the published papers examining mediators relied upon cross-sectional design, potentially generating biased estimates of longitudinal parameters (Maxwell & Cole, 2007). Shifting to longitudinal research designs will offer enhanced ability to understand mediating processes, as well as the role of time and the nature of variables that change over time (Bono & McNamara, 2011). This is especially important for leadership research due to the dynamic nature of leadership (Van Knippenberg & Sitkin, 2013) and paramount for theoretical precision and practical relevance (Fischer et al., 2017).

Rigor in Data Collection and Analysis
Further related to enhanced data quality offered by longitudinal designs, we echo the importance of recent movements towards collecting dyadic (e.g., Breevaart et al., 2016) and multisource data (e.g., Magalhães et al., 2019). Collecting data from only one party introduces simultaneity bias and amplifies existing concerns about endogeneity and confounded estimates in leadership research where outcomes are jointly influenced by the leader and follower (for a full discussion see Güntera et al., 2020). Recommendations to address simultaneity bias and endogeneity include increased use of experimental designs and rigorous analytical techniques such as two-stage least squares regression analysis (Güntera et al., 2020).

Multisource data offers an advantage over same source data because it provides a more balanced view in which multiple perspectives of the same reality are reflected in the data. Despite these advantages, this type of data can be more challenging to collect. Hence, our recommendation is tempered with this reality in mind. It may be more realistic in the study of destructive leadership where the source or event in which the untoward behavior occurs may be observed and reported by not only the perpetrator or the target, but also leaders, coworkers, or clients/customers (e.g., Beattie & Griffin, 2014). Thus, scholars could measure abusive supervision using supervisor self-reports, other reports, objective measures of well-being, and/or experimental designs in addition to follower self-reports (Tepper et al., 2017).

Organizational Context: Where to Situate Our Studies?
In our review, the majority of studies did not explicitly delineate the level of leadership being addressed. Similarly, from the perspective of

survey participants, it is uncertain whether they are responding to survey questions about 'your supervisor' or 'your leader' with reference to their direct supervisor, or a more remote supervisor without further specifications of the supervisor's role or proximity (Yagil et al., 2011). Hence, future work should aim to provide clear descriptions of the level of leadership under investigation and use analytical techniques that take into account the nested nature of the data at multiple levels. Leaders at many organizational levels may have a combined effect on employee well-being, and it will take a deliberate approach to parse out and understand the role and magnitude of various levels due to the interconnected nature of these relationships.

In addition to this issue of level, much of the published work we reviewed was nonspecific about the industry and cultural composition of the sample. Given the significant moderators discussed in the frameworks (Figures 5.1 and 5.2), this is an important consideration going forward and we would encourage researchers to report details on the context from which the sample is drawn, such as organizational characteristics, industry description, and timing of data collection(s), as well as relevant demographic, cultural and geographic information.

Promising Future Research Directions

In addition to our suggestions regarding future work provided above, we have identified three areas of fruitful focus for future work in this area.

Cooccurrence of Leadership Behaviors

Leaders are not all good or all bad, yet research on leadership styles and behaviors as they relate to well-being are typically framed as either constructive or destructive (as they are in this review) (Einarsen et al., 2007). The concept of individual leaders engaging in multiple styles of behavior simultaneously (i.e., code switching: Anicich & Hirsh, 2017) is not new; for example, Bass (1985) theorized an augmentation effect where transactional leadership behaviors would be augmented by enactment of transformational leadership. Line managers, in particular, may tweak their style multiple times in a day – sometimes in the course of a single situation (Anicich & Hirsh, 2017; Peterson et al., 2020). Nonetheless, studies that examine employee well-being outcomes based on exposure to multiple kinds of leader behavior from one leader, *both constructive and destructive*, are rare (e.g., Fiset et al., 2019).

Person-centered methodologies, such as latent profile analysis, are useful for examining this type of cooccurrence (e.g., Arnold et al., 2017). Studies might adopt this methodological approach as it allows researchers to test competing combinations of leadership approaches as they relate to employee well-being (Mäkikangas et al. 2016; Meuser et al., 2016). Furthermore, this approach may answer calls for leadership theory integration by examining whether certain combinations of leadership styles/behaviors are more effective in achieving positive employee well-being outcomes than others.

Virtual Leadership

In the midst of the Covid-19 global pandemic, many workplaces have shifted to virtual or remote models of work (Wong, 2020). Investigations of this shift and what it means for employee well-being would provide important information for both leaders and organizations. The research we reviewed has not yet initiated specific examinations of virtual leadership; however, some work on virtual communication can provide useful direction in this area. Diebig et al.'s (2017) study on types of communication that moderate the relationship between transformational leadership and stress found that employees perceived less stress when leaders used indirect forms of communication (i.e., email and messenger) compared to direct communication (i.e., face-to-face interactions or telephone). Future research that draws from construal level theory to enhance our understanding of near or far leaders operating virtually (Bligh & Riggio, 2013), and how this relates to employee well-being, could be beneficial.

Gender and Well-Being

Gender inequalities in the workplace have been exacerbated by disproportionate effects on women during the pandemic (McKinsey & Company, 2020). This recent realization may have shed light on the need to understand gender and gender identity as an important consideration in employee well-being research. Few studies in our review offered a gender-based examination of the link between leadership and employee well-being (N = 4), with only some controlling for gender in the analysis (N = 10). Future investigations would offer value through a greater focus on examining and reporting gendered effects and incorporating gender into research questions and designs. Future research could also examine how these trends affect gender-diverse individuals in the workplace with respect to leadership and employee well-being, reflecting current knowledge that gender is nonbinary (e.g., Hyde et al., 2019).

Conclusion

This chapter has reviewed the role of constructive and destructive leadership as predictors of employee context-free physical and psychological well-being and the theories, mediators, and moderators involved in these relationships. Key methodological issues were discussed and several areas have been suggested for future research. We look forward to an increase in robust research that is grounded in theory to further explain why, how, and when direct supervisors are important with regard to employee well-being, and the application of these findings to create healthier workplaces.

References

Abubakar, A. (2018). Linking work–family interference, workplace incivility, gender and psychological distress. *Journal of Management Development, 37*(3), 226–242.

Adams, G., & Buck, J. (2010). Social stressors and strain among police officers: It's not just the bad guys. *Criminal Justice and Behavior, 37* (9), 1030–1040.

Adil, A., & Kamal, A. (2016). Impact of psychological capital and authentic leadership on work engagement and job related affective well-being. *Pakistan Journal of Psychological Research, 31*(1), 1–21.

Agarwal, U. (2019). Examining links between abusive supervision, PsyCap, LMX and outcomes. *Management Decision, 57*(5), 1304–1334.

Alilyyani, B., Wong, C., & Cummings, G. (2018). Antecedents, mediators, and outcomes of authentic leadership in healthcare: A systematic review. *International Journal of Nursing Studies, 83*, 34–64.

Álvarez-Pérez, M., Carballo-Penela, A., & Rivera-Torres, P. (2020). Work–life balance and corporate social responsibility: The evaluation of gender differences on the relationship between family-friendly psychological climate and altruistic behaviors at work. *Corporate Social Responsibility and Environmental Management, 27*(2), 1–16.

Anicich, E. M., & Hirsh, J. (2017). The psychology of middle power: Vertical code-switching, role conflict, and behavioral inhibition. *Academy of Management Review, 42*(4). https://doi.org/10.5465/amr.2016.0002

Arnold, K. A. (2017). Transformational leadership and employee psychological well-being: A review and directions for future research. *Journal of Occupational Health Psychology, 22* (3), 381–393.

Arnold, K. A., Connelly, C. E., Gellatly, I. R., Walsh, M. M., & Withey, M. J. (2017). Using a pattern-oriented approach to study leaders: Implications for burnout and perceived role demand. *Journal of Organizational Behaviour, 38,* 1038–1056.

Audenaert, M., Vanderstraeten, A., & Buyens, D. (2017). When affective well-being is empowered: The joint role of leader–member exchange and the employment relationship. *The International Journal of Human Resource Management, 28*(15), 2208–2227.

Bakker, A. B., & Demerouti, E. (2007). The job demands-resources model: State of the art. *Journal of Managerial Psychology, 22*(3), 309–328. https://doi.org/10.1108/02683940710733115

Banks, G. C., Gooty, J., Ross, R. L., Williams, C. E., & Harrington, N. T. (2018). Construct redundancy in leader behaviors: A review and agenda for the future. *The Leadership Quarterly, 29,* 236–251.

Barling, J., Christie, A., & Hoption, C. (2011). Leadership. In S. Zedeck (Ed.), *Handbook of industrial and organizational psychology.* American Psychological Association.

Barling, J., & Frone, M. R. (2017). If only my leader would just do something! Passive leadership undermines employee well-being through role stressors and psychological resource depletion. *Stress & Health, 33,* 211–222.

Bass, B. (1985). *Leadership and performance beyond expectations.* Free Press.

Beattie, L., & Griffin, B. (2014). Day-level fluctuations in stress and engagement in response to workplace incivility: A diary study. *Work & Stress, 28*(2), 124–142.

Belschak, F., Muhammad, R., & Den-Hartog, D. (2018). Birds of a feather can butt heads: When Machiavellian employees work with Machiavellian leaders. *Journal of Business Ethics, 151*(3), 613–626.

Bligh, M., & Riggio, R. (2013). *Exploring distance in leader–follower relationships: When near is far and far is near* (Leadership: Research and practice series). Routledge.

Biron, M. (2013). Effective and ineffective support: How different sources of support buffer the short–and long–term effects of a working day. *European Journal of Work and Organizational Psychology, 22*(2), 150–164.

Blomberg, S., & Rosander, M. (2019). Exposure to bullying behaviours and support from co-workers and supervisors: A three-way interaction and the effect on health and well-being. *International Archives of Occupational and Environmental Health*, *93*, 479–490.

Bono, J. E., & McNamara, G. (2011). From the editors: Publishing in AMJ – Part 2: Research design [Editorial]. *Academy of Management Journal*, *54*(4), 657–660.

Booth, J., Shantz, A., Glomb, T., Duffy, M., & Stillwell, E. (2020). Bad bosses and self-verification: The moderating role of core self-evaluations with trust in workplace management. *Human Resource Management*, *59*(2), 135–152.

Breevaart, K., Bakker, A. B., Demerouti, E., & Derks, D. (2016). Who takes the lead? A multi-source diary study on leadership, work engagement, and job performance. *Journal of Organizational Behavior*, *37*(3), 309–325.

Busch, C., Koch, T., Clasen, J., Winkler, E., & Vowinkel, J. (2017). Evaluation of an organizational health intervention for low-skilled workers and immigrants. *Human Relations*, *70*(8), 994–1016.

Daniels, K., Russell, A., Michaelides, G., Nasamu, E., & Connolly, S. (2022). The measurement of well-being at work. In L. M. Lapierre & C. L. Cooper (Eds.), *Organisational stress and well-being*, Cambridge University Press.

Danna, K., & Griffin, R. W. (1999). Health and well-being in the workplace: A review and synthesis of the literature. *Journal of Management*, *25*, 357–384.

Diebig, M., Bormann, K., & Rowold, J. (2017). Day-level transformational leadership and followers' daily level of stress: A moderated mediation model of team cooperation, role conflict, and type of communication. *European Journal of Work and Organizational Psychology*, *26*(2), 234–249.

Dinh, J. E., Lord, R. G., Gardner, W. L., Meuser, J. D., Liden, R. C., & Hu, J. (2014). Leadership theory and research in the new millennium: Current theoretical trends and changing perspective. *Leadership Quarterly*, *25*(1), 36–62.

Dunkl, A., Jiménez, P., Žižek, S., Milfelner, B., & Kallus, W. (2015). Similarities and differences of health-promoting leadership and trans-formational leadership. *Naše gospodarstvo/Our Economy*, *61*(4), 3–13.

Einarsen, S., Aasland, M. S., & Skogstad, A. (2007). Destructive leadership behaviour: A definition and conceptual model. *Leadership Quarterly*, *18*, 207–216.

Ellis, A., Bauer, T., Erdogan, B., & Truxillo, D. (2019). Daily perceptions of relationship quality with leaders: Implications for follower well-being. *Work & Stress*, *33*(2), 119–136.

Fischer, T., Dietz, J., & Antonakis, J. (2017). Leadership process models: A review and synthesis. *Journal of Management, 43*(6), 1726–1753.

Fiset, J., & Boies, K. (2018). Seeing the unseen: Ostracism interventionary behaviour and its impact on employees. *European Journal of Work and Organizational Psychology, 27*(4), 403–417.

Fiset, J., Robinson, M. A., & Saffie-Robertson, M. C. (2019). Masking wrongs through brilliance: The moderating effect of vision on the relationship between abusive supervision and employee outcomes. *European Journal of Work and Organizational Psychology, 28*(6), 756–768. https://doi.org/10.1080/1359432X.2019.1637853

Ganster, D. C., & Rosen, C. C. (2013). Work stress and employee health. *Journal of Management, 39*(5), 1085–1122.

Gottfredson, R. K., Wright, S. L., & Heaphy, E. D. (2020). A critique of the Leader-Member Exchange construct: Back to square one. *The Leadership Quarterly, 31*, 101385.

Grant, A. M., Christianson, M. K., & Price, R. H. (2007). Happiness, health, or relationships? Managerial practices and employee well-being trade-offs. *Academy of Management Perspectives, 21*, 51–63.

Güntera, A. V., Klonek, F. E., Lehmann-Willenbrock, N., & Kauffeld, S. (2020). Follower behavior renders leader behavior endogenous: The simultaneity problem, estimation challenges, and solutions. *The Leadership Quarterly, 31*(101441).

Gurt, J., Schwennen, C., & Elke, G. (2011). Health-specific leadership: Is there an association between leader consideration for the health of employees and their strain and well-being? *Work & Stress, 25*(2), 108–127.

Hammer, L. B., Allen, S. J., & Leslie, J. J. (2022). Workplace interventions involving management. In L. M. Lapierre & C. L. Cooper (Eds.), *Organisational stress and well-being*. Cambridge University Press.

Hammer, L., Wan, W., Brockwood, K., Bodner, T., & Mohr, C. (2019). Supervisor support training effects on veteran health and work outcomes in the civilian workplace. *Journal of Applied Psychology, 104* (1), 52–69.

Harms, P. D, Credé, M., Tynan, M., Leon, M., & Jeung, W. (2017). Leadership and stress: A meta-analytic review. *The Leadership Quarterly, 28*(1), 178–194.

Herr, R., Van Harreveld, F., Uchino, B., Birmingham, W., Loerbroks, A., Fischer, J., & Bosch, J. (2019). Associations of ambivalent leadership with distress and cortisol secretion. *Journal of Behavioral Medicine, 42* (2), 265–275.

Hill, R., Morganson, V., Matthews, R., & Atkinson, T. (2016). LMX, breach perceptions, work–family conflict, and well-being: A mediational model. *The Journal of Psychology, 150*(1), 132–149.

Hobfoll, S. E. (1989). Conservation of resources. A new attempt at conceptualizing stress. *The American Psychologist*, 44(3), 513–524.

Howard, M. C., & Hoffman, E. F. (2018). Variable-centered, person-centered, and person-specific approaches: Where theory meets the method. *Organizational Research Methods*, 21, 846–876.

Huang, J., Wang, J., Wu, G., & You, X. (2016). Crossover of burnout from leaders to followers: A longitudinal study. *European Journal of Work and Organizational Psychology*, 25(6), 849–861.

Huyghebaert, T., Gillet, N., Becker, C., Kerhardy, S., & Fouquereau, E. (2017). Examining the effect of affective commitment to the supervisor on nurses' psychological health as a function of internal locus of control. *Journal of Nursing Management*, 25(4), 297–306.

Hyde, J., Bigler, R., Joel, D., Tate, C., & van Anders, S. (2019). The future of sex and gender in psychology: Five challenges to the gender binary. *American Psychologist*, 74(2), 171–193. https://doi.org/10.1037/amp0000307

Hartlaub, D., Inceoglu, I., Hernandez Bark, A., & Kark, R. (2022). Is it stressful at the top? The demands of leadership in times of stability and crisis. In L. M. Lapierre & C. L. Cooper (Eds.), *Organisational stress and well-being*. Cambridge University Press.

Inceoglu, I., Thomas, G., Chu, C., Plans, D., & Gerbasi, A. (2017). Leadership behavior and employee well-being: An integrated review and a future research agenda. *The Leadership Quarterly*, 29(1), 179–202.

Jimmieson, N. L., Tucker, M. K., & Campbell, J. L. (2017). Task conflict leads to relationship conflict when employees are low in trait self-control: Implications for employee strain. *Personality and Individual Differences*, 113, 209–218.

Kara, D., Uysal, M., Sirgy, M., & Lee, G. (2013). The effects of leadership style on employee well-being in hospitality. *International Journal of Hospitality Management*, 34, 9–18.

Karanika-Murray, M., Bartholomew, K., Williams, G., & Cox, T. (2015). Leader–member exchange across two hierarchical levels of leadership: Concurrent influences on work characteristics and employee psychological health. *Work & Stress*, 29(1), 57–74.

Keyes, C. L. M., Shmotkin, D., & Ryff, C. D. (2002). Optimizing well-being: The empirical encounter of two traditions. *Journal of Personality and Social Psychology*, 82(6), 1007–1022.

Kiersch, C. E., & Byrne, Z. S. (2015). Is being authentic being fair? Multilevel examination of authentic leadership, justice, and employee outcomes. *Journal of Leadership & Organizational Studies*, 22(3), 292–303.

Kozlowski, S. W. J., & Doherty, M. L. (1989). Integration of climate and leadership: Examination of a neglected issue. *Journal of Applied Psychology, 74*(4), 546–553.

Krasikova, D. V., Green, S. G., & LeBreton, J. M. (2013). Destructive leadership: A theoretical review, integration, and future research agenda. *Journal of Management, 39*(5).

Krasikova, D. V., & LeBreton, J. M. (2012). Just the two of us: Misalignment of theory and methods in examining dyadic phenomena. *Journal of Applied Psychology, 97*(4), 739–757.

Laschinger, H., Borgogni, L., Consiglio, C., & Read, E. (2015). The effects of authentic leadership, six areas of work-life, and occupational coping self-efficacy on new graduate nurses' burnout and mental health: A cross-sectional study. *International Journal of Nursing Studies, 52* (6), 1080–1089.

Li, Y., Wang, Z., Yang, L., & Liu, S. (2016). The crossover of psychological distress from leaders to subordinates in teams: The role of abusive supervision, psychological capital, and team performance. *Journal of Occupational Health Psychology, 21*(2), 142–153.

Liang, L. H., Hanig, S., Evans, R., Brown, D. J, & Lian, H. (2018). Why is your boss making you sick? A longitudinal investigation modeling time-lagged relations between abusive supervision and employee physical health. *Journal of Organizational Behavior, 39*(9), 1050–1065.

Liu, C., Yang, L., & Nauta, M. (2013). Examining the mediating effect of supervisor conflict on procedural injustice–job strain relations: The function of power distance. *Journal of Occupational Health Psychology, 18* (1), 64–74.

Lundmark, R., Hasson, H., von Thiele Schwarz, U., Hasson, D., & Tafvelin, S. (2017). Leading for change: Line managers' influence on the outcomes of an occupational health intervention. *Work & Stress, 31*(3), 276–296.

Mackey, J., Frieder, R., Brees, J., & Martinko, M. (2015). Abusive supervision: A meta-analysis and empirical review. *Journal of Management, 43* (6), 1940–1965.

Magalhães, A., Santos, N. R., & Pais, L. (2019). Multi-source research designs on ethical leadership: A literature review. *Business & Society Review* (00453609), *124*(3), 345–364.

Mäkikangas, A., Kinnunen, U., Feldt, T., & Schaufeli, W. (2016). The longitudinal development of employee well-being: A systematic review. *Work & Stress, 30*(1), 46–70.

Maxwell, S. E., & Cole, D. A. (2007). Bias in cross-sectional analyses of longitudinal mediation. *Psychological Methods, 12*(1), 23–44.

McKee, M., Driscoll, C., Kelloway, E., & Kelley, E. (2011). Exploring linkages among transformational leadership, workplace spirituality and well-being in health care workers. *Journal of Management, Spirituality & Religion, 8*(3), 233–255.

McKinsey & Company. (2020). *COVID-19 and gender equality: Countering the regressive effects.* www.mckinsey.com/featured-insights/future-of-work/covid-19-and-gender-equality-countering-the-regressive-effects

Meuser, J. D., Gardner, W. L., Dinh, J. E., Hu, J., Liden, R. C., & Lord, R. G. (2016). A network analysis of leadership theory: The infancy of integration. *Journal of Management, 42*(5), 1374–1403.

Miner, J. B. (2002). *Organizational behavior: Foundations, theories, and analyses.* Oxford University Press.

Mohr, G., & Wolfram, H. (2010). Stress among managers: The importance of dynamic tasks, predictability, and social support in unpredictable times. *Journal of Occupational Health Psychology, 15*(2), 167–179.

Molina-Azorin, J. F., Bergh, D. D., Corley, K. G., & Ketchen, D. J. (2017). Mixed methods in the organizational sciences: Taking stock and moving forward. *Organizational Research Methods, 20*(2), 179–192.

Montano, D., Reeske, A., Franke, F., & Huffmeir, J. (2017). Leadership, followers' mental health and job performance in organizations: A comprehensive meta-analysis from an occupational health perspective. *Journal of Organizational Behavior, 38*, 327–350.

Mullen, J., Fiset, J., & Rhéaume, A. (2018). Destructive forms of leadership. *Leadership & Organization Development Journal, 9*(8), 946–961. https://doi.org/10.1108/LODJ-06-2018-0203

Munir, F., Nielsen, K., Garde, A., Albertsen, K., & Carneiro, I. (2012). Mediating the effects of work–life conflict between transformational leadership and health-care workers' job satisfaction and psychological wellbeing. *Journal of Nursing Management, 20*(4), 512–521.

Nielsen, K. (2013). How can we make organizational interventions work? Employees and line managers as actively crafting interventions. *Human Relations, 66*(8), 1029–1050.

Nielsen, K., & Daniels, K. (2012). Does shared and differentiated transformational leadership predict followers' working conditions and well-being? *The Leadership Quarterly, 23*(3), 383–397.

(2016). The relationship between transformational leadership and follower sickness absence: The role of presenteeism. *Work & Stress, 30* (2), 193–208

Nielsen, K., & Randall, R. (2009). Managers' active support when implementing teams: The impact on employee well-being. *Applied Psychology: Health and Well-Being, 1*(3), 374–390.

Ogbonnaya, C., & Messersmith, J. (2019). Employee performance, well-being, and differential effects of human resource management subdimensions: Mutual gains or conflicting outcomes? *Human Resource Management Journal, 29*(3), 509–526.

Olinske, J., & Hellman, C. (2017). Leadership in the human service non-profit organization: The influence of the board of directors on executive director well-being and burnout. *Human Service Organizations: Management, Leadership & Governance, 41*(2), 95–105.

Pauli, J., Chambel, M., Capellari, M., & Rissi, V. (2018). Motivation, organisational support and satisfaction with life for private sector teachers in Brazilian higher education. *Higher Education Quarterly, 72*(2), 107–120.

Peltokorpi, V., & Ramaswami, A. (2019). Abusive supervision and subordinates' physical and mental health: The effects of job satisfaction and power distance orientation. *The International Journal of Human Resource Management, 32*(4), 893–919.

Peterson, S. J., Abramson, R., & Stutman, R. K. (2020, November/December). How to develop your leadership style. *Harvard Business Review.* https://hbr.org/2020/11/how-to-develop-your-leadership-style

Podsakoff, P. M., MacKenzie, S. B., & Podsakoff, N. P. (2012). Sources of method bias in social science research and recommendations on how to control it. *Annual Review of Psychology, 63*, 539–569.

Probst, T., Jiang, L., & Graso, M. (2016). Leader–member exchange: Moderating the health and safety outcomes of job insecurity. *Journal of Safety Research, 56*, 47–56. http://doi.org/10.1016/j.jsr.2015.11.003

Rafferty, A., Restubog, S., & Jimmieson, N. (2010). Losing sleep: Examining the cascading effects of supervisors' experience of injustice on subordinates' psychological health. *Work & Stress, 24*(1), 36–55.

Rahimnia, F., & Sharifirad, M. S. (2015). Authentic leadership and employee well-being: The mediating role of attachment insecurity. *Journal of Business Ethics, 132*(2), 363–377.

Rajesh, J., Prikshat, V., & Shum, P. (2019). Follower emotional intelligence: A mediator between transformational leadership and follower outcomes. *Personnel Review, 4*(5), 1239–1260.

Read, E., & Laschinger, H. (2015). The influence of authentic leadership and empowerment on nurses' relational social capital, mental health and job satisfaction over the first year of practice. *Journal of Advanced Nursing, 71*(7), 1611–1623.

Ryan, R. M., & Deci, E. L. (2001). On happiness and human potentials: A review of research on hedonic and eudaimonic well-being. *Annual Review of Psychology, 52*(1), 141–166.

Sallis, A., & Birkin, R. (2014). Experiences of work and sickness absence in employees with depression: An interpretative phenomenological analysis. *Journal of Occupational Rehabilitation*, 24(3), 469–483.

Schyns, B., & Schilling, J. (2013). How bad are the effects of bad leaders? A meta-analysis of destructive leadership and its outcomes. *The Leadership Quarterly*, 24, 138–158.

Sergent, K., & Stajkovic, A. D. (2020). Women's leadership is associated with fewer deaths during the COVID-19 crisis: Quantitative and qualitative analyses of United States governors. *Journal of Applied Psychology*, 105(8), 771–783.

Skakon, J., Nielsen, K., Borg, V., & Guzman, J. (2010). Are leaders' well-being, behaviours and style associated with the affective well-being of their employees? A systematic review of three decades of research. *Work & Stress*, 24(2), 107–139.

Spector, P. E. (2022). From occupational fatigue to occupational health. In L. M. Lapierre & C. L. Cooper (Eds.), *Organisational stress and well-being*, Cambridge University Press.

Steiner, B., & Wooldredge, J. (2015). Individual and environmental sources of work stress among prison officers. *Criminal Justice and Behavior*, 42 (8), 800–818.

Tepper, B. J. (2000). Consequences of abusive supervision. *Academy of Management Journal*, 43(2), 178–190.

Tepper, B. J., Simon, L., & Park, H. M. (2017). Abusive supervision. *Annual Review of Organizational Psychology of Organizational Behavior*, 4, 123–52.

The Lancet. (2020). The gendered dimensions of COVID-19. *The Lancet*, 395(10231), 1168.

Tripathi, N., & Ghosh, V. (2018). Gender differences in the effect of downward influence strategies on perceived stress and general-health: The mediating role of organizational justice. *Employee Responsibilities and Rights Journal*, 30(1), 1–35.

Van Knippenberg, D., & Sitkin, S. B. (2013). A critical assessment of charismatic -transformational leadership research: Back to the drawing board? *The Academy of Management Annals*, 7, 1–60.

Vignoli, M., Depolo, M., Cifuentes, M., & Punnett, L. (2018). Disagreements on leadership styles between supervisors and employees are related to employees' well-being and work team outcomes. *International Journal of Workplace Health Management*, 11(5), 274–293.

Vogel, R. M., Mitchell, M. S., Tepper, B. J., Restubog, S. L. D., Hu, C., Hua, W., & Huang, J. (2015). A cross-cultural examination of subordinates' perceptions of and reactions to abusive supervision. *Journal of Organizational Behavior, 36*(5), 720–745.

Walsh, M., & Arnold, K. (2020). The bright and dark sides of employee mindfulness: Leadership style and employee well-being. *Stress and Health, 36*(3), 287–298. http://doi.org/10.1002/smi.2926

Wang, Z., Xing, L., & Zhang, Y. (2019). Do high-performance work systems harm employees' health? An investigation of service-oriented HPWS in the Chinese healthcare sector. *The International Journal of Human Resource Management, 32*(10), 2264–2297. http://doi.org/10.1080/09585192.2019.1579254

Warr, P. (1999). Well-being and the workplace. In D. Kahneman, E. Diener, & N. Schwarz (Eds.), *Well-being: The foundations of hedonic psychology* (pp. 392–412). Russell Sage Foundation.

Weziak-Bialowolska, D., Bialowolski, P., Sacco, P. L., VanderWeele, T. J., & McNeely, E. (2020). Well-being in life and well-being at work: Which comes first? Evidence from a longitudinal study. *Frontiers in Public Health, 8*, 103. https://doi.org/10.3389/fpubh.2020.00103

Wong, M. (2020). Stanford research provides a snapshot of a new working-from-home economy, *Stanford News*. https://news.stanford.edu/2020/06/29/snapshot-new-working-home-economy/

Yagil, D., Ben-Zur, H., & Tamir, I. (2011). Do employees cope effectively with abusive supervision at work? An exploratory study. *International Journal of Stress Management, 18*(1), 5–23.

Yammarino, F. J., Dionne, S. D., Chun, J. U., & Dansereau, F. (2005). Leadership and levels of analysis: A state-of-the-science review. *The Leadership Quarterly, 16*, 879–919.

Yang, C. (2014). Does ethical leadership lead to happy workers? A study on the impact of ethical leadership, subjective well-being, and life happiness in the Chinese culture. *Journal of Business Ethics, 123*(3), 513–525.

Yang, L. Q., & Caughlin, D. E. (2017). Aggression-preventive supervisor behavior: Implications for workplace climate and employee outcomes. *Journal of Occupational Health Psychology, 22*(1), 1.

Zhang, S., & Tu, Y. (2018). Cross-domain effects of ethical leadership on employee family and life satisfaction: The moderating role of family-supportive supervisor behaviors. *Journal of Business Ethics, 152*(4), 1085–1097.

Zhang, Y., & Liao, Z. (2015). Consequences of abusive supervision: A meta-analytic review. *Asia Pacific Journal of Management, 32*(4), 959–987.

Zwingmann, I., Wegge, J., Wolf, S., Rudolf, M., Schmidt, M., & Richter, P. (2014). Is transformational leadership healthy for employees? A multilevel analysis in 16 nations. *German Journal of Human Resource Management, 28*(1–2), 2.

PART III

Major Issues Relating to Stress and Well-Being

6 Work–Nonwork Balance and Employee Well-Being

WENDY J. CASPER, JULIE HOLLIDAY
WAYNE, FREDERICK RICE, AND HODA
VAZIRI

Research on the interface between work and family dates back many years. One of the earliest discussions occurred in Pleck's (1977) analysis of the gendered work–family role system. These early discussions coincided with the rise of middle-class women's entrance into the workforce, such that more attention was placed on how parents – particularly working mothers – managed work and family roles (Cooke & Rousseau, 1984). Drawing from the scarcity perspective that time and energy are finite, research centered on how involvement in multiple roles creates challenges (Goode, 1974). In a key conceptual article drawing from Kahn et al.'s (1964) role theory, Greenhaus and Beutell (1985) defined work–family conflict as "a form of interrole conflict that occurs when work and family are mutually incompatible in some respect" (p. 77), including when the time, strain, or behavior of one role interferes with participation or functioning in the other role. Scholarly research on work–family conflict took off in the 1990s, and since that time, a mature literature has developed identifying its stressor antecedents and negative consequences (Eby et al., 2005). Around 2000, research began to focus on potential benefits of multiple roles and the concept of work–family enrichment, or when the positive gains, such as skills, mood, or other benefits, from one role improve satisfaction or functioning in the other (Carlson et al., 2006). Research has accumulated to demonstrate its resource antecedents and positive consequences (Lapierre et al., 2018). Yet, while academics talked about work–family conflict and enrichment, the popular vernacular that emerged to describe how people manage work and family was "work–family (or work–life) balance," resulting in a disconnect between the labels people used in practice ("balance") and what the scholarly literature discussed ("conflict" or "enrichment").

In this chapter, we review the history of the balance literature, including how it has been defined and measured, from its first mention

155

in the literature (Marks & MacDermid, 1996) until now (Wayne et al., 2021). In the first discussion of role balance, Marks and MacDermid (1996) posited that greater balance fosters better well-being. We review the limited literature that speaks to the relation between balance and well-being, and we note overall findings as well as trends in the way this research has been conducted. Finally, we conclude with recommendations for future theoretical and research development to enhance understanding of balance and its implications for the well-being of individuals, organizations, and their families.

The Meaning and Measurement of Balance

The first scholarly discussion occurred in the family studies literature in 1996 when Marks and MacDermid first used the term "balance" to denote a scholarly construct. They defined role balance as "The tendency to become fully engaged in the performance of every role in one's total role system, to approach every typical role and role partner with an attitude of attentiveness and care" (p. 421). They described role balance as focusing on all life roles, rather than only work and family, and theorized about the value of attending to one's entire role system in a balanced way, ensuring adequate attention and commitment to each role such that no one role is shortchanged. When people conscientiously attend to each role, role balance theory suggests they have more positive role experiences and experience less role stress, promoting well-being. Marks and MacDermid (1996) developed an 8-item scale to measure role balance, and their research found that greater role balance was linked to improved self-esteem, less depression and better functioning in work and school roles. Despite their important, seminal work on balance, Marks and MacDermid's definition and measure did not dominate the scholarly literature. A variety of other conceptualizations of balance and scales to measure it continued to emerge.

Around the turn of the twenty-first century, several researchers defined balance as an absence of work–family conflict (Buffardi et al., 1999; Clark, 2000), attempting to map the popular vernacular (i.e., balance) and the primary construct from the scholarly literature (i.e., conflict) onto one another. Meanwhile, another stream of research in the work–family literature began to examine the ways work and family might benefit one another and result in positive spillover

(Gryzwacz & Marks, 2000), which was later labeled work–family enrichment (Greenhaus & Powell, 2006; Wayne, 2009). Shortly after the emergence of this new positive construct, Frone (2003) defined work–family balance as a phenomenon that results from a combination of low conflict and high enrichment. Given conflict and enrichment were found to be bidirectional, Frone (2003) suggested four components were important to work–family balance. Work could hurt family (work-to-family conflict) and/or family could harm work (family-to-work conflict), or work could benefit family (work-to-family enrichment) and/or family could benefit work (family-to-work enrichment). Thus, Frone's (2003) work resulted in the fourfold taxonomy of work–family balance, and a number of researchers followed Frone's conceptualization of balance in their work (Aryee et al., 2005; Bulger et al., 2007; Gareis et al., 2009; Hennessy, 2007; Lu et al., 2009).

At the same time that Frone's (2003) definition emerged, a distinct conceptualization of balance was developed by Greenhaus et al. (2003). Drawing from a common meaning of the word "balance" to denote equality, Greenhaus et al. (2003) defined work–family balance as "The extent to which an individual is equally engaged in and equally satisfied with his or her work role and family role." These authors measured balance through a comparison of three facets: "(1) the amount of time spent at work with the amount of time spent on home and family activities, (2) involvement in work with involvement in family, and (3) satisfaction with work with satisfaction with family" (p. 518). Halpern and Murphy (2005) followed the lead of Greenhaus and colleagues (2003) to embrace the definition of equality across work and family roles by using the metaphor of a balance beam to describe work–family balance. These authors suggested that balance occurs when the investment in family on one side of the balance beam matches the investment in work on the other. However, Greenhaus and colleagues (2003) found that the equality-based operationalization of balance was not associated with better outcomes, but that greater involvement in family was, suggesting an equality conceptualization may not be the most relevant way to define balance.

In contrast to the equality notion embraced by Greenhaus et al. (2003), Voydanoff (2002) conceptualized work–family balance as a mechanism linking work and family domains. Drawing from the cognitive appraisal view of stress (Lazarus & Folkman, 1984), Voydanoff

(2005) positioned balance as a perception derived from the relative resources and demands in work and family experiences, defining it as "A global assessment that work and family resources are sufficient to meet work and family demands such that participation is effective in both domains" (p. 825). This view rejects the notion that balance requires equal time, involvement, and/or satisfaction across work and family roles and instead draws from a demands-resources person-environment fit perspective to conceptualize balance. Voydanoff (2005) theorized that balance appraisals developed as a result of perceptions of the degree to which work resources met family demands, family resources met work demands, and boundary-spanning resources generally help one manage work and family, resulting in "an overall appraisal of the extent of harmony, equilibrium, and integration of work and family" (p. 825).

In 2007, the debate around the meaning of balance shifted from a focus on whether balance required equality across work and family roles (Greenhaus et al., 2003) or was an assessment of fit between demands and resources within and across work and family domains (Voydanoff, 2005), to focus on whether balance was a psychological construct that involved a subjective appraisal of one's work and family experience (Valcour, 2007) or a social construct that reflects the views of role partners at work (e.g., supervisor, coworker) and home (e.g., spouse, children) (Grzywacz & Carlson, 2007). Drawing from Voydanoff (2005), Valcour (2007) defined balance as "An overall level of contentment resulting from an assessment of one's degree of success at meeting work and family role demands" (p. 1512), suggesting that balance is an attitude which includes affective (i.e., contentment) and cognitive (i.e., assessment of success) components. In contrast, that same year Grzywacz and Carlson (2007) defined balance as the "Accomplishment of role-related expectations that are negotiated and shared between an individual and his/her role-related partners in the work and family domain." Grzywacz and Carlson (2007) suggested that balance is more behavioral in nature, considering whether expectations that role partners have for the focal employee are met. Valcour's (2007) definition considered whether the focal employee feels successful, and balance was still defined as an attitudinal variable held in the mind of the focal employee. A self-report 5-item satisfaction-based scale was developed to assess it (i.e., rate your satisfaction with "the way you divide your time between work and personal or family life").

In contrast, by defining balance as a behavioral variable tapping into meeting expectations that are negotiated with role partners, Grzywacz and Carlson (2007) define balance as inextricably linked to social context, as views of role partners are central to the definition. Carlson et al. (2009) developed a 6-item scale to assess balance as they conceptualized it. While it was a self-report scale to be completed by the focal employee, it tapped into that employee's view of their effectiveness in the eyes of role partners (e.g., "I am able to accomplish the expectations that my supervisors and family have for me").

As the balance literature emerged over time, scholars began to coalesce around a view that balance was a distinct phenomenon from conflict and enrichment. This led to questions about how conflict and enrichment, which are directional constructs in which one domain impacts the other, might relate to balance, which was increasingly conceptualized as a global nondirectional assessment. In 2011, two important papers contributed to the conversation about how conflict and enrichment relate to balance. First, Greenhaus and Allen (2011) theorized about the personal and contextual conditions that give rise to a perception of work–family balance. In doing so, they defined work–family balance as "An overall appraisal of the extent to which individuals' effectiveness and satisfaction in work and family roles are consistent with their life values at a given point in time." They developed a theoretical model proposing that dispositional, work, and family characteristics lead to work–family conflict and enrichment which, in turn, foster satisfaction and effectiveness in work and family roles, which give rise to feelings of balance. In that same year, Maertz and Boyar (2011) distinguished conflict and enrichment, which could be studied as episodic variables that differ from day to day, from the global perception of balance, which they suggested may be less dynamic and referred to as a "levels" phenomenon. Like Greenhaus and Allen (2011), these authors conceptualized conflict and enrichment as antecedents to perceptions of balance, rather than variables that define what balance is. Yet, despite emerging consensus that conflict and enrichment were best conceptualized as antecedents of a more global perception called balance, there was still substantial disagreement about how to define balance.

In 2012, Allen et al. presented findings from a qualitative investigation of laypersons' definitions of work–family balance at the Work–Family Researchers Network conference. This qualitative study collected survey data from 783 employees of an engineering firm and asked: "When you think about work–family balance, what does that mean for you? How do YOU define work–family balance?" Participants were 80.3% male, 54.4% parents, and an average of 37.2 years old. Two researchers coded the themes that emerged in participants' definitions of work–family balance with 98% agreement. Eight themes emerged, suggesting that work–family balance does not mean the same thing to all people.

The most common definition of balance reported by 41.2% of participants was that balance means having adequate time to be with family as well as enough time to get work done (e.g., "Having time to be with my family that I want and having time to do my work"), indicating a form of behavioral involvement (time with family). The next most common definition, described by 32.4% of participants, was success and good performance in both work and family roles. For example, one participant said "I define work–family balance as successfully meeting the needs of one's career and the needs of family and home life." The next most common theme, reported by 15.5% of participants, was satisfaction (e.g., "To me it means being able to enjoy both work and family time"), which reflects the attitudinal view of Valcour (2007). A similar portion of people, 15.4% of the sample, reported being mentally present as indicative of balance. One participant noted, "My husband's work–life balance is out of whack… when he is not at work, he is still not fully present… he is checking email, fielding calls, thinking about projects, or actively working on projects." Mental engagement, along with the most common definition of temporal involvement, taps into the central role of involvement in balance, reflecting the conceptualization of Marks and McDermid (1996).

Low levels of conflict were described in defining balance for 12.7% participants (e.g., "A balance between work and family means that neither will suffer on the occasions when one or the other must be raised as the priority"), mirroring some researchers' view that balance is best defined as low conflict. Another 9.8% emphasized the notion of fit, indicating balance involved choices that fit one's priorities or values (e.g., "Family is priority one and work is two; Family needs and celebrations are first and foremost."), echoing Voydanoff's (2005) view. A handful of participants (3.6%) referenced energy in defining work–family balance (e.g., "Comfortable with the amount of energy spent in each area"). Finally, a small number of participants (3.3%) also referred to work–family enrichment – both family-to-work enrichment (e.g., "My family inspires me to do better at work") and work-to-family enrichment (e.g., "My work provides me with the means to give my family a good life"), as indicative of work–family balance. Thus, this research revealed that, much like the literature more generally, people have different meanings of balance.

In 2013, Casper et al., in their chapter on concepts and measures in the work–family interface, briefly reviewed the construct of balance to comment on the state of literature at that time. In addition to noting the tendency of some scholars to define balance as a function of conflict and/or enrichment (e.g., Frone, 2003), these authors described the primary scholarly definitions of balance. They noted three definitions of balance with scales associated with them (Carlson et al., 2009; Greenhaus et al., 2003; Valcour, 2007). They also mentioned the Greenhaus and Allen (2011) definition and noted that this definition could be operationalized by the interaction of life role values with role satisfaction and perceived role effectiveness, although at that time no empirical research had operationalized balance in this way.

In 2017, Wayne et al. differentiated and empirically examined various conceptualizations and measures of balance. To do so, Wayne and colleagues (2017) noted the various ways balance had been defined and suggested that the various definitions represented distinct forms of balance. Importantly, these authors differentiated the combined spillover approach to balance from a global approach. The combined spillover approach draws from Frone's (2003) fourfold taxonomy of balance such that the two directions of conflict and enrichment are components of balance. Wayne et al. (2017) differentiated the additive spillover approach from the multiplicative spillover approach, noting that most of the literature that draws from Frone (2003) operationalizes balance with the additive spillover approach, which examines the unique direct effects of four dimensions of balance (work-to-family conflict, family-to-work conflict, work-to-family enrichment, family-to-work enrichment). However, Wayne et al. (2017) argued that although the additive spillover approach had been used to operationalize Frone's (2003) definition of balance in several studies, it did not capture the true meaning of balance that is suggested by Frone (2003). They argue that Frone's definition of balance as "low levels of interrole conflict and high levels of interrole facilitation" (p. 145) suggests that "the synergistic effect of low conflict combined with high enrichment is greater than the sum of its individual parts" (Wayne et al., 2017, p. 171). Given this, Wayne et al. (2017) argue that an interaction effect better reflects the synergistic experience of low conflict with high enrichment that Frone (2003) defined as balance. Wayne et al. (2017) examined the effects of this multiplicative spillover approach (i.e., the interaction) on role attitudes and performance above and beyond the additive spillover effects. As expected, they found that multiplicative spillover predicted incremental variance in job satisfaction, family satisfaction, and turnover intentions, above and beyond additive spillover, suggesting the value of this multiplicative approach.

Wayne et al. (2017) labeled constructs that were gestalt, nondirectional perceptions of the interplay between work roles and family roles as "global approaches" to balance. Though various global approaches had been treated as if they were interchangeable with one another as balance constructs, Wayne and colleagues (2017) argued that there may be important conceptual and empirical differences between them. As such, they focused on two common global balance approaches for which there were established measures in the literature. The attitudinal construct developed by Valcour (2007) was labeled "balance satisfaction" and differentiated from the more social construct developed by Grzywacz and Carlson (2007), which was labeled "balance effectiveness." Despite the behavioral conceptual definition of this construct (accomplishing what is expected by role partners), Wayne and colleagues (2017) suggested that, given the self-report nature of this measure by the employee, balance effectiveness is best defined as a cognitive appraisal that involves self-evaluation of the interdependent self. That is, this self-evaluation takes into account not only general perceptions of the self (i.e., how well I think I am meeting expectations) but also perceptions of role partner views of the self (i.e., how well I think my supervisor and spouse think I am doing). Wayne et al. (2017) found that these two global balance perceptions (balance satisfaction and balance effectiveness) predicted additional variance in important outcomes above the effects of both additive and multiplicative spillover, but that these different forms of balance were predictive of distinct outcomes. Specifically, consistent with the compatibility principle (Ajzen & Fishbein, 1977), balance satisfaction was more strongly related to job and family attitudes whereas balance effectiveness was more strongly related to job and family performance. This demonstrates that, while they are related constructs that share variance (r = .74), balance effectiveness and balance satisfaction are distinct types of global balance that relate differently to correlates and, as such, should be distinguished in elaborations of the balance construct and theories regarding its processes.

Most recently, Casper et al. (2018) conducted a comprehensive review of the various conceptualizations and measures of balance in the work–nonwork literature. Across 290 articles, these authors identified 233 distinct conceptual definitions, which clustered into six higher order types of definitions which typically drew from multiple meanings within a single definition. The most common meanings evoked in defining balance in order of frequency were effectiveness, satisfaction, fit, conflict, and involvement, suggesting a variety of ways balance has been defined in the extant literature. Most of the operational definitions, which also clustered into six higher order definitions, were unidimensional or psychological (held in the mind of the focal person) and drew from multiple meanings. Operational and conceptual definitions frequently were not well aligned, with operational definitions most often using conflict or the term balance in items, followed by effectiveness, satisfaction, and involvement.

To examine the discriminant validity of distinct operationalizations of balance, Casper et al. (2018) meta-analyzed the unique operationalizations of balance with satisfaction-based correlates. Their analysis provided empirical evidence for the presence of operationalizations of balance that differ from conflict and enrichment and are more strongly correlated with job, family, and life satisfaction than are conflict and enrichment. These authors concluded that there is a unique construct called balance, which is conceptually and empirically distinguishable from conflict and enrichment and adds unique value to the literature. They suggested that, consistent with most of the balance literature, balance should be conceptualized as a psychological, attitudinal construct which is held in the mind of the focal person and as such, can be captured through self-report survey instruments. Given the various meanings which have been attributed to the term balance in the literature, Casper et al. (2018) argued that balance is best conceptualized as a multidimensional construct with multiple meanings, defining it as "The extent to which employees hold a favorable evaluation regarding their combination of work and nonwork roles, arising from the belief that their emotional experiences, involvement, and effectiveness in work and nonwork roles are commensurate (compatible) with the value they attach to the roles." (p. 197). Just as job satisfaction can be assessed using a global or facet approach, so can balance. They called for creation of a global balance scale as well as a scale which measures affective, effectiveness, and involvement facets.

Wayne et al. (2021) responded to these calls to develop a scale to measure Casper et al.'s (2018) multidimensional definition of balance, developing a 5-item global balance scale (e.g., "Overall, my work and nonwork roles fit together") and a 5-item measurement of the affective (e.g., "I am happy with the work and nonwork aspects of my life that are important to me."), effectiveness (e.g., "I perform well in my most highly valued work and nonwork roles"), and involvement (e.g., "I am able to devote enough attention to important work and nonwork activities") facets of balance. These authors explored the structure of the 20 items that measured balance. Consistent with Casper et al. (2018), they found that global balance was best represented as a general factor which could be measured with their five global balance items. Furthermore, the 15 items assessing each of the three dimensions of balance (involvement balance, effectiveness balance, and affective balance) all loaded significantly on the global balance as well as their intended factor, suggesting that global balance operates as a general factor that relates to the three dimensions of balance, and that each dimension represents a form of balance that is not fully picked up by global balance. Thus, it appears that, similar to job satisfaction, overall balance can be measured as a global construct, or a facet-based approach can be used. In a facet approach, distinct facets of balance are measured and can either be examined separately or can be combined to form an indicator of global balance that could be used instead of (or in addition to) the global balance items.

In addition to exploring the factor structure of balance, Wayne et al. (2021) also examined whether their new global and facet measures of balance predicted variance in important work-related and well-being variables, over and above the established measures of balance satisfaction (Valocur, 2007) and balance effectiveness (Carlson et al., 2009). All three facets and the global balance measure were all unique, incremental predictors of at least one important outcome variable, although there were some differences in which specific outcomes were predicted. The global measure of balance exhibited predictive validity across all the outcome variables that were examined, including work-related (organizational commitment, turnover intention, organizational citizenship behavior, OCBs) and well-being outcomes (vigor, emotional exhaustion, and general health). Affective balance was also associated with outcomes, predicting incremental variance in all the same variables with the exception of OCBs. Involvement and effectiveness facets of balance both predicted incremental variance in only work-related outcomes. Specifically, involvement balance was a unique predictor of organizational commitment, turnover intentions, and OCBs. In contrast, effectiveness balance was a unique predictor of only OCBs. This pattern of relationships highlights the important predictive role of the global balance construct, while also suggesting that a fine-grained examination of the facets of balance has important implications given distinct facets are linked to different outcomes.

In summary, though the balance literature began about 25 years ago, only recently has the research evolved to the point that there is clearer meaning and stronger measurement of the balance construct. In particular, balance is best considered a global appraisal of the combination of one's work and nonwork roles that is comprised of facets including the degree to which one's involvement, satisfaction, and effectiveness in roles is consistent with one's priorities (Casper et al., 2018). Wayne et al. (2021) have developed a reliable and valid measure of the global appraisal and involvement, effectiveness, and affective balance and demonstrated their relevance to work and well-being outcomes. A critical next step is that we urge scholars to consistently use these conceptual definitions and measures for research to accumulate in a meaningful way.

Work–Nonwork Balance and Well-Being

According to the Center for Disease Control (CDC, 2020), although there is no consensus around a singular definition of well-being, there is agreement that it "includes the presence of positive emotions and moods (e.g., contentment, happiness), the absence of negative emotions (e.g., depression, anxiety), satisfaction with life, fulfillment and positive functioning" as well as "physical well-being (e.g., feeling very healthy and full of energy)." Marks and MacDermid (1996) theorized that balance was associated with greater well-being, and this was supported by Wayne et al.'s (2021) research, linking balance with vigor, emotional exhaustion, and general physical health. Numerous other studies have examined this important connection, and in order to speak to the state of the literature, we conducted a literature review to examine the research linking balance to stress and well-being outcomes. Because our interest was to focus on holistic definitions of balance, we excluded articles that used a combined spillover approach in which balance was operationalized as conflict and enrichment, and only reviewed the literature on the well-being consequences of holistic balance (though we refer to these as "consequences," it is important to note that they are theorized as outcomes of balance, e.g., Marks & MacDermid, 1996, few studies appropriately use longitudinal studies to examine temporal order among these variables).

Our review searched for manuscripts through 2021 in PsycINFO and Business Source. To do so, we first used the keyword "work–family balance" along with each of the following keywords to search for articles: "well-being," "wellness," "stress," "anxiety," "thriving," "happiness," "health," and "depression." We then ran the same search using the keyword "work–life balance" instead. The search yielded a total of 140 references that used quantitative measures of balance, and 13 of them were empirical studies that examined well-being outcomes of a holistic balance construct. Examination of these studies revealed four distinct ways in which holistic balance was measured: fit-based balance, balance satisfaction, balance effectiveness, and balance involvement. Moreover, a separate group of studies was classified as overall balance because they used items that asked participants to rate their balance without invoking one of the meanings commonly attributed to balance like satisfaction, effectiveness, involvement, and fit (Casper et al., 2018). Table 6.1 provides information on the scales used to assess the various conceptualizations of balance. We clustered these scales according to four distinct primary meanings attributed to balance, drawing from the meanings of balance identified by Casper et al. (2018) – fit, satisfaction, effectiveness, and involvement. Scales that did not tap into a primary meaning identified by Casper et al. (2018) but that used the term "balance" in a scale item were classified as overall balance. Table 6.2 provides information on the 13 studies we identified that examined how balance was linked to indices of mental and/or physical well-being.

Table 6.1 *Instruments used to measure balance in studies*

Operationalization	Reference	Definition	Items	Sample Item
Fit-Based Balance				
Work–life balance	Eurofond (2012)	The extent to which one's working hours fit in with family and social commitments.	1	How do your working hours fit in with your family or social commitments outside work?
Work–life balance	Wu et al. (2013)	Worker's perception of how balanced his/her job is with his/her personal life.	8	There is a good fit between my personal life and work life.
Balance satisfaction				
Satisfaction with work–family balance	Valcour (2007)	The level of contentment resulting from one's success at meeting work and family role demands.	5	How satisfied are you with your ability to balance the needs of your job with those of your personal or family life?
Work–family balance	Greenhaus et al. (2004)	Effectively balancing work-related and nonwork-related demands.	6	I am satisfied with the balance I have achieved between my work life and my family life.
Work–family balance	Greenhaus et al. (2012)	The overall degree of balance individuals' experience between their work and family lives.	5	I am satisfied with the balance I have achieved between my work life and my nonwork life.
Affective balance	Wayne et al. (2021)	Experiencing pleasant emotions in work and nonwork roles consistent with the value attached to those roles.	5	I am happy with the work and nonwork aspects of my life that are important to me.
Balance effectiveness				
Work–family balance	Carlson et al. (2009)	The extent to which an individual is meeting negotiated role-related expectations in the work and family domains.	6	I do a good job of meeting the role expectations of critical people in my work and family life.

Table 6.1 (*cont.*)

Operationalization	Reference	Definition	Items	Sample Item
Fit-Based Balance				
Effectiveness balance	Wayne et al. (2021)	The perception that one's effectiveness in work and nonwork roles is consistent with the value attached to those roles.	5	I am able to effectively handle important work and nonwork responsibilities.
Balance involvement				
Involvement balance	Wayne et al. (2021)	The perception that one's involvement in work and nonwork roles is consistent with the value attached to the roles.	5	I am able to devote enough attention to important work and nonwork activities.
General balance				
Work–life balance	Bauld et al. (2009)	The degree to which employees believe they can achieve a satisfying mix of work and nonwork activities.	4	Overall, I believe my work and nonwork life are balanced.
Work–life balance	Haar (2013)	The overall level of enjoyment, satisfaction and management of all one's life roles, including work.	3	I manage to balance the demands of my work and personal/family life well.
Work–life balance	Brough et al. (2014)	The overall perception that one's work and nonwork life are balanced.	4	I feel that the balance between my work demands and nonwork activities is currently about right.
Global balance	Wayne et al. (2021)	The overall balance, harmony, fit, or integration of work and nonwork roles.	4	Overall, my work and nonwork roles are integrated.

Table 6.2 Studies linking balance to wellness-related factors

Construct name	Citation	Key consequences	Other consequences
Fit-based balance			
Work–life balance (Eurofond, 2012)	Lunau et al. (2014)	Well-being (+) Self-rated health (+)	
Work–life balance (Eurofond, 2012)	Lucia-Casademunt et al. (2018)	Well-being (+)	
Work–life balance (Wu et al., 2013)	Haider et al. (2018)	Psychological well-being (+)	
Balance satisfaction			
Satisfaction with work–family balance (Valcour, 2007)	Barnett et al. (2019)	Depression (−)	TI (−)
Satisfaction with work–family balance (Valcour, 2007)	Vanderpool & Way (2013)	Job anxiety (−)	Voluntary turnover (−) JS (+) OC (+)
Satisfaction with work–family balance (Valcour, 2007)	Odle-Dusseau et al. (2019)	Sleep disturbances (−) Musculoskeletal pain (−) General health perceptions (+)	Org justice perceptions (+)
Satisfaction with work–family balance (Valcour, 2007)	Wayne et al. (2021)	Vigor (+) Emotional exhaustion (−) Health (+)	JS (+), FS (+), LS (+), JI (+), FI (+), JP (+), FP (+), OC (+) OCB (+) TI (−)
Work–family balance (Greenhaus et al., 2004)	Rahim et al. (2020)	Psychological well-being (+)	Career satisfaction (+)
Work–family balance (Greenhaus et al., 2004)	Odle-Dusseau et al. (2012)	Stress (−) Depression (−) Quality of life (+)	OC (+) Intent to leave (−)

Table 6.2 (*cont.*)

Construct name	Citation	Key consequences	Other consequences
Fit-based balance			
Work–family balance (Greenhaus et al., 2012)	Wepfer et al. (2018)	Depression (-)	
Affective balance (Wayne et al., 2021)	Wayne et al. (2021)	Vigor (+) Emotional exhaustion (-) Health (+)	JS (+), FS (+), LS (+), JI (+), FI (+), JP (+), FP (+), OC (+) OCB (+) TI (−)
Balance effectiveness			
Work–family balance (Carlson et al., 2009)	Wayne et al. (2021)	Vigor (+) Emotional exhaustion (−) Health (+)	JS (+), FS (+), LS (+), JI (+), FI (+), JP (+), FP (+), OC (+) OCB (+) TI (−)
Effectiveness balance (Wayne et al., 2021)	Wayne et al. (2021)	Vigor (+) Emotional exhaustion (−) Health (+)	JS (+), FS (+), LS (+), JI (+), FI (+), JP (+), FP (+), OC (+) OCB (+) TI (−)
Balance involvement			
Involvement balance (Wayne et al., 2021)	Wayne et al. (2021)	Vigor (+) Emotional exhaustion (−) Health (+)	JS (+), FS (+), LS (+), JI (+), FI (+), JP (+), FP (+), OC (+) OCB (+) TI (−)

General balance

Global balance (Wayne et al., 2021)	Wayne et al. (2021)	Vigor (+) Emotional exhaustion (−) Health (+)	JS (+), FS (+), LS (+), JI (+), FI (+), JP (+), FP (+), OC (+) OCB (+) TI (−)
Work–life balance (Bauld et al., 2009)	Scanlan et al. (2013)	Vigor (+) Exhaustion (−)	JS (+) Disengagement (−)
Work–life balance (Brough et al., 2014)	Brough et al. (2014)	Psychological strain (−)	JS (+) FS (+) TI (−)
Work–life balance (Haar, 2013)	Haar et al. (2014)	LS (+) Anxiety (−) Depression (−)	JS (+)

Notes. JS = job satisfaction, LS = life satisfaction, FS = family satisfaction, JI = job involvement, FI = family involvement, JP = job performance, FP = family performance, OC = organizational commitment, TI = turnover intent, OCB = Organizational citizenship behavior

Fit-Based Balance and Well-Being

Three studies examined the association of fit-based balance with well-being. Using a single-item balance measure from the fifth European Working Conditions Survey in 2010 (EWCS; Eurofond, 2012), Lunau et al. (2014) found balance to be positively associated with both well-being and self-rated physical health. Similarly, Lucia-Casademunt et al. (2018) used data from the sixth EWCS in 2015 and found the same fit-based balance item was positively related to overall well-being, defined as having energy, positive affect, and interest (Eurofond, 2012). In the same year, Haider et al. (2018) found balance, assessed using a multi-item fit-based balance measure, was positively related to psychological well-being assessed 15 days later.

Satisfaction-Based Balance and Well-Being

Seven studies in our review use balance satisfaction measures as predictors of well-being. Odle-Dusseau et al. (2012) used a balance satisfaction measure developed by Greenhaus et al. (2004) to examine the link between work–family balance and well-being outcomes. They found that balance was negatively related to stress, depression, and intent to leave and positively related to quality of life and organizational commitment. Vanderpool and Way (2013) used Valcour's (2007) balance satisfaction measure and found that work–family balance was negatively associated with job anxiety and turnover intentions in a cross-sectional survey. Moreover, they followed participants over time and found work–family balance was also related to lower odds of actual voluntary turnover six months later. Also using Valcour's (2007) measure, Odle-Dusseau et al. (2019) found balance satisfaction was positively related to general health perceptions, job satisfaction, organizational commitment, and perceptions of organizational justice, and negatively associated with sleep disturbances and musculoskeletal pain. Wepfer et al. (2018) identified a negative relationship between work–family balance and depression using a scale from Greenhaus and colleagues (2012). In a recent study of hospice nurses, Barnett et al. (2019) found balance satisfaction (Valcour, 2007) was negatively associated with depression, and that work–family balance acted as a mediator between workplace social support and depression. Rahim et al. (2020) examined a sample of Malaysian university staff members and found a positive relationship of work–family balance with psychological well-being, as well as career satisfaction.

As mentioned previously, Wayne and colleagues (2021) recently developed and validated a scale to measure global balance and three facets (involvement, affective, and effectiveness). In their research, they included their newly developed measure, along with other measures of balance satisfaction (Valcour, 2007) and balance effectiveness (Carlson et al., 2009) and examined their relation to well-being as well as job attitudes and behaviors. They found balance satisfaction (Valcour, 2007) to be correlated with greater vigor and perceived physical health, less emotional exhaustion, more positive role attitudes (job, family and life satisfaction, job and family involvement, organizational commitment), greater self-reported role performance (job and family performance, citizenship behaviors), and fewer turnover intentions. When considered along with balance effectiveness (Carlson et al. 2009), balance satisfaction was uniquely related to greater vigor, less emotional exhaustion, greater perceived health, higher organizational commitment, and lower turnover intentions. Wayne et al.'s (2021) scale for affective balance shares some similar conceptual characteristics with balance satisfaction. Their affective balance scale was correlated with all the same outcomes as balance satisfaction and predicted an increment in perceived health, vigor, emotional exhaustion, organizational commitment, and turnover intent, above and beyond the effects of balance satisfaction (Valcour, 2007), balance effectiveness (Carlson et al., 2009), the other balance facets (effectiveness balance, involvement balance), and their global balance scale (Wayne et al., 2021).

Effectiveness-Based Balance and Well-Being

One study examined the link between balance effectiveness and well-being outcomes. Wayne et al. (2021) found that balance effectiveness (as measured by Carlson et al., 2009) was positively correlated with vigor and perceived health, negatively correlated with emotional exhaustion, and correlated with all the same role attitudes and behaviors as balance satisfaction. When effectiveness balance (Carlson et al., 2009) was considered along with balance satisfaction (Valcour, 2007), it was uniquely related to vigor, perceived health, organizational commitment, and OCBs. Wayne et al.'s effectiveness balance measure correlated with all the same variables as did the Valcour (2007) and Carlson et al. (2009) measures. When considered together, it was not incrementally related to vigor, emotional exhaustion, or perceived health above and beyond the Carlson measure, the Valcour measure, and Wayne et al.'s (2021) other measure (affective and effectiveness dimensions and global balance) but was incrementally associated with greater OCBs. It is important to note that these analyses examining the incremental validity of Wayne et al.'s balance effectiveness measure are conservative in that they are above and beyond five other balance scales or dimensions. Thus, when considered alone, their effectiveness balance facet may have unique relationships to these same well-being indicators.

Involvement-Based Balance and Well-Being

Based on the presence of involvement in the conceptual definitions of balance, Wayne and colleagues' (2021) multidimensional measure of balance has an involvement dimension, in addition to the affective and effectiveness dimensions. Their research found that the balance involvement dimension was correlated with all the same indices of well-being, role satisfaction, and role performance as the effectiveness and affective dimensions. After controlling for the Valcour (2007) and Carlson et al. (2009) scales as well as Wayne et al.'s (2021) affective balance, effectiveness balance, and global balance measure, the involvement balance predicted an increment in the variance of perceived health, organizational commitment, turnover intentions, and OCBs. It is important to note, however, that these relationships were opposite in sign to what was expected and to the bivariate relationships, suggesting suppression. This finding likely reflects the higher intercorrelations of balance involvement with Wayne et al.'s other balance measures (affective and effectiveness facets as well as global balance measure) as well as the Valcour (2007) and Carlson et al. (2009) measures. More research is critically needed to examine this facet and how it relates to indicators of well-being.

Overall Balance and Well-Being

Finally, we identified four studies that examined the link between overall balance and well-being. In their study assessing the well-being of Australian occupational therapists, Scanlan et al. (2013) found that work–life balance (Bauld et al., 2009) was linked to greater vigor and less emotional exhaustion, as well as greater job satisfaction and less work disengagement. A 4-item balance measure developed a year later by researchers in Australia and New Zealand (Brough et al., 2014) was linked to decreased psychological strain and lower turnover intentions, as well as greater job and family satisfaction in a cross-sectional survey. These relationships of balance with these outcomes were evident not only in the variables collected via a cross-sectional survey, but also when these same outcomes were measured a year later. In a sample from six nations, Haar et al. (2014) found that work–life balance (Haar, 2013) was negatively related to anxiety and depression and positively related to both job and life satisfaction. Finally, using their global balance measure, Wayne et al. (2021) found that global balance was correlated with indices of well-being as well as role satisfaction and performance. Especially notable, their global balance scale was incrementally related to more vigor, less emotional exhaustion, greater perceived health, more organizational commitment and OCBs, and lower turnover intentions above and beyond existing measures of balance satisfaction (Valcour, 2007), balance effectiveness (Carlson et al., 2009), and all three facets of balance developed by Wayne et al. (2021). This suggests that this global measure captures something unique and valuable in terms of the balance construct space.

Summary

Overall, these results suggest that, consistent with the theoretical tenets of Marks and MacDermid (1996), having balance across work and nonwork roles is linked to well-being. Across various measures, findings indicate that greater balance is associated with less stress, depression, emotional exhaustion, being more satisfied with life, and having better physical health. Though not the focus of this chapter, these studies also show a link between greater balance and job attitudes (e.g., organizational commitment) and behaviors (e.g., organizational citizenship behaviors). Yet, the research linking balance to well-being, as evident by this sparse review, is quite limited. Moreover, most of these studies were cross-sectional (for exceptions see Brough et al., 2014; Haider et al., 2018; Vanderpool & Way, 2013), making it difficult to disentangle true score variance from common method effects. In the next section, we discuss how scholars can expand upon theory and research linking balance and well-being.

Toward a Better Understanding of Work–Nonwork Balance and Its Link to Well-Being

Given the conceptual and measurement progress that has been made on the balance construct (Casper et al., 2018; Wayne et al., 2021), we encourage scholars to follow these suggestions and adopt the newly developed measures that capture the content domain and enable research to accumulate in a meaningful way. From this foundation, the time has come to enhance understanding of balance in general, including its link to well-being. There is little consensus around theory describing the key antecedents of balance, how and why people experience balance (or don't), and how it relates to outcomes such as well-being. For example, while role balance theory discusses the meaning and organization of the balance construct and how it relates to outcomes such as well-being (Marks & MacDermid, 1996), it does not discuss conflict, nor enrichment, nor other proximal antecedents. Voydanoff (2005) discusses demands and resources as antecedents of fit and, in turn, balance to outcomes, but also overlooks these central work–family constructs. Greenhaus and Allen's (2011) model of balance includes antecedents (work, family, and dispositional characteristics) and mediators (conflict and enrichment) as well as role satisfaction and performance, all as factors contributing to "feelings of balance." Most recently, Hirschi et al.'s (2019) action regulation model posits that balance is a function of attaining work and family goals. Hirschi et al. (2019) suggest that people attain balance through strategically engaging and disengaging in work and family roles to foster goal attainment, but do not speak to how balance relates to established work–family constructs (conflict and enrichment). As balance is the endpoint of the models proffered by both Greenhaus and Allen (2011) and Hirschi et al. (2019), neither speaks to how balance relates to indicators of well-being such as mental or physical health. This brief review highlights the need for greater consensus around theory describing how balance is linked to bidirectional conflict and enrichment, employee well-being, and role attitudes and behaviors.

Another limitation of existing theories of balance is that none of them account for current conceptualizations of balance as a multidimensional construct (Casper et al., 2018; Wayne et al., 2017; 2021). Theories are needed that explain how global balance and each dimension (involvement, affective, and effectiveness balance) relate to one another and to various indicators of well-being. Given global balance is defined as a favorable evaluation that arises from the three facets of balance (Casper et al., 2018), research could examine the assumption inherent in this definition that global balance is a mechanism that explains how the facets of balance relate to well-being outcomes. Moreover, research might also examine whether specific facets of balance are more closely linked to different indices of well-being. Based on the compatibility principle (Azjen & Fishbein, 1977), it may be that affective balance is more strongly related to subjective or hedonic well-being (e.g., life satisfaction; SWB) whereas effectiveness and/or involvement balance may relate more strongly to psychological or eudemonic well-being (e.g., a sense of purpose; growth or mastery; PWB; Ryan & Deci, 2001). Theory and research are needed that thoughtfully consider the facets of balance and how they connect to elements of well-being.

Theory and research should also take a broad view of well-being to include its numerous aspects such as physical, financial, social, and emotional/psychological (CDC, 2020). Within each type of well-being, scholars should study multiple indicators. For example, researchers might examine the link between balance and multiple indicators of physical health, including alcohol use, sleep duration, sleep quality, obesity, cardiovascular health, etc., and rely on biometric (e.g., sleep recordings via watch measurements) as well as self-report measures. Financial well-being has generally been overlooked and is also an important direction for future research. In a study that focused on work–family conflict rather than balance, Odle-Dusseau et al. (2018) quantitatively demonstrated that perceived financial insecurity predicts subsequent self-reports of physical health through increased work–family conflict and perceived stress. In a mixed method study, Odle-Dusseau et al. (2019) found that in critical incidents of financial hardship, financial insecurity was described as a cause of poor health, but poor health (and associated medical costs) was also described as a cause of financial insecurity, albeit to a lesser extent. Quantitatively, they demonstrated that financial insecurity related to greater stress and less balance satisfaction which, in turn, negatively related to health outcomes, including sleep disturbances, musculoskeletal pain, and general health perceptions, as well as organizational outcomes including job satisfaction, organizational commitment, and perceptions of organizational justice. This research tentatively suggests complex relationships among balance and financial, physical, and emotional well-being. More research is needed that gives these relationships deeper consideration theoretically and methodologically.

Following recent developments on balance as a multidimensional construct, empirical research is needed that offers theory-method fit (Allen et al., 2019). Allen and colleagues, in their review of the work–family conflict literature, concluded that there has been little theoretical attention to the role of time and not enough longitudinal designs to appropriately test theoretical assumptions. We urge researchers to explicitly consider the nature of the balance construct (as a stable or changing one) and consider how proposed relationships with well-being unfold over time (in the short-term and/or long-term). From this, it is essential that researchers employ experience sampling or longitudinal designs (in addition to cross-sectional ones) and use best practices in analytic techniques (e.g., fully autoregressive, cross-lagged panel designs; Orth, 2020; or latent growth curve modeling) to be able to gain insight into temporal precedence among variables. Extant theory implies, for example, that greater balance enables greater well-being (Marks & MacDermid, 1996). Perhaps, though, as tentatively suggested by Odle-Dusseau et al. (2019), having greater physical health, more energy, or better mental health may also provide someone the positive perspective needed to experience greater harmony across roles (global balance) or to be effective in valued roles, adequately involved in valued roles, and/or satisfied in valued roles – effectiveness, involvement, and affective balance. As also implied by Odle-Dusseau et al. (2019), rather than being unidirectional – as implied in previous theory – relationships between balance and various types of well-being may occur simultaneously and operate in feedback loops over time. Designs are needed that allow for examination of reciprocal relationships.

Beyond a focus on individual well-being, we encourage scholars to take a multilevel perspective. That is, well-being not only exists at the individual level but is also conceptualized and measured at levels of communities and/or countries and cultures (OECD, 2020). Research using local or state unemployment rates, for example, could explore the connection between community financial well-being, work–family balance, and individual-level well-being. This notion could also be used to examine whether national culture (and differences in country-level) well-being affects individual-level relationships. We see this as a ripe area for future research on the connection between the work–family interface and well-being.

In conclusion, theory and research linking balance and well-being are ripe for investigation. Here, we encourage theory development that will enhance understanding of the likely complex and multilevel relationships that exist between multiple types of balance and multiple indicators of individual and community-level well-being. We also encourage scholars to adopt a dynamic rather than static perspective to consider how these relationships unfold over time (Allen et al., 2019). Finally, we implore scholars to move beyond cross-sectional research to apply designs and analyses that enable appropriate conclusions regarding viability of dynamic theoretical explanations. In doing so, scholars can advance understanding will significantly advance of how, why, and when balance relates to well-being and better inform practice.

References

Allen, T. D., French, K. A., Braun, M. T., & Fletcher, K. (2019). The passage of time in work–family research: Toward a more dynamic perspective. *Journal of Vocational Behavior, 110*, 245–257.

Allen, T. A., Wayne, J. H., Casper, W. J., & Caza, B. (2012, June). *Work–family balance: A qualitative investigation.* Presented at the Inaugural Work–Family Researchers Network Conference, New York, NY.

Aryee, S., Srinivas, E. S., & Tan, H. H. (2005). Rhythms of life: Antecedents and outcomes of work–family balance in employed parents. *Journal of Applied Psychology, 90*, 132–146.

Ajzen, I., & Fishbein, M. (1977). Attitude–behavior relations: A theoretical analysis and review of empirical research. *Psychological Bulletin, 84*, 888–918.

Barnett, M. D., Martin, K. J., & Garza, C. J. 2019. Satisfaction with work–family balance mediates the relationship between workplace social support and depression among hospice nurses. *Journal of Nursing Scholarship, 51*(2), 187–94.

Bauld, R., Brough, P., & Timms, C. M. (2009). Working to live or living to work? The impact of time demands and preferred working hours on work and family outcomes. In P. H. Langford, N. J. Reynolds, & J. E. Kehoe (Eds.), *8th Industrial and Organisational Psychology Conference*

(IOP): Meeting the Future: Promoting Sustainable Organisational Growth (pp. 12–16). Australian Psychological Society.

Brough, P., Timms, C., O'Driscoll, M. P., Kalliath, T., Siu, O. L., Sit, C., & Lo, D. (2014). Work–life balance: A longitudinal evaluation of a new measure across Australia and New Zealand workers. *The International Journal of Human Resource Management, 25,* 2724–2744.

Buffardi, L. C., Smith, J. L., O'Brien, A. S., & Erdwins, C. J. (1999). The impact of dependent-care responsibility and gender on work attitudes. *Journal of Occupational Health Psychology, 4,* 356–367.

Bulger, C. A., Matthews, R. A., & Hoffman, M. E. (2007). Work and personal life boundary management: Boundary strength, work/personal life balance, and the segmentation-integration continuum. *Journal of Occupational Health Psychology, 12,* 365–375.

Carlson, D. S., Grzywacz, J. G., & Zivnuska, S. (2009). Is work–family balance more than conflict and enrichment? *Human Relations, 62(10),* 1459–1486.

Carlson, D. S., Kacmar, K. M., Wayne, J. H., & Grzywacz, J. G. (2006). Measuring the positive side of the work–family interface: Development and validation of a work–family enrichment scale. *Journal of Vocational Behavior, 68,* 131–164.

Casper, W. J., De Hauw, S., & Wayne, J. H. (2013). Concepts and measures in the work–family interface: Implications for work–family integration. In D. Major & R. Burke (Eds.), *Handbook of work–life integration of professionals: Challenges and opportunities.* Edward Elgar.

Casper, W. J., Vaziri, H. Wayne, J. H., De Hauw, S. & Greenhaus, J. (2018). The jingle-jangle of work–nonwork balance: A comprehensive and meta-analytic review of its meaning and measurement. *Journal of Applied Psychology, 103,* 182–214.

Centers for Disease Control and Prevention. (2020). *Well-being concepts.* www.cdc.gov/hrqol/wellbeing.htm

Clark, S. C. (2000). Work/family border theory: A new theory of work/family balance. *Human Relations, 53,* 747–770.

Cooke, R. A., & Rousseau, D. M. (1984). Stress and strain from family roles and work-role expectations. *Journal of Applied Psychology, 69,* 252–260.

Eby, L. T., Casper, W. J., Lockwood, A., Bordeaux, C., & Brinley, A. (2005). A retrospective on work and family research in IO/OB: A content analysis and review of the literature [Monograph]. *Journal of Vocational Behavior, 66,* 124–197.

Eurofond (2012). *Sixth European conditions survey: Overview report.* Publications Office of the European Union.

Frone, M. R. (2003). Work–family balance. In J. C. Quick and L. E. Tetrick (Eds.), *Handbook of Occupational Health Psychology* (pp. 143–162). American Psychological Association. http://doi.org/10.1037/10474-007

Gareis, K. C., Barnett, R. C., Ertel, K. A., & Berkman, L. F. (2009). Work–family enrichment and conflict: Additive effects, buffering, or balance? *Journal of Marriage and Family, 71,* 696–707.

Goode, W. J. (1974). A theory of strain. *American Sociological Review, 25,* 483–496.

Greenhaus, J. H. & Allen, T. D. (2011). Work–family balance: A review and extension of the literature. In J. C. Quick and L. E. Tetrick (Eds.), *Handbook of occupational health psychology* (pp. 165–183). American Psychological Association.

Greenhaus, J. H., Allen, T. D., & Foley, S. (2004 April 1–4). *Work–family balance: Exploration of a concept* [Conference presentation]. 19th Annual SIOP Conference, Chicago, IL, United States.

Greenhaus, J. H., & Beutell, N. J. (1985). Sources of conflict between work and family roles. *Academy of Management Review, 10,* 76–88.

Greenhaus, J. H., Collins, K. M., & Shaw, J. D. (2003). The relation between work–family balance and quality of life. *Journal of Vocational Behavior, 63,* 510–531.

Greenhaus, J. H., & Powell, G. N. (2006). When work and family are allies: A theory of work–family enrichment. *Academy of Management Review, 31,* 72–92.

Greenhaus, J. H., Ziegert, J. C., & Allen, T. A. (2012). When family-supportive supervision matters: Relations between multiple sources of support and work–family balance. *Journal of Vocational Behavior, 80* (2), 266–275.

Grzywacz, J. G., & Carlson, D. S. (2007). Conceptualizing work–family balance: Implications for practice and research. *Advances in Developing Human Resources, 9,* 455–471.

Grzywacz, J. G., & Marks, N. F. (2000). Reconceptualizing the work–family interface: An ecological perspective on the correlates of positive and negative spillover between work and family. *Journal of Occupational Health Psychology, 5,* 111–126.

Haar, J. (2013). Testing a new measure of work–life balance: A study of parent and non-parent employees from New Zealand. *International Journal of Human Resource Management, 24,* 3305–3324.

Haar, J., Russo, M., Suñe, A. & Ollier-Malaterre, A. (2014). Outcomes of work–life balance on job satisfaction, life satisfaction and mental health: A study across seven cultures. *Journal of Vocational Behavior, 85*(3), 361–373.

Haider, S., Jabeen, S., & Ahmad, J. (2018). Moderated mediation between work life balance and employee job performance: The role of psychological wellbeing and satisfaction with coworkers. *Journal of Work and Organizational Psychology, 34*(1), 29–37.

Halpern, D. F., & Murphy, S. E. (2005). From balance to interaction: Why the metaphor is important. In D. F. Halpern & S. E. Murphy (Eds.), *From work–family balance to work–family interaction*. Erlbaum.

Hennessy, K. D. (2007). Work–family balance: An exploration of conflict and enrichment for women in a traditional occupation. *Dissertation Abstracts International Section A: Humanities and Social Sciences, 68* (8-A), 3295.

Hirshi, A., Shockley, K. M., & Zacher, H. (2019). An action regulation model of work–family management. An action regulation model of work–family management. *Academy of Management Review, 44*(1), 150–171.

Kahn, R. L., Wolfe, D. M., Quinn, R., Snoek, J. D., & Rosenthal, R. A. (1964). *Organizational stress: Studies in role conflict and ambiguity.* Wiley.

Lapierre, L. M., Li, Y., Kwan, H. K., Greenhaus, J. H., DiRenzo, M. S., & Shao, P. (2018). A meta-analysis of the antecedents of work–family enrichment. *Journal of Organizational Behavior, 39*, 385–401.

Lazarus, R. S., & Folkman, S. (1984). *Stress, appraisal, and coping.* Springer.

Lucia-Casademunt, A. M., García-Cabrera, A. M., Padilla-Angulo, L., & Cuéllar-Molina, D. (2018). Returning to work after childbirth in Europe: Well-being, work–life balance, and the interplay of supervisor support. *Frontiers in Psychology, 6*, 1–30.

Lu, J., Siu, O., Spector, P. E., & Shi, K. (2009). Antecedents and outcomes of a fourfold taxonomy of work–family balance in Chinese employed parents. *Journal of Occupational Health Psychology, 14*, 182–192.

Lunau, T., Bambra, C., Eikemo, T. A., van der Wel, K. A., & Dragano, N. (2014). A balancing act? Work–life balance, health and well-being in European welfare states. *European Journal of Public Health, 24*(3): 422–427. https://doi.org/10.1093/eurpub/cku010

Maertz, C. P., Jr., & Boyar, S. L. (2011). Work–family conflict, enrichment, and balance under "levels" and "episodes" approaches. *Journal of Management, 37*, 68–98.

Marks, S. R., & MacDermid, S. M. (1996). Multiple roles and the self: A theory of role balance. *Journal of Marriage and the Family, 58*, 417–432.

Odle-Dusseau, H. N., Britt, T. W., & Bobko, P. (2012). Work–family balance, well-being, and organizational outcomes: Investigating actual versus desired work/family time discrepancies. *Journal of Business and Psychology*, 27, 331–343.

Odle-Dusseau, H. N., Matthews, R. A., & Wayne, J. H. (2018). Employees' financial insecurity and health: The underlying role of stress and work–family conflict appraisals. *Journal of Occupational and Organizational Psychology*, 91(3), 546–568.

Odle-Dusseau, H. N., Matthews, R. A., Wayne, J. H., & Huang, S. (2019). Critical incidents of financial hardship and worker health: A mixed-methods retrospective study. *Occupational Health Science*, 3, 145–165.

OECD. (2020). *Measuring well-being and progress: Well-being research.* www.oecd.org/statistics/measuring-well-being-and-progress.htm

Orth, U., Clark, D. A., Donnellan, M. B., & Robins, R. W. (2020). Testing prospective effects in longitudinal research: Comparing seven competing cross-lagged models. *Journal of Personality and Social Psychology*. Advance online publication. http://doi.org/10.1037/pspp0000358

Pleck, J. (1977). The work–family role system. *Social Problems*, 24, 417–427.

Rahim, N. B., Osman, I., & Arumugam, P. V. (2020). Linking work–life balance and employee well-being: Do supervisor support and family support moderate the relationship? *International Journal of Business and Society*, 21(2), 588–606.

Ryan, R. M., & Deci, E. L. (2001). On happiness and human potentials: A review of research on hedonic and eudaimonic well-being. *Annual Review of Psychology*, 52, 141–166.

Scanlan, J., Meredith, P., & Poulsen, A. (2013). Enhancing retention of occupational therapists working in mental health: Relationships between wellbeing at work and turnover intention. *Australian Occupational Therapy Journal*, 60(6), 395–403.

Sturges, J. & Guest, D. (2004). Working to live or living to work? Work/life balance early in the career. *Human Resource Management Journal*, 14, 5–20.

Vanderpool, C., & Way, S. A. (2013). Investigating work–family balance, job anxiety, and turnover intentions as predictors of health care and senior services customer contact employee voluntary turnover. *Cornell Hospitality Quarterly*, 54(2), 149–160.

Valcour, M. (2007). Work-based resources as moderators of the relationship between hours and satisfaction with work–family balance. *Journal of Applied Psychology*, 92, 1512–1523.

Voydanoff, P. (2005). Toward a conceptualization of perceived work–family fit and balance: A demands and resources approach. *Journal of Marriage and Family*, 67, 822–836.

(2002). Linkages between the work–family interface and work, family, and individual outcomes: An integrative model. *Journal of Family Issues*, 23, 138–164.

Wayne, J. H. (2009). Reducing conceptual confusion: Clarifying the positive side of the work–family interface. In D. R. Crane & J. Hill (Eds.), *Handbook of families and work: Interdisciplinary perspectives*. University Press of America.

Wayne, J. H., Butts, M., Casper, W. J. & Allen, T. D. (2017). In search of balance: A conceptual and empirical integration of multiple meanings of work–family balance. *Personnel Psychology*, 70, 167–210.

Wayne, J. H., Vaziri, H., & Casper, W. J. (2021). Work–nonwork balance: Development and validation of a global and multidimensional measure. *Journal of Vocational Behavior*, 127. https://doi.org/10.1016/j.jvb.2021.103565

Wepfer, A. G., Allen, T. D., Brauchli, R., Jenny, G. J., & Bauer, G. F. (2018). Work–life boundaries and well-being: Does work-to-life integration impair well-being through lack of recovery? *Journal of Business and Psychology*, 33, 727–740.

Wu, L., Rusyidi, B., Claiborne, N., & McCarthy, M. L. (2013). Relationships between work–life balance and job-related factors among child welfare workers. *Children and Youth Services Review*, 35, 1447–1454.

7 Understanding the Decision-Making Process for Presenteeism Behavior

An Integration and Conceptual Model

ZARA WHYSALL, MARIA KARANIKA-MURRAY, AND HUIJUN CHEN

Understanding how people make decisions to engage in presenteeism, defined as working while sick, is essential for advancing theory and informing practice in this field yet also an underdeveloped area. Research has identified a range of factors that impact upon presenteeism (see Lohaus & Habermann, 2019, for a review), along with a range of consequences of this behavior, but has neglected to unwrap the decision-making process via which these factors interact to give rise to presenteeism. Whilst little is known about *how* individuals make the decision to enact presenteeism, three notable contributions in the field provide a foundation from which to start. First, Johns (2010) outlined that the decision process is triggered initially by a health event and is then influenced by individual and contextual factors or considerations. Second, Lohaus and Haberman (2019) integrated the literature regarding antecedents and consequences of presenteeism into a framework outlining the "content of a decision-integrated model of presenteeism" (p. 53). Third, Cooper and Lu (2016) adopted social cognitive theory to explain how an individual's perceptions of their social environment may influence presenteeism behavior.

This chapter extends these foundations to propose a process model of presenteeism decision-making, encapsulating both sickness absenteeism and sickness presenteeism since both are potential outcomes of the same decision (Halbesleben et al., 2014; Hansen & Andersen, 2008; Patton & Johns, 2012). We draw upon the literatures relating to decision-making, sickness presenteeism, health behavior, and organizational behavior to outline the key decision-making principles and process steps likely to shape presenteeism decisions and therefore behavior.

The Importance of Understanding Presenteeism Decision-Making

A focus on understanding decision-making for presenteeism is timely for a number of reasons. First, definitions of presenteeism have evolved from simply attending work while ill (e.g., Aronsson & Gustafsson, 2005; Bergström et al., 2009; Cooper & Lu, 2016; Dew et al., 2005; Hansen & Andersen, 2009) to acknowledge presenteeism as a purposeful and adaptive behavior aimed at balancing conflicting health and work demands (Karanika-Murray & Biron, 2020). Viewing presenteeism as a purposeful and adaptive behavior implies an intention on the part of the presentee, who considers the options and consequences of their behavioral choices. As such, it becomes evident how understanding the decision process related to intentions and goals, weighing alternative options, enacting a chosen behavior, and even reviewing whether that behavior was appropriate or successful is essential to our understanding of presenteeism and work-related health and wellbeing.

A second fundamental development in our understanding of presenteeism is the notion that presenteeism is not inherently detrimental to health but has a range of potentially positive consequences (e.g., Johns, 2010; Karanika-Murray & Biron, 2020; Karanika-Murray & Cooper, 2018; Lohaus, Habermann et al., 2021; Whysall et al., 2018). Ill health and work are not mutually exclusive. Instead, it is the appropriateness of the choice between sickness absence and presenteeism and/or among various adjustment options, taking into account the nature of the illness and the work demands (including any adjustments that can be made to the work tasks and/or work environment), which determines whether presenteeism will be beneficial or detrimental to health (Karanika-Murray & Biron, 2020). In certain circumstances, taking sick leave could be beneficial for health (Bergström et al., 2009), yet under other circumstances, sickness presenteeism may provide a rehabilitative and restorative function (Karanika-Murray & Biron, 2020; Whysall et al., 2018). Indeed, the concept of vocational rehabilitation is based upon the understanding that when an employee's health condition permits, they should be supported to remain in or to (re-) enter work as soon as possible (Waddell & Burton, 2006). This positions presenteeism as a sustainable option and a means of facilitating a gradual return to full working capacity, if the work environment is supportive and adequate resources are provided to aid adaptation and maximize positive consequences (Karanika-Murray & Biron, 2020).

Third, there have been calls for a person-centered approach to understanding presenteeism behavior that can help to illuminate the variety of experiences, circumstances, and outcomes of presenteeism (Ruhle et al., 2019). Thus, leveraging the potential for presenteeism as an adaptive behavior that can help to balance and adjust to health and work demands and aid return to full working capacity require a better understanding of the decision-making process that underlies the presentees' intentions and behavior. The question becomes not *what* factors are associated with presenteeism but *how* individuals make the decision to adapt and potentially also benefit from presenteeism.

Finally, presenteeism has always been more difficult to detect than sickness absenteeism, since the most common ailments accounting for presenteeism are not necessarily visible (e.g., Aronsson et al., 2000). However, the widespread shift to home-working due to the Covid-19 global pandemic has further blurred the line between work and home, and in doing so, emphasizes the importance of definitions of presenteeism that avoid reference to presenteeism as *attending* work while sick. An individual does not have to attend a physical workplace to engage in presenteeism; they simply have to undertake work activities while sick, regardless of location. Remote working makes it more challenging for managers to spot and intervene when an imbalance between work demands and health needs arises, making presenteeism more likely (Ruhle et al., 2020). Uncertainty as to whether we will ever return to pre-Covid levels of office working places even greater importance on developing ways to manage presenteeism more effectively, which hinges upon understanding the decision-making process through which presenteeism arises.

The Importance of Understanding the *Process* of Presenteeism Decision-Making

Understanding of any phenomenon must answer both the *what* and, most importantly, *how* questions. Knowledge regarding the *what* of presenteeism is relatively more advanced, with numerous factors which impact on presenteeism having been identified (see Lohaus & Haberman, 2019), but we know little about how a choice to engage in sickness presenteeism is made or revised. Whilst categorical (or descriptive) theories aim to categorize the inputs for the end behavior and explain its variance, process theories formulate the range of inputs and its mediators into sequential steps (McGuire, 1983). In relation to presenteeism, Lohaus and Haberman (2019) describe these as content and process theories. Content models have their place but do not explain the psychological mechanisms and processes that can give rise to specific behaviors. Thus, a process approach would usefully augment existing knowledge by helping to explain the how and why of presenteeism behavior, also offering high practical value for supporting effective decision-making, maximizing benefits while minimizing negative impact of presenteeism on health or performance.

Current Understanding of Presenteeism Decision-Making

We put a decision-making lens on existing presenteeism literature to ask: what do we know about how people make the decision to abstain from work or continue to work when they are feeling unwell? We partition the current relevant knowledge into broad questions pertaining to the presenteeism decision: decision triggers, influences, consequences, and mechanisms, latterly integrating insights from the decision-making literature to build a more comprehensive understanding of the decision-making process for presenteeism.

Triggers of the Presenteeism Decision

Notable in the presenteeism literature is the idea that a health event triggers the need to decide between continuing to work in the face of compromised health or taking sickness absence (e.g., Aronsson & Gustafsson, 2005; Johns, 2010). Work attendance with 100% productivity is "interrupted by a 'health event' that is either acute (e.g., the flu), episodic (e.g., migraine), or chronic (e.g., the onset of diabetes)" (Johns, 2010, p. 531). Thus, the initial choice between absenteeism or presenteeism is determined by the nature and severity of the health event. In extreme medical cases, absence may be unavoidable regardless of the circumstances, whereas with less extreme medical conditions, contextual factors will be more salient and influential. For instance, Johns (2010) highlights that suffering from a sore throat may require absenteeism for a singer but allow presenteeism for a pianist. However, the model does not extend to explanation of how this decision is made, how individuals explore options, choose between alternatives, or review their decisions to adjust their behavior.

Central in the presenteeism literature is the notion that presenteeism and absenteeism are two potential outcomes of the same decision (Johns, 2010). However, rather than one being a direct substitution for the other (as in substitution hypothesis; Caverley et al., 2007), evidence suggests that the two tend to be highly correlated (Leineweber et al., 2012; Whysall et al., 2018) and even complementary (Gosselin et al., 2013). Critically, we suggest that the range of attendance behaviors and possible work adjustments in the face of ill-health imply that a binary choice is too simplistic. There a range of different types of presenteeism behavior, as illustrated in the health-performance framework (Karanika-Murray & Biron, 2020), depending on what adjustments can be made around or to the job, as job crafting theory suggests (Tims & Bakker, 2010), but also on the level of discretionary effort applied by each individual to their work whilst sick. This could range from attending to one's full range of tasks and maintaining 100% productivity, to being notionally "working" (irrespective of location) yet minimally productive. Furthermore, we previously acknowledged how increased home working blurs the line between work and home. In addition, we argue, it blurs the line between sickness absence and presenteeism. If an individual has officially taken sickness absence yet attends work during this time (e.g., checks their emails or attends to an urgent request), this immediately becomes presenteeism. To understand the complex evaluative processes involved, it is important to understand the stages and nuances of this decision process.

Influences on Presenteeism as Inputs for Decision-Making

A starting point to understanding how presenteeism decisions are made is to identify the influences on evaluation of decision options and the expected consequences. The dynamic model of presenteeism (Johns, 2010) lists work context-related factors (e.g., high job demands, low job security, strict absence policy) and person-related factors (e.g., work attitudes, health locus of control, personality, perceived absence legitimacy) as key influences on the choice between absenteeism and presenteeism behavior, to which Miraglia and

Johns's (2016) meta-analysis added mediating factors. Lohaus and Habermann (2019) comprehensively integrated the literature on these numerable influences into environmental (e.g., cultural norms, economic climate), organizational (e.g., absence policy, organizational support), job-related (e.g., role demands, adjustment latitude), and person-related (e.g., health, engagement). Macro-level influences (or environmental influences, as per Lohaus & Habermann, 2019) have received much less attention yet include economic circumstances such as recession (since absence rates are generally lower during recession), national unemployment rates (during which presenteeism rates tend to increase; Aronsson et al., 2000; Markham, 1985), cultural differences (such as the Confucius culture in which values of working long hours and working intensively are deep-rooted; Cooper & Lu, 2016), or dominant political systems (absenteeism rates differ between communist and capitalist countries; Patton & Johns, 2012). Macro factors shape the fundamental values, beliefs, and attitudes that underlie our work behavior and are therefore essential to presenteeism decision-making. Indeed, more distal influences on behavior are viewed as essential considerations within sickness absence research (Kristensen, 1991) and may be more salient for decision-making than we assume, as they define how important work centrality is for the individual (Addae et al., 2013).

It is important to understand not only the relative salience of each group of influences but also how they may interact to influence decision outcomes. It has been argued that work-related factors can be more important than personal factors in presenteeism decision-making (Hansen & Andersen, 2008). For example, whilst individual differences are likely to exist regarding perceived absence legitimacy, this is also likely to differ according to sick pay provisions, size of employer, and nature of work (Irvine, 2011). Similarly, larger organizations tend to provide more generous sick pay and may be perceived as able to carry the burden of their absence more readily than smaller organizations. In addition, work and environment-related factors and personal factors are likely to operate synergistically and bidirectionally, as opposed to independently of each other (Cooper & Lu, 2016; Karanika-Murray & Biron, 2020). For example, high neuroticism may mean that others' opinions have a stronger influence on one's decisions, or that we evaluate the environment more pessimistically (Cooper & Lu, 2016).

Consequences of Presenteeism as Outputs of Decision-Making

The decision to attend work when one is feeling unwell can have a range of consequences for the individual, their work team(s), and the organization. Lohaus and Habermann (2019) made a useful distinction between organizational vs. individual consequences, separately for presenteeism and absenteeism decisions. Most documented have been the negative consequences of presenteeism as a deleterious behavior due to its potentially high costs in terms of health and performance, to the extent that presenteeism research has been criticized for falling short in failing to acknowledge the benefits of presenteeism (Lohaus & Habermann, 2019). Recently, there has been an increasing focus on potentially positive outcomes (e.g. Karanika-Murray & Biron, 2020; Lohaus & Habermann, 2019; Lohaus et al., 2021; Whysall et al., 2018) and a "neutralization" of presenteeism as a work behavior that is not necessarily inherently positive or negative, instead seeking to understand the function of the behavior for the presentee (Karanika-Murray & Biron, 2020). Consequently, the health-performance framework of presenteeism (Karanika-Murray & Biron, 2020) identifies two key considerations for the presentee in view of their impaired health: to support their health and to attend to work commitments. Together, these considerations give rise to four types of presenteeism, each associated with different patterns of behavior and outcomes in terms of whether and how health and/or performance are impacted (functional, dysfunction, overcommitted, and therapeutic). Although the health-performance framework does not explicate how possible options and consequences are considered in presenteeism decision-making, it acknowledges that presenteeism involves a decision, driven by the need to balance health and performance.

Additionally, it is important to recognize that presenteeism behavior may have both intended and unintended consequences; presentees may have well-articulated goals and expectations (e.g., manage work demands in the immediate term) but experience unexpected or unforeseen consequences from their behavior (e.g., reduced ability to recover and longer-term sickness absence). Unintended consequences relate to both health and performance/productivity (Bergström et al., 2009), such as future sickness absenteeism or prolonged periods of rehabilitation (Bergström et al., 2009) or even a cycle of ill health (Johns, 2010). Unintended consequences may be both direct or indirect (e.g.,

impact on coworker or supervisor work or attributions of the presentee), as well as difficult to quantify or even identify. For example, a
presentee may decide to work whilst experiencing influenza or other
virus symptoms in order to maintain job security or financial stability,
but for their colleagues, being present at work with an infectious illness
may be perceived as irresponsible. Conversely, if a decision to take
sickness absence is perceived as demoting a lack of commitment and
receives backlash or disapproval from one's colleagues or manager, the
individual may be more likely to opt for presenteeism in future.

Mechanisms That Can Explain How Decisions to Enact Presenteeism Are Reached

Between inputs and outputs, influences and consequences, there is the
black box of presenteeism decision-making. Through what process is
the decision to enact presenteeism or sickness absenteeism is reached?

A Rational Evaluation Process

Classical decision theory, the most notable example of which is
expected utility theory (EUT, 1947, 2007), treats decision-making as
a rational, analytic process. It posits that decision-makers evaluate all
possible options in terms of perceived value or benefit, subsequently
selecting the option that offers the highest expected utility, defined as
its perceived value weighted by the probability that it will occur
(Mongin, 1997). Under EUT, therefore, all decisions are viewed as
rational, based on a comprehensive analysis of all potential options
in terms of expected value and likelihood, from which the optimal
option is selected. Similar principles are echoed in health behavior
theories such as the health belief model, for example, which holds
assessment of expected costs and benefits as core to health-related
behavioral outcomes (Janz & Becker, 1984). Applied to presenteeism,
the immediate question this raises is one of value or benefit (or, indeed,
costs) in relation to what or, indeed, whom. Value in terms of the
individual's job and financial security, potential future career progres-
sion, or work productivity? Or value in terms of the individual's own
health and wellbeing? However, such theories overlook the influence
of personal factors, which, as discussed above, appear to influence
presenteeism (Lohaus & Habermann, 2019; Miraglia & Johns,
2016). In terms of dispositional factors such as personality or work-

related values, for instance, it can be seen how an individual high in conscientiousness or with a strong work ethic would be likely to place a stronger weighting on the productivity benefits of presenteeism above the potential health benefits through absenteeism.

Psychological Influences, Motives, Biases, and Heuristics

Consequently, it is important to draw upon theories which acknowledge the influence of psychological factors such as an individual's values, preferences, and beliefs about their abilities, such as Vroom's (1964) expectancy theory and the work of Tversky and Kahneman (1974; Kahneman & Tversky, 1979). Vroom acknowledged that decisions arise from an evaluation of the anticipated consequences, but not in an entirely rational or objective way. Subjectivity is introduced in the individual's evaluation on three key dimensions: expectancy, instrumentality, and valence. Expectancy relates to the likelihood that the effort will lead to the intended goals. In presenteeism terms, this could relate to assessment of the likelihood that if one attempts to work, they will be able to do an acceptable job and/ or be perceived positively by their colleagues and/or line manager, for instance. This judgment is typically influenced by personal factors such as self-confidence (or self-efficacy, as referenced in social cognitive theory and applied to presenteeism by Cooper & Lu, 2016) and contextual factors such as the degree of control over their work tasks and/or environment. The second judgment is one of instrumentality, belief that the desired reward will be received if the performance expectations are met. In the context of presenteeism, this could include the belief that a strong attendance record is likely to lead to promotion or pay benefits or, conversely, that taking sickness absence will enhance recovery. Again, this judgment will be influenced by both personal factors (such as health locus of control) and contextual factors (such as organizational policies for pay increases and promotion). The third judgment is valence, the extent to which the individual values the reward/benefits and therefore introduces the influence of individual differences in goals, values, and preferences. Indeed, goals have been neglected in presenteeism research (Cooper & Lu, 2016), yet both expectancy theory and theories such as social cognitive theory (Bandura, 1986, 1997, 2001) highlight the important influences of personal goals in shaping behavior.

In terms of values and motives, it has been suggested that there are two motives which underlie presenteeism decision-making: approach and avoidance (or push and pull) motives (Cooper & Lu, 2016; Lu et al., 2013, 2014; Miraglia & Johns, 2016). Employees with approach motives will be more likely to choose presenteeism over absenteeism driven by the desire to "abide by one's work values and beliefs of achievement and loyalty to the profession and interested parties" (Cooper & Lu, 2016, p. 223). In contrast, employees with avoidance motives may engage in presenteeism to avoid potential social disapproval and financial loss as a consequence of taking sick leave. An important question is whether there is any systematic difference between approach or avoidance motives in terms of outcomes; for example, whether an avoidance motive is more likely to lead to dysfunctional presenteeism and thereby be detrimental to health, or an approach motive to functional presenteeism which is restorative to health.

Viewed in relation to decision-making theory, it is also reasonable to assume that avoidance motives may disproportionately guide behavior. Tversky and Kahneman (1974; Kahneman & Tversky, 1979) demonstrated that decision-making often violates the rules of rational decision-making in specific, systematic ways known as heuristics and cognitive biases (Kahneman et al., 1982; Kahneman & Tversky, 1973; Tversky & Kahneman, 1974). Kahneman and Tversky (1979) proposed prospect theory, which, like EUT, recognizes the evaluation of perceived value and weighting of likelihood as the foundation of decision-making but also acknowledges the influence of certain psychological features introducing a level of subjectivity and irrationality into decision-making. A key example is loss aversion: an exaggerated aversion to potential losses in comparison to equivalent potential gains and an overweighting of low probabilities and underweighting of high probabilities (Tversky & Kahneman, 1981). Expectancy and prospect theory, therefore, illustrate the ways in which work context-related factors (e.g., high job demands, low job security, strict absence policy) and person-related factors (e.g., work attitudes, health locus of control, personality, perceived absence legitimacy) outlined in Johns's (2010) dynamic model of presenteeism and Lohaus and Haberman's (2019) decision-making content framework may interact to influence the evaluation of options.

The Influence of Context

Tversky and Kahneman not only highlighted the influence of psychological factors on the evaluation of options but also demonstrated the influence of psychological and contextual factors on the options that are included for consideration in the first place. They demonstrated that decision options are framed by both intrinsic forces relating to the decision-maker such as temperament, emotional state and beliefs, and extrinsic influences such as the way decision options are presented (Tversky & Kahneman, 1981). Certain contexts are known to "prime" associated knowledge structures (schemas) to influence decision outcomes, similarly to the principles outlined in recognition-primed decision making (Klein, 1993). In these situations, decisions are made not as a result of different decision options being evaluated against one another; instead, previously established associations are automatically activated and acted upon (e.g., Cohen-Hatton et al., 2015; Doya, 2008).

The mechanics behind framing effects can be explained by dual-process theories, such as Wason and Evans's (1975) and Evans's (1984) dual process theory of reasoning distinguishing between heuristic processes and analytic processes, and Kahneman's (2003, 2012) distinction between system 1 (intuition) and systems 2 (reasoning) thinking. Wason and Evans identified heuristic processes as the means by which individuals select which information is relevant to the current situation, automatically filtering out irrelevant information. Kahneman (2003, 2012) built on this with his distinction between intuition and reasoning, whereby intuition (or system 1) is rapid and automatic, often influenced strongly by emotional states, and based on ingrained habits that are resistant to change. When experiencing psychological stress, decision-makers seek to resolve the decision as quickly as possible, increasing the likelihood of suboptimal decision-making (e.g., Janis & Mann, 1976). Indeed, the framing effect has been found to be associated specifically with amygdala activity, also inferring a key role for an emotional system in mediating decision biases (De Martino et al., 2006). Thus, with presenteeism, high levels of stress or strong emotional states may increase the likelihood that certain options are automatically filtered out of consideration and, as a result, suboptimal decisions.

Following the heuristic process, analytic processes are then employed to make judgments about the situation based on the information deemed relevant (Evans, 1984). Kahneman described this as reasoning (or system 2) thinking, considered to be slower, subject to more considered judgments and conscious evaluation. Generally, individuals adopt system 1 for making simple and quick decisions, and system 2 is for more complex decision-making. It is via system 2-driven reasoning processes, for example, that presenteeism decisions may become influenced by consideration of social norms and expectations.

The Role of Social Norms

Cultural and social norms are likely to have a strong influence on presenteeism decisions, since the coevolution process has

endowed us with preferences that go beyond the self-regarding concerns emphasised in traditional economic and biological theories, and embrace such other-regarding values as a taste for cooperation, fairness, and retribution; the capacity to empathize; and the ability to value such constitutive behaviors as honesty, hard work, toleration of diversity, and loyalty to one's reference group. (Gintis, 2007, p. 2)

Social and cultural norms typically influence behavior through conformity effects, as a result of which individuals accept the dominant cultural practices, which may then become internalized through social learning (Gintis, 2007). Indeed, research has shown that leaders' presenteeism has a positive effect on employee presenteeism (Dietz et al., 2020).

The influence of perceived societal norms is also acknowledged in the theory of planned behavior (TPB; Ajzen, 1988, 1985), perhaps the most widely researched model of health behavior, which outlines the key determinants of health-related behavior as: attitudes towards the behavior (involving beliefs about and evaluations of outcomes), perceived behavioral control (influenced by internal and external factors), and subjective norms (beliefs about significant others' attitudes towards the behavior, and motivation to comply with others). Together these influences combine to trigger a behavioral intention – in other words, a decision to act in a particular way; which may or may not translate into action, depending on the level of control, influenced by available resources, opportunities, and perceived barriers.

Social norms critical to presenteeism decision-making relate to the attendance culture of an organization (Ruhle & Süß, 2019), which integrates both absence culture, the beliefs and practices that influence absence frequency and duration (Martocchio, 1994), and presenteeism culture, the perceptions of attending work while ill (Dew et al., 2005). As emphasized by Ruhle and Süß, an integrated view of presenteeism and absenteeism norms is essential since the two behaviors are "not merely opposites but related phenomena and may be influenced by (and influence) a common attendance culture" (Ruhle & Süß, 2019, p. 242). The key variable shaping attendance culture is perceived legitimacy, of both sickness absence and presenteeism. A culture characterized by strong perceived legitimacy of sickness absence gives rise to a health-focused culture, whereas perceived legitimacy of sickness presenteeism gives rise to a "presentistic" culture, and one which perceived legitimacy in both behaviors denotes an individual decision culture (Ruhle & Süß, 2019). The key question, however, is how culture influences the decision process. Ruhle and Süß (2019) articulate two potential mechanisms: firstly, by indicating to individuals the type of attendance behavior that is considered legitimate in that particular context (Xie & Johns, 2000), and secondly, in moderating the relationship between attitudes and attendance behavior (Nicholson & Johns, 1985). Absence culture, the beliefs and practices that influence absence frequency and duration (Martocchio, 1994), describes a collective process in an organization and/or its subunits (e.g., groups, departments) that impacts the individuals' patterns of absence (Nicholson & Johns, 1985). Presenteeism culture describes the perceptions of attending work while ill (Dew et al., 2005; Simpson, 1998).

Applying social cognitive theory (Bandura, 1986) to presenteeism behavior, Cooper and Lu (2016) highlighted how individual-level constructs such as self-efficacy, outcome expectations, and goal representations are influenced, over time, through exposure to other people and events in their social context. This exposure differentially reinforces certain options above others, and through repeated exposure, people revise their self-efficacy beliefs, outcome expectations, and possibly even their goals. More recently, Miraglia and Johns's (2021) multilevel model of the social relational dynamics that impact on absenteeism linked the range of work and nonwork social influences via six paths. These six paths and related theories explain how these social factors operate, encompassing normative influence, social exchange, job resources, work attitudes, emotions, and ethics. As such, it posits the presenteeism decision in its important broader socio-psychological context.

The Role of Feedback

Considering presenteeism behavior as driven by the need to balance health status and work demands (Karanika-Murray & Biron, 2020), it is important to acknowledge that the decision to be present or absent will also be ongoing and revised as health status and work demands change. Indeed, Busemeyer and Townsend (1993) and Busemeyer and Johnson (2004) criticized the absence of attention to the deliberation process in decision-making theories, which involves indecisiveness, vacillation, inconsistency, lengthy deliberation, and distress. In response, they put forward decision field theory aimed at understanding the motivational and cognitive mechanisms that guide the deliberation process involved in decisions under uncertainty. Specifically, they highlighted that earlier theories do not account for why preferences may waver over time, nor do they explain why deliberation may be drawn out or how long it may last. Decision field theory (Busemeyer & Johnson, 2004; Busemeyer & Townsend, 1993) emphasizes the dynamic nature of decision-making process, stating that deliberate decision-making involves switching focus between alternatives, considering the consequences of each alternative over a period of time. As each possible consequence is brought to mind, it triggers different affective reactions, which are evaluated and compared in terms of desirability.

The consequences of presenteeism, in terms of both health consequences and experienced gains and losses in relation to one's goals, are likely to be an important source of feedback and to impact on both the current and subsequent presenteeism decisions (Cooper & Lu, 2016; Johns, 2010). For example, if an employee had a negative experience of taking sickness absence in the past, perhaps due to negative managerial attitudes, it may be more likely that they will opt to engage in presenteeism in the future. Indeed, the dynamic model of presenteeism (Johns, 2010) includes an important feedback loop that is created by the impact of the consequences of choosing between presenteeism or absenteeism on the original health event. Feedback is likely to create a learning loop during and/or after the presenteeism episode: was my decision to attend work appropriate, did I achieve/am I achieving what I was hoping to achieve, how did the decision affect my health, and do I need to revise my decision? In keeping with values-driven decision-making theory (e.g., Kahneman & Tversky, 1979; Tversky & Kahneman, 1974; Vroom, 1964), we propose that the impact of these different consequences – namely, on the individual in terms of their health or productivity, on colleagues/managers and their attitudes towards the individual, and on the organization in terms of results – will be differentially weighted according to the individual's own goals and values. For instance, an individual who values a good work–life balance would be expected to place more weight on feedback in terms of the impact on their health, compared to an individual who is driven by ambition and a desire for promotion, who would be expected to place more weight on feedback in relation to their manager's or other senior colleagues' reactions.

Busemeyer and Johnson (2004) contend that these comparisons of consequences are accumulated over time to form a preference state. Once the feeling of the desirability of action passes a threshold, this action is chosen. As a result, the threshold is a key parameter controlling the decision speed and quality trade-off; if the threshold is set low, only a weak preference is required to reach a choice, whereas if it is set to a very high threshold, a strong preference is required to make a decision. In this case, deliberation takes longer, but the decision is based on a more thoughtful evaluation of all the consequences (Busemeyer & Johnson, 2004). Echoing the highly interactive influence of individual and contextual influences on decision-making, Busemeyer and Johnson also acknowledge that impulsive individuals may tend to use lower thresholds, while perspicacious individuals may tend to use higher thresholds.

A Conceptual Model of the Decision-Making Process for Presenteeism

In the following section, we integrate and consolidate existing presenteeism research and decision-making theory, as outlined above, into a process model of presenteeism decision-making. We hope that this will provide a launchpad from which we can then test and refine our understanding of this critical process and transfer these insights into practice to support individuals to make better decisions and managers to support the employees. From our analysis of the available literature, we discern four potential stages of the decision-making process of presenteeism: (1) a trigger that necessitates the decision (what happened? how severely am I affected?), (2) perceived available options (what could I do? what is possible?), (3) evaluation of options

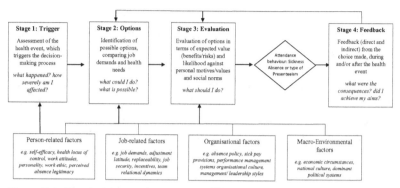

Figure 7.1 The decision-making process of presenteeism

in terms of perceived benefits/risks and potential consequences (what should I do?), and (4) seeking feedback and evaluating the decision (was this the right decision? did I achieve my aims?) (see Figure 7.1).

Stage 1: Trigger

Stage 1 concerns a self-assessment of the health event, which comprises the trigger for the decision-making process, focused narrowly around the question of illness severity (Johns, 2010). Given the subjectivity of health and illness (e.g., Johns, 2010; Van Hooft, 1997), personal factors are likely to influence each individual's appraisal of the severity of their health condition (e.g., pain thresholds, Jensen et al., 1993; genetics, Diatchenko et al., 2005; locus of control, Crisson & Keefe, 1988). Consequently, similar to Busemeyer and Johnson's (2004) concept of decision thresholds, there may be a threshold at which a health condition is automatically deemed to necessitate sickness absence, without deliberation. For some individuals and/or some health conditions, the threshold for deliberation may be very low, with very few health events automatically warranting sickness absence, whereas for others it may be high. Furthermore, given the that rapid and automatic processing is strongly influenced by emotional states (e.g. Kahneman, 2012), this threshold may also change situationally, for instance when individuals are experiencing stress or anger. Thus, if the health event is considered sufficiently serious that that absenteeism is immediately deemed the only option, then this behavior is selected without evaluation of the options.

Stage 2: Options

Stage 2 concerns the identification of perceived available response options. We know that identification of possible options is likely to be influenced by framing effects and other heuristics such as priming and availability bias (Tversky & Kahneman, 1973, 1981), which in turn are influenced by individual and situational factors. In some national or organizational cultures, for instance, sickness absence may not even be considered an option in relation to only mild health events. This stage reflects the "editing" stage of French and colleagues' two-stage editing and evaluation making theory (French et al., 2009), involving constructing a decision frame, influenced by personal values and normative or situational influences. Conversely, if an employer has recently run a health promotion campaign highlighting the importance of managing work–life balance, this may prime sickness absence as a feasible option.

Whilst automatic filtering of options via framing reflects what Kahneman referred to as intuitive, system 1 thinking, it is likely that the identification of options also involves more deliberate and considered cognitive processes associated with system 2 thinking. We propose that "options" here refer not only to a binary choice between absenteeism and presenteeism but also to different types of presenteeism: the range of options between full and partial productivity (e.g., attending to a limited range of tasks only, working but performing a poor job, or working reduced hours), which can be created through attempts to adjust work tasks to accommodate health limitations or capacities (health-performance framework of presenteeism; Karanika-Murray & Biron, 2020). Consequently, identification of options is likely to include considerations relating to how the health condition affects work capacity: what tasks am I able to carry out with my symptoms? and how can I adapt the tasks (both the associated demands and/or resources) until my health improves? This necessitates a more nuanced judgment, weighing up the symptoms (mental, physical, severe, less mild, etc.) against work-related variables such job demands (Demerouti et al., 2009; Kivimäki et al., 2005), ease of replacement (Aronsson & Gustafsson, 2005; Biron et al., 2006; Dew et al., 2005; Widera, et al., 2010), and adjustment latitude (Krohne & Magnussen, 2011). Indeed, these considerations echo the two-stage appraisal process captured within the cognitive-mediational theory of stress (Lazarus, 1993), which proposes that after evaluating a potential threat (i.e., primary appraisal, akin to stage 1 in this process) we then determine what resources we have at our disposal to manage a situation (i.e., secondary appraisal, stage 2 in this process). Once an individual has identified what they deem to be possible, we propose the decision process moves on to consider what is desirable, in relation both to their own goals and social norms and expectations.

Stage 3: Evaluation

Stage 3 is the evaluation of the options in terms of expected value and likelihood and is therefore focused less on what is possible and more on the individual's own wants and motivations, in addition to organizational factors and social norms and what they believe they "should" do. It reflects the second stage in French et al.'s (2009) decision-making process. Whilst editing involves constructing a decision frame, evaluation involves weighing the "framed" options against the individual's goals and objectives and anticipated outcomes. Consequently, this evaluation is likely to be influenced by the push and pull (Miraglia & Johns, 2016) or approach and avoidance motives (Cooper & Lu, 2016; Lu et al., 2013, 2014) of presenteeism. Low job satisfaction, for example, may lead individuals to place more weight on the benefits of sickness absence in terms of their own health and wellbeing than on productivity or work commitment from presenteeism when feeling dissatisfied with work.

It involves a series of judgments involving cognitive evaluation of expected value and likelihood, influenced by a range of factors identified in presenteeism research, from micro through to macro levels, which can be categorized into four main groups: personal, job-related, organizational, and environmental. Personal factors encompass factors such as work attitudes, self-efficacy (Cooper & Lu, 2016), perceived absence legitimacy, personality (Cooper & Lu, 2016; Johns, 2010), affective wellbeing such as depression (Burton et al., 2004; McTernan et al., 2013), stress, and past absenteeism/presenteeism experience (Matinez & Ferreira, 2012). Job-related variables include factors such as role demands, time pressure, and adjustment latitude, in addition to interpersonal factors such as supervisor support and work–family conflict (Lohaus & Habermann, 2019). Organizational factors include factors such as absence policy (Chatterji & Tilley, 2002; Irvine, 2011), reward systems, workplace norms (Dew et al., 2005; McKevitt & Morgan, 1997), and job security (Aronsson & Gustafsson, 2005; Prater & Smith, 2011; Widera et al., 2010). Finally, environmental factors include influences of macro factors such as national culture (Cooper & Lu, 2016) and economic climate (Kristensen, 1991).

Further research is needed to tease out the complex nature via which these factors influence the evaluation of options, but it is clear that some are antecedents (e.g., stress, depression) while others are likely to be moderators and/or mediators (e.g., self-efficacy, work attitudes, organizational commitment). Furthermore, it is feasible that some factors may act as an antecedent in one circumstance but a moderator in another, depending on the health condition. For instance, stress could be the trigger for presenteeism/absenteeism in some circumstances, or a moderator in another where the main trigger is another (e.g., physical) health condition, but the impact of stress reduces the threshold at which an individual deems absenteeism to be necessary. Equally, as already discussed, macro factors may have a stronger influence than we might assume. For example, individuals with high job security may still choose to go to work when they are experiencing ill health because cultural norms encourage working through illness. Furthermore, because many of these influencing variables are situational or context-specific, these judgments may vary between individuals and within individuals for different ill-health spells.

Following decision field theory (Busemeyer & Townsend, 1993; Busemeyer & Johnson, 2004), evaluation of each option in terms of desired and expected outcomes may involve switching between alternatives, considering the consequences of each alternative over a period of time. Given the importance of social norms, consequences (both positive and negative) will be evaluated with regard to one's self and in terms of others' interests. For example, sickness absence would give me time to rest and may speed my recovery; however, this may result in additional workload for my colleagues which may cause animosity, which is then compared against the individual's motives and goals.

Arguably, this is the stage where decision-making theory has most to offer, with a number of theories offering insights into how such judgments are influenced. Prospect theory (Kahneman & Tversky, 1979), for instance, suggests that people are likely to choose certain gains over the probability of losses if the difference between gains and losses is relatively small (risk aversion), whilst if facing certain losses, they will choose the probability of losses over the certain losses (risk seeking). In addition, expectancy theory helps us to understand how anticipated outcomes might combine with an individual's goals and objectives to form the judgments which lead to determination of the final choice. In simplistic terms, for instance, employees who value financial stability or favorable relationships with colleagues and supervisors as desired outcomes are likely to choose presenteeism. However, given those desired outcomes, this may potentially become dysfunctional presenteeism (Karanika-Murray & Biron, 2020), depending on the health condition and nature of the work demands. In contrast, individuals who place recovery as the primary desired outcome may enact absenteeism, in order to provide rest in order to recover from their illnesses, if their stage 2 assessment concluded that their work demands were insufficiently adaptable. The individual-desired outcomes differentiate the courses of action, informed by personal values. It is important to note that macro-level influences such as national culture and work climate norms also influence outcomes, whether this is directly through internalization of these values or indirectly through conformity. For example, individuals who work within countries or even organizations where long working hours and commitment to work (above all) are valued highly are more likely to select presenteeism, as a responsible act towards their employer and their colleagues (Cooper & Lu, 2016; Ruhle et al., 2019).

Comparisons of likely consequences will reach a preference state once the desirability of action passes a threshold (Busemeyer & Johnson, 2004), and consequently this action is chosen. As discussed, given the range of potential options resulting from different levels of role/work adaptability, the discretionary amount of employee effort exerted, or even time spent working during any given working day, there are a range of different types of presenteeism (as characterized in the health-performance framework of presenteeism; Karanika-Murray & Biron, 2020) that may be enacted. Thus, this is not a simple binary decision between absenteeism and presenteeism, but one between sickness absence without any work engagement (bearing in mind that some individuals may still undertake some work duties, such as checking emails, despite officially having taken sickness absence, thereby enacting presenteeism whilst on sick leave) and a range of sickness presenteeism behaviors, from working while ill yet maintaining full productivity, to working at limited capacity and/or on limited duties/ hours, to being physically present but completely unproductive.

Stage 4: Feedback

Stage 4 is characterized by an evaluation of the efficacy of the choice made, which depending on the duration of illness may take place during illness and/or after the health event has subsided: did I make the right decision? and/or do I need to reconsider my decision? As discussed, feedback plays an important role in effective decision-making, in terms of evaluating the appropriateness of the selected option for the situation, assessing the extent to which the intended outcomes were achieved, and identifying links between actions and consequences. Feedback is essential in order to adapt behavior (Hardman, 2009) to external demands and changing circumstances, helping the individual to learn through this process and reinforce (positive feedback) or inhibit (negative feedback) specific decisions in the future (Verharen et al., 2019). This is consistent with evidence that people make decisions based on their past experience in similar situations (Verharen et al., 2019), with reinforced behaviors being most likely to be repeated while punished behaviors would be ceased. Evaluating the trade-offs between resources, demands, and expected outcomes is an essential part of the feedback mechanism for presenteeism. Intended and unintended consequences (at both the individual and organizational level, Lohaus & Habermann, 2019) will feed into the decision-making process in different ways, consciously and prospectively or unconsciously and retrospectively. Critically, feedback may help to adjust dysfunctional behavior towards more functional presenteeism. It is possible that through self and/or others' feedback, individuals reconsider their health capacities and work tasks and through this process move between the quadrants described in the health-performance framework (Karanika-Murray & Biron, 2020) .

Directions for Further Research

As described at the outset, with this process model, we hope to help build the foundations and empirical work that will enrich our understanding of presenteeism behavior, support evidence-based practice, and offer directions for further research. Consequently, we offer an initial integration of presenteeism research and decision-making theory, which requires empirical testing and subsequent honing to validate and refine the clustering of the key elements of the decision-making process into the stages outlined.

First, further research is needed to understand which and how the range of inputs identified in presenteeism research (i.e., from micro through to macro levels, and as four main groups of personal, interpersonal, organizational, and environmental factors) impact on each of the stages of decision-making. For example, how do different factors inform judgments around expected value and likelihood in the evaluation of options? Or how does the interaction between work demands and health condition shape the importance placed on different consequences?

In addition, we feel that future research would advantageously be directed towards exploring the extent to which instinctive (system 1) and more analytical thinking (system 2) (Kahneman, 2012) influences the decision-making process, at which stage(s), and to what effect. For instance, the influence of heuristics on the framing of alternatives is particularly important. Specifically, the influence of deep-rooted assumptions or attributions held by individuals regarding the reciprocal relationship between work and health (for instance, an implicit belief that work is detrimental to health), which is likely to influence whether both options are even given due consideration in certain circumstances.

Furthermore, we also recognize that these modes of thinking are likely to combine personal preferences, attitudes, and values, on the one hand, against what the individual believes that they should do according to formal and informal rules, norms, and expectations. Thus, although the presenteeism behavior is preceded by a decision-making process and although presenteeism is a voluntary behavior (Karanika-Murray et al., 2015), external pressures such as punitive attendance policies or an attendance culture of the workplace may make this choice "imposed". Further research, therefore, should explore the interaction between internal (individual) and external (e.g., organizational or cultural) influences on the presenteeism decision-making process.

Finally, as the health-performance framework of presenteeism (Karanika-Murray & Biron, 2020) suggests, depending on whether the concern is weighted more towards supporting health or supporting performance, different types of presenteeism may emerge. The essential choice between prioritizing health or performance may be a most immediate concern that has implications for both recovery and performance. Consequently, further research should explore the decision-making process in relation not only to presenteeism–absenteeism, but also at the more nuanced level of functional, dysfunction, and therapeutic types of presenteeism and how these evolve until the presentee is ready to engage with work at full capacity.

Conclusions

The question of *how* individuals make decisions to attend or not to attend work when they are experiencing ill health is critical to effective management of employee health and productivity, providing the basis for understanding when and how one might intervene to help maximize those decisions. Thus, we hope that this model of the absenteeism–presenteeism decision-making process will help to build upon the limited amount of conceptual work in the field and help not only to explain but also to optimize the decision-making process. Greater understanding of the decision-making process regarding presenteeism is of not only high practical value, empowering better interventions to promote health in the workplace, but also of theoretical significance. By integrating presenteeism research with decision-making theory, we provide the foundations of a process model that outlines how the decision to enact presenteeism may unfold, incorporating the factors and correlates influencing this decision and evaluation of alternatives and consequences. Consequently, in outlining this conceptual model, we hope to enrich understanding of the decision-making process of presenteeism, as well as inspire future empirical research to test these propositions. Ultimately, these will help to promote work-related health and wellbeing, facilitate a more positive work experience for employees, and, by optimizing the health-productivity trade-off, promote organizational productivity.

References

Addae, H. M., Johns, G., & Boies, K. (2013). The legitimacy of absenteeism from work: A nine nation exploratory study. *Cross Cultural Management: An International Journal, 20*(3), 402–428.

Ajzen, I. (1985). From intentions to actions: A theory of planned behavior. In J. Kuhl & J. Beckmann (Eds.), *Action-control: From cognition to behavior* (pp. 11–39). Springer.

(1988). *Attitudes, Personality, and behavior.* Dorsey.

Aronsson, G., & Gustafsson, K. (2005). Sickness presenteeism: Prevalence, attendance-pressure factors, and an outline of a model for research. *Journal of Occupational and Environmental Medicine, 47*(9), 958–966.

Aronsson, G., Gustafsson, K., & Dallner, M. (2000). Sick but yet at work: An empirical study of sickness presenteeism. *Journal of Epidemiology & Community Health, 54*(7), 502–509.

Bandura, A. (1986). *Social foundations of thought and action: A social cognitive theory.* Prentice- Hall.

Baxter, L. A. (1990). Dialectic contradictions in relationships development. *Journal of Social and Personal Relationships, 7,* 69–88.

Baxter, L. A., & Montgomery, B. M. (1996). *Relating: Dialogues and dialectics.* Guilford Press.

Bergström, G., Bodin, L., Hagberg, J., Aronsson, G., & Josephson, M. (2009). Sickness presenteeism today, sickness absenteeism tomorrow? A prospective study on sickness presenteeism and future sickness absenteeism. *Journal of Occupational and Environmental Medicine, 51*(6), 629–638.

Biron, C., Brun, J.-P., Ivers, H., & Cooper, C. L. (2006). At work but ill: Psychosocial work environment and wellbeing determinants of presenteeism propensity. *Journal of Public Mental Health, 5*(4), 26–37.

Burton, W. N., Pransky, G., Conti, D. J., Chen, C-Y., & Edington, D. W. (2004). The Association of Medical Conditions and Presenteeism. *Journal of Occupational and Environmental Medicine, 46*(6), S38–S45.

Busemeyer, J. R., & Johnson, J. G. (2004). Computational models of decision making. In D. J. Koehler & N. Harvey (Eds.), *Blackwell handbook of judgment and decision making* (pp. 133–154). Blackwell Publishing.

Busemeyer, J. R., & Townsend, J. T. (1993). Decision field theory: A dynamic-cognitive approach to decision making in an uncertain environment. *Psychological Review, 100* (3), 432–459.

Caverley, N., Cunningham, J. B., & MacGregor, J. N. (2007). Sickness presenteeism, sickness absenteeism, and health following restructuring in a public service organisation. *Journal of Management Studies, 44,* 304–319.

Chatterji, M., & Tilley, C. J. (2002). Sickness, absenteeism, presenteeism, and sick pay. *Oxford Economic Papers, 54*(4), 669–687.

CIPD. (2019). *Health and well-being at work* [online]. London: CIPD. www .cipd.co.uk/Images/health-and-well-being-at-work-2019.v1_tcm18-55881.pdf.

Cohen-Hatton, S. R., Butler, P. C., & Honey, R. C. (2015). An investigation of operational decision making in situ: Incident command in the U.K. fire and rescue service. *Human Factors, 57*(5), 793–804.

Cooper, C., & Lu, L. (2016). Presenteeism as a global phenomenon. *Cross Cultural & Strategic Management, 23*(2), 216–231.

Crisson, J. E., & Keefe, F. J. (1988). The relationship of locus of control to pain coping strategies and psychological distress in chronic pain patients. *Pain, 35*(2), 147–154.

Deloitte. (2017). *Mental health and employers: The case for investment* [online]. London: Deloitte. https://www2.deloitte.com/content/dam/ Deloitte/uk/Documents/public-sector/deloitte-uk-mental-health-employ ers-monitor-deloitte-oct-2017.pdf.

De Martino, B., Kumaran, D., Seymour, B., & Dolan, R.J. (2006). Frames, biases, and rational decision-making in the human brain. *Science, 313* (5787), 684–687.

Demerouti, E., Le Blanc, P. M., Bakker, A. B., Schaufeli, W. B., & Hox, J. (2009). Present but sick: A three-wave study on job demands, presenteeism and burnout. *Career Development International, 14*(1), 50–68.

Dew, K., Keefe, V., & Small, K. (2005). "Choosing" to work when sick: Workplace presenteeism. *Social Science & Medicine, 60*(10), 2273–2282.

Diatchenko, L., Slade, G. D., Nackley, A. G., Bhalang, K., Sigurdsson, A., Belfer, I., Goldman, D., Xu, K., Shabalina, S. A., Shagin, D., Max, M. B., Makarov, S. S. & Maixner, W. (2005). Genetic basis for individual variations in pain perception and the development of a chronic pain condition. *Human Molecular Genetics, 14*(1), 135–143.

Dietz, C., Zacher, H., Scheel, T., Otto, K., & Rigotti, T. (2020). Leaders as role models: Effects of leader presenteeism on employee presenteeism and sick leave. *Work & Stress, 34*(3), 300–322.

Eurofound. (2012). *Health and well-being at work: A report based on the fifth European Working Conditions Survey* [online]. Dublin: Eurofound. www.eurofound.europa.eu/sites/default/files/ef_publica tion/field_ef_document/ef1302en.pdf.

Evans, J. (1984). Heuristic and analytic processes in reasoning. *British Journal of Psychology, 75*(4), 451–468.

French, S., Maule, J., & Papamichail, N. (2009). *Decision behavior, analysis and support.* Cambridge University Press.

Gintis, H. (2007). A framework for the unification of the behavioral sciences. *Behavioural & Brain Sciences, 30*(1), 1–16.

Gosselin, E., Lemyre, L., & Corneil, W. (2013). Presenteeism and absenteeism: Differentiated understanding of related phenomena. *Journal of Occupational Health Psychology, 18*(1), 75–86.

Halbesleben, J. R. B., Whitman, M. V., & Crawford, W. S. (2014). A dialectical theory of the decision to go to work: Bringing together absenteeism and presenteeism. *Human Resource Management Review, 24* (2), 177–192.

Hansen, C. D., & Andersen, J. H. (2008). Going ill to work – what personal circumstances, attitudes and work-related factors are associated with sickness presenteeism? *Social Science & Medicine, 6*(6), 956–964.

(2009). Sick at work – a risk factor for long-term sickness absence at a later date? *Journal of Epidemiology & Community Health, 63*(5), 397–402.

Hardman, D. (2009). *Judgment and decision making.* BPS Blackwell.

Hemp, P. (2004). *Presenteeism: At work – but out of it* [online]. Harvard Business Review. https://hbr.org/2004/10/presenteeism-at-work-but-out-of-it.

Irvine, A. (2011). Fit for work? The influence of sick pay and job flexibility on sickness absence and implications for presenteeism. *Social Policy & Administration, 45*(7), 752–769.

Janis, I. L., & Mann, L. (1976). Coping with decisional conflict: An analysis of how stress affects decision-making suggests interventions to improve the process. *American Scientist, 64*(6), 657–667.

Janz, N. K., & Becker, M. H. (1984). The health belief model: A decade later. *Health Education Quarterly, 11*(1), 1–47.

Jensen, R., Rasmussen, B. K., Pedersen, B., & Olesen, J. (1993). Muscle tenderness and pressure pain thresholds in headache. A population study. *Pain, 52*(2), 193–199.

Johansen, V., Aronsson, G., & Marklund, S. (2014). Positive and negative reasons for sickness presenteeism in Norway and Sweden: A cross-sectional survey. *BMJ Open, 4*(2).

Johns, G. (2010). Presenteeism in the workplace: A review and research agenda. *Journal of Organizational Behavior, 31*(4), 519–542.

Kahneman, D. (2003). A perspective on judgment and choice: Mapping bounded rationality. *American Psychologist, 58*(9), 697–720.

(2012). *Thinking, fast and slow.* Penguin.

Kahneman, D., & Tversky, A. (1979). Prospect theory: An analysis of decision under risk. *Econometrica, 47*(2), 263–292.

Karanika-Murray, M., & Biron, C. (2020). The health-performance framework of presenteeism: Towards understanding an adaptive behavior. *Human Relations, 73*(2), 242–261.

Karanika-Murray, M., & Cooper, C. L. (2018). Presenteeism: An introduction to a prevailing global phenomenon. In C. L. Cooper & L. Lu (Eds.), *Presenteeism at work* (pp. 9–34). Cambridge University Press.

Karanika-Murray, M., Pontes, H. M., Griffiths, M. D., & Biron, C. (2015). Sickness presenteeism determines job satisfaction via affective-motivational states. *Social Science & Medicine, 139*, 100–106.

Kivimäki, M., Head, J., Ferrie, J. E., Hemingway, H., Shipley, M. J., Vahtera, J., & Marmot, M. G. (2005). Working while ill as a risk factor for serious coronary events: The Whitehall II study. *American Journal of Public Health*, 95(1), 98–102.

Klein, G. A. (1993). A recognition-primed decision (RPD) model of rapid decision making. In G. A. Klein, J. Orasanu, R. Calderwood, & C. E. Zsambok (Eds.), *Decision making in action: Models and methods* (pp. 138–147). Ablex Publishing.

Kristensen, T. S. (1991). Sickness absence and work strain among Danish slaughterhouse workers: An analysis of absence from work regarded as coping behavior. *Social Science & Medicine*, 32(1), 15–27.

Krohne, K., & Magnussen, L. H. (2011). Go to work or report sick? A focus group study on decisions of sickness presence among offshore catering section workers. *BMC Research Notes*, 4(1), 70–76.

Lazarus, R. S. (1993). From psychological stress to the emotions: A history of changing outlooks. *Annual Review of Psychology*, 44, 1–21.

Leineweber, C., Westerlund, H., Hagberg, J., Svedberg, P., & Alexanderson, K. (2012). Sickness presenteeism is more than an alternative to sickness absence: results from the population-based SLOSH study. *International Archives of Occupational & Environmental Health*, 85, 905–914.

Lohaus, D., & Habermann, W. (2019). Presenteeism: A review and research directions. *Human Resource Management Review*, 29(1), 43–58.

Lohaus, D., Habermann, W., Kertoubi, I. E., & Röser, F. (2021). Working while ill is not always bad – positive effects of presenteeism. *Frontiers in Psychology*, 11, 4059.

Lu, L., Lin, H. Y., & Cooper, C. L. (2013). Unhealthy and present: Motives and consequences of the act of presenteeism among Taiwanese employees. *Journal of Occupational Health Psychology*, 18(4), 406–416.

Lu, L., Peng, S. Q., Lin, H. Y., & Cooper, C. L. (2014). Presenteeism and health over time among Chinese employees: The moderating role of self-efficacy. *Work & Stress*, 28(2), 165–178.

Markham, S. E. (1985). An investigation of the relationship between unemployment and absenteeism: A multi-level approach. *The Academy of Management Journal*, 28(1), 228–234.

Martinez, L. F., & Ferreira, A. I. (2012). Sick at work: Presenteeism among nurses in a Portuguese public hospital. *Stress and Health*, 28(4), 297–304.

Martocchio, J. J. (1994). The Effects of Absence Culture on Individual Absence. *Human Relations*, 47(3), 243–262.

McGuire, W. J. (1983). A contextualist theory of knowledge: Its implications for innovation and reform in psychological research. *Advances in Experimental Social Psychology*, 16, 1–47.

McKevitt, C., & Morgan, M. (1997). Illness doesn't belong to us. *Journal of the Royal Society of Medicine*, 90(9), 491–495.

McTernan, W. P., Dollard, M. F., & LaMontagne, A. D. (2013). Depression in the workplace: An economic cost analysis of depression-related productivity loss attributable to job strain and bullying. *Work & Stress*, 27 (4), 321–338.

Miraglia, M., & Johns, G. (2021). The social and relational dynamics of absenteeism from work: A multilevel review and integration. *Academy of Management Annals*, 15, 37–67.

(2016). Going to work ill: A meta-analysis of the correlates of presenteeism and a dual-path model. *Journal of Occupational Health Psychology*, 21(3), 261–283.

Mongin, P. (1997) Expected utility theory. In J. Davis, W. Hands, W. & U. Maki (Eds.), *Handbook of economic methodology* (pp. 342–350). Edward Elgar.

Ozernoy, V.M. (1985). Generating alternatives in multiple criteria decision making problems: A survey. In Y. Y. Haimes & V. Chankong (Eds.), *Decision making with multiple objectives: Lecture notes in economics and mathematical systems* (Vol. 242, pp. 322–330). Springer.

Nicholson, N., & Johns, G. (1985). The absence culture and the psychological contract – Who's in control of absence? *The Academy of Management Review*, 10(3), 397–407.

Nickerson, R. S. (1990). William James on reasoning. *Psychological Science*, 1(3), 167–171.

Patton, E., & Johns, G. (2012). Context and the social representation of absenteeism: Absence in the popular press and in academic research. *Human Relations*, 65(2), 217–240.

Prater, T., & Smith, K. (2011). Underlying factors contributing to presenteeism and absenteeism. *Journal of Business & Economics Research*, 9(6), 1–14.

Ruhle, S., Breitsohl, H., Aboagye, E., Baba, V., Biron, C., Correia-Leal, A. C., Dietz, C., Ferreira, A., Gerich, J., Johns, G., Karanika-Murray, M., Lohaus, D., Løkke, A., Lopes, S. L., Martinez, L. F., Miraglia, M., Muschalla, B., Poethke, U., Sarwat, N., Schade, H., Steidelmüller, C., Vinberg, S., Whysall, Z., & Yang, T. (2019). "To work, or not to work, that is the question" – Recent trends and avenues for research on presenteeism. *European Journal of Work and Organizational Psychology*.

Ruhle, S. A., & Süß, S. (2020). Presenteeism and absenteeism at work – An analysis of archetypes of sickness attendance cultures. *Journal of Business Psychology*, 35, 241–255. https://doi.org/10.1007/s10869-019-09615-0.

Saaty, T. L. (1980). *The analytic hierarchy process: Planning, priority setting, resource allocation*. McGraw-Hill.

(2008). Decision making with the analytic hierarchy process. *International Journal of Services Sciences*, 1(1), 83–98.

Schultz, A. B., & Edington, D. W. (2007). Employee health and presenteeism: A systematic review. *Journal of Occupational Rehabilitation*, 17(3), 547–579.

Simpson, R. (1998). Presenteeism, power and organizational change: Long hours as a career barrier and the impact on the working lives of women managers. *British Journal of Management*, 9, 37–50.

Tims, M., & Bakker, A. B. (2010). Job crafting: Towards a model of individual job redesign. *Journal of Industrial Psychology*, 36, 1–9.

Tversky, A., & Kahneman, D. (1973). Availability: A heuristic for judging frequency and probability. *Cognitive Psychology*, 5(2), 207–232.

(1974). Judgment under uncertainty: Heuristics and biases. *Science, 185* (4157), 1124–1131. www.jstor.org/stable/1738360

(1981). The framing of decisions and the psychology of choice. *Science, 211*(4481), 453–458.

Van Hooft, S. (1997). Health and subjectivity. *Health*, 1(1), 23–36.

Verharen, J. P. H., Adan, R. A. H., & Vanderschuren, L. J. M. J. (2019). How reward and aversion shape motivation and decision making: A computational account. *The Neuroscientist*, 26(1), 87–99.

Von Neumann, J., & Morgenstern, O. (1947). *Theory of games and economic behavior* (2nd rev. ed.). Princeton University Press.

(2007). *Theory of games and economic behavior*. Princeton University Press. https://doi.org/10.1515/9781400829460

Vroom, V. H. (1964). *Work and motivation*. Wiley.

Waddell, G., & Burton, A. K. (2006). Is work good for your health and well-being? *TSO*.

Wason, P. C., & Evans, J. St. B. T. (1975). Dual processes in reasoning? *Cognition*, 3, 141–154.

Whysall, Z., Bowden, J., & Hewitt, M. (2018). Sickness presenteeism: Measurement and management challenges. *Ergonomics*, 61(3), 341–354.

Widera, E., Chang, A., & Chen, H. L. (2010). Presenteeism: A public health hazard. *Journal of General Internal Medicine*, 25(11), 1244–1247.

Xie, J. L., & Johns, G. (2000). Interactive effects of absence culture salience and group cohesiveness: A multi-level and cross-level analysis of work absenteeism in the Chinese context. *Journal of Occupational and Organizational Psychology*, 73(1), 31–52.

Zhou, Q., Martinez, L. F., Ferreira, A. I., & Rodrigues, P. (2016). Supervisor support, role ambiguity and productivity associated with presenteeism: A longitudinal study. *Journal of Business Research*, 69(9), 3380–3387.

8 Burnout
A Critical Overview

WILMAR SCHAUFELI

Burnout is a stark metaphor that refers to the loss of mental energy. It is commonly used to describe a state or process of mental exhaustion, similar to the smothering of a fire, the extinguishing of a candle, or the draining of a battery. The Merriam-Webster dictionary describes it as 'exhaustion of physical or emotional strength or motivation usually as a result of prolonged stress or frustration' (noun) and 'to cause to fail, wear out, or become exhausted especially from overwork or overuse' (verb). Introduced in the 1970s and initially ridiculed in academia and ignored as pop psychology, burnout is currently a well-respected scholarly topic. This is evidenced by the fact that, according to PsycLit, over 13,000 scientific publications about burnout have appeared. Moreover, year after year more papers on burnout are published; for instance, between 1991 and 2010, publications rose by a factor of 7.7 (Heinemann & Heinemann, 2017). So, it does not seem that burnout is a fad as initially believed; rather, it is here to stay. As we will see below, this is unsurprising as burnout can be seen as a modern, global affliction. First introduced in the United States, it readily expanded internationally. Tellingly, burnout originally appeared as a social problem, particularly in human services such as education, health care, and social work and was then taken up by academia. This means that initially it was a practical rather than a scholarly challenge because it comes with huge costs, for the individual as well as organizations. In addition, societal costs occur because of increased health care expenditure and income compensation for those suffering from burnout. In order to ameliorate these costs, an extensive burnout industry has emerged. Today, many professionals earn a living by treating burnout victims, offering workshops on burnout, or assisting organizations on how to prevent it. In this sense, burnout has boosted professional practice, thereby closing the vicious circle of supply and demand.

The current chapter sets out to present a state-of-the-art overview about our scientific knowledge on burnout, thereby also addressing some criticisms and ongoing debates. Clearly, it is beyond the scope of the chapter to review all scientific publications, but fortunately many useful meta-analyses have appeared that summarize research findings. This chapter is structured as follows. The second section explains the history and background of burnout, which illustrates that various forerunners exist. The third section focuses on the concept and definition and how these developed. The fourth section is about the assessment of burnout, discussing not only popular self-report questionnaires but also diagnostic criteria that are used by practitioners in clinical interviews. The fifth section addresses the prevalence of burnout and also includes a critical discussion about the criteria for proper epidemiological research that are often not met in burnout research. In the sixth section, a brief overview is presented about the antecedents, consequences, and correlates of burnout, thereby focusing on the individual as well as the organizational level. The seventh section is about various psychological explanations of burnout, whereas the eighth section discusses the effectiveness of individual, team, and organizational interventions to prevent and combat burnout. The chapter closes with a final section that summarizes the main conclusions and presents an outlook on the challenges of burnout research and practice that lie ahead.

History and Background

Although the term burnout as we know it today was first coined in the 1970s, the use of the metaphor is much older. Almost four hundred years ago William Shakespeare wrote: 'She burnt with love, as straw with fire flameth. She burnt out love, as soon as straw out burneth'. Instead of hard work, Shakespeare associated burning love with an unfeeling of burnout. It was Herbert Freudenberger (1974) who borrowed the term 'burnout' from the illicit drug scene, where it colloquially referred to the devastating effect of chronic drug abuse. He employed the metaphor to describe the gradual emotional depletion, loss of motivation, and reduced commitment among volunteers who worked with drug addicts. Not unimportantly, Freudenberger himself fell victim to burnout twice, which increased his credibility in spreading the message of burnout in the media, turning it soon into a buzzword. Independently and almost simultaneously, Christina Maslach (1976) and her colleagues came across 'burnout' in California as well when interviewing a variety of human services workers. As a social psychological researcher, she was interested in how these workers coped with their emotional arousal using cognitive strategies such as detached concern. Through these interviews, she learned that these workers often felt emotionally exhausted, that they developed negative perceptions and feelings about their clients or patients, and that they experienced a crisis in professional competence as a result of the emotional turmoil. These practitioners referred to this syndrome as 'burnout'. So, in fact, both Freudenberger and Maslach stumbled simultaneously and more or less accidently across the same colloquial term; apparently, burnout was in the air.

At a closer look, though, many cases of burnout *avant la lettre* have been documented, such as 'acedia' in Medieval monasteries and 'melancholy' among the nobility of the 15th and 16th century (Schaffner, 2017). However, particularly interesting is the parallel with 'neurasthenia' – literally nervous weakness (Schaufeli, 2017). Neurasthenia emerged at the end of the 19th century and was seen as the result of modern, hectic life. It was believed that continuous overstimulation by artificial light, telephone and telegraph use, newspapers, ads, and steam trains weakens the nerves. This results in extreme fatigue, demotivation, and an inability to work, the reasoning went. Busy business people in particular used to fall victim to neurasthenia. Please note the striking similarity to the current public debate linking burnout with overstimulation due to the 24/7 economy, social media, mobile phones, and the Internet. In retrospect, one could say that the rise of neurasthenia was related to the transition from an agricultural to an industrial society, while burnout coincides with the transformation from an industrial to a postindustrial, service-oriented society. While in neurasthenia the businessman is the embodiment of the dynamic, overstimulated modern human being, in burnout, this is the emotionally overloaded human services professional. The businessman is the victim of hectic pace of life, the professional of psychosocial demanding life.

It has been argued that a particular social, cultural, and economic constellation existed in the United States that led to the 'discovery' of burnout the 1970s (Schaufeli et al., 2009). For example, President Lyndon B. Johnson's 'War on Poverty' caused a large influx of idealistically motivated young people into human services professions.

However, after struggling to reduce poverty for over a decade, they found themselves increasingly disillusioned. Their frustrated idealism was critical to the concept's momentum: the experience of burnout was not merely an inconvenience or an occupational hazard but rather a damaging attack on their professional identity. Second, starting in the late 1950s, human services rapidly professionalized and bureaucratized because of increasing government and state influence. Particularly, small-scale, traditional agencies where work was considered a calling changed into largescale formalized organizations. The frustration and disillusionment resulting from the clash of utilitarian organizational values with providers' professional values further contributed to the spread of burnout. Third, the cultural revolution of the 1960s and 1970s weakened professionals' authority so that their traditional prestige was no longer self-evident. At the same time, entitled and empowered recipients expected much more than ever before. Together, these two trends increased the emotional demands of professional work considerably, hence contributing to burnout as well.

The three factors mentioned above are more or less specific for human services, the occupational group where burnout was observed first. However, other sociocultural developments also seem to have contributed to the emergence and proliferation of burnout. Notably, since the World War II, a process of social fragmentation unfolded whereby traditional social communities and networks such as the church, neighborhood, community, and family have gradually eroded. This resulted in increased individualization and decreased community support, thereby fostering the 'corrosion of character' (Sennett, 1998), a notion similar to burnout. In parallel, a 'narcissistic culture' (Lasch, 1979) developed, characterized by transient, unrewarding social relationships which produce self-absorbed, manipulative individuals who remain perpetually unsatisfied. As Farber (1983, p. 11) noted, the combination of these trends toward social fragmentation, individualization, and narcissism produces 'a perfect recipe for burnout'.

After its initial emergence in the United States, the concept of burnout rapidly spread across the globe. First it was introduced in Europe, followed by all other continents. Roughly speaking, the order in which the interest in burnout seems to have spread corresponds with the country's socioeconomic development. For instance, currently, the economies of and China and India are booming, and burnout attracts attention in these countries as well. It has been suggested that global-ization, privatization, and liberalization cause rapid changes in modern working life, such as learning new skills, new types of work, pressure of higher productivity and quality of work, and hectic, time-pressured jobs, which, in their turn, may produce burnout – particularly in rapidly developing countries (Kulkarni, 2006). In addition, social frag-mentation, individualization, empowerment of recipients and custom-ers, and the rise of 'me-culture' are pervasive in not only the United States and Europe but also other countries in the world.

Yet, 'burnout' does not necessarily mean the same thing in different countries. For instance, in North America it signifies a crisis in the relationship of employee with their jobs, whereas in welfare states in continental Europe, burnout is considered a psychological disorder. In other words, in North America burnout is a nonmedical, psychological term that is colloquially used, but in many European countries it is also used as a medical diagnosis that serves as an entry ticket which legit-imizes the use of public social and health services. In some European countries, burnout is used as an officially recognized occupational disease (Lastovkova et al., 2018). That means that workers suffer from it are eligible for treatment and financial compensation in case of sickness absence or work.

Concept and Definition

Initially, in the pioneering phase of burnout research, attempts were made to characterize burnout by means of careful but unstandardized observations and case studies. This resulted in a laundry list of 132 symptoms associated with burnout that ranged from A (anxiety) to Z (loss of zeal) (Schaufeli & Enzmann, 1998). These symptoms can be grouped into affective (e.g., anxiety, depressed mood), cognitive (e.g., forgetfulness, intellectualization), physical (e.g., headaches, muscle pain), behavioral (e.g., impulsivity, procrastination), and motivational (e.g., loss of zeal and interest) symptoms. Moreover, burnout symptoms were identified at not only the individual level but also the interpersonal (e.g., stereotyping recipients, blaming the victim) and organizational level (e.g., poor work performance, absenteeism). This laundry list approach is not very helpful because it is overinclusive; by listing all conceivable symptoms, the concept itself becomes meaningless. Yet, it gives an impression of the kind of symptoms that are involved.

In addition to identifying its symptoms in this pioneering phase, burnout was also considered as a process that unfolds across time. For instance, Edelwich and Brodsky (1980) described burnout as a process of increasing disillusionment; that is, as a '...progressive loss of idealism, energy and purpose experienced by people in the helping professions as a result of conditions in their work' (p. 14). More specifically, they distinguished four progressive stages: enthusiasm, stagnation, frustration, and apathy. In the final stage, a full-blown burnout developed that includes symptoms like those listed above. Although such stage models have an intuitive appeal and therefore tend to be popular, they have not been confirmed empirically and are only based on anecdotal evidence.

The most influential definition of burnout originates from Maslach and Jackson (1981), which marks the start of a next empirical phase: 'Burnout is a syndrome of emotional exhaustion, depersonalization, and reduced personal accomplishment that occurs frequently among individuals who do "people work" or some kind' (p. 99). In addition to emotional exhaustion and depersonalization (i.e., an impersonal attitude toward recipients), a third factor was distinguished: reduced personal accomplishment, or the tendency to judge oneself negatively in contact with recipients with whom one works professionally. The basic assumption was that working with people requires a lot of energy, effort, attention, and empathy and is therefore emotionally demanding. It was argued that high emotional demands are the root cause of burnout (see also 'Explanations').

Soon after the introduction of the Maslach Burnout Inventory (MBI) – a short, easy-to-administer self-report questionnaire – burnout research started to boom. Please note that initially – *by definition* – burnout could only occur among those who work with other people. So, basically, the massive use MBI fueled the self-fulfilling prophecy that burnout is limited to the human services and cannot be found in other occupational groups. This changed in the mid-1990s with the introduction of the general version of the MBI (Maslach et al., 1996). From then on, burnout could be assessed in *any* occupational group. In the process the original three constituting components of burnout were relabeled: emotional exhaustion turned into exhaustion, depersonalization into cynicism, and reduced personal accomplishment into lack of professional efficacy. The exhaustion component represents the stress dimension of burnout and refers to feelings of being overextended and depleted of one's mental and physical resources. The cynicism component represents the attitudinal dimension of burnout and refers to a negative or excessively detached attitude to various aspects of the job. Finally, reduced efficacy represents the self-evaluation dimension of burnout, referring to feelings of incompetence and a lack of achievement and productivity at work.

Soon after its introduction in the early 1980s, the MBI became the gold standard to assess burnout. It was used in 93% of all scientific papers on burnout that appeared until 1996 (Schaufeli & Enzmann, 1998, p. 71). Almost two decades later, the MBI continues to dominate the field; it still is the instrument of choice in 88% of all scientific papers (Boudreau et al., 2015). This supremacy has the undesirable side effect that the concept of burnout corresponds with the way in which it is assessed. In other words, burnout is what the MBI measures, and vice versa. Needless to say, that this circularity is undesirable because it impedes new and innovative research that leads to a better understanding of burnout. On a positive note, the supremacy the MBI is conducive for conducting meta-analyses.

The conceptualization of burnout from Maslach and her colleagues is not completely uncontested. A discussion raged about its dimensionality from the outset. For instance, Pines et al. (1981) described burnout as 'a state of physical, emotional and mental exhaustion caused by long-term involvement in situations that are emotionally demanding' (p. 9). In other words, burnout was reduced to mere exhaustion, and consequently their Burnout Measure yields a single score. In a similar vein, Shirom and Melamed (2006) distinguished between physical fatigue, emotional exhaustion, and cognitive weariness, and Kristensen et al. (2005) between physical and psychological exhaustion. Also, their 'burnout' measures produce a single, overall exhaustion score. All authors above argue that the correlations among the three dimensions of the MBI are not strong enough to justify calling them a syndrome. In other words, they consider the dimensions of cynicism and inefficacy as incidental and therefore unnecessary for understanding the presumed unitary nature of burnout. Exhaustion is indeed a hallmark of burnout. However, although it is a necessary criterion, it is not sufficient. If it were, then it should be recognized for what it is and plainly labeled 'exhaustion'. In short, it would not make much sense to use a novel label ('burnout') for an already existing construct ('exhaustion').

Also, Schaufeli and Taris (2005) criticized the approach of Maslach and her colleagues on conceptual grounds. In their view, the essence of fatigue is both the inability and the unwillingness to spend effort, which is reflected by the energetic and motivational components of burnout, respectively. The unwillingness to perform manifests itself by increased resistance, reduced commitment, lack of interest, disengagement, and so on – in short, mental distancing. Thus, inability (exhaustion) and unwillingness (mental distancing) constitute two sides of the same burnout coin. Moreover, they argued that in the case of normal, occasional occupational fatigue, the unwillingness to spend effort is functional because it fosters taking a break to recuperate or switching to another task and will therefore reduce fatigue. In chronic fatigue (burnout), however, the protective distancing mechanism is dysfunctional because it has habituated into relatively permanent impaired motivation. Mental distancing has become part and parcel of occupational life: instead of a solution, it is now part of the problem.

Furthermore, Schaufeli and Taris (2005) argue that instead of a constituting component of burnout, inefficacy should be considered a consequence. As such, personal accomplishment or professional efficacy can be seen as a consequence of being unable and unwilling to no longer spend effort at work. After all, because people cannot and no longer want to perform at work, they feel inefficacious. This view is supported by two longitudinal studies that showed that exhaustion leads to depersonalization and depersonalization leads, in turn, to reduced personal accomplishment (Taris et al., 2005).

Most recently, building on (1) the theorizing of Schaufeli and Taris (2005), (2) a review of current burnout instruments, and (3) in-depth interviews with professionals who deal with burned-out employees on a daily basis, burnout was reconceptualized as 'a work-related state of exhaustion that occurs among employees, which is characterized by extreme tiredness, reduced ability to regulate cognitive and emotional processes, and mental distancing' (Schaufeli, De Witte, & Desart, 2020a, p. 4). In addition to the inability (exhaustion) and unwillingness (distancing) to perform, cognitive and emotional impairment are added as distinct components that, for instance, refer to poor concentration and overreacting emotionally, respectively. As a result of exhaustion, the person's functional capacity to regulate cognitive and emotional processes is deteriorated. Seen from that perspective, cognitive and emotional impairment are specific types of exhaustion that manifest themselves in the cognitive and emotional domain, respectively. Clearly, there is a certain parallel with the approaches of Pines et al. (1981) and Shirom and Melamed (2006), who also distinguished between various forms of exhaustion. As in the definition of Maslach and her colleagues, exhaustion and cynicism (mental distancing) are included, but reduced professional efficacy is excluded for conceptual reasons (see above). Besides, it was also not mentioned in the in-depth interviews with professionals (Schaufeli et al., 2020a).

A recurrent theme in the discussion whether or not burnout is 'old wine in new bottles' is its relationship with depression. A seminal review and meta-analyses including 92 studies on the burnout–depression overlap (Bianchi et al., 2015) concluded that: (1) most burned-out employees also exhibit depressive symptoms; (2) burnout and depression scores are moderately to highly correlated, particularly as far as the exhaustion component is concerned; (3) results regarding the causal link between burnout and depression are heterogeneous; (4) somatic and biological levels of analysis seem to suggest some degree of distinctiveness; and (5) burnout and depression associate differently with both job-specific (burnout) and generic (depression) factors. Hence, it seems that the distinction between burnout and depression is – at least to some extent – supported by empirical research. This is also confirmed by a more recent meta-analysis that revealed no conclusive overlap between burnout and depression, '...indicating that they are different and robust constructs' (Koutsimani et al., 2019, p. 1).

Assessment

Basically, burnout can be assessed in two ways: by using self-report questionaries and by means of a structured, clinical interview. Most psychological researchers use the former, considering burnout a continuous variable, whereas occupational physicians and occupational health psychologists prefer the latter, considering it a dichotomous variable. Psychological research focusing on working and relatively healthy employees with only mild burnout symptoms is abundant. In contrast, research is relatively scarce among those with a burnout disorder who suffer from severe symptoms and are not able to work. Below, the assessment of burnout with self-reports is discussed first, followed by diagnostic guidelines that are employed to assess burnout as a mental disorder.

Self-Reports

As noted previously, the MBI is the gold standard to assess burnout and was developed during the late 1970s, based on a program of field research within the human services (Maslach & Jackson, 1981). The original version is known as the MBI-Human Services Survey (MBI-HSS), and several years later, a specific version was developed for use in educational settings (MBI-Educators Survey, or MBI-ES). In the mid-1990s a third, general version of the MBI was developed (MBI-General Survey, or MBI-GS) that can be used in all occupations and work settings (Maslach et al., 1996). Finally, a student version of the MBI is now available (Schaufeli et al., 2002).

Instead of a single, common burnout score, all versions of the MBI produce three subscale scores: (1) *exhaustion* – feelings of being emotionally overextended and exhausted by one's work (e.g., 'I feel burned out from my work'); (2) *depersonalization* – an unfeeling and impersonal response toward recipients of one's care or service (e.g., 'I've become more callous toward people since I took this job') – or *cynicism* – a negative or distant attitude toward the job (e.g., 'I have become less enthusiastic about my work'); and (3) *professional efficacy* – feelings of competence and successful achievement in one's work (e.g., 'At my work, I feel confident that I am effective at getting things done'). High scores on exhaustion and depersonalization/cynicism, and low scores on professional efficacy, are indicative for burnout.

Generally speaking, the psychometric quality of the MBI is good. A meta-analysis across 221 studies shows that the internal consistency (coefficient α) of the three MBI subscales generally falls within the .70–.80 range (Wheeler et al., 2011). More specifically, in 98% of the studies, values of α for the exhaustion scale exceed .80. However, it is also concluded that mean α-values for depersonalization and professional efficacy 'were well below recommended levels for high-stakes decisions, such as the diagnosis of burnout syndrome' (Wheeler et al., 2011, p. 232). Such decisions would require α values of at least .90. Another meta-analysis by the same authors examined the dimensionality of the MBI, using 35 exploratory and 28 confirmatory factor-analytic studies (Worley et al., 2008). Although the three-factor model of the MBI is generally supported, a two-factor solution is also found occasionally with exhaustion and depersonalization/cynicism collapsing into one factor (sometimes called the core of burnout) and professional efficacy as the second factor. This is not surprising because the mean correlation between exhaustion and depersonalization/cynicism (r = .57) is much higher than that between exhaustion and professional efficacy (r = −.30) and depersonalization/cynicism and professional efficacy (r = −.25).

As far as discriminant validity is concerned, a meta-analysis including over 60 studies (Koutsimani et al., 2019) shows that burnout as assessed with the MBI, is moderately related to anxiety (r = .45) as well as depression (r = .47). Consistently, relationships with the exhaustion scale are higher than with the other two burnout scales. According to the authors, these effect sizes are not so strong that it would suggest they are the same constructs. Hence, they conclude that '. . . burnout and anxiety appear to be different constructs that share some common characteristics and they probably develop in tandem, rather they fall into the same category with different names being used to describe them' (Koutsimani et al., 2019, p. 14). In a similar vein, MBI-burnout can also be discriminated from work addiction, a compulsive tendency to work excessively hard (Schaufeli et al., 2008) as well as boredom, a low degree of activation due to a lack of stimulation at work (Reijseger et al., 2013).

Despite these positive psychometric features, the MBI is also criticized on conceptual grounds (Schaufeli et al., 2020a). As mentioned above, it is doubted that reduced professional efficacy is a constituting element of burnout because it may be better interpreted as a *consequence* of burnout (Schaufeli & Taris, 2005). Furthermore, it is shown that reversing the positively worded professional efficacy items in order to tap a *lack* of professional efficacy – as is the standard procedure for the MBI – creates an artifact. Results of confirmatory factor analyses show that the professional efficacy scale of the MBI loads on a positive work engagement factor instead of a negative burnout factor, whereas the reverse is true for a scale with negatively worded inefficacy items (Schaufeli & Salanova, 2007). Hence, MBI-efficacy loads on the 'wrong' factor – work engagement – considered to be the positive antipode of burnout. So, all in all, it seems that professional efficacy competence is the odd one out, meshing with the idea of exhaustion and depersonalization/cynicism both constituting the core of burnout.

A multidimensional questionnaire that that not includes professional efficacy is the Oldenburg Burnout Inventory (OLBI – Demerouti et al., 2003). The OLBI comprises two dimensions – exhaustion and disengagement – that are similar but somewhat broader defined as compared to the MBI. That is, exhaustion includes not only affective but also physical and cognitive aspects, whereas the disengagement items refer to the lack of interest and meaning of the job. A distinctive feature of the OLBI is that both subscales also include reversed, *positively* formulated items. Using the Multi-Trait–Multi-Method (MTMM) approach in a German sample, convergent and discriminant validity of the OLBI vis-à-vis the MBI-GS is demonstrated. Both instruments correlate .74, thus sharing 55% of their variance (Demerouti et al., 2003). Subsequent research using two US samples corroborates these results and demonstrates acceptable reliability (test–retest reliability and internal consistency) as well as factorial validity (Halbersleben & Demerouti, 2005).

Recently, the Burnout Assessment Tool (BAT – Schaufeli et al., 2020a, 2020b) was introduced, specifically with the aim of supporting practitioners with diagnosing burnout. In addition to the four core dimensions of burnout (exhaustion, mental distancing, emotional impairment, and cognitive impairment), a scale with secondary distress symptoms (e.g., irritability, sleeping problems, and tension headaches) is also included. Using the MTMM approach, convergent and discriminant validity of the BAT vis-à-vis the MBI-GS and the OLBI is demonstrated (Schaufeli et al., 2020a). Moreover, it appears that a second-order factor model including the four core dimensions of the BAT is invariant across national representative samples from seven different countries (De Beer et al., 2020). Finally, using Rasch analysis, it is shown that the core dimensions constitute a unidimensional scale so that a single composite BAT-score can be computed, which is indicative for a person's level of burnout; the higher the score, the higher the level of burnout (Hadzibajramovic et al., 2020).

Taken together, it seems that the OLBI and the BAT are viable alternatives for the MBI. The former has the advantage that it is more concise conceptually because it does not include the disputed professional efficacy dimension, whereas the latter produces a single, overall score that can be used to assess burnout comprehensively as a syndrome incorporating four core symptoms.

In addition to these three multidimensional burnout questionnaires, one-dimensional questionnaires also exist that reduce burnout to mere exhaustion. The most used and best validated questionnaires are the Burnout Measure (BM; Pines et al., 1981), the Shirom Melamed

Burnout Measure (SMBM; Shirom & Melamed, 2006) and the Copenhagen Burnout Inventory (CBI; Kristensen et al., 2005).

Diagnostic Guidelines

Burnout is not included in the DSM-V, but it is mentioned in the latest version of the International Classification of Diseases (ICD-11) of the WHO (2019). Instead of a disease that should be diagnosed, burnout is considered an 'occupational phenomenon'. As a consequence, the ICD-11 does not include specific diagnostic criteria for burnout.

In countries like Sweden (Hasselberg et al., 2014) and the Netherlands (Van der Klink & Van Dijk, 2003), officially sanctioned guidelines exist for the assessment of burnout that are used in clinical interviews by physicians and psychologists. Both countries' diagnostic criteria for burnout (in Sweden called 'exhaustion disorder') largely overlap and include:

- Physical and mental exhaustion (even after minimal effort), which is considered the hallmark of burnout;
- Loss of control or ineffectiveness of the usual coping strategies;
- Loss of work and/or social roles by at least 50%;
- Core symptoms (daily):
  - Cognitive (lack of concentration, memory deficits, inefficient thinking);
  - Emotional (irritability, emotional instability);
- Supplemented by (daily) secondary distress symptoms (e.g., palpitations, muscle aches, dizziness, nervousness, worrying, inability to relax, sleep problems, gloomy mood);
- Symptoms should be present for at least six months.

Exclusion criteria are:

- Psychiatric disorders such as mood disorder, anxiety disorder, or PTSD;
- The symptoms should not be due to substance abuse, medication, or a somatic disease (e.g., diabetes, hyperthyroidism, arthritis, chronic fatigue syndrome, or fibromyalgia).

Based on these inclusion and exclusion criteria, burnout is diagnosed as an occupational disease by medical professionals such as occupational physicians and general practitioners. These criteria were also used for selecting employees that suffer from severe burnout who were used to establish clinically validated cut-off scores for the BAT (Schaufeli et al., 2020b). Based on the criteria above, a self-rating scale was developed in Sweden (Besèr et al., 2003). Hence, this self-rated questionnaire can be used by professionals to validate the outcome of their clinical interview.

Prevalence

For proper epidemiological research to estimate the prevalence of burnout, two requirements need to be met: (1) the use of a valid and reliable questionnaire with appropriate cut-off values; and (2) a representative sample. Although the MBI can be considered a valid and reliable burnout measure, cut-off values to discriminate burnout cases from noncases are lacking. The current MBI test-manual even explicitly warns against using cut-off values by including a note of caution that reads: 'It is important to understand that there is no definitive score that "proves" a person is "burned out"' (Maslach, Jackson & Leiter, 2016, p. 23). In other words, the MBI should *not* be used to estimate the prevalence of burnout. Nevertheless, previous versions of the test-manual (Maslach & Jackson, 1986; Maslach et al., 1996) specified cut-off values that have been used extensively for that very purpose. Those cut-off values corresponded with the upper third of the score distribution of particular reference groups from previous test-manuals such as teachers and medical and social services professionals. Unfortunately, these were nonrepresentative samples and data were gathered in the late 1970s, which, in fact, makes the MBI cut-offs useless and outdated.

Given the problematic nature of the MBI cut-offs, it is not surprising that estimates of the prevalence of burnout are uninformative. For instance, a systematic review that includes 131 studies among physicians concludes that the prevalence of burnout ranges from 0% to 87% (Rotenstein et al., 2018). Hence, the authors conclude: 'These findings preclude definitive conclusions about the prevalence of burnout' (p. 1145). In a similar vein, Adriaenssens et al. (2015) found that the prevalence of burnout among emergency nurses ranges across 17 studies from 9% to 76%. Another systematic review including 113 studies reports an overall pooled prevalence of 11% among nurses from 49 different countries (Woo et al., 2020). However, significant heterogeneity exists in the estimated burnout rates so that the pooled prevalence is not very informative, as the authors note.

Proper epidemiological research was carried out in Sweden's two most northern counties using a large random sample (Norlund et al., 2010). To assess burnout, the SMBM was employed with validated cut-offs that were based on a reference group that meets the Swedish diagnostic criteria for exhaustion disorder (see above). This study revealed that 13% had a high level of burnout – or, more precisely, show elevated exhaustion levels. Moreover, exhaustion is more prevalent among women (16%) compared to men (10%), is observed most frequently in the age group between 35 and 44 years, and decreases with age in both sexes. The latter might point to the so-called healthy worker effect: a selection bias whereby the least healthy workers have left their jobs, thus leaving their healthier colleagues.

The results of this Swedish study are remarkably similar to that of the Dutch Annual Working Conditions Survey, which is carried out among a large, representative sample of the working population. This survey uses the exhaustion scale of the MBI with cut-offs that are based on a reference group that meets the Dutch diagnostic criteria for burnout (see above). It was estimated in 2019 that 17% experience severe exhaustion, 18% among women and 16% among men (Houtman, 2020). Exhaustion is most prevalent among those aged between 25 and 34 years and rates for both sexes decrease with age. Moreover, exhaustion is most prevalent in teaching (23%), followed by health care (19%) and industry (18%). Finally, the prevalence of severe work-related exhaustion appears to be more or less stable across time, initially fluctuating around 11% from 1997 till 2012, after which it increased gradually to 17% in 2019.

The only study so far that compares national representative samples from various countries (De Beer et al., 2020) showed that, using the BAT, burnout levels in Japan are significantly higher compared to six European countries (Austria, Belgium, Finland, Germany Ireland, the Netherlands).

In conclusion, the MBI is not suitable for epidemiological research, and when it is nonetheless used, the prevalence of burnout varies too much across studies to draw any meaningful conclusions. Employing questionnaires that tap exhaustion only, it was estimated in Sweden and the Netherlands that between 13% and 17% of the working population suffer from this hallmark of burnout. In both countries, exhaustion was more prevalent in women and younger age groups and decreased with age.

Antecedents, Consequences, and Correlates

The main antecedents, consequences, and correlates of burnout, which emerged mostly from systematic reviews and meta-analyses, are summarized below. The Job Demands-Resources (JD-R) model is used to structure this section (Bakker & Demerouti, 2016). Before discussing the main empirical findings, two notes should be made.

First, the vast majority of empirical burnout studies is cross-sectional in nature, which precludes drawing any conclusions about its causes and effects. Using the JDR-model, Lesener et al. (2019) analyzed the results of 74 longitudinal samples and found that job characteristics (i.e., job demands and job resources) are *reciprocally* related to burnout. This means, for instance, that work overload leads to burnout, but also the other way around, that employees who feel burned out at a certain point in time are likely to perceive a higher future workload. Hence, perceived work overload may act as an antecedent as well as a consequence of burnout.

Second, various antecedents may interact with each other. Negative effects of job demands, such as work overload or role problems, may be compensated or buffered by job resources, such as job control and social support (Xanthopoulou et al., 2007). These may mitigate these effects and thus protect employees from burning out. Recently, a meta-analysis of 48 longitudinal studies found that the 'stressor-effect' (job demands → burnout) is smaller than the reverse 'strain-effect' (burnout → job demands) and that the latter is moderated (i.e., reduced) by job control and social support (Guthier et al., 2020). Supplementary analyses suggest that the reciprocal relations are mainly driven by exhaustion and that exhaustion and depersonalization/cynicism are reciprocally related across time.

Hence, it can be concluded that the longitudinal relationships between job characteristics and burnout are more complex and go beyond the simple idea that job stressors and lack of job resources 'cause' burnout. Hence, the phrase *potential* antecedents and consequences is used below. First, potential antecedents and consequences of burnout are discussed, followed by its correlates, such as person and sociographic factors. Next, the potential consequences and correlates of burnout will be examined, respectively.

Potential Antecedents

Table 8.1 summarizes the most important potential causes of burnout and is based on various qualitative reviews (Halbesleben & Buckley, 2004; Schaufeli & Taris, 2014; Shirom, 2002) as well as three meta-analyses (Alarcon, 2011; Aronsson et al., 2017; Crawford et al., 2010).

The most consistent finding is that *quantitative* job demands, such as work overload (i.e., too much work to do), time pressure, long work hours, and frequent contact with customers or clients (caseload) are positively related to burnout. The same applies for *qualitative* job demands, such as conflicting work roles and inadequate information to fulfill one's work role (role problems), being involved in emotionally charged situations (emotional demands), and interference between work and nonwork roles (work–nonwork conflict). The reason is that such job demands spark an energy depletion process whereby an employee's sustained effort to meet these demands may drain his or her energy backup. An illustrative study on the impact of objectively assessed quantitively job demands was carried out in over 200 Pennsylvania hospitals (Aiken et al., 2020). It shows that an unfavorable patient-to-nurse ratio, which causes nurses to spend more

Table 8.1 *Main potential antecedents of burnout*

Job demands	Work overload
	Time pressure
	Number of work hours
	Caseload
	Role problems
	Work–nonwork conflict
	Emotional demands
Job resources	Lack of social support from colleagues and supervisor
	Lack of feedback
	Poor participation in decision making
	Lack of job control
	Absence of transformational leadership

effort on their job, is positively related to burnout; an increase of one patient per nurse to a hospital's staffing level increases nurse burnout by 23% and patient mortality by 7%, after controlling for patient and hospital characteristics. An example of a specific emotional demand is emotional dissonance, which occurs when expressed emotions are in conformity with organizational norms but clash with one's true feelings. A meta-analysis using 52 studies found a medium-sized, positive relationship between emotional dissonance and emotional exhaustion (Kenworthy et al., 2014). As far as work–nonwork conflict is concerned, a meta-analysis including 91 studies revealed that work to nonwork conflict is more strongly related to emotional exhaustion and cynicism as compared to nonwork to work conflict, with ρs of .61 and .41 vs. .34 and .34, respectively (Reichl et al., 2014).

Moreover, burnout is also related to lacking job resources. More specifically, burnout is likely to occur when interpersonal resources (e.g., social support from colleagues and supervisors) or resources that refer to the content of the job (e.g., performance feedback, participation in decision making, and job control) are lacking, both of which are instrumental in achieving one's work goals. For instance, Neveux (2007) found among French correctional officers that depletion of resources, such as coworker support and participation in decision making, leads to burnout and, in turn, to depression and sickness absence. Leadership plays a special role because leaders are supposed to balance the job demands and job resources of their followers in order to prevent them from burning out. The majority of studies focus on transformational leadership. According to a review by Arnold (2017), most studies find a negative relationship with burnout. Yet, study results are equivocal because different results are obtained for different aspects of transformational leadership. For instance, burnout is reduced when supervisors are perceived to be charismatic and individually considerate (negative relationship), but it is higher when supervisors are perceived as intellectually stimulating (positive relationship).

Generally speaking, associations with job demands are somewhat stronger than with job resources. Typically, associations with the former vary between .35 and .45, and with the latter between .25 and .30. Moreover, associations with the exhaustion component of burnout are more consistent and usually also stronger, as compared to both other burnout dimensions.

Potential Consequences

Table 8.2 summarizes the most important possible consequences of burnout and is based on the same reviews and meta-analyses as Table 8.1, supplemented by more specific overviews and studies mentioned below.

Potentially, burnout has negative consequences for the individual employee as well as for the organization they are working for. Individual consequences pertain particularly to the employee's physical and mental health. A systematic review of 61 prospective studies found that the most frequently investigated physical outcomes of burnout are cardiovascular diseases (i.e., coronary heart disease (CHD) and hospitalization for cardiovascular diseases) and risk factors for these diseases, such as obesity, hyperlipidemia, type 2 diabetes, large waist circumference, high body mass index (BMI), metabolic syndrome, hypertension, high triglycerides, low HDL cholesterol, and high LDL cholesterol (Salvagioni et al., 2017). In addition, this review also found that musculoskeletal disorders, pain (overall pain, neck–shoulder pain, back pain, and pain-related disability), and psychosomatic complaints (headaches, insomnia, gastrointestinal and respiratory problems) are prospectively related to burnout. As far as mental health is concerned, burnout may lead to anxiety and depression (Koutsimani et al, 2019). For instance, using a three-wave longitudinal design spanning seven years, it was shown that burnout leads to depression, rather than the other way around (Hakanen & Schaufeli, 2012). Moreover, it

Table 8.2 *Main potential consequences of burnout*

Employee health	Coronary heart disease (incl. its risk factors)
	Musculoskeletal disorders
	Psychosomatic complaints
	Insomnia
	Anxiety and depression
	Hospital admissions and mortality
Organizational outcomes	Poor organizational commitment
	Turnover (intention)
	Sickness absence and disability pension
	Occupational injuries
	Job performance

appeared that work engagement acted as a protective factor for burn-out (Hakanen et al., 2018). Finally, at the behavioral level, two larges-cale Finnish studies showed that burnout is a predictor of hospital admissions due to mental disorders over a ten-year period (Toppinen-Tanner et al., 2009), as well as a significant predictor of mortality in the next decade among those aged 45–65 years (Ahola et al., 2010).

Although burnout has been related to poor physical and mental health, as well as behavioral outcomes, the underlying physiological mechanisms are still largely uncovered. This is illustrated by a meta-analysis of 31 studies that includes 36 different biomarkers and con-cludes that 'no potential biomarkers for burnout were found' (Danhof-Pont et al., 2011, p. 505). This conclusion was confirmed by a more recent narrative review by Jonsdottir and Dahlman (2019), who wrote: '… albeit the large body of studies, it cannot be concluded that clear effects are seen on HPA-axis function in people with burnout' (p. 147). The hypothalamic–pituitary–adrenal (HPA) axis is a major neuroen-docrine system that controls reactions to stress and regulates many body processes, including mood and emotions and energy expenditure. So, obviously, burnout does not lead to poor health via physiological changes that are indicated by biological markers such as particular hormones like cortisol, or immune parameters such as cytokines.

Negative consequences of burnout for the organization (see Table 8.2) typically reflect employee withdrawal, either mentally (e.g., poor organizational commitment; Alarcon, 2011) or physically (e.g., turnover, and frequency and duration of sickness absence; Swider & Zimmerman, 2010). In addition, a large Finnish population study (Ahola et al., 2009) that spanned eight years found that workers with severe burnout have a greater likelihood of receiving a new disability pension (15%) compared to those with mild (8%) or no burnout (5%). Furthermore, Nahrgang et al. (2011) tested a meta-analytic model that was based on over 200 studies and showed that burnout played a mediating role between safety demands (e.g., risks and hazards) and lacking safety recourses (e.g., poor safety climate), on the one hand, and safety outcomes like accidents, adverse events, and unsafe behav-iors, on the other. More specifically, a meta-analysis of 82 studies carried out among nurses and physicians showed that both quality of care and patient safety decrease as burnout complaints of these health care providers increase (Salyers et al., 2017). Finally, a meta-analysis of

20 studies showed that burnout is negatively related to task perform-ance as well as contextual work performance (Swider & Zimmerman, 2010). Generally speaking, this association is rather weak with ρs between .20 and .35 depending on the burnout dimension, and appears to be somewhat stronger for other-rated performance compared to self-rated performance.

Correlates

Two kinds of correlates will be discussed below: sociobiographical characteristics (gender and age) and personality factors. These factors may have a direct impact on burnout as well as moderate the negative effect of job demands or a lack of resources on burnout. In the former case, they can be interpreted as personal vulnerability factors, whereas in the latter case they act as stress buffers. Finally, personality factors may also influence the way the job is perceived. For instance, optimists may perceive their jobs as less demanding than pessimists and may therefore less likely fall victim to burnout.

A meta-analysis including 183 studies shows that women feel slightly more exhausted, while men exhibit somewhat more mental distance (Purvanova, 2010). These differences are very small, though, with effect sizes lower than .20. Moderator analyses revealed that gender differences in the USA are larger as compared to Europe, but do not vary significantly in male- typed vs. female-typed occupations. Gender may also act as a moderator: work to nonwork conflict seems to have a stronger impact on women than on men (Reichl et al., 2014). Another meta-analysis covering 35 studies supported a negative cor-relation between age and burnout, meaning that older employees experience less burnout than younger employees (Brewer & Shapard, 2004). Also, a negative correlation was found between work experi-ence in a particular job and burnout; i.e., more seasoned employees experience less burnout. Associations with age and work experience are rather weak (r's < .20) and might reflect a heathy worker effect. Please note that the results of the Dutch and Swedish epidemiological studies discussed above agree with these meta-analyses.

The most important personality factors that are associated with burnout are shown in Table 8.3. Research has unequivocally shown that burnout is associated with all Big Five personality traits, except openness. A meta-analysis that includes 66 studies shows that

Table 8.3 *Main person factors*

Big Five personality traits	Emotional stability
	Extroversion
	Agreeableness
	Conscientiousness
Core self-evaluation	Self-efficacy
	Self-esteem
	Locus of control
Other personality traits	Positive and negative affectivity
	Hardiness
	Dispositional optimism
	Proactive personality
	Perfectionism

emotional stability and extroversion are moderately and negatively associated with burnout, followed by conscientiousness and agreeableness, which are somewhat less strongly and also negatively related with burnout (Swider & Zimmerman, 2010). This means that especially persons who are less emotionally stable, extroverted, conscientious, and agreeable are more likely to burn out. Overall, these four personality traits explain between 21% and 32% of the variance, depending on the burnout dimension. Finally, a path model was successfully tested in which burnout mediated the relationship between the Big Five personality traits and three outcomes (i.e., absenteeism, turnover, and job performance). Neuroticism and extroversion in particular were indirectly related to these outcomes via burnout.

It is not surprising that another meta-analysis that included 144 samples confirmed this picture because it is largely based on the same Big Five studies (Alarcon, 2009). However, this meta-analysis provides more detailed information about the unique contribution of each of the Big Five personality traits in explaining the variance of each burnout dimension separately. It appears that emotional stability has especially strong unique, negative relationships with emotional exhaustion and depersonalization, whereas extroversion has an especially strong unique negative relationship with lack of personal accomplishment.

The meta-analysis of Alarcon et al. (2009) also includes another set of personality traits known as core self-evaluation (CSE), which represents an individual's fundamental beliefs about competence and self-worth. This higher-order construct consists of four traits: self-esteem, self-efficacy, internal locus of control, and emotional stability. All components of CSE are negatively associated with burnout. Taken together, they explain 26%, 17%, and 30% of the variance in exhaustion, cynicism/depersonalization, and professional efficacy, respectively. Emotional stability explains most unique variance in exhaustion and cynicism/depersonalization, whereas self-efficacy explains most unique variance in professional efficacy.

According to the meta-analysis of Alarcon et al. (2009), four more specific personality characteristics are related to burnout. First, positive affectivity and negative affectivity, whereby the former refers to a general tendency to experience positive emotional states (i.e., happiness, excitement, and energy), whereas the latter is the tendency to experience negative emotional states (i.e., sadness, anxiety, and hostility). Not surprisingly, positive affectivity is moderately negatively related to burnout, and negative affectivity moderately positively. Second, hardiness reflects the extent to which a person is able to endure stressors without experiencing negative effects and includes three dimensions: control, challenge, and commitment. It appears that individuals who (1) tend to believe that they can control the events that happen to them; (2) perceive stressors as challenges rather than as threats; and (3) are committed to several life domains (e.g., family, friends, religion) are less likely to burn out. Third, dispositional optimism – the general tendency to believe that good things will occur in the future and that bad things will not occur – is moderately negatively related to burnout. Fourth, burnout is negatively associated with a proactive personality, which takes action, shows initiative, and perseveres. This meshes with the results of a meta-analysis of 36 studies that showed that active, problem-focused coping correlated negatively with all three dimensions of burnout (Shin et al., 2014).

Finally, according to a meta-analysis of 43 studies, burnout also appears to be related to perfectionism; more particularly, perfectionistic concerns but *not* perfectionistic strivings are positively related to burnout (Hill & Curran, 2016). The former refers to concerns over making mistakes, fear of negative social evaluation, and feelings of discrepancy between one's expectations and performance, whereas the latter refers to striving for perfection and the setting of very high personal performance standards.

Taken together, a more or less consistent pattern emerges of personality characteristics that can be considered as risk factors for burnout. It may not come as a surprise that emotional stability and (positive and negative) affectivity show the most consistent and strongest relationships with burnout, notably exhaustion. The reason is that neuroticism, affectivity, and burnout overlap, albeit burnout symptoms refer to *current* experiences, while emotional stability and affectivity refer to how someone *generally* feels.

Explanations

To date, a specific overall psychological theory that explains burnout does not exist. Instead, the picture is rather scattered when it comes to explaining the underlying psychological processes that play a role in burnout. Early explanations focused on the individual, interpersonal, or organization factors as the main causal agents (for an overview, see Schaufeli & Enzmann, 1998, pp. 100–142). But most of these theoretical explanations are speculative and lack sufficient empirical support. This section discusses three theoretical explanations that can draw on empirical evidence and in which emotional overload, lack of reciprocity, and emotional contagion play a key role, respectively. Two descriptive frameworks are considered that are helpful for integrating the results from burnout research discussed in the previous section.

Descriptive Models

Crawford et al. (2010) used the JD-R model for testing a meta-analytic model in which they differentiated between challenging and hindrance stressors. The former tend to be appraised as stressful demands that have the potential to promote mastery, personal growth, or future gain (e.g., high workload and time pressure). The latter tend to be appraised as stressful demands that have the potential to thwart personal growth, learning, and goal attainment (e.g., role conflict and work–nonwork conflict). Their results showed that, in addition to lack of resources, hindrance demands were more strongly related to burnout than challenge demands. In other words, it matters how demands are appraised; when this occurs in terms of situational constraints, this has a stronger negative impact on burnout than when this is done in terms of opportunities.

Another descriptive framework is the Six Areas of Working Life approach (Leiter & Maslach, 1999). Based on the person–environment fit-principle, this framework describes the interplay of stressors and resources in relation to burnout. As a result of maladjustment or adaption of the employee's needs and expectations, a stressful person–job incongruity develops in six critical areas of working life which may threaten well-being. These six areas are: workload, job control, community, reward, fairness, and values. When a mismatch in each of these areas occurs, burnout is likely to result; this is the case when the workload is too high, job control is lacking, the sense of community and fairness among employees is eroded, intrinsic and extrinsic rewards are poor, and personal values of employees do not correspond with those of the organization. A study among Spanish hospitality workers shows that together these six areas explained 23% of the variance in exhaustion, 8% in cynicism, and 18% in professional efficacy (Gascón et al., 2019). By far the most important area for exhaustion is workload, whereas community explains most variance in cynicism, community, and values in professional efficacy. Apparently, mismatches in different areas are associated with different aspects of burnout. Moreover, a German study among nurses suggests that these six mismatches constitute a more complex pattern (Brom et al., 2015). This study successfully tested a model in which reward, community, and fairness mediated the relationship between control and values, and values, in turn, was associated with burnout. Hence, control and values play a crucial role as antecedent and mediator, respectively. In addition, it was found that workload mediated the relationship between control and exhaustion, thus emphasizing the key role of exhaustion in the development of burnout.

Emotional Overload

According to Maslach (1993), interpersonal demands resulting from the helping relationship are considered to be the root cause of burnout. Please note that initially burnout was restricted to human services professions in which this helping relationship is pivotal. Maslach (1993) argued that contacts with service recipients are, by their very nature, emotionally charged because human services professionals deal with troubled people who are in need. In addition, human service workers often experience emotional dissonance that may lead to emotional exhaustion (Kenworthy et al., 2014). In order to deal with emotional demands at work and avoid emotional exhaustion, human service workers detach themselves from their recipients. When they are treated in a more remote, objective way, it is easier to do one's job without psychological discomfort. A functional way is to develop an attitude of detached concern, the ideal blending of compassion with emotional distance. However, detached concern may turn into dysfunctional depersonalization: that is, a persistent callous, indifferent, and cynical attitude. As a result of depersonalization, performance and service quality are likely to deteriorate because the major vehicle for occupational success – compassion with and concern for others – has been destroyed in an attempt to protect one's psychological integrity. So, due to depersonalization, successes at work diminish so that the professional's sense of personal accomplishment erodes and feelings of insufficiency and self-doubt develop.

Based on the theoretical approach of Maslach, Leiter (1993) conducted a series of studies among health care workers in which he distinguished quantitative job demands (e.g., work overload, hassles), qualitative job demands (e.g., interpersonal conflict), and lack of resources (e.g., lack of social support, poor patient cooperation, lack of autonomy, and poor participation in decision making). Both types of demands were expected to be related with emotional exhaustion, whereas lacking resources was expected to be related with depersonalization and lack of personal accomplishment. Indeed, these hypothesized relationships were observed in Leiter's (1993) mixed sequential and parallel development model of burnout. As expected, this model found that emotional exhaustion leads to depersonalization, but contrary to expectations, reduced personal accomplishment seems to develop rather independently from both other burnout dimensions. Based on meta-analytic data, Swider and Zimmerman (2010) confirmed the sequence of the three burnout dimensions as hypothesized by Maslach, at least as far as the prediction of job performance is concerned. When other outcomes such as absenteeism and turnover were used, a different sequence emerged (reduced accomplishment → depersonalization → exhaustion and exhaustion → reduced accomplishment → depersonalization, respectively). It should be noted that Maslach's reasoning primarily pertained to job performance and not to absenteeism or turnover, which can be seen as withdrawal behaviors.

Although Maslach's (1993) explanation, in which emotional over-load plays a key role as a root cause of burnout, originally focused on human professionals, the same logic may be applied for explaining burnout in other job contexts (Maslach et al., 2001). Accordingly, exhaustion develops primarily in reaction to job demands, including interpersonal demands, and to a somewhat lesser extend in reaction to lack of resources. This concurs with the results of various meta-analyses that have been discussed in the previous section. As a means of self-protection, mental distancing develops not only from the people one is working with but also from the job as a whole. In turn, this mental distancing undermines the employee's capacity to perform, leading to a feeling of reduced professional efficacy.

Lack of Reciprocity

Although emotionally demanding interpersonal relationships may be seen as the root cause of burnout, it is not clear *why* these relationships are so stressful. As Buunk and Schaufeli (1993) have pointed out, lack of reciprocity – an unbalanced relationship between service provider and recipient – drains the professionals' emotional resources and even-tually leads to emotional exhaustion. By definition, relationships with service recipients are complementary; service workers are assumed to 'give', whereas patients, clients, students, and customers – in short recipients – 'receive' care, assistance, education, counseling, advise, support, and so on. Yet, service workers expect 'rewards' in return for their efforts, like gratitude, recognition, appreciation, respect, improvement, or perhaps just a smile. But often such expectations are not fulfilled so that, over time, a lack of reciprocity develops: professionals feel that they continuously put much more in relation-ships with their recipients than they receive back in return. As Buunk and Schaufeli (1993) argued, this is typically dealt with by decreasing one's investments in relationships with others; that is, by responding to recipients in a callous, depersonalized way instead of expressing genu-ine empathic concern. From a social exchange perspective, depersonal-ization – or cynicism, for that matter – may be regarded as a way of restoring reciprocity by withdrawing psychologically. However, as was outlined above, this dysfunctional way of coping fosters a sense of diminished professional efficacy.

Indeed, positive relationships were found between lack of reciprocity at the interpersonal level and all three dimensions of burnout among various service professionals, such as nurses, physicians, teachers, police officers, and correctional officers (for an overview, see Schaufeli, 2006). Moreover, there is some longitudinal evidence for a curvilinear relationship between lack of reciprocity and emotional exhaustion: feeling more deprived as well as feeling more advantaged may result in higher levels of exhaustion (Van Dierendonck et al., 2001). Another longitudinal study showed that depersonalizing patients at Time 1 increases the likelihood of feeling harassed by them five years later, which, in turn, fostered a lack of reciprocity, eventually leading to burnout (Bakker et al., 2000). Thus, a lack of reciprocity in interpersonal relationships at work seems to play an important role in the development of burnout.

Similar social exchange processes also govern the relationships of employees with their teams and the organization. Employees have a so-called psychological contract with the organization they work for which entails expectations about the nature of the exchange with that organization (Rousseau, 2011). Expectations concern concrete issues such as an acceptable workload and career advancement, as well as less tangible matters such as esteem and dignity at work and support from supervisors and colleagues. In other words, the psychological contract reflects the employees' subjective notion of reciprocity, whereby the expected gains or outcomes from the team and the organization are expected to be proportional to the investments or inputs. When the psychological contract is violated because experience does not match expectancies, reciprocity is corroded. A series of studies among nurses, medical specialists, psychotherapists, teachers, and bus drivers showed that in addition to burnout, violation of the psychological contract may also lead to withdrawal from the team (e.g., reduced involvement, social isolation) and the organization (e.g., reduced organizational commitment and sickness absence) (for an overview, see Schaufeli, 2006).

So, taken together, it seems that a disturbed balance of give and take at the interpersonal, team, and organizational levels plays a major role in the development of burnout. This may lead not only to exhaustion and mental distancing (i.e., burnout) but also to withdrawal from the team and the organization.

Emotional Contagion

It has been suggested that colleagues may act as role models whose symptoms are imitated through a process of emotional contagion (Hatfield et al., 1993). That is, individuals under stress may perceive symptoms of burnout in their colleagues and automatically take on these symptoms. In addition to this nonconscious emotional contagion, an alternative pathway may exist through which people may catch the emotions of others (Bakker et al., 2006). Namely, contagion may also occur through a conscious cognitive process by 'tuning in' to the emotions of others. This is the case when an individual shows empathic concern and tries to imagine how they would feel in the position of another and, as a consequence, experiences the same feelings.

The contagious nature of burnout was demonstrated in nearly 80 European Intensive Care Units (Bakker et al., 2005). It was observed that burnout tends to cluster in particular units, whereas it is virtually absent in others – also after controlling for job autonomy and subjective and objectively assessed workload. Moreover, as expected, nurses from units in which burnout clusters observe more burnout complaints among their colleagues then their fellow nurses do in the other units. In a similar vein, it was found among professionals who work with homeless people that emotional contagion is directly as well as indirectly – through communicative responsiveness – related to burnout (Miller et al., 1995). Another study (Bakker et al., 2001) shows that general practitioners who perceive burnout complaints among their colleagues reported higher levels of burnout than those who did not perceive such complaints. In addition, individual susceptibility to emotional contagion is positively related to burnout, particularly in combination with the perception of burnout symptoms in their colleagues. That is, doctors who perceive burnout complaints among colleagues *and* who are susceptible to emotional contagion report the highest exhaustion scores. Instead of using peer ratings of other's levels of burnout as in the previous studies, Meredith et al. (2020) used social network analysis to study burnout contagion among teachers. Their results show that social interactions between teachers act as conduits for burnout contagion, particularly when: (1) teachers have frequent contact; (2) they are reciprocally and strongly tied to each other; and (3) their interactions are instrumental (i.e., aimed at achieving work-related goals) as well as expressive (i.e., include a strong affective,

emotional component). Moreover, it appears that these three characteristics of teachers' social interactions predict their levels of emotional
exhaustion (but not depersonalization and reduced professional efficacy) two years later. Hence, it seems that specific characteristics of
social relationships matter as they relate to the strength of the burnout
contagion process.

In summary, these three psychological explanations are, in a way,
complementary. The first approach assumes that burnout results from
emotionally charged relationships between service providers and
recipients and stipulates a dynamic process in which depersonalization
is considered to be a dysfunctional attempt to deal with feelings of
emotional exhaustion. However, it remains unclear why this relationship is so demanding. This is where the second approach kicks in by
emphasizing that this relationship may be characterized by a lack of
reciprocity. This lack of reciprocity, which may exist in not only
interpersonal relationships with recipients but also the relationship
with the team and with organization, lies at the core of the burnout
syndrome. This is also recognized by the heuristic Six Areas of
Working Life approach, three of which (i.e., reward, fairness, and
values) have to do with reciprocity, in one way or another. It appears
that the balance between give and take at various levels is crucial for
the development of burnout. Finally, once burnout has occurred
among individual team members, a group-based process of emotional
contagion seems to play a role in spreading it amongst other team
members.

Interventions

A curious discrepancy exists regarding interventions to reduce burnout. On the one hand, a true burnout industry has emerged over the
years with countless providers of just as many different, sometimes
even very exotic, interventions. Yet, on the other hand, relatively few
solid, well-designed studies on their effectiveness have been carried out.
Based on the systematic reviews and meta-analyses discussed below, it
is estimated that only .004% of all publications evaluate the effectiveness of burnout interventions.

In principle, burnout interventions may target either the individual
or the organization. Most interventions, by far, focus on the individual, probably because organizational interventions are more difficult to

244 Wilmar Schaufeli

implement as they may interfere with work and interpersonal processes at the shop floor. Examples of individual approaches are cognitive-behavioral interventions (e.g., stress inoculation training, rational emotive therapy), time-management training, and relaxation, mindfulness, and interpersonal skills training, whereas examples of organizational interventions include the introduction of new human resources (HR) practices, job redesign (e.g., task restructuring), time rescheduling, and management development (for more detailed descriptions, see Schaufeli & Enzmann, 1998, pp. 143–183).

The picture that emerges from various meta-analyses is rather unambiguous and consistent: burnout interventions have a statistically significant, small positive effect with effect sizes (Cohen's d about .20) This is illustrated by a meta-analysis of 47 controlled studies among different occupational groups, of which 96% focus on individual interventions (Marțicuroiu, 2014). Results show significant but small effects on general burnout (Cohen's d = .22) and exhaustion (d = .17), but *not* on cynicism/depersonalization (d = .04) or reduced professional efficacy (d = −.02). The strongest positive effect is found for relaxation, followed by learning new role behavior and cognitive-behavioral interventions, respectively.

More or less similar results are obtained by various meta-analyses that focused on specific occupational groups. For instance, a meta-analysis of 23 controlled intervention studies among teachers (Iancu et al., 2018) shows small yet statistically significant positive effects on overall burnout (d = .18), exhaustion (d = .18), and reduced efficacy (d = .14), but *not* on depersonalization (d = .03). The strongest effects are found for cognitive–behavioral approaches, mindfulness and stimulating professional development, and, to a somewhat lesser extent, learning how to organize social support. A meta-analysis of 27 controlled intervention studies among mental health professionals performed by Dreison et al. (2018) shows small, positive effects on overall burnout (Hedges' g = .13), exhaustion (g = .20), and depersonalization (g = .15), but *not* on reduced efficacy (g = .08). Subsequent moderator analyses shows that the effect of person-oriented interventions is stronger than that of organization-oriented interventions.

Physicians are the most often studied occupational group. A meta-analysis identified 15 randomized clinical trials (RCTs) and 37 controlled cohort studies carried out among physicians and find significant intervention effects on overall burnout, emotional exhaustion, and depersonalization, with absolute symptom levels decreasing on average 10%, 14%, and 4%, respectively (West et al., 2016). Lack of efficacy is not considered in this study. Most interventions focus on individual physicians (e.g., mindfulness, stress management and self-care training, communication skills training). Another meta-analysis including 20 interventions analyzed interventions to reduce physician burnout (Panagioti et al., 2017). The database of this analysis partly overlapped with the previous meta-analysis but only focused on emotional exhaustion, and, most importantly, additional subgroup analyses were carried out. First, and not surprising, a small but significant positive intervention effect was found (d = .29). Second, this effect appeared to be stronger for organization-oriented interventions (d = .45), such as rescheduling hourly shifts, reducing workload, discussion meetings to enhance teamwork, leadership, and structural changes than for physician-oriented interventions (d = .18), such as mindfulness, stress reduction techniques, exercise, and educational interventions targeting physicians' self-confidence and communication skills. Third, no difference in effectiveness of interventions was shown for more vs. less experienced physicians or for those working in primary vs. secondary care settings.

Typically, all meta-analyses discussed above include *preventive* interventions among those without or with mild burnout complaints who are still working. But what about the effectiveness of treating those with severe burnout symptoms? Ahola et al. (2017) identified 18 studies, of which four were RCTs, that evaluated the effectiveness of burnout treatment programs. Mostly this involved individual cognitive–behavioral therapy, but also group interventions based on psycho- and sociodrama methods. Unfortunately, their meta-analysis did *not* show a significant decrease in burnout complaints across the intervention groups compared to the waitlist control groups. A disappointing result indeed, in terms of both the number of studies and their effect. A Swedish follow-up study showed that seven years after burnout treatment finished, only 16% fully recovered, whereas 73% reported reduced stress tolerance, 46% extreme fatigue, and 43% problems with memory (Glise et al., 2020). So, it seems that residual symptoms are very persistent in burnout disorder.

In addition to symptom reduction, return to work is another important outcome of burnout interventions. Although both are related, they do not completely overlap. For instance, even if burnout symptoms have not completely disappeared, gradual return to work is possible. Indeed, modern disability management approaches assume that return to work fosters symptom reduction (Waddell & Burton, 2006). This view contradicts the traditional approach, in which return to work should only be considered after all symptoms have disappeared.

How effective are interventions that foster return to work after burnout? A meta-analysis of eight interventions that are targeted at return to work among those with clinically significant burnout do *not* find significant results compared to a waitlist control group (Perski et al., 2017). The extent to which burned-out employees fully returned to work does *not* differ whether they had received treatment, were on the waiting list, or received 'treatment as usual'. However, compared to the control group, the intervention group returns to work *partially* more quickly. Remarkably, burnout, anxiety, and depression symptoms do *not* decrease significantly as a result of return-to-work interventions. So, despite the fact that symptom levels do not decrease, interventions lead to faster *partial* but not full return to work. This illustrates that symptom reduction and return to work are indeed two relatively independent outcomes.

In conclusion, it seems that burnout symptoms can be decreased, particularly as a result of person-oriented interventions, such as relaxation, mindfulness, and cognitive–behavioral approaches. This is most convincingly shown for general burnout and exhaustion, and less so for cynicism/depersonalization and personal efficacy. This pattern is similar across various occupational groups, such as teachers, mental health care workers, and physicians. One meta-analysis found that organization-oriented interventions were more effective than interventions that were targeted to individual physicians. It is important to note that these positive intervention effects apply to those with relatively mild complaints. It seems that interventions for those with severe burnout symptoms are less effective, though. In addition to symptom reduction, some interventions also explicitly aim to foster return to work. These interventions are partly successful because they lead to partial work resumption but not to symptom reduction or full work resumption.

Conclusions and Outlook

Burnout – a metaphor that refers to a severe loss of mental energy – can be seen as a modern affliction that emerged in the 1970s due the transformation from an industrial into a postindustrial society. In a way, this parallels the rise of neurasthenia – a syndrome akin to burnout – at the end of the 19th century when the agricultural society transformed into an industrial society. Originally, it seemed that burnout occurred exclusively among human services professionals who work with other people, but this resulted from the fact that the questionnaire for measuring burnout was designed to be used in this occupational group only. Once a general version of the MBI – the leading questionnaire that serves as the gold standard to assess burnout – was developed, burnout was also observed in other occupational groups. The MBI, which boasts good psychometric qualities, has been challenged by other questionnaires that reduce burnout to mere exhaustion. However, this boils down to throwing the baby out with the bath water because it denies the specificity of burnout. After all, conceptually speaking, burnout is a chronic, work-related state of fatigue that is characterized by the inability and the unwillingness to spend effort, representing its energetic and motivational component, respectively. Hence, inability (exhaustion) and unwillingness (mental distancing) are two sides of the same burnout coin.

Throughout this chapter, it became clear that mild burnout symptoms have to be distinguished from severe symptoms that are indicative for a burnout disorder. On the one hand, burnout may be considered a multidimensional phenomenon that can be measured using continuous scales, while on the other hand, it may also be considered dichotomously in terms of a diagnosis that is based on a clinical interview. Typically, most psychological research focuses on mild burnout symptoms – as assessed by self-reports – among those who are working. This means that our current knowledge of burnout is mainly based on workers with mild symptom levels. This knowledge can be used to prevent the development of burnout. Indeed, various successful interventions have been developed, at both the individual and the organizational level. In contrast, research among those who suffer from severe burnout and therefore dropped out of work is relatively scarce. Hence, more research is needed on severe burnout. An important prerequisite is that agreement exists about the diagnostic guidelines for burnout disorder that goes beyond the mere description that is included in the ICD-11, which is essentially based on the original definition of Maslach and Jackson (1981). In order to boost research on severe burnout, clinically validated cut-off values should be available, as for instance, in the BAT; Schaufeli et al., 2020b).

Unfortunately, our current knowledge on the prevalence of burnout is rather limited because proper epidemiological studies are lacking. It seems that about 15% of the working population shows elevated levels of exhaustion. But, as was noticed above, burnout goes beyond mere exhaustion. Estimates of burnout prevalence in various occupational groups vary for 0% to almost 90%, which, of course, is rather uninformative (see 'Prevalence'). The reason for this exceptionally wide range is that virtually all studies use neither representative samples nor validated cut-off values so that results cannot be compared. Representativity and the use of similar, valid cut-offs are necessary for a reliable estimation of the prevalence of burnout. Unfortunately, the MBI cannot be used for epidemiological research because it was not designed for that purpose; it yields three scores that should not be combined into a single, overall burnout score (Maslach et al., 2017). In addition, the MBI lacks validated cut-off scores to discriminate between burnout 'cases' and 'noncases'. Although the MBI can be used to separately assess and compare mean levels of exhaustion, cynicism/depersonalization, and reduced efficacy between groups, it cannot establish level of burnout as such. This points to a fundamental ambiguity of the MBI: burnout is defined as a 'syndrome', yet only its components can be measured separately. The recently developed BAT overcomes this problem as it produces a single burnout score (Hadzibajramovic et al., 2020).

A host of potential antecedents, consequences, and correlates of burnout has been uncovered (see 'Interventions'), but it also appears that the idea that burnout mediates the effects of unfavorable job characteristics on negative personal and organizational outcomes is an oversimplification. Instead, it seems that reciprocal causation plays a role as well. For instance, particular job demands, such as work overload, may act as not only antecedents but also consequences of burnout, thus pointing at a dynamic and bidirectional rather than a one-directional process. To further complicate the picture, person characteristics may play a moderating role in this process, for instance by buffering or exacerbating the negative impact of job characteristics on burnout. Taken together, it seems that the burnout process is dynamic and rather complex. Although the different elements of that process have been identified (job demands, lacking job resources, person factors, individual and organizational outcomes), future research should uncover how these elements are linked and how the process unfolds across time.

It seems that, unfortunately, the quest for biomarkers that can be linked to burnout has been in vain so far. Perhaps this might be due to a lack of sensitivity of the physiological measures applied or to poor sampling of burnout cases, so that it makes sense to continue research in this area with better measures and samples (Danhof-Pont et al., 2011). But it might also be that we are simply on the wrong track by studying peripheral biomarkers and a better way forward would be to explore other biological pathways, such as brain activity or epigenetics. For instance, Van Luijtelaar et al. (2010) found different electrophysiological brain activity in burnout patients compared to health controls that also differs from patterns found in the literature for depression and chronic fatigue syndrome. Moreover, it is found that burnout severity of medical professionals can be explained by reduced empathy-related brain activity (Tei et al., 2014) and that burnout severity is related to epigenetic changes (Bakusic et al., 2020). Hence, it seems worthwhile to further explore these avenues.

As far as the psychological explanations for burnout are concerned, the picture is somewhat scattered. No overarching burnout theory exists and probably never will, given the complexity of the phenomenon. However, two handy heuristic frameworks exist that allow for the integration of most burnout research; the Job-Demands Resources model and the Six Areas of Working Life approach (see 'Explanations'). Although useful for practitioners who look for possible drivers of burnout, these frameworks do not explain the underlying psychological mechanisms of burnout. Three theoretical approaches supported by empirical evidence have been discussed in 'Explanations', in which emotional overload, lack of reciprocity in social exchange relations, and emotional contagion play a key role. However important these processes may be, given the nature of burnout as energetic and motivational dysfunction, it makes sense to also consider theories of work effort (Hockey, 2013) and motivation, such as conservation of resources theory (Hobfoll, 2011) or self-determination theory (Deci & Ryan, 2012), for explaining burnout.

There is considerable empirical evidence for the effectiveness of burnout interventions, at the individual as well as the organizational level. Although the effects are small, they are consistent across various occupational groups and work settings and are relevant for preventing burnout. However, most interventions are targeted at the individual and carried out among relatively healthy workers with only mild burnout symptoms. Research on organizational interventions is scarce, as is research on the effectiveness of interventions for severe burnout. Clearly, more intervention studies are needed, particularly focusing on the organization and on those with severe burnout.

So, taken together, in order to increase our understanding of burnout, future research should focus on (1) severe burnout, using clinical interviews as well as clinically validated cut-offs; (2) the prevalence of burnout across various occupational groups, industries, and countries; (3) the dynamic nature of burnout and its development across time; (4) alternative biological pathways that go beyond peripheral biomarkers; (5) explanatory frameworks using theories on work effort and motivation; and (6) burnout interventions, particularly regarding severe burnout. Burnout is here to stay, as is burnout research.

References

Adriaenssens, J., De Gucht, V., & Maes, S. (2015). Determinants and prevalence of burnout in emergency nurses: A systematic review of 25 years of research. *International Journal of Nursing Studies*, 52, 649–661.

Ahola K., Gould R., Virtanen M., Honkonen T., Aromaa A., & Lönnqvist J. (2009). Occupational burnout as a predictor of disability pension: A population-based cohort study. *Occupational and Environmental Medicine*, 66, 84–90.

Ahola, K., Toppinen-Tanner, S., & Seppänen, J. (2017). Interventions to alleviate burnout symptoms and to support return to work among employees with burnout: Systematic review and meta-analysis. *Burnout Research*, 4, 1–11.

Ahola K., Väänänen A., Koskinen A., Kouvonen A., & Shirom A. (2010). Burnout as a predictor of all-cause mortality among industrial employees: A 10-year prospective register-linkage study. *Journal of Psychosomatic Research*, 69, 51–57.

Aiken, L. H., Clarke, S. P., Sloane, D. M., Sochalski, J., & Silber, J. H. (2002). Hospital nurse staffing and patient mortality, nurse burnout, and job dissatisfaction. *Journal of the American Medical Association*, *288*, 1987–1993.

Alarcon, G. M. (2011). A meta-analysis of burnout with job demands, resources, and attitudes. *Journal of Vocational Behavior*, *79*, 549–562.

Alarcon, G., Eschleman, K. J., & Bowling, N. A. (2009). Relationships between personality variables and burnout: A meta-analysis. *Work & Stress*, *23*, 244–263.

Arnold, K. A. (2017). Transformational leadership and employee psychological well-being: A review and directions for future research. *Journal of Occupational Health Psychology*, *22*, 381–393.

Aronsson, G., Theorell, T., Grape, T., Hammerström, A., Hogstedt, C., Marteinsdottir, I., Skoog, I., Träskman-Bendz, L., & Hall, C. (2017). A systematic review including meta-analysis of work environment and burnout symptoms. *BMC Public Health*, *17*, 2642–77.

Bakker, A. B., & Demerouti, E. (2016). Job Demands-Resources Theory: Taking stock and looking forward. *Journal of Occupational Health Psychology*, *22*, 273–285.

Bakker, A. B., Le Blanc, P. M., & Schaufeli, W. B. (2005). Burnout contagion among intensive care nurses. *Journal of Advanced Nursing*, *51*, 276–287.

Bakker, A. B., Schaufeli, W. B., Demerouti, E., & Euwema, M. C. (2006). An organizational and social psychological perspective on burnout and work engagement. In M. Hewstone, H. Schut, J. de Wit, K. Van den Bos, & M. Stroebe (Eds.), *The scope of social psychology: Theory and applications* (pp. 229–252). Psychology Press.

Bakker, A. B., Schaufeli, W. B., Sixma, H., & Bosveld, W. (2001). Burnout contagion among general practitioners. *Journal of Social and Clinical Psychology*, *20*, 82–98.

Bakker, A., Schaufeli, W. B., Sixma, H. J., Bosveld, W., & Van Dierendonck, D. (2000). Patient demands, lack of reciprocity, and burnout: A five-year longitudinal study among general practitioners. *Journal of Organizational Behavior*, *21*, 425–441.

Bakusic, J., Manosij, G., Polli, A., Bekaert, B., Schaufeli, W. B., Claes, S., & Godderis, L. (2020). Epigenetic perspective on the role of brain-derived neurotrophic factor in burnout. *Translational Psychiatry*, *10*, 354. https://doi.org/10.1038/s41398-020-01037-4

Besèr, A., Sorjonen, K., Wahlberg, K., Peterson, U., Nygren, Å., & Åsberg, M. (2014). Construction and evaluation of a self-rating scale for stress-induced Exhaustion Disorder, the Karolinska Exhaustion Disorder Scale. *Scandinavian Journal of Psychology*, *55*, 72–82.

Bianchi, R., Schonfeld, I. S., & Laurent, E. (2015). Burnout–depression overlap: A review. *Clinical Psychology Review*, *36*, 28–41.

Boudreau, R. A., Boudreau, W. F., & Mauthe-Kaddoura, A. J. (2015). *From 57 for 57: A bibliography of burnout citations.* Poster presented at the 17th Conference of the European Association of Work and Organizational Psychology (EAWOP), Oslo, Norway.

Brewer, E. W., & Shapard, L. (2004). Employee burnout: A meta-analysis of the relationship between age or years of experience. *Human Resource Development Review, 3,* 102–123.

Brom, S. S., Buruck, G., Horváth, I., Richter, P., & Leiter, M. P. (2015). Areas of worklife as predictors of occupational health – A validation study in two German samples. *Burnout Research, 2,* 60–70.

Buunk, A. P., & Schaufeli, W. B. (1993). Burnout from a social comparison perspective. In W. B. Schaufeli, C. Maslach, & T. Marek (Eds.). *Professional burnout: Recent developments in theory and research* (pp. 53–69). Taylor & Francis.

Cherniss, C. (1980). *Professional burnout in human services organizations.* Praeger.

Crawford, E. R., LePine, J. A., & Rich, B. L. (2010). Linking job demands and resources to employee engagement and burnout: A theoretical extension and meta-analytic test. *Journal of Applied Psychology, 95,* 834–848.

Danhof-Pont, M. B., Van Veen, T., & Zitman, F. G. (2011). Biomarkers in burnout: A systematic review. *Journal of Psychosomatic Research, 70,* 505–524.

De Beer, L. T., Schaufeli, W. B., De Witte, H., Hakanen, J., Shimazu, A., Glaser, J., Seubert, C., Bosak, J., Sinval, J., & Rudnev, M. (2020). Measurement invariance of the Burnout Assessment Tool (BAT) across seven cross-national representative samples. *International Journal of Environmental Research and Public Health, 17,* 4604. https://doi.org/10.3390/ijerph17155604

Deci, E. L., & Ryan, R. M. (2012). Self-determination theory. In P. A. M. Van Lange, A. W. Kruglanski, & E. T. Higgins (Eds.), *Handbook of theories of social psychology* (pp. 416–436). Sage.

Demerouti, E., Bakker, A. B., Vardakou, I., & Kantas, A. (2003). The convergent validity of two burnout instruments. *European Journal of Psychological Assessment, 18,* 296–307.

Dreison, K. C., Luther, L., Bonfils, K. A., Sliter, M. T., McGrew, J. H., & Salyers, M. P. (2018). Job burnout in mental health providers: A meta-analysis of 35 years of intervention. *Journal of Occupational Health Psychology, 23,* 18–30.

Edelwich, J., & Brodsky, A. (1980). *Burn-out: Stages of disillusionment in the helping professions.* Human Sciences Press.

Farber, B. A. (1983). Introduction: A critical perspective on burnout. In B. A. Farber (Ed.), *Stress and burnout in the human services professions* (pp. 1–20). Pergamon.

Freudenberger, H. J. (1974). Staff burnout. *Journal of Social Issues*, *30*, 59–65.

Gascón, S., Masluk, B., Montero-Marin, J., Leiter, M. P., Herrera, P., & Albesa, A. (2019). Areas of work-life in Spanish hostelry professionals: Explanatory power on burnout dimensions. *Health and Quality of Life Outcomes*, *17*, 1–11.

Glise, K., Wiegner, L., & Jonsdottir, I. H. (2020). Long-term follow-up of residual symptoms in patients treated for stress-related exhaustion. *BMC Psychology*, *8*, 26. https://doi.org/10.1186/s40359-020-0395-8

Guthier, C., Dormann, C., & Voelkle, M. C. (2020). Reciprocal effects between job stressors and burnout: A continuous time meta-analysis of longitudinal studies. *Psychological Bulletin.* https://doi.org/10.1037/bul0000304

Hadzibajramovic, E., Schaufeli, W. B., & De Witte, H. (2020). A Rasch analysis of the Burnout Assessment Tool. *PLoS ONE*, *15*(11): e0242241. https://doi.org/10.1371

Hakanen, J. J., & Schaufeli, W. B. (2012). Do burnout and work engagement predict depressive symptoms and life satisfaction? A three-wave seven-year prospective study. *Journal of Affective Disorders*, *141*, 415–424.

Hakanen, J. J., Peeters, M. C. W., & Schaufeli, W. B. (2018). Different types of employee wellbeing across time and their relationships with job crafting. *Journal of Occupational Health Psychology*, *23*, 289–301.

Halbesleben, J. R. B., & Buckley, M. R. (2004). Burnout in organizational life. *Journal of Management*, *30*, 859–879.

Halbesleben, J. R. B., & Demerouti, E. (2005). The construct validity of an alternative measure of burnout: Investigating the English translation of the Oldenburg Burnout Inventory. *Work and Stress*, *19*, 208–220.

Hasselberg, K., Jonsdottir, I. H., Ellbin, S., & Skagert, K. (2014). Self-reported stressors among patients with Exhaustion Disorder: An exploratory study of patient records. *BMC Psychiatry*, *14*, 66. https://doi.org/10.1186/1471-244X-14-66

Hatfield, E., Cacioppo, J. T., & Rapson, R. L. (1993). *Emotional contagion.* Cambridge University Press.

Heinemann, L. V., & Heinemann, T. (2017). Burnout research: Emergence and scientific investigation of a contested diagnosis. *SAGE Open*, *7*(1). https://doi.org/10.1177/2158244017697154

Hill, A. P., & Curran, Th. (2016). Multidimensional perfectionism and burnout: A meta-analysis. *Personality and Social Psychology Review*, 20, 269–288.

Hobfoll, S. E. (2011). Conservation of resources theory: Its implication for stress, health, and resilience. In S. Folkman (Ed.), *The Oxford handbook of stress, health, and coping* (pp. 127–147). Oxford University Press.

Hockey, G. R. J. H. (2013). *The psychology of work fatigue: Work, effort and control.* Blackwell.

Houtman, I. (2020). De epidemiologie van werkgerelateerde psychische aandoeningen en klachten [The epidemiology of work related mental disorders and complaints]. In W. B. Schaufeli & A. B. Bakker (Eds.), *De psychologie van arbeid en gezondheid* [*Occupational health psychology*] (pp. 259–278). Bohn Stafleu van Loghum.

Iancu, A. E., Rusu, A., Mǎroiu, C., Pǎcurar, R., & Maricuţoiu, L. P. (2018). The effectiveness of interventions aimed at reducing teacher burnout: A meta-analysis. *Educational Psychology Review*, 30, 373–396.

Jonsdottir, I. H., & Dahlman, A. S. (2019). Mechanisms in endocrinology: Endocrine and immunological aspects of burnout: A narrative review. *European Journal of Endocrinology*, 180, 147–158.

Kenworthy, J., Fay, C., Frame, M., & Petree, R. (2014). A meta-analytic review of the relationship between emotional dissonance and emotional exhaustion. *Journal of Applied Social Psychology*, 44, 94–105.

Kim, H. J., Shin, K. H., & Swanger, N. (2009). Burnout and engagement: A comparative analysis using the Big Five personality dimensions. *International Journal of Hospitality Management*, 28, 96–104.

Koutsimani, P., Montgomery, A., & Georganta, K. (2019). The relationship between burnout, depression, and anxiety: A systematic review and meta-analysis. *Frontiers in Psychology*, 10, 1–19.

Kristensen, T. S., Borritz, M., Villadsen, E., & Christensen, K. B. (2005). The Copenhagen Burnout Inventory: A new tool for the assessment of burnout. *Work and Stress*, 19, 92–207.

Kulkarni, G. K. (2006). Burnout (Editorial). *Indian Journal of Occupational and Environmental Medicine*, 10, 3–4.

Lasch, C. (1979). *The culture of narcissism: American life in an age of diminishing returns.* Norton.

Lastovkova, A., Carder, M., Rasmussen, H. M., Sjoberg, L., Groene, G. J., Sauni, R., Vevoda, J., Vevodoca, S., Lasfargues, G., Svartengren, M., Varga, M., Colosio, C., & Pelclova, D. (2018). Burnout syndrome as an occupational disease in the European Union: An exploratory study. *Industrial Health*, 56, 160–165.

Leiter, M. P., & Maslach, C. (1999). Six areas of worklife: A model of the organizational context of burnout. *Journal of Health and Human Services Administration, 21*, 472–489.

Lesener, T., Gusy, B., & Wolter, C. (2019). The job demands-resources model: A meta-analytic review of longitudinal studies. *Work and Stress, 33*, 76–103.

van Luijtelaar, G., Verbraak, M., van den Bunt, M., Keijsers, G., & Arns, M. (2010). EEG findings in burnout patients. *The Journal of Neuropsychiatry and Clinical Neurosciences, 22*, 208–217.

Maricuțoiu, L. P., Sava, F. A., & Butta, O. (2014). The effectiveness of controlled interventions on employees' burnout: A meta-analysis. *Journal of Occupational and Organizational Psychology, 89*, 1–27.

Maslach, C. (1976). Burned-out. *Human Behavior, 9*, 16–22.

  (1993). Burnout: A multidimensional perspective. In W. B. Schaufeli, C. Maslach, & T. Marek (Eds.), *Professional burnout: Recent developments in theory and research* (pp. 19–32). Taylor & Francis.

Maslach, C., & Jackson, S. E. (1981). The measurement of experienced burnout. *Journal of Occupational Behavior, 2*, 99–113.

  (1986). *Maslach Burnout Inventory Manual* (2nd ed.). Consulting Psychologists Press.

Maslach, C., Jackson, S. E., & Leiter, M. P. (1996). *Maslach Burnout Inventory Manual* (3rd ed.). Consulting Psychologists Press.

Maslach, C., & Leiter, M. P. (1993). Burnout: A multidimensional perspective. In W. B. Schaufeli, C. Maslach, & T. Marek (Eds.), *Professional burnout: Recent developments in theory and research* (pp. 19–32). Taylor & Francis.

Maslach, Ch., Leiter, M. P., & Jackson, S. (2017). *Maslach Burnout Inventory Manual* (4th ed.). Mind Garden.

Maslach, C., Schaufeli, W. B., & Leiter, M. P. (2001). Job burnout. *Annual Review of Psychology, 52*, 397–422.

Meredith, C., Schaufeli, W. B., Struyve, C., Vandecandelaere, M., Gielen, S., & Kyndt, E. (2020). 'Burnout contagion' among teachers: A social network approach. *Journal of Occupational and Organizational Psychology, 93*, 328–352.

Miller, K., Birkholt, M., Scott, C., & Srage, C. (1995). Empathy and burnout in human service work: An extension of a communication model. *Communication Research, 22*, 123–147.

Nahrgang, J. D., Morgeson, F. P., & Hofmann, D. (2011). Safety at work: A meta-analytic investigation of the link between job demands, job resources, burnout, engagement, and safety outcomes. *Journal of Applied Psychology, 96*, 71–94.

Neveux, J. P. (2007). Jailed resources: Conservation of resources as applied to burnout among prison guards. *Journal of Organizational Psychology, 28*, 21–42.

Norlund, S., Reuterwall, C., Höög, J., Lindahl, B., Janlert, U., & Birgander, L. S. (2010). Burnout, working conditions and gender: Results from the northern Sweden MONICA Study. *BMC Public Health, 10*. https://doi .org/10.1186/1471-2458-10-326

Panagioti, M., Panagopoulou, E., Bower, P., Lewith, G., Kontopantelis, E., Chew-Graham, C., Dawson, S., van Marwijk, H., Geraghty, K., & Esmail, A. (2017). Controlled interventions to reduce burnout in physicians: A systematic review and meta-analysis. *JAMA Internal Medicine, 177*, 195–205.

Perski, O., Grossi, G., Perski, A., & Niemi, M. (2017). A systematic review and meta-analysis of tertiary interventions in clinical burnout. *Scandinavian Journal of Psychology, 58*, 551–561.

Pines, A., Aronson, E., & Kafry, D. (1981). *Burnout: From tedium to personal growth*. Free Press.

Purvanova, R. K., & Muros, J. P. (2010). Gender differences in burnout: A meta-analysis. *Journal of Vocational Behavior, 77*, 168–185.

Reichl, C., Leiter, M. P., & Spinath, F. M. (2014). Work–nonwork conflict and burnout: A meta-analysis. *Human Relations, 67*, 979–1005.

Reijseger, G., Schaufeli, W. B., Peeters, M. C. W., Taris, T. W., Van Beek, I., & Ouweneel, E. (2013). Watching the paint dry: Validation of the Dutch Bore-out Scale. *Anxiety, Stress & Coping, 26*, 508–525.

Rotenstein, L. S., Torre, M., Ramos, M. A., Rosales, R. C., Guille, C., Sen, S., & Mata, D. A. (2018). Prevalence of burnout among physicians a systematic review. *Journal of the American Medical Association, 320*, 1131–1150.

Rousseau, D. M. (2011). The individual–organization relationship: The psychological contract. In S. Zedeck (Ed.), *APA handbook of industrial and organizational psychology: Vol. 3. Maintaining, expanding, and contracting the organization* (pp. 191–220). American Psychological Association.

Salvagioni, D. A. J., Melanda, F. N., Mesas, A. E., González, A. D., Gabani, F. L., & De Andrade, S. M. (2017). Physical, psychological and occupational consequences of job burnout: A systematic review of prospective studies. *PLoS ONE, 12*, 1–29.

Salyers, M. P., Bonfils, K. A., Luther, L., Firmin, R. L., White, D. A., Adams, E. L., & Rollins, A. L. (2017). The relationship between professional burnout and quality and safety in healthcare: A meta-analysis. *Journal of General Internal Medicine, 32*, 475–482.

Schaffner, A. K. (2017). Pre-modern exhaustion: On melancholia and acedia. In S. Neckel, A. K. Schaffner, & G. Wagner (Eds.), *Burnout, fatigue, exhaustion. An interdisciplinary perspective on a modern affliction* (pp. 27–50). Springer Nature.

Schaufeli, W. B. (2006). The balance of give and take: Toward a social exchange model of burnout. *The International Review of Social Psychology, 19*, 87–131.

Schaufeli, W. B., & Salanova, M. (2007). Efficacy or inefficacy, that's the question: Burnout and work engagement, and their relationships with efficacy Beliefs. *Anxiety, Stress Coping, 20*, 177–196.

Schaufeli, W. B. (2017). Burnout: A short socio-cultural history. In S. Neckel, A. K. Schaffner, & G. Wagner (Eds.), *Burnout, fatigue, exhaustion: An interdisciplinary perspective on a modern affliction* (pp. 105–127). Springer Nature.

Schaufeli, W. B., & Enzmann, D. (1998). *The burnout companion to study & practice: A critical analysis.* Taylor & Francis.

Schaufeli, W. B., & Taris, T. W. (2005). The conceptualization and measurement of burnout: Common ground and worlds apart. *Work & Stress, 19*, 356–262.

Schaufeli, W. B., & Taris, T. W. (2014). A critical review of the Job Demands-Resources Model: Implications for improving work and health. In G. Bauer & O. Hämmig (Eds.), *Bridging occupational, organizational and public health* (pp. 43–68). Springer.

Schaufeli, W. B., Taris, T. W., & Van Rhenen, W. (2008). Workaholism, burnout and engagement: Three of a kind or three different kinds of employee well-being. *Applied Psychology: An International Review, 57*, 173–203.

Schaufeli, W. B., Desart, S., & De Witte, H. (2020a). Burnout Assessment Tool (BAT): Development, validity and reliability. *International Journal of Environmental Research and Public Health, 17*, 94–95. https://doi.org//10.3390/ijerph17249495

Schaufeli, W. B., De Witte, H., & Desart, S. (2020b). *Manual Burnout Assessment Tool (BAT) – Version 2.0.* KU Leuven, Belgium: Unpublished internal report. www.burnoutassessmenttool.be

Schaufeli, W. B., Leiter, M. P., & Maslach, C. (2009). Burnout: 35 years of research and practice. *Career* Development International, *14*, 204–220.

Schaufeli, W. B., Martínez, I. M., Marques-Pinto, A., Salanova, M., & Bakker, A. B. (2002). Burnout and engagement in university students: A cross-national study. *Journal of Cross-Cultural Psychology, 33*, 464–481.

Sennett, R. (1998). *The corrosion of character: The personal consequences of work in the new capitalism.* Norton.

Shin, H., Park, Y. M., Ying, J. Y., Kim, B., Noh, H., & Lee, S. M. (2014). Relationships between coping strategies and burnout symptoms: A meta-analytic approach. *Professional Psychology: Research and Practice, 45*, 44–56.

Shirom, A. (2002). Job-related burnout: A review. In J. C. Quick & L. R. Tetrick (Eds.), *Handbook of occupational health psychology* (pp. 245–264). American Psychological Association.

Shirom, A., & Melamed, S. (2006). A comparison of the construct validity of two burnout measures in two groups of professionals. *International Journal of Stress Management, 13*, 176–200.

Swider, B. W., & Zimmerman, R. D. (2010). Born to burnout: A meta-analytic path model of personality, job burnout, and work outcomes. *Journal of Vocational Behavior, 76*, 847–506.

Taris, T. W., Le Blanc, P. M., Schaufeli, W. B., & Schreurs, P. J. G. (2005). Are there causal relationships between the dimensions of the Maslach Burnout Inventory? A review and two longitudinal tests. *Work & Stress, 19*, 241–258.

Tei, S., Becker, C., Kawada, R., Fujino, J., Jankowski, K. F., Sugihara, G., Muria, T., & Takahashi, H. (2014). Can we predict burnout severity from empathy-related brain activity? *Translational Psychiatry, 4*(6), e393. https://doi.org/10.1038/tp.2014.34

Toppinen-Tanner, S., Ahola, K., Koskinen, A., & Väänänen, A. (2009). Burnout predicts hospitalization for mental and cardiovascular disorders: 10-year prospective results from industrial sector. *Stress & Health, 25*, 287–96.

Van Dierendonck, D., Schaufeli, W. B., & Buunk, A. P. (2001). Burnout and inequity among human service professionals: A longitudinal study. *Journal of Occupational Health Psychology, 6*, 43–52.

Van der Klink, J. J., & Van Dijk, F. J. (2003). Dutch practice guidelines for managing adjustment disorders in occupational and primary health care. *Scandinavian Journal of Work, Environment and Health, 29*, 478–487.

Waddell, G., & Burton, A. K. (2006). *Is work good for your mental health and well-being?* Stationary Office.

West, C. P., Dyrbye, L. N., Erwin, P. J., & Shanafelt, T. D. (2016). Interventions to prevent and reduce physician burnout: A systematic review and meta-analysis. *The Lancet, 388*, 2272–2281.

Wheeler, D., Vassar, M., Worley, J., & Barnes, L. (2011). A reliability generalization meta-analysis of coefficient alpha for the Maslach Burnout Inventory. *Educational and Psychological Measurement, 71*, 231–244.

WHO. (2019). *International Classification of Diseases (ICD-11).* World Health Organization.

Woo, T., Ho, R., Tang, A., & Tam, W. (2020). Global prevalence of burnout symptoms among nurses: A systematic review and meta-analysis. *Journal of Psychiatric Research, 123,* 9–20.

Worley, J. A., Vassar, M., Wheeler, D. L., & Barnes, L. L. B. (2008). Factor structure of scores from the Maslach Burnout Inventory: A review and meta-Analysis of 45 exploratory and confirmatory factor-analytic studies. *Educational and Psychological Measurement, 68,* 797–823.

Xanthopoulou, D., Bakker, A. B., Dollard, M. F., Demerouti, E., Schaufeli, W. B., Taris, T. W., & Schreurs, P. J. G. (2007). When do job demands particularly predict burnout? The moderating role of job resources. *Journal of Managerial Psychology, 22,* 766–785.

9 | Work Engagement and Organizational Well-Being

MARISA SALANOVA

What Is Work Engagement?

Organizations and workplaces have the potential to influence employees' health and well-being, which accounts for the numerous definitions, theories, and measures about health and well-being. Some inconsistences also exist among the terms that researchers use to refer to psychological and/or physical health/well-being, such as "psychological well-being", "subjective well-being", "mental health", and "physical health", among others. Moreover "health" and "well-being" are considered as equivalents, but at times health has a more physical component and well-being a more psychological one.

The World Health Organization defines *health* as "a state of complete physical, mental and social *well-being*, not merely absence of disease or infirmity" (WHO, 1946). Moreover, the Organization for Economic Cooperation and Development (OECD) defines health as "a physical, psychological, mental, and social state of tolerance and compensation outside the limits of which any situation is perceived by the individual ...as the manifestation of a morbid state ...[so] as far as the individual is concerned, his opinion is the only one that counts" (cited in Emmet, 1991, p. 40). The OECD developed the Better Life project that includes objective well-being variables and also subjective well-being defined as "good mental states, including all the various evaluations, positive and negative, that people make of their lives, and the affective reaction of people to their experiences" (OECD, 2013, p. 29).

Thus, it is important to differentiate different facets of health/well-being, such as: physical health/well-being of workers (e.g., physical symptoms and physical illnesses and diseases); psychological health/well-being (mental/emotional), addressing topics such as positive/negative emotional states, satisfaction, strain, burnout, engagement, thriving, and so on; and social/societal facets, such as connectedness, giving/receiving help, and prosocial motivation. These three levels refer

260

to health/well-being related to the presence of positive states (e.g., satisfaction) and the absence of negative states (e.g., anxiety). However, whereas the WHO or OECD health definitions address general well-being, our concern is with workplace well-being, which Grant et al. (2007, p. 52), drawing on the work by Warr (1987), define as "the overall quality of an employee's experience and functioning at work". In 1999, Danna and Griffin proposed several definitions of health and well-being in the workplace, indicating that "health" "generally appears to encompass both physiological and psychological symptomology within a more medical context (e.g., reported symptomology or a diagnosis of illness or disease)" (p. 364). Furthermore, "well-being" is rooted in the concept of "affective well-being" by Warr (1987, 1990), which is broader and views the person as a whole that includes context-free measures such as life satisfaction and home–work relations.

Building on the literature, although in previous research health is usually linked to physical symptoms, I agree more with the WHO definition of "*health*" as a state of complete physical, mental, and social "*well-being*", which is conceptually similar. Moreover, health and well-being "are not the mere absence of illness", which coincides with the positive psychology perspective, according to which well-being and happiness are not simply the absence of negative functions but rather something more. In other words, a lack of job burnout among employees of a company is not the same thing as the presence of work engagement among them. Therefore, well-being is a complex psychosocial construct that is not only the absence of negative psychological constructs but also includes different life domains and comprises multiples physical, psychological, and social dimensions as well (e.g., Forgeard et al., 2011; Friedman & Kern, 2014; Huppert & So, 2013; Ryff & Keyes, 1995).

In the specific arena of work and organizations, we could extrapolate that there are three main facets of work-related well-being concerned with physical, psychological, and social functioning in the workplace and in organizations. I will adapt this approach by referring to organizational well-being as a multilevel construct that includes individual, group, leader, and organizational (IGLO) levels (Nielsen et al., 2018) of different facets (i.e., physical, psychological-mental/emotional, and social) of well-being in a reciprocal, nutritive, and sustainable relationship over time (Salanova, 2020a). I suggest that there is no unique model of organizational well-being, but that there are rather different ones that consider "well-being" in organizations with multiple facets that can be measured and enhanced over time.

With this broad background in mind, I consider work engagement (WE) as an indicator of psychological well-being. In this regard, although past research has shown different approaches to work engagement, such as need satisfaction (Kahn, 1990), satisfaction-engagement (Harter et al., 2002), multidimensional (Saks, 2006), and burnout-engagement (Maslach & Leiter, 1997; Schaufeli et al., 2002; see Shuck, 2017 for a review), in this chapter, work engagement will be considered within the burnout-engagement approach, due to its predominance in the research on work engagement (see Schaufeli & Bakker, 2022, for a review). The work engagement concept is rooted in occupational health psychology (OHP) and positive organizational psychology (POP) as a distinct concept but is negatively related to burnout, and in turn it is defined in its own right as a fully motivational (affective-cognitive) experience, a kind of psychological *well-being* at work. For example, one of the most widespread definitions of WE (Schaufeli et al., 2002) views it as a "positive, fulfilling, work-related state of mind that is characterized by vigor, dedication, and absorption" (p. 74). Moreover, Bakker et al. (2008) define work engagement as "a positive, fulfilling affective-motivational state of work-related *well-being* that is characterized by vigor, dedication, and absorption" (p. 187).

Rather than a momentary and specific state, work engagement refers to a more persistent and psychological state that is not focused on any particular object, event, individual, or behavior. Vigor is characterized by high levels of energy and mental resilience while working, the willingness to invest effort in one's work, and persistence even in the face of difficulties. Dedication is characterized by a sense of significance, enthusiasm, inspiration, pride, and challenge. Dedication has a wider scope because it not only refers to a particular cognitive or belief state but also includes the affective dimension as well. The final dimension of engagement, absorption, is characterized by being fully concentrated and deeply engrossed in one's work, where time passes quickly and one finds it difficult to detach from work. Sometimes engagement has been considered as "flow" (Csikszentmihalyi, 1990), but while both are related, they are not the same. Specifically, the subdimension of absorption is very close to flow experiences because both are related

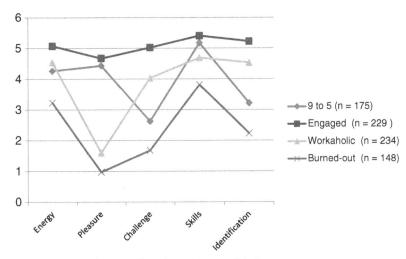

Figure 9.1 The four profiles of employee well-being

to focused attention, clear mind, unison of mind and body, effortless concentration, complete control, loss of self-consciousness, distortion of time, and intrinsic enjoyment. However, flow is temporary and related to the specific task or activity that you are doing, and engagement is a more pervasive and persistent positive state of mind.

Based on previous research, in Salanova (2021), I define work engagement as a key indicator of employee health/well-being, specifically *organizational well-being* at all IGLO levels, as well as a core dimension of a healthy organization, as in the healthy and resilient organization (HERO) model (Salanova et al., 2012, 2019). Thus, employees with high levels of work engagement (i.e., vigor, dedication, and absorption) are characterized by a positive pattern of psychological well-being at work, and team engagement or collective engagement exists at different levels in organizations (Salanova et al., 2003) and is an indicator of a healthy organization.

Furthermore, employee engagement is a complex well-being psychological construct that coexists in organizations with other constructs such as employee burnout. In other places (Salanova et al., 2014), we provided evidence of a parsimonious, theory-based classification of profiles of employee well-being: burnout, work engagement, and other less well-known profiles such as workaholism and 9-to-5 employees (see Figure 9.1). We contributed to the discussion (Avey et al., 2010) about the conceptualization and measurement of employee well-being by suggesting a new combination of motivational, affective, and cognitive dimensions with which to interpret differences in patterns of employee well-being. Specifically, we showed that engaged workers have high levels of energy while working, take pleasure in and are challenged by jobs where they can use their skills and energy, and feel good at work. They also identify with their work and their organization. In sum, the concept of engaged employees consists of a pattern of psychological well-being characterized by high levels of positive drive and energy, pleasure, work identification, and feeling challenged to have good job skills. Moreover, despite being heavy work investors, this "investment" is positive, due to their subjective perceptions of high levels of well-being and favorable job characteristics (medium job demands and high job resources), according to the predictions of the JD-R Model (Bakker & Demerouti, 2017; Schaufeli & Bakker, 2022), which will be described in the next section.

How and Why Do Employees Experience Work Engagement?

Mainly, research has focused on the way workplaces influence employees' stress and strain and how organizational/job characteristics are potential stressors with a negative impact on employee life and societies (see Chapters 1–3 of this book). However, organizations can also influence employees in a positive way by reducing job stress and illness and enhancing work-related psychological well-being, as in work engagement, allowing employees to experience these positive feelings in healthy organizations (Salanova et al., 2012) and psychologically healthy workplaces (Day & Nielsen, 2017; Kelloway & Day, 2005). We defined HERO as

those organizations that make systematic, planned, and proactive efforts to improve employees' and organizational processes and outcomes such as work engagement... [and] that involve carrying out healthy organizational resources and practices aimed at improving the work environment at the levels of (a) the task (autonomy, feedback), (b) the interpersonal (social relationships, transformational leadership), and (c) the organization (HR practices), especially during turbulence and times of change. (Salanova et al., 2012, p. 788)

In a similar way, the idea of a psychologically healthy workplace (PHW) refers to a workplace that aims to foster employee health by

reducing negative stressors and demands and promoting organizational resources to enhance well-being (Kelloway & Day, 2005). Day
and Randell (2014) defined PHW as workplaces that "are dedicated
to promoting and supporting the physical and psychological health
and well-being of their employees while simultaneously incorporating solid business practices to remain an efficient and productive
business entity and having a positive impact on their clients and
community" (p. 10).

These nutritive workplace environments provide employees with job
resources, not only material ones, such as salaries, time structure, etc.,
but also the satisfaction of basic psychological needs so that employees
feel more engaged and motivated in the workplace. According to self-
determination theory (SDT; Deci & Ryan, 2000), humans are basically
motivated and experience psychological well-being (such as work
engagement) when three basic psychological needs are satisfied, i.e.,
the need for autonomy, competence, and relatedness. In the workplace,
for example, employees can experience autonomy by making decisions
about their tasks, competence by using signature strengths in different
work areas, and relatedness by cultivating social relationships and
having leaders' social support, in addition to contributing to coworkers' personal grow and development. In these inspiring work atmos-
pheres, work is meaningful and engaging and leads employees to thrive
and flourish as human beings.

The job demands-resources (JD-R) model (Bakker & Demerouti,
2017; Schaufeli & Bakker, 2022) is a good theoretical framework to
explain how job resources together with job demands influence work
engagement and reduce job burnout (see Chapter 8 in this book for a
more detailed overview of burnout). According to the JD-R model, job
resources contribute to an intrinsic motivational process because they
help employees to obtain personal and professional growth, learning,
and development. They also play a role in extrinsic motivational
because they are instrumental for achieving different goals at work.
In addition, the JD-R model postulates that job resources are even
more relevant when job demands are higher, such as work overload,
role conflicts, and emotional demands (Bakker et al., 2007).

Different meta-analyses on work engagement have shown its
uniqueness and relationships with job demands and (job and personal)
resources. Halbesleben (2010) carried out a meta-analysis that
included 74 unique samples and 45,683 participants, in order to assess

the associations between work engagement and job demands and resources. As expected, job resources (i.e., social support, job control, feedback, and climate) were positively related to work engagement (ρ = .35), whereas job demands (i.e., work overload and work–family conflict) were weakly and negatively associated with it (ρ = −.09). However, although resources are usually strongly related to work engagement, this is not always true for job demands. For example, in a recent study, Lesener et al. (2019) carried out a meta-analysis that included 77 longitudinal samples, and they showed that job demands were not related to work engagement over time, whereas job resources were reciprocally related to work engagement. Thus, it seems that resources and work engagement could have a kind of reciprocal effect on each other over time, and so the idea of positive gain cycles emerged in past research. Resources have motivational power as drivers of work engagement, which, in turn, leads to the accumulation of more resources, and so on (Salanova et al., 2010). Recently, DeCuypere and Schaufeli (2020) also showed in their meta-analysis (k = 69, N = 32,924) that work engagement was positively correlated with a very important job social resource, that is, positive leadership styles, including transformational (ρ = .45), servant (ρ = .40), and authentic (ρ = .35) leadership.

Personal resources are mutually related to job resources and appear to influence work engagement and, in turn, job performance. Recent research showed that relatively permanent personal resources (e.g., personality traits such as extraversion, positive affectivity, conscientiousness; see meta-analysis by Young et al., 2018) and more state-like and temporary personal resources (i.e., resilience, self-efficacy, emotional intelligence, psychological capital; see systematic review by Bailey et al., 2017; Carmona et al., 2020; Peláez et al., 2020) are strongly related to work engagement. Research suggests that these personal and job resources have effects on WE, which in turn influences job attitudes and behaviors, business outcomes, and *health and well-being* (see Figure 9.2), as described recently by Schaufeli and Bakker (2022). Figure 9.2 also reflects research suggesting that WE can influence job resources (see above) and be influenced by employees' health and well-being, job attitudes, and work behaviors (explained in greater detail below). The arrows therefore depict *reciprocal* relationships between WE and those other constructs.

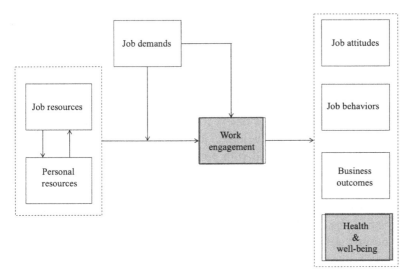

Figure 9.2 Integrative model of work engagement

In sum, work engagement occurs in the context of (healthy) organizations at different IGLO levels as a positive well-being psychological experience, due to the influence of personal and job resources and job demands. In turn, work engagement has a positive effect on positive attitudes, behaviors, and "other facets of health and well-being", as described in the following sections. As mentioned above, health and well-being "are not the mere absence of illness"; they do not simply involve an absence of negative symptoms but rather something more. A lack of burnout or depression symptoms is not the same thing as the presence of engagement, happiness, trust, thriving, and so on, because well-being is a complex psychosocial construct. In this chapter, I consider work engagement to be an indicator of psychological well-being, and according to the JD-R and HERO models, it is also related to other well-being facets, such as physical, psychological, and social well-being.

Work Engagement and Physical Well-Being

Physical well-being catches physiological markers of health and sickness in organizations; it is normally investigated through feelings of health, including positive markers, such as a feeling of energy, and negative ones, such as lack of fatigue, strain, and psychosomatic complains (i.e., headaches, sleep problems, musculoskeletal disorders). According to predictions of the JD-R model, employees working in environments where they experience higher levels of WE draw on positive psychological spiral gains that positively influence their health (Xanthopoulou et al., 2009). For example, in a sample of older employees, a study with a one-year longitudinal design showed that physical load, higher psychological job demands, and lower autonomy at baseline were associated with *poorer physical health* at follow-up, but higher WE at baseline was related to better physical and, especially, mental health over time, showing this kind of positive spiral (Leijten et al., 2015). Moreover, in a recent meta-analytic structural equation model (MASEM), Goering et al. (2017) found that there was a positive relationship between WE and physical health (ß = 0.08), albeit weaker in magnitude. Regarding *medical indicators of physical health*, prospective cohort studies showed that engaged employees had low levels of C-reactive protein, which is an established risk factor for cardiovascular disease (Eguchi et al., 2016). Work engagement is also associated with healthy cardiac autonomic activity (Seppälä et al., 2012). These last two studies seem to suggest that WE fosters cardiovascular health as well.

Work engagement has been researched in terms of its relationship with *sleep quality* and as an indirect measure of physical health. The idea is that good sleep quality is an indicator of physical health and improves levels of WE among employees because it is a vital resource that fills people with positive energy. Thus, in a sample of 328 workers, Barber et al. (2013) observed that people who are frequently engaged in poor sleeping behaviors had lower self-regulatory competence, suffered depletion of energy, and showed less work engagement. A daily diary study with 107 employees (Kühnel et al., 2017) provided data showing that sleep quality was beneficial for employees' daily work engagement. After nights when employees slept better, they indicated higher WE during the next day. In a similar vein and considering that *recovery* could be a kind of marker of sleep quality, Sonnentag et al. (2012) found that when individuals were more sleep recovered in the morning, they experienced more engagement at the workplace. Moreover, using a diary study (N = 63), Diestel et al. (2015) tested the moderating effect of sleep quality between emotional dissonance and daily work engagement, showing that the negative relationship between them was mitigated by increasing daily sleep quality. However, the work engagement–sleep quality relationship seems to be complex. Sheng et al. (2019) showed that chronic sleep quality moderated the relationship between daily time pressure (as a type of challenge demand) and daily engagement. Thus, when the sleep quality at person-level is high, then a curvilinear relationship exists between time pressure experienced and WE that increases moderately day by day.

Finally, it is interesting to report research results about the way WE is related to *physical energy* while working, and that WE could have a limit in terms of workers' *depletion of energy* or *exhaustion* over work days and weeks, with potential negative long-term effects. WE involves resource investment each day at work, and it is accumulative over time. Therefore, WE physiologically depletes resources, causing employees to feel exhausted. In this regard, research has shown, on the one hand, that WE may increase feelings of exhaustion over time (Byrne et al., 2016, Hakanen et al., 2018, Schaufeli et al., 2002), but this engagement–exhaustion relationship is even more complex. For example, from a temporal perspective, Junker et al. (2020) investigated how exhaustion develops over time as a function of WE. In two samples, they showed that WE may be positive in the short term (in the beginning, high levels of engagement are associated with less exhaustion), but more harmful in the long term by increasing exhaustion over time.

Mäkikangas et al. (2016) showed that the association between changes in WE and changes in exhaustion is not identical in every individual; instead, subgroups exist (i.e., moderating variables) where increases in WE are unrelated to decreases in exhaustion, for example. Thus, one study (Chen et al., 2020) showed that WE predicts exhaustion when individuals score lower on the conscientiousness and emotional stability personality traits. They found a three-way interaction where WE increased emotional exhaustion in less conscientious individuals who were also neurotic or emotionally unstable, whereas it decreased emotional exhaustion in more conscientious individuals who were emotionally stable. Finally, WE also mediated the effect of the toxic relationship between emotional exhaustion and negative affect on productivity loss in employees due to their presenteeism. In a sample of 42 employees (Ferreira et al., 2019) who completed a ten-day diary survey (420 diary tasks), multilevel linear modeling showed this mediating effect of WE, pointing to the relevance of promoting WE to reduce the effects of negative affect and emotional exhaustion on productivity.

Depletion of physical energy and feelings of exhaustion in highly engaged employees can be explained physiologically. In a recent study, Baethge et al. (2020) showed that WE was related to high sympathetic arousal (heart rate variation, HRV) in a sample of 118 public office employees on five working days, and multilevel analyses showed that elevated WE during one work week was associated with higher sympathetic activation, which is a health risk. Thus, a positive subjective construct (i.e., work engagement) does not always match objective indicators of well-being, as other research has also shown (Feldman et al., 1999; Jackowska et al., 2011). Schwerdtfeger and Gerteis (2014) found that daily activated engagement was related to less momentary HRV and, therefore, stronger sympathetic activation. Their absorption on that day may further reduce their perception of early signs of fatigue (Sonnentag et al., 2010) and then negatively affect their levels of well-being in the long run. Because prolonged sympathetic activation has been associated with severe physiological consequences, including cardiovascular and metabolic diseases (Grassi et al., 2005), it could be an indicator of a "negative side" of work engagement, at least in terms of the long-term physiological costs of a highly engaged work workforce.

Work Engagement and Psychological Well-Being

Psychological (mental and emotional) well-being comprises both the absence of negative mind states and the presence of positive ones. Past research has shown that WE is related to an absence of anxiety, depression (Shuck et al., 2017), and burnout (Schaufeli & Bakker, 2022). For example, Innstrand et al. (2012), in a two-year longitudinal study, examined the dynamic relationships between WE (i.e., vigor and dedication) and symptoms of *anxiety* and *depression* in a sample of 3,475 respondents from different occupational groups in Norway. The results showed that WE is more likely to be the antecedent of low symptoms of depression and anxiety than the other way around. In particular, the vigor dimension of WE predicts lower levels of depression and anxiety two years later. Moreover, WE not only predicts future self-reported outcomes such as low levels of depressive symptoms (Hakanen & Schaufeli, 2012) and low levels of psychological distress (Hakanen et al., 2018) but is also an important predictor of the nonoccurrence of a major depression diagnosis (Imamura et al., 2016). In the recent systematic review about how WE, along with work vigor, is related to physical and psychological health, Cortés-Denia et al. (2021) found, in the final 70 papers reviewed, that WE is mostly related to a lower risk of suffering from stress, anxiety, depression, fatigue, and psychological tension.

Regarding the relationship between engagement and *burnout*, research is intense and very productive (see Chapter 8 in this book), although there is still an ongoing debate about the relationships between the two, i.e., whether they are identical and opposite constructs (Maslash & Leiter, 1997) or whether WE does not add anything beyond burnout. Abundant research and meta-analyses on WE (shown in this chapter) show that engagement is a psychological construct that adds something to the research. Even the burnout and engagement dimensions are placed on two distinct and bipolar dimensions (i.e., energy with vigor and exhaustion; and identification with dedication and cynicism) (González-Romá et al., 2006; Schaufeli & Salanova, 2007). In that sense, an absence of one (e.g., low engagement) does not necessarily imply that the other is high (e.g., high burnout).

The bipolar dimension of energy seems to be more prominent, and, in any case, both terms refer to energy, with energy depletion (burnout) and increased energy (engagement) being related to each other. In a recent MASEM, Goering et al. (2017) concluded that burnout and engagement manifested different relationships with drivers and antecedents proposed by the JD-R model. For example, challenge demands are related to both engagement and burnout. However, hindrance demands have a stronger relationship with burnout, whereas job resources relate more strongly to WE. Burnout and engagement have different attitudinal, emotional, and behavioral consequences as well.

From a temporal perspective, longitudinal analyses of burnout and engagement could answer some questions about the way these two constructs develop over time, i.e., how engagement influences burnout and vice versa. Because well-being levels can fluctuate over time (Mäkikangas et al., 2016), employees can move from feeling engaged to feeling burnout, and vice versa. Depending on specific organizational characteristics, WE can be an antecedent of burnout (e.g., due to impaired social exchange processes; Schaufeli & Salanova, 2011), but it is also possible that initial levels of burnout can develop into more engagement over time if personal and job resources also change. For example, in the study by Mäkikangas et al. (2016), the authors concluded that well-being tends to vary over time, especially in younger employees. Considering changing job environments, they argue that an increase in resources is related to a boost in well-being, and that the opposite is also true.

But what influences what? Research on the way burnout is related to engagement over time (Hakanen & Schaufeli, 2012) showed that burnout at Time 1 is negatively related to engagement at Time 2 (after three years) and Time 3 (four years after Time 2). Experiencing burnout seems to deplete resources and hamper engagement over time. In a sample of 274 secondary-school teachers, Llorens and Salanova (2014) found, in a two-wave longitudinal study, that exhaustion and cynicism negatively predicted vigor and dedication over time (eight months later). We considered that these findings tested the conservation of resources theory (Hobföll, 1989), in the sense that when people lost some valued resources, they try to minimize the possibility of losing even more. However, this relationship between burnout and engagement over time seems to be moderated by the time lag. For example, in the systematic review by Maricuṭoiu et al. (2017) with 25 longitudinal studies (N = 13.271 participants), they did not find a significant temporal order between burnout and engagement, taking into account all the time intervals. However, when considering a specific timeframe, i.e., a 12-month time lag, the results showed a reciprocal, negative relationship between exhaustion (the energy dimension of burnout) and work engagement. The other interesting result is that the effect of burnout on engagement seems to be stronger than the effect of engagement on burnout.

Based on previous research on the relationship between engagement and burnout over time, this relationship is complex and depends, among other things, on the time lag. Moreover, it could also depend on the level of analysis used to examine engagement and burnout. For example, an interesting theoretical approach is defended by Sabine Sonnentag's studies showing that engagement and burnout differ at a deeper psychological level because they are related to each other at different levels of analysis (i.e., WE occurs at the task level and burnout at the job level). Work engagement fluctuates from task to task during a workday, whereas burnout is a chronic state that is more lasting over time, more pervasive, and affected more by job characteristics than by specific tasks.

However, psychological well-being is not only the absence of negative mental constructs such as anxiety, depression, or burnout. From a positive psychological approach, well-being includes not only the mere absence of illness but also the presence of positive states of mind such as positive emotions or work engagement, among others. Ryan and Deci (2002), for example, noted that (1) two types of psychological well-being can be differentiated: hedonic and eudaimonic well-being; and (2) although the relations between the two are still unclear and more research is needed (Heintzelman, 2018), it is interesting to clarify how work engagement is related to each of them.

Hedonic Well-Being

Hedonic well-being involves "feeling good", and the concept most frequently used to measure it is subjective well-being, which consists of high levels of positive affect together with low levels of negative affect, and life satisfaction (Diener & Emmons, 1984). The term "affect" is often used as a broad concept to refer to discrete emotions (e.g., joy or curiosity) and moods that are not specifically related to a concrete stimulus, such as feeling happy or feeling sad. Regarding positive and negative affect, it is typically assessed by asking people how often they have experienced concrete emotions (joy, contentment, anger, worry, etc.).

Work engagement seems to be associated with affect. In this regard, Erdil and Müceldili (2014) found that envy, which is a characteristic of negative affect in the workplace, is negatively associated with WE, whereas Kong and Li (2018) found that negative affect does not predict WE, but positive affect does. Moreover, positive affect is proposed as a psychological mechanism to buffer the costs associated with stressors, such as job insecurity, in terms of reduced work engagement. Vander Elst et al. (2013) found empirical evidence in a sample of 296 employees from a South African institution, based on the COR theory. They explain that people with high positive affect cope better when they experience stressful situations in their lives, suffering less from the negative consequences of job insecurity, and they are even more engaged in their work. In addition, Ouweneel et al. (2012), using a diary study with Dutch university employees, found that positive affect after a working day was positively related to the levels of engagement in the next day when employees experienced hope before working.

This relationship could be explained from the broad-and-build theory (Fredrickson, 2001), where the positive emotions (i.e., joy, enthusiasm) broaden people's thought-action repertories and build their personal resources, which in turn may promote well-being (e.g., work engagement). Positive emotions and work engagement could have a reciprocal relationship, with WE being both a driver and a consequence of them. First, feeling positive emotions at work leads employees to have higher levels of work engagement, but feeling engaged is also a pleasant experience that elicits future positive emotional states. Furthermore, positive emotions/affect also increase WE indirectly via personal resources such as self-efficacy, optimism, and resilience (Salanova et al., 2010), which have strong motivational potential and are important predictors of WE (Bakker & Demerouti, 2007. In other studies, these personal (or job) resources predicted WE through positive affect. For example, in a sample of 422 employees at a large IT company, Wang et al. (2017) showed that positive affect partially mediates the relationships between resilience, transformational leadership, and WE. In addition, Malinowski and Lim (2015), in a sample of 299 adults with full-time employment, showed that positive affect mediates the relationship between (dispositional) mindfulness and WE. The reciprocal nature of the relationship between emotions and WE was also tested in a cross-lagged study with a sample of 941 teachers in Croatia (Burić & Macuka, 2018). They showed that the more engaged teachers at Time 1 also showed higher levels of positive emotions (joy, pride) and lower levels of negative emotions (anger, fatigue) at Time 2; and teachers with more positive emotions (and low negative emotions) at T1 were also more engaged in their work six months later.

However, although positive emotions have a clear and direct effect on WE, not all kinds of positive emotions/affect are related to WE in the same way. In a two-way longitudinal study with a sample of 274 secondary-school teachers, Salanova et al. (2011) found more complex temporal relationships between positive affect and WE over time. More enthusiasm, satisfaction, and comfort predict higher WE over time, but positive affect characterized by high activation (i.e., enthusiasm) had a stronger effect on engagement than does positive affect with lower levels of activation (i.e., comfort). In turn, WE predicts positive emotions with high levels of activation (i.e., enthusiasm), but it negatively predicts emotions with low levels of energy, such as comfort.

Thus, the more engaged teachers feel, the more enthusiasm and the less comfort they will feel over time.

Positive/negative affect and emotions seem to have a complex relationship with WE. Using a longitudinal design, Clark et al. (2014), in a sample of 340 working adults, showed that positive emotions – specially joviality and self-assurance – mediated the relationship between WE and work–home enrichment. Wu and Wu (2019), in 263 supervisor–employee dyads (131 supervisors plus 263 employees) in a Chinese company, showed that employees' positive (but not negative) emotions mediated the positive effect of supervisors' expression of positive emotions on WE; and this engagement mediated the positive effect of employees' positive emotions on their innovative behavior. In this direction, Miralles et al. (2015) analyzed the mediating role of positive and negative affect between work event appraisals and daily work engagement, using a ten-day diary study with 117 workers (1,203 observations). Multilevel analysis showed that positive and negative affect partially mediated the relationship between daily event appraisal and WE, but the effect of positive affect was greater than the effect of negative affect.

These results could be explained in the lens of the affective events theory (AET) proposed by Weiss and Cropanzano (1996), where the positive or negative events the employees have at work trigger affective reactions (e.g., curiosity, anger), which in turn influence employees' work attitudes and behaviors, such as work engagement. Following the assumptions of AET and based on spillover theory (Edwards & Rothbard, 2000), which considers that psychological states can transfer from one life domain (e.g., family) to another (e.g., work), Gkorezis et al. (2016), in a four-week diary study (N = 164 observations), showed a spillover effect from football games to negative affective events at work domain, which mediated between satisfaction with the football game and work engagement. Another theory that explains the complex relationships between positive/negative affect, and WE comes from the self-regulation affective shift model of work engagement developed by Bledow et al. (2011). This model asserts that WE emerges from the dynamic interplay between positive and negative affect, in the sense that negative affect is positively related to WE if negative affect is followed by positive affect. In their study, they tested this hypothesis in a sample of 55 software developers, collecting data twice a day on nine working days. Hence, negative mood and negative events experienced in the morning of a workday were positively related to WE in the afternoon, but that occurs only if positive mood was high in the time interval between morning and afternoon.

The last indicator of hedonic or subjective well-being is *satisfaction*, which, according to Diener and Emmons (1984), could also be called "cognitive well-being" because it is based on an evaluation or appraisal of how well one's life is going relative to an ideal state of affairs and the person's appraisal of his or her overall degree of life contentment (Pavot & Diener, 1993). People with high cognitive well-being should judge that their goals, desires, and standards are largely met by the current conditions of their life; i.e., they are satisfied with their life. However, it also includes satisfaction with specific life domains, such as work (i.e., domain satisfactions). In this sense, job satisfaction was defined as "a pleasurable or positive emotional state resulting from the appraisal of one's job" (Locke, 1976, p. 1300). In this regard, relationships between WE and job satisfaction proliferate (Judge et al., 2017) in past research on the psychological understanding of work in people's lives, and they seem to be related but empirically distinguishable dimensions of employee well-being, as Rothmann (2008) showed. Thus, job satisfaction indicates pleasure experienced, whereas WE is a more complex construct that refers to positive energy, dedication, and absorption of employees in their work. Job satisfaction has a more "satiated" nature and is based on the past, whereas WE is a more "motivating" construct and oriented toward the future, bringing employees to initiate positive behavior.

Some studies have shown that WE and life/job satisfaction are both outcome indicators of well-being and positively related to each other. Cortés-Denia et al. (2021), in their recent systematic review, found that WE is related to life satisfaction, but what is the causal link between the two? Does WE predict satisfaction or vice versa? For example, in the study by Dugan and Barnes-Farrell (2020) with 440 working mothers, life satisfaction and WE were significatively correlated (.32), and both were positive well-being consequences of engaging in self-care behaviors and experiencing less stress due to the second shift workload. Extremera et al. (2005) also found, in a sample of 112 employees who work with mentally handicapped people, that emotional intelligence (as a personal positive resource) predicted both life satisfaction and WE as intercorrelated outcome variables. Job satisfaction and WE are sometimes considered psychological mechanisms that explain how some workplace drivers influence employee behaviors. For example, Wang et al. (2020), in a sample of 1,312 Chinese hotel employees, recently showed the mediating role of both of these constructs between professional identity and turnover intention as important ways to associate professional identity with turnover intention.

However, different meta-analytic studies have provided more empirical evidence that WE is positively related to satisfaction. For example, Goering et al. (2017) found that WE relates positively to job satisfaction (ß = 0.24), and the meta-analytic study by Christian et al. (2011) with a sample of 9,712 employees (k = 4) found a correlation between engagement and job satisfaction of .53. In some studies, WE is a kind of mediator variable between different job/personal resources and job/life satisfaction. The idea here is that WE, which includes positive, meaningful, and extraordinary work experiences, could generate positive thinking, experiences, and feelings, helping individuals to achieve their personal goals and aspirations and improving their life/job satisfaction. Thus, Ariza-Montes et al. (2018), in a study with 142 Spanish religious workers, found that WE mediated the relationship between authenticity (as a personal resource) and subjective well-being, considering life satisfaction as an outcome of WE. Considering emotional intelligence as a personal resource, Butakor et al. (2021), in a sample of 260 teachers, showed that job satisfaction mediated the relationship between teachers' emotional intelligence and WE. Liu et al. (2019) found that WE directly affected life satisfaction in 760 police officers ($\beta = 0.58$, $p < 0.001$), and it indirectly influenced their life satisfaction through work–family conflict ($\beta = -0.07$, $p < 0.05$). A study by Eldor et al. (2016), using multilevel models in a sample of 554 employees from different occupational sectors, found that WE was strongly related to job satisfaction (r = .55***), but also to life satisfaction (r = .44***). Furthermore, their findings stressed that WE offers a significant added value above and beyond job satisfaction in predicting work and nonwork positive attitudes such as life satisfaction. Based on the JD-R model, Salmela-Aro and Upadyaya (2018) examined, among others, how personal and job demands and resources of 1,415 employees were related to their life satisfaction, as well as the full mediating role of WE during different career stages, again finding this relationship: higher work engagement was related to greater life satisfaction.

Longitudinal studies also provide empirical evidence about the link between WE and satisfaction. For example, in a three-wave seven-year follow-up design with a national sample of 1,964 Finnish dentists, Hakanen and Schaufeli (2012) found that WE spills over to general, context-free well-being, such as life satisfaction over time (from T1 to T2 and from T2 to T3), but not the other way around, i.e., life satisfaction only predicted life satisfaction over time, not WE. In addition, Karatepe and Karadas (2015), using a time lag of two weeks in three waves with 285 frontline employees, found that WE partially mediated the relationship between psychological capital (as a personal resource) and job, career, and life satisfaction.

Eudaimonic Well-Being

Eudaimonia was introduced by Aristotle to describe human flourishing as a kind of virtue that influences one's own potential and development and is different from the pleasurable experiences that define hedonic well-being. Virtue is a type of activity directed toward some sort of universal completeness or perfection according to our human nature, such as personal growth and development, accomplishment, thriving, and self-determination, among others (Ryan et al., 2008; Vittersø, 2004). With eudaimonic well-being, the existence of positive emotions and positive attitudes toward one's life or work is less important that the process of having a good life and a positive psychological functioning (Jayawickreme et al., 2012; Ryff, 1989).

Carol Ryff suggests that the psychological well-being (PWB) construct is based on individuals' growth and fulfillment in six main dimensions (i.e., positive relations, autonomy, mastery, life purpose, self-acceptance, and personal growth). These dimensions are drawn from self-determination theory (Ryan & Deci, 2000), which considers eudaimonia to be a kind of "self-realization" focusing on what processes can be achieved through self-actualization. These Ryff dimensions are self-acceptance, positive social relationships, and autonomy. The others are more associated with personal growth and fulfillment. According to Ryft, engagement in important work (in our case, work engagement) means that people make relevant contributions to society.

Eudaimonic theories of well-being and happiness can also be applied at work and in organizations, making it possible for employees to cultivate psychological competencies such as virtuosity, autonomy, and positive relations with colleagues and clients, regardless of whether they feel good or feel like it (Kesevir, 2018). Bartels et al. (2019) recently developed a measure of workplace eudaimonic well-being based on the eudaimonic perspective of Ryft's general well-being (1989) and Keyes' social context theory (1998). They defined it as "an employee's subjective evaluation of his or her ability to develop and optimally function within the workplace" (p. 3). Eudaimonic workplace well-being considers Ryft's six dimensions of general well-being together with Keyes' five social dimensions of well-being (i.e., social integration, social acceptance, social contribution, social actualization, and social coherence). Bartels et al. (2019) showed sufficient discriminant validity between the two dimensions of eudaimonic well-being and employee engagement in their study. On a three-wave questionnaire with 338 Chinese employees, Yang et al. (2019) showed that career adaptability has a significant effect on WE, which in turn predicts eudaimonic well-being as a kind of antecedent or driver. However, other studies showed that WE is also a consequence of eudaimonic well-being. For example, Aiello and Tesi (2017, in a sample of 140 social workers, provided evidence for a mediational model where job resources fully mediate the association between eudaimonic well-being and WE. In this study, eudaimonic well-being endorses the perception, identification, and promotion of job resources, which in turn were associated with WE.

The psychological construct(s) that constitutes the core of eudaimonic well-being is still an under-researched topic. For example, Kashdan et al. (2008) noted that there is greater consensus about the dimensions of hedonic well-being, but not those of eudaimonic well-being. However, some eudaimonic well-being dimensions such as meaning, self-determination, or flourishing appear more frequently in research (Huta & Waterman, 2014; Kahn & Fellows, 2013; Keyes, 2007; Steger et al., 2012).

Meaningfulness has been quite researched as a component of eudaimonic well-being, as a kind of feeling that one's life is meaningful (Baumeister, 1995). If the activities that we are doing are related to our own personal mission/vision and we believe we are contributing to something larger than (i.e., transcend) ourselves, then we can experience higher levels of psychological meaningfulness (Hitge & Van Schalkwyk, 2018; Olivier & Rothmann, 2007), which implies positive psychological experiences. In the arena of work and organizations, meaningful work has been suggested as crucial for the psychological experience of engagement (Chalofsky, 2010; Fairle, 2011). Meaningfulness further aids in the enhancement and mainten-ance of general mental health, life satisfaction, and WE (Glazer et al., 2014). The psychological meaningfulness of work represents the employee's cognitive assessment of work as significant and meaningful. So far, you can expect that when employees have these feelings, they will invest energy at work and feel vigorous, dedicated, and fully absorbed in their tasks. It is easy to imagine that if the work context is not meaningful (does not fit one's values, boring tasks, etc.), employ-ees simply are not engaged at work. We rarely put energy into activities if they have no personal meaning or if we believe our efforts will ultimately result in fruitless results and consequences.

However, meaningfulness at work and the meaning of work are not the same thing. Pratt and Ashforth (2008) suggested that meaningful-ness is related to subjective evaluations of the amount of meaning something holds, whereas the "meaning of work" refers to the individ-uals' interpretation of the role work plays in their lives (e.g., salary, calling, social relevance). Meaning seems to be "psychological" in nature and derived from individual values, beliefs, and personal atti-tudes. Meaningful work tries to respond to questions such as: does my work have significance and purpose for me? Does it contribute to finding a broader meaning in my life? Does it make a positive contri-bution to the greater good? These conditions of meaningful work seem to be drivers of WE; thus, the extent to which workers experience meaningfulness at work is a necessary condition for experiencing engagement (Kahn & Fellows, 2013). Meaningfulness is a consequence of different drivers such as purpose (viewing one's circumstances like connected to the future), personal control and efficacy (being cause for some particular fact), and belonging (due to nutritive connections to others) (Baumeister & Leary, 1995).

Vogt et al. (2013) suggested that meaningfulness is the extent to which one's work is seen as worthy of commitment and involvement. Therefore, the meaningfulness of a job is a kind of personal resource that employees have available to put toward work tasks (Kahn, 1992). Perceiving work as meaningful denotes an important connection between employees and their work, which stimulates them to go a step forward the usual job requirements. For example, the meta-analysis by Christian et al. (2011) shows that a general sense of meaningfulness in one's work increases employee engagement. The recent study by Van Zyl et al. (2020) with a sample of 274 South African industrial psychologists found three mental health profiles (languishing, moderately mentally healthy, and flourishing) that significantly differ in their levels of meaningful work and WE. Flourishers showed higher levels of both. Research demonstrated that employees with a high psychological experience of meaningful work are more committed to the organization and less likely to leave it, feeling more engaged than employees who do not consider their work to be particularly meaningful (May et al., 2004; Olivier & Rothmann, 2007). Moreover, meaningful work and WE are connected via psychological mechanisms such as the use of strengths by employees. In this regard, Van Wingerden and Van der Stoep (2018) found, in a sample of 459 employees, that multiple factors such as strength use and WE mediated the impact of meaningful work on performance. In addition, interestingly, meaningful work influences WE not only directly but also indirectly via the use of character strengths by employees. Thus, when employees perceive their work as meaningful, they are more likely to use their strengths and feel more work engaged.

Steger et al. (2012), in a sample of 252 white-collar employees, found that meaningful work was an even better predictor of WE than affective disposition. Individuals that feel that their work is meaningful are more engaged, regardless of their affective disposition. Moreover, in a sample of 194 employees in a two-wave longitudinal study, Matthew and Jiang (2017) found that meaningful work is positively related to enrichment of work-to-life over time. In addition, WE mediated, but did not moderate, the relationship between meaningful work at Time 1 and work-to-life enrichment at Time 2. Hence, it seems that meaningful work is associated with benefits that transfer from work to nonwork areas, such as the full experience of work-to-life enrichment. These enriching benefits of meaningful work appear only when people invest in their work role by using their personal strengths, thus experiencing their work activities with vigor, absorption, and dedication (i.e., work engaged). However, it seems that the relationship between meaningful work and work engagement depends on the focus on between-or-within-person. Recently, Vogel et al. (2020), in a daily within-person examination of 86 employees (N = 804 observations), found that when there is a misfit in one day between received and needed meaningful work, it could be related with a lower engagement this day.

Regarding *self-determination* as a (multi-)component of eudaimonic well-being, we would expect employees who report being fully engaged in their work to also have a strong intrinsic work motivation (Meyer, 2014). In this direction, SDT (Deci & Ryan, 1985; Ryan & Deci, 2000) explains why employees have intrinsically motivated behaviors such as an "inherent tendency to seek out novelty and challenges, to extend and exercise one's capacities, to explore, and to learn" (Ryan & Deci, 2000, p. 70). Intrinsic motivation is related to three basic psychological needs fulfillment: autonomy, competence, and relatedness. When these needs are met, employees feel intrinsically motivated to perform a specific behavior, and they feel good and engaged in their work.

Research on the mediating role of these basic psychological needs and work engagement is quite fruitful. For instance, Van den Broeck et al. (2008) found that basic psychological need satisfaction explains the influence of job demands on WE and is a mediator between the two. Schreurs et al. (2014) also found that need satisfaction was positively associated with WE. Goodboy et al. (2020), in a study about the negative effects of workplace bullying on work engagement in a sample of 243 full-time employees, showed an indirect relationship between workplace bullying and WE that was mediated by basic psychological needs satisfaction. Thus, workplace bullying indirectly and negatively affects employees' WE, denying them their autonomy and relatedness needs and decreasing their motivation to perform work in a fulfilling way. Recently, Zeijen et al. (2020) carried out a multilevel study with 97 police officers' dyads (N = 194 participants) during two-time blocks on one working day (N = 227–491 episodes). They showed that episodic need satisfaction influences work engagement when police officers satisfy their own daily needs showing support, and it also depends on when the support is given and also to who is provided. This study expands the SDT by showing the relevance of social support in the relationship between need satisfaction and WE. From a within-person approach, and considering daily work engagement (i.e., transient state of mind that exists at a given moment and fluctuates within the same individual over short periods of time) instead of work engagement (i.e., how engaged employees feel in relation to their work in general and over longer periods of time), Bakker et al. (2019) used a diary study with a multilevel approach (N = 66 employees who responded to a daily diary questionnaire,

N = 261; as well as momentary, task-related items, N = 1,539) to show that daily job crafting was positively related to daily work engagement through momentary need satisfaction and momentary engagement. This episodic and momentary engagement is more likely when employees satisfy their basic needs for relatedness, autonomy, and competence.

Finally, from the area of positive psychology, Hursthouse (1999) argued that a *flourishing* life (just as adopting a healthy lifestyle) is the best bet for being healthy and happy, even though it does not guarantee perfect health or longevity. Flourishing seems to be an umbrella psychological construct that contains different dimensions of well-being, such as hedonic, eudaimonic, and social well-being. It is a state of optimal mental health in individuals who feel good, not only about themselves but also about their potential to (socially) contribute to the world around them in positive ways (Keyes, 2007). Flourishing is on one end of a mental health continuum, with languishing on the opposite end as the absence of mental health. Seligman (2018) presented a similar flourishing model called PERMA: positive emotion, engagement (flow), (positive) relationships, meaning, and achievement. According to Seligman, these five elements of well-being are pursued for their own sake and not necessarily to increase other well-being elements. It is interesting that the PERMA model includes (life) engagement and flow as dimensions of flourishing in life.

Research has shown that WE predicts flourishing and acts as a mediating variable between job/personal resources and flourishing. For example, Diedericks and Rothmann (2013), in a sample of 205 technology professionals, found that work engagement (together with job satisfaction) partially mediated between personal and job resources (supervisor relations and work role fit) and flourishing (considered a complex indicator of emotional, psychological, and social well-being). In addition, in a sample of 142 nuns, Ariza-Montes et al. (2018) found that the more engaged nuns are in their work (social action to serve the poorest and most disadvantaged people), the more they flourish in their working environment and in their personal lives. However, in other studies, flourishing mediated between job/personal resources and work engagement. In a sample of 229 employees and using structural equation modeling (SEM), Shao-mei Zheng et al. (2018) showed that psychological flourishing partially mediated the relationship between mindfulness and work engagement.

Therefore, although flourishing could be considered an umbrella construct that includes psychological (hedonic and eudaimonic) and social well-being, I think it is important to consider its unique contribution to the relationship between work engagement and social well-being.

Work Engagement and Social Well-Being

In a more general view of well-being, Keyes (2007) noted that social well-being refers to a psychosocial experience where individuals are socially accepting, believe in the others' potential, feel that the society is meaningful and their own activities are meaningful for others, and experience psychological relatedness with other people. In this regard, engagement is associated with social well-being because it contributes to a meaningful life, making the person feel part of society (Keyes, 2007). Moreover, social well-being could be experienced in the workplace because it is associated with strong feelings of social connection with others, such as coworkers, leaders, customers, etc. For example, *giving and receiving help* to people in the workplace could guard against job demands (Teng et al., 2018; Uy et al., 2017), and *prosocial motivations,* such as the desire to exert effort to benefit others or social collectives, are potential indicators of social well-being that could be related to a strong sense of energy at work and being dedicated to and absorbed in tasks, that is, work engagement. For example, in a study about the relationship between job insecurity and work engagement and performance, Shin and Hur (2020) found that the negative relationship between job insecurity and work engagement was weakest when employees' help-giving and prosocial motivations were both high. Thus, giving/receiving help and prosocial behavior are potential psychosocial mechanisms of social well-being that alleviate work engagement when employees suffer from job insecurity.

Furthermore, when interactions and relationships with others, such as coworkers, leaders, and customers, shape how people think, feel, and behave, they can potentially affect meaningfulness if they provide the opportunity to reinforce valued identities at work (Kahn, 2007). These relational sources of meaning could be, for example, voices that are heard, important work social connections, or even competent and inspirational supervision by leaders. When these social sources of meaning are present in the workplace, they can cause employees to think about relevant questions, such as whether it is worthwhile for them to be fully engaged at this moment in their work/task/teamwork (Kahn & Fellows, 2013). In this context, the construct of *team/collective work engagement* and its relationship with indicators of social well-being makes sense. Work engagement can also be shared by team members as an index of (collective) team engagement (Salanova et al., 2003; Schaufeli & Salanova, 2011; Torrente et al., 2012). This sharedness of engagement can occur through an emotional contagion process defined as "the tendency to automatically imitate and synchronize facial expressions, vocalizations, postures, and movements with those of another person and, therefore, to converge together" (Hatfield et al., 1994). We have shown the existence of team engagement in studies with more than 200 work units and their leaders. This research reveals that team engagement is activated by the presence of social resources shared by the team (i.e., team coordination, teamwork, shared social support), and it results in high in-role and extra-role performance (Cruz et al., 2013; Gracia et al., 2013; Salanova et al., 2011; Torrente et al., 2012, 2013). To date, *team/group cohesion* could be an indicator of social well-being because it can be understood as the extent to which team members are committed to their team and how well the team is integrated as it pursues its goals (Kozlowski & Ilgen, 2006). Members of teams with high cohesion are more motivated to contribute to the team's collective goal and engage in collective work as a team. For example, in a longitudinal three-wave study with 118 project teams (605 individuals) that performed three creativity tasks, we showed (Rodriguez-Sánchez et al., 2017) that team cohesion leads to collective team engagement, which in turn has a positive effect on team creative performance.

A psychosocial construct that is close to cohesion is *organizational connectedness* (Huynh, 2012a), a collective positive state of well-being that people experience when they feel a strong sense of belonging in the workplace or even with customers, clients, and recipients of their service. People with high organizational connectedness manifest human striving for interpersonal attachments through positive feelings of appreciation and respect as part of the relationship with the client, through feelings such as compassion and altruistic behaviors, and in turn they experience satisfaction due to the feelings of appreciation and gratitude received from others (Dein & Abbas, 2005). Moreover, organizational connectedness could be related to an individual's sense of connection to the values of an organization where employees feel appreciated, recognized, and treated fairly, as well as connection to their own tasks when they are motivating and inspiring. Studies by Huynh and colleagues (Huynh et al., 2012a, 2012b) have shown that organizational connectedness is related to desirable outcomes for people doing voluntary tasks, including work engagement. For example, Huynh et al. (2014), in a sample of 887 volunteers, and based on the JD-R model framework, showed that WE and organizational connectedness were positive mechanisms that explain how job resources are related to turnover. These well-being psychological constructs are also highly intercorrelated ($r = .61$); however, in this study, no specific relationships between the two were proposed.

Social well-being could also be experienced with people from other life domains outside the workplace, such as family, friends, community, society, etc., thus affecting work engagement and vice versa. For example, engagement in the workplace may provide benefits for individuals' positive social contacts and interactions, which are valuable social resources that lead to a positive social connection with others at work and successful communal and social functioning. According to the spillover theory (Wilensky, 1960), attitudes and behaviors experienced in a social domain (i.e., work) could be transferred to other life contexts, showing a kind of effect on one's skills and psychological experience. For example, engaged employees could express a desire to be useful and contribute to other social contexts related to social life (Vigoda-Gadot et al., 2008). This spillover is defined by Greenhaus and Powell (2006, p. 73) as "the extent to which experiences in one role improve the quality of life in the other role". In this regard, WE has been related to *community social involvement*, referred to as activities of individual citizens, such as belonging to community associations and school committees and taking part in cultural activities aimed at influencing the community (Verba & Nie, 1972). Moreover, Eldor et al. (2016) found in their multilevel study that WE is also related to employees' levels of community involvement, creating added value beyond the work area and enriching other social domains of their lives outside the workplace. At the societal level, the European Working Conditions Survey has shown that work engagement at the national level is curvilinearly related to a country's gross domestic product and linearly related to various indicators of *good governance*, such as *public integrity*, *quality of democracy*, and *gender equality* as societal indicators of social well-being (Schaufeli, 2018).

Finally, it is important to note that social well-being is processed differently by individuals and groups. It also depends on cultural and societal norms and is different, for example, in collectivistic or individualistic cultures. The Chinese term *"guanxi"* is related to personal connections from the implicit psychological contracts reciprocity exchanged, and also nurture mutual commitment and the desire for relationships in the long term (Chen et al., 2013) as the general quality of "informal" relationships rather than formal relationships (Wong et al., 2003). Guanxi can be built and used to progress through life and work (Chen et al., 2013; Xin & Pearce, 1996). However, guanxi in HRM practices is negatively perceived by employees when they observe other colleagues with more guanxi-based preferential treatment and, thus, perceive them as guanxi beneficiaries. Thus, studies have shown the negative effects of employees' perceptions of guanxi HRM practices on employee outcomes, such as in-role and extra-role performance (Hsu & Wang, 2007), management trust (Chen et al., 2011), and even work engagement. For example, in a three-wave study with 338 employees on how career adaptability affects eudaimonic well-being and work engagement, Yang et al. (2018) found that career adaptability has a significant effect on work engagement, which, in turn, predicts EWB, with these effects being stronger when guanxi is low. Moreover, in a double study with (1) a three time-lagged sample of 45 work groups and 205 employees in a state-owned organization and another (2) cross-sectional study of 101 work groups and 413 employees in 101 different organizations, Yang et al. (2018) showed that supervisors' perceptions of guanxi HRM practices were positively related to subordinates' perceptions of guanxi HRM practices, which, in turn, negatively affected subordinates' work engagement.

Conclusions

I would like to end the chapter by making some theoretical and practical concluding remarks and describing current insights about what WE is, how and why employees experience it, how WE is related to other indicators of organizational well-being, and some notes for a future research agenda on work engagement and organizational well-being.

Throughout the chapter, work engagement is considered a key element of organizational well-being, a multilevel construct (IGLO) presenting different facets or areas of well-being, such as physical, psychological, and social well-being, which are reciprocally related over time (Salanova, 2020a). Work engagement could be considered a "psychological" indicator of organizational well-being. Of course, there are different definitions of work engagement, as I noted in this chapter. However, from my point of view, an integrative vision of WE is rooted in OHP and POP, as a concept distinct from but negatively related to burnout. Defined in its own right, WE is considered a fully motivational (affective-cognitive) experience, a kind of psychological *well-being in the workplace,* characterized by vigor, dedication, and absorption. Furthermore, WE is contextualized in a broader picture as a core dimension of a HERO, where the incidence of WE in an organization coexists with other patterns of employee well-being, such as burnout, workaholics, and 9-to-5 employees.

Work-engaged employees usually work in nutritive workplace environments that provide them with enough job resources and healthy organizational practices to not only satisfy their basic physical and psychological needs but also provide them with future positive and inspirational scenarios so that they can prosper and flourish. This chapter showed empirical evidence about the way employees experience work engagement in these HERO environments, where job resources may play either an intrinsic motivational role because they foster employees' growth, learning, and development, or an extrinsic motivational role because they are instrumental in achieving work goals. Moreover, resources and work engagement seem to work together and have a reciprocal interinfluence on each other over time, forming positive gain cycles and spirals. Resources have motivational power as drivers of work engagement, which, in turn, leads to the accumulation of more resources, and so on. Employees feel motivated when resources are available in the workplace, and different meta-analyses have shown that job demands and job and personal resources are linked to work engagement, which in turn has consequences for employees' work attitudes (i.e., organizational commitment), behaviors (i.e., job performance), or health/well-being.

This chapter examined the relationships between work engagement and other facets of well-being at work. The well-being concept is viewed in different ways in the research literature. My goal was to clarify this point and propose a trilogy of facets of well-being (i.e., physical, psychological, and social) from research on POP. From this perspective, health and well-being "are not the mere absence of illness"; there is not simply an absence of negative symptoms but rather something else, i.e., positive states of mind where the presence of engagement, positive affect, connectedness, and flourishing, among other indicators, make well-being a complex psychosocial construct.

Without trying to be exhaustive, we learn some of the following lessons from past research about how work engagement and organizational well-being are related. First, being more engaged at work seems to protect the employee by providing positive psychological gains and then better physical well-being as indicated by less risk of cardiovascular disease, better sleep quality, and healthier job recovery, as well as higher physical energy and less exhaustion while working. I presented evidence about differences in these results based on personal, temporal, and contextual factors, with moderating and mediating variables that explain unexpected results. We have to consider these factors for both theoretical and practical reasons, in order to invest in positive psychological interventions in the workplace.

Second, work-engaged workers also manifest less anxiety, depression, and burnout as main indicators of negative psychological well-being. Thus, WE seems to help prevent or reduce anxiety and depression, rather than the other way around. The latest and most recent systematic review by Cortés-Denia et al. (2021) shows that WE is mostly related to a lower risk of suffering from stress, anxiety, depression, fatigue, and psychological tension. Among all these negative indicators of psychological well-being, it is clear that the most researched question has to do with the way WE is related to burnout in the workplace. The chapter shows how the two constructs are connected, and that work engagement research started due to results from burnout studies, as a kind of antipode of burnout. Abundant research compiled in systematic and meta-analytic studies demonstrates that WE adds something to burnout. The two concepts display empirically distinct relationships within the JD-R model, particularly in terms of drivers (i.e., challenge or hindrance demands, or job resources), but they also predict different consequences. Interestingly, the time and level of analysis are important variables, and recent results show that these constructs are reciprocally related over time, but the effect of burnout on engagement seems to be stronger than the effect of engagement on burnout. Moreover, engagement and burnout differ at a deeper psychological level because they are related to each other at "different levels of analysis". Hence, WE seems to occur at the task level, and burnout at the job level of analysis.

The relationship between WE and hedonic (psychological) well-being is fascinating as well. For example, WE has a causal temporal sequence where the more engaged employees are with their work, the more positive (and the less negative) affect they feel over time, such as greater hope and less envy. Feeling positive emotions at work leads employees to have higher levels of work engagement, but feeling engaged is also a pleasant experience that elicits future positive emotional states over time. In these relationships, personal resources such as self-efficacy, optimism, resilience, etc., interact with positive affect in the prediction of work engagement as important moderators in the development of WE over time. However, positive and negative emotions and affect have a complex relationship with WE, as described in the chapter. Recent research on this topic calls for more research to obtain a clearer picture of what it is happening in the world of emotions and work engagement relationships.

Further insights stem from research on how satisfaction and engagement are related to each other. They seem to be related but empirically distinguishable dimensions of employee well-being. Satisfaction indicates more pleasure, is past oriented, and shows need/expectation satiation, whereas WE is a multidimensional construct, future oriented, and more "motivational".

As far as psychological well-being is concerned, WE is considered a kind of "eudaimonic psychological well-being indicator". As documented in the chapter, the psychological construct(s) that make up the core of eudaimonic well-being are still an under-researched topic, mainly because they consist of a range of constructs that vary across researchers. Without trying to mention all of them, I focused on the three most researched constructs: meaningfulness, self-determination, and flourishing. In sum, although differences exist when considering time frames and between-and-within-person approaches, research shows that when employees feel that their work is meaningful to them, they invest energy in their work activity, feeling vigorous, dedicated, and fully absorbed in their tasks. In addition, when employees have their psychological needs of competence, autonomy, and relatedness satisfied, they feel intrinsically motivated by their work and fully work engaged. Regarding flourishing in the workplace, the research shows that, despite its umbrella nature, flourishing seems to be reciprocally related to WE.

Finally, the area of social well-being and its relationship with work engagement has been less researched compared to other facets of well-being. We know that the social context in organizations (i.e., social support from colleagues and supervisors) is a strong driver of work engagement. However, social well-being is not a job (social) resource; instead, it is related to the psychosocial experience of being socially accepted and coherent, finding society meaningful, and experiencing connection and relatedness with others. Research on giving and receiving help, prosocial motivation, group cohesion, and organizational connectedness has shown that these social well-being indicators are related to work engagement at the individual and the collective levels, such as teams and groups.

To end the chapter, I would like to present some ideas for a future research agenda about the relationships between WE and organizational well-being indicators. Much research has addressed links between WE and negative well-being (e.g., anxiety, depression, burnout). However, new changes in societies and the labor market, such as more digital societies or overqualified employees, require research on other negative indicators of psychological well-being, such as technostress, techno-aholism, and boredom at work, and their relationships with work engagement. Can WE protect against these negative psychological consequences of new changes in the labor market, or will WE simply suffer as a result?

Recent research on the way time and levels of analysis act on burnout and engagement relationships calls for more studies on the interaction between time and levels of analysis in predicting the development of burnout (at the job level) and engagement (at the task level). Furthermore, research on collective levels of work engagement, in other words team engagement, complicates the equation, which should be a new area of future research as well. Do team-engaged groups develop over time with different patterns of psychological well-being based on previous levels of burnout (at the job level) and task engagement?

The complex and fascinating results about how emotions/affect are related to WE call for more longitudinal and multilevel studies to obtain a clearer picture of this relationship, as well as more studies

with physiological measures of emotions/affect facets and their consequences for WE. No studies were found using these techniques that
could clarify the sometimes-contradictory results. For example, based
on the self-regulation affective shift model of work engagement
developed by Bledow et al. (2011), we could obtain greater knowledge
about the way WE emerges from the dynamic interplay between positive and negative affect over time, which neurological areas and mechanisms are activated in our brain, and so on.

More research is needed on the reciprocal relationships between
work engagement and other well-being constructs outside the workplace, considering the permeable nature of the boundaries between
work and beyond-work domains, by considering research on the spillover theory and expanding its implications.

Although social well-being and work engagement seem to be related,
there is a need for more research on how different indicators of social
well-being are related and how and under what conditions they are
related to engagement. This is interesting because the idea that one's
own happiness and well-being can be linked to the perception of
others' well-being is called "psychological interconnection of happiness", and it has been researched in cultural psychology by Uchida and
colleagues in the Japanese context. For example, Hitokoto and Uchida
(2018) standardized a self-report scale called the "interdependent happiness scale" to measure individual perceptions of the interpersonally
harmonized, quiescent, and ordinary nuances of happiness that represent the shared meaning of happiness in an interdependent cultural
context. Research on work engagement (at different levels of analysis)
and the psychological interconnection of happiness would be an interesting and inspiring area of research, as shown with other psychosocial
constructs such as social capital (Fukushima et al., 2021).

Finally, longitudinal studies should consider levels of analysis (i.e.,
individual, group, leader, and organization) in the explanation of the
way individual and team engagement develop over time in organizations, in order to clarify these complex relationships over time and across
different levels and their effects on different facets of well-being (physical, psychological, and social). Moreover, this new research will be
useful for designing workplace interventions to increase work engagement (at different levels) and its effects on organizational well-being.

References

Aiello, A., & Tesi, A. (2017). Psychological well-being and work engagement among Italian social workers: Examining the mediational role of job resources. *Social Work Research*, *41*(2), 73–84. https://doi.org/10.1093/swr/svx005.

Ariza-Montes, A., Molina-Sánchez, H., & Ramirez-Sobrino, J. G. (2018). Work engagement and flourishing at work among nuns: The moderating role of human values. *Frontiers in Psychology*, *9*, 1874. https://doi.org/10.3389/fpsyg.2018.01874.

Avey, J. B., Luthans, F. L., Smith, R. M., & Palmer, N. F. (2010). Impact of positive psychological capital on employee well-being over time. *Journal of Occupational Health Psychology*, *15*, 17–28.

Baethge, A., Junker, N. M., & Rigotti, T. (2020) Does work engagement physiologically deplete? Results from a daily diary study. *Work & Stress*, *35*(3), 283–300. https://doi.org//10.1080/02678373.2020.1857466.

Bailey, C., Madden, A., Alfes, K., & Fletcher, L. (2017). The meaning, antecedents and outcomes of employee engagement: A narrative synthesis. *International Journal of Management Reviews*, *19*(1), 31–53. https://doi.org/10.1111/ijmr.12077.

Bakker, A. B., & Demerouti, E. (2007). The job demands-resources model: State of the art. *Journal of Managerial Psychology*, *22*(3), 309–328. https://doi.org/10.1108/02683940710733115.

(2017). Job demands–resources theory: Taking stock and looking forward. *Journal of Occupational Health Psychology*, *22*(3), 273–285. https://doi.org/10.1037/ocp0000056.

Bakker, A. B., & Oerlemans, W. G. M. (2019). Daily job crafting and momentary work engagement: A self-determination and self-regulation perspective. *Journal of Vocational Behavior*, *112*, 417–430. https://doi.org/10.1016/j.jvb.2018.12.005.

Bakker, A. B., Schaufeli, W. B., Leiter, M. P., & Taris, T. W. (2008). Work engagement: An emerging concept in organizational psychology. *Work and Stress*, *22*, 187–200.

Barber, L., Grawitch, M. J., & Munz, D. C. (2013). Are better sleepers more engaged workers? A self-regulatory approach to sleep hygiene and work engagement. *Stress & Health*, *29*, 307–316. https://doi.org/10.1002/smi.2468.

Bartels, A. L., Peterson, S. J., & Reina, C. S. (2019). Understanding well-being at work: Development and validation of the eudaimonic workplace well-being scale. *PLoS ONE*, *14*(4), e0215957. https://doi.org/10.1371/journal.pone.0215957.

Baumeister, R. F., & Leary, M. R. (1995). The need to belong: Desire for interpersonal attachments as a fundamental human motivation. *Psychological Bulletin, 117*(3), 497–529.

Bledow, R., Schmitt, A., Frese, M., & Kühnel, J. (2011). The affective shift model of work engagement. *Journal of Applied Psychology, 96*(6), 1246–1257. https://doi.org/10.1037/a0024532.

Burić, I., & Macuka, I. (2018). Self-efficacy, emotions and work engagement among teachers: A two wave cross-lagged analysis. *Journal of Happiness Studies, 19,* 1917–1933. https://doi.org/10.1007/s10902-017-9903-9.

Butakor, P. K., Guo, Q., & Adebanji, A. O. (2021). Using structural equation modeling to examine the relationship between Ghanaian teachers' emotional intelligence, job satisfaction, professional identity, and work engagement. *Psychology in the Schools, 58*(3), 534–552. https://doi.org/10.1002/pits.22462.

Byrne, Z. S., Peters, J.M., & Weston, J. W. (2016). The struggle with employee engagement: Measures and construct clarification using five samples. *Journal of Applied Psychology, 101*(9), 1201–1227.

Carmona-Halty, M., Salanova, M., Llorens, S., & Schaufeli, W. B. (2021). Linking positive emotions and academic performance: The mediated role of academic psychological capital and academic engagement. *Current Psychology: A Journal for Diverse Perspectives on Diverse Psychological Issues, 40*(6), 2938–2947. https://doi.org/10.1007/s12144-019-00227-8.

Chalofsky, N. (2010). *Meaningful workplaces.* Jossey-Bass.

Chen, C. C., Chen, X. P., & Huang, S. (2013). Chinese guanxi: An integrative review and new directions for future research. *Management and Organization Review, 9,* 167–207. https://doi.org/10.1111/more.12010.

Chen, H., Richard, O. C., Boncoeur, O. D., & Ford, D. L. (2020). Work engagement, emotional exhaustion, and counterproductive work behavior. *Journal of Business Research, 114,* 30–41. https://doi.org/10.1016/j.jbusres.2020.03.025.

Chen, Y., Friedman, R., Yu, E., & Sun, F. (2011). Examining the positive and negative effects of guanxi practices: A multi-level analysis of guanxi practices and procedural justice perceptions. *Asia Pacific Journal of Management, 28,* 715–735.

Christian, M. S., Garza, A. S., & Slaughter, J. E. (2011). Work engagement: A quantitative review and test of its relations with task and contextual performance. *Personnel Psychology, 64*(1), 89–136. https://doi.org/10.1111/j.1744-6570.2010.01203.x.

Clark, M. A., Michel, J. S., Stevens, G. W., Howell, J. W., & Scruggs, R. S. (2014). Workaholism, work engagement and work–home outcomes: Exploring the mediating role of positive and negative emotions. *Stress* and Health: *Journal of the International Society for the Investigation of Stress*, *30*(4), 287–300. https://doi.org/10.1002/smi.2511.

Cortés-Denia, D., Lopez-Zafra, E., & Pulido-Martos, M. (2021). Physical and psychological health relations to engagement and vigor at work: A PRISMA-compliant systematic review. *Current Psychology*, first online. https://doi.org/10.1007/s12144–021-01450-y.

Cruz, V., Salanova, M., & Martínez, I. M. (2013). Liderazgo transformacional y desempeño grupal: unidos por el engagement grupal. *Revista de Psicología Social*, *28*(2), 183–196.

Csikszentmihalyi. M. (1990). *Flow: The psychology of optimal experience.* Harper & Row.

Danna, K., & Griffin, R. W. (1999). Health and well-being in the workplace: A review and synthesis of the literature. *Journal of Management*, *25*(3), 357–384. https://doi.org/10.1177/014920639902500305.

Day, A., & Nielsen, K. (2017). What does our organization do to help our well-being? Creating healthy workplaces and workers. In N. Chmiel, F. Fraccaroni, & M. Sverke (Eds.), *An introduction to work and organizational psychology: An international perspective* (pp. 295–314). John Wiley & Sons.

Day, A., & Randell, D. (2014). Building a foundation for psychologically healthy workplaces and well-being. In A. Day, E. K. Kelloway, & J. J. Hurrell Jr. (Eds.), *Workplace wellbeing: How to build psychologically healthy workplaces* (pp. 3–26). John Wiley & Sons.

Deci, E. L., & Ryan, R. M. (1985). *Intrinsic motivation and self-determination in human behavior.* Plenum.

(2000). The "what" and "why" of goal pursuits: Human needs and the self determination of behavior. *Psychological Inquiry*, *11*, 227–268. https://doi.org/10.1207/S15327965PLI1104_01.

Decuypere, A., & Schaufeli, W. (2020). Leadership and work engagement: Exploring explanatory mechanisms. *German Journal of Human Resource Management*, *34*(1), 69–95. https://doi.org/10.1177/2397002219892197.

Dein, S., & Abbas, S. Q. (2005). The stresses of volunteering in a hospice: A qualitative study. *Palliative Medicine*, *19*, 58–64. https://doi.org/10.1191/0269216305pm969oa.

Diedericks, E., & Rothmann, S. (2013). Flourishing of information technology professionals: The role of work engagement and job satisfaction. *Journal of Psychology in Africa*, *23*(2), 225–234.

Diener, E., & Emmons, R. A. (1984). The independence of positive and negative affect. *Journal of Personality and Social Psychology*, *47*(5), 1105–1117. https://doi.org/10.1037/0022-3514.47.5.1105.

Diestel, S., Rivkin, W., & Schmidt, K. H. (2015). Sleep quality and self-control capacity as protective resources in the daily emotional labor process: Results from two diary studies. *Journal of Applied Psychology*, *100*, 809–827. https://doi.org/10.1037/a0038373.

Dugan, A. G., & Barnes-Farrell, J. L. (2020). Working mothers' second shift, personal resources, and self-care. *Community, Work & Family*, *23*(1), 62–79, https://doi.org/10.1080/13668803.2018.1449732.

Edwards, J. R., & Rothbard, N. P. (2000). Mechanisms linking work and family: Specifying the relationships between work and family constructs. *Academy of Management Review*, *25*, 178–199. https://doi.org/10.5465/AMR.2000.2791609.

Eguchi, H., Shimazu, A., Kawakami, N., Inoue, A., Nakata, A., & Tsutsumi, A. (2015). Work engagement and high-sensitivity C-reactive protein levels among Japanese workers: A 1-year prospective cohort study. *International Archives of Occupational Environmental Health*, *88*, 651–658. https://doi.org/10.1007/s00420-014-0995-9.

Eldor, L., Harpaz, I., & Westman, M. (2016). The work/nonwork spillover: The enrichment role of work engagement. *Journal of Leadership and Organizational Studies*, *27*(1), 21–34. https://doi.org/10.1177/1548051816647362.

Emmet, E. A. (1991). Physical and chemical agents at the workplace. In G. M. Green & F. Baker (Eds.), *Work, health, and productivity* (pp. 35–44). Oxford University Press.

Erdil, O., & Müceldili, B. (2014). The effects of envy on job engagement and turnover intention. *Procedia – Social and Behavioral Sciences*, *150*, 447–454. https://doi.org/b68h.

Extremera, N., Durán, A., & Rey, L. (2005). La inteligencia emocional percibida y su influencia sobre la satisfacción vital, la felicidad subjetiva y el "engagement" en trabajadores de centros para personas con discapacidad intelectual. *Ansiedad y Estrés*, *11*(1), 63–73.

Fairle, P. (2011). Meaningful work, employee engagement, and other key employee outcomes: Implications for human resource development. *Advances in Developing Human Resources*, *13*, 508–525. https://doi.org/10.1177/1523422311431679.

Feldman, P. J., Cohen, S., Lepore, S. J., Matthews, K. A., Kamarck, T. W., & Marsland, A. L. (1999). Negative emotions and acute physiological responses to stress. *Annals of Behavioral Medicine*, *21*(3), 216–222. https://doi.org/10.1007/BF02884836DO.

Ferreira, A. I., da Costa Ferreira, P., Cooper, C. L., & Oliveira, D. (2019). How daily negative affect and emotional exhaustion correlates with work engagement and presenteeism-constrained productivity. *International Journal of Stress Management*, *26*(3), 261–271. https://doi.org/10.1037/str0000114.

Forgeard, M. J. C., Jayawickreme, E., Kern, M., & Seligman, M. E. P. (2011). Doing the right thing: Measuring wellbeing for public policy. *International Journal of Wellbeing*, *1*(1), 79–106. https://doi.org/10 .5502/ijw.v1i1.15.

Fredrickson, B. L. (2001). The role of positive emotions in positive psychology: The broaden-and-build theory of positive emotions. *American Psychologist*, *56*(3), 218–226. https://doi.org/10.1037/0003-066x.56.3 .218.

Friedman, H. S., & Kern, M. L. (2014). Personality, well-being, and health. *Annual Review of Psychology*, *65*, 719–42. https://doi.org/10.1146/ annurev-psych-010213-115123.

Fukushima, S., Uchida, Y., & Takemura, K. (2021). Do you feel happy when other members look happy? Moderating effect of community-level social capital on interconnection of happiness. *International Journal of Psychology*. http://doi.org/10.1002/ijop.12744.

Gkorezis, P., Bellou, V., Xanthopoulou, D., Bakker, A. B., & Tsiftsis, A. (2016). Linking football team performance to fans' work engagement and performance: Test of a spillover model. *Journal of Occupational and Organizational Psychology*, *89*(4), 791–812. https://doi.org/10 .1111/joop.12155.

Glazer, S., Kozusznik, M. W., Meyers, J. H., & Ganai, O. (2014). Meaningfulness as a resource to mitigate work stress. *Contemporary Occupational Health Psychology: Global Perspectives on Research and Practice*, *3*, 114–130. https://doi.org/10.1002/9781118713860.ch8.

Goering, D. D., Shimazu, A., Zhou, F., Wada, T., & Sakai, R. (2017). Not if, but how they differ: A meta-analytic test of the nomological networks of burnout and engagement. *Burnout Research*, *5*, 21–34. https://doi.org/ 10.1016/j.burn.2017.05.003.

González-Romá, V., Schaufeli, W. B., Bakker, A., & Lloret, S. (2006). Burnout and work engagement: Independent factors or opposite poles? *Journal of Vocational behavior*, *68*(1), 165–174. https://doi.org/10 .1016/j.jvb.2005.01.003.

Goodboy, A. K., Martin, M. M., & Bolkan, S. (2020). Workplace bullying and work engagement: A self-determination model. *Journal of Interpersonal Violence*, *35*(21–22), 4686–1708. https://doi.org/10 .1177/0886260517717492.

Gracia, E., Salanova, M., Grau, R., & Cifre, E. (2013). How to enhance service quality through organizational facilitators, collective work engagement, and relational service competence. *European Journal of Work and Organizational Psychology*, *22*(1), 42–55.

Grant, A., Christianson, M., & Price, R. (2007). Happiness, health, or relationships? Managerial practices and employee well-being tradeoffs. *Academy of Management Executive*, *21*(1), 51–63.

Grassi, G., Dell'Oro, R., Quarti-Trevano, F. et al. (2005). Neuroadrenergic and reflex abnormalities in patients with metabolic syndrome. *Diabetologia*, 48, 1359–1365. https://doi.org/10.1007/s00125-005-1798-z.

Greenhaus, J. H., & Powell, G. N. (2006). When work and family are allies: A theory of work–family enrichment, 31(1). https://doi.org/10.5465/amr.2006.19379625.

Hakanen, J. J., Peeters, M. C. W., & Schaufeli, W. B. (2018). Different types of employee well-being across time and their relationships with job crafting. *Journal of Occupational Health Psychology*, 23(2), 289–301.

Hakanen, J. J., & Schaufeli, W. B. (2012). Do burnout and work engagement predict depressive symptoms and life satisfaction? A three-wave seven-year prospective study. *Journal of Affective Disorders*, 141, 415–424. https://doi.org/10.1016/j.jad.2012.02.043.

Halbesleben, J. R. B. (2010). A meta-analysis of work engagement: Relationships with burnout, demands, resources, and consequences. In A. B. Bakker & M. P. Leiter (Eds.), *Work engagement: A handbook of essential theory and research* (pp. 102–117). Psychology Press.

Harter, J. K., Schmidt, F. L., & Hayes, T. L. (2002). Business unit-level relationship between employee satisfaction, employee engagement, and business outcomes: A meta-analysis. *Journal of Applied Psychology*, 87(2), 268–279.

Hatfield, E., Cacioppo, J. T., & Rapson, R. L. (1994). *Emotional contagion.* Cambridge University Press.

Heintzelman, S. J. (2018). Eudaimonia in the contemporary science of subjective well-being: Psychological well-being, self-determination, and meaning in life. In E. Diener, S. Oishi, & L. Tay (Eds.), *Handbook of well-being*. DEF Publishers. https://doi.org/nobascholar.com.

Hitge, E., & Van Schalkwyk, I. (2018). Exploring a group of South African psychologists' well-being: Competencies and contests. *South African Journal of Psychology*, 48(4), 553–566.

Hitokoto H., & Uchida Y. (2018). Interdependent happiness: Progress and implications. In M. Demir & N. Sümer (Eds.), *Close relationships and happiness across cultures: Cross-cultural advancements in positive psychology* (Vol. 13). Springer. https://doi.org/10.1007/978-3-319-89663-2_2.

Hobföll, S. E. (1989). Conservation of resources. A new attempt at conceptualizing stress. *American Psychologist*, 44, 513–524. https://doi.org/10.1037//0003-066X.44.3.513

Hsu, W., & Wang, A. (2007). Downsides of guanxi practices in Chinese organizations. Paper presented at the 68th Annual Academy of Management Meeting, Philadelphia, PA, August.

Huppert, F. A., & So, T. T. C. (2013). Flourishing across Europe: Application of a new conceptual framework for defining well-being. *Social Indicators Research*, *110*, 837–861. https://doi.org/10.1007/s11205-011-9966-7.

Hursthouse, R. (1999). *On virtue ethics*. Oxford University Press.

Huta, V., & Waterman, A. S. (2014). Eudaimonia and its distinction from hedonia: Developing a classification and terminology for understanding conceptual and operational definitions. *Journal of Happiness Studies*, *15*, 1425–1456. https://doi.org/10.1007/s10902–013-9485-0.

Huynh, J. Y., Metzer, J. C., & Winefield, A. H. (2012a). Validation of the four dimensional connectedness scale in a multisample volunteer study: A distinct construct from work engagement and organizational commitment. *Voluntas: International Journal of Voluntary and Nonprofit Organizations*, *23*, 1056–1082. https://doi.org/10.1007/s11266-011-9259-4.

(2012b). Engaged or connected? A perspective of the motivational pathway of the job demands-resources model in volunteers working for nonprofit organizations. *Voluntas: International Journal of Voluntary and Nonprofit Organizations*, *23*, 870–898. https://doi.org/10.1007/s11266-011-9233-1.

Huynt, J. Y., Xanthopoulou, D., & Winefield, A. H. (2014). The job demands-resources model in emergency service volunteers: Examining the mediating roles of exhaustion, work engagement and organizational connectedness. *Work & Stress: An International Journal of Work, Health & Organizations*, *28*(3), 305–322. https://doi.org/10.1080/02678373.2014.936922.

Imamura, K., Kawakami, N., Inoue, A., Shimazu, A., Tsutsumi, A., Takahashi M. et al. (2016). Work engagement as a predictor of onset of major depressive episode (MDE) among workers, independent of psychological distress: A 3-year prospective cohort study. *PLoS ONE*, *11*(2), e0148157. https://doi.org/10.1371/journal.pone.0148157.

Innstrand, S. T., Langballe, E. M., & Falkum, E. (2012). A longitudinal study of the relationship between work engagement and symptoms of anxiety and depression. *Stress & Health*, *28*(1), 1–10. https://doi.org/10.1002/smi.1395.

Jackowska, M., Dockray, S., Hendrickx, H., & Steptoe, A. (2011). Psychosocial factors and sleep efficiency: Discrepancies between subjective and objective evaluations of sleep. *Psychosomatic Medicine*, *73*(9), 810–816. https://doi.org/10.1097/PSY.0b013e3182359e77.

Jayawickreme, E., Forgeard, M. J. C., & Seligman, M. E. P. (2012). The engine of well-being. *Review of General Psychology*, *16*(4), 327–342. https://doi.org/10.1037/a0027990.

Judge, T. A., Weiss, H. M., Kammeyer-Mueller, J. D., & Hulin, C. L. (2017). Job attitudes, job satisfaction, and job affect: A century of continuity and of change. *Journal of Applied Psychology*, *102*(3), 356–374. https://doi.org/10.1037/apl0000181.10.1037/apl0000181.supp.

Junker, N. M., Kaluza, A. J., Häusser, J. A., Mojzisch, A., van Dick, R., Knoll, M., & Demerouti, E. (2020). Is work engagement exhausting? The longitudinal relationship between work engagement and exhaustion using latent growth modeling. *Applied Psychology: An International Review*, first online. https://doi.org/10.1111/apps.12252.

Kahn, W. A. (1990). Psychological conditions of personal engagement and disengagement at work. *Academy of Management Journal*, *33*, 692–724.

(1992). To be fully there: Psychological presence at work. *Human Relations*, *45*(4), 321–349. https://doi.org/10.1177/001872679204500402

(2007). Meaningful connections: positive relationships and attachments at work. In J. E. Dutton & B. R. Ragins (Eds.). *Exploring positive relationships at work: Building a theoretical and research foundation* (pp. 189–206). Lawrence Erlbaum Associates.

Kahn, W. A., & Fellows, S. (2013). Employee engagement and meaningful work. In B. J. Dik, Z. S. Byrne, & M. F. Steger (Eds.), *Purpose and meaning in the workplace* (pp. 105–126). American Psychological Association. https://doi.org/10.1037/14183-006.

Karatepe, O. M., & Karadas, G. (2015). Do psychological capital and work engagement foster frontline employees' satisfaction? A study in the hotel industry. *International Journal of Contemporary Hospitality Management*, *27*(6), 1254–1278. https://doi.org/10.1108/IJCHM-01-2014-0028.

Kashdan, T. B., Biswas-Diener, R., & King, L. A. (2008). Reconsidering happiness: the costs of distinguishing between hedonics and eudaimonia. *The Journal of Positive Psychology*, *3*(4), 219–233. https://doi.org/10.1080/17439760802303044.

Kelloway, E. K., & Day, A. L. (2005). Building healthy workplaces: What we know so far. *Canadian Journal of Behavioral Science*, *37*(4), 223–235.

Kesebir, P. (2018). Scientific answers to the timeless philosophical question of happiness. In E. Diener, S. Oishi, & L. Tay (Eds.), *Handbook of well-being*. DEF Publishers. https://doi.org/nobascholar.com.

Keyes, C. L. M. (1998). Social well-being. *Social Psychology Quarterly*, 121–40.

(2007). Promoting and protecting mental health as flourishing: A complementary strategy for improving national mental health. *American Psychologist*, *62*, 95–108.

King, R. B., Pitliya, R. J., & Datu, J. A. (2020). Psychological capital drives optimal engagement via positive emotions in work and school contexts. *Asian Journal of Social Psychology*, 23(4), 457–468. https://doi.org/10 .1111/ajsp.12421.

Kong, Y., & Li, M. (2018). Proactive personality and innovative behavior: The mediating roles of job-related affect and work engagement. *Social Behavior and Personality: An International Journal*, 46(3), 431–446. https://doi.org/10.2224/sbp.6618.

Kozlowski, S. W. J., & Ilgen, D. R. (2006). Enhancing the effectiveness of work groups and teams. *Psychological Science in the Public Interest.*, 7 (3), 77–124. https://doi.org/10.1111/j.1529-1006.2006.00030.x.

Kühnel, J., Zacher, H., Bloom, J., & Bledow, R. (2017). Take a break! Benefits of sleep and short breaks for daily work engagement, *European Journal of Work and Organizational Psychology*, 26(4), 481–491. https://doi.org/10.1080/1359432X.2016.1269750.

Leijten, F. R. M., van den Heuvel, S. G., van der Beek, A. J. et al. (2015). Associations of work-related factors and work engagement with mental and physical health: A 1-year follow-up study among older workers. *Journal of Occupational Rehabilitation*, 25, 86–95. https://doi.org/10 .1007/s10926-014-9525-6.

Lesener, T., Gusy, B., Jochmann, A., & Wolter, C. (2019). The drivers of work engagement: A meta-analytic review of longitudinal evidence. *Work & Stress*, 1–20. https://doi.org/10.1080/02678373.2019 .1686440.

Liu, T., Zeng, X., Chen, M., & Lan, T. (2019). The harder you work, the higher your satisfaction with life? The influence of police work engagement on life satisfaction: A moderated mediation model. *Frontiers in Psychology*, *10*, 826. https://doi.org/10.3389/fpsyg.2019.00826.

Llorens, S., & Salanova, M. (2014). Loss and gain cycles? A longitudinal study about burnout, engagement and self-efficacy. *Burnout Research*, 1, 3–11. https://doi.org/10.1016/j.burn.2014.02.001.

Locke, E. A. (1976). The nature and causes of job satisfaction. In M. D. Dunnette (Ed.), *Handbook of industrial and organizational psychology*. Rand McNally.

Mäkikangas, A., Hyvönen, K., & Feldt, T. (2016). The energy and identification continua of burnout and work engagement: Developmental profiles over eight years. *Burnout Research*, *5*, 44–54. https://doi.org/10 .1016/j.burn.2017.04.002.

Malinowski, P., & Lim, H. J. (2015). Mindfulness at work: Positive affect, hope, and optimism mediate the relationship between dispositional mindfulness, work engagement, and well-being. *Mindfulness*, *6*, 1250–1262. https://doi.org/10.1007/s12671–015-0388-5.

Maricuțoiu, L. P., Sulea, C., & Iancu, A. (2017). Work engagement or burnout: Which comes first? A meta-analysis of longitudinal evidence. *Burnout Research*, *5*, 35–43. https://doi.org/10.1016/j.burn.2017.05 .001.

Maslach, C., & Leiter, M. P. (1997). *The truth about burnout*. Jossey-Bass.

Matthew, J. J., & Jiang, L. (2017). Reaping the benefits of meaningful work: The mediating versus moderating role of work engagement. *Stress and Health*, *33*(3), 288–297. http://doi.org/10.1002/smi.2710.

May, D. R., Gilson, R. L., & Harter, L. M. (2004). The psychological conditions of meaningfulness, safety and availability and the engagement of the human spirit at work. *Journal of Occupational and Organizational Psychology*, *77*, 11–37.

Meyer, J. P. (2014). Employee commitment, motivation, and engagement: Exploring the links. In M. Gagné (Ed.), *The Oxford handbook of work engagement, motivation, and self-determination theory* (pp. 33–49). Oxford University Press.

Miralles, C., Navarro, J., & Unger, D. (2015). Daily work events and state work engagement: the mediating role of affect. *International Journal of Social Psychology*, *30*(2), 264–294. https://doi.org/10.1080/21711976 .2015.1016755.

Nielsen, K., Yarker, J., Munir, F., & Bültmann, U. (2018). IGLOO: An integrated framework for sustainable return to work in workers with common mental disorders. *Work Stress*, *32*, 400–417.

OECD (2013). *Guidelines on measuring subjective well-being*. OECD.

Olivier, A. L., & Rothmann, S. (2007). Antecedents of work engagement in a multinational oil company. *South African Journal of Industrial Psychology*, *33*(3), 49–56. www.ianrothmann.com/pub/engagement_ olivier.pdf.

Ouweneel, E., Le Blanc, P. M., Schaufeli, W. B., & van Wijhe, C. I. (2012). Good morning, good day: A diary study on positive emotions, hope, and work engagement. *Human Relations*, *65*(9), 1129–1154. https://doi .org/10.1177/0018726711429382.

Pavot, W., & Diener, E. (1993). The affective and cognitive context of self-reported measures of subjective well-being. *Social Indicators Research*, *28*, 1–20. https://doi.org/10.1007/BF01086714.

Peláez, M. J., Coo, C., & Salanova, M. (2020). Facilitating work engagement and performance through strengths-based micro-coaching: A controlled trial study. *Journal of Happiness Studies*, *21*, 1265–1284. https://doi.org/10.1007/s10902–019-00127-5.

Pratt, M. G., & Ashforth, B. E. (2008). Fostering meaningfulness in working and at work. In K. Cameron, J. E. Dutton, & R. E. Quinn (Eds.), *Positive Organizational Scholarship Foundation of a New Discipline* (pp. 309–327). Berett-Koehler Publishers.

Rodríguez-Sánchez, A. M., Devloo, T., Rico, R., Salanova, M., & Anseel, F. (2017). What makes creative teams tick? Cohesion, engagement, and performance cross creativity tasks: A three-wave study. *Group & Organization Management, 42*(4), 521–547. https://doi.org/10.1177/1059601116636476.

Rothmann, S. (2008). Occupational stress, job satisfaction, burnout and work engagement as components of work-related well-being. *South African Journal of Industrial Psychology, 34*(3), 11–16.

Ryan, R. M., & Deci, E. L. (2000). Self-determination theory and the facilitation of intrinsic motivation, social development, and well-being. *American Psychologist, 55*, 68–78. https://doi.org/10.1037//0003-066x .55.1.68.

(2002). Overview of self-determination theory: An organismic dialectical perspective. In E. L. Deci & R. M. Ryan (Eds.), *Handbook of self-determination research* (pp. 3–36). University of Rochester Press.

Ryan, R., Huta, V., & Deci, E. L. (2008). Living well: a self-determination theory perspective on eudaimonia. *Journal of Happiness Studies, 9*, 139–170. https://doi.org/10.1007/s10902–006-9023-4.

Ryff, C. D. (1989). Happiness is everything, or is it? Explorations on the meaning of psychological well-being. *Journal of Personality and Social Psychology, 57*(6), 1069.

Ryff, C. D., & Keyes, C. L. M. (1995). The structure of psychological well-being revisited. *Journal of Personality and Social Psychology, 69*(4), 719–727. https://doi.org/10.1037//0022-3514.69.4.719.

Saks, A. M. (2006). Antecedents and consequences of employee engagement. *Journal of Managerial Psychology, 21*, 600–619.

Salanova, M. (2020a). *Cultivar el Bienestar Organizacional (BO) en tiempos de la Covid-19* [Cultivate organizational wellbeing in times of Covid-19]. Capital Humano.

(2020b). How to survive COVID-19? Notes from organizational resilience. In Moya et al., Social Psychology in the face of COVID-19 (special issue), *International Journal of Social Psychology*, first online. https://doi.org/10.1080/02134748.2020.1795397.

(2021). Work engagement: A key to HEROs – healthy and resilient organizations. In J. P. Meyer & B. Schneider (Eds.), *Research agenda for employee engagement in the changing world of work*. Edward Elgar. *(p. 53–65)* https://doi.org/10.4337/9781789907858.00011

Salanova, M., Del Libano, M., Llorens, S., & Schaufeli, W. B. (2014). Engaged, workaholic, burned-out or just 9-to-5? Toward a typology of employee well-being. *Stress & Health, 30*(1), 71–81. https://doi.org/ 10.1002/smi.2499.

Salanova, M., Llorens, S., Cifre, E., & Martínez, I. M. (2012). We need a HERO! Towards a validation of the healthy & resilient organization

(HERO) model. *Group & Organization Management, 37*, 785–822. https://doi.org/10.1177/1059601112470405.

Salanova, M., Llorens, S., Cifre, E., Martínez, I. M., & Schaufeli, W. B. (2003). Perceived collective efficacy, subjective well-being and task performance among electronic work groups: An experimental study. *Small Group Research, 34*, 43–73.

Salanova, M., Lorente, L., Chambel, M. J., & Martínez, I. M. (2011). Linking transformational leadership to nurses' extra-role performance: The mediating role of self-efficacy and work engagement. *Journal of Advanced Nursing, 67*(10), 2256–2266.

Salanova, M., Llorens, S., & Martínez, I. M. (2019). *Organizaciones Saludables. Una mirada desde la psicología positiva [Healthy organizations: A look from positive psychology]* (1st ed.). Aranzadi.

Salanova, M., Llorens, S., & Schaufeli, W. B. (2011). "Yes, I can, I feel good, and I just do it!" On gain cycles and spirals of efficacy beliefs, affect, and engagement. *Applied Psychology, 60*, 255–285. https://doi.org/cn5mk4.

Salanova, M., Schaufeli, W. B., Xanthopoulou, D., & Bakker, A. B. (2010). The gain spiral of resources and work engagement: Sustaining a positive worklife. In A. B. Bakker & M. P. Leiter (Eds.), *Work engagement: A handbook of essential theory and research* (pp. 118–131). Psychology Press.

Salmela-Aro, A., & Upadyaya, K. (2018). Role of demands-resources in work engagement and burnout in different career stages, *Journal of Vocational Behavior, 108*, 190–200. https://doi.org/10.1016/j.jvb.2018.08.002.

Schaufeli, W., & Salanova, M. (2011). Work engagement: On how to better catch a slippery concept. *European Journal of Work and Organizational Psychology, 20*(1), 39–46. https://doi.org/10.1080/1359432X.2010.515981.

Schaufeli, W. B. (2018). Work engagement in Europe: Relations with national economy, governance and culture. *Organizational Dynamics, 47*, 99–106.

Schaufeli, W. B. & Bakker, A. B. (2022). Work engagement: A critical assessment of concept and measurement. In W. R. Tuch, A. B. Bakker, L. Tay, & F. Gander (Eds.), *Handbook of positive psychology assessment.* (pp. 273–295) Göttingen: Hogrefe.

Schaufeli, W. B., & Salanova, M. (2007). Efficacy or inefficacy, that's the question: Burnout and work engagement, and their relationships with efficacy beliefs, *Anxiety, Stress & Coping, 20*(2), 177–196. https://doi.org/10.1080/10615800701217878.

Schaufeli, W. B., Salanova, M., González-Romá, V., & Bakker, A. B. (2002). The measurement of engagement and burnout: A two sample confirmatory factor analytic approach. *Journal of Happiness Studies, 3*, 71–92.

Schreurs, B., van Emmerick, I. H., Van den Broeck, A., & Guenter, H. (2014). Work values and work engagement within teams: The mediating role of need satisfaction. *Group Dynamics: Theory, Research, and Practice, 18*, 267–281. https://doi.org/10.1037/gdn0000009.

Schwerdtfeger, A. R., & Gerteis, A. K. S. (2014). The manifold effects of positive affect on heart rate variability in everyday life: Distinguishing within-person and between-person associations. *Health Psychology, 33* (9), 1065–1073. https://doi.org/10.1037/hea0000079.

Seligman, M. (2018). PERMA and the building blocks of well-being. *The Journal of Positive Psychology, 13*(4), 333–335. https://doi.org/10.1080/17439760.2018.1437466.

Seppälä, P., Mauno, S., Kinnunen, M., Feldt, T., Juuti, T. Tolvanen. A., & Rusko, H. (2012). Is work engagement related to healthy cardiac autonomic activity? Evidence from a field study among Finnish women workers, *The Journal of Positive Psychology, 7*(2), 95–106. https://doi.org/10.1080/17439760.2011.637342.

Shao-mei Zheng, C., Gunasekara, A., & Blaich, S. (2018). Mindfulness and work engagement: The mediating effect of psychological flourishing. *Academy of Management Annual Meeting Proceedings*, (1), 12210. https://doi.org/10.5465/AMBPP.2018.12210abstract.

Sheng, X., Wang, Y., Hong, W., Zhu, Z., & Zhang, X. (2019). The curvilinear relationship between daily time pressure and work engagement: The role of psychological capital and sleep. *International Journal of Stress Management, 26*(1), 25–35. https://doi.org/10.1037/str0000085/.

Shin, Y., & Hur, W.-M. (2020). When do job-insecure employees keep performing well? The buffering roles of help and prosocial motivation in the relationship between job insecurity, work engagement, and job performance. *Journal of Business and Psychology*. https://doi.org/10.1007/s10869-020-09694-4.

Shuck, B., Alagaraja, M., Rose, K., Owen, J., Osam, K., & Bergman, M. (2017). The health-related upside of employee engagement: Exploratory evidence and implications for theory and practice. *Performance Improvement Quarterly, 30*(3), 165–178. http://doi.org/10.1002/piq.21246.

Sonnentag, S., Binnewies, C., & Mojza, E. J. (2010). Staying well and engaged when demands are high: The role of psychological detachment. *Journal of Applied Psychology, 95*(5), 965–976. https://doi.org/10.1037/a0020032.

Sonnentag, S., Dormann, C., & Demerouti, E. (2010). Not all days are created equal: The concept of state work engagement. In A. B. Bakker

& M. P. Leiter (Eds.), *Work engagement: Recent developments in theory and research* (pp. 25–38). Psychology Press.

Sonnentag, S., Mojza, E. J., Demerouti, E., & Bakker, A. B. (2012). Reciprocal relations between recovery and work engagement: The moderating role of job stressors. *Journal of Applied Psychology*, *97*(4), 842–853. https://doi.org/10.1037/a0028292.

Steger, M. F., Littman-Ovadia, H., Miller, M., Menger, L., & Rothmann, S. (2012). Engaging in work even when it is meaningless: Positive affective disposition and meaningful work interact in relation to work engagement. *Journal of Career Assessment*, *21*(2), 348–361. http://doi.org/10 .1177/1069072712471517.

Teng, E., Zhang, L., & Qiu, Y. (2018). Always bad for creativity? An affect-based model of job insecurity and the moderating effects of giving support and receiving support. *Economic and Industrial Democracy*, 1–27.

Torrente, P., Salanova, M., & Llorens, S. (2013). Spreading engagement: On the role of similarity in the positive contagion of teamwork engagement. *Journal of Work and Organizational Psychology*, *29*, 153–159.

Torrente, P., Salanova, M., Llorens, S., & Schaufeli, W.B. (2012). Teams make it work: How teamwork engagement mediates between social resources and performance in teams. *Psicothema*, *24*(1), 106–112.

Uy, M., Lin, K., & Ilies, R. (2017). Is it better to give or receive? The role of help in buffering the depleting effects of surface acting. *Academy of Management Journal*, *60*, 1442–1462.

Van den Broeck, A., Vansteenkiste, M., De Witte, H., Soenens, B., & Lens, W. (2010). Capturing autonomy, competence, and relatedness at work: Construction and initial validation of the work-related basic need satisfaction scale. *Journal of Occupational and Organizational Psychology*, *83*, 981–1002. https://doi.org/10.1347/096317909X481382.

Van Wingerden, J., & Van der Stoep, J. (2018). The motivational potential of meaningful work: Relationships with strengths use, work engagement, and performance. *PLoS ONE*, *13*(6), e0197599. https://doi.org/ 10.1371/journal.pone.0197599.

Van Zyl, L. E., Rothmann, S., & Nieman, C. (2020). Mental health, work engagement and meaningful work–role fit of industrial psychologists: A latent profile analysis. *Psychological Studies*, *65*, 199–213. https://doi .org/10.1007/s12646–019-00544-9.

Vander Elst, T., Bosman, J., De Cuyper, H., Stouten, J., & De Witte, H. (2013). Does positive affect buffer the associations between job insecurity and work engagement and psychological distress? A test among South African workers. *Applied Psychology: An International Review*, *62*(4), 558–570. https://doi.org/10.1111/j.1464-0597.2012.00499.x.

Verba, S., & Nie, N. H. (1972). *Participation in America*. Harper and Row.

Vigoda-Gadot, E., Mizrahi, S., Miller-Mor, R., & Tevet, E. (2008). The bureaucracy–democracy tango: A dual-source empirical revalidation by structural equation modeling in the Israeli public sector. *Politics & Policy, 36*, 431–448.

Vittersø, J. (2004). Subjective well-being versus self-actualization: Using the flow-simplex to promote a conceptual clarification of subjective quality of life. *Social Indicators Research, 65*(3), 299–331. https://doi.org/10.1023/B:SOCI.0000003910.26194.ef.

Vogel, R. M., Rodell, J. B., & Sabey, T. B. (2020). Meaningfulness misfit: Consequences of daily meaningful work needs–supplies incongruence for daily engagement. *Journal of Applied Psychology, 105*(7), 760–770.

Vogt, K., Jenny, G. J., & Bauer, G. F. (2013). Comprehensibility, manageability and meaningfulness at work: Construct validity of a scale measuring work related sense of coherence. *Journal of Industrial Psychology, 39*(1), 1–8. http://doi.org/10.4102/sajip.v39i1.1111.

Wang, C., Xu, J., Zhang, T. C., & Li, Q. M. (2020). Effects of professional identity on turnover intention in China's hotel employees: The mediating role of employee engagement and job satisfaction, *Journal of Hospitality and Tourism Management, 45*, 10–22. https://doi.org/10.1016/j.jhtm.2020.07.002.

Wang, Z., Li, C., & Li, X. (2017). Resilience, leadership and work engagement: The mediating role of positive affect. *Social Indicators Research, 132*, 699–708. https://doi.org/10.1007/s11205-016-1306-5.

Warr, P. (1987). *Work, unemployment and mental health*. Clarendon Press. (1990). The measurement of well-being and other aspects of mental health. *Journal of Occupational Psychology, 63*(3), 193–210.

Weiss, H. M., & Cropanzano, R. (1996). Affective events theory: A theoretical discussion of the structure, causes and consequences of affective experiences at work. In B. M. Staw & L. L. Cummings (Eds.), *Research in Organizational Behavior* (pp. 1–74). JAI Press.

Wilensky, H. L. (1960). Work, careers, and social integration. *International Social Science Journal, 12*, 543–560.

Wong, Y.-T., Ngo, H.-Y., & Wong, C. S. (2003). Antecedents and outcomes of employees' trust in Chinese joint ventures. *Asia Pacific Journal of Management, 20*, 481–499. https://doi.org/10.1023/A:1026391009543.

World Health Organization (WHO). (1946). *Preamble to the Constitution of the World Health Organization*. WHO.

Wu, T. J., & Wu, Y. J. (2019). Innovative work behaviors, employee engagement, and surface acting: A delineation of supervisor-employee emotional contagion effects. *Management Decision, 57*(11), 3200–3216. https://doi.org/10.1108/MD-02-2018-0196.

Xanthopoulou, D., Bakker, A. B., Demerouti, E., & Schaufeli, W. B. (2009). Reciprocal relationships between job resources, personal resources, and work engagement. *Journal of Vocational Behavior, 74*, 235–244. https://doi.org/10.1016/j.jvb.2008.11.003.

Xin, K., & Pearce, J. L. (1996). Guanxi: connections as substitutes for formal institutional support. *Academy of Management Journal, 39*, 1641–1658. https://doi.org/10.2307/257072.

Yang, F., Qian, J., Liu, J., Huang, X., Chau, R., & Wang, T. (2018). Bridging the gap: How supervisors' perceptions of guanxi HRM practices influence subordinates' work engagement. *Applied Psychology: An International Review, 67*(4), 589–616. http://doi.org/10.1111/apps.12144.

Yang, X., Feng, Y., Meng, Y., & Qiu, Y. (2019). Career adaptability, work engagement, and employee well-being among Chinese employees: The role of guanxi. *Frontiers in Psychology, 10*, 1029. http://doi.org/10.3389/fpsyg.2019.01029.

Young, H. R., Glerum, D. R., Wang, W., & Joseph, D. (2018). Who are the most engaged at work? A meta-analysis of personality and employee engagement. *Journal of Organizational Behavior, 39*(10), 1330–1346. https://doi.org/10.1002/job.2303.

Zeijen, M. E. L., Petrou, P., Bakker, A. B., & van Gelderen, B. R. (2020). Dyadic support exchange and work engagement: An episodic test and expansion of self-determination theory. *Journal of Occupational and Organizational Psychology, 93*(3), 687–711. http://doi.org/10.1111/joop.12311.

10 How and Why Gender Relates to Workplace Stress and Well-Being

HOPE DODD, ROSE LEFEVRE-LEVY,
AND KRISTEN M. SHOCKLEY

Just less than 200 years ago, the biggest trials women were faced with were that of fighting for their fundamental civil rights. The right to vote, attend university, a pension, play contact sports, earn minimum wage, and the list goes on. Today, despite being the closest we have ever been to equality in North American history, women are now fighting an entirely different battle against an often silent killer, whose effects are becoming increasingly prevalent in our gender: stress.

—Kang (2015) in *Psychology Today*

As the quote above illustrates, there is a prevalent belief that the experiences of stress for men and women are unique. Indeed, gender differences in many facets of life are frequently discussed by the popular press (e.g., Cook, 2019; Schmitt, 2017) and academics alike (e.g., Ellemers, 2018; Hyde, 2014). Such discussions even prompted a best-selling book in the 1990s proclaiming men and women were from different planets altogether (*Men Are From Mars and Women Are From Venus*, Gray, 1995)! In this chapter, we aim to address the veracity of assumptions regarding gender differences in the specific area of workplace stress and well-being. In doing so, we summarize theoretical notions that have been used to explain and predict gender differences as well as empirical research that has examined mean differences in stressors and well-being across men and women. We also consider how gender functions as a moderator in the relationship between stressors and strain or well-being outcomes. Lastly, we use this information to guide suggestions for future research on the topic.

Before diving into the literature, it is important to address the topic of what we are actually studying when we study "gender" differences. The first germane point to this argument revolves around what gender is. Gender is a social construction and is inextricably intertwined with societal expectations and social roles (Lorber & Farrell, 1991). As such, the meaning of gender and how gender is perceived (e.g., what it means to be "male" or "female" in society) is subject to change. This is in contrast to the term "sex," which refers to biological and genetic differences. Biological sex is determined by anatomical and physiological differences between the male and female sexes. Much of the current chapter will focus on gender, as most researchers within industrial-organizational psychology and related fields conceptualize their work as a study of gender rather than biological sex. However, we will also touch upon the influence of biological sex as this is a perspective that has also been studied, albeit to a lesser extent.

Second, it is important to note that in many cases gender seems to be a proxy for other constructs rather than a substantive variable in and of itself. That is, it is not a person's sex per se that biologically impacts their experiences; rather, gender is often used as a proxy for other important factors that vary systematically with gender (e.g., life role values, gendered socialization). In practice, these effects can be difficult to disentangle, which often results in authors invoking a theoretical perspective that relies on more substantive variables than gender but ultimately falling back on the use of demographic gender in their analyses instead of measuring the substantive variable itself.

In addition, it is important to clarify the concepts of workplace stress and well-being. Broadly, the stress process is comprised of two main components: the *stressor* – the stressful event or circumstances individuals experience (e.g., low job control, poor interpersonal relationships, incompatibility of work and home roles) – and the *strain* – the negative outcome that results from the stressor (e.g., burnout, low motivation, low job satisfaction). The relationship between a stressor and strain can be influenced by several factors, including the use of coping strategies and social support. Throughout the chapter, we review research focused on individual stressors and strains as well as the full stress process.

Common Theoretical Perspectives Regarding Gender Differences

The Differential Exposure Perspective

The *differential exposure perspective* suggests that gender is an exogenous variable that predicts workplace stressors. This perspective rests on the assumption that differences in the way men and women are socialized and the roles they are traditionally expected to inhabit in society influence their work (and nonwork) situations, which in turn exposes them to different types of stressors or to different levels of the same stressors (Jick & Mintz, 1985). For example, women might be more likely than men to experience stressors that are related to their upward career mobility as occupations associated with higher pay and greater opportunities for career advancement are often dominated by men (e.g., mechanical engineers are 91.3% male, surgeons are 73.7% male; U.S. Bureau of Labor Statistics, 2021), while women are over-represented in caregiving and administrative roles (e.g., nurses are 87.4% female, administrative assistants are 72.7% female; U.S. Bureau of Labor Statistics, 2021) that tend to offer fewer opportunities for upward mobility (Cohen, 2013; International Labour Organization, 2019; Stroh & Reilly, 1999). Gender differences in the levels of the same stressors can stem from the fact that different occupations are associated with varying levels of work stressors. To the extent that these occupations are stratified by gender, it may appear there are gender differences in mean levels of work stressors when, in actuality, this relationship is due to characteristics of the types of occupations men and women tend to hold. For example, Mazzola et al. (2011) found clerical workers (e.g., administrative staff) experience particularly high levels of stress in the form of low job control, while engineers tend to experience stress much more frequently in the form of underload (too few job demands). Given that there is a gender skew in each of these occupations, one could falsely draw the conclusion that women experience low job control, when in reality it is people in certain types of jobs, regardless of gender, who experience low job control.

The Psychological/Coping Perspective

The *psychological/coping* framework suggests that gender influences experiences of work stress not by influencing the type and frequency of stressors men and women experience, but instead through the way in which they cope with these stressors. In other words, gender acts as a moderator in the stress process, altering the strength of the relationship between a stressor and strain outcome. Two prevalent theories within this framework include *gender socialization theory* and *role constraint theory*. Although these two theories predict similar patterns of gender-based coping (that men generally use problem-focused coping and women generally use emotion-focused coping), they suggest that different mechanisms underlie coping differences between men and women (Narayanan et al., 1999; Tamres et al., 2002).

Gender socialization theory (sometimes referred to as the socialization hypothesis or the dispositional hypothesis) proposes that men and women are socialized from a young age to cope with stressors in different ways. The theory suggests men are taught to deal with problems in an active manner and therefore tend to use problem-focused or action-oriented coping strategies (Tamres et al., 2002). On the other hand, because women are taught to be more passive and to engage with their emotions, they will tend to use socially or emotionally oriented coping strategies (Folkman & Lazarus, 1980).

Role constraint theory, which was first conceptualized (albeit informally) by Folkman and Lazarus (1980) and later expanded by Rosario et al. (1988), takes a slightly different approach. Gender socialization still influences coping behavior. However, this perspective argues that it primarily influences the types of jobs men and women hold, and these jobs are associated with different environments and situational factors that constrain the coping behaviors that are possible and/or acceptable in a given work context. According to this perspective, women have historically occupied jobs that lend themselves towards more emotion-focused coping, while men have historically occupied jobs in which problem-focused coping is more appropriate (Rosario et al., 1988). For example, an individual (most likely a woman) whose job is in childcare may have a greater tendency to use emotion-focused coping strategies at work as it may be futile to try to deal with the regular stressors associated with taking care of small children (e.g., tantrums) solely through problem-focused coping strategies. In contrast, in other types of jobs (i.e., those that tend to be male-dominated) such as consulting, it may be more effective to deal with stressors encountered on the job (e.g., delivering to clients on a tight timeline) with problem-focused coping. Role constraint theory would suggest that gender differences in coping strategies will persist to the degree that men and women are differentially represented in these two types of roles. Gender differences in coping should disappear as men and women engage in the same societal roles (i.e., are equally represented across professions) (Sigmon et al., 1995).

Biological Sex Differences Perspective

The *biological sex differences* perspective postulates that males and females have biological differences in their reactivity at the neuroendocrine level. Specifically, this perspective emphasizes that by virtue of the levels of varying hormones in the male and female body or by direct genetic effects stemming from the X and Y chromosomes, there is a biologically determined difference in how the body deals with stressors. Although there is a large body of research on biological differences in stress reactivity in the medical and biological sciences (Kajantie & Phillips, 2006), the topic has not been studied extensively in the workplace context specifically. One issue in this area of research generally is that it is difficult to isolate the role of biological sex; measurable differences in physiological stress reactivity for men and women could be attributed to the different psychological or social factors they have experienced throughout life as a result of their sex.

Summary

Within the industrial-organizational literature, most of the research regarding gender differences in workplace stress has been guided by the differential exposure and psychological/coping perspectives. Relatively less attention has been paid to potential biological explanations that align with the biological sex differences perspective. However, it is important to note that, while generally studied independently, each of the perspectives covered are not mutually exclusive. Each proposes a different mechanism responsible for gender differences in workplace stress. Because these mechanisms impact the stress process at different stages – some directly influencing men and women's exposure to stress, others influencing how individuals cope with and appraise stressful experiences, and still others influencing the body's physiological reaction to stress – it is possible that several of these perspectives, taken together, could explain gender differences in the stressor–strain relationship.

Empirical Evidence Regarding Gender Differences in Work Stressors

In the following section, we review research on the work stressors that have received the most empirical attention with regard to gender

differences, including work–family conflict, job demands, job auton-
omy/decision latitude, work hours, and career concerns.

Work–Family Conflict

Out of all the work-related stressors, gender differences are perhaps
most frequently discussed and studied in the context of work–family
conflict, a stressor that occurs when work and family are mutually
incompatible in some respect (Greenhaus & Beutell, 1985). This is not
surprising given the historically gendered nature of social roles
involved in the work and family domains. In this section, we discuss
theoretical ideas put forth to explain gender differences in mean levels
of work–family conflict specifically before diving into empirical analyses of mean differences as well as the veracity of these theoretical
perspectives. First, it is important to note that work–family conflict can
occur in two distinct directions – work-interference-with-family (WIF)
and family-interference-with-work (FIW) – and most theories and
research have focused on each direction distinctly.

The *rational view* (Gutek et al., 1991) proposes that work–family
conflict is largely due to the amount of time spent in a given domain;
the more hours spent in a particular role, the higher the chance that
conflict will occur. Because men tend to spend more time in the work
domain, they should experience greater WIF than women. On the
other hand, women should experience more FIW than men because
they typically spend more time in the family domain. Alternatively, the
sensitization perspective (also called the *gender role view*; Pleck, 1977,
1979) posits that males and females differentially value work and
family roles in accordance with gender socialization processes.
Gender norms suggest that in comparison to women, men's identities
are more closely tied to their work roles than to their family roles.
Accordingly, men should place a greater value on the work role and be
more sensitive to intrusions into this role, specifically FIW, because
these intrusions pose a threat to a highly valued identity (Stryker,
1968, 1980). The inverse of these relationships is true for women, such
that the family role is a highly valued and integral aspect of their self-
concept so women would be expected to perceive and recall more
instances of WIF.

According to the *asymmetrical boundary perspective*, women construct stronger boundaries around the family domain and subsequently

experience less WIF than men, while men form stronger boundaries around the work domain, which would reduce the amount of FIW they experience in comparison to women (Pleck, 1977). However, other researchers have suggested women tend to have more permeable boundaries across all roles, and men are better able to separate their various life roles (Andrews & Bailyn, 1993; Crosby, 1991). This perspective is referred to as the *male segmentation perspective* and would suggest women experience greater WIF and FIW compared to men due to the weaker boundaries they form around both the work and family domains.

In summary, these perspectives often conflict and predict various patterns of gender differences. As a way to bring consensus to the field, Shockley et al. (2017) used meta-analytic path analysis to test competing hypotheses based on the various theoretical perspectives described above. In line with the rational view, results indicated support for mediated models that suggested gender did relate to time spent in a given domain (work/family), which in turn related to WIF/FIW. There was also partial support for the asymmetrical boundary perspective in that gender (being female) related to stronger boundaries around family, which was associated with lower WIF. Counter to this theory, results revealed women also created stronger boundaries around the work domain, which was negatively related to FIW. The mediated models suggested no support for the sensitization nor the male segmentation perspective. However, these findings must be interpreted in light of the main effects. The overall effect sizes for gender differences in WIF and FIW were very small ($rs = -.011$ for WIF and $-.015$ for FIW). This was despite the fact that the rational view and the asymmetrical boundary perspective were supported and thus there *should* have been gender differences. It ultimately implies there are other unmeasured factors at play that have not been clearly implicated in work–family theory, essentially canceling out these effects.

Moreover, various work and family characteristics (e.g., part-time vs. full-time employees, parental status) can have a substantial impact on how one deals with work–family conflict and may vary systematically by gender. Thus, holding these characteristics constant within subsamples could alter the strengths of the gender–work–family conflict relationships. Accordingly, Shockley et al. (2017) also tested for moderating variables that might alter the strengths of the relationships between WIF and FIW among various subgroups. While there were no gender differences in samples consisting of only full-time employees, they found evidence for several small effects in other subgroups. Among samples where men and women were employed in the same job (i.e., studies that included all people in the same occupation), there were no differences in FIW, but women experienced slightly more WIF than men. Parent-only samples, where family demands and gendered division of labor may be exacerbated due to the presence of children, only exhibited gender differences in FIW, such that mothers reported higher conflict than fathers. Among the last type of subgroup, samples of matched dual-earner couples (i.e., the men and women were a part of the same couple, allowing some family factors to be held constant), women reported slightly more FIW than men, but men reported slightly more WIF than women. Lastly, given arguments in the work–family literature that the broader social and cultural context can influence work–family experiences, Shockley and colleagues evaluated whether cultural values and publication date moderated their findings. However, neither cultural gender egalitarianism nor publication date was found to be a significant moderator of the relationships between gender and WIF or FIW.

What this comprehensive review of gender and work–family conflict suggests is that contrary to popular perception, men and women tend to experience similar levels of work–family conflict, with some situational factors causing slight variation in effect sizes. With that being said, we encourage readers to consider the manner in which work–family research is generally conducted and interpret the previous statement in light of this. The meta-analysis is only as strong as its primary studies and the manner in which work–family conflict is typically measured (through subjective Likert scales with questions such as "My work keeps me from my family activities more than I would like"). The meta-analysis was not able to tease apart if gender socialization has caused men and women to interpret similar work–family conflict situations differently. For example, a woman and man might face very similar situations but respond differently when translating these experiences to a Likert scale response. Women are socialized to anticipate work–family conflict (Weer et al., 2006) and may have become accustomed to it over time, distorting their perceptions of it. In that case, a woman might describe one situation as translating to "a fair amount" of work–family conflict, whereas a man would consider the same situation as representing "a great deal" of conflict. These response patterns would in turn distort any true differences. More nuanced research with different types of measurement is needed to test the veracity of these ideas. Episodic research where men and women report work–family conflict situations as they occur, describe them, and report their well-being reactions would be useful. Experimental research where men and women are exposed to similar work–family stressors and their reactions are measured could be enlightening as well.

The Nature of Work

Aspects of the job related to the demands and stress imposed on workers as well as employees' abilities to control how they complete their work have been a point of focus throughout the literature. This is due in large part to the connections between job demands and job autonomy with one's general physical and mental health (Clark et al., 2012; Nixon et al., 2011). Researchers who have focused on gender differences in these specific job characteristics typically invoke the differential exposure perspective noted above, arguing that men and women's tendencies to inhabit different types of jobs impact the nature of their work and their subsequent stress experiences.

Job Demands

Job demands refer to any "physical, psychological, social, or organizational aspects of the job that require sustained physical and/or psychological effort or skills and are therefore associated with certain physiological and/or psychological costs" (Demerouti & Bakker, 2011, p. 2). When assessing changes in the nature of work throughout the late 1900s, Tausig et al. (2004) found women reported experiencing greater job demands in the first wave of the study (1972), but this difference appears to have been eliminated by 2002. This finding is bolstered by more recent research which indicates there are not substantial gender differences in job demands (Grönlund & Öun, 2018; Haines et al., 2019; Hwang & Ramadoss, 2017).

However, some empirical findings indicate there may be factors that moderate this relationship. One such factor is gender segregation within an occupation. When representation within a role or occupation is skewed toward one gender, the broader work context and environment may elicit behavioral expectations or take on characteristics associated with that gender's role (e.g., Eagly et al., 1995; Gutek & Cohen, 1987). As a result, members of the minority gender may be seen as role deviants, which creates additional or unique work stress (Gutek et al., 1988). For example, among a sample of South African construction professionals, a traditionally male-dominated occupation, women reported greater levels of job pressure than men (Bowen et al., 2018). This could be attributable to the fact that women feel an additional pressure to "prove themselves" in an industry where the culture is very masculine and the perception of the ideal worker is likewise masculine.

Job Autonomy/Decision Latitude

One particularly important aspect of work relates to an employee's ability to make decisions regarding their work and how they will perform various job tasks. This characteristic of work has been studied under a variety of different construct names, most commonly job autonomy or decision latitude. Both *skill discretion*, the level of skill required on the job and the employee's flexibility in deciding which skills to employ, as well as *decision authority*, the latitude provided by the organization to the employee in terms of making decisions regarding their work, are components of decision latitude (Karasek et al., 1998). Across a variety of countries and occupations, women report experiencing less skill discretion and decision authority in comparison to men (Grönlund & Öun, 2018; Haines et al., 2019; Hochwarter et al., 1995; Karasek et al., 1998; Li et al., 2006; Matijaš et al., 2018; Roxburgh, 1996). While there is some evidence that this gender gap has decreased over time (Tausig et al., 2004), it is evident that significant gender differences remain.

Two general arguments have been put forth regarding why this gender gap exists. The first points toward gender segregation in the workplace. Female-dominated occupations have been associated with less favorable work conditions, which often include limited job autonomy (Glass, 1990; Stier & Yaish, 2014). Others have argued that organizational level is a more important predictor of job autonomy than occupational type (Adler, 1993). Accordingly, men should be more likely to report higher levels of job autonomy because they are more likely to hold higher ranking roles in organizations, such as supervisors or policy makers (Catalyst, 2021). The empirical evidence is mixed regarding support for both positions. To evaluate the different explanations for the gender gap in job autonomy, researchers have compared the relative effects of both occupational segregation and authoritative positions on job autonomy. Some researchers have found occupational segregation to be more predictive of job autonomy (Glass, 1990; Jaffee, 1989), while others contend that authoritative positions are the dominant force driving the gender gap in autonomy (Adler, 1993; Petrie & Roman, 2004).

In sum, historical reports and evidence of gender differences in job demands seem to have largely dissipated over time. However, this may not apply equally to all occupations, particularly those that remain highly segregated by gender. On the other hand, gender differences in job autonomy continue to persist such that men generally report higher levels of skill discretion and decision authority. Future research might investigate these potential explanations in order to understand why differences along certain work characteristics have been eliminated while others have persisted given that men and women's gender roles have become more similar over time.

Work Hours

A common source of work-related stress pertains to the amount of time one spends working. Working excessive hours detracts from the time spent in other life roles and activities and can negatively impact one's physical and mental health (Wong et al., 2019). Despite women's increasing participation in the labor force, many researchers continue to find evidence that, compared to men, women spend fewer hours in paid labor (e.g., Erosa et al., 2017; Lozano et al., 2016). These findings can be attributed in part to differences in employment status (e.g., part-time vs. full-time), as women are much more likely than men to be employed part-time (U.S. Bureau of Labor Statistics, 2020). However, even among full-time employees, women work fewer hours than men (Beckhusen, 2019; Haines et al., 2019). Additionally, even though women are more likely than men to take a second job, male multiple jobholders are more likely to be employed full-time across all jobs, whereas female multiple jobholders are more likely to be employed part-time across all jobs (Beckhusen, 2019). Men may average a higher number of work hours because they are more likely to work more overtime (Bolotnyy & Emanuel, 2018; Li et al., 2006) or have employers who require longer hours (whether it be in the form of requiring a willingness to work overtime, unpredictable schedules, or constant availability; Grönlund & Öun, 2018) compared to women.

Career Concerns

Changes in the nature of work and the broader composition of the workforce have prompted concerns regarding employees' job prospects (Chui et al., 2016; Davis, 2013). Such concerns can be studied in the context of job insecurity. There are two types of job insecurity: quantitative job insecurity, which reflects a threat to the continuity of the job itself, and qualitative job insecurity, which reflects a threat to the continuity of important features associated with the job (Hellgren et al., 1999). Recent comprehensive meta-analytic work did not find evidence for gender differences in mean levels of overall job insecurity, quantitative job insecurity, or qualitative job insecurity (Jiang et al., 2020; Keim et al., 2014). In addition to investigating gender differences in mean levels of job insecurity, another major point of focus in this area of literature has been on gender differences in the reaction to job insecurity. Gender differences in the reaction to job insecurity stem from gender role theory. However, gender role ideologies would suggest there is not a straightforward influence of gender on one's reaction to this stressor. The male gender role is strongly associated with employment and their role as a provider (Kimmel, 1993, 1996). Because men's identities are so intertwined with work, it has been suggested that men should have a more negative response to job insecurity than women. However, men also tend to have greater occupational mobility and pay than women (Bukodi & Dex, 2010; Graf et al., 2019; Hughes, 2019). This could mean they perceive job insecurity as less distressing than women because men might be more financially secure or have more optimistic job prospects (see job dependence perspective; Greenhalgh & Rosenblatt, 1984). Given these competing arguments, it is not surprising that evidence has been found for men having a stronger negative reaction to job insecurity (e.g., Cheng et al., 2005; Rugulies et al., 2006; Wang et al., 2008) and women having a stronger negative reaction (e.g., Rosenblatt et al., 1999; Rugulies et al., 2008), as well as no gender differences in the response to job insecurity (e.g., Cheng & Chan, 2008; László et al., 2010). Future research focused on identifying the factors that make one more or less vulnerable to the impact of job insecurity and the resources one utilizes to cope with job insecurity would be helpful in delineating these discrepant findings.

Gender Influences on the Relationship of Stressors with Strain and Well-Being Outcomes

Having reviewed the evidence for mean gender differences in specific work stressors, we now turn our attention to the various ways gender can influence the process through which stressors effectuate strain and well-being. There are several paths by which gender might influence this relationship: gender may influence how certain stressors are perceived, men and women may cope with the same stressors differently, or there may be sex differences in the biological response to stress.

Gender Differences in the Perception of Stressors

The basis for this argument is built primarily on gender socialization theory and the social roles that men and women are prescribed. This perspective argues that one's experiences and expectations are so intertwined with the gendered nature of social roles that men and women react differently to workplace stressors (Bem, 1981; Davis et al., 2011). Theoretically, this can manifest in a few ways. First, men are socialized to be tough and stoic, and reacting to stressors may be viewed as a sign of weakness or a threat to masculinity (e.g., Pleck, 1976; Vandello & Bosson, 2013), especially when those stressors originate in the workplace, a traditionally masculine domain. On the other hand, women are socialized to be more expressive (Brody & Hall, 2008). As such, when examining self-report reactions to job stressors, we may see a stronger strain reaction in women compared to men. The main way researchers have tested this idea is by examining the moderating role of gender in the relationship between job stressors and strain reactions. Because of the variety of specific stressors as well as specific strain outcomes that have been examined, this literature is difficult to synthesize. However, some insights can be gleaned from meta-analytic work. Specifically, Fila et al. (2017) meta-analyzed the relationships between job demands (broadly defined to include numerous types of demands) and job satisfaction and emotional exhaustion and conducted subgroup analyses by gender. The trend was such that the relationships were stronger for women than men, suggesting women are more reactive to job demands; however, the statistical significance of this effect depended on how it was tested meta-analytically (overlapping confidence intervals vs. meta regression).

Second, men and women might perceive job stressors differently based on the stressors they are also experiencing in other life roles (Vagg et al., 2002). In support of this, using a large sample of Swedes matched on occupational level, age, and parental status, Krantz et al. (2005) found women's physical health symptoms were best predicted by an interaction of conditions at work and at home (i.e., high work-load in each role), whereas men's physical health was best predicted by only work conditions. Similarly, also based on Swedish data, Boye (2010) found that time spent on housework explains part of the observed gender differences in psychological distress. In a less direct but nonetheless informative test of this idea, Backhans et al. (2007) found that as indicators of equality (i.e., similarity in percentage of men and women in part-time jobs, income similarity) increased in a given Swedish municipality, health outcomes for men and women also became more similar.

Third, women are socialized to be empathetic and nurturing, meaning they may place significant value on interpersonal relationships (Cross & Madson, 1997; Stewart & Lykes, 1985). Therefore, women may be more sensitive to interpersonal conflict in the workplace and subsequently report this particular stressor more often or as more distressing than men. On the other hand, men often ascribe to the male breadwinner role, which may provoke greater feelings of the associated "breadwinner burden" (Gerson, 1993; Gilbert, 1985; Meisenbach, 2010). The breadwinner aspect of their identity would be threatened if they were unemployed, meaning men may perceive job insecurity, job loss, or lack of promotion as more stressful and experience more severe well-being outcomes compared to women. These findings are in line with gendered social norms which suggest men are primarily concerned with factors related to their provider role and ability to work, while women tend to focus on interpersonal relationships.

We highlight a few empirical studies that support these claims. In a qualitative study of types of stressors experienced by men and women in academia and sales (Narayanan et al., 1999), women in both pro-fessions cited interpersonal conflict as the most frequent source of stress, and it was significantly higher than men's reports of stressor frequency. For sales associates, men reported lack of reward and recognition as the biggest stressor and it was significantly higher than female sales associates' reports. In a sample of police officers, Violanti et al. (2016) compared how stressful men and women perceived different stressors to be. Significant differences were observed for situations requiring use of force, insufficient manpower to adequately handle a job, fellow officers not doing their job, inadequate support by supervisor, and inadequate or poor-quality equipment. In all cases, female officers perceived these stressors are more distressing. Although not all deal with interpersonal situations, several do (i.e., the support-related topics). Lastly, as noted in the section on career concerns, there is some evidence that men may demonstrate a more negative reaction to unemployment (Artazcoz et al., 2004; Cheng et al., 2005; Rugulies et al., 2006; Wang et al., 2008). Interestingly, Gaunt and Benjamin (2007) extended this idea to also consider the gender ideology (the extent to which one endorses traditional gender roles) of men and women. They found the relationship between job insecurity and three types of stress were positive for egalitarian and traditional men as well as egalitarian-minded women. However, they were not significant for traditional women, potentially suggesting women with traditional gender role ideologies do not internalize their view as a breadwinner and thus are not as affected by threats to it.

Gender Differences in Coping

Coping refers to the cognitive and behavioral efforts that an individual makes in response to a stressor (Folkman & Lazarus, 1980). There are many different coping strategies one may choose from, but each strategy serves two main functions: "[to manage or alter] the person–environment relationship that is the source of stress (problem-focused coping) and [to regulate] stressful emotions (emotion-focused coping)" (Folkman & Lazarus, 1980, p. 223). When faced with a stressor, the selection of a particular coping strategy as well as the efficacy of that strategy can depend on individual and contextual characteristics (Edwards, 1992; Mauno & Rantanen, 2013; Nandkeolyar et al., 2014). This suggests no one strategy is inherently more effective than another; rather, the efficacy of a strategy depends on the alignment between the demands imposed by the stressor and a combination of the coping strategy, the individual, and the situation (Edwards, 1992; Thoits, 1995).

In light of these complexities, gender has been proposed to be a relevant individual difference factor that could influence the coping process (Thoits, 1995). Subsequent gender differences in well-being might occur as a function of variation in coping styles and resources. As discussed at length in the section on theoretical perspectives, differences in coping styles may stem from the unique ways in which men and women are socialized to cope with stress (i.e., the gender socialization hypothesis; Pearlin & Schooler, 1978). Alternatively, gendered differences in coping behaviors may be due to the different social roles men and women occupy, which determine the stressors one experiences and constrain coping behaviors (i.e., the role constraint hypothesis; Folkman & Lazarus, 1980). Empirical evidence comparing the two perspectives has been quite mixed, as both have received support (Ptacek et al., 1994; Rosario et al., 1988; Sigmon et al., 1995).

Crucial to this discussion is the precise nature of the questions being asked regarding gender differences in coping. Researchers have compared gender differences in men versus women's absolute use of a particular type of coping strategy (e.g., women engage in more emotional support-seeking than do men). Alternatively, researchers have also compared within each gender how much a given coping strategy is used relative to other coping strategies (e.g., women tend to use emotional support-seeking more than they use avoidance coping). These are distinct questions that have sometimes been muddied in the literature.

As referenced above, Tamres et al. (2002) aimed to address both types of comparison through meta-analysis (although notably this only includes studies published between 1990 and 2000) and primary studies. In the meta-analytic part of their study, Tamres et al. compared mean gender differences in the use of 17 different coping strategies. They found women used 11 of these strategies (active problem-focused, seeking instrumental social support, general problem-focused coping, seeking emotional social support, avoidance coping, positive reappraisal, rumination, wishful thinking, positive self-talk, seeking nonspecific support, and religion) more often than did men and found no significant differences in the other six (planning, denial, isolation, venting, self-blame, and exercise). This suggests women generally tend to engage in more coping, regardless of the type of coping, than do men.

Using a sample of college students and a sample of cardiac patients, Tamres et al. (2002) also examined whether there were relative differences in the types of coping strategies used. To do so, they subtracted the mean coping score across all 17 types for each individual from the coping score on an individual dimension. Thus, higher scores meant that relative to all other types of coping, a person used that method more. A different pattern emerged than in the meta-analysis. In the student sample, they found men were more likely than women to use active coping, denial, and distraction relative to other strategies (i.e., these were the strategies of choice more for men than women), whereas women were more likely to use seeking instrumental and emotional support ahead of other strategies. In the cardiac patients, men were more likely than women to use active coping, relative to other strategies, whereas women were more likely to seek emotional support and use religion ahead of other strategies. Taken together, these findings suggest it is important to examine precisely how gender differences are assessed in relation to the exact question being asked when drawing conclusions.

Additionally, Tamres et al. (2002) aimed to use meta-analytic data to speak to the gender socialization versus role constraint debate. To do so, they examined whether the nature of the stressor influenced the type of coping that men and women used, which would be indicative of role constraint theory. In some cases, there was support for this – women engaged in more coping when facing personal health and others' health stressors. These are stressors that women may experience more than men. On the other hand, other stressors where we might expect differential exposure did not show gender differences in coping. Moreover, the authors also claim to find some support for the gender socialization perspective. Specifically, men were more likely than women to use avoidant and withdrawal strategies to cope with relationship issues and others' health, which may speak to the fact that men generally feel pressure to adhere to the masculine gender role by using strategies that do not convey a sense of control loss. Ultimately, it seems it is difficult to truly disentangle these perspectives.

An additional point of focus in the coping literature has been on the role of social support. Social support has been conceptualized as three different types of support: instrumental, informational, and emotional support. Social support can originate from many different sources. Most relevant to this chapter is job support, or social support stemming from the work domain, and its impact on positive and negative indicators of employee well-being. It is commonly thought that women tend to have higher levels of job support and that job support has a more positive impact on well-being among women than among men. While some empirical evidence supports these ideas (Drummond et al., 2017; Haines et al., 2019; Olson & Shultz, 1994), evidence for mean gender differences in received job support is quite mixed, and apparent differences may be declining over time (Tausig et al., 2004). In terms of coworker support, some researchers have noted higher mean levels among female employees (Hwang & Ramadoss, 2017; Matijaš et al., 2018; Roxburgh, 1996; Thompson & Cavallaro, 2007), while others have found no gender differences (Baruch-Feldman et al., 2002; Haines et al., 2019; Li et al., 2006) or that men report higher levels of coworker support (Attell et al., 2017; Ramadoss & Rajadhyaksha, 2012). Empirical findings on mean differences in supervisor support received has also been mixed but tends to favor either no gender differences (Baruch-Feldman et al., 2002; Haines et al., 2019; Hwang & Ramadoss, 2017; Li et al., 2006; Thompson & Cavallaro, 2007) or that men encounter greater levels of supervisor support (Olson & Shultz, 1994; Ramadoss & Rajadhyaksha, 2012). However, there are apparent gender differences in the amount and types of support that are sought out (Tamres et al., 2002). Compared to men, women tend to prefer to utilize support-seeking coping strategies more often than other coping behaviors. In particular, women are more likely to engage in emotional support-seeking behaviors.

Evidence regarding gender differences in the impact of job support on well-being have also been mixed and can vary widely according to the type and source of support as well as the well-being outcome of interest. For example, Perrewé and Carlson (2002) found job support was more positively related to work satisfaction among women than among men, while other researchers failed to find evidence that gender influenced the relationships between job support and burnout, satisfaction, productivity, and perceptions of the family environment (Baruch-Feldman et al., 2002; Thompson & Cavallaro, 2007). These conflicting findings might be indicative of meaningful differences in the efficacy of job support depending on job characteristics as well as the type and source of support (Hwang & Ramadoss, 2017; Vermeulen & Mustard, 2000). As an example of this, Vermeulen and Mustard

(2000) evaluated gender differences in the efficacy of social support across environments with varying levels of job control and psychological demands. They noted that in high strain (i.e., low job control and high psychological demands) and active (i.e., high job control and high psychological demands) work environments, a supportive work environment effectively mitigated psychological distress in women but not in men.

In summary, the question of whether there are gender differences in coping strategies is deceptively complex. In general, it appears that when compared to men, women tend to utilize more coping strategies overall. It is also clear that women engage in more support-seeking behaviors, particularly emotional support (see Greenglass, 2002, for a review). The assumed ideas involving men engaging in more problem-focused coping have not been generally supported meta-analytically in direct gender comparisons. However, there is some evidence that this may be the type of strategy men tend to use most, although women still use it in addition to other strategies. Beyond just examining gender differences in coping, what may be more informative in future work is to focus on whether there are gender differences in well-being *because* of differences in the usage of coping strategies. Said otherwise, are certain coping strategies more or less efficacious and does this efficacy differ by gender?

Sex-Based Differences in Biological Stress Reactions

Another consideration in understanding how stressor–strain relationships may be different for men and women is the role of biological sex. As touched upon earlier in our discussion of the biological sex differences perspective, research in the medical and biological sciences suggest there may be physiological differences in how men and women react to stress. Researchers have suggested that gender differences in the prevalence of stress-related diseases and disorders (e.g., hypertension, depression, anxiety) are likely, at least in part, due to these differences (Verma et al., 2011). Below, we provide a general overview of the physiological stress process and describe a few studies from the small body of research that has examined gender differences in these processes in relation to the workplace.

In simplified terms, there are two neuroendocrine systems related to the stress response, the sympathetic adrenomedullary (SAM) system and the hypothalamic–pituitary–adrenal (HPA) axis (Charmandari et al., 2005; Koolhaas et al., 2011). The SAM system is fast acting and responsible for the production of epinephrine and norepinephrine, catecholamines that are responsible for mobilizing energy in preparation for the "fight or flight" response to stressors. With the activation of these hormones comes associated increases in other physiological systems, including heart rate, blood pressure, and the galvanic skin response aimed at facilitating quick reactivity. The HPA axis also responds to stressors but is a much slower acting system and only responds when exposure is long term or more chronic. This system is responsible for triggering a biological process that ultimately triggers the adrenal release of cortisol, which facilitates energy to continue the fight or flight response. Researchers use indicators from this process, such as catecholamine levels, cortisol, blood pressure, heart rate, and galvanic skin response, to assess a participant's stress reactivity (e.g., Eatough et al., 2016).

Researchers have found some differences in physiological markers of stress in reaction to workplace stressors when comparing men and women. Frankenhaeuser et al. (1989) measured blood pressure and norepinephrine levels, both indicators of stress, in male and female managers throughout the course of several days. Both male and female managers exhibited high blood pressure and norepinephrine during the day, but only for female managers did the levels remain high after work. This pattern was not observed on nonwork days. In a similar study, Lundberg and Frankenhaeuser (1999) found women had significantly higher norepinephrine levels during and after work, and men showed a quicker decline in the secretion of catecholamines after work. The authors attributed these differences to gender differences in responsibility for household duties; the women did not have the same opportunity to "unwind" as the men did.

There are considerably more studies, conducted both in lab and field settings, focused on cortisol. One review, which was not limited to work stressors, summarized the literature by stating that women appear more reactive to stressors involving social rejection, whereas men are more reactive to those that involve threats to achievement (Stroud et al., 2002). In a study more specific to the workplace, Kunz-Ebrecht et al. (2004) examined one type of cortisol reaction – the cortisol awakening response (the change in cortisol that occurs in the first hour after awakening from sleep, which is thought to capture the reactivity of the

HPA axis) – and found results that paralleled those of Frankenhaeuser and colleagues noted above. Women exhibited a greater cortisol awakening response than men on workdays, but there were no gender differences on nonwork days. Interestingly, there are not marked gender differences in cortisol reactivity in young children, which further suggests these differences may be due to socialization and gender role fulfillment that tend to occur later in life, rather than a genetic predisposition based on X and Y chromosomes (cf. Theorell et al., 2014).

Lastly, a study conducted on nonprofessional workers is worth mentioning. Persson et al. (2009) focused on a small sample of 17 men and 20 women who were matched in terms of the precise tasks that were performed on the job (production work on an assembly line). They found no differences between men and women in any of the physiological indicators tested at the end of the day (cortisol, adrenaline, noradrenaline, and heart functioning). Thus, this study suggests there do not seem to be marked gender differences in reactivity stemming from tasks that are physical and routine, although this study did not measure reactivity in the evening to determine longer-term effects.

The results summarized above should be interpreted with a few caveats. First, some of these studies were conducted several decades ago, and the extent to which they replicate in the modern world of work and gender roles is unclear. Additionally, as with other areas of inquiry, isolating the biological role of sex is challenging given the number of covariates that must be taken into account. With research involving biomarkers, this is also made more challenging by methodological concerns. For example, eating, smoking habits, BMI, and even the hormonal status of study participants (e.g., phase of menstrual cycle) can impact physiological measurements, and perfect participant compliance with data collection procedures is challenging (e.g., Kudielka & Kirschbaum, 2005). Nonetheless, isolating physiological reactions from subjective self-report reactions is an area we see as worthy of inquiry and one likely to continue to expand in the future with the advent of increasingly affordable and ambulatory measurement devices (cf. Eatough et al., 2016).

Discussion of Gaps in the Literature and Future Research Ideas

As is evident from the preceding review, the answer to the question of whether there are gender differences in work stressors and strain experiences is not straightforward and depends greatly on the particular variables of focus as well as the design of the study. In many cases, this makes drawing overall conclusions challenging. The areas of work where there are recent meta-analyses help overcome these challenges in synthesis, but meta-analyses that explicitly focus on gender differences in work stressors are quite rare (for an exception, see Shockley et al., 2017) or are somewhat dated given the changing nature of gender roles (Tamres et al., 2002). Interestingly, in the most recent comprehensive meta-analysis on gender issues of which we are aware, Shockley et al. (2017), found negligible gender differences in work–family conflict, which is a main stressor invoked in the context of workplace gender differences. This certainly calls into question whether we would see similar trends with other stressors, especially those where there is less theoretical rationale to expect differences in the first place.

Despite the difficulties in clearly synthesizing the literature, our review highlights several clear gaps and subsequent ideas for future research. First, there are very few individual empirical studies that take a comprehensive view of stress processes. It would be useful if authors tested (a) gender differences in work stressors and strain outcomes as well as variables that may correlate with stressors, such as job conditions, (b) whether men and women differ in the relationships between job conditions and stressors as well as in the relationships between stressors and strains, and (c) whether there are mean differences in coping strategies used and whether the relationships between coping strategies and strain or well-being varies by gender. Including all of these variables within single studies would help for syntheses of results. As is, when various components of the process are tested in different studies that employ different measures and designs, it is difficult to draw comprehensive conclusions. Relatedly, as we have alluded to several times above, researchers should measure additional process variables that overlap more closely with the theoretical ideas behind their predictions. For example, if women are hypothesized to experience more strain as a result of long work hours due to traditional gender roles, researchers should actually measure to what extent women in their study have responsibility for labor at home or feel guilty about working long hours. This would help the field to move beyond assumptions about gender and actually test some of those assumptions that are driving results.

Second, the role of time generally is neglected in this literature. We see time as playing a role in at least two distinct ways. Gender roles have changed considerably over time and are likely to continue shifting. In fact, the Families and Work Institute found that 58% of people responded somewhat or strongly agree to the item "A mother who works outside the home can have just as good a relationship with her children as a mother who does not work" in 1977, and that number rose to 73% in 2008 (Galinsky, 2009). Many of the theoretical perspectives underlying gender differences rely on notions of distinct gender roles. As these gender roles change, so too should gender differences in work stress experiences. To our knowledge, this idea has not been comprehensively tested. It would be very useful, perhaps in the context of meta-analytic work, to examine how gender differences have changed over time (see Wegman et al.'s 2018 meta-analysis for a similar example with how work characteristics have changed over time). This would help researchers better understand the veracity of certain theories (i.e., if there is no substantial change in gender differences but there has been a substantial change in role occupation and gender views, these variables are likely not main drivers of gender effects) as well as interpret mixed findings (i.e., provide insight into how much weight we should place on older studies in this area to inform current knowledge). Another time factor is related to the lack of consideration of the life stage of participants in most research. This seems like an important oversight in that gender differences in work stress experiences might be most pronounced around the time when families have young children. Although men are undoubtedly affected by the transition to parenthood, the process of pregnancy, childbirth, and breastfeeding falls on mothers. Thus, we might expect gender differences in work stress to be particularly strong around this time when women, especially those in countries with minimal structural-level support, are juggling very high family demands that are not easily outsourced. On the other hand, before children are born or once children have left the house, gender differences may be minimal as family demands during these times might allow for more equal roles.

The notion of unique experiences for women brings up a third point. Rather than focus on explicit comparisons in stress experiences between men and women, we think the field would benefit from a further exploration of stressors that are unique to each gender. Grandey et al. (2020) provide numerous compelling ideas related to this notion, highlighting the roles the "Three Ms" – menstruation, maternity, and menopause – play in women's work lives. Each of these processes is vastly understudied and has key insights for the stress process. For example, all involve fluctuations in women's hormones, which can impact stress reactivity, mood, and fatigue. They are also taboo to discuss in the workplace, which can have additional repercussions in terms of stress associated with feeling the need to hide these experiences as well as negative emotions such as shame or embarrassment. The Three Ms, particularly maternity, can even create new stressors in and of themselves, such as the need to manage breastfeeding/pumping or infertility treatments while at work (see Gabriel et al. 2020 for a rare study of the challenges of continuing to breastfeed while returning to work). While the Three Ms are only biologically possible for females, other stressors that disproportionately affect woman also merit greater research attention, namely sexual harassment in the workplace (83.2% of the sexual harassment charges filed to the U.S. Equal Employment Opportunity Commission in 2019 were made by women). While there is a substantial body of research on the consequences of sexual harassment (cf. Willness et al., 2007), there is considerably less work focused on effective coping strategies (for exceptions, see Buchanan et al., 2007; Morganson & Major, 2014), which is critical practical information.

As there are fewer bodily changes that occur in men after puberty, highlighting biological situations specific to them is more challenging. However, there are aspects of masculinity that may create stressors that almost exclusively affect men (although we acknowledge that the downstream effects of masculinity also affect women). Specifically, precarious manhood, the idea that the state of manhood is a precarious social status that is difficult to attain but easy to lose (Vandello & Bosson, 2013) has workplace implications. Studies have found men are less likely to use available flexible benefits, even when they want to, for fear these often female-branded policies will make them appear less masculine (Vandello et al., 2013). This may, in part, explain the general underutilization of paternity policies as well (e.g., U.S. Department of Labor, n.d.). Aspects of masculinity that involve not appearing weak can also negatively impact men; for example, Motro and Ellis (2017) found men who cried in reaction to performance feedback received biased evaluations from the feedback giver. This need to appear strong may also have stress implications in terms of men being less willing to address unfavorable work conditions or use employee assistance programs. Other potential topics include visible erections in the workplace, male pattern baldness, andropause, and male specific cancers such as prostate cancer, where treatments can affect urinary and bowel function as well as hormonal changes (Pupco & Barling, 2021). In summary, we urge researchers to consider focusing on issues that are relevant only or primarily to one gender in addition to those with commonalities in order to give a comprehensive picture of workplace stressors.

A fourth area in need of future research is to take into account the role of gender in nonbinary people. Many gender theories rely on prescribed social roles for men and women in society generally as well as within their own households. Given that the division of labor tends to be more equal in same-sex compared to different-sex couples (Evertsson & Boye, 2018), those same assumptions about gender as it relates to household roles may not apply. Furthermore, there is evidence same-sex male couples divide paid and unpaid labor differently than same-sex female couples, further complicating the interaction between sexual orientation and/or gender identity and gender (Jaspers & Verbakel, 2013). Relatedly, the main aspect of identity that seems to be taken into account in gender research is gender role ideology or masculine/feminine identity. Clearly, there are other meaningful identities that likely intersect with gender (e.g., race, religion, subjective social status), and their general omission could be causing us to overlook important intersectionality effects (Sawyer et al., 2013).

Lastly, we offer a few methodological insights we believe can help advance the field. We urge researchers to carefully consider precisely what questions they aim to answer when designing studies. For example, is the interest in sex (biology driving differences) or gender (social roles driving differences)? If the interest is in gender, it is worth considering the underlying assumptions driving the theoretical rationale for expecting gender differences. That is, are differences expected because of the varying salience of work and nonwork roles to women, or pressures to engage in masculine behaviors for men, etc.? When possible, these process variables should then be directly measured to more accurately test hypotheses. Erdogan et al.'s (2019) study exemplifies this idea; rather than assuming gender differences in work–family conflict based on identity salience, they actually measured identity salience and used latent cluster analysis to identify unique configurations of various role saliences within individuals to predict work–family conflict. We view this as increasingly important, particularly with role salience, given the continual changing nature of gender roles in society coupled with the fact that Shockley et al. (2017) found quite small meta-analytic gender differences in both career and family salience. Another critical methodological recommendation is to take into account confounding variables and attempt to match samples on these or control for them in analyses to better isolate the role of gender. That is, comparing samples of men and women who are in vastly different occupations does little to speak to the true source of any stress differences.

For better or for worse, gender is clearly ingrained in our society. While its presence appears to be a relatively permanent fixture, the meanings attached to gender and the adoption of gender ideologies are less rigid. Changes in gender ideologies, the demographic composition of the workforce, and the nature of work have prompted interesting lines of research regarding gender differences in work stressors. There are many commonalities between men and women in terms of their experiences with work stressors. That being said, meaningful gender differences certainly exist and are in large part driven by gender socialization processes. As iterated above, exactly how these processes develop and exert their influence on the entirety of the stress process is a ripe area for future research. Such an approach would significantly build on existing theoretical models and deepen our understanding of how gender shapes work stress. A comprehensive understanding of this process would be beneficial in terms of reducing any gender disparities in stressors and well-being and could be used to inform organizational practices.

References

Adler, M. A. (1993). Gender differences in job autonomy: The consequences of occupational segregation and authority position. *The Sociological Quarterly, 34*(3), 449–465. https://doi.org/10.1111/j.1533-8525.1993.tb00121.x.

Andrews, A., & Bailyn, L. (1993). Segmentation and synergy: Two models of linking work and family. In J. C. Hood (Ed.), *Men, work, and family* (pp. 262–275). Sage.

Artazcoz, L., Benach, J., Borrell, C., & Cortes, I. (2004). Unemployment and mental health: Understanding the interactions among gender, family roles, and social class. *American Journal of Public Health*, *94*(1), 82–88. https://doi.org/10.2105/AJPH.94.1.82.

Attell, B. K., Kummerow Brown, K., & Treiber, L. A. (2017). Workplace bullying, perceived job stressors, and psychological distress: Gender and race differences in the stress process. *Social Science Research*, *65*, 210–221. https://doi.org/10.1016/j.ssresearch.2017.02.001.

Backhans, M. C., Lundberg, M., & Månsdotter, A. (2007). Does increased gender equality lead to a convergence of health outcomes for men and women? A study of Swedish municipalities. *Social Science and Medicine*, *64*(9), 1892–1903. https://doi.org/10.1016/j.socscimed.2007.01.016.

Baruch-Feldman, C., Brondolo, E., Ben-Dayan, D., & Schwartz, J. (2002). Sources of social support and burnout, job satisfaction, and productivity. *Journal of Occupational Health Psychology*, *7*(1), 84–93. https://doi.org/10.1037/1076-8998.7.1.84.

Beckhusen, J. (2019). *Multiple jobholders in the United States: 2013*. United States Census Bureau. www.census.gov/content/dam/Census/library/publications/2019/demo/P70BR-163.pdf.

Bem, S. L. (1981). Gender schema theory: A cognitive account of sex typing. *Psychological Review*, *88*(4), 354–364. https://doi.org/10.1037/0033-295X.88.4.354.

Bolotnyy, V., & Emanuel, N. (2018). Why do women earn less than men? Evidence from bus and train operators [Working paper]. https://scholar.harvard.edu/files/bolotnyy/files/be_gendergap.pdf.

Bowen, P., Govender, R., Edwards, P., & Cattell, K. (2018). Work-related contact, work–family conflict, psychological distress and sleep problems experienced by construction professionals: An integrated explanatory model. *Construction Management and Economics*, *36*(3), 153–174. https://doi.org/10.1080/01446193.2017.1341638.

Boye, K. (2010). Time spent working: Paid work, housework and the gender difference in psychological distress. *European Societies*, *12*(3), 419–442. https://doi.org/10.1080/14616691003716928.

Brody, L. R., & Hall, J. A. (2008). Gender and emotion in context. In M. Lewis, J. M. Haviland-Jones, & L. F. Barrett (Eds.), *Handbook of emotions* (pp. 395–408). The Guilford Press.

Buchanan, N. T., Settles, I. H., & Langhout, R. D. (2007). Black women's coping styles, psychological well-being, and work-related outcomes following sexual harassment. *Black Women, Gender Families*, *1*(2), 100–120. www.jstor.org/stable/10.5406/blacwomegendfami.1.2.0100.

Bukodi, E., & Dex, S. (2010). Bad start: Is there a way up? Gender differences in the effect of initial occupation on early career mobility in Britain. *European Sociological Review*, *26*(4), 431–446. https://doi.org/10.1093/esr/jcp030.

Catalyst. (2021, February 11). *Women in the workforce – Global: Quick take*. www.catalyst.org/research/women-in-the-workforce-global/.

Charmandari, E., Tsigos, C., & Chrousos, G. P. (2005). Neuroendocrinology of stress response. *Annual Review of Physiology*, 67, 259–284. https://doi.org/10.1146/annurev.physiol.67.040403 .120816.

Cheng, G. H. L., & Chan, D. K. S. (2008). Who suffers more from job insecurity? A meta-analytic review. *Applied Psychology*, 57(2), 272–303. https://doi.org/10.1111/j.1464-0597.2007.00312.x.

Cheng, Y., Chen, C. W., Chen, C. J., & Chiang, T. L. (2005). Job insecurity and its association with health among employees in the Taiwanese general population. *Social Science and Medicine*, 61(1), 41–52. https:// doi.org/10.1016/j.socscimed.2004.11.039.

Chui, M., Manyika, J., & Miremadi, M. (2016). Where machines could replace humans—and where they can't (yet). *McKinsey Quarterly*, 30 (2), 1–9. www.mckinsey.de/~/media/McKinsey/Business%20Functions/ McKinsey%20Digital/Our%20Insights/Where%20machines%20could %20replace%20humans%20and%20where%20they%20cant/Where-machines-could-replace-humans-and-where-they-cant-yet.pdf.

Clark, C., Pike, C., McManus, S., Harris, J., Bebbington, P., Brugha, T., Jenkins, R., Meltzer, H., Weich, S., & Stansfeld, S. (2012). The contribution of work and nonwork stressors to common mental disorders in the 2007 Adult Psychiatric Morbidity Survey. *Psychological Medicine*, 42(4), 829–842. https://doi.org/10.1017/S0033291711001759.

Cohen, P. N. (2013). The persistence of workplace gender segregation in the U.S. Sociology *Compass*, 7(11), 889–899. https://doi.org/10.1111/soc4 .12083

Cook, J. (2019, October 18). *How stress hits women's brains harder and why men don't always get it*. Prevention. hwww.prevention.com/health/ mental-health/a26678044/women-and-stress/.

Crosby, F. (1991). *Juggling: The unexpected advantages of balancing career and home for women and their families*. Free Press.

Cross, S. E., & Madson, L. (1997). Models of the self: Self-construals and gender. *Psychological Bulletin*, 122(1), 5–37. https://doi.org/10.1037/ 0033-2909.122.1.5.

Davis, G. F. (2013). After the corporation. *Politics and Society*, 41(2), 283–308. https://doi.org/10.1177/0032329213483110.

Davis, M. C., Burleson, M. H., & Kruszewski, D. M. (2011). Gender: Its relationship to stressor exposure, cognitive appraisal/coping processes, stress responses, and health outcomes. In R. Contrada & A. Baum (Eds.), *The handbook of stress science: Biology, psychology, and health* (pp. 247–261). Springer Publishing Company.

Demerouti, E., & Bakker, A. B. (2011). The job demands–resources model: Challenges for future research. *SA Journal of Industrial Psychology, 37* (2), 1–9. https://doi.org/10.4102/sajip.v37i2.974.

Drummond, S., O'Driscoll, M. P., Brough, P., Kalliath, T., Siu, O. L., Timms, C., & Riley, D. (2017). The relationship of social support with well-being outcomes via work–family conflict: Moderating effects of gender, dependants and nationality. *Human Relations, 70*(5), 544–565. https://doi.org/10.1177/0018726716662696.

Eagly, A. H., Karau, S. J., & Makhijani, M. G. (1995). Gender and the effectiveness of leaders: A meta-analysis. *Psychological Bulletin, 117*(1), 125–145. https://doi.org/10.1037/0033-2909.117.1.125.

Eatough, E. M., Shockley, K. M., & Yu, P. (2016). A review of ambulatory health data collection methods for employee daily diary research. *Applied Psychology: An International Review, 65*(2), 322–354. https://doi.org/10.1111/apps.12068.

Edwards, J. R. (1992). A cybernetic theory of stress, coping, and well-being in organizations. *Academy of Management Review, 17*(2), 238–274. https://doi.org/10.5465/amr.1992.4279536.

Ellemers, N. (2018). Gender stereotypes. *Annual Review of Psychology, 69,* 275–298. https://doi.org/10.1146/annurev-psych-122216-011719.

Erdogan, I., Ozcelik, H., & Bagger, J. (2019). Roles and work–family conflict: How role salience and gender come into play. *The International Journal of Human Resource Management,* 1–23. https://doi.org/10.1080/09585192.2019.1588346.

Erosa, A., Fuster, L., Kambourov, G., & Rogerson, R. (2017). *Hours, occupations, and gender differences in labor market outcomes* (No. w23636; p. w23636). National Bureau of Economic Research. https://doi.org/10.3386/w23636.

Evertsson, M., & Boye, K. (2018). The transition to parenthood and the division of parental leave in different-sex and female same-sex couples in Sweden. *European Sociological Review, 34*(5), 471–485. https://doi.org/10.1093/esr/jcy027.

Fila, M. J., Purl, J., & Griffeth, R. W. (2017). Job demands, control and support: Meta-analyzing moderator effects of gender, nationality, and occupation. *Human Resource Management Review, 27*(1), 39–60. https://doi.org/10.1016/j.hrmr.2016.09.004.

Folkman, S., & Lazarus, R. S. (1980). An analysis of coping in a middle-aged community sample. *Journal of Health and Social Behavior, 21*(3), 219–239. https://doi.org/10.2307/2136617.

Frankenhaeuser, M., Lundberg, U., Fredrikson, M., Melin, B., Tuomisto, M., Myrsten, A. L., Hedman, M., Bergman-Losman, B., & Wallin, L. (1989). Stress on and off the job as related to sex and occupational status in white-collar workers. *Journal of Organizational Behavior, 10* (4), 321–346. https://doi.org/10.1002/job.4030100404.

Gabriel, A. S., Volpone, S. D., MacGowan, R. L., Butts, M. M., & Moran, C. M. (2020). When work and family blend together: Examining the daily experiences of breastfeeding mothers at work. *Academy of Management Journal, 63*(5), 1337–1369. https://doi.org/10.5465/amj .2017.1241.

Galinsky, E. (2009). *Times are changing: Gender and generation in the workplace.* Families and Work Institute. https://blog.shrm.org/sites/ default/files/reports/TimesAreChanging_EGalinsky_FWI.pdf.

Gaunt, R., & Benjamin, O. (2007). Job insecurity, stress and gender: The moderating role of gender ideology. *Community, Work and Family, 10* (3), 341–355. https://doi.org/10.1080/13668800701456336.

Gerson, K. (1993). *No man's land: Men's changing commitments to family and work.* Basic Books.

Gilbert, L. A. (1985). *Men in dual-career families: Current realities and future prospects.* Lawrence Erlbaum Associates.

Glass, J. (1990). The impact of occupational segregation on working conditions. *Social Forces, 68*(3), 779–796. https://doi.org/10.1093/sf/68.3 .779.

Graf, N., Brown, A., & Patten, E. (2019, March 22). *The narrowing, but persistent, gender gap in pay.* Pew Research Center. www.pewresearch .org/fact-tank/2019/03/22/gender-pay-gap-facts/.

Grandey, A. A., Gabriel, A. S., & King, E. B. (2020). Tackling taboo topics: A review of the Three Ms in working women's lives. *Journal of Management, 46*(1), 7-35. https://doi.org/10.1177/0149206319857144.

Gray, J. (1995). *Men are from Mars, women are from Venus.* HarperCollins.

Greenglass, E. R. (2002). Work stress, coping, and social support: Implications for women's occupational well-being. In D. L. Nelson & R. J. Burke (Eds.), *Gender, work stress and health* (pp. 85–96). American Psychological Association. https://doi.org/10.1037/10467-006.

Greenhalgh, L., & Rosenblatt, Z. (1984). Job insecurity: Toward conceptual clarity. *Academy of Management Review, 9*(3), 438–448. www.jstor .org/stable/258284.

Greenhaus, J. H., & Beutell, N. J. (1985). Sources of conflict between work and family roles. *Academy of Management Review, 10*(1), 76–88. https://doi.org/10.5465/amr.1985.4277352.

Grönlund, A., & Öun, I. (2018). In search of family-friendly careers? Professional strategies, work conditions and gender differences in work–family conflict. *Community, Work and Family, 21*(1), 87–105. https://doi.org/10.1080/13668803.2017.1375460.

Gutek, B. A., & Cohen, A. G. (1987). Sex ratios, sex role spillover, and sex at work: A comparison of men's and women's experiences. *Human Relations*, 40(2), 97–115. https://doi.org/10.1177/001872678704000202.

Gutek, B. A., Repetti, R., & Silver, D. (1988). Nonwork roles and stress at work. In C. Cooper & R. Payne (Eds.), *Current concerns in occupational stress* (pp. 141–174). Wiley.

Gutek, B. A., Searle, S., & Klepa, L. (1991). Rational versus gender role explanations for work-family conflict. *Journal of Applied Psychology*, 76(4), 560–568. https://doi.org/10.1037/0021-9010.76.4.560.

Haines, V. Y., Bilodeau, J., Demers, A., Marchand, A., Beauregard, N., Durand, P., & Blanc, M. E. (2019). Sex, gender dynamics, differential exposure, and work–family conflict. *Journal of Family Issues*, 40(2), 215–239. https://doi.org/10.1177/0192513X18806945.

Hellgren, J., Sverke, M., & Isaksson, K. (1999). A two-dimensional approach to job insecurity: Consequences for employee attitudes and well-being. *European Journal of Work and Organizational Psychology*, 8(2), 179–195. https://doi.org/10.1080/135943299398311.

Hochwarter, W. A., Perrewe, P. L., & Dawkins, M. C. (1995). Gender differences in perceptions of stress-related variables: Do the people make the place or does the place make the people? *Journal of Managerial Issues*, 7(1), 62–74. www.jstor.org/stable/40604050.

Hughes, R. C. (2019). *Gender-based pay equity differences and upward occupational mobility through the lens of comparable worth*. World at work. www.worldatwork.org/journal/articles/gender-based-pay-equity-differences-and-upward-occupational-mobility-through-the-lens-of-comparable-worth.

Hwang, W., & Ramadoss, K. (2017). The job demands–control–support model and job satisfaction across gender: The mediating role of work–family conflict. *Journal of Family Issues*, 38(1), 52–72. https://doi.org/10.1177/0192513X16647983.

Hyde, J. S. (2014). Gender similarities and differences. *Annual Review of Psychology*, 65, 373–398. https://doi.org/10.1146/annurev-psych-010213-115057.

International Labour Organization. (2019, May). *Women in business and management: The business case for change*. www.ilo.org/wcmsp5/groups/public/—dgreports/—dcomm/—publ/documents/publication/wcms_700953.pdf.

Jaffee, D. (1989). Gender inequality in workplace autonomy and authority. *Social Science Quarterly*, 70(2), 375–389. www.academia.edu/download/34348092/Jaffee-Gender_Inequality_in_Worplace.pdf.

Jaspers, E., & Verbakel, E. (2013). The division of paid labor in same-sex couples in the Netherlands. *Sex Roles, 68*, 335–348. https://doi.org/10.1007/s11199-012-0235-2.

Jiang, L., Xu, X., & Wang, H. J. (2020). A resources–demands approach to sources of job insecurity: A multilevel meta-analytic investigation. *Journal of Occupational Health Psychology.* https://doi.org/10.1037/ocp0000267.

Jick, T. D., & Mitz, L. F. (1985). Sex differences in work stress. *Academy of Management Review, 10*(3), 408–420. https://doi.org/10.2307/258124.

Kajantie, E., & Phillips, D. I. (2006). The effects of sex and hormonal status on the physiological response to acute psychosocial stress. *Psychoneuroendocrinology, 31*(2), 151–178. https://doi.org/10.1016/j.psyneuen.2005.07.002.

Kang, S. (2015, March 31). *Stress and the gender gap.* Psychology Today. www.psychologytoday.com/us/blog/the-dolphin-way/201503/stress-and-the-gender-gap.

Karasek, R., Brisson, C., Kawakami, N., Houtman, I., Bongers, P., & Amick, B. (1998). The job content questionnaire (JCQ): An instrument for internationally comparative assessments of psychosocial job characteristics. *Journal of Occupational Health Psychology, 3*(4), 322–355. https://doi.org/10.1037/1076-8998.3.4.322.

Keim, A. C., Landis, R. S., Pierce, C. A., & Earnest, D. R. (2014). Why do employees worry about their jobs? A meta-analytic review of predictors of job insecurity. *Journal of Occupational Health Psychology, 19*(3), 269–290. https://doi.org/10.1037/a0036743.

Kimmel, M. S. (1993). What do men want? *Harvard Business Review, 71*(6), 50–63.

(1996). *Manhood in America: A cultural history.* Free Press.

Koolhaas, J. M., Bartolomucci, A., Buwalda, B., de Boer, S. F., Flügge, G., Korte, S. M., Meerlo, P., Murison, R., Oliver, B., Palanza, P., Richter-Levin, G., Sgoifo, A., Steimer, A., Stiedl, O., van Dijk, G., Wohr, M., & Fuchs, E. (2011). Stress revisited: A critical evaluation of the stress concept. *Neuroscience and Biobehavioral Reviews, 35*(5), 1291–1301. https://doi.org/10.1016/j.neubiorev.2011.02.003.

Krantz, G., Berntsson, L., & Lundberg, U. (2005). Total workload, work stress and perceived symptoms in Swedish male and female white-collar employees. *The European Journal of Public Health, 15*(2), 209–214. https://doi.org/10.1093/eurpub/cki079.

Kudielka, B. M., & Kirschbaum, C. (2005). Sex differences in HPA axis responses to stress: A review. *Biological Psychology, 69*(1), 113–132. https://doi.org/10.1016/j.biopsycho.2004.11.009.

Kunz-Ebrecht, S. R., Kirschbaum, C., Marmot, M., & Steptoe, A. (2004). Differences in cortisol awakening response on work days and weekends in women and men from the Whitehall II cohort. *Psychoneuroendocrinology*, *29*(4), 516-528. https://doi.org/10.1016/S0306-4530(03)00072-6.

László, K. D., Pikhart, H., Kopp, M. S., Bobak, M., Pajak, A., Malyutina, S., Salavecz, G., & Marmot, M. (2010). Job insecurity and health: A study of 16 European countries. *Social Science and Medicine*, *70*(6), 867–874. https://doi.org/10.1016/j.socscimed.2009.11.022.

Li, J., Yang, W., & Cho, S. (2006). Gender differences in job strain, effort-reward imbalance, and health functioning among Chinese physicians. *Social Science and Medicine*, *62*(5), 1066–1077. https://doi.org/10.1016/j.socscimed.2005.07.011.

Lorber, J., & Farrell, S. A. (Eds.). (1991). *The social construction of gender*. Sage.

Lozano, M., Hamplová, D., & Bourdais, C. L. (2016). Non-standard work schedules, gender, and parental stress. *Demographic Research*, *34*, 259–284. https://doi.org/10.4054/DemRes.2016.34.9.

Lundberg, U., & Frankenhaeuser, M. (1999). Stress and workload of men and women in high-ranking positions. *Journal of Occupational Health Psychology*, *4*(2), 142–151. https://doi.org/10.1037/1076-8998.4.2.142.

Matijaš, M., Merkaš, M., & Brdovčak, B. (2018). Job resources and satisfaction across gender: The role of work–family conflict. *Journal of Managerial Psychology*, *33*(4–5), 372–385. https://doi.org/10.1108/JMP-09-2017-0306.

Mauno, S., & Rantanen, M. (2013). Contextual and dispositional coping resources as predictors of work-family conflict and enrichment: Which of these resources or their combinations are the most beneficial? *Journal of Family and Economic Issues*, *34*(1), 87–104. https://doi.org/10.1007/s10834-012-9306-3.

Mazzola, J. J., Schonfeld, I. S., & Spector, P. E. (2011). What qualitative research has taught us about occupational stress. *Stress and Health*, *27*(2), 93–110. https://doi.org/10.1002/smi.1386.

Meisenbach, R. J. (2010). The female breadwinner: Phenomenological experience and gendered identity in work/family spaces. *Sex Roles*, *62*(1–2), 2–19. https://doi.org/10.1007/s11199-009-9714-5.

Morganson, V. J., & Major, D. A. (2014). Exploring retaliation as a coping strategy in response to customer sexual harassment. *Sex Roles: A Journal of Research*, *71*(1–2), 83–94. https://doi.org/10.1007/s11199-014-0373-9.

Motro, D., & Ellis A. P. J. (2017). Boys, don't cry: Gender and reactions to negative performance feedback. *Journal of Applied Psychology, 102*(2), 227–235. https://doi.org/10.1037/apl0000175.

Nandkeolyar, A. K., Shaffer, J. A., Li, A., Ekkirala, S., & Bagger, J. (2014). Surviving an abusive supervisor: The joint roles of conscientiousness and coping strategies. *Journal of Applied Psychology, 99*(1), 138–150. https://doi.org/10.1037/a0034262.

Narayanan, L., Menon, S., & Spector, P. E. (1999). Stress in the workplace: A comparison of gender and occupations. *Journal of Organizational Behavior, 20*(1), 63–73. https://doi.org/10.1002/(SICI)1099-1379(199901)20:1<63::AID-JOB873>3.0.CO;2-J.

Nixon, A. E., Mazzola, J. J., Bauer, J., Krueger, J. R., & Spector, P. E. (2011). Can work make you sick? A meta-analysis of the relationships between job stressors and physical symptoms. *Work and Stress, 25*(1), 1–22. https://doi.org/10.1080/02678373.2011.569175.

Olson, D. A., & Shultz, K. S. (1994). Gender differences in the dimensionality of social support. *Journal of Applied Social Psychology, 24*(14), 1221–1232. https://doi.org/10.1111/j.1559-1816.1994.tb00555.x.

Pearlin, L. I., & Schooler, C. (1978). The structure of coping. *Journal of Health and Social Behavior, 19*(1), 2–21. https://doi.org/10.2307/2136319.

Perrewé, P. L., & Carlson, D. S. (2002). Do men and women benefit from social support equally? Results from a field examination within the work and family context. In D. L. Nelson & R. J. Burke (Eds.), *Gender, work stress, and health* (pp. 101–114). American Psychological Association. https://doi.org/10.1037/10467-007.

Persson, R., Hansen, A., Ohlsson, K., Balogh, I. Nordander, C., & Ørbæk, P. (2009). Physiological and psychological reactions to work in men and women with identical job tasks. *European Journal of Applied Physiology, 105*(4), 595–606. https://doi.org/10.1007/s00421–008-0939-8.

Petrie, M., & Roman, P. M. (2004). Race and gender differences in workplace autonomy: A research note. *Sociological Inquiry, 74*(4), 590–603. https://doi.org/10.1111/j.1475-682X.2004.00106.x.

Pleck, J. H. (1976). The male sex role: Definitions, problems, and sources of change. *Journal of Social Issues, 32*(3), 155–164. https://doi.org/10 .1111/j.1540-4560.1976.tb02604.x.

(1977). The work–family role system. *Social Problems, 24*(4), 417–427. https://doi.org/10.2307/800135.

(1979). Men's family work: Three perspectives and some new data. *Family Coordinator, 28*(4), 481–488. https://doi.org/10.2307/583508.

Ptacek, J. T., Smith, R. E., & Dodge, K. L. (1994). Gender differences in coping with stress: When stressor and appraisals do not differ.

Personality and Social Psychology Bulletin, 20(4), 421–430. https://doi .org/10.1177/0146167294204009.

Pupco, S., & Barling, J. (2021). Leadership and well-being. In E. K. Kelloway & C. L. Cooper (Eds.), *A research agenda for workplace stress and well-being* (pp. 53–72). Edward Elgar Publishing. https://doi.org/10.4337/ 9781789905021.00012

Ramadoss, K., & Rajadhyaksha, U. (2012). Gender differences in commitment to roles, work–family conflict and social support. *Journal of Social Sciences, 33*(2), 227–233. https://doi.org/10.1080/09718923 .2012.11893101.

Rosario, M., Shinn, M., Mørch, H., & Huckabee, C. B. (1988). Gender differences in coping and social supports: Testing socialization and role constraint theories. *Journal of Community Psychology, 16*(1), 55–69. https://doi.org/10.1002/1520-6629(198801)16:1<55::AID-JCOP2290160108>3.0.CO;2-U.

Rosenblatt, Z., Talmud, I., & Ruvio, A. (1999). A gender-based framework of the experience of job insecurity and its effects on work attitudes. *European Journal of Work and Organizational Psychology, 8*(2), 197–217. https://doi.org/10.1080/135943299398320.

Roxburgh, S. (1996). Gender differences in work and well-being: Effects of exposure and vulnerability. *Journal of Health and Social Behavior, 37* (3), 265–277. https://doi.org/10.2307/2137296.

Rugulies, R., Aust, B., Burr, H., & Bültmann, U. (2008). Job insecurity, chances on the labour market and decline in self-rated health in a representative sample of the Danish workforce. *Journal of Epidemiology and Community Health, 62*(3), 245–250. https://doi .org/10.1136/jech.2006.059113.

Rugulies, R., Bültmann, U., Aust, B., & Burr, H. (2006). Psychosocial work environment and incidence of severe depressive symptoms: Prospective findings from a 5-year follow-up of the Danish work environment cohort study. *American Journal of Epidemiology, 163*(10), 877–887. https://doi.org/10.1093/aje/kwj119.

Sawyer, K., Salter, N., & Thoroughgood, C. (2013). Studying individual identities is good, but examining intersectionality is better. *Industrial and Organizational Psychology, 6*(1), 80–84. https://doi.org/10.1111/ iops.12012.

Schmitt, D. P. (2017, November 7). *The truth about sex differences.* Psychology Today. www.psychologytoday.com/us/articles/201711/the-truth-about-sex-differences.

Shockley, K. M., Shen, W., DeNunzio, M. M., Arvan, M. L., & Knudsen, E. A. (2017). Disentangling the relationship between gender and work–family conflict: An integration of theoretical perspectives using meta-analytic methods. *Journal of Applied Psychology, 102*(12), 1601–1635. https://doi.org/10.1037/apl0000246.

Sigmon, S. T., Stanton, A. L., & Snyder, C. R. (1995). Gender differences in coping: A further test of socialization and role constraint theories. *Sex Roles, 33*(9–10), 565–587. https://doi.org/10.1007/BF01547718.

Stewart, A. J., & Lykes, M. B. (Eds.). (1985). *Gender and personality: Current perspectives on theory and research.* Duke University Press.

Stier, H., & Yaish, M. (2014). Occupational segregation and gender inequality in job quality: A multi-level approach. *Work, Employment, and Society, 28*(2), 225–246. https://doi.org/10.1177/0950017013510758.

Stroh, L. K., & Reilly, A. H. (1999). Gender and careers: Present experiences and emerging trends. In G. N. Powell (Ed.), *Handbook of gender and work* (pp. 307–324). Sage.

Stroud, L. R., Salovey, P., & Epel, E. S. (2002). Sex differences in stress responses: Social rejection versus achievement stress. *Biological Psychiatry, 52*(4), 318–327. https://doi.org/10.1016/S0006–3223(02) 01333-1.

Stryker, S. (1968). Identity salience and role performance: The relevance of symbolic interaction theory for family research. *Journal of Marriage and Family, 30*(4), 558–564. https://doi.org/10.2307/349494.

(1980). *Symbolic interactionism: A social structural version.* Benjamin/ Cummings.

Tamres, L. K., Janicki, D., & Helgeson, V. S. (2002). Sex differences in coping behavior: A meta-analytic review and an examination of relative coping. *Personality and Social Psychology Review, 6*(1), 2–30. https://doi.org/10.1207/S15327957PSPR0601_1.

Tausig, M., Fenwick, R., Sauter, S. L., Murphy, L. R., & Corina, G. (2004). The changing nature of job stress: Risk and resources. In P. L. Perrewé & D. C. Ganster (Eds.), *Exploring Interpersonal Dynamics* (Vol. 4, pp. 93–126). Emerald Group Publishing Limited. https://doi.org/10.1016/S1479–3555(04)04003-X.

Theorell, T., Hammarström, A., Gustafsson, P. E., Hanson, L. M., Janlert, U., & Westerlund, H. (2014). Job strain and depressive symptoms in men and women: A prospective study of the working population in Sweden. *Journal of Epidemiol Community Health, 68*(1), 78–82. http://doi.org/10.1136/jech-2012-202294.

Thoits, P. A. (1995). Stress, coping, and social support processes: Where are we? What next? *Journal of Health and Social Behavior, 35*, 53–79. https://doi.org/10.2307/2626957.

Thompson, B. M., & Cavallaro, L. (2007). Gender, work-based support and family outcomes. *Stress and Health, 23*(2), 73–85. https://doi.org/10.1002/smi.1122.

U.S. Bureau of Labor Statistics. (2020). *Full-time/part-time employment.* www.bls.gov/cps/cpsaat08.pdf.

(2021). *Labor force statistics from the current population survey.* www .bls.gov/cps/cpsaat11.htm.

U.S. Department of Labor. (n.d.). *DOL policy brief. Paternity leave: Why parental leave for fathers is so important for working families.* www.dol .gov/sites/dolgov/files/OASP/legacy/files/PaternityBrief.pdf.

U.S. Equal Employment Opportunity Commission. (2019). *Charges alleging sex-based harassment (charges filed with EEOC) FY 2010–FY 2019.* www.eeoc.gov/statistics/charges-alleging-sex-based-harassment-charges-filed-eeoc-fy-2010-fy-2019.

Vagg, P. R., Spielberger, C. D., & Wasala, C. F. (2002). Effects of organizational level and gender on stress in the workplace. *International Journal of Stress Management, 9*(4), 243–261. https://doi.org/10.1023/ A:1019964331348.

Vandello, J. A., & Bosson, J. K. (2013). Hard won and easily lost: A review and synthesis of research on precarious manhood. *Psychology of Men and Masculinity, 14*(2), 101–113. https://doi.org/10.1037/a0029826.

Vandello, J. A., Hettinger, V. E., Bosson, J. K., & Siddiqi, J. (2013). When equal really isn't equal: The masculine dilemma of seeking work flexibility. *Journal of Social Issues, 69*(2), 303–321. https://doi.org/10.1111/ josi.12016.

Verma, R., Balhara, Y. P. S., & Gupta, C. S. (2011). Gender differences in stress response: Role of developmental and biological determinants. *Industrial Psychiatry Journal, 20*(1), 4–10. https://doi.org/10.4103/ 0972-6748.98407.

Vermeulen, M., & Mustard, C. (2000). Gender differences in job strain, social support at work, and psychological distress. *Journal of Occupational Health Psychology, 5*(4), 428–440. https://doi.org/10 .1037/1076-8998.5.4.428.

Violanti, J. M., Fekedulegn, D., Hartley, T. A., Charles, L. E., Andrew, M. E., Ma, C. C., & Burchfiel, C. M. (2016). Highly rated and most frequent stressors among police officers: Gender differences. *American Journal of Criminal Justice, 41*(4), 645–662. https://doi.org/10.1007/ s12103-016-9342-x.

Wang, J. L., Lesage, A., Schmitz, N., & Drapeau, A. (2008). The relationship between work stress and mental disorders in men and women: Findings from a population-based study. *Journal of Epidemiology and Community Health, 62*(1), 42–47. https://doi.org/10.1136/jech.2006 .050591.

Weer, C. H., Greenhaus, J. H., Colakoglu, S. N., & Foley, S. (2006). The role of maternal employment, role-altering strategies, and gender in college students' expectations of work–family conflict. *Sex Roles*, *55*(7–8), 535–544. https://doi.org/10.1007/s11199-006-9107-y.

Wegman, L. A., Hoffman, B. J., Carter, N. T., Twenge, J. M., & Guenole, N. (2018). Placing job characteristics in context: Cross-temporal meta-analysis of changes in job characteristics since 1975. *Journal of Management*, *44* (1), 352–386. https://doi.org/10.1177/0149206316654545.

Willness, C. R., Steel, P., & Lee, K. (2007). A meta-analysis of the antecedents and consequences of workplace sexual harassment. *Personnel Psychology*, *60*(1), 127–162. https://doi.org/10.1111/j.1744-6570 .2007.00067.x.

Wong, K., Chan, A. H., & Ngan, S. C. (2019). The effect of long working hours and overtime on occupational health: A meta-analysis of evidence from 1998 to 2018. *International Journal of Environmental Research and Public Health*, *16*(12), 2102. https://doi.org/10.3390/ijerph16122102.

11 | *The Measurement of Well-Being at Work*

KEVIN DANIELS, EMMA RUSSELL,
GEORGE MICHAELIDES, EMIKE
NASAMU, AND SARA CONNOLLY

Well-being has a prominent profile in many academic disciplines. For example, in philosophy, there is Aristotle's conception of well-being as associated with human flourishing or 'eudaimonia'. In political theory, Utilitarianism defines the main goals of policy as maximising pleasure and minimising gain (Bache & Reardon, 2016). Much more recently, some national political leaders, as well as political theorists/scientists, have become interested in well-being as an alternative marker of national progress to economic measures such as gross domestic product. Although there are many debates on the nature of well-being, the dominant view is that well-being is inherently a psychological construct (O'Donnell et al., 2014). Thus, psychological approaches to measuring well-being provide a platform for indexing the effectiveness of policy decisions made at all levels, from workplaces through to nation states (Layard, 2016). In relation to the workplace, such policies may include those directed at reducing absence rates or securing sustainable productivity gains without threatening worker health, wherein psychological well-being may serve as a leading indicator. At regional, national or even supra-national level, relevant policies pertain to labour market regulation and workplace health and safety.

As such, the purpose of this chapter is to outline some of the main and emerging issues in the measurement of workplace well-being. We consider both positive markers of well-being (e.g., job satisfaction) and markers developed from research focused on indexing psychologically harmful effects of working practices. As we shall see, research on positive markers pre-dates by some decades the emergence of positive psychology (Seligman, 2002), which sought to direct researchers away from a primary focus on negative states and psychopathology. Moreover, measures of the major well-being concepts developed reflect not just psychological constructs *per se* but overlap considerably with lay/public views on what constitutes workplace well-being

(Daniels et al., 2018), namely around job satisfaction, happiness, absence of psychological ill-health and a sense of meaning and purpose in life. This overlap is important for two reasons. First, measures of the major concepts have a starting point to establish face validity. Second, the reasons for policies and practices developed from research on workplace well-being can be conveyed with relative ease by reference to scientific concepts that are easily translated into everyday language.

At a theoretical level, the overlap is also important. There are concerns that well-being is a social construction that needs to be understood from the point of view of research participants and their specific contexts (White et al., 2014). This contrasts with the dominant approach in the psychological (and economic) sciences, wherein well-being comprises a series of more specific constructs that can be measured using quantitative rating scales that apply across all contexts. The overlap between the theoretical constructs and corresponding measures developed in the psychological literature and lay/public conceptions of well-being considerably lessens concerns over the ontological/epistemological status of well-being.

There are concepts we do not cover in the chapter. We do not consider measures of potential workplace causes of well-being (e.g., job demands, resources, person–environment fit) or consequences (in-role performance, organisational citizenship, absence, presenteeism). Neither do we consider indicators of well-being that relate to physiology (e.g., heart rate) or expression of felt emotions (e.g., facial expressions of feelings of happiness that an individual may or may not choose to suppress). Rather, we concentrate on the psychological aspects of well-being. Although there is overlap, physiological, expressive and psychological aspects of well-being are only loosely coupled (Lang, 1988).

Psychological well-being has two major components (Waterman, 1993). The first, subjective well-being, consists of summative assessments of one's life (e.g., life satisfaction) or life domain (e.g., job satisfaction) and affective well-being, which is the experience of positive affective states (e.g., joy, enthusiasm) and the relative absence of negative affective states (e.g., lack of anxiety, feeling calm) (Diener, 1984). The second component is eudaimonic well-being, which includes feelings of autonomy, mastery, personal growth, positive relations with others, purpose in life and self-acceptance (Ryff & Keyes, 1995).

Following a brief history of major developments in the measurement of well-being, the chapter will then consider current issues and complexities in well-being assessment. The first of these is one not traditionally of much concern to researchers into workplace well-being, namely, how to establish accepted monetary thresholds for changes in well-being to inform those who take decisions about well-being. For organisational decision makers and policy makers, this is a critical practical issue as it informs investment decisions: If one option returns more well-being gains than another for a lower price, then the former option should be chosen. Monetisation is also important for researchers to draw out the practical implications of their research more fully. We then consider the dynamics of well-being. As noted above, a central element of well-being relates to affective states, which are themselves highly volatile, and so capturing this element of well-being in particular has raised many issues relating to the design of measurement instruments. Looking forward, we then consider emerging issues in the dynamic assessment of well-being. One key element here is indexing variability in well-being in the same person over time. This leads to the final substantive section on considering variability in well-being between people and considering how to index well-being inequalities and why well-being inequalities might matter.

Some Highlights in the Measurement of Well-Being

The purpose of this brief section is not to provide a comprehensive listing of every measure of worker well-being, or indeed every concept. Rather, it is to give the reader an overview of the major concepts that have emerged and some of the measures of those concepts. The choices are subjective and based on the authors' personal favourites from their combined years of researching in this field.

One of the earliest formal, quantitative measures is that of job satisfaction. In 1951, Brayfield and Rothe published an 18-item measure of job satisfaction that included items pertaining to how interesting workers found their jobs, boredom at work, enthusiasm for their job, liking for the job and how satisfied they are at work. Job satisfaction, most generally defined as the extent to which people like or derive pleasure from their jobs (Locke, 1976), has remained as one of the key indicators of workplace well-being used in work psychology and employment relations research. Multiple measures have been developed, tapping into generalised assessments of how much people like their work or satisfaction with specific facets of their work (e.g., job security, pay, supervision, development opportunities), which are then summed into an overall score. Hackman and Oldham's Job Diagnostic Survey (1974) includes examples of both kinds of job satisfaction scale, although many researchers appear to use generalised assessments and summations of satisfaction with specific facets interchangeably. Generalised assessments of job satisfaction appear to confer two key benefits for the assessment of well-being. First, they provide a summative assessment of well-being in relation to work. Second, they can be assessed with just one, or a small number, of items (e.g., Eurofound, 2015).

Given the growth of models of occupational stress in the 1960s and 1970s (e.g., French et al., 1974; Kahn et al., 1964), typologies of occupational stressors (e.g., Cooper & Marshall, 1976) and measures of those stressors (e.g., House & Rizzo, 1972), researchers needed to incorporate measures of strain as well as satisfaction in their studies. In the UK, the 12-item measure of mental health, the GHQ12 (Goldberg, 1972), became championed as a short, unidimensional measure for workplace studies (Banks et al., 1980) that could potentially capture the influence of workplaces on clinical and subclinical mental health outcomes. The Maslach Burnout Inventory (MBI, Maslach et al., 1986) has been a popular measure to gauge the impact of workplace stressors on well-being, especially in human service work. The MBI assesses burnout across three dimensions of emotional exhaustion, depersonalisation and reduced personal accomplishment.

To capture both negative and positive well-being reactions to work, measurement developed further in two complementary ways. One line of research sought to augment measurement in studies of burnout, and the concept and measurement of work engagement were developed (Schaufeli et al., 2002), which positions positive work-related well-being to consist of three elements of vigour, dedication and absorption in work activities. Although burnout and engagement are considered to be distinct concepts, they are highly correlated (Schaufeli & De Witte, 2017).

Another line of research on negative and positive well-being took as its starting point debates concerning the dimensional structure of affect. On the one hand, Russell (1980) argued for a two-dimensional structure of affect, with dimensions of pleasantness–unpleasantness and arousal. On the other, Watson and Tellegen (1985) argued for two alternative dimensions of negative and positive affect, representing the degree to which highly activated pleasant (e.g., enthusiasm) and unpleasant (e.g., anxiety) affective states are experienced. Larsen and Diener (1992) argued that the difference between Russell's and Watson and Tellegen's models reflected the choice of rotation in factor analytic models.

Research building on models of the dimensional structure of affect has produced a range of measures of workplace affective well-being. Some of these measures (Van Katwyk et al., 2000; Warr et al., 2014) have assessed affective well-being as a composite for four unipolar 'facets' on well-being: i) high pleasure/high arousal (e.g., enthusiastic); ii) high pleasure/low arousal (e.g., relaxed); iii) low pleasure/high arousal (e.g., anxious); and iv) low pleasure/low arousal (e.g., depressed). Others have argued that differential tendencies to response to positively or negatively items obscures the true bipolarity of dimensions of affective states in conventional factor analytic models. Correspondingly, these researchers sought to assess affective well-being through measures assessing bipolar dimensions and sophisticated factor analytic methods (Daniels, 2000; Warr, 1990). Warr's measures capture two bipolar elements of well-being (depressed to enthusiastic, corresponding most closely to positive affect, and anxious to contented, corresponding to {low} negative affect). Daniels' measures capture five bipolar dimensions that have two bipolar second order factors corresponding to negative and positive affect, with high and low arousal states.

In concluding this section on some but not all major developments, in the measurement of well-being, there is one omission. Measures of eudaimonic well-being have historically attracted less attention in much work psychology research, possibly because of the focus on stress and/or health outcomes, including mental health outcomes. One measure developed for use in general populations, rather than working populations, is that developed by Ryff and Keyes (1995). This measure assessed six dimensions of eudaimonic well-being, namely autonomy, mastery, personal growth, positive relations with others, purpose in life and self-acceptance. In an analysis of indicators of psychological and eudaimonic well-being used in the European Social Survey, Huppert and So (2013) found support for two separate dimensions, with one reflecting items with a greater affective content (labelled 'positive characteristics') and another reflecting items with a greater eudaimonic content (learning new things, sense of meaning, sense of accomplishment, positive social relationships). Nevertheless, to date, there is no widely accepted and comprehensive measure of eudaimonic well-being in relation to work.

Common Metrics and Conversion Rates across Measures

As discussed above, there are many conceptions, as well as different measures, of well-being. The choice of well-being measure will depend on the use of relevant stakeholders. Within the domain of policy making and at a macro-economic level, Stiglitz et al. (2009) and Coyle (2014) highlighted the importance of using statistical metrics which can capture aspects of social progress and quality of life, which are absent in traditional economic indicators such as GDP (see Wallace et al., 2020, for how gross domestic well-being might be monitored across domains). In particular policy domains, such as health, there was also a dissatisfaction with reliance upon cost–benefit analysis which required monetising all elements when justifying policy choices or evaluating policy outcomes. Evaluation techniques have now been developed which compared costs in monetary terms and benefits in quality adjusted life years, and these are now embedded in health decision making (NICE, 2013). A similar approach is now being applied for evaluating workplace well-being initiatives where benefits are captured in terms of well-being (Bryce et al., 2020). These techniques of well-being cost-effectiveness analysis can be applied at a policy level (e.g., employment legislation, health and safety regulation) but have been developed primarily for use by employers faced with making choices between different workplace health and well-being initiatives.

As discussed above, well-being is multi-dimensional and may correlate with key indicators such as health, education, material living standard, social connections and so on. Layard (2016) argues that having a singular well-being metric which serves as a common currency is necessary for ease of comparison across policy domains or types of intervention. Measures of well-being need to be meaningful to individuals, in terms of providing a summary or an overview measure of their quality of life. Similarly, there needs to be a clear metric for decision makers who monitor well-being and thereby compare the well-being outcomes of various interventions or activities associated with workforce development for transformation.

National statistical agencies (e.g., UK Office of National Statistics (ONS), 2011) and international organisations (e.g., Eurostat, 2010) responded to the recommendations of Stiglitz et al. (2009),[1] by undertaking research on what meaningful and reliable data on well-being could be collected, and which of these could measure people's quality of life and inform decision making. In the UK, the national statistical agency (ONS) identified four questions, reflecting psychological well-being (summative, affective and eudaimonic components): 'Overall, how satisfied are you with your life nowadays?' (summative); 'Overall, to what extent do you think the things you do in your life are worthwhile?' (eudaimonic); 'Overall, how happy did you feel yesterday?' (affective); and 'Overall, how anxious did you feel yesterday?' (affective). The latter two are clearly sensitive to changing events and the second reflects the respondent's value judgement on what is/ not worthwhile. Layard (2016) recommended the first question 'Overall, how satisfied are you with your life nowadays?' be used as a common currency in measuring well-being. Responses to the question are made on a scale of 0–10, where 0 is not at all and 10 is completely. In relation to the workplace, the choice of a life satisfaction measure may seem unusual, when an index of job satisfaction may appear more relevant to workplace initiatives and policies. However, a metric that captures the entire life experience has the advantage of reflecting the effects of workplace initiatives and policies that reach beyond the workplace, such as flexible working practices that enhance family life or make caring responsibilities less demanding.

In the field of health, a medical intervention which yields an additional quality of life adjusted year is deemed to be cost effective if it costs less than £20–30,000 (or equivalent). Building upon this, Layard (2016) proposes that an extra unit of life satisfaction over a year converts to a threshold benefit of between £2,000 and £3,000. The use of a common well-being metric – a additional unit of life satisfaction over a year – alongside a monetary benchmark of acceptable costs not only enables comparisons between different workplace well-being interventions but also well-being interventions in other domains of life.

In practice, however, individuals may be interested in other aspects of well-being and researchers or organisations may monitor other variables of interest such as job satisfaction, engagement, mental

Table 11.1 *Conversion rates for different measures of well-being into life satisfaction*

Well-being measure	Range	Exchange rate
Life satisfaction (ONS[a])	0–10	1
Satisfaction with Life Scale[b]	5–35	0.24
Worthwhile (ONS)	0–10	0.75
Happy (ONS)	0–10	0.72
Anxious (ONS)	0–10	0.35
General Health Questionnaire[c]	0–36	−0.21
Short Warwick Edinburgh Mental Well-Being Scale[d]	7–35	0.25
Satisfaction with job (BHPS[e])	1–7	0.49
Satisfaction with income (BHPS)	1–7	0.61
Satisfaction with amount of leisure time (BHPS)	1–7	0.57
Satisfaction with use of leisure time (BHPS)	1–7	0.62
Satisfaction with social life (BHPS)	1–7	0.60
Satisfaction with health (BHPS)	1–7	0.63

[a] Office of National Statistics (ONS, 2011).
[b] Pavot and Diener (2008).
[c] Goldberg and Williams (1988).
[d] Kammann and Flett (1983); Stewart-Brown et al. (2009).
[e] British Household Panel Survey (Taylor et al., 2018).
Source: Bryce et al. (2020)

health, self-esteem and social support. In such cases, Layard (2016) proposes 'converting' values of other metrics into a corresponding value for the ONS life satisfaction by making use of conversion rates, as in Table 11.1. The conversion rates in Table 11.1 are based on empirical estimates from the analyses of Mukuria et al. (2016) and Powdthavee (2012), where panel data has been used to examine the impact of changes in each of the well-being measures upon life satisfaction.

The use of life satisfaction as a single-item metric measuring well-being is not uncontroversial. Huppert (2017) returns to the argument that well-being is a multi- dimensional construct which requires measurement of both the internal and external factors which influence it. Recent research (Marsh et al., 2020; Ruggeri et al., 2020) has sought ways to bridge theory, evidence and practice by developing a composite score based on more complex multi-item psychological measures. For decision makers – whether they be HR managers or policy makers – this approach may still be unwieldy and the simplicity of a single-item metric such as life satisfaction remains a more pragmatic route to embedding well-being into organisational practice, and does not preclude using other measures in surveys of well-being.

The Measurement of Affective Well-Being at Work

Affective well-being (AWB) involves a person's evaluation of the valence and activation of their feelings, to constitute an emotional expression that has value or meaning within a specific context. AWB will be higher if a person considers their emotional experience to be positive, meaningful and valuable (Frijda, 2008). A person's AWB may or may not be tied to a particular event or stimulus, is differently structured depending on the duration and intensity of emotions experienced and reflects an individual's interaction with their environment (Bliese et al., 2017; Frijda, 2008; Wright & Cropanzano, 2000). As such, measures of AWB involve more than just reports of sensations, responses or feelings; AWB is imbued with meaning according to the individual's evaluation of their affective experience. It is therefore important that both the structure of affect, and the context within which it is being considered (time, place, etc.), be appropriately captured and represented, in AWB measurement.[2]

In work contexts, AWB is increasingly recognised as a salient predictor *and* outcome of job-relevant metrics and initiatives. For example, AWB has been found to predict work outcomes such as satisfaction (Hoffmann et al., 2014; Ilies & Judge, 2004) and success (Lyubomirsky et al., 2005). It is also a significant outcome of work-based predictors such as goal conflict (Hoffmann et al., 2014) and provision of job resources (e.g., coaching and autonomy) (Xanthopoulou et al., 2012a). Because of these relationships, measuring AWB at work has become a necessary feature of much organisational-based research and is likely to influence the extent to which work policies and initiatives are sustained in the long term (Diener et al., 2015). Moreover, AWB is a key element of well-being and, being highly volatile (Xanthopoulou et al., 2012b), measures of AWB are well placed to capture short-term and dynamic influences on changes in a person's well-being whilst still retaining the ability to capture longer-term and more stable differences between people (Xanthopoulou et al., 2020).

Levels of AWB

Much organisational research concerned with measuring AWB, as either a predictor or outcome of work-related variables and stimuli, is also concerned with how AWB is constructed. AWB can be hierarchically arranged as representing three broad levels relating to the duration and stability of the construct (Frijda, 1993; Russell & Daniels, 2018). At the most stable level, trait-based characteristics of a person and their propensity to appraise emotions in a particular way, or express a particular emotional style over time, are represented (Beal & Ghandour, 2011; de Neve & Cooper, 1998; Steel et al., 2008). The level down from this involves relatively changeable aspects of emotional experience, usually framing generalised 'mood', or a sum of a person's affective response over a briefer, aggregated period of time (e.g., last week, last month, yesterday) (Brief & Weiss, 2002; Weiss & Cropanzano, 1996). At the lowest, most transitory level, AWB is represented as a momentary construct that fluctuates in terms of discrete emotional expression, often in response to a specific event or stimulus (Frijda, 1993).

Measuring AWB at any of these levels requires an adaptation in approach. For example, the focal instruction used with the respondent must make clear which time period is of interest. Asking how someone feels 'right now' will not capture stable, trait-based affect, although it is likely to be influenced by this. Further, the terms used to capture and rate the affective experience need to be carefully considered and scored to reflect the level of interest. For example, asking if a person feels 'good' or 'bad' is more likely to capture a mood construct. Rating discrete emotions, such as how 'angry' or 'calm' a person feels, is likely to be momentary-based or would need to be aggregated with other items in a composite score if it is to represent an overall trait-based characteristic such as 'hostility' or 'neuroticism'. To provide a reliable measure of AWB, researchers also need to weigh up how long an AWB scale needs to be, to capture the construct effectively and reliably without causing survey fatigue, which can invalidate outcomes (Gable et al., 2000; Stanton et al., 2002). For example, in measuring momentary AWB, respondents may need to complete an AWB scale several times a day over a period (Xanthopoulou et al., 2012b). Such scales need to be shorter, so that response rates are not undermined (Cranford et al., 2006; Ouweneel et al., 2012). However, if respondents only need to complete a one-off measure (e.g., to measure trait-based AWB), longer scales can be justified. Table 11.2 summarises some of these issues.

Considerations in the Measurement of AWB at Work

Balancing the issues outlined above requires careful evaluation for the organisational researcher. In measuring AWB at work, we suggest that there are seven key elements to consider.

Context

The *context* of the affective experience needs to be captured via the use of appropriate focal instructions and scoring bands. When the temporality of the experience is of interest, then the scoring band needs to include options of frequency (e.g., Always to Never) and focal instructions need to refer to the time boundedness. For example, if the researcher is interested in momentary AWB, then the focal instruction needs to ask the respondent to reflect on how they feel 'right now' or 'at the present moment'. In considering mood, the focal instruction will ask the respondent to sum their experience over 'today' or 'the past week', for example. For stable traits, the focal instruction needs to look at 'how you generally/typically feel', or what one would 'usually' do or feel. Apart from temporality, context may involve understanding the intensity of the emotion, so focal instructions may ask about the 'extent to which' the affect was experienced, using scoring bands that refer to 'not at all' to 'very much'. Further, the focal instruction can draw out whether AWB in relation to an event, experience or domain is relevant, e.g., 'in relation to your last customer interaction', or 'when at work'. The Job Affective Well-Being Scale (JAWS: van Katwyk et al., 2000) provides a focal instruction that asks participants to think about their job environment, e.g., 'my job made me feel...'. Choosing a focal instruction that represents the context is therefore significant, and researchers would be well placed to utilise AWB scales that allow for the focal instructions to be adapted for context (without undermining the reliability and validity of the measure).

Table 11.2 *Measuring AWB at different levels*

Level	Affective structure	Duration of affective experience	Example	Suggested focal instruction	Suggested scoring approach	Recommended scale length
1	Trait-based	Stable	Optimism; neuroticism	'To what extent are you generally...'	Summing/averaging scale items to provide an overall score representing each trait-based factor (potentially bipolar)	Can be lengthier; usually a one-off administration
2	Summative, aggregate of emotion	Fluctuates somewhat	Positive affect (PA); bad mood	'Over the past week, to what extent have you felt...'	Summing/averaging scale items of discrete emotional terms (potentially related to valence and/or arousal) OR using individual scores from aggregated item terms (such as bad/ good, positive/negative mood states) Several factors may be represented (potentially bipolar)	Can be one-off or repeated administration (e.g., every day for 10 working days), so needs to be shorter
3	Discrete emotions or feelings	Momentary fluctuation	Tired; enthusiastic	'At the present time, to what extent do you feel...'	Individual item scores or summing/averaging item scores to represent discrete affective clusters of items (potentially bipolar)	Repeated administrations likely (e.g., in response to daily events), so needs to be shortest form with the fewest scale items

Length

The *length* of the AWB measure needs to be appropriate for the frequency with which the respondent is expected to rate their affective experiences. This is especially relevant when the respondent is completing measures alongside normal, day-to-day work/life tasks (Russell & Daniels, 2018). Too much cognitive load on the participant is likely to negatively impact response rates and create invalid responses or even dropouts from studies (Gable et al., 2000; Scollon et al., 2003). If the respondent is frequently rating their momentary AWB in relation to a specific experience (e.g., over several times a day), the length of the AWB scale needs to be short and convenient with few items (Cranford et al., 2006). A one-off measure, specifically if stable AWB is being captured, can afford to be longer and include more items without creating survey fatigue or invalidating responses.

Affective Structure

The nature of the '*affective*' structure of well-being needs to be balanced across the scale. Although other areas of psychology have been concerned with understanding the broad, universal categories of emotional expression (e.g., Ekman, 1992; Izard, 1977), psychologists concerned with measuring AWB have generally overlooked this (Frijda, 2008). As such, AWB measures can include an array of terms that vary in terms of categorisation, representation, activation, specificity and valence.

For example, the 20-item Positive and Negative Affect Schedule (PANAS) (Watson et al., 1988) includes states that are not feelings (e.g., strong and alert), motivational terms (e.g., determined, inspired) and emotional feelings (e.g., afraid, nervous) (Diener et al., 2009). Items are considered to be of negative or positive valence, but there are more negatively valenced terms relating to categories of anxiety (e.g., jittery, nervous), none relating to sadness and few representing hostility (Diener et al., 2009). Low activation emotions are also omitted; however, when these are added to the newer 60-item version of PANAS (Watson & Clark, 1999), the factor structure of the PANAS is compromised, no longer cleanly representing two factors of AWB (a positive and a negative factor). Rather, a positive affect factor emerges (with only highly activated positive affect items loading strongly onto this) and a range of negative affect factors representing hostility, fear, low activation, low self-esteem and other categories.

Relatedly, a bias towards negative items is seen in both the long and short versions of the Profile of Mood States (POMS: Cranford et al., 2006; McNair et al., 1992). The POMS captures emotional terms that represent negatively valenced items across categories of anxiety, depression, anger/hostility and fatigue. Positive affect is captured with just a fifth of its items, primarily representing vigour.

In other models of affect, the valence and activation of the emotional term has been balanced equally in representations. Russell (1980), Feldman-Barrett and Russell (1998) and Larsen and Diener (1992) present circumplex models where there are two orthogonal factors representing high to low activation and positive to negative valence. So, 'calm' represents positive valence and low activation, whereas 'angry' represents negative valence and high activation. Any term can be plotted along both factors on a continuum, and scales attempt to provide a balance of items accordingly (Daniels, 2000; Diener et al., 2009). The circumplex model does not necessarily specify from which emotional categories of affect each term should herald (representation of 'fear', 'joy', 'disgust', 'regret', etc.). Some circumplex scales, such as the Scale of Positive and Negative Experience (SPANE: Diener et al., 2009, 2010), include terms that represent both discrete emotional terms and also broad categories of 'mood' (e.g., good, negative, pleasant) to overcome the context-dependency of items which, they argue, bias existing AWB measures towards certain groups.

Researchers choosing which AWB measures to use should therefore consider whether the terms used to represent affect in the scale also represent their position as to how affect is structured. If a circumplex structure is favoured, then scales need to represent hedonic tone (valence) and activation (arousal). Whether terms should reflect discrete emotions or broader mood items probably depends on the level of affect being considered (e.g., using general or 'mood' terms at level 3 (Table 11.2) is possibly not advisable). Further, although there is no existing measure of AWB that claims to have captured the breadth of relevant emotions that emerge in the workplace, researchers should consider whether the emotions that are referenced are appropriate for predicting (or being predicted by) their contingent variables in the focal research design. For example, using the PANAS to index 'frustration' may not be helpful, as anger items are poorly represented. Scales such as JAWS (Van Katwyk et al., 2000) include terms such as 'satisfied' and 'inspired', which other authors suggest should be considered separately to AWB (Diener et al., 2009; Ilies et al., 2007; Wright & Cropanzano, 2000) and potentially could create a conceptual contamination or tautology if used to predict, for example, job satisfaction.

Scope

Relatedly, the terms used in an AWB scale need to represent the broad *scope* of emotional experiences felt in relation to human activity, without being biased towards particular cultures, age-groups (Diener et al., 2009) or other demographically relevant groups. For example, if a measure includes more 'energy'-related terms, Diener et al. (2009) argue that these will be biased towards younger people who are more likely to agree that they are feeling 'active', 'alert', etc. This would result in younger people potentially being misconstrued as having higher levels of well-being in a context, compared with older responders. Across organisational research, many AWB scales have been validated and trialled in other national cultures (Schimmack et al., 2002). This is to be encouraged, but scale developers need to make clear the scope of their scale for use in different organisational and national settings, by clarifying from which dictionaries original scale terms have been derived (and their embeddedness in the culture in question), and with which sample groups scales have been validated (as per Van Katwyk et al., 2000). Further, there is evidence that there are gender differences in the rating of emotions and tendency towards positive response bias which is not necessarily reflected in the actuality of experience (Fujita et al., 1991). More research is needed to ascertain whether ratings of AWB are biased towards people from certain groups or categories, and the extent to which this impacts the significance of findings. Researchers are encouraged to return to the original papers that detail scale development to understand whether validity and reliability data can applicably relate to the scope of the studies they wish to undertake, and the people with whom AWB will be sampled.

Scoring

The *scoring* approach applied to the AWB measure needs to represent the hierarchical level of the affective experience of interest. For example, assuming AWB can be expressed as a fluctuating, transitory state at the most volatile level, then momentary AWB is likely to best be captured by scoring affective terms as discrete items or small clusters of items (anxious, sad, etc.). At the next level, AWB may be experienced as a more stable but still fluctuating state, such as a mood state. Scoring may therefore focus on summing or averaging discrete affective term items into broader mood-based categories (e.g., happy plus enthusiastic plus joyful may result in a generalised 'positive' mood). It is also possible that at this level, terms could themselves provide an affective summary by directly asking respondents if they feel in a 'pleasant' mood or a 'negative' mood. Thus, single scores for such aggregated terms may be sufficient for capturing mood-based AWB. It is unclear whether summing discrete terms or using single-item aggregate terms are synonyms for capturing 'mood'-based AWB. At the highest, most stable level, AWB may be expressed as a trait – a representation of how one usually feels. Optimism and neuroticism are often considered to be personality-based reflections of durable AWB (Brief & Weiss, 2002). These constructs would usually be 'scored' by utilising scales of multiple items reflective of the stable construct, which are then summed or averaged.

Along with the level of affect under consideration, scoring needs to appropriately represent factor structures. For example, when SPANE (Diener et al., 2009) is scored as an overall measure of well-being (taking negative items away from positive items), the two-factor positive and negative factor structure is disrupted. In using the 20-item PANAS, only independent positive and negative valence is captured with the scoring approach; no unique activation factor is scored. Daniels' (2000) scale can be used to represent different levels and factor structures, depending on how it is scored. Using Daniels' 10-item measure, momentary AWB is best scored using five 2-item factors, whereas longer-term, mood-based AWB (past week) is best scored across 2–3 factors (one PA and two NA factors) (Russell & Daniels, 2018). It is also apparent that if a longer-form scale is used to measure AWB, but only items relating to specific scales are scored, then the factor structure breaks down, as the original contextualisation of terms has not been accounted for (Russell & Daniels, 2018). Researchers are therefore encouraged either to use standalone short scales when brevity is needed, *or*, if using items extracted from long-form scales, to undertake reliability, validity and factor analysis checks of the reduced range of items before applying them (Boyle, 1991; Kline, 1986; Stanton et al., 2002). Attending to the scoring of scales reveals that it is not just the upfront scale design and validation that matters when using AWB measures; the end-user scoring of scales is equally vital, to ensure that measures retain their worth in application.

Inter and Intra-Individual Measurement

At levels 2 and 3 (Table 11.2), AWB can be measured as both an inter-individual or intra-individual construct. Dynamic, within-person measures of AWB have been enabled by the increased use of experience sampling methods (ESM) and the analytical tools (such as hierarchical linear modelling) that can examine how variables impact, or are impacted by, repeated measures of AWB (Brief & Weiss, 2002; Ilies et al., 2007; Schimmack, 2003; Xanthopoulou et al., 2012b, 2020). This has been advantageous as work-related AWB involves understanding both the transient, fleeting feelings associated with work events and outcomes, alongside more enduring (between-person) affective tendencies. By positioning within-person ratings at a moment in time, research into the conceptualisation of AWB has developed substantially, not least because prior ratings can be used as lagged measures or predictors of subsequent ratings, enabling researchers to better understand cycles and fluctuations in affect in relation to other variables and stimuli (e.g., Park et al., 2011). In particular, using within-person measures means that changes in AWB can be directly related to events, especially when measures are captured directly before and directly after the event in question (Zhu et al., 2019).

Further, by moving beyond between-person measurement of affect, discrete item measurement and specificity in terms can be enabled, which allows for greater conceptual concordance with contextual stimuli (e.g., job events) (Brief & Weiss, 2002). Finally, including intra-individual measures in analyses can overcome some of the measurement biases that beset any form of self-report construct. By centring repeated measures data to the individual's mean, variations in AWB can be more accurately related to each participant's specific experience, rather than confounded by personal biases in comparison to the overall group or sample (Schimmack, 2003). In designing studies of AWB, researchers are therefore advised to integrate both inter- and intra-individual measurement, in order to better understand the dynamic relationship between the construct and other variables, and in terms of individual participant experiences across a period (Ilies et al., 2007).

Ethics and the Participant Experience

In addition to the above considerations, relating to the structural and environmental issues involved in scale measurement, perhaps the most significant consideration in rating any psychological construct is the respondent. Much has been written about respondent biases (Schimmack et al., 2002), when it comes to response styles brought about by insufficient motivation, honesty or self-awareness (Scollon et al., 2003) or a general tendency to more positive or negative responding (Gotlib & Meyer, 1986; Schimmack et al., 2002). These all need to be attended to in the design of any scale.

Further, researchers can adhere to certain principles in designing their studies to ensure that AWB ratings consider the participant experience. First, researchers need to consider the time of day and week when respondents are asked to complete measures, as AWB tends to show different patterns according to when it is recorded. For example, PA scores appear to rise throughout the day before dropping in the evening (Clarke et al., 1989), suggesting that afternoon ratings of AWB will be more positive than morning ratings, which is important to acknowledge when using daily ratings to capture whole day effects. There are also day-of-week effects. For example, AWB (particularly 'mood') is rated lowest at the beginning of the working week, with positive valence more likely to be reported on weekends – specifically Saturdays (Kennedy-Moore et al., 1992; Ryan et al., 2010). Despite this general trend, asking people to rate AWB in relation to work, in their own time (e.g., after work or on the weekend), could feasibly produce more negative ratings from those who do not wish to be disturbed by thoughts of work in their time off (Derks et al., 2016; Park et al., 2011).

Thinking about affect, and rating one's affect, could also feasibly alter the affective experience. This can mean that a measure designed to capture AWB in relation to a work event may actually have low fidelity as the feelings being captured are – in reality – related to the process of rating them. Although this interference effect has not been examined in empirical research (to the authors' knowledge), it would be useful to understand the extent to which ratings of AWB can – in and of themselves – create an 'intervention' that impacts ecological validity. With other variables, using objective measures can be useful for validating self-reports. However, in rating AWB, which involves a value-laden evaluation or emotion, objective measures may not be helpful.

Physiological measures could provide some construct validity for arousal ratings but cannot suggest how meaning and valence were imbued in the level of arousal.

There are also issues in terms of participant memory recall (Fisher et al., 2016). Because momentary or mood-based AWB (levels 2 and 3) can be transient constructs, asking people to recall in the evening how they felt earlier on that morning can be problematic. People may end up 'summing' their emotions (Reis & Gable, 2000), or being unduly affected by the memory of a particular strong emotion, depending on their own trait-based AWB (e.g., pessimists may focus more on negative events and show bias towards recalling these) (Taylor, 1991). Finally, we have the issue of measurement fatigue for participants (Stanton et al., 2002, Xanthopoulou et al., 2012b). Repeated or lengthy administrations of AWB scales can be demotivating and tiring (Gable et al., 2000; Scollon et al., 2003). This can result in response styles emerging (careless or random responding; central tendency bias, etc.) which then invalidate the study design. The message of this section is to consider the psychology of participant responding and to show due ethical concern to respondents in designing any study that requires use of AWB measures.

The CLASSIE Framework for Measuring AWB at Work

For ease of reference, we have organised the above elements into a CLASSIE framework. This provides a summary of the issues that researchers would do well to consider prior to designing their studies of AWB and engaging in AWB measurement at work. It could also serve as a tool for researchers interested in advancing understanding of the structure and conceptualisation of the AWB construct at work, as the discussion above highlights areas that are still unclear and require further elucidation. Table 11.3 provides an overview of the framework.

Emotion Dynamics

Further to the assessment of emotional experiences, patterns of emotion fluctuation over time can be important markers of psychological functioning and AWB (Davidson, 2015; Hollenstein, 2015; Houben et al., 2015; Koval et al., 2016). As we react emotionally to different

Table 11.3 *The CLASSIE framework for measuring AWB at work*

	Measurement issue	Consideration	Future research
C	Context	The focal instruction (and scoring bands) should be made relevant to the temporality and intensity of the construct and/or the event, experience or domain (e.g., work) of interest.	Does the reliability and validity of the scale change when the focal instruction is changed to reflect a different context?
L	Length	Inclusion of the number of items must consider the participants' available time and cognitive load in rating (e.g., the frequency with which the scale is administered, concurrent use of other scales and engagement with other tasks).	Ensure short-form measures are valid and reliable in their own right.
A	Affect structure	Choose scales that reflect the theoretical affective structure of interest. Ensure concordance of scales with associated variables of interest.	What are the broad, universal categories of AWB in relation to valence and arousal constructs at work?
S	Scope	Check the scope of the sample used in the original scale development, and check that scale items will not adversely bias results from any demographic group or culture.	More research is needed to ascertain how scale items may bias well-being ratings for different groups.

Table 11.3 (*cont.*)

Measurement issue	Consideration	Future research
S Scoring	Ensure hierarchical levels and factor structures of AWB is appropriately represented by the aggregation or summation of item scores.	Do aggregate terms (e.g., positive) capture level 2 mood in the same way as summing discrete terms (e.g., joy, enthusiasm, vigour)?
I Inter- and intra-individual measurement	Use within- and between-measures and analyses of AWB, wherever possible. Measure affect change by taking pre-event ratings.	Continue to investigate work-based relationships between inter- and intra-individual AWB and work activity (including cyclical or longitudinal fluctuations).
E Ethics and the participant	Capture variations in participant responding that may be due to response bias, time of day or week effects, memory recall biases, etc.	Examine interference effects in studies and how rating affect can change the affective experience, potentially negating ecological validity.

affective events, our AWB shifts away from our normal baseline levels, and at the same time our emotional system tries to regulate our emotions and return them back to baseline levels (Kuppens et al., 2010b). To explore individual differences in the degree to which we react to external stimuli and how quickly or efficiently we return to baseline, Kuppens and Verduyn (2015) propose a 2×2 taxonomy of dynamic features. This taxonomy differentiates between those features that focus on variability of affective states within a specific time period, and other features concerned with time dependency or whether affective states carry over or are sustained over time. Each of these can also be applied to individual discrete emotions or dimensions of AWB, or can be applied to combinations of emotions or multiple AWB dimensions simultaneously. This suggests a combination of four potential dynamic signatures that relate to AWB and emotional regulation in different ways, each of which is discussed below.

Emotional Inertia

Emotional inertia was first introduced by Suls et al. (1998) and refers to the persistence of affective states and whether these are sustained for a long time once they are experienced. Such lingering affective states are considered to be a failure in regulating emotions and their homeostatic return back to baseline levels (Houben et al., 2015; Kuppens et al., 2010a). As such, high emotional inertia implies that the emotional system is subject to a self-perpetuating process of affective states that is less open to external influences. High levels of inertia can be evidence of psychological maladjustment, and different studies have shown that it is related to other measures of AWB and eudaimonic well-being (Houben et al., 2015), depression (Koval et al., 2016; Kuppens et al., 2010a), onset of depression in adolescence (Kuppens et al., 2012) and rumination (Koval et al., 2012). It should be noted that inertia is not indicative of lower well-being only for negative affective states. Although it is more intuitive to think of inertia of negative emotions as an indicator of low AWB, persistence of positive emotions is also considered as an indication of maladaptive emotional regulation and has been associated with lower AWB (Houben et al., 2015; Trull et al., 2015). Nevertheless, this association tends to be weaker for inertia of positive emotions and stronger for negative emotions (Koval et al., 2016).

Emotional inertia is typically captured as the auto-correlation coefficient from successive measurements of emotions (e.g., Koval et al., 2013) and can easily be applied to discrete emotions, or to individual dimensions of AWB such as those discussed earlier. More elaborate approaches use a multi-level model to estimate auto-regressive effects as random slopes of lagged consecutive measures of affect (Jongerling et al., 2015; Koval et al., 2016). Although more complex, this approach has the benefit of being integrated into a bigger model that allows controlling for other time-dependent and time-independent covariates. It is also possible to use this approach to model predictors of affect inertia by testing cross-level interactions between lagged effects with person-level covariates (Kuppens et al., 2010b).

A key issue for the measurement of inertia is that the actual estimate may change according to the study design and the interval at which the successive measurements of emotions are collected (Ebner-Priemer & Sawitzki, 2007; Koval et al., 2013). One specific concern is that auto-correlation coefficients tend to wane for longer time intervals, so shorter intervals would produce higher and incomparable estimates to longer intervals. This can potentially be addressed through the adoption of continuous time models that take into account the length of each time interval in the estimation of inertia (Oravecz et al., 2011). Such models are in effect the equivalent of a random effect auto-regressive slope for continuous time (Oravecz & Tuerlinckx, 2011) and can be ideal for capturing inertia in experience sampling studies with random or unequally spaced data collection. Nevertheless, the link between lower well-being and emotional inertia has been established for different timescales varying from seconds to minutes or days (Koval et al., 2013; Kuppens et al., 2012; Neumann et al., 2011).

Emotional Cross-Lags

Emotional cross-lags encapsulate a similar idea as emotional inertia but apply to different discrete emotions or different dimensions and how they influence and perpetuate each other over time. Thus, cross-lagged effects reflect how different emotions can increase or decrease the experience of other emotions. This is referred to as emotional augmentation or blunting and, similar to affect inertia, at high levels can signify a self-contained system that is less open to external stimuli – which is characteristic of mood disorders. Combining emotional inertia with emotional cross-lags can allow the construction of an emotion network to represent the dynamic relationships between different discrete emotions over time. The auto-regressive and cross-regressive estimates for these emotion networks can be obtained as random slopes from a series of multi-level regressions (one for each emotion) or by estimating a multi-level vector auto-regressive model for all the emotions or dimensions simultaneously (Bringmann et al., 2016, 2013). The strength of the auto-regressive and cross-regressive relationships is typically referred to as the emotional density of the network and reflects the degree to which the whole emotional system is more resistant to change and has been associated with mood disorders (Pe et al., 2015). More complex metrics can be obtained from the emotional network by applying network analysis to further understand the resulting architecture of the networks.

Emotional Variability

Emotional variability captures the degree to which emotions fluctuate over time, and it is considered to be indicative of the degree to which individuals are more or less sensitive to external stimuli (Kuppens & Verduyn, 2015). High levels of variability, which imply stronger emotional reactions, are generally considered to be maladaptive, and meta-analytic evidence suggests that variability is related to numerous indicators of well-being, including negative AWB and eudaimonic well-being as well as a number of disorders such as depression, bipolar disorder, anxiety and borderline personality disorder (Houben et al., 2015). Similar to inertia, variability is considered to be maladaptive regardless of whether it is variability of positive or negative emotions (Gruber et al., 2013). Moreover, whilst it is high variability that is typically associated with low well-being, very low variability or reactivity can be equally problematic. For example, depression is associated with a decrease in emotional responsiveness to either positive or negative stimuli (Rottenberg et al., 2005).

Variability can be easily estimated by calculating dispersion of within-person measures using standard deviation or variance (e.g., Eaton & Funder, 2001; Eid & Diener, 1999). This can be applied to either measures of discrete emotions or affect dimensions based on the circumplex model. More sophisticated approaches are founded on modelling variability as latent constructs using multi-level innovation variance. Innovation variance simply refers to the model residual from a time series model and can be estimated per person as a random model parameter using multi-level location scale models of repeated measures (Jongerling et al., 2015; Schuurman & Hamaker, 2019; Wang et al., 2012). The advantage of using this more complex approach is that these estimates of variability are based on the residual or what cannot be explained by the rest of the model. Thus, these latent estimates exclude any potential emotional inertia or effects of time-dependent and time-independent covariates.

A related concept to variability is that of instability, which refers to the magnitude of change from one point in time to the next. Thus, in contrast to variability, which focuses solely on the amplitude of changes in affective states, instability combines variability with temporal dependency (Trull et al., 2015, 2008). To capture this construct, a number of different indices have been proposed, including the mean squared successive difference between consecutive measurements of affective states, the proportion of acute changes in affect over total changes (Jahng et al., 2008) and aggregate point by point changes (Santangelo et al., 2014). The mean squared successive difference is the most common approach, and although it is treated as a separate construct from measures of either variability or temporal variability, it is closely related to both, and it is possible to express instability as a formula of variance and auto-correlation of within-person measures of affect (Jahng et al., 2008). It is no surprise, then, that similar to emotional variability, instability has also been linked to negative AWB and eudaimonic well-being, as well as numerous psychological disorders (Houben et al., 2015; Trull et al., 2015).

Emotional Covariation

Emotional covariation transposes the idea of affect variability to multiple dimensions and examines the degree to which different emotions or different dimensions of within-person AWB covary. The substantive meaning of such contemporaneous associations of within-person variability is that they reflect an inability to differentiate between different discrete emotions or affect dimensions. This is also referred to as emotional differentiation and is considered to be necessary for emotional regulation (Barrett et al., 2001). Individuals with difficulties in differentiating between emotions tend to experience more negative affect, depression and reduced self-esteem (Erbas et al., 2014).

The simplest way through which emotional differentiation can be estimated is via within-person bivariate correlations of different affect dimensions or emotions. More sophisticated approaches are based on estimating the intra-class correlation coefficient to represent agreement between different emotions over the duration of a study (Tomko et al., 2015; Tugade et al., 2004). A more elaborate approach is to estimate emotional differentiation as a latent variable from the residual covariance matrix of a multi-variate multi-level location scale model. Similar to estimating variability as a residual that varies per person, in a multi-variate model it is possible do the same for the covariance residual matrix (Jongerling et al., 2015). Although this is a complex approach, it has the benefits of i) estimating both variability and emotional differentiation as latent parameters simultaneously and ii) that estimating these constructs from a full model allows for controlling for other momentary, personal or contextual variables or for other dynamic processes such as inertia and cross-lagged effects at the same time.

Two related concepts that also capture variability in multiple dimensions using the core affect model are affect pulse and affect spin (Kuppens et al., 2007; Moskowitz & Zuroff, 2004). These measures are based on representing affect scores on the two-dimensional circumplex. Affect pulse, which captures the intensity of changes in affective states, is estimated as the within-person standard deviation of the distance of each affect score on the circumplex and the neutral midpoint position. Affect spin, or affect quality variability, is calculated as the standard deviation of the angular displacement of each emotion experienced on the circumplex model (Beal et al., 2013; Kuppens et al., 2007). Thus, pulse captures variability of the intensity of emotions whilst remaining agnostic to the specific emotions, and spin captures the circular variability of changing emotions regardless of their intensity. Similar to other measures of variability and differentiation, high pulse and spin are also considered to be maladaptive and have been positively associated with borderline personality disorder (Russell et al., 2007), and personality traits such as neuroticism and pessimism and negatively with extroversion and optimism (Kuppens et al., 2007) .

Assessing Inequalities in Well-Being between People

Inequalities matter for health and well-being. One of the most widely studied types of inequality is inequalities in income. Studies have consistently found an inverse correlation between country level income inequality and a range of health and social problem indicators, such that countries or regions with the highest levels of income inequality also tend to have worse health and social outcomes (Pickett & Wilkinson, 2015). Recorded outcomes include educational attainment, teenage birth rates, social mobility, crime rates, mental health problems and a range of other physical health outcomes. These associations are explained through social comparison processes, in which inequality is a social stressor that undermines interpersonal trust and social cohesion.

A smaller research stream has examined well-being inequalities across countries, often using life satisfaction as a summative index of well-being. This research stream also indicates well-being inequalities are inversely associated with well-being (Goff et al., 2016). This association holds after taking into account factors that reflect any artefactual influence on the size of the correlation brought about by range restriction (i.e., the measure of well-being is bounded by the extremes of the rating scale, meaning people with very high/low and moderately high/low levels of well-being will tend to bunch at the extremes of the rating scale rather than being differentiated). Moreover, where people have poor levels of well-being, social and health outcomes may be even worse for some groups that others (e.g., differentiation by gender and socio-economic class; Linder et al., 2020).

We know of no research on inequalities in well-being in work organisations, although there is a well-developed stream of research on inequalities in how leaders treat subordinates (Martin et al., 2018). There are many reasons why investigating well-being inequalities in organisations is potentially important. If inequalities in well-being are causal in reducing average levels of well-being in an organisation, then there are important implications for health and social outcomes of workers. If inequalities in well-being in an organisation undermine trust between co-workers and/or managers, then there are important implications for co-operation and conflict. In both cases, there are potential consequences for organisational performance, for example through higher absence rates (health and well-being path), reduced organisational citizenship or industrial disputes and grievances (trust and social cohesion path).

The question then becomes one of deciding on the best means of assessing well-being inequalities. Asides from deciding on the best aspect of well-being to use (life satisfaction, job satisfaction, affective well-being), there are choices concerning the best means of assessing inequality through the distribution of well-being scores in a given unit (country, organisation, team). Quick and Devlin (2018) reviewed a number of ways of assessing well-being inequalities. They divided these into measures of dispersion (e.g., standard deviation, variance, coefficient of variation, Gini coefficient) and measures based on a threshold (e.g., average well-being of the bottom 20% of the well-being distribution compared to average well-being of the top 80% of the distribution, percentage of the distribution falling below a given well-being score).

Quick and Devlin (2018) note that measures based on dispersion each have their own weaknesses. However, one critical weakness shared by most measures of dispersion is that they do not capture the difference in well-being between the best and worst off in well-being terms. Put another way, interventions focused on reducing well-being inequalities through minimising the standard deviation of well-being could work just as easily through reducing the well-being of the best off as increasing the well-being of the worst off. In policy terms at least, this would make very little sense. Measures based on thresholds can capture differences between the best and worst off, but the choice of thresholds would appear to be arbitrary. This could be especially problematic in policy applications, where the choice of threshold could be manipulated to suit some rather than other policy options. However, the relative advantages and disadvantages of different approaches to assessing well-being inequalities in organisational research have yet to be investigated.

Conclusions

Theoretical approaches to understanding well-being have a long history, and research on the assessment of psychological well-being has produced an enormous volume of research that includes the assessment of workplace well-being. This has led to a range of different instruments, some more suited to some theoretical approaches, methodologies and applications than others. Notwithstanding, although we have well-developed knowledge of how to assess the level of someone's well-being at a given moment in time, there are four clear conclusions. First, making an assessment of well-being is not straightforward and involves a number of design choices (see Table 11.3). Second, far less research has examined variability in markers of workplace well-being and the implications of variability, whether variability relates to patterns in the dynamics of well-being over time or variability relates to inequalities in well-being within social groups. Third, although recent developments in well-being economics have provided a way of monetising well-being policy options for (managerial) decision makers, this is a relatively new field of research that has yet to come fully to terms with the multi-dimensional and dynamic nature of well-being and how to incorporate concerns about minimising well-being inequalities between people into the calculations. Fourth, and summarising the first three conclusions, there is much we know but much we still do not know about the measurement of workplace well-being.

Notes

1 Their report resulted from the Commission on the Measurement of Economic Performance and Social Progress.
2 This is not to say that AWB is contained enough as a construct to only represent affect experienced within that context. We recognise that there are clear spill-over effects of AWB, whereby how a person feels in relation to work will also impact their feelings at home, and vice versa (Ilies et al., 2014).

References

Bache, I., & Reardon, L. (2016). *The politics and policy of well-being: Understanding the rise and significance of a new agenda*. Edward Elgar Publishing.

Banks, M. H., Clegg, C. W., Jackson, P. R., Kemp, N. J., Stafford, E. M., & Wall, T. D. (1980). The use of the General Health Questionnaire as an indicator of mental health in occupational studies. *Journal of Occupational Psychology, 53*, 187–194.

Barrett, L. F., Gross, J., Christensen, T. C., & Benvenuto, M. (2001). Knowing what you're feeling and knowing what to do about it: Mapping the relation between emotion differentiation and emotion regulation. *Cognition & Emotion, 15*, 713–724.

Beal, D. J., & Ghandour, L. (2011). Stability, change, and the stability of change in daily workplace affect. *Journal of Organizational Behavior, 32*, 526–546.

Beal, D. J., Trougakos, J. P., Weiss, H. M., & Dalal, R. S. (2013). Affect spin and the emotion regulation process at work. *Journal of Applied Psychology, 98*, 593–605.

Bliese, P. D., Edwards, J. R., & Sonnentag, S. (2017). Stress and well-being at work: A century of empirical trends reflecting theoretical and societal influences. *Journal of Applied Psychology, 102*, 389–402

Boyle, G. J. (1991). Does item homogeneity indicate internal consistency or item redundancy in psychometric scales? *Personality and Individual Differences, 12,* 291–294.

Brayfield, A. H., & Rothe, H. F. (1951). An index of job satisfaction. *Journal of Applied Psychology, 35,* 307–311.

Brief, A. P., & Weiss, H. M. (2002). Organizational behavior: Affect in the workplace. *Annual Review of Psychology, 53,* 279–307.

Bringmann, L. F., Pe, M. L., Vissers, N., Ceulemans, E., Borsboom, D., Vanpaemel, W., ... Kuppens, P. (2016). Assessing temporal emotion dynamics using networks. *Assessment, 23,* 425–435.

Bringmann, L. F., Vissers, N., Wichers, M., Geschwind, N., Kuppens, P., Peeters, F., ... Tuerlinckx, F. (2013). A network approach to psychopathology: New insights into clinical longitudinal data. *PLoS ONE, 8,* e60188.

Bryce, A., Bryan, M., Connolly, S., & Nasamu, E. (2020). *Workplace cost effectiveness analysis (CEA) calculator: User manual.* What Works Centre for Well-Being.

Clark, L. A., Watson, D., & Leeka, J. (1989). Diurnal variation in the positive affects. *Motivation and Emotion, 13,* 205–234.

Cooper, C. L., & Marshall, J. (1976). Occupational sources of stress: A review of the literature relating to coronary heart disease and mental ill health. *Journal of Occupational Psychology, 49,* 11–28.

Coyle, D. (2014). *GDP: A brief but affectionate history.* Princeton University Press.

Cranford, J. A., Shrout, P. E., Iida, M., Rafaeli, E., Yip, T., & Bolger, N. (2006). A procedure for evaluating sensitivity to within-person change: Can mood measures in diary studies detect change reliably? *Personality and Social Psychology Bulletin, 32,* 917–929.

Daniels, K. (2000). Measures of five aspects of affective well-being at work. *Human Relations, 53,* 275–294.

Daniels, K., Connolly, S., Ogbonnaya, C., Tregaskis, O., Bryan, M. L., Robinson-Pant, A., & Street, J. (2018). Democratisation of well-being: Stakeholder perspectives on policy priorities for improving national well-being through paid employment and adult learning. *British Journal of Guidance & Counselling, 46,* 492–511.

Davidson, R. J. (2015). Comment: Affective chronometry has come of age. *Emotion Review, 7,* 368–370.

De Neve K. M., & Cooper, H. (1998). The happy personality: A meta-analysis of 137 personality traits and subjective well-being. *Psychological Bulletin, 124,* 197–229.

Derks, D., Bakker, A. B., Peters, P., & van Wingerden, P. (2016). Work-related smartphone use, work–family conflict and family role performance: The role of segmentation preference. *Human Relations*, 69, 1045–1068.

Diener, E. (1984). Subjective well-being. *Psychological Bulletin*, 95, 542–575.

Diener, E., Oishi, S., & Lucas, R. E. (2015). National accounts of subjective well-being. *American Psychologist*, 70, 234–242.

Diener, E., Wirtz, D., Biswas-Diener, R., Tov, W., Kim-Prieto, C., Choi, D. W., & Oishi, S. (2009). New measures of well-being. In E. Diener (Ed.), *Assessing well-being: Social indicators research series* (Vol. 39, pp. 247–266). Springer.

Diener, E., Wirtz, D., Tov, W., Kim-Prieto, C., Choi, D. -W., Oishi, S., & Biswas-Diener, R. (2010). New well-being measures: Short scales to assess flourishing and positive and negative feelings. *Social Indicators Research*, 97(2), 143–156.

Eaton, L. G., & Funder, D. C. (2001). Emotional experience in daily life: Valence, variability, and rate of change. *Emotion*, 1, 413.

Ebner-Priemer, U. W., & Sawitzki, G. (2007). Ambulatory assessment of affective instability in borderline personality disorder: The effect of the sampling frequency. *European Journal of Psychological Assessment*, 23, 238.

Eid, M., & Diener, E. (1999). Intraindividual variability in affect: Reliability, validity, and personality correlates. *Journal of Personality and Social Psychology*, 76, 662.

Ekman, P. (1992). Facial expressions of emotion: An old controversy and new findings. *Philosophical Transactions of the Royal Society of London. Series B: Biological Sciences*, 335, 63–69.

Erbas, Y., Ceulemans, E., Lee Pe, M., Koval, P., & Kuppens, P. (2014). Negative emotion differentiation: Its personality and well-being correlates and a comparison of different assessment methods. *Cognition & Emotion*, 28, 1196–1213.

Eurofound. (2015). *6th European working conditions survey – technical report*. Eurofound.

Eurostat. (2010). *Feasibility study for well-being indicators. Task 4: critical review*. Office for Official Publications of the European Communities.

Feldman Barrett, L., & Russell, J. A. (1998). Independence and bipolarity in the structure of current affect. *Journal of Personality and Social Psychology*, 74, 967–984.

Fisher, G. G., Matthews, R. A., & Gibbons, A. M. (2016). Developing and investigating the use of single-item measures in organizational research. *Journal of Occupational Health Psychology*, 21, 3.

French, J. R. P., Rodgers, R., & Cobb, S. (1974). Adjustment as person environment fit. In G. V. Coelho, D. A. Hamburg, & J. E. Adams (Eds.), *Coping and adaptation* (pp. 316–333). Basic Books.

Frijda, N. H. (1993). Moods, emotion episodes, and emotions. In M. Lewis & J. M. Haviland (Eds.) *Handbook of emotions* (pp. 381–403). Guilford Press.

(2008). The psychologists' point of view. In M. Lewis, J. M. Haviland-Jones, & L. Feldman Barrett (Eds.) *Handbook of emotions* (3rd ed., pp. 68–87). Guilford Press.

Fujita, F., Diener, E., & Sandvik, E. (1991). Gender differences in negative affect and well-being: The case for emotional intensity. *Journal of Personality and Social Psychology, 61*, 427–434.

Gable, S. L., Reis, H. T., & Elliot, A. J. (2000). Behavioral activation and inhibition in everyday life. *Journal of Personality and Social Psychology, 78*, 1135–1149.

Goff, L., Helliwell, J. F., & Mayraz, G. (2016). The welfare costs of well-being inequality. NBER Working Paper Series, 27. https://faculty.arts .ubc.ca/jhelliwell/papers/w21900.pdf

Goldberg, D. P. (1972). *The detection of psychiatric illness by questionnaire.* Oxford University Press.

Goldberg, D., & Williams, P. (1988). *A user's guide to the General Health Questionnaire.* nferNelson.

Gotlib, I. H., & Meyer, J. P. (1986). Factor analysis of the Multiple Affect Adjective Check List: A separation of positive and negative affect. *Journal of Personality and Social Psychology, 50*, 1161–1165.

Gruber, J., Kogan, A., Quoidbach, J., & Mauss, I. B. (2013). Happiness is best kept stable: Positive emotion variability is associated with poorer psychological health. *Emotion, 13*, 1–6.

Hackman, J. R., & Oldham, G. R. (1974). *The Job Diagnostic Survey: An instrument for the diagnosis of jobs and the evaluation of job redesign projects.* Yale University School of Organization and Management.

Hofmann, W., Luhmann, M., Fisher, R. R., Vohs, K. D., & Baumeister, R. F. (2014). Yes, but are they happy? Effects of trait self-control on affective well-being and life satisfaction. *Journal of Personality, 82*, 265–277.

Hollenstein, T. (2015). This time, it's real: Affective flexibility, time scales, feedback loops, and the regulation of emotion. *Emotion Review, 7*, 308–315.

Houben, M., Van Den Noortgate, W., & Kuppens, P. (2015). The relation between short-term emotion dynamics and psychological well-being: A meta-analysis. *Psychological Bulletin, 141*, 901–930.

House, R. J., & Rizzo, J. R. (1972). Toward the measurement of organizational practices: Scale development and validation. *Journal of Applied Psychology, 56*, 388–396.

Huppert, F. A. (2017). *Measurement really matters.* What Works Centre for Well-Being.

Huppert, F. A., & So, T. T. (2013). Flourishing across Europe: Application of a new conceptual framework for defining well-being. *Social Indicators Research, 110,* 837–861.

Ilies, R., Aw, S. S., & Pluut, H. (2015). Intraindividual models of employee well-being: What have we learned and where do we go from here? *European Journal of Work and Organizational Psychology, 24,* 827–838.

Ilies, R., & Judge, T. A. (2004). An experience-sampling measure of job satisfaction and its relationships with affectivity, mood at work, job beliefs, and general job satisfaction. *European Journal of Work and Organizational Psychology, 13,* 367–389.

Ilies, R., Schwind, K. M., & Heller, D. (2007). Employee well-being: A multilevel model linking work and nonwork domains. *European Journal of Work and Organizational Psychology, 16,* 326–341.

Izard, C. E. (1977). *Human emotions.* Plenum Press.

Jahng, S., Wood, P. K., & Trull, T. J. (2008). Analysis of affective instability in ecological momentary assessment: Indices using successive difference and group comparison via multilevel modeling. *Psychological Methods, 13,* 354–375.

Jongerling, J., Laurenceau, J.-P., & Hamaker, E. L. (2015). A multilevel ar (1) model: Allowing for inter-individual differences in trait-scores, inertia, and innovation variance. *Multivariate Behavioral Research, 50,* 334–349.

Kahn, R. L., Wolfe, D. M., Quinn, R. P., Snoek, J. D., & Rosenthal, R. A. (1964). *Organizational stress: Studies in role conflict and ambiguity.* Wiley.

Kammann, R., & Flett, R. (1983). Affectometer 2: A scale to measure current level of general happiness. *Australian Journal of Psychology, 82,* 1007–1022.

Kennedy-Moore, E., Greenberg, M. A., Newman, M. G., & Stone, A. A. (1992). The relationship between daily events and mood: The mood measure may matter. *Motivation and Emotion, 16,* 143–155.

Kline, P. (1986). *A handbook of test construction: Introduction to psychometric design.* Methuen.

Koval, P., Kuppens, P., Allen, N. B., & Sheeber, L. (2012). Getting stuck in depression: The roles of rumination and emotional inertia. *Cognition & Emotion, 26,* 1412–1427.

Koval, P., Pe, M. L., Meers, K., & Kuppens, P. (2013). Affect dynamics in relation to depressive symptoms: Variable, unstable or inert? *Emotion, 13,* 1132–1141.

Koval, P., Sütterlin, S., & Kuppens, P. (2016). Emotional inertia is associated with lower well-being when controlling for differences in emotional context. *Frontiers in Psychology, 6,* 1997.

Kuppens, P., Allen, N. B., & Sheeber, L. B. (2010a). Emotional inertia and psychological maladjustment. *Psychological Science, 21,* 984–991.

Kuppens, P., Oravecz, Z., & Tuerlinckx, F. (2010b). Feelings change: Accounting for individual differences in the temporal dynamics of affect. *Journal of Personality and Social Psychology, 99,* 1042–1060.

Kuppens, P., Sheeber, L. B., Yap, M. B., Whittle, S., Simmons, J. G., & Allen, N. B. (2012). Emotional inertia prospectively predicts the onset of depressive disorder in adolescence. *Emotion, 12,* 283.

Kuppens, P., Van Mechelen, I., Nezlek, J. B., Dossche, D., & Timmermans, T. (2007). Individual differences in core affect variability and their relationship to personality and psychological adjustment. *Emotion, 7,* 262.

Kuppens, P., & Verduyn, P. (2015). Looking at emotion regulation through the window of emotion dynamics. *Psychological Inquiry, 26,* 72–79.

Lang, P. J. (1988). What are the data of emotion. In V. Hamilton, G. H. Bower, & N. Frijda (Eds.), *Cognitive perspectives on emotion and motivation* (NATO ASI Series D, Vol. XXXXIV, pp. 173–191). Kluwer.

Larsen, R. J., & Diener, E. (1992). Promises and problems with the circumplex model of emotion. *Review of Personality and Social Psychology, 13,* 25–29.

Layard, R. (2016). *Measuring well-being and cost-effectiveness analysis using subjective well-being,* What Works Centre for Well-Being.

Locke, E. A. (1976). The nature and causes of job satisfaction. In M. D. Dunnette (Ed.), *Handbook of industrial and organizational psychology* (pp. 1297–1343). Rand McNally.

Linder, A., Gerdtham, U. G., Trygg, N., Fritzell, S., & Saha, S. (2020). Inequalities in the economic consequences of depression and anxiety in Europe: A systematic scoping review. *European Journal of Public Health, 30,* 767–777.

Lyubomirsky, S., King, L., & Diener, E. (2005). The benefits of frequent positive affect: Does happiness lead to success? *Psychological Bulletin, 131,* 803–855.

Marsh H. W., Huppert, F. A., Donald, J. N., Horwood, M. S., & Sahdra, B. K. (2020). The well-being profile (WB-Pro): Creating a theoretically based multidimensional measure of well-being to advance theory, research, and practice. *Psychological Assessment, 32,* 294–313.

Martin, R., Thomas, G., Legood, A., & Dello Russo, S. (2018). Leader–member exchange (LMX) differentiation and work outcomes: Conceptual clarification and critical review. *Journal of Organizational Behavior, 39,* 151–168.

Maslach, C., Jackson, S. E., Leiter, M. P., Schaufeli, W. B., & Schwab, R. L. (1986). *Maslach burnout inventory* (Vol. 21). Consulting Psychologists Press.

McNair, D. M., Lorr, M., & Droppleman, L. F. (1992). *EdITS manual for the Profile of Mood States*. Educational and Industrial Testing Service.

Moskowitz, D., & Zuroff, D. C. (2004). Flux, pulse, and spin: Dynamic additions to the personality lexicon. *Journal of Personality and Social Psychology*, *86*, 880.

Mukuria, C., Rowen, D., Peasgood, T., & Brazier, J. (2016). *An empirical comparison of well-being measures used in UK*. Research Interim Report RR0027: University of Sheffield and the University of York.

Neumann, A., Van Lier, P. A., Frijns, T., Meeus, W., & Koot, H. M. (2011). Emotional dynamics in the development of early adolescent psychopathology: A one-year longitudinal study. *Journal of Abnormal Child Psychology*, *39*, 657–669.

NICE (2013). *Guide to the methods of appraisal*. National Institute of Health and Care Excellence.

O'Donnell, G., Deaton, A., Durand, M., Halpern, D., & Layard, R. (2014). *Well-being and Policy*. Legatum Institute.

ONS. (2011). *Initial investigation into subjective well-being from the opinions survey*. Cardiff: Office for National Statistics.

Oravecz, Z., & Tuerlinckx, F. (2011). The linear mixed model and the hierarchical Ornstein–Uhlenbeck model: Some equivalences and differences. *British Journal of Mathematical and Statistical Psychology*, *64*, 134–160.

Oravecz, Z., Tuerlinckx, F., & Vandekerckhove, J. (2011). A hierarchical latent stochastic differential equation model for affective dynamics. *Psychological Methods*, *16*, 468–490.

Ouweneel, E., Le Blanc, P. M., Schaufeli, W. B., & van Wijhe, C. I. (2012). Good morning, good day: A diary study on positive emotions, hope, and work engagement. *Human Relations*, *65*, 1129–1154.

Park, Y., Fritz, C., & Jex, S. M. (2011). Relationships between work–home segmentation and psychological detachment from work: The role of communication technology use at home. *Journal of Occupational Health Psychology*, *16*, 457–467.

Pavot, W., & Diener, E. (2008). The satisfaction with life scale and the emerging construct of life satisfaction. *The Journal of Positive Psychology*, *3*, 137–152.

Pe, M. L., Kircanski, K., Thompson, R. J., Bringmann, L. F., Tuerlinckx, F., Mestdagh, M. … Gotlib, I. H. (2015). Emotion-network density in major depressive disorder. *Clinical Psychological Science*, *3*, 292–300.

Pickett, K. E., & Wilkinson, R. G. (2015). Income inequality and health: A causal review. *Social Science & Medicine, 128,* 316–326.

Powdthavee, N. (2012). Jobless, friendless and broke: What happens to different areas of life before and after unemployment? *Economica, 79,* 557–575.

Quick, A. & Devlin, S. (2018). *Measuring well-being inequality: Working paper on the selection of a headline indicator.* New Economics Foundation.

Reis, H. T., & Gable, S. L. (2000). Event-sampling and other methods for studying everyday experience. In H. T. Reis & C. M. Judd (Eds.), *Handbook of research methods in social and personality psychology* (pp. 190–222). Cambridge University Press.

Rottenberg, J., Gross, J. J., & Gotlib, I. H. (2005). Emotion context insensitivity in major depressive disorder. *Journal of Abnormal Psychology, 114,* 627–639.

Ruggeri, K., Garcia-Garzon, E., Maguire, A., Matz, S., & Huppert. F. A. (2020). Well-being is more than happiness and life satisfaction: A multidimensional analysis of 21 countries. *Health and Quality of Life Outcomes, 18,* 1–16.

Russell, J. A. (1980). A circumplex model of affect. *Journal of Personality and Social Psychology, 39,* 1161–1178.

Russell, E., & Daniels, K. (2018). Measuring affective well-being at work using short-form scales: Implications for affective structures and participant instructions. *Human Relations, 71,* 1478–1507.

Russell, J. J., Moskowitz, D., Zuroff, D. C., Sookman, D., & Paris, J. (2007). Stability and variability of affective experience and interpersonal behavior in borderline personality disorder. *Journal of Abnormal Psychology, 116,* 578–588.

Ryan, R. M., Bernstein, J. H., & Brown, K. W. (2010). Weekends, work, and well-being: Psychological need satisfactions and day of the week effects on mood, vitality, and physical symptoms. *Journal of Social and Clinical Psychology, 29,* 95–122.

Ryff, C. D., & Keyes, C. L. M. (1995). The structure of psychological well-being revisited. *Journal of Personality and Social Psychology, 69,* 719–727.

Santangelo, P., Reinhard, I., Mussgay, L., Steil, R., Sawitzki, G., Klein, C. … Ebner-Priemer, U. W. (2014). Specificity of affective instability in patients with borderline personality disorder compared to posttraumatic stress disorder, bulimia nervosa, and healthy controls. *Journal of Abnormal Psychology, 123,* 258–272.

Schaufeli, W., & De Witte, H. (2017). Outlook work engagement in contrast to burnout: Real and redundant! *Burnout Research, 5,* 58–60.

Schaufeli, W. B., Salanova, M., Gonzalez-Roma, V., & Bakker, A. B. (2002). The measurement of engagement and burnout: A two sample confirmatory factor analytic approach. *Journal of Happiness Studies*, 3, 71–92.

Schimmack, U. (2003). Affect measurement in experience sampling research. *Journal of Happiness Studies*, 4, 79–106.

Schimmack, U., Radhakrishnan, P., Oishi, S., Dzokoto, V., & Ahadi, S. (2002). Culture, personality, and subjective well-being: Integrating process models of life satisfaction. *Journal of Personality and Social Psychology*, 82, 582–593.

Schuurman, N. K., & Hamaker, E. L. (2019). Measurement error and person-specific reliability in multilevel autoregressive modeling. *Psychological Methods*, 24, 70–91.

Scollon, C. N., Kim-Prieto, C., & Diener, E. (2003). Experience sampling: Promises and pitfalls, strengths and weaknesses. *Journal of Happiness Studies*, 4, 5–34.

Seligman, M. E. P. (2002). Positive psychology, positive prevention, and positive therapy. In C. R. Snyder & S. J. Lopez (Eds.), *Handbook of positive psychology* (pp. 3–9). Oxford University Press.

Stanton, J. M., Sinar, E. F., Balzer, W. K., & Smith, P. C. (2002). Issues and strategies for reducing the length of self-report scales. *Personnel Psychology*, 55, 167–194.

Steel, P., Schmidt, J., & Shultz, J. (2008). Refining the relationship between personality and subjective well-being. *Psychological Bulletin*, 134, 138–161.

Stewart-Brown, S., Tennant, A., Tennant, R., Platt, S., Parkinson, J., & Weich, S. (2009). Internal construct validity of the Warwick–Edinburgh mental well-being scale (WEMWBS): A Rasch analysis using data from the Scottish health education population survey. *Health and Quality of Life Outcomes*, 7, 15–22.

Stiglitz, J. E., Sen, A., & Fitoussi, J. P. (2009). *Report by the commission on the measurement of economic performance and social progress.* Commission on the Measurement of Economic Performance and Social Progress.

Suls, J., Green, P., & Hillis, S. (1998). Emotional reactivity to everyday problems, affective inertia, and neuroticism. *Personality and Social Psychology Bulletin*, 24, 127–136.

Taylor, M. F., Brice, J., Buck, N., & Prentice-Lane, E. (2018). *British Household Panel Survey user manual volume A: Introduction, technical report and appendices.* University of Essex.

Taylor, S. E. (1991). Asymmetrical effects of positive and negative events: the mobilization-minimization hypothesis. *Psychological Bulletin*, 110, 67–85.

Tomko, R. L., Lane, S. P., Pronove, L. M., Treloar, H. R., Brown, W. C., Solhan, M. B. . . . Trull, T. J. (2015). Undifferentiated negative affect and impulsivity in borderline personality and depressive disorders: A momentary perspective. *Journal of Abnormal Psychology*, *124*, 74 –753.

Trull, T. J., Lane, S. P., Koval, P., & Ebner-Priemer, U. W. (2015). Affective dynamics in psychopathology. *Emotion Review*, *7*, 355–361.

Trull, T. J., Solhan, M. B., Tragesser, S. L., Jahng, S., Wood, P. K., Piasecki, T. M., & Watson, D. (2008). Affective instability: Measuring a core feature of borderline personality disorder with ecological momentary assessment. *Journal of Abnormal Psychology*, *117*, 647–661.

Tugade, M. M., Fredrickson, B. L., & Feldman Barrett, L. (2004). Psychological resilience and positive emotional granularity: Examining the benefits of positive emotions on coping and health. *Journal of Personality*, *72*, 1161–1190.

Van Katwyk, P. T., Fox, S., Spector, P. E., & Kelloway, E. K. (2000). Using the Job-Related Affective Well-Being Scale (JAWS) to investigate affective responses to work stressors. *Journal of Occupational Health Psychology*, *5*, 219–230.

Wallace, J., Ormston, H., Thurman, B., Diffley, M., McFarlane, M., & Zubairi, S. (2020). *Gross domestic well-being (GDWe): An alternative measure of social progress.* Carnegie UK Trust.

Wang, L. P., Hamaker, E., & Bergeman, C. (2012). Investigating inter-individual differences in short-term intra-individual variability. *Psychological Methods*, *17*, 567–581.

Warr, P. (1990). The measurement of well-being and other aspects of mental health. *Journal of Occupational Psychology*, *63*, 193–210.

Warr, P., Bindl, U. K., Parker, S. K., & Inceoglu, I. (2014). Four-quadrant investigation of job-related affects and behaviors. *European Journal of Work and Organizational Psychology*, *23*, 342–363.

Waterman, A. S. (1993). Two conceptions of happiness: Contrasts of personal expressiveness (eudaimonia) and hedonic enjoyment. *Journal of Personality and Social Psychology*, *64*, 678–691.

Watson, D., & Clark, L. A. (1999). *The PANAS-X: Manual for the positive and negative affect schedule – expanded form.* Department of Psychology Publications.

Watson, D., Clark, L. A., & Tellegen, A. (1988). Development and validation of brief measures of positive and negative affect: The PANAS scales. *Journal of Personality and Social Psychology 54*, 1063–1070.

Watson, D., & Tellegen, A. (1985). Toward a consensual structure of mood. *Psychological Bulletin*, *98*, 219–235.

Weiss, H. M., & Cropanzano, R. (1996). Affective events theory: A theoretical discussion of the structure, causes, and consequences of affective experiences at work. *Research in Organizational Behavior 18*, 1–74.

White, S. C., Gaines, Jr., S. O. & Jha, S. (2014). Inner well-being: Concept and validation of a new approach to subjective perceptions of well-being. *Social Indicators Research*, 119, 723–746.

Wright, T. A., & Cropanzano, R. (2000). Psychological well-being and job satisfaction as predictors of job performance. *Journal of Occupational Health Psychology*, 5(1), 84–94.

Xanthopoulou, D., Bakker, A. B., Demerouti, E., & Schaufeli, W. B. (2012a). A diary study on the happy worker: How job resources relate to positive emotions and personal resources. *European Journal of Work and Organizational Psychology*, 21, 489–517.

Xanthopoulou, D., Bakker, A. B., & Ilies, R. (2012b). Everyday working life: Explaining within-person fluctuations in employee well-being. *Human Relations*, 65, 1051–1069.

Xanthopoulou, D., Daniels, K., Sanz-Vergel, A. I. (2020). The temporal perspective on well-being at work: Lessons learned and future trends. In Y. Griep, S. Hansen, T. Vantilborgh, & J. Hofmans (Eds.), *Handbook of dynamic organizational behavior. Volume 1: A dynamic look at organizational behavior topics* (pp. 290–303). Elgar.

Zhu, Z., Kuykendall, L., & Zhang, X. (2019). The impact of within-day work breaks on daily recovery processes: An event-based pre-/post-experience sampling study. *Journal of Occupational and Organizational Psychology*, 92, 191–211.

PART IV

Workplace Interventions Addressing Stress and Well-Being

12 | Occupational Stress and Well-Being

Workplace Interventions Involving Managers/Supervisors

LESLIE B. HAMMER, SHALENE J. ALLEN,
AND JORDYN J. LESLIE

Overview

This chapter is based on a systematic review of 29 randomized controlled trials published between the years 2000 and 2020 evaluating the effectiveness of workplace interventions involving manager/supervisors aimed at reducing occupational stress and improving well-being of workers. Only studies where the authors reported that they used a randomized controlled trial (RCT) were included for the purposes of this chapter. As suggested by Eden (2020) in his review of leadership research, using RCT designs is best poised to lead to causal conclusions that provide practitioners with useful tools to move science to practice. Throughout this chapter we use the terms "manager", "supervisor", and "leader" interchangeably because of the relevance of research in each area (see Chapter 5 in this book for a discussion of the conceptual clarity in the use of these terms). To understand the types of occupational stress and well-being interventions that are the focus of this review and that involve managers and supervisors, it is first important to clarify what we mean by occupational stress, well-being, and the critical role of leaders in impacting employee stress and well-being outcomes.

What Is Occupational Stress?

Occupational stress refers to those physical or psychosocial conditions in the workplace environment that lead to physical or psychological strain outcomes. Given early knowledge of the effects of stress on the body (Selye, 1946) and increased understanding of the negative impact of workplace psychosocial conditions, such as long work hours, low control over work, and role stress (e.g., Katz & Kahn, 1978), on both worker health and organizational outcomes, addressing workplace stress is important to both organizational scholars and practitioners. Workplace stress is closely related to worker well-being and costs up to $190 billion annually in the United States (Goh et al., 2015). This is consistent with Ganster and Rosen's (2013) review of work stress and health, with evidence that job stressors predict several indicators of cardiovascular disease, depression, type 2 diabetes, and higher employee healthcare costs (Ganster & Rosen, 2013). Given that the impact of occupational stress on individual and organizational costs is high, it is vital for organizational scholarship and practice to investigate and understand interventions that may reduce such costs.

What Is Well-Being?

Warr (2011) defines well-being as a combination of physical, mental, and social health. More recently, Chari et al. (2018) defined worker well-being as "an integrated concept that characterizes quality of life with respect to an individual's health and work-related environmental, organizational, and psychosocial factors" (p. 590). Well-being is characterized by positive experiences and emotions and reflected in such outcomes as life satisfaction, positive health, and happiness. In this chapter, we focus on worker physical and psychological health that is impacted by manager interventions. Given researchers have grouped together and examined health, safety, and well-being as similar constructs (Zwetsloot et al., 2013), we also believe that perceived safety is an aspect of worker well-being and therefore have included interventions that impact worker safety outcomes in this review. With reports of extreme levels of psychological distress among the general population in relation to the COVID-19 pandemic (American Psychological Association, 2020), there has never been a more important time to pay attention to the psychological health and well-being of employees. Managers may be the best positioned to have a significant impact on employees (see Chapters 5 and 15 in this book), yet only recently has employee well-being been given serious attention in the leadership literature (Inceoglu et al., 2018).

Occupational Stress and Well-Being Interventions

The need for primary prevention interventions has been clearly discussed in the public health and occupational safety and health fields for some time. These are also considered as primary prevention/proactive interventions and what the National Institute for Occupational Safety and Health (NIOSH) would call environmental/organizational level interventions. Primary prevention interventions are those that pro-actively eliminate the hazard or occupational stress before it has a chance to occur. Such interventions are at the top of the NIOSH hierarchy of controls. In the public health field, primary interventions are seen as preventative and, thus, when it comes to occupational stress, involve the prevention of such stress through changes in the physical or psychosocial work environment. Examples of primary prevention interventions shown to impact employee stress reduction include organizational strategies to increase social support and job redesign (LaMontagne et al., 2007). These types of organizational level preventative interventions are reported to be the most effective com-pared to secondary (e.g., screening to detect existing stressors that can be targeted for reduction) or tertiary (e.g., managing stress such as individual stress management practices) reactive interventions (LaMontagne et al., 2007). Below we discuss job stress interventions and Total Worker Health® (TWH) interventions, both aimed at under-standing ways of reducing occupational stress and improving the well-being of workers.

Job Stress Interventions

Job stress interventions refer to those implemented with the explicit focus of reducing exposures to stressors in the workplace. We have not seen a systematic review of job stress interventions since the LaMontagne et al. (2007) review that included both organizational level and individual level interventions. LaMontagne et al. (2007) reviewed interventions involving both organizational level and individual level approaches (e.g., employee-level personal changes to reduce stressors such as personal coping strategies) and rated these interventions in terms of the degree to which a systems approach was applied to job stress reduction. A high systems approach was defined as both organization-ally and individually focused, versus moderate (organizational only) and low (individual only). Moderate ratings were those interventions that only used primary prevention/organizational approaches. With the focus on employee job stress as the outcome, LaMontagne identified 30 studies rated as a high systems organizational level interventions approach (30/90 = 33%); 17 moderate (19%), and 43 low (48%). These high systems approach interventions included managerial interventions, which are a subset of organizational level interventions and the focus of this chapter. The most effective interventions were those that were either organizationally focused or *both* organizationally and individually focused (LaMontagne et al., 2007), a conclusion consistent with that of Semmer (2007), who characterized job stress interventions as those that were focused on improving employee health and well-being by changing task characteristics, work conditions, or social aspects of work.

Total Worker Health Interventions

Total Worker Health® (TWH) is a program that was launched by NIOSH in 2011 (Schill & Chosewood, 2013) and is based on the premise that individuals' experiences, exposures, health, and well-being both affect and are affected by their work (Feltner et al., 2016). TWH is defined as policies, programs, and practices that integrate protection from work-related safety and health hazards with promotion of injury and illness prevention efforts to advance worker well-being (Tamers et al., 2019). The TWH approach is focused on workplace hazard reduction and its impact on employee health, safety, and well-being. While such hazards can come in the form of safety hazards that are part of the physical work environment, they can also be psychosocial stress hazards associated with unhealthy work that directly affects employee health and well-being (Schnall et al., 2009). TWH approaches emphasize the importance of inter- ventions that integrate changing the employee, other people in the employee's workplace (supervisors or coworkers), the employee's job characteristics, or the organization's climate. Managers and super- visors can be the target of interventions in any of these areas, but most commonly the last three (i.e., other people in the employee's workplace, the employee's job characteristics controlled by managers, or the organization's climate impacted by managers). While much evidence points to the critical role of managers, supervisors, and leaders in impacting employee well-being (Chapter 5 in this book; Arnold, 2017; Hammer et al., 2007; Inceoglu et al., 2018; Kelloway & Barling, 2010), there is less systematic research on the effectiveness of such approaches.

Managerial/Leadership Behavior and Employee Occupational Stress and Well-Being

A recent meta-analysis based on longitudinal studies linking job resources at organizational, group, and leader levels to employee work engagement demonstrated the importance of managerial resources in predicting employee well-being over time (Lesener et al., 2020). In fact, the meta-analysis suggested that managerial/leader-level resources such as supervisor social support that have the power to increase organizational level resources, such as autonomy, create both manager level and organizational level resources to improve employee well-being. Given manager discretion to enact formal and informal organizational policies that lead to the distribution of organizational resources, their role is critical when it comes to employee stress and well-being. This is consistent with conservation of resources (COR) theory (Hobfoll, 1989), although the loss of resources seems more detrimental to well-being than the positive gain of resources would be (Halbesleben et al., 2014). Thus, managers have control over resources and the power to implement organizational policies to varying degrees. Furthermore, research on idiosyncratic deals (i-deals) suggests that managers are key to employees' negotiations to allow for flexible scheduling and developmental opportunities (Hornung et al., 2008), which in turn can impact employee stress and well-being. Thus, we argue that managers and supervisors are key to understanding employee stress and well-being and, thus, the focus of intervention targets in this review.

Recognizing the critical role of leadership behavior in employee well-being is the focus of Chapters 5 and 15 of this book. The present chapter specifically identifies those leader interventions that have promise for reducing stress and improving well-being of employees. However, as indicated by both the Arnold (2017) and Inceoglu et al. (2018) reviews, much of this work is based on cross-sectional research designs, and there is a need for rigorous studies to investigate, using RCTs, the types of leadership interventions that pave the way to improvements in employee stress and well-being and suggest clear strategies for organizational practitioners.

In their earlier review of leadership interventions, Avolio et al. (2009) noted that the most common leadership intervention was leadership training and development. They defined a leadership intervention study as "one in which the researcher overtly manipulated leadership to examine its impact on some specific intermediate process variables or outcomes" (Avolio et al., 2009, p. 765). Focusing on experimental and quasi-experimental designs, the authors meta-analyzed leadership interventions and their effects on affective, cognitive, and behavioral leader and employee outcomes and organizational performance. From our assessment, it was not clear whether the effects were differentiated based on leader or follower outcome reports. Most of the training and development research that exists has focused on training context, trainee characteristics, and training design and delivery, with most criteria at the individual trainee level of analysis. With the advent of hierarchical multilevel modeling techniques, training effects on team performance emerged (Bell et al., 2017). We found very little scholarly work on the impact of manager training on employee outcomes, let alone on employee occupational stress and well-being outcomes.

Managerial training can be broadly categorized as focused on general management development, self-awareness programs, problem-solving/decision-making programs, rater training programs, motivation/values training, or human relations/leadership training programs, according to Burke and Day (1986). Leadership training effectiveness has been documented most recently in a meta-analysis by Lacerenza et al. (2017). The present review is focused on managerial/leadership training and other intervention programs that impact employee occupational stress and well-being. The goal of this chapter is to provide a general review that can serve as a rubric for scholars to use when summarizing information on effectiveness of leadership interventions and training impacting employee occupational stress and well-being.

Review Methodology

Search Procedure

We conducted an initial search in PsycINFO, PubMed, Medline, and Google Scholar between the years 2000 and 2020 using the search terms "manager", "supervisor", "leader", "occupational stress", "well-being", "intervention", "training", and "program" combined with "workplace" or "occupation". Any abstract that suggested the article contained an occupational stress and well-being intervention, training, or program in which managers/supervisors/leaders played a critical role and reported occupational stress and well-being outcomes for employees was then reviewed in detail and coded by at least one of the authors. A total of 106 articles met these criteria and hence were reviewed in detail. After reviewing the articles, duplicates were removed, as well as review articles, interventions that were not RCTs, interventions that did not examine employee outcomes, and any interventions that did not explicitly have supervisors/managers/leaders as a main part of the intervention. We were left with a total of 29 articles that met the final inclusion criteria of being an RCT involving a manager/leadership intervention that was designed to impact employee occupational stress and well-being outcomes (see Table 12.1). Such interventions can be both proactive/preventative and reactive/responsive. We coded for type of intervention, type of employee outcome, type of primary effect (main, mediation, moderation), and significance of the effects.

Type of Leadership Intervention

In the present review, all intervention programs are categorized as managerial training and educational programs. Five broad categories were identified based on the substantive content focus of the training program and the outcomes the intervention was expected to impact for employees. These include managerial training and educational programs that were focused on improving: (a) *job design/ergonomic workplace conditions* (N = 3) (i.e., Eklöf et al., 2006; Kajiki et al., 2017; Linton et al., 2015); (b) *employee psychological health* (N = 5) (i.e., Dimoff & Kelloway, 2019; Kawakami et al., 2005, 2006; Milligan-Saville et al., 2017; Takao et al., 2006); (c) *employee physical health* (N = 4) (i.e., Karlqvist & Gard, 2013; Ketelaar et al., 2017; Morken et al., 2002; Stansfeld et al., 2015); (d) *employee safety* (N = 7) (i.e., Amiri et al., 2018; Hammer & Truxillo et al., 2019; Hammer et al., 2015; Mullen & Kelloway, 2009; Shaw et al., 2006; Zohar, 2002; Zohar & Polachek, 2014); and (e) *employee received and perceived supervisor social support* (N = 10) (i.e., Crain et al., 2019; Hammer et al., 2011, 2016, 2020; Hammer & Wan et al., 2019; Hurtado et al., 2016; Kelly et al., 2014; Kossek et al., 2019; Moen et al., 2016; Olson et al., 2015). It should also be noted that some of

Table 12.1 *Summary of occupational stress and well-being interventions involving managers/supervisors*

Citation	Intervention type	Employee outcome type	Type of effect	Significant findings (Y/N)
Eklöf & Hagberg (2006)	Job design/ergonomic	Psychological health	Main	N
Kajiki et al. (2017)	Job design/ergonomic	Physical health	Main	Y
Linton et al. (2016)	Job design/ergonomic	Physical health	Main	Y
Dimoff & Kelloway (2019)	Psychological health	Psychological health	Main	Y
Kawakami et al. (2005)	Psychological health	Psychological health	Main	Y
Kawakami et al. (2006)	Psychological health	Psychological health	Main	Y
Milligan-Saville et al. (2017)	Psychological health	Physical health	Main	Y
Takao et al. (2006)	Psychological health	Psychological health	Main, moderation	Y
Karlqvist & Gard (2013)	Physical health	Physical health	Main	Y
Ketelaar et al. (2017)	Physical health	Physical health	Main	N
Morken et al. (2002)	Physical health	Psychological health	Main, mediation, moderation	N
Stansfeld et al. (2015)	Physical health	Physical health	Main	N
Amiri et al. (2018)	Safety	Safety	Main	Y
Hammer et al. (2015)	Safety	Physical health	Main	Y
Hammer & Truxillo et al. (2019)	Safety	Psychological health	Moderation	Y
Mullen & Kelloway (2009)	Safety	Safety	Main	Y
Shaw et al. (2006)	Safety	Safety	Main	Y
Zohar (2002)	Safety	Safety	Main	Y
Zohar & Polachek (2014)	Safety	Safety	Main	Y
Crain et al. (2019)	Supervisor social support	Physical health	Main, mediation	Y

Hammer et al. (2020)	Supervisor social support	Physical health	Main, moderation	Y
Hammer et al. (2016)	Supervisor social support	Safety	Main, moderation	Y
Hammer et al. (2011)	Supervisor social support	Physical health	Mediation, moderation	Y
Hammer & Wan et al. (2019)	Supervisor social support	Physical health	Moderation	Y
Hurtado et al. (2016)	Supervisor social support	Physical health	Main	Y
Kelly et al. (2014)	Supervisor social support	Psychological health	Main, moderation	Y
Kossek et al. (2019)	Supervisor social support	Psychological health	Moderation	Y
Moen et al. (2016)	Supervisor social support	Psychological health	Mediation, moderation	Y
Olson et al. (2015)	Supervisor social support	Physical health	Main, mediation	Y

these programs were also designed to affect what we refer to as secondary outcomes of leader knowledge and organizational climate outcomes, which are addressed later in our review.

Type of Employee Outcomes

We identified the general employee outcome categories of physical health, psychological health, and safety, consistent with our focus on occupational stress and well-being interventions. While most intervention evaluation studies included multiple outcomes at multiple levels, our interest was in employee outcomes that are indicators of reduced occupational stress and improved well-being. Also, given the vast number of outcomes included in many studies, we focused on the key or primary employee outcome that was of interest as noted by the authors. Within these three categories, employee outcomes included a number of *physical health* outcomes, including sleep – actigraphic total sleep time, actigraphic wake after sleep onset (WASO), insufficiency, insomnia (i.e., Crain et al., 2019; Olson et al., 2015); musculoskeletal symptoms; and eye discomfort. *Psychological health* outcomes include emotional distress, willingness to use resources, employee perceptions of leaders' communication about mental health and resources, and employee perceptions of leader consideration for struggling employees, all of which lead to improved psychological health outcomes for employees (e.g., Dimoff & Kelloway, 2019; Moen et al., 2016). *Safety and ergonomic* outcomes include support for patient safety and employee perceptions of patient safety. Ergonomic outcomes include quality of modifications in the ergonomic and psychosocial environment and modification activity.

Type of Effect

In addition to intervention main effects, which are very difficult to detect in intervention research (e.g., Adler et al., 2015), we were interested in noting intervention mediators that provide information on the process by which the intervention impacts employee outcomes, and moderators which provide information on the contextual conditions under which interventions impact employee outcomes. Examples of potential mediators and moderators are provided in Chapter 5 of this book.

Findings on Leadership Training Effectiveness

All 29 of the included supervisor intervention studies (as shown in Table 12.1) examined effects on employee occupational stress and well-being outcomes. Notably, there has been little systematic research examining causal effects of stress and well-being interventions involving managers and supervisors, primarily because of the complexity and cost of implementing such interventions, with fewer research efforts being able to examine these interventions in randomized controlled trials. Thus, this section of the chapter aims to summarize the effects of varying categories of supervisor/manager stress and well-being interventions on the primary employee physical health, psychological health, and safety outcomes identified in each study.

Employee Physical Health Outcomes

Employee physical health outcomes were investigated in 11 articles (Crain et al., 2019; Hammer et al., 2011, 2015, 2019b, Hurtado et al., 2016; Kajiki et al., 2017; Karlqvist & Gard, 2013; Ketelaar et al., 2017; Linton et al., 2015; Milligan-Saville et al., 2017; Olson et al., 2015). These included both objective and subjective reports of employee *sleep-related outcomes, incident rates for lower back pain, physical fitness, smoking, blood pressure, perceived overall health, sick leave utilization,* and *absenteeism.*

In terms of *sleep-related outcomes,* a work–family and educational intervention, as part of the Work, Family, and Health Network (WFHN), used supervisor and employee facilitated sessions aimed at identifying ways of increasing control over work, in addition to a supportive supervisor training program. Results demonstrated significant direct effects of the intervention on employee total sleep duration at 12 months, with approximately 8 minutes of more sleep per night compared to the control condition (Olson et al., 2015). Furthermore, researchers using data from the WFHN expanded upon the prior intervention by Olson and colleagues (2015) and demonstrated significant intervention effects on sleep quality and sleep quantity at both 6 months and 18 months postintervention, with individuals in the treatment group experiencing approximately 9 minutes more sleep per night at 6 months and approximately 13 minutes more sleep per night at 18 months (Crain et al., 2019).

Research also provides evidence for improvements in employee physical health outcomes unrelated to sleep such as *decreased incident rate ratios for lower back pain* shortly after a participatory workplace intervention where leaders were trained in methods of ergonomic improvement and assessment (Kajiki et al., 2017). However, these effects did not endure over time at the 10-month follow-up. Additionally, a supervisor coaching intervention found that employee *physical fitness* levels increased from baseline to follow-up after supervisors were coached on promoting employee health through organizational and lifestyle factors (Karlqvist & Gard, 2013). This study also found significant effects of supervisor stress and well-being interventions on objective health measures. Another study based on data from the WFHN showed direct effects of the supervisor training intervention on employees who were identified as smokers, *reducing cigarette consumption* by about seven cigarettes per week (Hurtado et al., 2016). Notably, this intervention prevented declines in employee perceptions of family-supportive supervisor behaviors (FSSBs) at 6 months, specifically among employees who categorized themselves as smokers (Hurtado et al., 2016). Researchers examining the Safety and Health Improvement Program (SHIP) among construction workers reported significant positive intervention effects for employee *objective blood pressure* at 12 months postintervention (Hammer et al., 2015). Both Hammer et al. (2011) and Hammer et al. (2019b) showed significant intervention effects on employee reports of *perceived physical health*.

Finally, three different studies found significant supervisor training intervention effects on employee-reported sick day use and absenteeism, purportedly due to poor physical health. Linton and colleagues (2015) implemented a supervisor worker and workplace intervention aimed at minimizing the impact of workplace psychosocial risk factors and creating a more supportive workplace. The intervention resulted in significant differences in *employee work absences due to pain* at follow-up. Additionally, employees in the treatment as usual condition were also four times more likely to seek out healthcare compared to the intervention group, and those participants in the intervention group reported *fewer healthcare visits* and *improvement in perceived health* at follow-up (Linton et al., 2015). Mental health training for managers demonstrated *reduced sickness absence* reports for the intervention group compared to the control group of employees (Milligan-Saville et al., 2017). In addition, although not approaching significance, another intervention found greater *reductions in average employee sick days* in the intervention condition from baseline (i.e., 4.6 days) to follow-up (i.e., 2.4 days) compared to the control group at baseline (i.e., 3.8 days) to follow-up (i.e., 3.6 days), after a multifaceted supervisor intervention involving supervisor training on employee sick leave and supervisor coaching (Ketelaar et al., 2017).

Overall, leadership intervention studies aimed at improving physical health of employees ranged from supervisor social support training interventions (N = 4) to safety-related supervisor training (2), job design/ergonomic training (2), manager physical health-related training (1), and manager mental health training (2). These interventions were effective at improving employee sleep, pain, cigarette smoking, physical fitness, blood pressure, missing work, and perceived health. Many of these physical health outcomes are critically linked to employee outcomes. For example, sleep has been identified as a major contributor to a variety of employee outcomes such as job strain, work–family conflict, engagement, job satisfaction, turnover, cognition, counterproductive work behavior, hostility, positive affect, and relaxation (Litwiller, 2017), and thus, they have broader implications beyond physical health.

Employee Psychological Health Outcomes

Employee psychological health outcomes were examined in 11 supervisor intervention studies (Dimoff & Kelloway, 2019; Eklöf et al., 2006; Kawakami et al., 2005, 2006; Kelly et al., 2014; Kossek et al., 2019; Milligan-Saville et al., 2017; Moen et al., 2016; Morken et al., 2002; Stansfeld et al., 2015; Takao et al., 2006). These employee outcomes tend to be self-reported and include reports of *perceived control, perceived supervisor support for family and for mental health,* and *psychological distress.* Note that each of these could also serve as mediators to explain the effects of supervisor interventions on employee psychological or physical health outcomes.

The WFHN study focused on training supervisors to be more supportive of employees who were managing work and family demands and involved facilitated sessions prompting employees to discuss where and when they work in two different industry sectors: information technology and healthcare. Researchers found that the intervention *increased employees' schedule control and significantly increased employee perceptions of their supervisor eliciting supervisor support for family and personal life* and decreased *work–family conflict and family time adequacy* reported by information technology employees (Kelly et al., 2014). Likewise, Moen et al. (2016) found that the WFHN intervention had significant effects on *reduced burnout, perceived stress,* and *psychological distress,* as well as *increased job satisfaction* among information technology workers. Kossek et al. (2019) evaluated the effects of the WFHN intervention among healthcare workers and found that it decreased *psychological distress* for employees with elder care responsibilities. Thus, this leader intervention with a primary component focused on improving social support provided by managers and supervisors demonstrated significant effects on employee psychological health outcomes, hence improving well-being.

Furthermore, a web-based training for supervisors on workplace mental health was found to provide significant effects on *employee perceptions of their supervisor eliciting greater supervisor support for mental health* and *reduced employee psychological distress* (Kawakami et al., 2005). Similarly, another leader-focused mental health training showed improvements in *employees' willingness to use and seek out available mental health resources* (Dimoff & Kelloway, 2019). Manager mental health training given to firefighter supervisor leads showed significant decreases in *employee work-related sick leave use* by approximately 6.45 hours per employee and reduced the overall levels of employees taking standard sick leave at 6 months following the intervention (Milligan-Saville et al., 2017). Additionally, employee reports of their leaders' communication about mental health and subsequent mental health resources significantly increased at both follow-up time points of 6 and 12 weeks postintervention. Employees also reported their *leaders as being more considerate toward employees who were struggling,* showing significant increases at the time three 12-week follow-up (Dimoff & Kelloway, 2019). Finally, Takao and colleagues (2006) found significant intervention effects on employee *psychological distress* postimplementation of an educational program for supervisors centered around mental health workplace manager responsibilities aimed at reducing stress among subordinate employees. Notably, however, this was only significant for young white-collar male subordinates.

Although no statistically significant intervention effects were found, a few interventions have demonstrated improvements in employee psychological health outcomes via occupational stress and well-being interventions involving managers and/or supervisors. For example, organizations can implement one-hour feedback sessions (i.e., evaluative information is provided about specific behaviors or events in one-on-one or group-based discussions) with their supervisors to potentially and positively impact employees' and workgroups' perceptions of social support (Eklöf et al., 2006). Additionally, Stansfeld and colleagues (2015) found employees whose manager completed an online educational well-being intervention had higher well-being scores at baseline and follow-up, suggesting that intervention group supervisors already had employees who exhibited higher levels of well-being to begin with. Similarly, Morken and colleagues (2002) found that a musculoskeletal health intervention program improved coping strategies among employees with musculoskeletal disorders and injuries (e.g., working more slowly, taking more or longer breaks, asking colleagues for help with strenuous tasks) as well as social support from both coworkers and supervisors. Overall, past occupational stress and well-being interventions involving managers or supervisors have provided important evidence that utilizing supervisors as a point of intervention can have beneficial downstream outcomes for employee psychological health and well-being.

Employee Safety Outcomes

Six studies were identified that evaluated the effects of leadership training on employee safety outcomes (Amiri et al., 2018; Hammer et al., 2016; Mullen & Kelloway, 2009; Shaw et al., 2006; Zohar, 2002; Zohar & Polachek, 2014). The studies include examination of managerial/supervisor training effects on employee *safety behavior, reports of safety compliance, reports of injuries, use of personal protective equipment,* and *improved safety communication.*

For example, feedback sessions with supervisors regarding safety, productivity, and teamwork showed significant improvements on *employee safety behavior* (Zohar & Polachek, 2014). Similarly, the WFHN study, examining the intervention aimed at improving supervisor support for work and family among healthcare workers, showed significant effects on *employee self-reports of safety compliance* at 6 months postintervention (Hammer et al., 2016). This finding is consistent with prior correlational studies showing a relationship between work–family conflict and safety (e.g., Smith et al., 2018). Furthermore, Mullen and Kelloway (2009) implemented a transformational leadership-based intervention in the healthcare setting focusing on safety-specific aspects of transformational leadership and found significant improvements in *employee ratings of leader's safety-specific transformational leadership.* Another safety-based intervention supports this argument as employees were also shown to have *higher rates of earplug use* in their organizational subunits after the supervisory safety intervention improved supervisory safety practices (Zohar, 2002). An intervention aimed at improving safety culture via supervisor training in intensive care units found significant improvements in teamwork within specific units, such as *increased communication openness* (i.e., ability to question decisions and speak up when concerns arise), as well as *improved handoffs and transitions of patient care,* which was the weakest component of the safety culture prior to the intervention (Amiri et al., 2018). Effective safety-specific interventions are crucial, as the National Safety Council estimates that worker injury costs reached $170.8 billion in 2018 (National Safety Council, 2020). Thus, interventions including supervisors may be an effective approach to improving employee safety and preventing subsequent costs to organizations.

Overall, supervisors play a crucial role in the health, well-being, and safety of employees, especially through workplace stress and well-being interventions aimed at improving employee outcomes. Employee-level outcomes range from physical health such as improved sleep and psychological health such as decreased burnout and distress, to safety-related employee outcomes such as safety compliance. Thus, this review demonstrates that managerial occupational stress and well-being interventions have been successful in directly impacting employees' occupational stress and well-being outcomes.

Moderators and Mediators of Stress and Well-Being Interventions on Employee Outcomes

As mentioned previously, main effects, as well as moderating effects and mediational effects, were observed in the studies included in this review. Specifically, research has examined variables that may influence the strength of the relationship between interventions and subsequent outcomes as well as specific mediating variables that determine the process through which interventions are effectively impacting employee stress and well-being outcomes. Mediators help explain *how* the training impacted employee outcomes (e.g., mediators captured in our review include control over work schedule, FSSB, work–family conflict, family–work conflict, family time adequacy, control over work time, emotional exhaustion (burnout), return to work practices, and immediate supervisor–subordinate relationships). Intervention moderators help explain under what conditions the interventions are effective, such as organizational context (e.g., Bell et al., 2017). Given the difficulty in detecting main intervention effects, these mediators and moderators are important to consider. Intervention moderators were grouped into five overarching categories of work-specific variables (i.e., control over work time, team cohesion, schedule control, job demands, job insecurity, organization, being at risk for sick leave at baseline, decision authority, managerial status, occupation, and supervisors' self-reported job demands), work–family variables (i.e., work–family climate, work–family conflict, family–work conflict, child at home, care for adults, and family caregiving structure), work attitudes and behaviors (i.e., supervisor attitudes, FSSBs, general supervisor support, and perceptions of supervisor leadership style), health-specific variables (i.e., general health, psychological distress, and need for recovery), and demographic variables (i.e., age, sex, gender, and level of education). These moderation and mediation variables shed light on the importance of examining the organizational context and other contextual factors that have the ability to influence supervisor stress and well-being intervention effects on various employee outcomes. When considering these effects, we found that examination by research program was most effective.

Practical Implications

As demonstrated by this review, there is little evidence of manager/ leader interventions that improve employee occupational stress and well-being. This is consistent with the Inceoglu et al. (2018) review, which noted most leadership research had focused on employee performance as opposed to employee well-being. Based on our review, we have identified the following three key leadership intervention areas that are most suggestive of future targets for impacting employee occupational stress and well-being: (a) relational leadership training that includes transformational leadership (e.g., Arnold, 2017) and supervisor support training (e.g., Hammer et al., 2007); (b) leader awareness training to improve knowledge related to employee physical and psychological health of employees, such as leader mental health awareness training (e.g., Dimoff & Kelloway, 2019); and (c) leader training to improve the safety culture (e.g., Mullen & Kelloway, 2009). This is hopefully useful information for organizational practitioners who see value in placing an emphasis on employee stress and well-being over that of job performance.

Relational Leadership Training

We refer to relational leadership training as specifically targeting leader people-skills and improving upon how they relate to employees. This includes both transformational leadership training as well as supervisor social support training. Arnold (2017) provided an excellent review of the research on the relationship between transformational leadership and employee health and well-being. Unfortunately, most of the existing research on transformational leadership is based on cross-sectional research designs, and little is known about the effects of transformational leadership training on employee outcomes (for an exception, see Mullen & Kelloway, 2009). In her review of transformational leadership and well-being studies, Arnold (2017) identified 40 empirical papers published between January 1980 and December 2015. An earlier review of transformational leadership and employee well-being by Kelloway and Barling (2010) demonstrated this positive relationship. While transformational leadership theory is one of the most highly studied leadership theories (Arnold, 2017), we have not found many studies on how to enact such leadership, as 80% of the studies noted in the Arnold review are cross-sectional studies. Furthermore, there have been serious critiques of transformational leadership theory (e.g., Van Knippenberg & Sitkin, 2013) raising serious concerns about the measurement, partially due to the conceptual confusion around the definition of charismatic-transformational leadership theory. Furthermore, Arnold also noted that we need not only rigorous studies that do not employ a cross-sectional design as to enable cause and effect relationships to be determined, but a better understanding of how, through mediation, and when, through moderation, regarding the relationship between transformational leadership and employee well-being outcomes.

We suggest that supervisor support can be considered a special case of relational transformational leadership, and it may be the key ingredient that is related to employee well-being outcomes. For example, the Hammer et al. (2007) review identified the critical role of supervisor support for family in impacting employee psychological health, physical health, safety, and workplace outcomes, as they argued that the supervisor has the ability to enact both formal and informal organizational policies that support workers. Again, this review was based primarily on correlational studies. What followed the Hammer et al. review was a program of research on FSSB training interventions. A recent systematic review of social support in the management sciences points to the role of social support as a positive catalyst that can facilitate employee well-being (Bavik et al., 2020). It is important to note that each of these reviews identified the critical role of the leader in impacting health, safety, and well-being of employees and called for more systematic study of the causal effects of leadership on employee well-being outcomes.

Leadership Awareness Training

We found several of the articles in our review were specifically focused on improving supervisor knowledge and behaviors that could impact employee occupational stress and well-being. Below we discuss knowledge, attitudes, and behaviors that impact employee occupational stress and well-being outcomes. For example, Dimoff and Kelloway (2019) implemented workplace mental health training specifically for those in leadership positions. Their findings suggest mental health awareness training for supervisors significantly improved a multitude of supervisor outcomes, such as leader communication about mental health and mental health resources provided to their employees, leader actions to encourage employee mental health resource use, and leader warning sign recognition of deteriorating mental health among their subordinate employees. Interestingly, leader warning sign recognition was not significant at baseline or 6-week follow-up, but was significant at 12 weeks postintervention, suggesting delayed but longitudinal effects of the leadership mental health training on these supervisor outcomes (Dimoff & Kelloway, 2019). Similarly, Milligan-Saville and colleagues (2017) implemented manager mental health training with the goal of improving managers' behavior toward mental health as well as improving employees' willingness to take sickness absence. Results indicated managers in the intervention group reported significantly higher levels of mental health knowledge, knowledge of the role of a manager in mental health promotion, and confidence in communicating with their employees regarding mental illness in the workplace. Notably, however, the intervention's effects on manager confidence in communicating with their employees regarding mental illness was the only enduring significant outcome, as no other outcomes were found to be significant at 6 months postintervention (Milligan-Saville et al., 2017). These mental health focused supervisor trainings, which were shown to positively influence supervisory outcomes, have the ability to then influence the willingness for employees to be able to capitalize on these intervention resources to improve their overall well-being.

Leadership Training to Improve Safety Culture

Two occupational stress and well-being interventions involving managers/supervisors have also found significant effects related to supervisor safety knowledge. Amiri and colleagues (2018) implemented an educational empowerment program for nurses and supervisors in adult intensive care units with the aim of improving patient safety culture. With regard to behavioral outcomes, the intervention had significant effects on *manager expectations* and *actions promoting patient safety*, which was a key dimension of patient safety culture as identified by the authors. Furthermore, Mullen and Kelloway (2009) implemented a transformational leadership-based intervention with a focus on the difference between general transformational leadership and safety-specific transformational leadership. Researchers found that the intervention had a significant effect on *manager safety attitudes, intent to promote safety,* and *manager self-efficacy* (Mullen & Kelloway, 2009). Specifically, those supervisors randomized to the safety-specific transformational leadership group had significantly improved safety attitudes and self-efficacy compared to the general transformational leadership group and the control group. Intentions to promote safety were also higher in the safety-specific group than the general group, but this intervention effect was not statistically significant (Mullen & Kelloway, 2009).

We identified five leader training intervention studies that included outcomes focused specifically on changing the safety culture and one that was focused on changing the health culture, all with the aim of improving stress and well-being of employees. Kawakami and colleagues (2006) implemented a web-based supervisor training aimed at improving health and support outcomes. Researchers found that the intervention significantly improved the friendliness of the worksite atmosphere (e.g., increased mutual support, respect, teamwork, etc.; Kawakami et al., 2006). For example, a safety-leadership intervention aimed at providing supervisors with weekly personal feedback on safety-related interactions with subordinates found that the intervention led to a significant decrease in micro accidents and injuries post-intervention, as well as significant improvements in group safety climate (Zohar, 2002). Similarly, a discourse-based intervention modified daily communication messages between supervisors and subordinates to include more safety and productivity-related issues (Zohar & Polachek, 2014). This intervention found that the communication modification significantly improved safety climate, safety audits performed by external safety consultants, and overall heightened perceptions of teamwork (Zohar & Polachek, 2014). Another study aimed to examine the impact of an intervention for both general and safety-specific transformational leadership on an array of organizational outcomes (Mullen & Kelloway, 2009). This intervention found significant effects for perceptions of safety climate in the safety-specific transformational leadership intervention group as compared to the control group (Mullen & Kelloway, 2009). Furthermore, a study conducted by Amiri and colleagues (2018) employed an education empowerment program for nurses and supervisors which significantly improved patient safety culture among adult intensive care units (ICUs), with specific improvements in dimensions of patient safety culture that were previously weak prior to the intervention, such as organizational learning, organizational continuous improvement, and teamwork within units (Amiri et al., 2018).

Need for Future Research

A limitation of this review is that we are not comparing apples to apples, and therefore, caution needs to be maintained in drawing conclusions that cut across different studies. For example, interventions vary greatly in terms of dose and whether they have a single component or multiple components. For example, the WFHN intervention was a multicomponent intervention where supervisor training was one aspect. Similarly, the Safety and Health Improvement project was multicomponent. These are compared to other interventions that are based on single-component supervisor training alone, such as Milligan-Saville et al. (2017). Additionally, most effects noted were significant, pointing to publication bias in the social and behavioral sciences and our lack of investigation of unpublished research. Thus, another limitation of this review is that it is based only on published research, which tends to be biased toward those studies showing significant results, as can be seen by the high proportion of significant effects. We also note that most studies in our reviews did not include particularly diverse samples, reflecting a general bias in organizational research that lacks attention to diversity and, thus, makes generalization of such interventions to a wide variety of employees and workplaces questionable. There is a need for more research on such sectors of the population that tend to be disproportionately represented in low-wage, service, farm, and food processing jobs where we see some of the highest levels of occupational stress and threats to well-being due to hazardous job conditions.

Clearly, there is a need for methodologically strong leadership training intervention research designs that lead to causal conclusions and are focused on employee occupational stress and well-being, given our search only revealed 29 such studies between the years 2000 and 2020. As Eden (2020) argued, we must be using the gold standard RCT to effectively arrive at sound practical recommendations for leadership on how to improve stress and well-being of employees. Given the current estimated cost of stress is over $190 billion annually (Goh et al., 2015), and given that the COVID-19 pandemic has taken workplaces to a new level of psychological distress among employees (i.e., APA 2020 Stress in America report that 6 in 10 employees reported extreme psychological distress), there is renewed interest for organizational scholars to implement supervisor-focused training interventions that are evidence-based and known to improve the health and well-being of employees.

Finally, what was clear from the Anger et al. (2015, 2019) reviews was the lack of dissemination and implementation of effective interventions. In fact, they found that only 1 intervention out of 17 was even available to the general public. Moreover, occupational safety and health intervention research is extremely limited in translation–

dissemination–implementation. What good is an evidence-based leadership training intervention that is not available? Thus, we believe that more research is needed in the area of dissemination and implementation science to better understand how to improve the sharing, marketing, and organizational reception and buy-in of stress and well-being interventions. This is a difficult challenge, as most leadership training is focused on improving performance, not health and well-being. Thus, this requires a change in priorities, and perhaps now, in the midst and aftermath of the COVID-19 pandemic, there is no better time to make the case for the importance of improving occupational stress and well-being of employees.

References

Adler, A. B., Bliese, P. D., Pickering, M. A., Hammermeister, J., Williams, J., Harada, C., … Ohlson, C. (2015). Mental skills training with basic combat training soldiers: A group-randomized trial. *Journal of Applied Psychology, 100*, 1752–1764. https://doi.org/10.1037/apl0000021

American Psychological Association (APA). (2020, December). Stress in America™ 2020: A National Mental Health Crisis. www.apa.org/news/press/releases/stress/2020/report-october

Amiri, M., Khademian, Z., & Nikandish, R. (2018). The effect of nurse empowerment educational program on patient safety culture: A randomized controlled trial. *BMC Medical Education, 18*(1), 158. https://doi.org/10.1186/s12909-018-1255-6

Anger, K., Rameshbabu, A., Parker, K., Wan, W., Hurtado, D., Olson, R., Rohlman, D., Wipfli, B., & Bodner, T. (2019). Effectiveness of total worker health interventions: A systematic review. In H. L. Hudson, J. A. Nigam, S. L. Sauter, L. C. Chosewood, A. L. Schill (Eds.), *Total worker health* (pp. 61–90). American Psychological Association.

Anger, W. K., Elliot, D. L., Bodner, T., Olson, R., Rohlman, D. S., Truxillo, D. M., Kuehl, K. S., Hamer, L. B., & Montgomery, D. (2015). Effectiveness of total worker health interventions. *Journal of Occupational Health Psychology, 20*(2), 226. https://doi.org/10.1037/a0038340

Arnold, K. A. (2017). Transformational leadership and employee psychological well-being: A review and directions for future research. *Journal of Occupational Health Psychology, 22*(3), 381–393. https://doi.org/10.1037/ocp0000062

Avolio, B. J., Reichard, R. J., Hannah, S. T., Walumbwa, F. O., & Chan, A. (2009). A meta-analytic review of leadership impact research:

Experimental and quasi-experimental studies. *The Leadership Quarterly, 20*(5), 764–784.

Bavik, Y. L., Shaw, J. D., & Wang, X. H. (2020). Social support: Multi-disciplinary review, synthesis, and future agenda. *Academy of Management Annals, 14*(2). https://doi.org/10.5465/annals.2016.0148

Bell, B. S., Tannenbaum, S. I., Ford, J. K., Noe, R. A., & Kraiger, K. (2017). 100 years of training and development research: What we know and where we should go. *Journal of Applied Psychology, 102*(3), 305.

Biron, C., & Karanika-Murray, M. (2014). Process evaluation for organizational stress and well-being interventions: Implications for theory, method, and practice. *International Journal of Stress Management, 21*, 85–111. http://doi.org/10.1037/a0033227

Burke, M. J., & Day, R. R. (1986). A cumulative study of the effectiveness of managerial training. *Journal of Applied Psychology, 71*(2), 232.

Chari, R., Chang, C. C., Sauter, S. L., Sayers, E. L. P., Cerully, J. L., Schulte, P., Schill, A. L., & Uscher-Pines, L. (2018). Expanding the paradigm of occupational safety and health: A new framework for worker well-being. *Journal of Occupational and Environmental Medicine, 60*(7), 589–593. https://doi.org/10.1097/JOM.0000000000001330

Crain, T. L., Hammer, L. B., Bodner, T., Olson, R., Kossek, E. E., Moen, P., & Buxton, O. M. (2019). Sustaining sleep: Results from the randomized controlled work, family, and health study. *Journal of Occupational Health Psychology, 24*(1), 180. https://doi.org/10.1037/ocp0000122

Dimoff, J. K., & Kelloway, E. K. (2019). With a little help from my boss: The impact of workplace mental health training on leader behaviors and employee resource utilization. *Journal of Occupational Health Psychology, 24*(1), 4. https://doi.org/10.1037/ocp0000126

Eden, D. (2020). The science of leadership: A journey from survey research to field experimentation. *The Leadership Quarterly*, 101472. https://doi.org/10.1016/j.leaqua.2020.101472

Eklöf, M., & Hagberg, M. (2006). Are simple feedback interventions involving workplace data associated with better working environment and health? A cluster randomized controlled study among Swedish VDU workers. *Applied Ergonomics, 37*(2), 201–210. https://doi.org/10.1016/j.apergo.2005.04.003

Feltner, C., Peterson, K., Palmieri Weber, R., Cluff, L., Coker-Schwimmer, E., Viswanathan, M., & Lohr, K. N. (2016). The effectiveness of total worker health interventions: A systematic review for a national institutes of health pathways to prevention workshop. *Annals of Internal Medicine, 165*, 262. https://doi.org/10.7326/M16-0626

Ganster, D. C., & Rosen, C. C. (2013). Work stress and employee health: A multidisciplinary review. *Journal of Management, 39*(5), 1085–1122. https://doi.org/10.1177/0149206313475815

Goh, J., Pfeffer, J., Zenios, S. A., & Rajpal, S. (2015). Workplace stressors & health outcomes: Health policy for the workplace. *Behavioral Science & Policy, 1,* 43–52. https://doi.org/10.1353/bsp.2015.0001

Halbesleben, J. R. B., Neveu, J.-P., Paustian-Underdahl, S. C., & Westman, M. (2014). Getting to the "COR": Understanding the role of resources in conservation of resources theory. *Journal of Management, 40,* 1334–1364. http://doi.org/10.1177/0149206314527130

Hammer, L. B., Brady, J. M., & Perry, M. L. (2020). Training supervisors to support veterans at work: Effects on supervisor attitudes and employee sleep and stress. *Journal of Occupational and Organizational Psychology, 93*(2), 273–301. https://doi.org/10.1111/joop.12299

Hammer, L. B., Johnson, R. C., Crain, T. L., Bodner, T., Kossek, E. E., Davis, K. D., ... & Berkman, L. (2016). Intervention effects on safety compliance and citizenship behaviors: Evidence from the work, family, and health study. *Journal of Applied Psychology, 101*(2), 190. http://doi.org/10.1037/apl0000047

Hammer, L. B., Kossek, E. E., Anger, W. K., Bodner, T., & Zimmerman, K. L. (2011a). Clarifying work–family intervention processes: The roles of work–family conflict and family-supportive supervisor behaviors. *Journal of Applied Psychology, 96*(1), 134. https://doi.org/10.1037/a0020927

Hammer, L. B., Kossek, E. E., Zimmerman, K., & Daniels, R. (2007). Clarifying the construct of family-supportive supervisory behaviors (FSSB): A multilevel perspective. In P. L. Perrewé & D. C. Ganster (Eds.), *Research in occupational stress and well-being: Vol. 6. Exploring the work and nonwork interface* (pp. 165–204). Elsevier Science/JAI Press.

Hammer, L. B., Truxillo, D. M., Bodner, T., Pytlovany, A. C., & Richman, A. (2019b). Exploration of the impact of organisational context on a workplace safety and health intervention. *Work & Stress, 33*(2), 192–210. https://doi.org/10.1080/02678373.2018.1496159

Hammer, L. B., Truxillo, D. M., Bodner, T., Rineer, J., Pytlovany, A. C., & Richman, A. (2015). Effects of a workplace intervention targeting psychosocial risk factors on safety and health outcomes. *BioMed Research International.* https://doi.org/10.1155/2015/836967

Hammer, L. B., Wan, W. H., Brockwood, K. J., Bodner, T., & Mohr, C. D. (2019). Supervisor support training effects on veteran health and work outcomes in the civilian workplace. *Journal of Applied Psychology, 104* (1), 52. https://psycnet.apa.org/doi/10.1037/apl0000354

Hobfoll, S. E. (1989). Conservation of resources: A new attempt at conceptualizing stress. *American Psychologist, 44*(3), 513.

Hornung, S., Rousseau, D. M., & Glaser, J. (2008). Creating flexible work arrangements through idiosyncratic deals. *Journal of Applied Psychology, 93*(3), 655. https://doi.org/10.1037/0021-9010.93.3.655

Hurtado, D. A., Okechukwu, C. A., Buxton, O. M., Hammer, L., Hanson, G. C., Moen, P., Klein, L. C., & Berkman, L. F. (2016). Effects on cigarette consumption of a work–family supportive organisational intervention: 6-month results from the work, family and health network study. *Journal of Epidemiol Community Health, 70*(12), 1155–1161. http://doi.org/10.1136/jech-2015-206953

Inceoglu, I., Thomas, G., Chu, C., Plans, D., & Gerbasi, A. (2018). Leadership behavior and employee well-being: An integrated review and a future research agenda. *The Leadership Quarterly, 29*(1), 179–202. https://doi.org/10.1016/j.leaqua.2017.12.006

Kajiki, S., Izumi, H., Hayashida, K., Kusumoto, A., Nagata, T., & Mori, K. (2017). A randomized controlled trial of the effect of participatory ergonomic low back pain training on workplace improvement. *Journal of Occupational Health*, 16-0244. https://doi.org/10.1539/joh .16-0244-OA

Karlqvist, L., & Gard, G. (2013). Health-promoting educational interventions: A one-year follow-up study. *Scandinavian Journal of Public Health, 41*(1), 32–42. https://doi.org/10.1177/1403494812467504

Katz, D., & Kahn, R. L. (1978). *The social psychology of organizations* (Vol. 2). Wiley.

Kawakami, N., Kobayashi, Y., Takao, S., & Tsutsumi, A. (2005). Effects of web-based supervisor training on supervisor support and psychological distress among workers: A randomized controlled trial. *Preventive Medicine, 41*(2), 471–478. https://doi.org/10.1016/j.ypmed.2005.01 .001

Kawakami, N., Takao, S., Kobayashi, Y., & Tsutsumi, A. (2006). Effects of web-based supervisor training on job stressors and psychological distress among workers: A workplace-based randomized controlled trial. *Journal of Occupational Health, 48*(1), 28–34. https://doi.org/10.1539/ joh.48.28

Kelly, E. L., Moen, P., Oakes, J. M., Fan, W., Okechukwu, C., Davis, K. D., Hammer, L. B., Kossek, E. E., King, R. B., Hanson, G. C., Mierzwa, F., & Casper, L. M. (2014). Changing work and work–family conflict: Evidence from the work, family, and health network. *American*

Sociological Review, 79(3), 485–516. https://doi.org/10.1177/0003122414531435

Kelloway, E. K., & Barling, J. (2010). Leadership development as an intervention in occupational health psychology. *Work & Stress*, 24, 260–279. https://doi.org/10.1080/02678373.2010.518441

Ketelaar, S. M., Schaafsma, F. G., Geldof, M. F., Kraaijeveld, R. A., Boot, C. R. L., Shaw, W. S., Bültmann, U., & Anema, J. R. (2017). Implementation of the participatory approach for supervisors to increase self-efficacy in addressing risk of sick leave of employees: Results of a cluster-randomized controlled trial. *Journal of Occupational Rehabilitation*, 27(2), 247–257. https://doi.org/10.1007/s10926-016-9652-3

Kossek, E. E., Thompson, R. J., Lawson, K. M., Bodner, T., Perrigino, M. B., Hammer, L. B., Buxton, O. M., Almeida, D. M., Wipfli, B., Berkman, L. F., & Bray, J. W. (2019). Caring for the elderly at work and home: Can a randomized organizational intervention improve psychological health? *Journal of Occupational Health Psychology*, 24(1), 36–54. https://doi.org/10.1037/ocp0000104

Lacerenza, C. N., Reyes, D. L., Marlow, S. L., Joseph, D. L., & Salas, E. (2017, July 27). Leadership training design, delivery, and implementation: A meta-analysis. *Journal of Applied Psychology*. Advance online publication. http://doi.org/10.1037/apl0000241

LaMontagne, A. D., Keegel, T., Louie, A. M., Ostry, A., & Landsbergis, P. A. (2007). A systematic review of the job-stress intervention evaluation literature, 1990–2005. *International Journal of Occupational and Environmental Health*, 13(3), 268–280. https://doi.org/10.1179/oeh.2007.13.3.268?

Lesener, T., Gusy, B., Jochmann, A., & Wolter, C. (2020). The drivers of work engagement: A meta-analytic review of longitudinal evidence. *Work & Stress*, 34(3), 259–278. https://doi.org/10.1080/02678373.2019.1686440

Linton, S. J., Boersma, K., Traczyk, M., Shaw, W., & Nicholas, M. (2016). Early workplace communication and problem solving to prevent back disability: Results of a randomized controlled trial among high-risk workers and their supervisors. *Journal of Occupational Rehabilitation*, 26(2), 150–159. https://doi.org/10.1007/s10926-015-9596-z

Litwiller, B., Snyder, L. A., Taylor, W. D., & Steele, L. M. (2017). The relationship between sleep and work: A meta-analysis. *Journal of Applied Psychology*, 102(4), 682. https://doi.org/10.1037/apl0000169

Milligan-Saville, J. S., Tan, L., Gayed, A., Barnes, C., Madan, I., Dobson, M., Bryant, R. A., Christensen, H., Mykletun, A., & Harvey, S. B.

(2017). Workplace mental health training for managers and its effect on sick leave in employees: A cluster randomised controlled trial. *The Lancet Psychiatry*, *4*(11), 850–858. https://doi.org/10.1016/S2215-0366(17)30372-3

Moen, P., Kelly, E. L., Fan, W., Lee, S. R., Almeida, D., Kossek, E. E., & Buxton, O. M. (2016). Does a flexibility/support organizational initiative improve high-tech employees' well-being? Evidence from the work, family, and health network. *American Sociological Review*, *81*(1), 134–164. https://doi.org/10.1177/0003122415622391

Morken, T., Moen, B., Riise, T., Hauge, S. H. V., Holien, S., Langedrag, A., Olson, H.-O., Pedersen, S., Saue, I. L. L., Seljebø, G. M., & Thoppil, V. (2002). Effects of a training program to improve musculoskeletal health among industrial workers – effects of supervisor's role in the intervention. *International Journal of Industrial Ergonomics*, *30*(2), 115–127. https://doi.org/10.1016/S0169-8141(02)00090-2

Mullen, J. E., & Kelloway, E. K. (2009). Safety leadership: A longitudinal study of the effects of transformational leadership on safety outcomes. *Journal of Occupational and Organizational Psychology*, *82*(2), 253–272. https://doi.org/10.1348/096317908X325313

National Safety Council. (2020, February 20). *Work injury costs*. https://injuryfacts.nsc.org/work/costs/work-injury-costs/

Olson, R., Crain, T. L., Bodner, T. E., King, R., Hammer, L. B., Klein, L. C., Erickson, L., Moen, P., Berkman, L. F., & Buxton, O. M. (2015). A workplace intervention improves sleep: Results from the randomized controlled Work, Family, and Health Study. *Sleep Health*, *1*(1), 55–65. https://doi.org/10.1016/j.sleh.2014.11.003

Schill, A. L., & Chosewood, L. C. (2013). *The NIOSH total worker health™ program: An overview*. https://doi.org/10.1097/JOM.0000000000000037

Schnall, P. L., Dobson, M., & Rosskam, E. (2009). *Unhealthy work: Causes, consequences, cures*. Baywood Pub. Co.

Selye, H. (1946). The general adaptation syndrome and the diseases of adaptation. *The Journal of Clinical Endocrinology*, *6*(2), 117–230. https://doi.org/10.1210/jcem-6-2-117

Semmer, N. K. (2007). *Recognition and respect (or lack thereof) as predictors of occupational health and well-being*. Paper presentation at World Health Organization, Geneva.

Shaw, W. S., Robertson, M. M., McLellan, R. K., Verma, S., & Pransky, G. (2006). A controlled case study of supervisor training to optimize response to injury in the food processing industry. *Work*, *26*(2), 107–114. https://doi.org/1051-9815/06/517.00

Smith, T. D., Hughes, K., DeJoy, D. M., & Dyal, M. A. (2018). Assessment of relationships between work stress, work–family conflict, burnout and firefighter safety behavior outcomes. *Safety Science, 103*, 287–292.

Stansfeld, S. A., Kerry, S., Chandola, T., Russell, J., Berney, L., Hounsome, N., Lanz, D., Costelloe, C., Smuk, M., & Bhui, K. (2015). Pilot study of a cluster randomised trial of a guided e-learning health promotion intervention for managers based on management standards for the improvement of employee well-being and reduction of sickness absence: GEM Study. *BMJ Open, 5*(10). https://doi.org/10.1136/bmjopen-2015-007981

Takao, S., Tsutsumi, A., Nishiuchi, K., Mineyama, S., & Kawakami, N. (2006). Effects of the job stress education for supervisors on psychological distress and job performance among their immediate subordinates: A supervisor-based randomized controlled trial. *Journal of Occupational Health, 48*(6), 494–503. https://doi.org/10.1539/joh.48.494

Tamers, S., Chosewood, L., Childress, A., Hudson, H., Nigam, J., & Chang, C.-C. (2019). Total Worker Health® 2014–2018: The novel approach to worker safety, health, and well-being evolves. *International Journal of Environmental Research and Public Health, 16*, 321. https://doi.org/10.3390/ijerph16030321

Van Knippenberg, B., & Sitkin, S. B. (2013). A critical assessment of charismatic–transformational leadership research: Back to the drawing board? *Academy of Management Annals, 7*, 1–60.

Warr, P. B. (2011). *Work, happiness, and unhappiness*. Taylor & Francis.

Zohar, D. (2002). Modifying supervisory practices to improve subunit safety: A leadership-based intervention model. *Journal of Applied Psychology, 87*(1), 156. https://doi.org/10.1037//0021-9010.87.1.156

Zohar, D., & Polachek, T. (2014). Discourse-based intervention for modifying supervisory communication as leverage for safety climate and performance improvement: A randomized field study. *Journal of Applied Psychology, 99*(1), 113. https://doi.org/10.1037/a0034096

Zwetsloot, G. I., Van Scheppingen, A. R., Bos, E. H., Dijkman, A., & Starren, A. (2013). The core values that support health, safety, and well-being at work. *Safety and Health at Work, 4*(4), 187–196. https://doi.org/10.1016/j.shaw.2013.10.001

13 | Effective Employee-Targeted Stress and Well-Being Interventions

KIMBERLY E. O'BRIEN AND TERRY A. BEEHR

Employee health is a concern for both financial and moral reasons. In 2020, US employers spent an average of $21,342 on annual health insurance premiums per employee (KFF et al., 2020). Likewise, workplace accidents (largely preventable) resulted in direct and indirect costs (e.g., legal, investigation, replacement, productivity) of $151 billion in 2016 (OSHA, 2018). Employee wellness also has less visible costs, such as cognitive withdrawal and mood disturbance. Depression, for example, is responsible for 67% of global disability and may be tied to workplace conditions. Because of these costs, both tangible and intangible, employers have sought interventions to increase worker well-being. In this chapter, we review job stress interventions directly involving employees that are intended to prevent or remedy their health and well-being problems. These are to be distinguished from interventions targeting employees' managers, which are the subject of Chapter 12.

The earliest worksite health interventions have been traced to on-site gyms for management and executive employees shortly after World War II (Sparling, 2010). Now, approximately 90% of US workplaces with at least 50 employees have some form of health promotion program (Aldana et al., 2005). Workplace health interventions are quite varied in terms of audience (e.g., all employees versus at-risk employees, or certain industries), format (e.g., length), delivery (e.g., face to face, online), and goal (e.g., weight loss, stress management). Some workplace interventions even target the worker's family (Goetzel et al., 2014). The specific goal and breadth of these interventions also vary, ranging from narrow programs (e.g., stress resilience) to comprehensive workplace health promotion programs focused on general lifestyle as it relates to premature death and disability.

The goal of the current chapter is to review the research on the effectiveness of stress and well-being interventions. Program evaluation, in general, can be complicated due to conceptual ambiguities.

For example, when a program has multiple goals (e.g., stress reduction and smoking cessation), or multiple delivery formats (e.g., some volunteers attend weight management meetings, whereas all employees are eligible for a bonus if they complete bloodwork), it becomes difficult to identify specific interventions or program components that are effective. Herein, we first describe specific characteristics of effective interventions as best as possible and best practices when developing interventions. Next, we review empirically supported job stress interventions. Finally, we conclude with practical concerns.

Characteristics of Effective Interventions

Outcome Goals Drive Evaluations of Effectiveness

One measure of effectiveness is return on investment (ROI). Depending on metrics and program characteristics, these interventions may elicit a positive ROI. Many corporate benefits, such as health insurance, do not return an obvious fiscal gain and are instead offered because of corporate social responsibility or common labor market practices that improve organizational attractiveness to employees and job applicants. That said, a large assessment of workplace health programs shows generally positive ROI with a mean weighted ROI of 1.38–1.80. In other words, for each dollar spent on comprehensive workplace health promotion programs, at least $1.38 was received back due to reduced turnover and other costs (Baxter et al., 2015). While the cost of more narrow stress resilience programs is likely much lower than general workplace health promotion, the returns would likely be lower as well, such that the ROI might be less visible. In addition, as a form of reciprocity, employees who are appreciative of their employer's help with stress may work harder or perform extra helping behaviors for the organization, and it is difficult to know if these behaviors are attributable to the stress program.

That said, effectiveness of wellness programs is infrequently measured in terms of ROI, due to the excessive cost, time, and expertise (e.g., measurement and statistics, health, economics, program evaluation skills are needed) required to make these calculations. Program evaluation is difficult in general, and in this case, many well-being interventions target more than one goal (e.g., to decrease task errors and increase safety) or use multiple methods (e.g., survey feedback followed by stress management training), complicating and confounding attempts to measure effectiveness and compare one program with another. In these settings, even the best study design cannot prevent attrition from the study or workplace, low power due to the number of employees available, data with very low variance, or practical constraints prohibiting random assignment in a field setting.

ROI is not only difficult to measure but is also an overly restrictive way of considering an intervention's value. Not all benefits will be dollar for dollar. An effective program that has a negative ROI might be useful, for example, if it improves perceptions of corporate social responsibility, or just because management or owners care about the health of their employees. Previous research has found that the most common goals include

improvements in the health and well-being of workers; cost savings through appropriate use of health care services; and enhanced individual and business performance metrics. Other key human capital outcomes may include improved quality of life; a more engaged and motivated workforce; increased worker retention and attraction; improved safety performance; improved manufacturing reliability; and a healthier company culture. (Goetzel et al., 2014)

Consequently, when we consider the effectiveness of a well-being intervention, we consider success in the broader sense.

Primary Prevention Is Most Effective

Interventions are often described from a timing perspective as primary, secondary, or tertiary (LaMontagne et al., 2007). Primary prevention is oriented toward reducing hazards and supporting a healthy work environment or by improving individuals' coping skills before they have suffered from stress. These interventions prevent problems before they occur by including broad groups of employees instead of targeting those who already have a health concern. Primary interventions might attempt to improve social support or identify the source of potential workplace stressor. Interventions that target the job (e.g., job control, job demands) would usually be considered primary prevention because not all workers on that job have had stress reactions yet. We note, however, exhortations to remove job stressors can be of limited value due to practical complications, and therefore employees should also receive training in coping or stress management to achieve the best prevention (Semmer, 2003).

Secondary prevention includes management of well-being decrements (e.g., depressed mood) and improving health behavior adherence after employees have had stress-related problems. This includes training and education on stress management. Tertiary interventions are similar to secondary interventions, but a distinguishing factor is how chronic the employees' problems, like depression or hypertension, have become. They involve harm mitigation, recovery, and rehabilitation, often conducted through an employee assistance program (EAP). EAPs are worksite programs designed to help workplaces address productivity issues and help employees resolve personal problems (e.g., legal, financial, substance use; Cooper & Cartwright, 1994). These are typically delivered by external agencies. Such tertiary interventions are usually effective for alleviating individual employee's problems, but they often appear to provide negative ROI and few visible organization-level benefits.

The efficacy of prevention over treatment is echoed in a very large study of 2 million employees across 18 years (Edington, 2001). In this study, the average healthcare cost increased with each risk factor gained (e.g., obesity, smoking; $350), whereas the benefit when eliminating a risk factor was less (only $150). In other words, fixing problems was less profitable than preventing them in the first place, and programs that target prevention will therefore have better ROI. In general, behavioral medicine shows that prevention is more efficient than rehabilitation and cures.

Training "Dose"

Interventions have a training component in most cases. Consequently, we can consider the dose of training, reflected in terms of quantity (e.g., length, intensity) and quality (e.g., fidelity) of the training session(s). Training outcomes are reflected in a dose–response relationship, such that better training programs have better outcomes (Goetzel et al., 2014). However, the wide variance in intervention formats makes research difficult, as training characteristics tend not to be methodically manipulated, or even measured, making it difficult to separate and investigate characteristics such as management support or the employee's prior experience in wellness programs. With that said, employee-targeted interventions often take the form of specific types of training that could have different effects (e.g., safety, stress management, communication, health behaviors). Thus, well-being interventions that adhere to the guidelines for effective training in general are more likely to be successful.

Healthy People, a US initiative to provide science-based decade-long objectives for improving health, provides a set of training guidelines for comprehensive workplace health promotion programs. These include health education, supportive social and physical environments, integration of the worksite program into organizational infrastructure, links between health promotion and related programs (e.g., EAPs), and health screenings with follow-up. However, even more narrow wellness programs (e.g., tailored to job stress) benefit from incorporating these qualities when possible, adapting screenings to match employee needs to program goals.

In another perspective, O'Donnell (1997) emphasizes the sustainability of programs and suggests ten principles, including (1) linking of program to business objectives; (2) executive management support; (3) multiyear strategic planning; (4) employee input when developing goals and objectives; (5) a wide variety of program offerings; (6) effective targeting of high-risk individuals; (7) incentives to motivate employees to participate in the program, leading to high participation rates; (8) program accessibility; (9) effective communications; and (10) evaluation of effectiveness.

Effective Intervention Practices

The characteristics of effective trainings described above are rather idealistic. In many conditions, wellness interventions may have limited resources, and the goals and components listed to this point are not all appropriate given organizational resources. That said, small interventions may still have a small benefit when adhering to best practices. Poorly planned interventions waste employee time and management resources. We adapt a training perspective here to describe important considerations that have been shown to be useful in health promotion and job stress trainings (e.g., Driskell et al., 2001). Readers are referred to Noe (2020) for a comprehensive, empirically supported, readable guide to training implementation.

Diagnosis or Needs Assessment

Delivering training to employees who will never use the training or already have those skills wastes their time and organizational resources. These employees may lose productivity due to time spent in the inappropriate training, experience frustration and decreased morale, and still have skill deficits due to not receiving training that they actually need. Most (73%) training programs skip a needs assessment and do not bother to target the appropriate employees or establish what trainings are already provided (Saari et al., 1988) and may therefore overlap with existing training or otherwise target inappropriate goals.

Efficient training must target the gap between what employees have and what employees need, and a simple needs assessment can be used to measure employee skill levels relative to skills required. A Shortened Stress Evaluation Tool (ASSET; Cooper & Cartwright, 1994) is a self-report survey that can be used to measure job stress, identify those vulnerable, measure job attitudes and coping skills, and evaluate physical and psychological health. It also provides norms, allowing better assessment of where training is most needed. Carefully randomized and structured focused groups, representing a variety of employees, can also be useful. See Simpson et al. (2017) for more information on diagnosing organizational wellness problems.

Needs assessment should also consider management and executive priorities. Buy-in from upper levels of the organization provides boosters over time for the trained employees, supporting long-term outcomes, and ensures better resources for the intervention delivery.

Objectives

The objective of the training should be distilled from the needs assessment by identifying the gap between the existing employee competencies, relative to what is needed. For example, when interpersonal conflict is a central complaint, conflict negotiation or communication interventions would be more beneficial than a general stress management workshop. Conversely, if work overload is a problem, then stress management, time management, job crafting, or empowerment might be a better objective. In sum, interventions should be designed specifically to address the gap identified in the diagnosis. Specific, measurable goals should be established based on the objectives (e.g., a significant decrease in reported job stress or an increase in healthy coping behaviors). Interventions should be designed to improve these specific metrics.

Design

In-house or external training experts can design an intervention around the program objective, considering the costs and benefits of different training features. The goal is the best transfer of training (ensuring that the skills trained are able to be applied later to relevant tasks and situations on the job) given available resources (see Baldwin & Ford, 1988, for more detail). For example, because training dose is such an important predictor of effectiveness, a spaced (rather than massed) intervention might be preferable. However, if resources are unavailable, then a well-designed massed intervention will likely be more effective than limited spaced delivery. Design features should also reflect employee characteristics (e.g., how they prefer to learn) and the work environment (e.g., empowerment interventions will not be successful if the managers do not allow autonomy). Training transfer is best when the intervention includes feedback, teaches general principles about why something is done (as opposed to only how to do it, so that employees know when to apply their new skills), features identical elements (e.g., a role play is more effective when acted out by two people, rather than imagined), provides overlearning to achieve automaticity, and considers the best sequencing (e.g., part versus whole instruction, spaced versus massed delivery). Delivery methods, such as online tutorial, lecture, role play, or on-the-job training, should be considered in terms of what will provide the best transfer of training (via identical elements, overlearning, etc.) given the employee learning style and workplace environment.

Delivery

After the intervention is designed to provide best transfer of training, it is delivered by an expert. Within the field of health and wellness, there may be legal considerations regarding who can deliver the training. Some benign online trainings exist and can be administered without hiring a consultant; however, the most effective interventions are be delivered by an experienced consultant or licensed health professional.

Evaluation

The final step is to evaluate the effectiveness of the program, although preparation, planning, and pretests for the evaluation need to be performed at the beginning. During the "objectives" step of the intervention design, metrics should be chosen by which to evaluate the program. By measuring the amount that employees learned from the training, or how much they liked it, intervention personnel can quickly assess if the training was effective at a superficial level. Later on, health evaluations closely tied to the objectives may be appropriate. Likewise, behaviors (e.g., number of views on a breathing app provided in a stress management workshop) can be applicable, partly to understand dosage. Whatever the evaluation chosen, it should be closely tied to the objective and solicit feedback from a diverse group of employees.

Existing Well-Being Interventions

Moving away from ideal intervention components, this section describes existing evidence-based workplace interventions that aim to help individual employees reduce any harmful effects of their own workplace stress experiences. Specifically, we review programs and interventions with recent, rigorous, peer-reviewed research that found them to be successful for at least some stress-relief purposes (e.g., Bostock et al., 2019; Ebert et al., 2018; Foa et al., 2018; McGonagle et al., 2020; Sianoja et al., 2018). There are other treatments available, but we did not find them relevant for the chapter using these criteria. These are psychological rather than comprehensive or medical interventions and can be adapted for most workplace situations and employees. Most are likely to be best applied by professionals who have specialized training, and a few are designed in ways that could be used to approximate self-help programs (e.g., those at least partially led by recorded programming).

Mindfulness

Mindfulness is a relatively recent approach to treating occupational stress, but it has seen rapidly increasing usage and research evaluation in recent years. It is now becoming one of the single most used and evaluated individual treatments for occupational stress. Mindfulness treatment does not have a very narrow and concrete definition but typically involves focusing on the present moment and recognizing one's internal states (e.g., thoughts, feelings, bodily sensations). Although it consists of a set of mental and physical activities that an employee can learn on their own with the help of freely available, often online, learning materials, it is probably more effectively learned from an expert professional mindfulness trainer. The mental activities involve concentration, awareness, calmness, and acceptance, and the physical activities can include types of breathing, relaxation, and, often implicitly, posture. Body scans are often a part of the instruction, involving concentrating on parts of the body (e.g., from head to toe) in order to become more cognitively aware of how each part of the body feels at the present moment (e.g., Crain et al., 2017; Krick & Felfe, 2020).

The historical background of mindfulness meditation comes from Asia and includes Buddhism (especially Zen) and yoga (especially breathing) meditation techniques (e.g., Slutsky et al., 2019). It seems to be widely useful for many types of employees, although there is at least some weak evidence that social or cultural norms of acceptance of this kind of treatment might influence how effective it is (Krick & Felfe, 2020). In employee treatments in the United States, however, the Eastern elements are usually deemphasized, and the interventions typically mix in elements of progressive relaxation (Benson & Klipper, 1975) and cognitive-behavioral therapy (e.g., Cherkin et al., 2016) from Western psychology. A common theme when used for occupational stress is to have employees recall past stressful situations that they handled poorly and to learn to accept and be at ease with their thoughts and feelings about them (e.g., self-forgiveness; Webb et al., 2013). They then learn how to reduce those aversive thoughts and feelings in the future by engaging in mindfulness meditation.

Forms of mindfulness training especially used in employment settings include mindfulness-based cognitive training (MBCT) and its offshoot, mindfulness-based stress reduction (MBSR; e.g., Crain et al., 2017; Slutsky et al., 2017; Smith et al., 2020). The object of the intervention is for the employees to learn mindfulness meditation techniques through a time-limited set of training sessions, but the training educates employees on how to continue their own use of mindfulness techniques indefinitely. The time involved in mindfulness training varies greatly. It is common to attend short weekly sessions for approximately six to eight weeks, often with one or two "retreat" sessions mixed in. Whereas the weekly sessions might range from one-half hour to two and one-half hours and can be on or off the worksite, the retreats are longer in duration (up to a full day) and held at a more remote off-site location. The retreats are sometimes in a setting evoking the historical roots of mindfulness meditation, such as Buddhist and/or Tibetan pictures, objects, tapestries, and so forth. The total time involved in many of the formal mindfulness meditation employee interventions is often about 35–40 hours, with longer sessions including more periods of silent meditation (e.g., Bostock et al., 2019; Crain et al., 2017), although very short single sessions may have some effectiveness (e.g., Slutsky et al., 2019).

The following describes example topics of mindfulness training sessions in a typical program (e.g., Crain et al., 2017): understanding what mindfulness is and what the objectives of the program are; learning kindness, compassion, and forgiveness; becoming more aware of pleasant, unpleasant, and neutral internal and external stimuli; learning how to respond to those stimuli with calmness and acceptance; dealing with interpersonal conflict; becoming aware of and dealing with negative emotions; and instruction in future practice by oneself. These topics are learned in separate sessions of a couple of hours each and reinforced with longer retreats. The content of the mindfulness training sessions are usually very experiential, although short lectures and one-on-one and/or group discussions are common forms of instruction during at least parts of the sessions.

In mindfulness training programs, the trainer may use a standard manual prepared by someone else for instructions to deliver the training. Technology has become part of some modern mindfulness training sessions, with video and audio instruction being very common (e.g., Crain et al., 2017). More unusual, however, are some approaches that incorporate the use of moderate amounts of biofeedback, usually with wearable devices (e.g., Bostock et al., 2019; Smith et al., 2020). Finally, people also can learn to become mindfulness trainers through train-the-trainer type of sessions, and having a qualified mindfulness trainer in-house might be useful for some organizations (e.g., Slutsky et al., 2017).

Psychotherapy and Counseling

Formal counseling or psychotherapy is also used for treating individuals experiencing occupational stress. We assume that most employees experiencing occupational stress do not have a clinically diagnosable psychological disorder, and so the use of psychotherapy in this case is normally for prevention and growth rather than for remediating or restoring damaged mental health. However, some wellness programs, and EAPs in particular, contract with local therapists to provide clinical mental health treatment. In the United States, even for the specific purpose of treating occupational stress, professionals who offer any treatment legally classified as psychotherapy are usually required to be licensed in their state. As noted above, principles and techniques used in mindfulness meditation can overlap with some forms of psychotherapy, especially cognitive-behavioral therapy approaches (e.g., Cherkin et al., 2016), or any approaches that emphasize physical and psychological calmness, cognitive thought, and sometimes mental imagery. When mindfulness training includes present-moment thinking about stressful work situations, being nonjudgmental about them and letting feelings about them go, it resembles some types of cognitive-behavioral therapy, especially exposure therapy.

Acceptance and commitment therapy (embracing uncomfortable internal states; e.g., Finnes et al., 2019; Lloyd et al., 2017; Wersebe, 2018) varies in length, from days of training to months. Homework and practice between sessions is important. Some of it strongly resembles mindfulness training, with acceptance of thoughts and situations being a part of it, but it is usually followed by some goal-setting and concrete action planning by the employee.

Exposure therapy, or stress inoculation, is used for treating occupational stress and is based on principles of learning to be calm rather than distressed while exposed to work demands. For example, in nursing, this might include communicating with a distressed family or a patient, or for law students may include speaking in front of a judge. Developed and used primarily for anxiety disorders, exposure therapy is most effective when employees' anxiety (rather than, for example, behavioral withdrawal or burnout) is their predominant stress response or drives the experience of other strains. Exposure therapy consists of specific techniques derived from cognitive-behavioral approaches, mainly including types of exposure (e.g., viewing images) to anxiety-arousing situations. Treatment can include cognitive reassessment of the situation and problem-solving with the goal of allowing the employee to have practiced working in stressful situations, circumventing the automatic stress responses that accompany these workplace events.

In terms of delivery format, some form of relaxation training (e.g., progressive muscle relaxation) is often used in conjunction with exposure therapies (or can be used independently) to develop a skill the employees can use to calm their bodies and minds while exposed to the stressors. Exposure therapy can occur on different time schedules, such as 10 or 12 weekly sessions of 40–60 minutes each, or the same number of sessions collapsed into two weeks (e.g., Bryant et al., 2019; Finnes et al., 2019; Foa et al., 2018). Spacing the sessions over a longer time period versus massing them into a shorter time may not matter in terms of effectiveness. The contents of the sessions can include education and skill-building (regarding thinking and relaxing), exposure by remembering and imagining the stressful work events, and sometimes homework and actual experience of the work situation. One study's results showed the effects on severe problems like PTSD may be weak, however (e.g., Foa et al., 2018) .

Mild Physical Activity

Structured strenuous aerobic or anaerobic physical exercise is often recommended for increasing physical strength, stamina, and general health that might help in stress resilience (e.g., Emerson et al., 2017), but not everyone will faithfully participate in that approach to exercise. Some encouragement and support are therefore needed for many employees. Programs can enhance the psychology of employees' exercise engagement, however, by offering multiple sessions focusing not on exercising itself but on how to get oneself and one's coworkers to exercise consistently (e.g., Pedersen et al., 2019). This creates an environment that encourages and is supportive of employee exercise, by providing sessions with information about the benefits of and how to exercise, sessions with reflection by one's self and with coworkers, and training in how to provide support for coworkers continuing to exercise.

In addition to strenuous exercise, milder but regular exercise is also an option that more people might be willing to try, and some forms of it can even be done while at work. Examples include engaging in more standing, walking, and moving around while doing everyday tasks.

One such form of exercise is walking during breaks at work. A 15-minute walk every day during an employee's lunch break can be beneficial and requires no particular training (e.g., Sianoja et al., 2018). Some add-on recommendations that may or may not be necessary are (1) to walk in a park or "green" area where natural surroundings might bring feelings of peace and satisfaction and (2) to avoid talking to others while walking, even when not walking alone. Talking, especially to coworkers, might become a source of stress if the topics are work-related problems, for example (e.g., Beehr et al., 2010). In addition to mild exercise during breaks, mild exercise while working is also possible. Some jobs inherently require mild-to-strong physical labor, but many modern jobs are sedentary, sometimes due to advanced technology helping reduce physical burdens. An example of technology that reverses this trend is the sit–stand desk, which makes it possible to do deskwork in a less sedentary manner. Office technology is usually designed to make it easier to accomplish most work while seated in a chair, but some office work can be done while standing or even engaging in small amounts of walking (e.g., talking on the telephone). Many office tasks can be accomplished while standing, if equipment is designed differently. Sit–stand desks are adjustable, so that an employee can use them from either a sitting or standing position. In addition to installing the adjustable equipment, a small amount of advice and training can be presented with these desks (e.g., to adjust them just right for the specific person, to arrange arm locations to avoid repetitive motion injuries, to vary standing and sitting periods, and to space out work breaks; e.g., Konradt et al., 2020).

In addition to employees' mild exercise while at work, they can also be encouraged to engage in such activity during their off-work time. A simple aid is to offer employees some activity trackers that give them feedback on how active versus sedentary their off-work behavior is. Feedback alone is likely to encourage employees to move around a little more, if they see such activity as a positive thing. The trackers can take the form of a wristband-mounted device, and employees can also set them to emit a reminder sound after a certain amount of nonactive time. In addition, programs can be offered with the device, such as online contact with a coach who can offer information and advice, goal-setting features, and group challenges with incentives (e.g., Lennefer et al., 2020).

Mild physical activity is more utilized when it is the default option. For example, keeping popular equipment (e.g., printers or coffee machines) in a centralized location can encourage walking at low cost. Reserving the closest parking for customers or guests can likewise increase physical activity. Informational interventions, such as providing maps to local parks for newcomers, or posting directions to the stairs near elevators, can help employees find or remember to use these options.

Coaching

Definitions of coaching can be ambiguous. Some other techniques include coaches as a small part of their program (e.g., Ebert et al., 2020; Lennefer, 2020), but some programs are primarily based on coaching. Coaches come from a variety of backgrounds, education, and training, and there are multiple coaching credentials and certifications. Historically, coaching tends to include some one-on-one interactions, maybe making it expensive, so that it is often used for "expensive" employees, like managers and professionals. It is not possible to fully and accurately describe coaching interventions in a way that would be accurate for all of them because they vary in goals and tools with the specific setting, job, and person. They are, however, usually client-centered and involve the use of self-regulation (e.g., Bandura, 1991) or related theories (e.g., selection, optimization, and compensation theory; Müller et al., 2016), with principles like developing and acting on action plans that incorporate the goals of the coachee.

One example, based on positive psychology, was coaching primary care physicians over a three-month period with meetings every two weeks (McGonagle et al., 2020). Because of schedule constraints of the physicians, the coaching meetings after the first one were conducted by telephone. Activities included assessing strengths, reflection and mindfulness, ways of thinking, identification of one's ideal self, and prework or homework between sessions, among others. Each physician's coaching experience could be different, using different activities or tools, because it is tailored to meet their needs. In a sense, many activities could be considered manualized, but the whole coaching experience was not. That is, interaction between the coach and coachee would determine which "manual" or tool was most appropriate for that particular coachee. Multiple coaches were used to coach the different physicians, and they met frequently to have discussions about how the project was going and to keep the coaching principles consistent across coaches.

A second example was of military personnel who were attending college, so that a common issue was balancing military jobs with student demands (Ebner et al., 2018). Coachees chose to work on specific topics that were most relevant to themselves, such as work–life balance, time management, or general academic challenges. There were four 2-hour sessions over an 8- to 10-week period. Coaches used manuals to lead the coachee to examine problem issues, set goals, and make plans for reaching them. Homework between sessions was part of the process. Each session focused on a specific topic, including setting goals for the future, fleshing out ways to reach the goals, including necessary intermediate steps, and evaluation of the degree of success in reaching intermediate steps. Some group contexts also were used so that coaches could learn from each other.

Other Occupational Stress Treatments

There are many treatments for occupational stress that are simply called stress treatments, and they include both narrower, single method approaches and eclectic approaches using multiple methods. Sometimes these "other" treatments were developed for a specific organization or set of employees, but they could also be tailored to other sites.

The methods can include relaxation and yoga- or mindfulness-like experiential methods, self-help methods that rely on self-regulation principles like coaching does, off-shoots of cognitive-behavior therapy principles, job crafting, and time management. For example, resilience training can train employees to anticipate stressors and prepare for them in advance as well as to treat stress issues after they arise. This has been done in group sessions totaling 20 hours a few times per week for two months that included activities like work-value assessment, role play, case studies, chart presentations, positive affirmations, and homework assignments with a goal of enabling the employees to fend off the ill effects of work stressors by themselves (e.g., Chitra & Karunanidhi, 2018).

In contrast to such general treatments for occupational stress, some other treatments are very narrow and specific. For example, nonviolent communication training was developed to enhance employee skills in acting calmly, rationally, and effectively in tense situations of potential conflict (Wacker & Dziobek, 2018). The program was administered in groups and lasted three full days. It included education and practice through role play, verbal and nonverbal communication training, and listening skills. Another example of a specific treatment is job redesign, that is, changing the job's tasks, the way of doing tasks, the order of tasks, or the control of these tasks' characteristics. One program focused on giving groups of employees training on some new tasks while also giving them more control over the tasks. The sessions consisted of a two-day workshop and follow-up meetings two weeks later that could help clarify and solve problems, and weekly discussions could continue as needed (Holman & Axtell, 2016).

Finally, we note that many types of occupational stress treatments and training have steadily become more technology-based (and we suspect the COVID-19 pandemic might have strengthened that trend). Several of the occupational stress treatments described above use technology for communication, education, or skill-practice delivery (e.g., Crain et al., 2017; Konradt et al., 2020). One intervention lasted several weeks with multiple e-sessions per week (Ebert et al., 2018). Heavily supported by internet-based technology, it used 11 modules (e.g., time management, detaching from work, nutrition, and exercise) available to choose from, for use in the sessions, with written feedback from an e-coach (following manualized instructions) after each session. It also used texts and exercises that included interactive audio and video.

Accessing Wellness Interventions

There are many more treatments available commercially as well as some that can be accessed free on online. Mindfulness training is readily available from many consulting sources. Basic do-it-yourself principles and practices can be obtained through books and internet searches, but the research we found showed that successful treatments have usually been led by professional trainers. Like mindfulness training, the acceptance and commitment therapy and exposure therapy techniques can use manuals or take the form of self-help books or recordings, although more so for acceptance and commitment than exposure therapies, which may require a licensed professional. Similarly, coaching tends to be professionally led and individualized for each coachee, but there are many standardized techniques or tools to choose from when the coachee's situation and goals become understood. Some are commercially available, and others are freely available online. Perhaps the easiest and least expensive to enact would be mild physical activity, in which walking maps could be printed from the internet or group leaders could encourage walking microbreaks.

Concluding Thoughts

In this chapter, we reviewed promising job stress interventions, describing the effectiveness of workplace wellness programs, characteristics that drive effectiveness, and best practices. We did neglect the topic of employee participation and incentivization because the recommendations are less clear there. Training is certainly least effective when it is not administered, but requiring participation or overly incentivizing participation can cause frustration or interfere with other organizational goals. While well-intentioned and competent wellness interventions following a satisfactory needs assessment are generally well received, forced participation in these programs has been a source of litigation. Employees might feel that the organization is being inappropriately invasive, and insensitive solicitation of employees into, say, a weight loss program are obviously unwelcome. Privacy, while not protected by HIPAA except for healthcare professions, can still be a source of threats of legal action. Without the oversight of an experienced consultant, voluntary programs with moderate incentives are likely to be well received. Overall, wellness programs are supported for financial, health, and moral reasons, but steps should be taken to maintain this goodwill created by these programs.

References

Aldana, S. G., Merrill, R. M., Price, K., Hardy, A., & Hager, R. (2005). Financial impact of a comprehensive multisite workplace health promotion program. *Preventive Medicine*, *40*(2), 131–137.

Baldwin, T. T., & Ford, J. K. (1988). Transfer of training: A review and directions for future research. *Personnel Psychology*, *41*(1), 63–105.

Bandura, A. (1991). Social cognitive theory of self-regulation. *Organizational Behavior and Human Decision Processes*, 50(2), 248–287.

Baxter, S., Campbell, S., Sanderson, K., Cazaly, C., Venn, A., Owen, C., & Palmer, A. J. (2015). Development of the Workplace Health Savings Calculator: A practical tool to measure economic impact from reduced absenteeism and staff turnover in workplace health promotion. *BMC Research Notes*, 8(1), 457–469.

Beehr, T. A., Bowling, N. A., & Bennett, M. M. (2010). Occupational stress and failures of social support: When helping hurts. *Journal of Occupational Health Psychology*, 15(1), 45–59.

Benson, H., & Klipper, M. Z. (1975). *The relaxation response* (pp. 1–158). Morrow.

Bostock, S., Crosswell, A. D., Prather, A. A., & Steptoe, A. (2019). Mindfulness on-the-go: Effects of a mindfulness meditation app on work stress and well-being. *Journal of Occupational Health Psychology*, 24(1), 127–138.

Bryant, R. A., Kenny, L., Rawson, N., Cahill, C., Joscelyne, A., Garber, B., Tockar, J., Dawson, K., & Nickerson, A. (2019). Efficacy of exposure-based cognitive behavior therapy for post-traumatic stress disorder in emergency service personnel: A randomised clinical trial. *Psychological Medicine*, 49(9), 1565–1573.

Cherkin, D. C., Sherman, K. J., Balderson, B. H., Cook, A. J., Anderson, M. L., Hawkes, R. J., Hansen, K. E., & Turner, J. A. (2016). Effect of mindfulness-based stress reduction vs cognitive behavioral therapy or usual care on back pain and functional limitations in adults with chronic low back pain: A randomized clinical trial. *Journal of the American Medical Association*, 315(12), 1240–1249.

Chitra, T., & Karunanidhi, S. (2018). The impact of resilience training on occupational stress, resilience, job satisfaction, and psychological well-being of female police officers. *Journal of Police and Criminal Psychology*, 36(8), 1–16.

Cooper, C. L., & Cartwright, S. (1994). Healthy mind; healthy organiza-tion – a proactive approach to occupational stress. *Human Relations*, 47(4), 455–471.

Crain, T. L., Schonert-Reichl, K. A., & Roeser, R. W. (2017). Cultivating teacher mindfulness: Effects of a randomized controlled trial on work, home, and sleep outcomes. *Journal of Occupational Health Psychology*, 22(2), 138–152.

Driskell, J. E., Johnston, J. H., & Salas, E. (2001). Does stress training generalize to novel settings? *Human Factors*, 43(1), 99–110.

Ebert, D. D., Kählke, F., Buntrock, C., Berking, M., Smit, F., Heber, E., Baumeister, H., Funk, B., Riper, H., & Lehr, D. (2018). A health economic outcome evaluation of an internet-based mobile-supported stress management intervention for employees. *Scandinavian Journal of Work, Environment & Health, 44*(2), 171–182.

Ebner, K., Schulte, E. M., Soucek, R., & Kauffeld, S. (2018). Coaching as stress-management intervention: The mediating role of self-efficacy in a framework of self-management and coping. *International Journal of Stress Management, 25*(3), 209–233.

Edington, D. W. (2001). Emerging research: A view from one research center. *American Journal of Health Promotion, 15*(5), 341–349.

Emerson, N. D., Merrill, D. A., Shedd, K., Bilder, R. M., & Siddarth, P. (2017). Effects of an employee exercise programme on mental health. *Occupational Medicine, 67*(2), 128–134.

Finnes, A., Ghaderi, A., Dahl, J., Nager, A., & Enebrink, P. (2019). Randomized controlled trial of acceptance and commitment therapy and a workplace intervention for sickness absence due to mental disorders. *Journal of Occupational Health Psychology, 24*(1), 198–212.

Foa, E. B., McLean, C. P., Zang, Y., Rosenfield, D., Yadin, E., Yarvis, J. S., Mintz, J., Young-McCaughan, S., Borah, E. V., Dondanville, K. A., Fina, B. A., Hall-Clark, B. N., Lichner, T., Litz, B. T., Roache, J., Wright, E. C., Peterson, A. L., & STRONG STAR Consortium. (2018). Effect of prolonged exposure therapy delivered over 2 weeks vs 8 weeks vs present-centered therapy on PTSD symptom severity in military personnel: A randomized clinical trial. *Journal of the American Medical Association, 319*(4), 354–364.

Goetzel, R. Z., Henke, R. M., Tabrizi, M., Pelletier, K. R., Loeppke, R., Ballard, D. W., Grossmeier, J., Anderson, D. R., Yach, D., Kelly, R. K., McCalister, T., Serxner, S., Selecky, C., Shallenberger, L. G., Fries, J. F., Baase, C., Isaac, F, Crighton, K. A., Wald, P., . . . Metz, R. D. (2014). Do workplace health promotion (wellness) programs work? *Journal of Occupational and Environmental Medicine, 56*(9), 927–934.

Holman, D., & Axtell, C. (2016). Can job redesign interventions influence a broad range of employee outcomes by changing multiple job characteristics? A quasi-experimental study. *Journal of Occupational Health Psychology, 21*(3), 284–295.

KFF. (2020). *2020 employer health benefits survey.* www.kff.org/health-costs/report/2020-employer-health-benefits-survey/

Konradt, U., Heblich, F., Krys, S., Garbers, Y., & Otte, K. P. (2020). Beneficial, adverse, and spiraling health-promotion effects: Evidence from a longitudinal randomized controlled trial of working at sit–stand desks. *Journal of Occupational Health Psychology, 25*(1), 68–81.

Krick, A., & Felfe, J. (2020). Who benefits from mindfulness? The moderating role of personality and social norms for the effectiveness on psychological and physiological outcomes among police officers. *Journal of Occupational Health Psychology, 25*(2), 99–112.

LaMontagne, A. D., Keegel, T., Louie, A. M., Ostry, A., & Landsbergis, P. A. (2007). A systematic review of the job-stress intervention evaluation literature, 1990–2005. *International Journal of Occupational and Environmental Health, 13*(3), 268–280.

Lennefer, T., Lopper, E., Wiedemann, A. U., Hess, U., & Hoppe, A. (2020). Improving employees' work-related well-being and physical health through a technology-based physical activity intervention: A randomized intervention-control group study. *Journal of Occupational Health Psychology, 25*(2), 143–158.

Lloyd, J., Bond, F. W., & Flaxman, P. E. (2017). Work-related self-efficacy as a moderator of the impact of a worksite stress management training intervention: Intrinsic work motivation as a higher order condition of effect. *Journal of Occupational Health Psychology, 22*(1), 115–127.

McGonagle, A. K., Schwab, L., Yahanda, N., Duskey, H., Gertz, N., Prior, L., Roy, M., & Kriegel, G. (2020). Coaching for primary care physician well-being: A randomized trial and follow-up analysis. *Journal of Occupational Health Psychology, 25*(5), 297–314.

Müller, A., Heiden, B., Herbig, B., Poppe, F., & Angerer, P. (2016). Improving well-being at work: A randomized controlled intervention based on selection, optimization, and compensation. *Journal of Occupational Health Psychology, 21*(2), 169–181.

Noe, R. (2020). *Employee training and development* (8th ed.). McGraw Hill.

O'Donnell, M. P. (1997). *Characteristics of the best workplace health promotion programs.* Wellness Management: Newsletter of the National Wellness Association, 3–4.

OSHA. (2018). *Business Case for Safety and Health.* United States Department of Labor. www.osha.gov/businesscase#:~:text=The%20National%20Safety%20Council%20estimated,individuals%20%24151%20billion%20in%202016

Pedersen, C., Halvari, H., & Olafsen, A. H. (2019). Worksite physical activity intervention and somatic symptoms burden: The role of coworker support for basic psychological needs and autonomous motivation. *Journal of Occupational Health Psychology, 24*(1), 55–65.

Saari, L. M., Johnson, T. R., McLaughlin, S. D., & Zimmerle, D. M. (1988). A survey of management training and education practices in US companies. *Personnel Psychology, 41*(4), 731–743.

Semmer, N. K. (2003). Job stress interventions and organization of work. In J. C. Quick & L. E. Tetrick (Eds.), *Handbook of occupational health psychology* (pp. 325–353). American Psychological Association.

Sianoja, M., Syrek, C. J., de Bloom, J., Korpela, K., & Kinnunen, U. (2018). Enhancing daily well-being at work through lunchtime park walks and relaxation exercises: Recovery experiences as mediators. *Journal of Occupational Health Psychology, 23*(3), 428–442.

Simpson, D. A., O'Brien, K. E., & Beehr, T. A. (2017). Assessing workplace stress: Diagnosing the problem. In A. M. Rossi, J. A. Meurs, & P. L. Perrewé (Eds.), *Stress and quality of working life: Conceptualizing and assessing stress* (pp. 185–202). Information Age Publishing.

Slutsky, J., Chin, B., Raye, J., & Creswell, J. D. (2019). Mindfulness training improves employee well-being: A randomized controlled trial. *Journal of Occupational Health Psychology, 24*(1), 139–149.

Slutsky, J., Rahl, H., Lindsay, E. K., & Creswell, J. D. (2017). Mindfulness, emotion regulation, and social threat. In J. C. Karremans & E. K. Papies (Eds.), *Mindfulness in social psychology* (pp. 79–93). Routledge.

Smith, E. N., Santoro, E., Moraveji, N., Susi, M., & Crum, A. J. (2020). Integrating wearables in stress management interventions: Promising evidence from a randomized trial. *International Journal of Stress Management, 27*(2), 172–182.

Sparling P. B. (2010). Worksite health promotion: Principles, resources, and challenges. *Preventing Chronic Disease, 7*(1), A25.

Wacker, R., & Dziobek, I. (2018). Preventing empathic distress and social stressors at work through nonviolent communication training: A field study with health professionals. *Journal of Occupational Health Psychology, 23*(1), 141–150.

Webb, J. R., Phillips, T. D., Bumgarner, D., & Conway-Williams, E. (2013). Forgiveness, mindfulness, and health. *Mindfulness, 4*, 235–245.

Wersebe, H., Lieb, R., Meyer, A. H., Hofer, P., & Gloster, A. T. (2018). The link between stress, well-being, and psychological flexibility during an Acceptance and Commitment Therapy self-help intervention. *International Journal of Clinical and Health Psychology, 18*(1), 60–68.

PART V

Emerging Issues

14 | *Mitigating the Adverse Effects of Technostress*

MONIDEEPA TARAFDAR, HENRI
PIRKKALAINEN, AND MARKUS SALO

The current pandemic-shaped times poignantly demonstrate the immutable and entangled role of information technology (IT) in our lives. The necessity of remote work has forced organizations to implement fast-paced roll-outs of remote working IT infrastructures without carefully considering the well-being–related implications of what, for both companies and individuals, is a vast digital leap (Waizenegger et al., 2020). Our work lives are now mediated by the sustained and relentless use of both asynchronous (e.g., email, ERP/CRM, One Drive) and synchronous (e.g., Teams, Zoom, and Slack) IT devices and applications. Moreover, once we are done with work, a key (and, for many, perhaps the defining) feature of our nonwork lives involves consuming digital content, using ever-present social media applications (e.g., Facebook, Instagram, Twitter, TikTok) and engaging in virtual meet-ups, games, cocktails, and quizzes with friends and family (e.g., Zoom, WhatsApp, Google Meet, Kahoot) for keeping abreast on what is going in the world and lives of others. Not only that, our children are 'going' to school through virtual classrooms (e.g., Zoom), virtual projects (e.g., Google Meet, Google Docs, Google Slides), and virtual libraries (e.g., Epic). It is not expected that once the Covid-19 pandemic is over, we will drop these new practices altogether, because, among other things, they bring convenience and fun.

However, what is sobering and should give pause for thought is the extensive literature that suggests that use of IT can form a source of stress for users – *technostress*. The phenomenon of technostress has emerged as a prominent 'dark side' of the use of IT, both in the workplace and outside it. Although stress can also have a positive side (e.g., by challenging individuals to achieve difficult goals), technostress creates many adverse effects for individuals, spanning the worlds of work and nonwork. Our stance is that technostress is inevitable, even more so now and in the new normal that will emerge. IT is inextricable from our lives. Therefore, it is critical to alleviate and inhibit the adverse effects of technostress. The objective of this chapter is *to examine the mitigation of technostress*.

Technostress: Work and Nonwork Domains

In the workplace, IT users experience technostress because they perceive the demands created by IT use – such as constant connectivity, interruptions, and availability, as well as dealing with continual newness of features and functionalities (Ayyagari et al., 2011; Galluch et al., 2015) – as threatening to their well-being at work. A number of conditions, referred to as *technostress creators* or *technostressors*, can lead to technostress (Tarafdar et al., 2019). Techno-invasion embodies the invasive effect of IT in situations where employees can be reached anytime and anywhere by office colleagues. The constantly accessibility of work through IT can mean that employees are tethered to work and the workday gets longer and may 'never' end (Eurofound and the International Labour Office, 2017). Techno-overload refers to facing too much technology, multitasking, and/or information, creating potentially additional effort for employees just to keep up with the use of IT. Research shows that IT can increase the pace of work interactions because digital and asynchronous work communication through emails and text messages can take place rapidly (Barley et al., 2011). Further, even if synchronous applications are used (e.g., video-conferencing), demands from asynchronous applications (e.g., email) do not reduce (Stich et al., 2017). Techno-complexity emerges when employees feel pressured because they have to understand and learn how to use various devices and applications that are difficult for them. Such work is usually not part of their direct work, and yet they have to do it in order to get their work done. For example, studies on professional sales persons show that requirements for learning how to use various customer relationship management (CRM) applications adversely affects their ability to achieve sales quota (Tarafdar et al., 2015). Even worse, such applications tend to change with every successive upgrade so that employees have to install and update applications or new additions, such as security-related patches and upgrades. As a result, they come up against what is known as techno-uncertainty, a stressor experienced when feeling unsettled because of constant changes.

Individuals experiencing technostress in the workplace face a plethora of strains and negative work-related outcomes, such as reduced job satisfaction, task performance, innovation, and organizational commitment, as well as increased exhaustion, job-related anxiety, turnover intentions, and even burnout (Tarafdar et al., 2019). Furthermore, security-related stress increases workers' reluctance to comply with organizational IT requirements such as appropriate IT security behaviors (D'Arcy et al., 2014).

Technostress in nonwork activities can emerge from the constant availability of digital content, perhaps most prominently from the use of social networking services (SNS). In addition to stressors similar to techno-complexity, techno-invasion, and techno-uncertainty, there are several stress-creating conditions distinct to SNS. SNS overdependence refers to the users' excessive reliance on SNS in one's daily activities (Salo et al., 2019). Social overload describes the demand of responding to excessive SNS-mediated requests for social actions and support (e.g., helping one's contacts look for a house or giving travel related advice) (Maier et al., 2015b). Disclosure refers to the condition of individuals feeling that they are exposed to too much information on SNS, which prevents them from effectively processing it (Maier et al., 2015a). Life comparison discrepancy refers to the users' unpleasant feelings when contrasting one's life to the lives of others via SNS (Salo et al., 2019). Other SNS stressors include online discussion conflicts, conformity to one's friends' use practices, and privacy/security concerns (Fox & Moreland, 2015; Maier et al., 2015a; Salo et al., 2019).

What distinguishes IT use in personal and nonwork activities from that of the work context is that it is undertaken voluntarily, ostensibly for hedonic and social purposes. Indeed, we use SNS for entertainment, leisure, and staying in touch with friends. SNS use does bring convenience and fun when individuals actualize the action possibilities (i.e., SNS affordances) of these applications. For example, it can be pleasurable to keep up with friends on Facebook, by actualizing the affordance provided by the 'post' feature. However, each interaction with the features of Facebook also creates small, almost hidden 'actualization costs'. That is, the user has to expend resources such as effort, attention, and time during the interaction (Salo et al., 2021) while using the feature. For example, 'liking' a message notification is done at the cost of shifting attention away from other ongoing activities. Over multiple interactions, these costs accumulate and exceed the individual's resources for dealing with them. Such incremental actualization, building up gradually, can cause technostress (Salo et al.,

2021). In this way, initially enjoyable interactions with IT can turn gradually to technostress experiences (e.g., being incapable of handling constant bombardment from SNS notifications). Despite the hedonic aspects of SNS use, it can also generate negative feelings such as envy, worry, and depression (Krasnova et al., 2015) and fear of missing out on what friends do (Fox & Moreland, 2015), as borne out by a glut of observations by both researchers and commentators. This has caught the attention of policy makers as well. For example, in 2020, the UK government released an 'Online Harms White Paper',[1] which lays out different types of harmful effects from the use of the Internet and SNS and identifies those that need regulatory attention by way of mitigation.

Negative outcomes from SNS-related technostress include exhaustion, dissatisfaction, and discontinuance of use (Maier et al., 2015a; 2015b) as well as problems related to concentration, sleep, identity, and social relationships (Salo et al., 2019). Ironically, SNS stressors can also make individuals use SNS even more, leading to addiction to the same SNS (Tarafdar et al., 2020b). The relationships between technostress, excessive use, and technology addiction are multifaceted and complex. They deserve more attention from researchers in the future. Finally, work and nonwork contexts can converge, creating technostress that spills over from work to home or vice versa (Benlian, 2020).

Technostress Mitigation

So, how can we mitigate the adverse effects of technostress? We look at studies that have addressed technostress mitigation, at both the organizational and individual levels. Most mitigation studies have focused on technostress at work, but there are also some studies on technostress mitigation in the nonwork context.

Organizational Mechanisms and Individual Factors That Inhibit the Effects of Technostress

Organizations can help mitigate technostress at least in three ways. First, remote and prompt technical helpdesk support can address many concerns and technical problems that individuals encounter when working with IT (Ragu-Nathan et al., 2008). Second, it is important that organizations frame explicit guidelines for technology use. Such technology manuals for employees to access can help employees avoid technostress (Tarafdar et al., 2015). Third, they can involve employees in IT implementation decisions by encouraging them to shape their own work patterns with IT (Ragu-Nathan et al., 2008). This can help employees avoid technostress-creating conditions (Tarafdar et al., 2015) and increase their job satisfaction and job commitment (Ragu-Nathan et al., 2008). However, organizations can also do things to make it worse. For example, there are examples of companies mandating email bans after 6 p.m.[2] Such policies do not work for everyone and indeed can backfire because they curtail employee flexibility and choice. The tendency has been for organizations to assume that 'less' is better. Research shows that this is not always the case. For example, employees can appraise their use of email as being stressful when they perceive that they get too much email as well as too little email (Stich et al., 2019). Thus, measures such as banning email outside certain hours can lead to stressful work relationships and low work satisfaction.

Factors relating to the individual can inhibit the effects of technostress. When managing technostress at work, being 'good at using IT' helps; employees with high IT self-efficacy experience lower technostress in the first place and perform better at work even when they do (Shu et al., 2011; Tams et al., 2018; Tarafdar et al., 2015). Similarly, users who are mindful about what IT features they use experience lower levels of technostress-creating conditions (Maier et al., 2019). Further, while organizations have certain policies for IT use, employees still have possibilities to shape their own IT use practices. For example, employees can develop their own email management strategies and take temporary breaks from IT (Soucek & Moser, 2010) in response to technostress. In nonwork contexts, studies show that users have various options, such as modifying the features and applications in their smartphones or changing their IT use routines and the features of an IT to reduce their exposure to technostressors. Success or failure in such actions depends on the extent to which users can monitor and regulate their use. However, monitoring one's use realistically is particularly difficult because use occasions are frequent and of short duration in such nonwork contexts. Further, the user tends to be absorbed in their IT use (Salo et al., 2021). In addition to monitoring, other important self-regulatory components in technostress mitigation include the awareness of the norms to which people are held while using IT, motivation for use, and the capacity to change. Each of these components also reflect potential pitfalls. For example, bias toward particular norms leads to a tendency for a socially promoted and over-positive perception of IT use and, hence, neglect of its potential negative sides (Salo et al., 2021).

Coping with Technostress

Ultimately, however, IT users will need to take charge of their relationship with technology, their IT use practices, and, hence, technostress. Our lives are irreversibly intertwined with IT, and we cannot rely solely on others to make us feel better about it. An individual's ability to tackle stress depends considerably on how well they can cope with it. Coping refers to individuals' cognitive and behavioral efforts to manage demands that are appraised as taxing (cf., Lazarus, 1993; Lazarus & Folkman, 1984). This means that an individual's evaluation of a certain demanding situation (i.e., appraisal) triggers and shapes their coping actions (Folkman & Moskowitz, 2004). Literature has identified key appraisals that influence coping. Commonly discussed appraisals include the perceived importance of the situation and its consequences as a primary appraisal and one's control over the situation as a secondary appraisal (Folkman & Moskowitz, 2004). Appraisal in the context of stress from email applications suggests that employees appraise email use as stressful when it is in both excess and deficit of what they feel comfortable with (Stich et al., 2019).

The focus of coping is on alleviating the intensity and effects of stressors perceived by the individual. Seminal studies on stress note that individuals cope with stress by exercising many kinds of cognitive and behavioral efforts to respond to the demands they appraise as threatening to their well-being (cf., Lazarus, 1993; Lazarus & Folkman, 1984). One extensively used approach is to differentiate between problem-focused and emotion-focused coping. Problem-focused ways of coping are aimed at handling the source of stress (Carver et al., 1989). Individuals adopt this approach when they want to do something concrete about the situations that create stress for them (Carver et al., 1989). Emotion-focused ways of coping include behaviors aimed at handling and regulating emotions associated with a stressful situation and feeling better about it (Carver et al., 1989). Both problem-focused and emotion-focused coping have been studied in the IT context. This brings us to the subject of the individual's coping responses to IT in general and technostress in particular.

Coping with the Demands of IT Use

Before we get to coping with technostress, we note that both work-related requirements and nonwork-related personal circumstances for using IT applications place demands on individuals that can hinder their use of these applications.

Individuals cope with these demands in a number of ways. Researchers have investigated coping for various IT applications, such as bank systems (Beaudry & Pinsonneault, 2005), enterprise resource planning systems (Elie-Dit-Cosaque & Straub, 2011), administrative software packages (Stein et al., 2015), and mobile applications (Salo et al., 2020). Studies have found that employees who have high IT self-efficacy or control over how they use IT tend to respond with problem-focused coping strategies, while those with low IT self-efficacy or control tend to engage in emotion-focused strategies (Beaudry & Pinsonneault, 2005; Elie-Dit-Cosaque & Straub, 2011; Liang & Xue, 2009; Stein et al., 2015). Despite these broad patterns, it is important to note that coping is influenced by many factors and, hence, IT self-efficacy or control do not fully determine the employed coping strategies (Salo et al., 2020). On a general level, those who appraise the requirements for using new IT applications as an opportunity for improving their work and have high levels of latitude in their IT use can maximize benefits to themselves by exploring different features and incorporating them in their work processes. They tend to experience emotions such as satisfaction and excitement. On the other hand, employees who appraise such requirements as a threat to their established ways of working, and do not have leeway in how they use IT, are more likely to find that they can preserve their emotional stability by using the applications minimally or not at all. They can experience emotions such as anger and anxiety (Beaudry & Pinsonneault, 2005, 2010). In general, employees may have emotions that are similar/uniform (e.g., loss or achievement) or mixed (e.g., both loss and achievement) toward IT use situations (Stein et al., 2015). The former are associated with focused and converging coping strategies and the latter with combinations of different coping strategies.

In nonwork settings, particularly in the use of mobile applications, users are found to engage in more than one type of coping behavior (i.e., both problem- and emotion-focused), often engaging in complex sequences of different behaviors involving reappraisals. For example, users may respond to outstandingly negative mobile application experiences by first trying to soothe their emotions by venting, then attempting several IT-related workarounds to solve the problem, and finally switching to an alternative application. In such coping efforts, experiencing intense momentary emotions such as frustration or anger (i.e., a high momentary emotional load) can steer users toward emotion-focused strategies (Salo et al., 2020).

Coping Behaviors and Approaches for Technostress

Interestingly, but not surprisingly, individuals exert a number of distinctive coping behaviors and approaches for addressing technostress, as we describe in Table 14.1.

The first group includes those that help individuals proactively prepare themselves for apparent and upcoming technostress situations that they cannot fully avoid (Schwarzer & Taubert, 2002). They do this in order to build resilience against ongoing stressful events relating to the use of IT. *IT control* (Pirkkalainen et al., 2019) is one such coping approach. IT control is about developing autonomy and competence in the use of IT which gives the individual the confidence to tackle ongoing technostress situations such that, when faced with a problem in the use of IT, they can find alternative ways or tools to work through it. Another coping approach is *positive reinterpretation,* which is about equipping oneself with an optimistic mindset about technostress situations and infusing them with a positive meaning (Pirkkalainen et al., 2019).

A second set of coping behaviors includes strategies to act on technostress situations after they have actualized. These ways of coping include *timing control, work and nonwork IT use separation, instrumental support,* and *distraction.* Timing control refers to setting aside certain times for particular types of IT use, such as deciding when to read work-related emails and when to search for information related to ongoing work tasks. Work and nonwork IT use separation is about setting boundaries regarding when to use IT for work or nonwork purposes (Tarafdar et al., 2020a). Instrumental support refers to seeking help from others to accomplish IT-related tasks at work (Weinert

Table 14.1 *Coping behaviors for technostress*

Coping type	Coping behavior/approach	Description	References
Preparing for apparent technostress situations	IT control	Developing confidence in own IT use capabilities by focusing on certain IT use skills and autonomy that help master IT	Pirkkalainen et al. (2019); Tarafdar et al. (2020a)
	Positive reinterpretation	Developing a positive mindset about stressful situations with IT by infusing them with a positive meaning	Pirkkalainen et al. (2019); Tarafdar et al. (2020a)
Acting in actualized technostress situations	Timing control	Deciding when to use IT for a certain purpose, such as accessing and reading emails	Tarafdar et al. (2020a)
	Work and nonwork IT use separation	Demarcating times regarding when to use IT for work or nonwork purposes	Tarafdar et al. (2020a)
	Instrumental support	Seeking help from others for IT use-related tasks and problems	Weinert et al. (2020)
	Distraction	Diverting attention from the technostress-creating situation	Tarafdar et al. (2020b)
Relying on emotions in technostress situations	Seeking emotional support	Seeking sympathy, understanding, and encouragement from others in the case of IT use-related concerns	Weinert et al. (2020)
	Venting	Venting negative emotions related to stressful IT use situations	Pirkkalainen et al. (2019); Tarafdar et al. (2020a)
	Distancing	Avoiding thinking about the stressful situation with IT and switching to other tasks	Pirkkalainen et al. (2019); Tarafdar et al. (2020a)

et al., 2020). Distraction consists of diverting attention away from the technostress creating situation and focusing on something different (Tarafdar et al., 2020b).

The third set of coping behaviors relies primarily on emotions. These behaviors are activated when the individual perceives that the technostress situation cannot be avoided or that they have limited ways to deal with the threats (Carver et al., 1989). Such strategies include *emotional support*, *venting*, and *Distancing*. The first of these emotional supports refers to seeking sympathy, understanding, and encouragement (e.g., from coworkers) to restore emotional stability in technostress situations (Weinert et al., 2020). Venting is about expressing negative emotions in the technostress situation, such as letting out frustration regarding IT, in interactions with colleagues or friends (Tarafdar et al., 2020a). Distancing is about diverting from the stressful situation and switching to other work or nonwork-related activities to create a temporary break from the stressful situation with IT (Tarafdar et al., 2020a).

Coping Outcomes for Technostress

Coping with technostress is a nuanced and complex matter and one of individual choice and action; one size does not fit all individuals (Tarafdar et al., 2020a). Different coping strategies can be activated singly or in combination. Further, different coping behaviors may lead to different outcomes. Some outcomes are positive and favorable for the individual. Others are mixed and may not be healthy for the individual.

Positive Outcomes of Coping. Building up resilience against ongoing stressful events has been shown to be an effective way to combat technostress (Pirkkalainen et al., 2019). For instance, IT control and positive reinterpretation can help individuals avert the negative outcomes that are commonly witnessed for technostress, such as reduced work-related performance with IT (Pirkkalainen et al., 2019). Similarly, timing control as well as work and nonwork IT use separation, and instrumental support has been found helpful in retaining individuals' IT-enabled productivity at work (Tarafdar et al., 2020a; Weinert et al., 2020). Further, timing control may even prevent certain technostressors from emerging in the first place. For instance, it can reduce the number of IT-related interruptions and help individuals avoid feelings of overload from IT use (Galluch et al., 2015). Relying on emotions for coping can also lead to positive results. For example, emotional support can help individuals avoid exhaustion from the use of IT when facing computer bugs and freezes (Weinert et al., 2020).

Mixed Outcomes of Coping. Some coping behaviors that rely on emotion, such as venting and distancing, may lead to mixed results. On the one hand, they can be constructive and have positive results, because handling one's emotions effectively can help individuals maintain their work performance with IT (Pirkkalainen et al., 2019). However, they may also be maladaptive because they can increase emotional strain (Pirkkalainen et al., 2017). In particular, feelings of anger, often associated with venting, draw from negative emotions that are toxic for the individual's mental well-being. Denial, often associated with distancing, can prevent the individual from confronting the issues that create technostress. Such feelings can be particularly harmful in long-term if the individual continuously faces technostress but does not seek to address the root causes.

In the context of SNS, coping through distraction can be linked with maladaptive behaviors such as addiction to SNS (Tarafdar et al., 2020b). Those habituated in the use of Facebook, for example, when faced with technostress while using the application, gravitate toward using it even more as a means to cope with the stress. What they do is switch to a different activity from the one that causes them stress, all the time staying on Facebook and not leaving it. Thus, they fall into a vicious cycle of feeling stressed from and yet being unable to leave Facebook.[3] Such people, ironically, see SNS use as both a stressor and a means to cope with the stress, engaging in maladaptive coping that can actually strengthen addiction to the social networking site. On the other hand, those whose use habits for SNS are not as strong manage to get away from Facebook altogether and do something different as a means of coping.

Combinations of Coping Behaviors Leading to Positive Outcomes. Interestingly, recent findings show that combinations of multiple coping strategies can foster positive outcomes and lessen the potential maladaptive aspects of coping. For example, coping behaviors/ approaches that help individuals proactively prepare for apparent and upcoming technostress situations (i.e., IT control, positive reinterpretation) can be effectively combined with emotion-based strategies (i.e., venting, distancing). The potential negative effects of venting can be countered by high levels of IT control and strong positive reinterpretation. While the former can create emotion strain due to anger, for example, the latter can act as a balancing factor by equipping the individual with confidence in their own IT use capabilities and optimism regarding IT use (Pirkkalainen et al., 2019). Similarly, coping behavior that seeks high levels of emotional support can be more effective for those with high IT self-efficacy, and that which seeks high levels of instrumental and technical support is more effective for those with low IT self-efficacy in lowering the levels of technostress creating conditions experienced by individuals (Weinert et al., 2020) .

Conclusion

Technostress, having become a pervasive and global phenomenon due to wide-ranging digitalization of work over the past decade and in the pre-Covid era can only increase its import for the way we work and live in the even more digitally infused world that is expected to emerge post-Covid. While we know a lot about conditions that create technostress and the outcomes they engender, the time has come for scholars to pay attention to the mitigation of technostress. Our stance is that mitigation of technostress needs to occur at both the organizational and individual levels. While organizations can and do provide technical support, IT involvement, and technical training and education, individuals are eventually responsible for managing and mitigating the effects of their own technostress because IT is infused in almost every work and nonwork activity.

In presenting this review of technostress mitigation and coping, it occurs to us that certain areas stand out in terms of their importance for further research. One is the intertwining of work and nonwork settings for example, via remote work at home or using personal devices and applications at work. Research needs to examine how technostress can be alleviated in the context of the combination and convergence of work and nonwork, such as spillovers from work to home or vice versa (cf. Benlian, 2020). Addressing this area is important because such spillovers influence work and nonwork domains. Another area to focus on is the individual's IT use practices and modifications of IT features for technostress mitigation and changes in these practices over time (cf. Salo et al., 2021). Understanding such details can help to tailor interventions to help technostressed users and find suitable mitigation options. Third, given the plethora of existing and emerging technostress coping behaviors and mitigation mechanisms, we suggest scholars continue investigating the combined effects of different mitigation mechanisms and/or coping approaches in different contexts of work (Tarafdar et al., 2020a).

Notes

1 See www.gov.uk/government/consultations/online-harms-white-paper/out come/online-harms-white-paper-full-government-response
2 www.bbc.co.uk/news/technology-50073107
3 See for example, M. Tarafdar (2018, May), Social media: Six ways to take back control, *The Conversation*, https://theconversation.com/social-media-six-steps-to-take-back-control-95814

References

Ayyagari, R., Grover, V., & Purvis, R. (2011). Technostress: Technological antecedents and implications. *MIS Quarterly*, *35*(4), 831–858.

Barley, S. R., Meyerson, D. E., & Grodal, S. (2011). E-mail as a source and symbol of stress. *Organization Science*, 22(4), 887–906.

Beaudry, A., & Pinsonneault, A. (2005). Understanding user responses to information technology: A coping model of user adaption. *MIS Quarterly*, *29*(3), 493–524.

(2010). The other side of acceptance: Studying the direct and indirect effects of emotions on information technology use. *MIS Quarterly*, *34* (4), 689–710.

Benlian, A. (2020). A daily field investigation of technology-driven stress spillovers from work to home. *MIS Quarterly*, *44*(3), 1259–1300.

Carver, C., Scheier, M., & Weintraub, J. (1989). Assessing coping strategies: A theoretically based approach. *Journal of Personality and Social Psychology*, *56*, 267–283.

D'Arcy, J., Herath, T., & Shoss, M. (2014). Understanding employee responses to stressful information security requirements: A coping perspective. *Journal of Management Information Systems*, *31*(2), 285–318.

Elie-Dit-Cosaque, C. M., & Straub, D. W. (2011). Opening the black box of system usage: User adaptation to disruptive IT. *European Journal of Information Systems*, *20*(5), 589–607.

Eurofound and the International Labour Office. (2017). *Working anytime, anywhere: The effects on the world of work.* Publications Office of the

European Union, Luxembourg, and the International Labour Office, Geneva. Fairweather.

Folkman, S., & Moskowitz, J. T. (2004). Coping: Pitfalls and promise. *Annual Review of Psychology, 55,* 745–774.

Fox, J., & Moreland, J. J. (2015). The dark side of social networking sites: An exploration of the relational and psychological stressors associated with Facebook use and affordances. *Computers in Human behavior, 45,* 168–176.

Galluch, P., Grover, V., & Thatcher, J. (2015). Interrupting the workplace: Examining stressors in an information technology context. *Journal of the Association for Information Systems, 16*(1), 1–47.

Krasnova. K., Widjaja. T., Buxmann, P., Wenninger, H., & Benbasat, I. (2015). Research note – why following friends can hurt you: An exploratory investigation of the effects of envy on social networking sites among college-age users. *Information Systems Research, 26*(3), 585–605.

Maier, C., Laumer, S., Eckhardt, A., & Weitzel, T. (2015b). Giving too much social support: Social overload on social networking sites. *European Journal of Information Systems, 24*(5), 447–464.

Maier, C., Laumer, S., Weinert, C., & Weitzel, T. (2015a). The effects of technostress and switching stress on discontinued use of social networking services: A study of Facebook use. *Information Systems Journal, 25* (3), 275–308.

Maier, C., Laumer, S., Wirth, J., & Weitzel, T. (2019). Technostress and the hierarchical levels of personality: A two-wave study with multiple data samples. *European Journal of Information Systems, 28*(5), 496–522. https://doi.org/10.1080/0960085X.2019.1614739

Lazarus, R. S. (1993). From psychological stress to the emotions: A history of changing outlooks. *Annual Review of Psychology, 44,* 1–21.

Lazarus, R. S., & Folkman, S. (1984). *Stress, appraisal and coping.* Springer.

Liang, H., & Xue, Y. (2009). Avoidance of information technology threats: A theoretical perspective. *MIS Quarterly, 33*(1), 71–90.

Pirkkalainen, H., Salo, M., & Makkonen, M. (2020). IT engagement as a blessing and a curse? Examining its antecedents and outcomes in organizations. *International Journal of Information Management, 53*(April), 102130.

Pirkkalainen, H., Salo, M., Makkonen, M., & Tarafdar, M. (2017). Coping with technostress: When emotional responses fail. *Proceedings of the 38th International Conference on Information Systems (ICIS).*

Pirkkalainen, H., Salo, M., Tarafdar, M., & Makkonen, M. (2019). Deliberate or instinctive? Proactive and reactive coping for technostress. *Journal of Management Information Systems, 36*(4), 1179–1212.

Ragu-Nathan, T. S., Tarafdar, M., Ragu-Nathan, B. S., & Tu, Q. (2008). The consequences of technostress for end users in organizations: Conceptual development and validation. *Information Systems Research*, 19(4), 417–433.

Salo, M., Makkonen, M., & Hekkala, R. (2020). The interplay of IT users' coping strategies: Uncovering momentary emotional load, routes, and sequences. *MIS Quarterly*, 44(3), 1143–1175.

Salo, M., Pirkkalainen, H., Chua, C., & Koskelainen, T. (2021). Formation and mitigation of technostress in the personal use of IT. *MIS Quarterly*, 46(2), 1073–1108.

Salo, M., Pirkkalainen, H., & Koskelainen, T. (2019). Technostress and social networking services: Explaining users' concentration, sleep, identity, and social relation problems. *Information Systems Journal*, 29(2), 408–435.

Schwarzer, R., & Taubert, S. (2002). Tenacious goal pursuits and striving toward personal growth: Proactive coping. In E. Frydenberg (Ed.), *Beyond coping: Meeting goals, visions and challenges* (pp. 19–35). Oxford University Press.

Shu, Q., Tu, Q., & Wang, K. (2011). The impact of computer self-efficacy and technology dependence on computer-related technostress: A social cognitive theory perspective. *International Journal of Human–Computer Interaction*, 27(10), 923–939.

Stein, M., Newell, S. M., Wagner, E. L., & Galliers, R. D. (2015). Coping with information technology: Mixed emotions, vacillation, and nonconforming use patterns. *MIS Quarterly*, 39(2), 367–392.

Stich, J.-F., Tarafdar, M., Cooper, C. L., & Stacey, P. (2017). Workplace stress from actual and desired computer-mediated communication use: A multimethod study. *New Technology, Work and Employment*, 32(1), 84–100.

Stich, J.-F., Tarafdar, M., Stacey, P., & Cooper, C. L. (2019). Appraisal of email use as a source of workplace stress: A person–environment fit approach. *Journal of the Association for Information Systems*, 20(2), article 2.

Tams, S., Thatcher, J. B., & Grover, V. (2018). Concentration, competence, confidence, and capture: An experimental study of age, interruption-based technostress, and task performance. *Journal of the Association for Information Systems*, 19(9), 857–908.

Tarafdar, M., Bolman Pullins, E., & Ragu-Nathan, T. S. (2015). Technostress: Negative effect on performance and possible mitigations. *Information Systems Journal*, 25(2), 103–132.

Tarafdar, M., Cooper, C. L., & Stich, J. F. (2019). The technostress trifecta – techno eustress, techno distress and design: Theoretical directions and an agenda for research. *Information Systems Journal, 29*(1), 6–42.

Tarafdar, M., Maier, C., Laumer, S., & Weitzel, T. (2020b). Explaining the link between technostress and technology addiction for social networking sites: A study of distraction as a coping behavior. *Information Systems Journal, 30*(1), 96–124.

Tarafdar, M., Pirkkalainen, H., Salo, M., & Makkonen, M. (2020a). Taking on the 'dark side' – coping with technostress. *IEEE IT Professional, 22* (6), 82–89.

Waizenegger, L., McKenna, B., Cai, W., & Bendz, T. (2020). An affordance perspective of team collaboration and enforced working from home during COVID-19. *European Journal of Information Systems, 29*(4), 429–442.

Weinert, C., Maier, C., Laumer, S., & Weitzel, T. (2020). Technostress mitigation: An experimental study of social support during a computer freeze. *Journal of Business Economics, 90*(8), 1199–1249.

15 | *What Can Management Do about Employee Mental Health?*

LAURENT M. LAPIERRE, E. KEVIN
KELLOWAY, AND DANIEL
QUINTAL-CURCIC

The likelihood that companies employ an individual with a mental health challenge is high. For example, in any given year, one in five working-age Canadians experiences a mental health illness, such as an anxiety disorder, major depression, or bipolar disorder (Smetanin et al., 2011). In England, one in four people experience a mental health problem of some kind each year, and one in six people experience a common mental health problem (e.g., anxiety, depression) in any given week (McManus et al., 2009). Similarly, one in five adults in the United States experience mental illness each year (Substance Abuse and Mental Health Services Administration, 2019).

Mental health problems are among the leading causes of the overall disease burden worldwide (Vos et al., 2015). Major depression has been said to be the second leading cause of disability worldwide and a major contributor to suicide and ischemic heart disease (Whiteford et al., 2013). Data collected in 2010 estimated the global cost of mental disorders at US$2.5 trillion, which is expected to double by 2030 (Bloom et al., 2012). The economic toll of mental health disorders is partially explained by their direct costs (e.g., diagnosis and treatment in the healthcare system, medications, physician visits, psychotherapy sessions, etc.). However, their indirect costs have a far greater economic impact (Trautmann et al., 2016). These include losses due to mortality, disability, care-seeking, and hampered production due to work absenteeism, presenteeism, and turnover. Considering the prevalence and costliness of mental health problems, it behooves organizations to take at least some responsibility for protecting, if not enhancing, the mental health of those they employ.

Attention given to mental health has seemingly risen among Western organizations. Several corporations have implemented mental health awareness campaigns, such as Bell Canada's "Let's talk," Maybelline's "Brave together," and Jan Sport's "#LightenTheLoad." Although many organizations now put health and wellness initiatives in place for their employees, such as lunch-and-learns and ergonomic assessments (e.g., Human Resources Professionals Association of Ontario, 2021), it is doubtful that the most commonly used ones are sufficient to effectively support employees' mental health. Evidence points to managers within the organization as having a central role to play.

Empirical research over the last several decades has made it abundantly clear that workplace experiences can significantly affect employees' mental health, both positively and negatively. Managers (i.e., individuals in formal positions of leadership) typically have a profound influence over employees' experiences. Senior managers (e.g., executives, directors) do so through the internal policies they put in place and the interpersonal behaviors they model for those lower in the organizational hierarchy. Immediate managers (those to whom employees report directly) can have a particularly strong influence on employees' mental health given the greater frequency with which they interact and the more immediate consequences of their behavior on employees' daily or weekly experiences.

This chapter aims to provide a greater understanding of the utility and shortcomings of scholarly literature addressing how managers can support employees' mental health. We begin by clarifying the notion of "mental health" among employed individuals. This should help the reader understand conceptual parallels with terminology used elsewhere in this book. It is also meant to guide how employees' mental health can be measured, particularly when gauging the need for, and effectiveness of, mental-health-supportive management practices. We then review scholarly literature on how senior and immediate managers can each support employees' mental health. More attention is given to immediate managers, not only because of their more direct influence on employees, but also because they have more frequently been the subject of scholarship. That sizable literature falls short of specifying a comprehensive set of behaviors with which immediate managers can support their employees' mental health. To help address this gap, we finish the chapter by integrating useful empirical insights and proposing a behavioral taxonomy of "mental-health-supportive supervision."

What Is Meant by Employee "Mental Health"?

Many terms used throughout this book, such as "well-being," "strain," "engagement," and "burnout," are conceptually related to, and likely indicators of, the broader notion of "mental health." The World Health Organization (WHO) proposes that mental health is more than the absence of mental disorders, illness, or disabilities. It is a "state of well-being in which an individual realizes his or her own abilities, can cope with the normal stresses of life, can work productively and is able to make a contribution to his or her community" (World Health Organization, 2018). As such, mental health is not simply the absence of strain, burnout, or any other negative indicator of mental health. It must also include positive manifestations indicative of a person's hedonic (good feelings and attitudes) and eudaimonic (positive functioning) well-being, such as positive affect and engagement across life roles and social settings. Examples of umbrella terms used to capture various positive indicators of mental health include "flourishing" (Keyes, 2007) and "thriving" (Spreitzer et al., 2005).

Mental health exists along a continuum ranging from good to poor. Because mental health can be manifested positively (well-being) and negatively (illness), each end of the continuum would involve opposing patterns of *positive* and *negative* indicators of mental health. Thus, where good mental health would involve high levels of positive indicators and low levels of negative indicators, poor mental health would involve the reverse pattern. Considering both positive and negative indicators of mental health implies that they each provide unique information rather than simply being complete opposites of one another. There are empirical reasons to hold such a view, such as positive affectivity not being the complete opposite of negative affectivity (e.g., Watson et al., 1988), and work engagement not being the complete opposite of burnout (Cole et al., 2012). Accordingly, considering positive and negative indicators should provide a more comprehensive understanding of individuals' mental health.

Indicators of mental health can be quite varied in nature. Evidence suggests that they can be psychological, physiological, and behavioral (e.g., American Psychiatric Association, 2013; Banks et al., 1980; Newcomer & Hennekens, 2007), which mirrors the three types of stress-induced strain (Jex & Beehr, 1991; Spector et al., 1988).

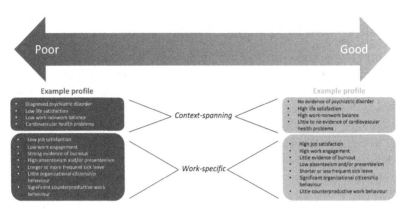

Figure 15.1 A continuum of mental health among employed individuals

Consequently, any single indicator would fail to comprehensively capture a person's mental health. Presumably, this is why germane concepts such as flourishing involve multiple indicators (Colbert et al., 2016; Keyes, 2007).

When measuring employees' mental health, researchers and practitioners should consider indicators that span multiple contexts as well as those that are specific to the work context. *Context-spanning indicators* speak to a person's overall mental health across life domains (work, family, etc.). Examples include symptoms of a psychiatric disorder (e.g., major depressive disorder), overall life satisfaction, cardiovascular health (e.g., blood pressure, cholesterol), and work–nonwork balance (Banks et al., 1980; Cohen et al., 2015; Diener et al., 1985; Wayne et al., 2021). *Work-specific indicators* denote the ways people manifest their mental health at (or in relation to) work. As such, they should be of particular interest to managers. Examples can include overall job satisfaction (an affect-laden appraisal of one's overall job experience), work engagement (see Chapter 9 of this book for more information), job burnout (see Chapter 8 for more information), turnover intentions, absenteeism, presenteeism (see Chapter 7 for more information), the frequency and/or duration of sick leave, and discretionary performance-related behavior, namely organizational citizenship and counterproductive work behavior (described as consequences of positive and negative employee affect, respectively; Spector & Fox, 2002). Figure 15.1 provides an overview of the mental health continuum among employed individuals with opposing profiles of context-spanning and work-specific indicator levels at both extremes. Please note that the list of indicators is not meant to be exhaustive. It aims to reflect variables commonly measured in organizational and occupational health psychology that, together, exemplify the view that mental health involves psychological, physiological, and behavioral manifestations of a positive and negative nature. Although the indicators listed are expected to covary, there is little reason to believe that some would be made completely redundant by others. Accordingly, measuring several indicators (i.e., context-spanning *and* work-specific; positive *and* negative; psychological, physiological, *and* behavioral) should be more revealing of an individuals' overall mental health than measuring few. Most of the research addressing managers' impact on their employees' mental health have relied on very few indicators (sometimes only one).

How Can Senior Managers Support Employees' Mental Health?

There are at least two ways that senior managers (e.g., C-suite members, directors) can affect employees' mental health: the formal human resource (HR) policies they put in place and the leadership example they set for those below them in the hierarchy. HR policies supportive of employees' mental health can include employee assistance programs, sufficient health insurance to cover mental-health-related expenses, mental health training and promotion programs, and selection and promotion policies that emphasize interpersonal skills.

Implementing Mental-Health-Supportive HR Policies

Employee Assistance Programs (EAPs)
EAPs are employer-sponsored benefit programs that provide employees with free access to various resources, such as short-term counseling and referrals. They are designed to help employees deal with personal and/or work-related problems, including those involving their mental health. Evidence suggests that EAP-provided counseling services can be effective in helping employees overcome mental health struggles, as shown by reductions in presenteeism, absenteeism, life satisfaction, and workplace distress (Attridge et al., 2018; Joseph et al., 2018). However, despite EAPs offering viable support for employees, only

about 4% of employees use them (Attridge et al., 2013). A lack of EAP utilization may be due to a lack of awareness of their existence, a lack of understanding of how to use them, and/or a failure to grasp how they can help those who experience mental health challenges (Dimoff & Kelloway, 2018). Thus, in addition to instituting EAPs that offer mental-health-supportive resources (e.g., counseling), senior leaders should develop and implement communication strategies to promote available EAP-related resources to employees. They should also consider measuring employees' satisfaction with EAP features and soliciting ways to improve its offerings and accessibility (e.g., via smartphones).

Sufficient Health Insurance Coverage for Mental Health Expenses
National healthcare programs often fall short of providing people with the professional mental health support they need. For example, Canada's universal healthcare system covers most physician and hospital-related expenses. Still, it does not provide coverage for services provided by (nonmedical) mental health professionals (e.g., psychologists, social workers), nor does it cover prescribed medication for mental health treatment (Mulvale & Hurley, 2008). The 2020 Canada Life and Health Insurance Association report suggests that 80% of working Canadians are protected by private insurance plans offered by their employer, professional association, or union. These insurance plans are offered to employees as part of their compensation and rewards package to help pay for expenses not covered by universal healthcare. However, insurance coverage for mental health services in Canada and in the United States is often limited in terms of the breadth of services covered and the maximum expenses that can be claimed per year (Mulvale & Hurley, 2008; Reinert et al., 2020). In the United States, health insurance coverage has increased, yet coverage for mental health services has remained limited. According to a Mental Health America report (Reinert et al., 2020), 45% of Americans receive inadequate mental health service coverage from their employer.

The Kaiser Family Foundation report on employer health benefits (2020) suggests that employees disproportionally use mental-health-related services not covered by their employer-provided health insurance, causing them added financial and psychological strain (Barry et al., 2019). Insurance coverage for mental-health-related services varies depending on job type, industry, and the organization's financial position. According to the 2020 Sanofi Canada Healthcare Survey, the current median dollar amount for mental-health-related services, such as counseling and therapy, is $1,011 per year. Yet, 68% of Canadians have an annual maximum coverage for mental health services of less than $1,000 per year (Sanofi, 2020). In comparison, Manulife offers its employees $10,000 per year for mental health services, and employee's spouse/dependents can utilize this benefit as well (The Manufacturers Life Insurance Company, 2021). To prevent their employees from seriously struggling with their mental health, senior managers should determine how their employees' health insurance can be made to sufficiently cover mental-health-related expenses.

Mental Health Training and Promotion Programs

By implementing training programs for managers (see Chapter 12 in this book) and employees (see Chapter 13) on matters relating to mental health, senior managers convey their genuine commitment to maintaining a supportive work setting. Of note, manager training programs expressly designed to give them the knowledge and skills to help direct reports seriously struggling with their mental health have only recently been developed. Examples include the four-hour RESPECT program (Milligan-Saville et al., 2017) and the three-hour Mental Health Awareness Training program (MHAT; Dimoff et al., 2016; Dimoff & Kelloway, 2018). Each has been shown to be beneficial in randomized controlled trials. Despite some differences in content, both aim to bolster managers' mental health knowledge (e.g., key features, risk factors, warning signs, the effects of the most common serious mental health problems or illnesses, the role of leaders as sources of support for struggling employees) and improve their skill at supporting their employees' mental health (e.g., how to promote mental health in the workplace, reduce workplace stressors, approach and assist employees showing signs of struggling). Evidence of the effectiveness of these programs has been shown among participating managers in terms of improved skill at recognizing employees' mental health struggles, greater self-efficacy in supporting mental health, increased sharing of information on mental health and mental-health-supportive resources (e.g., EAP), and being more supportive of employee mental health issues. Positive effects have also been shown among trained managers' employees, such as being more willing to use mental-health-supportive resources and being less absent due to sickness). Considering these findings, senior leaders need to ensure that mental health training needs are evaluated annually and that required training is offered.

Selection and Promotion Policies That Emphasize Interpersonal Skills
Historically, organizations have largely focused on evaluating candidates' technical ("hard") skills when deciding whether to promote them into management positions. However, interpersonal ("soft") skills, such as being courteous, flexible, personable, friendly, and empathetic, have increasingly been recognized as crucial and often lacking among managers and employees (Bedwell et al., 2014; Clarke, 2016; Robles, 2012). There is a looming belief that employees quit their bosses rather than their jobs. This can be due to their immediate manager severely lacking in interpersonal skills. Strong interpersonal skills make the difference between successful and unsuccessful managerial leadership (Bedwell et al., 2014). Senior managers should therefore implement selection and promotion policies that give much greater attention to interpersonal skills. That said, it is not necessarily evident which specific behaviors exemplify such skills, making it difficult to know exactly what to assess (measure) among candidates in a selection or promotion context. We further elucidate the specific nature of these behaviors when discussing how immediate managers can support their employees' mental health.

Leading by Example

Much of human behavior is learned through observation. When observing how others behave, individuals may imitate behaviors they perceive as acceptable or appropriate (Bandura, 1977). Senior leaders can foster greater support for mental health in their organization by demonstrating such support in the ways they interact with managers directly reporting them. At least some of those managers would emulate similar types of supportive behavior with their own staff, who in turn would do so with theirs, and so on. As such, senior leaders' display of supportive behavior would "trickle down" into the organization. Various studies have provided evidence of this phenomenon. For example, Tepper and Taylor (2003) found that managers' perceptions of procedural justice (how fair they consider the organization's decision-making procedures) positively related to how helpful they were with their subordinates, which in turn related to subordinates' own procedural justice perceptions, and ultimately to how helpful those subordinates were with others. Similarly, Shanock and Eisenberger (2006) showed that managers' perceptions of how supportive their organization is of them positively related to how supportive they were viewed by their immediate staff, which in turn related to how helpful those staff members were with others. Such findings imply that senior managers would be wise to display the types of supportive behavior they wish to have emulated further down in the organization. The next section delves into the specific types of supportive behavior that could be modeled if mental health is to be best supported in organizations.

How Can Immediate Managers Support Their Employees' Mental Health?

What Does Research on Leadership Behavior Tell Us?

Compared to more senior managers, employees' immediate managers can more easily influence their day-to-day work experiences, thus having a more proximal impact on their mental health. The actions immediate managers take to shape their direct reports' work experiences can be viewed as their leadership style or behavior. Some of these work experiences can benefit employees' mental health, while others can seriously harm it. For example, employees' mental health would presumably be strengthened when their manager makes changes that render the nature of employees' work more intrinsically motivating and helps them overcome personal obstacles at work and/or in their personal lives. Conversely, their mental health would likely suffer the more their manager makes their work experience strenuous, such as failing to provide needed direction or throwing insults at them.

The positive and negative ways immediate managers can influence their employees' mental health correspond to the constructive and destructive forms of managerial leadership described in Chapter 5 of this book. While no single conceptualization of leadership behavior is perfect, empirical research has offered a relatively more straightforward understanding of the behaviors exemplifying destructive leadership than of those illustrating its constructive counterpart.

Destructive Leadership behaviors

Kelloway et al. (2005) proposed that destructive ("poor") leadership can be either passive or active ("abusive") in nature. Passive destructive leadership denotes a deficiency in the competencies required for a leadership role and frequent failure to live up to one's leadership responsibilities. Laissez-faire leadership and the more passive type of management-by-exception (Bass & Avolio, 1994) typify passive leadership. Behavioral examples include showing a lack of caring of what happens, avoiding taking responsibility, being indecisive, failing to provide employees with feedback and/or reward their contributions, and being satisfied to wait for someone else to step up to a challenge (Avolio, 2011). Conversely, active destructive leadership involves being overly punitive or aggressive, such as yelling at, insulting, belittling, and/or threatening employees with job loss or pay cuts (e.g., Tepper, 2000). Such passive and active forms of destructive leadership delineate concrete types of behavior that immediate managers must undoubtedly *refrain from displaying*, lest they seriously impair their employees' mental health (e.g., higher levels of burnout, depression, counterproductive work behavior; Mackey et al., 2017).

Constructive Leadership behaviors

Constructive leadership behaviors remain somewhat more elusive. This is at least partly attributable to the popularity of the charismatic–transformational leadership (e.g., Bass & Avolio, 1994; Conger & Kanungo, 1987) and leader–member exchange (Graen & Uhl-Bien, 1995) models of leadership, which have dominated organizational scholarship since the 1980s. Despite significant associations reported between measures of those leadership constructs and indicators of employee mental health (see Chapter 5 for an overview), each model has received considerable criticism. We discuss some of these criticisms below, as well as research on other (less popular) conceptualizations of constructive leadership that have offered more useful insights.

The "Full Range" Model of Leadership. Avolio (2011) suggested that the "full range" model of leadership involves transformational and transactional styles of leadership, both of which are distinct from passive leadership (e.g., laissez-faire leadership; see above). Transformational leadership has been said to be more effective/positive than the more managerial and less stimulating style of transactional leadership (Avolio, 2011; Bass & Avolio, 1994). Yet, transformational leadership (and similar leadership conceptualizations involving charisma) has attracted the fiercest criticism. Van Knippenberg and Sitkin (2013) provided a detailed explanation of its major shortcomings. Perhaps most damning is the fact that the commonly used measures of charismatic–transformational leadership (e.g., the Multifactor Leadership Questionnaire [MLQ]; Bass & Avolio, 1990) fail to yield factor analytic results consistent with the multidimensional conceptualizations they aim to capture (e.g., Bycio et al., 1995). For instance, transformational leadership purportedly involves at least four distinct dimensions, including idealized influence, inspirational motivation, intellectual stimulation, and individualized consideration (Bass, 1985). However, correlations among dimension scores are so strong that researchers often sum across them and use a single "transformational leadership" score. With little to no idea how to convincingly measure charismatic–transformational leadership, we are ill equipped to offer immediate managers concrete guidance on how they can display such leadership, let alone explain why and in which circumstances such behaviors would be particularly beneficial to employees' mental health. The implication is not that charismatic–transformational leadership does not exist, only that more research is necessary to clearly understand the distinct behaviors it truly involves. To that end, van Knippenberg and Sitkin (2013) proposed that scholars isolate elements of charismatic–transformational leadership (e.g., how leaders communicate an inspiring vision) without being confined by commonly used dysfunctional frameworks and operationalizations.

Transactional leadership would involve the use of contingent rewards (i.e., rewarding employees when they meet performance expectations) and the more active (timely) type of management-by-exception (i.e., monitoring employees and taking corrective action to prevent serious difficulties when their behavior deviates from expectations). Such behaviors seem relatively more concrete and easily distinguishable than those supposedly comprising transformational leadership.

The use of contingent rewards merits particular attention when considering its potential positive effects on employees' mental health. An immediate manager using such rewards clarifies the reward that will be given for meeting designated performance standards, makes sure employees receive appropriate rewards when they achieve performance targets, and/or expresses his/her satisfaction when they do a good job. The importance of using contingent rewards is not to be underestimated. Judge and Piccolo's (2004) meta-analytic review revealed that their use relates to employee job satisfaction and motivation as much as, if not more than, transformational leadership. People generally want to feel valued or appreciated for their contributions, making contingent rewards an important way of satisfying socioemotional needs. In fact, a large German study showed that immediate managers' use of contingent rewards can relate quite strongly to employees' mental and physical health (Zwingmann et al., 2014).

It is important to distinguish between formal contingent rewards, which usually have financial implications for employees (e.g., performance-based pay increases, promotions) and informal ones (e.g., expressing satisfaction to well-performing employees). Informal rewards lie outside the bureaucratic machinery of the organization. They can be equally if not more effective at satisfying employees' socioemotional needs, such as their need to belong, be cared about, be valued, feel competent, have personally meaningful work, have autonomy in how they do their work, and have influence over their broader social context (Deci & Ryan, 2000; Maslow, 1943; McClelland, 1987; Michaelson et al., 2014; Spreitzer, 1995). Work experiences that better satisfy such needs can be seen as more *intrinsically* motivating (Deci et al., 1989; Deci & Ryan, 1985; Spreitzer, 1995) and hence more conducive to better mental health (Caesens et al., 2020; Marin-Garcia & Bonavia, 2021). Examples of informal rewards helping to satisfy socioemotional needs include explaining to more highly performing employees *why* their contributions are so valuable and appreciated (to increase how meaningful they consider their work; Spreitzer, 1995), praising them for a job well-done (to give them a greater sense of competence, of feeling valued; Deci & Ryan, 1985; Spreitzer, 1995), giving them more latitude in choosing the best way to carry out their work (to give them greater autonomy; Deci & Ryan, 1985; Spreitzer, 1995), and soliciting as well as implementing their ideas for how the unit should operate (to help them realize they have impact; Spreitzer, 1995). Immediate managers who value their employees' mental health would do well to consider using such informal rewards alongside those integral to their organization's formal reward policies (Gilbert & Kelloway, 2018).

Of course, making employees' work more intrinsically motivating does not *only* have to be done as an informal reward for their work contributions. Organizational job redesign interventions aiming to enrich the characteristics of employees' jobs by making them less stressful and more intrinsically motivating have been shown to bolster employee mental health according to various indicators (Holman & Axtell, 2016; Holman et al., 2018). We urge immediate managers to involve their employees in determining how to make their jobs as intrinsically motivating as possible (Sorensen & Holman, 2014). At least some of the behaviors associated with empowering leadership would be useful to consider (Arnold et al., 2000).

The Leader–Member Exchange (LMX) Model of Leadership. For decades, LMX research has addressed dyadic (one-on-one) relational dynamics between managers (leaders) and their direct reports (members). Despite its impressive size, this literature has been heavily criticized. Most recently, Gottfredson et al. (2020) pointed out that there remains little consensus on best defining the LMX construct. Does it describe the differentiation of relationships and/or exchanges between managers and their different subordinates, the quality of the exchange and/or relationship between a manager and a subordinate, or some combination of the above? Definitional difficulties make it hard to develop a broadly endorsed LMX measure with compelling construct validity. Moreover, Gottfredson and colleagues argue that LMX measures do not adequately capture the notion of exchange, which appears in the title of the construct and is at the core of LMX theory. It can also be difficult to easily distinguish them from other measures, such as proposed antecedents and outcomes of LMX. However it is defined, the LMX construct has much more to do with describing the nature of manager–employee relationships than with delineating a comprehensive set of specific leadership behaviors. As such, neither LMX theory nor its measures appear particularly useful for clearly understanding the range of distinct behaviors that immediate managers should use to support their direct reports' mental health.

Consideration and Initiating Structure. Over half a century ago, leadership studies conducted at the Ohio State University identified and distinguished between two fundamental leadership styles, initiating structure and consideration (Fleishman, 1995; Stogdill, 1950). As interest in charismatic–transformational models of leadership gained popularity in the 1980s, organizational scholars eventually lost interest in initiating structure and consideration styles of leadership, condemning them as outdated and of little validity or utility. Yet, a meta-analytic review of those two rather discernable types of leadership behavior revealed that they both meaningfully relate to important outcomes, such as employee satisfaction, motivation, and group-organization performance (Judge et al., 2004). They also differ in the strength with which they relate to those outcomes, with consideration being more strongly related to employee satisfaction and motivation, and initiating structure more strongly related to group-organization performance.

Initiating structure denotes the degree to which immediate managers clarify and organize their role and those of their employees, are concerned with task accomplishment, and establish clear patterns and channels of communication (Fleishman, 1973). Examples include letting employees know what is specifically expected of them, making sure they understand the manager's role in the group, deciding what will be done and how it will be done, assigning specific tasks to employees, and scheduling the work to be done (Stogdill, 1963). Such a style of leading is clearly focused on ensuring employees have the necessary knowledge to accomplish their tasks, without necessarily trying to make them feel good or enjoy their work (although one does not have to preclude the other – more on that below). It is conceptually germane to active management-by-exception, although the latter only focuses on correcting employee mistakes. By clarifying roles and ways of achieving success, initiating structure can potentially reduce strain-inducing role ambiguity (Lee & Schuler, 1980) and help employees reap the (contingent) rewards of achieving higher levels of performance. As such, use of initiating structure can support employees' mental health, assuming it is used in ways that *they* consider helpful. Excessive use of initiating structure (used when employees do not need it) has been associated with unfavorable employee attitudes (Lambert et al., 2012). Giving structure in ways that ignore employees' needs could explain why that style of leadership, when compared to leader consideration, is less strongly related to employee satisfaction and motivation. For instance, employees will likely be frustrated (if not infuriated) when their managers insist on work methods that they consider overly cumbersome or bureaucratic. If those methods are warranted, then immediate managers could avoid frustrating their employees by providing a clearer rationale for insisting upon them.

Consideration involves showing concern for employees, respecting them, and looking out for their personal welfare. It therefore focuses on trying to satisfy employees' socioemotional needs, such as those noted earlier (e.g., to be cared about, to be valued, etc.). Unsurprisingly, consideration seems relatively more consequential than initiating structure to employees' mental health, as suggested by differences in their relationships with employee satisfaction and motivation (Judge et al., 2004). Examples include doing little things to make it pleasant for employees to be members of the group, doing personal favors for group members, finding time to listen to them, putting their suggestions into action, being willing to make changes, and giving advance notice of changes (Halpin, 1957; Stogdill, 1963). Such actions seem to be manifestations of empathy (i.e., the capacity and willingness to understand others' perspectives and experience emotions similar to theirs; Cuff et al., 2016) and altruism (i.e., selflessness and concern for others; Costa et al., 1991). The examples provided above also imply that being considerate of employees means being attuned to their socioemotional needs, whether they are exhibiting clear signs of poor mental health *or not*. We revisit this point later when discussing the social support literature.

There are some conceptual parallels between leader consideration and the full range leadership model discussed earlier. The use of contingent rewards evokes a considerate way of leading, in that the manager is concerned with satisfying employees' needs (e.g., for recognition). As such, use of contingent rewards could be considered an example of leader consideration, not simply a ploy to coax the highest level of performance out of employees. In fact, research has shown that the use of contingent rewards is more indicative of managers' efforts to nurture good relationships with their staff than of their efforts to ensure tasks are accomplished (Yukl, 1999). Also, leader consideration resembles the transformational leadership dimension of individualized consideration, although questionnaire items purportedly capturing that dimension make it unclear *how* consideration is actually shown (e.g., "Treats me as an individual rather than just a member of a group," "Treats each of us as individuals with different needs, abilities, and aspirations"; Bass & Avolio, 1990).

Leader consideration and, to some degree, initiating structure imply the provision of social support. Below, we delve into the workplace social support literature, especially work addressing supervisor-provided support, which further elucidates ways that immediate managers can benefit their employees' mental health.

Supervisor-Provided Social Support. Social support refers to psychological or material resources provided to a focal individual (e.g., the employee) by partners in some form of social relationship (e.g., the immediate manager; Jolly et al., 2021). It has been linked to both positive (e.g., work engagement) and negative (e.g., burnout) manifestations of mental health (Sarti, 2014; Viswesvaran et al., 1999). Despite the social support literature's limitations (e.g., fragmented conceptual development, inconsistent definitions and operationalizations, lack of fit between studied supports and stressors; Jolly et al., 2021), it has helped distinguish between at least two broad types of socially supportive behavior that immediate managers (and others) can display: *emotional* and *instrumental* support.

Whereas emotional support involves trying to satisfy employees' socioemotional needs by showing empathy, caring, love, and trust, instrumental support does so by providing more tangible resources (e.g., time, schedule flexibility, task-specific knowledge) that employees can use to address a specific problem or challenge (House, 1981). Although other general types of social support have been proposed (e.g., informational, appraisal; House, 1981), emotional and instrumental support have been those most often studied (Jolly et al., 2021).

Examples of emotional support include paying attention to employees' feelings, making the time to listen to their work-related or personal problems, showing an interest in their opinions, trying to make their job as interesting as possible, saying things that would raise their self-confidence, helping them move up the ranks, and speaking highly of them when they have significantly contributed to the group (Caplan et al., 1975; Eisenberger et al., 1986; Peeters et al., 1995; Vinokur et al., 1987). The last example denotes the use of a contingent reward, further reinforcing our earlier point that such rewards can be used to show consideration for employees' socioemotional needs.

Examples of instrumental support include finding ways to give them more time when they feel overloaded (extending a deadline and/or reducing workload), helping them when they need a special favor, granting a reasonable request for changes in their working conditions, showing them how to more easily or successfully accomplish tasks they are struggling with, and giving them advice on how to handle specific challenges (Eisenberger et al., 1986; Peeters et al., 1995). The latter two examples evoke the initiating structure style of leadership. *Thus, task-focused leadership does not necessarily imply a lack of consideration of employees' socioemotional needs.* Providing structure that they appreciate will presumably be taken as a sign of consideration. It therefore seems of limited value to focus on the distinction between consideration and initiating structure when it comes to employees' mental health. Instead, we suggest that managers hold a broader view of leader consideration that involves emotional and instrumental types of social support, the latter of which can involve the provision of structure that employees endorse.

The examples of support given above reveal that employee distress is not a necessary condition to provide either emotional or instrumental types of support. Some measures of social support (e.g., most of the items in the commonly used Caplan et al. [1975] measure) imply that struggling employees are those who need support, which is misleading. For example, although employees may not be in distress, they could still very much appreciate a manager who shows interest in their opinions, tries to make their job more interesting, or provides guidance on how to overcome specific challenges at work. Unless they are experiencing serious mental health problems, employees will not necessarily make their socioemotional needs obvious or apparent. Thus, to help them have the best possible mental health (beyond an absence of mental illness), immediate managers should regularly consider how their employees could be perceiving and reacting to workplace circumstances, be mindful of their more subtle nonverbal cues (e.g., those signaling disappointment, frustration), and proactively engage them in conversations meant to explore their specific needs and determine how they could be satisfied.

The workplace social support literature has also examined how immediate managers can lend support to employees on issues that transcend the workplace. Examples include "family-supportive supervisor behaviors" and "healthy leadership," each of which is salient to employees' mental health.

Family-Supportive Supervisor Behaviors (FSSBs). These behaviors aim to help employees more successfully manage the intersection of their work and family lives. Employees who experience greater conflict between both domains tend to report poorer mental health (Amstad et al., 2011; Greenhaus et al., 2006; Shockley & Allen, 2013). FSSBs can involve emotional support (e.g., being willing to listen to

employees' problems in juggling work and family demands), instrumental support (e.g., helping employees with work–family scheduling
conflicts), as well as role-modeling (e.g., displaying how to balance
work and family roles) and creative work–family management (e.g.,
soliciting and implementing employee suggestions that would facilitate
work–family balance; Hammer et al., 2009). Although similar in
nature to previously discussed examples of considerate leadership
(e.g., emotional support, instrumental support, and soliciting/imple-
menting employees' ideas), FSSBs explicitly focus on helping employees
more successfully deal with competing work and family role demands.
This probably explains why they relate more strongly than supportive
supervision of a more general nature to reduced work–family conflict
(Kossek et al., 2011). FSSBs have also been shown to relate more
strongly than perceived managerial effectiveness to higher levels of
employee work engagement and subjective well-being, particularly
among employees with dependent care responsibilities and no family-
friendly benefits available (Matthews et al., 2014). Several studies have
reported positive relationships of FSSBs with employees' mental and
physical health (for a review, see Crain & Stevens, 2018). The seemingly unique value of FSSBs to employees' capacity to successfully
juggle work and family demands highlights the idea that managers
must provide employees with the specific type of support they need to
overcome their particular challenge (i.e., support-stressor match;
Jolly et al., 2021; Viswesvaran et al., 1999). We revisit this point
further on.

Healthy leadership. Several models of healthy leadership have been
introduced over the past decade to address the health-specific effects
that leaders (immediate managers) can have on employees' physical,
mental, and social well-being. These models have sought to overcome
the vagueness with which more "established" models of leadership
(e.g., transformational, LMX) address employee health (Franke et al.,
2011). Among the various models proposed (for a review, see Rudolph
et al., 2020), two have received significantly more research attention:
"health-promoting" and "health-oriented" leadership.

Health-promoting leadership purportedly involves having a supportive leadership style, organizing health-promoting activities, and
developing a health-promoting workplace (Eriksson et al., 2011).
However, its measurement emphasizes the types of considerate leadership behavior described earlier in this chapter over behaviors explicitly

addressing employees' health. For example, most of the 21-item Health-Promoting Leadership Conditions questionnaire (HPLC; Dunkl et al., 2015) captures efforts to provide emotional and instrumental types of social support. Only three items mention health (e.g., "My leader takes care that the health of all employees is promoted"). Although this measure's item content reinforces the value of emotional and instrumental types of supervisor-given social support to employee (mental) health, it does little to clearly distinguish so-called health-promoting leadership from previously studied considerate leadership behaviors.

In contrast, health-oriented leadership is more explicitly health-focused. It is said to encompass leaders' health-promoting communication and design of working conditions, as well as their values toward, and awareness of, their followers' health (Franke & Felfe, 2011). Its operationalization (Franke et al., 2014) involves manager self-ratings and employee-provided ratings of the immediate manager's *self-care* (i.e., health-oriented self-leadership) and *staff-care* (i.e., health-oriented leadership of employees). Self-care and staff-care would both involve the manager's health-oriented *awareness* (i.e., awareness of own health and of that of staff members), *values* (i.e., prioritizes own health and that of staff members), and *behavior* (i.e., makes decisions that benefit own health and that of staff members).

Advocating the use of two rating sources (managers and their direct reports) can be useful for examining rater agreement and for improving health-oriented communication between managers and their staff. The distinction between managers' self-care and staff-care is particularly interesting in that it stresses the idea that managers would be ill positioned to care for their employees if they lack the capacity or desire to care for themselves (Franke et al., 2015).

A few studies report that ratings of managers' health-oriented leadership relate to indicators of employee mental health, including less irritation and fewer somatic complaints, as well as lower levels of burnout and depression (Franke & Felfe, 2011; Santa Maria et al., 2019), and seem to do so above and beyond the variance explained by transformational leadership (Franke et al., 2014). Despite some limitations (e.g., several items failing to capture concrete behaviors, some items confounding support with outcomes of support), evidence to date suggests that healthy leadership could be of unique benefit to employees' mental health.

Summary of Insights from Constructive Leadership Research. The literature addressing constructive forms of leadership provides several insights into how immediate managers can sustain or even enhance their employees' mental health. First, in addition to avoiding displays of destructive leadership, being considerate of employees' socioemotional needs appears key. Consideration can involve the provision of emotional and instrumental types of social support. Emotional support involves communicating to employees that they are cared about, valued, respected, and trusted. This can involve a variety of behaviors (see examples above), including the use of contingent rewards, assuming those rewards satisfy socioemotional needs. Instrumental support involves providing employees with resources that directly help them overcome specific challenges. Examples include providing more time, money, and/or people to accomplish a task, as well as providing structure (e.g., information, guidance) on how to overcome a specific challenge.

Second, immediate managers can benefit their employees' mental health by taking care of their own mental health. This is exemplified by research on FSSBs ("role-modeling") and on health-oriented leadership ("self-care"). Given the near ubiquitous challenge of having conflicting work and nonwork role demands and its negative association with mental health (Allen et al., 2020), modeling how to effectively balance work and nonwork aspects of one's life could be viewed as part of the broader notion of manager self-care. It is plausible that managers who look after their own mental health would experience less stress that would otherwise curtail their capacity to support their employees (Harms et al., 2017). Also, social learning theory (Bandura, 1977) suggests that observing how managers look after their own health could give employees greater comfort and/or motivation to do the same for themselves.

Third, consistent with the "matching hypothesis" (Viswesvaran et al., 1999), it seems important to ensure that employees receive the support that is most salient to their needs. For instance, FSSBs have been shown to explain variance in employees' work–family conflict above and beyond general supervisor support, and health-oriented leadership would explain incremental variance in employee mental health beyond the effects of transformational leadership (though for reasons unknown given the challenges with current conceptualizations and operationalizations of transformational leadership – see above).

This further supports our earlier suggestion that managers must take the time to become keenly aware of their employees' specific challenges, whether they are work-related *or not*, if they are to provide them with the most beneficial support. What remains unanswered is whether the types of supervisor support discussed so far are sufficient to help employees maintain the best possible mental health. Are additional or more specific supportive behaviors needed to achieve this aim?

Supporting Employees *Who* Seriously *Struggle with Their Mental Health*

None of the empirical literature we reviewed addresses how immediate managers can support employees experiencing particularly poor mental health. When employees show signs of a serious mental health problem or illness, such as symptoms of a major depressive episode (e.g., displaying over several weeks a depressed mood, a markedly diminished interest or pleasure in all or most activities, indecisiveness; American Psychiatric Association, 2013), managers can feel ill equipped to be supportive (Thorpe & Chenier, 2011). This is not surprising since mental illnesses are rather poorly understood among the public, concealable to some degree (especially when they are experienced more episodically than chronically), and often stigmatized.

Stigmatized views of mental illness are varied. Examples include believing the mentally ill are difficult to interact with, that their illness is a sign of weakness, or that they will have the illness for life (Jones et al., 1984; Smith, 2019). One can only assume that managers holding such views would be less disposed to helping mentally ill employees, if not more likely to treat them poorly (e.g., ostracizing them, belittling them). In fact, beliefs that others could hold such stigmatized views and discriminate against the mentally ill is one of the key reasons why struggling employees conceal rather than disclose what they are living with (Brohan et al., 2012; Hastuti & Timming, 2021). However, although disclosure can lead to unfair treatment, it can also be a necessary step to receive the most beneficial support (Bonaccio et al., 2019; Hastuti & Timming, 2021). Thus, to make employees in crisis sufficiently comfortable to confide in them and seek their help, managers would *first* need to provide compelling evidence (e.g., prior displays of support) that they would likely help rather than harm mentally ill employees.

Although symptoms of a serious mental health problem may not have an obvious triggering event, let alone one tied to work, immediate managers can still provide support that would help reduce their severity and/or duration. "Mental Health First Aid" training, which is currently offered in several countries and has been shown to be effective (Hadlaczky et al., 2014), describes behaviors that anyone (including immediate managers) can use to support a person experiencing a mental health crisis, such as having a panic attack or feeling suicidal. These include listening nonjudgmentally, giving reassurance, offering practical help to overcome the crisis, encouraging appropriate professional help, and encouraging self-help (National Council for Mental Wellbeing, 2021). Such actions seem to require at least some understanding of mental illnesses, such as how and why symptoms manifest, and what specific types of support could help. Many managers seem to lack this knowledge (Dimoff & Kelloway, 2019), which is what prompted the development of the RESPECT and MHAT training programs discussed earlier.

Toward a More Comprehensive Conceptualization of Mental-Health-Supportive Supervision

To guide future work on how immediate managers can best support their employees' mental health, we propose a taxonomy of behaviors exemplifying mental-health-supportive supervision (MHSS). This taxonomy integrates research-based insights highlighted in the preceding pages and specific behaviors advocated by Mental Health First Aid. We include actions that should be avoided (destructive leadership) and those that should be enacted (constructive leadership) as they are not mutually exclusive (e.g., a manager can be destructive on one day and constructive on another).

Our MHSS behavioral taxonomy includes six different types of behavior. Two describe destructive leadership (active and passive) and four describe constructive leadership. The four types of constructive leadership reflect a broader conceptualization of leader consideration. They are rooted in House's (1981) seminal work distinguishing between emotional, instrumental, informational, and appraisal types of social support. As explained below, including the latter two types enabled us to better integrate actions promoted by Mental Health First Aid into our taxonomy.

The range of behaviors denoting emotional and instrumental types of support would include those described earlier as well as those promoted by Mental Health First Aid. For instance, MHSS can include emotionally supportive actions such as nonjudgmental listening and the provision of encouragement when an employee is experiencing a severe mental health problem. Similarly, instrumental support can involve practical ways of overcoming a particular mental health crisis.

Informational support involves providing information that is not immediately instrumental in solving an employee's problem but can potentially lead to useful resources. Examples salient to MHSS include providing information on resources accessible through the organization's EAP and, as advocated by Mental Health First Aid, encouraging employees to seek professional help if they are seriously struggling. Like informational support, appraisal support only involves the transmission of information. This type of information would facilitate employee self-evaluation by providing them with a point of social comparison. Examples consistent with Mental Health First Aid could include encouraging employees to use specific self-care strategies and providing feedback on their self-care behaviors, both of which could help them better understand their own self-care. Although more implicit in nature, managers could also offer appraisal support by serving as self-care role models (Franke et al., 2014).

Table 15.1 includes, for each of the six types of behavior included in our taxonomy, a range of examples drawn from our literature review. All are worded from the employee perspective. They can be used in a questionnaire asking employees to rate the frequency with which their immediate manager engages in each by using the MLQ's five-point frequency response scale (0 – Not at all; 1 – Once in a while; 2 – Sometimes; 3 – Fairly often; 4 – Frequently, if not always). To minimize ambiguity, we worded the behaviors as concretely as possible by focusing on observable actions, avoiding double-barreling and any mention of the effects of the behavior on employee mental health, and sometimes specifying the circumstances in which the behavior is displayed (e.g., "when...," "if..."). Research suggests that concretely worded behavioral scale items facilitate respondents' access to episodic memory, meaning the recollection of incidents involving specific behaviors displayed by their manager (Hansbrough et al., 2021). The

480

Table 15.1 *Proposed behavioral taxonomy for mental-health-supportive supervision*

Type of behavior	Definition	Behavioral examples	Sources[a]
Destructive leadership – Active (*to be avoided*)	Being overly punitive or aggressive.	Excludes me from work group activities.	Einarsen (2000)
		Tells me my thoughts or feelings are stupid or ridiculous.	Tepper (2000)
			Rospenda (2002)
		Threatens to punish me if I don't do what is asked.	Duffy et al. (2002)
		Puts me down when I question decisions or work procedures.	Tepper (2000)
		Blames me for problems that I am not responsible for.	Rospenda (2002)
		Yells or swears at me.	
Destructive leadership – Passive (*to be avoided*)	Failing to live up to one's leadership responsibilities.	Waits for a problem to get very serious before acting.	Bass and Avolio (1990, 1994)
		Waits for a problem to occur several times before trying to address it.	Bass and Avolio (1990, 1994)
		Is unavailable when needed.	Bass and Avolio (1990, 1994)
		Takes too long to respond to an urgency.	Bass and Avolio (1990, 1994)
		Delays making up his/her mind.	Bass and Avolio (1990, 1994)
Constructive leadership – Emotional support	Showing empathy, caring, love, and trust toward the employee.	Asks me for my opinion.	Eisenberger et al. (1986)
		Puts my suggestions into action.	Stogdill (1963)
		Considers my personal needs or preferences when making decisions.	Eisenberger et al. (1986)
		Explains his/her decisions and actions to me.	Arnold et al. (2000)
		Speaks highly of me when I make a strong contribution.	Bass and Avolio (1990, 1994)
		Ensures I get appropriate credit for my contributions.	Bass and Avolio (1990, 1994)
		Tells me *why* my work is important.	Spreitzer (1995)
			Eisenberger et al. (1986)

	Item	Reference
	Gives me the freedom to decide how I do my work.	Dunkl et al. (2015)
	Remains respectful/polite with me when I make a mistake.	Eisenberger et al. (1986)
	Checks in with me when I show a change in my emotions or mood.	Franke et al. (2014)
	Invites me to talk about what is troubling me.	Caplan et al. (1975)
	Takes the time to patiently discuss my concerns.	Arnold et al. (2000)
	Makes sure he/she clearly understands what I am saying.	Vinokur et al. (1987)
	Tells me I have nothing to be ashamed of when I am very depressed or anxious.	National Council for Mental Wellbeing (2021)
	Reassures me when I am feeling very depressed or anxious, such as telling me that it's going to be alright.	National Council for Mental Wellbeing (2021)
Constructive leadership – Instrumental support: Giving employees what they need to overcome a specific work-related or personal challenge.	Clarifies what I need to achieve (specific goals, deadlines, quality standards, etc.) when I am uncertain.	Stogdill (1963)
	Helps me prioritize tasks or projects when I have too much on my plate.	Franke et al. (2014)
	Helps me coordinate more effectively with others.	Stogdill (1963)
	Shows me how to better perform a task that I struggle with.	Peeters et al. (1995)
	Gives me additional time to complete my work when I need it.	Dunkl et al. (2015)
	Proposes practical solutions for reducing my stress.	Franke et al. (2014)
	Reduces my workload when it is more than I can manage.	Peeters et al. (1995)
	Gives me flexibility in my work schedule when I need it.	Hammer et al. (2009)

Table 15.1 (*cont.*)

Type of behavior	Definition	Behavioral examples	Sources[a]
Constructive leadership – Informational support	Giving employees information on resources that could potentially benefit their mental health.	Makes it easy for me to work from home when I need to.	Hammer et al. (2009)
		Gives me useful advice for solving personal problems.	McMullan et al. (2018)
		Grants my requests for special accommodations.	Eisenberger et al. (1986)
		Speaks highly of our EAP.	Dimoff and Kelloway (2018)
		Clarifies what my health benefits include.	Dimoff and Kelloway (2018)
		Encourages me to use my health benefits.	Dimoff and Kelloway (2018)
		Encourages me to seek the help of a professional if I am seriously struggling with my mental health.	National Council for Mental Wellbeing (2021)
Constructive leadership – Appraisal support	Helping employees evaluate how well they care for their own mental health.	Demonstrates how to put healthy limits on work.	Franke et al. (2014)
		Is a good role model for work and nonwork balance.*	Hammer et al. (2009)
		Demonstrates how to stay healthy.	Peeters et al. (1995)
		Praises my efforts to take care of my mental health.	National Council for Mental Wellbeing (2021)
		Encourages me to take better care of my mental health.	National Council for Mental Wellbeing (2021)

[a] These sources provide conceptualizations and/or scale items used as a basis for the behavioral examples included. The list of sources is not exhaustive. Several behaviors were based on multiple sources. Those marked with an asterisk were taken verbatim from the source.

more abstract or vague the wording, the more respondents would base their ratings on general impressions (e.g., how much they like their manager overall). To further increase respondents' use of episodic memory, we suggest that survey instructions include a lay distinction between episodic and semantic memory, and encourage respondents to rely on the former (for more information, see study one of Hansbrough et al., 2021). With respect to the behaviors denoting constructive leadership, we strongly recommend that the response scale include a sixth option letting respondents indicate that they have not been in circumstances calling for such behavior (e.g., "Not applicable to me" or "There has not been any need for my manager to display this behavior") .

We cannot presume that the six types of behavior included in our taxonomy are clearly distinct from each other. Some may covary to such a degree as to be deemed reflective of a common, broader type of support. Empirical work is therefore required to examine the factor structure underlying observed relationships among these behaviors.

Conclusion

Drawing from considerable academic literature, this chapter high-lighted specific ways managers can act to protect, if not enhance, their employees' mental health. Senior managers can do so through the specific HR policies and practices they institute, and by serving as MHSS role models for those below them in the organization. Irrespective of the example set by their superiors, immediate managers must strive to exemplify MHSS. In addition to avoiding passive and abusive leadership, MHSS can involve showing care and consideration of employees' needs or preferences, directly helping them overcome specific challenges, giving them information on potentially useful mental-health-supportive resources, and helping them see how they can better take care of their mental health. Managers' propensity to provide MHSS to all employees, including those seriously struggling with their mental health, is likely to increase with their understanding of mental illnesses.

The importance for managers to maintain their own mental health cannot be overstated. Doing so should facilitate their capacity to display MHSS. As such, they need to know how to look after them-selves. This can involve various tactics, such as seeking support themselves, making time for their personal life, and setting limits on work demands. Sometimes, setting limits can involve the cessation of attempts to support an unreasonably needy employee.

We encourage scholars to empirically test the validity of our proposed taxonomy of MHSS behaviors. Efforts should also be made to elucidate the personal and contextual factors explaining why managers vary in their display of MHSS, either over time or relative to each other. Furthermore, we need to understand *why* MHSS would benefit employees' mental health. Is it solely due to socioemotional needs being satisfied? If so, which specific needs are most important to satisfy and which types of MHSS would best satisfy them? If not, what other mediating mechanisms are at play? Lastly, future research must identify circumstances in which different types of MHSS would be of greatest benefit. Until then, we will be ill positioned to provide evidence-based guidance on *when* to offer certain types of support to employees.

References

Allen, T. D., French, K. A., Dumani, S., & Shockley, K. M. (2020). A cross-national meta-analytic examination of predictors and outcomes associated with work–family conflict. *Journal of Applied Psychology, 105,* 539–576.

American Psychiatric Association. (2013). *Diagnostic and statistical manual of mental disorders* (5th ed.). American Psychiatric Publishing.

Amstad, F. T., Meier, L. L., Fasel, U., Elfering, A., & Semmer, N. K. (2011). A meta-analysis of work–family conflict and various outcomes with a special emphasis on cross-domain versus matching-domain relations. *Journal of Occupational Health Psychology, 16,* 151–169.

Arnold, J., Arad, S., Roades, J. A., & Drasgow, F. (2000). The empowering leadership questionnaire: The construction and validation of a new scale for measuring leader behaviors. *Journal of Organizational Behavior, 21,* 249–269.

Attridge, M., Cahill, T., Granberry, S. W., & Herlihy, P. A. (2013). The National Behavioral Consortium Industry Profile of External EAP Vendors. *Journal of Workplace Behavioral Health, 28,* 251–324.

Attridge, M., Sharar, D. A., DeLapp, G. P., & Veder, B. (2018). EAP Works: Global results from 24,363 counseling cases with pre–post data on the Workplace Outcome Suite (WOS). *International Journal of Health & Productivity.* https://archive.hshsl.umaryland.edu/handle/10713/8962

Avolio, B. J. (2011). *Full range leadership development* (2nd ed.). Sage.

Bandura, A. (1977). *Social learning theory.* Prentice-Hall.

Banks, M. H., Clegg, C. W., Jackson, P. R., Kemp, N. J., Stafford, E. M., & Wall, T. D. (1980). The use of the General Health Questionnaire as an indicator of mental health in occupational studies. *Journal of Occupational Psychology, 53,* 187–194.

Barry, M. M., Clarke, A. M., Petersen, I., & Jenkins, R. (Eds.). (2019). *Implementing mental health promotion* (2nd ed.). Springer.

Bass, B. M. (1985). *Leadership and performance beyond expectations.* Free Press.

Bass, B. M., & Avolio, B. J. (1990). *Transformational leadership development: Manual for the multifactor leadership questionnaire.* Consulting Psychologists Press.

(1994). *Improving organizational effectiveness through transformational leadership.* Sage.

Bedwell, W. L., Fiore, S. M., & Salas, E. (2014). Developing the future workforce: An approach for integrating interpersonal skills into the MBA classroom. *Academy of Management Learning & Education, 13,* 171–186.

Bloom, D. E., Cafiero, E., Jané-Llopis, E., Abrahams-Gessel, S., Bloom, L. R., Fathima, S., . . . Weiss, J. (2012). The global economic burden of non-communicable diseases. In *PGDA Working Papers* (No. 8712). Program on the Global Demography of Aging.

Bonaccio, S., Lapierre, L. M., & O'Reilly, J. (2019). Creating work climates that facilitate and maximize the benefits of disclosing mental health problems in the workplace. *Organizational Dynamics, 48,* 113–122.

Brohan, E., Henderson, C., Wheat, K., Malcolm, E., Clement, S., Barley, E. A., . . . Thornicroft, G. (2012). Systematic review of beliefs, behaviors and influencing factors associated with disclosure of a mental health problem in the workplace. *BMC Psychiatry, 12,* 11.

Bycio, P., Hackett, R. D., & Allen, J. S. (1995). Further assessments of Bass's (1985) conceptualization of transactional and transformational leadership. *Journal of Applied Psychology, 80,* 468–478.

Caesens, G., Bouchat, P., & Stinglhamber, F. (2020). Perceived organizational support and psychological empowerment: A multi-sample study. *Journal of Occupational and Environmental Medicine, 62,* 526–531.

Caplan, R. D., Cobb, S., French, J. P. R., Harrison, R. V., & Pinneau, S. R. (1975). *Job demands and worker health: Main effects and occupational differences.* National Institute for Occupational Safety and Health.

Clarke, M. (2016). Addressing the soft skills crisis. *Strategic HR Review, 15,* 137–139.

Cohen, B. E., Edmondson, D., & Kronish, I. M. (2015). State of the art review: Depression, stress, anxiety, and cardiovascular disease. *American Journal of Hypertension, 28*, 1295–1302.

Colbert, A. E., Bono, J. E., & Purvanova, R. K. (2016). Flourishing via workplace relationships: Moving beyond instrumental support. *Academy of Management Journal, 59*, 1199–1223.

Cole, M. S., Walter, F., Bedeian, A. G., & O'Boyle, E. H. (2012). Job burnout and employee engagement: A meta-analytic examination of construct proliferation. *Journal of Management, 38*, 1550–1581.

Conger, J. A., & Kanungo, R. N. (1987). Toward a behavioral theory of charismatic leadership in organizational settings. *Academy of Management Review, 12*, 637–647.

Costa, P. T., McCrae, R. R., & Dye, D. A. (1991). Facet scales for agreeableness and conscientiousness: A revision of the NEO Personality Inventory. *Personality and Individual Differences, 12*, 887–898.

Crain, T. L., & Stevens, S. C. (2018). Family-supportive supervisor behaviors: A review and recommendations for research and practice. *Journal of Organizational Behavior, 37*(7), 869–888. https://doi.org/10.1002/job.2320

Cuff, B. M. P., Brown, S. J., Taylor, L., & Howat, D. J. (2016). Empathy: A review of the concept. *Emotion Review, 8*, 144–153.

Deci, E. L., Connell, J. P., & Ryan, R. M. (1989). Self-determination in a work organization. *Journal of Applied Psychology, 74*, 580–590.

Deci, E. L., & Ryan, R. M. (1985). *Intrinsic motivation and self-determination in human behavior*. Plenum Press.

(2000). The "what" and "why" of goal pursuits: Human needs and the self-determination of behavior. *Psychological Inquiry, 11*, 227–268.

Diener, E., Emmons, R. A., Larsen, R. J., & Griffin, S. (1985). The Satisfaction With Life Scale. *Journal of Personality Assessment, 49*, 71.

Dimoff, J. K., & Kelloway, E. (2018). With a little help from my boss: The impact of workplace mental health training on leader behaviors and employee resource utilization. *Journal of Occupational Health Psychology*, n.p.

Dimoff, J. K., & Kelloway, E. K. (2019). Mental health problems are management problems: Exploring the critical role of managers in supporting employee mental health. *Organizational Dynamics, 48*, 105–112.

Dimoff, J. K., Kelloway, E. K., & Burnstein, M. D. (2016). Mental health awareness training (MHAT): The development and evaluation of an intervention for workplace leaders. *International Journal of Stress Management, 23*, 167–189.

Duffy, M. K., Ganster, D. C., & Pagon, M. (2002). Social undermining in the workplace. *Academy of Management Journal, 45*, 331–351.

Dunkl, A., Jiménez, P., Šarotar Žižek, S., Milfelner, B., & Kallus, W. K. (2015). Similarities and differences of health-promoting leadership and transformational leadership. *Naše Gospodarstvo/Our Economy, 61*, 3–13.

Einarsen, S. (2000). Harassment and bullying at work: A review of the Scandinavian approach. *Aggression and Violent Behavior, 5*, 379–401.

Eisenberger, R., Huntington, R., Hutchison, S., & Sowa, D. (1986). Perceived organizational support. *Journal of Applied Psychology, 71*, 500–507.

Eriksson, A., Axelsson, R., & Axelsson, S. B. (2011). Health promoting leadership – different views of the concept. *Work, 40*, 75–84.

Fleishman, E. A. (1973). Twenty years of consideration and structure. In E. A. Fleishman & J. G. Hunt (Eds.), *Current developments in the study of leadership* (pp. 1–40). Southern Illinois University Press.

(1995). Consideration and structure: Another look at their role in leadership research. In F. Dansereau & F. J. Yammarino (Eds.), *Leadership: The multiple-level approaches* (pp. 51–60). JAI Press.

Franke, F., Ducki, A., & Felfe, J. (2015). Gesundheitsförderliche Führung. *Trends der psychologischen Führungsforschung* (pp. 253–264). Scopus.

Franke, F., & Felfe, J. (2011). Diagnose gesundheitsförderlicher Führung – Das Instrument "Health-oriented Leadership." In B. Badura, A. Ducki, H. Schröder, J. Klose, & K. Macco (Eds.), *Fehlzeiten-Report 2011: Führung und Gesundheit: Zahlen, Daten, Analysen aus allen Branchen der Wirtschaft* (pp. 3–13). Springer.

Franke, F., Felfe, J., & Pundt, A. (2014). The impact of health-oriented leadership on follower health: Development and test of a new instrument measuring health-promoting leadership. *Zeitschrift Für Personalforschung, 28*, 139–161.

Franke, F., Vincent, S., & Felfe, J. (2011). Gesundheitsbezogene führung. In E. Bamberg, A. Ducki, & A.-M. Metz (Eds.), *Gesundheitsförderung und Gesundheitsmanagement in der Arbeitswelt. Ein Handbuch* (pp. 371–392). Hogrefe.

Gilbert, S. L., & Kelloway, E. K. (2018). Leadership, recognition and well-being: A moderated mediational model. *Canadian Journal of Administrative Sciences / Revue Canadienne Des Sciences de l'Administration, 35*, 523–534.

Gottfredson, R. K., Wright, S. L., & Heaphy, E. D. (2020). A critique of the leader–member exchange construct: Back to square one. *The Leadership Quarterly*, 101385.

Graen, G. B., & Uhl-Bien, M. (1995). Development of leader–member exchange (LMX) theory of leadership over 25 years: Applying a multi-level multi-domain perspective. *Leadership Quarterly, 6*, 219–247.

Greenhaus, J. H., Allen, T. D., & Spector, P. E. (2006). Health consequences of work–family conflict: The dark side of the work–family interface. In P. L. Perrewé & D. C. Ganster (Eds.), *Research in occupational stress and well-being* (Vol. 5, pp. 61–98). Emerald Group.

Hackman, J. R., & Oldham, G. R. (1980). *Work redesign.* Addison-Wesley.

Hadlaczky, G., Hökby, S., Mkrtchian, A., Carli, V., & Wasserman, D. (2014). Mental Health First Aid is an effective public health intervention for improving knowledge, attitudes, and behavior: A meta-analysis. *International Review of Psychiatry, 26*, 467–475.

Halpin, A. W. (1957). *Manual for the LEADER BEHAVIOR DESCRIPTION QUESTIONNAIRE.* Fisher College of Business, The Ohio State University.

Hammer, L. B., Kossek, E. E., Yragui, N. L., Bodner, T. E., & Hanson, G. C. (2009). Development and validation of a multidimensional measure of family supportive supervisor behaviors (FSSB). *Journal of Management, 35*, 837–856.

Hansbrough, T. K., Lord, R. G., Schyns, B., Foti, R. J., Liden, R. C., & Acton, B. P. (2021). Do you remember? Rater memory systems and leadership measurement. *The Leadership Quarterly, 32*, 101455.

Harms, P. D., Credé, M., Tynan, M., Leon, M., & Jeung, W. (2017). Leadership and stress: A meta-analytic review. *The Leadership Quarterly, 28*, 178–194.

Hastuti, R., & Timming, A. R. (2021). An inter-disciplinary review of the literature on mental illness disclosure in the workplace: Implications for human resource management. *The International Journal of Human Resource Management, 32*(15), 3302–3338.

Holman, D., & Axtell, C. (2016). Can job redesign interventions influence a broad range of employee outcomes by changing multiple job character-istics? A quasi-experimental study. *Journal of Occupational Health Psychology, 21*, 284–295.

Holman, D., Johnson, S., & O'Connor, E. (2018). Stress management interventions: Improving subjective psychological well-being in the workplace. In E. Diener, S. Oishi, & L. Tay (Eds.), *Handbook of well-being* (pp. 754–766). DEF Publishers.

House, J. S. (1981). *Work stress and social support.* Addison-Wesley.

Human Resources Professionals Association of Ontario. (2021). HRPA 2020 Trends Survey report. www.hrpa.ca/hrpa-2020-trends-survey-gate-2021-03-24/

Jex, S. M., & Beehr, T. A. (1991). Emerging theoretical and methodological issues in the study of work-related stress. *Research in Personnel and Human Resources Management, 9,* 311–365.

Jolly, P. M., Kong, D. T., & Kim, K. Y. (2021). Social support at work: An integrative review. *Journal of Organizational Behavior, 42,* 229–251.

Jones, E. E., Farina, A., Hastorf, A. H., Markus, H., Miller, D. T., & Scott, R. A. (1984). *Social stigma: The psychology of marked relationships.* Freeman.

Joseph, B., Walker, A., & Fuller-Tyszkiewicz, M. (2018). Evaluating the effectiveness of employee assistance programmes: A systematic review. *European Journal of Work and Organizational Psychology, 27,* 1–15.

Judge, T. A., & Piccolo, R. F. (2004). Transformational and transactional leadership: A meta-analytic test of their relative validity. *Journal of Applied Psychology, 89,* 755–768.

Judge, T. A., Piccolo, R. F., & Ilies, R. (2004). The forgotten ones? The validity of consideration and initiating structure in leadership research. *Journal of Applied Psychology, 89,* 36–51.

Kaiser Family Foundation. (2020, October 8). 2020 Employer Health Benefits Survey. www.kff.org/health-costs/report/2020-employer-health-benefits-survey/

Kelloway, E. K., Sivanathan, N., Francis, L., & Barling, J. (2005). Poor leadership. In J. Barling & E. K. Kelloway (Eds.), *Handbook of work stress* (pp. 89–112). Sage.

Keyes, C. L. M. (2007). Promoting and protecting mental health as flourishing: A complementary strategy for improving national mental health. *American Psychologist, 62,* 95–108.

Kossek, E. E., Pichler, S., Bodner, T., & Hammer, L. B. (2011). Workplace social support and work–family conflict: A meta-analysis clarifying the influence of general and work-family specific supervisor and organizational support. *Personnel Psychology, 64,* 289–313.

Lambert, L. S., Tepper, B. J., Carr, J. C., Holt, D. T., & Barelka, A. J. (2012). Forgotten but not gone: An examination of fit between leader consideration and initiating structure needed and received. *Journal of Applied Psychology, 97,* 913–930.

Lee, C., & Schuler, R. S. (1980). Goal specificity and difficulty and leader initiating structure as strategies for managing role stress. *Journal of Management, 6,* 177–187.

Mackey, J. D., Frieder, R. E., Brees, J. R., & Martinko, M. J. (2017). Abusive supervision: A meta-analysis and empirical review. *Journal of Management, 43,* 1940–1965.

Marin-Garcia, J. A., & Bonavia, T. (2021). Empowerment and employee well-being: A mediation analysis study. *International Journal of Environmental Research and Public Health, 18,* 5822.

Maslow, A. H. (1943). A theory of human motivation. *Psychological Review, 50,* 370–396.

Matthews, R. A., Mills, M. J., Trout, R. C., & English, L. (2014). Family-supportive supervisor behaviors, work engagement, and subjective well-being: A contextually dependent mediated process. *Journal of Occupational Health Psychology, 19,* 168–181.

McClelland, D. C. (1987). *Human motivation.* Cambridge University Press.

McManus, S., Meltzer, H., Brugha, T. S., Bebbington, P. E., & Jenkins, R. (2009). Adult psychiatric morbidity in England – 2007, results of a household survey. https://digital.nhs.uk/data-and-information/publica tions/statistical/adult-psychiatric-morbidity-survey/adult-psychiatric-morbidity-in-england-2007-results-of-a-household-survey

McMullan, A. D., Lapierre, L. M., & Li, Y. (2018). A qualitative investigation of work-family-supportive coworker behaviors. *Journal of Vocational Behavior, 107,* 25–41.

Michaelson, C., Pratt, M. G., Grant, A. M., & Dunn, C. P. (2014). Meaningful work: Connecting business ethics and organization studies. *Journal of Business Ethics, 121,* 77–90.

Milligan-Saville, J. S., Tan, L., Gayed, A., Barnes, C., Madan, I., Dobson, M., . . . Harvey, S. B. (2017). Workplace mental health training for managers and its effect on sick leave in employees: A cluster randomised controlled trial. *The Lancet Psychiatry, 4,* 850–858.

Mulvale, G., & Hurley, J. (2008). Insurance coverage and the treatment of mental illness: Effect on medication and provider use. *The Journal of Mental Health Policy and Economics, 11,* 177–199.

National Council for Mental Wellbeing. (2021). Mental health first aid. www.mentalhealthfirstaid.org/

Newcomer, J. W., & Hennekens, C. H. (2007). Severe mental illness and risk of cardiovascular disease. *JAMA, 298,* 1794–1796.

Peeters, M. C. W., Buunk, B. P., & Schaufeli, W. B. (1995). Social interactions and feelings of inferiority. *Journal of Applied Social Psychology, 25,* 1073–1089.

Reinert, M., Nguyen, T., & Fritze, D. (2020). 2021: The state of mental health in America. www.mamh.org/assets/files/2021-State-of-Mental-Health-in-America.pdf

Robles, M. M. (2012). Executive perceptions of the top 10 soft skills needed in today's workplace. *Business Communication Quarterly, 75,* 453–465.

Rospenda, K. (2002). Workplace harassment, services utilization, and drinking outcomes. *Journal of Occupational Health Psychology, 7,* 141–155.

Rudolph, C. W., Murphy, L. D., & Zacher, H. (2020). A systematic review and critique of research on "healthy leadership." *The Leadership Quarterly*, *31*, 101335.

Sanofi. (2020). *Sanofi Canada Healthcare Survey*, *40*.

Santa Maria, A., Wolter, C., Gusy, B., Kleiber, D., & Renneberg, B. (2019). The impact of health-oriented leadership on police officers' physical health, burnout, depression and well-being. *Policing: A Journal of Policy and Practice*, *13*, 186–200.

Sarti, D. (2014). Job resources as antecedents of engagement at work: Evidence from a long-term care setting. *Human Resource Development Quarterly*, *25*, 213–237.

Shanock, L. R., & Eisenberger, R. (2006). When supervisors feel supported: Relationships with subordinates' perceived supervisor support, perceived organizational support, and performance. *Journal of Applied Psychology*, *91*, 689–695.

Shockley, K. M., & Allen, T. D. (2013). Episodic work–family conflict, cardiovascular indicators, and social support: An experience sampling approach. *Journal of Occupational Health Psychology*, *18*, 262–275.

Skogstad, A., Einarsen, S., Torsheim, T., Aasland, M. S., & Hetland, H. (2007). The destructiveness of laissez-faire leadership behavior. *Journal of Occupational Health Psychology*, *12*, 80–92.

Smetanin, P., Stiff, D., Briante, C., Adair, C., Ahmad, S., & Khan, M. (2011). *The life and economic impact of major mental illnesses in Canada: 2011 to 2041*.

Smith, N. (2019). *Development and validation of the Workplace Mental Illness Stigma Scale (W-MISS)* (Unpublished doctoral dissertation). Portland State University.

Sorensen, O. H., & Holman, D. (2014). A participative intervention to improve employee well-being in knowledge work jobs: A mixed-methods evaluation study. *Work & Stress*, *28*, 67–86.

Spector, P. E., Dwyer, D. J., & Jex, S. M. (1988). Relation of job stressors to affective, health, and performance outcomes: A comparison of multiple data sources. *Journal of Applied Psychology*, *73*, 11–19.

Spector, P. E., & Fox, S. (2002). An emotion-centered model of voluntary work behavior: Some parallels between counterproductive work behavior and organizational citizenship behavior. *Human Resource Management Review*, *12*, 269–292.

Spreitzer, G. M. (1995). Psychological empowerment in the workplace: Dimensions, measurement, and validation. *Academy of Management Journal*, *38*, 1442–1465.

Spreitzer, G. M., Sutcliffe, K., Dutton, J., Sonenshein, S., & Grant, A. M. (2005). A socially embedded model of thriving at work. *Organization Science*, *16*, 537–549.

Stogdill, R. M. (1950). Leadership, membership and organization. *Psychological Bulletin, 47*, 1–14.

(1963). *Manual for the leader behavior description questionnaire, form XII*. Bureau of Business Research, Ohio State University.

Substance Abuse and Mental Health Services Administration. (2019). 2019 National Survey of Drug Use and Health (NSDUH) releases. www.samhsa.gov/data/release/2019-national-survey-drug-use-and-health-nsduh-releases

Tepper, B. J. (2000). Consequences of abusive supervision. *Academy of Management Journal, 43*, 178–190.

(2007). Abusive supervision in work organizations: Review, synthesis, and research agenda. *Journal of Management, 33*, 261–516.

Tepper, B. J., & Taylor, E. C. (2003). Relationships among supervisors' and subordinates' procedural justice perceptions and organizational citizenship behaviors. *Academy of Management Journal, 46*, 97–105.

The Manufacturers Life Insurance Company. (2021). $10,000 mental health benefit for our employees in Canada. www.manulife.com/en/about/sustainability/10000-dollar-mental-health-benefit-for-our-employees-in-canada.html

Thorpe, K., & Chenier, L. (2011). *Building mentally healthy workplaces: Perspectives of Canadian workers and front-line managers*. The Conference Board of Canada.

Trautmann, S., Rehm, J., & Wittchen, H. (2016). The economic costs of mental disorders. *EMBO Reports, 17*, 1245–1249.

Van Knippenberg, B., & Sitkin, S. B. (2013). A critical assessment of charismatic–transformational leadership research: Back to the drawing board? *Academy of Management Annals, 7*, 1–60.

Vinokur, A., Schul, Y., & Caplan, R. D. (1987). Determinants of perceived social support: Interpersonal transactions, personal outlook, and transient affective states. *Journal of Personality and Social Psychology, 53*, 1137–1145.

Viswesvaran, C., Sanchez, J. I., & Fisher, J. (1999). The role of social support in the process of work stress: A meta-analysis. *Journal of Vocational Behavior, 54*, 314–334.

Vos, T., Barber, R. M., Bell, B., Bertozzi-Villa, A., Biryukov, S., Bolliger, I., … Murray, C. J. (2015). Global, regional, and national incidence, prevalence, and years lived with disability for 301 acute and chronic diseases and injuries in 188 countries, 1990–2013: A systematic analysis for the Global Burden of Disease Study 2013. *The Lancet, 386*, 743–800.

Watson, D., Clark, L. A., & Tellegen, A. (1988). Development and validation of brief measures of positive and negative affect: The PANAS scales. *Journal of Personality and Social Psychology, 54*, 1063–1070.

Wayne, J. H., Vaziri, H., & Casper, W. J. (2021). Work–nonwork balance: Development and validation of a global and multidimensional measure. *Journal of Vocational Behavior*, 103565.

Whiteford, H. A., Degenhardt, L., Rehm, J., Baxter, A. J., Ferrari, A. J., Erskine, H. E., ... Vos, T. (2013). Global burden of disease attributable to mental and substance use disorders: Findings from the Global Burden of Disease Study 2010. *The Lancet, 382*, 1575–1586.

World Health Organization. (2018, March 30). Mental health: Strengthening our response. www.who.int/news-room/fact-sheets/detail/mental-health-strengthening-our-response

Yukl, G. (1999). An evaluative essay on current conceptions of effective leadership. *European Journal of Work and Organizational Psychology, 8*, 33–48.

Zwingmann, I., Wegge, J., Wolf, S., Rudolf, M., Schmidt, M., & Richter, P. (2014). Is transformational leadership healthy for employees? A multilevel analysis in 16 nations. *German Journal of Human Resource Management, 28*, 24–51.

Subject Index

Printed in the United States
by Baker & Taylor Publisher Services